TECH EDGE SERIES

COMPUTERS

Understanding Technology
second edition

INTRODUCTORY

FLOYD FULLER

Appalachian State University
Boone, North Carolina

BRIAN LARSON

Modesto Junior College
Modesto, California
California State University–Stanislaus
Turlock, California

EMCParadigm

P U B L I S H I N G

Senior Editor	Sonja M. Brown
Consulting Editor	Deborah Merz
Cover Designer	Leslie Anderson
Text Design and Page Layout	ImageSmythe
Illustrator	Colin Hayes
Copyeditor	Rosemary Wallner
Editorial Assistant	Susan Capecchi
Proofreader	Teresa Hudoba
Indexer	Nancy Fulton

Publishing Team: George Provol, Publisher; Janice Johnson, Director of Product Development; Tony Galvin, Acquisitions Editor, Lori Landwer, Marketing Manager; Shelley Clubb, Electronic Design and Production Manager

---

Library of Congress Cataloging-in-Publication Data

Fuller, Floyd.

Computers : understanding technology : introductory / Floyd Fuller, Brian Larson.-- 2nd ed.

p.cm. -- (Tech edge series)

Includes index.

ISBN 0-7638-2093-8 (text & cd)

1. Computer science. 2. Computers. I. Larson, Brian. II. Title. III. Series.

QA76.F8145 2005

004--dc22   2003064287

Text + Multimedia CD-ROM: ISBN 0-7638-2093-8

© 2005 by Paradigm Publishing Inc.

Published by **EMC**Paradigm Publishing

875 Montreal Way

St. Paul, MN 55102

(800) 535-6865

E-mail: educate@emcp.com

Web site: www.emcp.com

10   9   8   7   6   5   4   3   2

contents

* These activities appear at the end of every chapter.

preface

For millions of people worldwide, the computer and the Internet have become an integral and essential part of life. In the home, we use computers to communicate quickly with family and friends, manage our finances more effectively, enjoy music and games, shop online for products and services, and much more. In the workplace, computers have become an almost indispensable tool. With them, workers can become more efficient, productive, and creative, and companies can connect almost instantly with suppliers and partners on the other side of the world.

Studying this book will help prepare you for the workplace of today—and tomorrow—in which some level of computer skills is often an essential requirement for employment. Employees who continually try to improve their skills have an advantage over those who do not. Some would even argue that understanding technology has become a survival skill. This book will help you become a survivor.

WHAT'S NEW IN THE SECOND EDITION?

As with the first edition, the goal of this new edition of *Computers: Understanding Technology* is to introduce you to the key information technology concepts and the vital technical skills that can help improve your personal and professional lives. In planning the changes for the second edition, we conducted focus groups and used their input to create a state-of-the-art computer concepts product that will enhance the teaching and learning experience.

A major change with the second edition is that the three books in the series represent divisions of the identical chapter content into groups to match the three most common computer concepts course lengths. The Comprehensive book consists of chapters 1-15, the Introductory book consists of chapters 1-9, and the Brief book includes chapters 1-5. Additionally, the order of chapters has changed minimally and the two e-commerce chapters from the first edition have been combined into one. The new topic order is as follows:

Chapter 1: Our Digital World
Chapter 2: Input and Processing
Chapter 3: Output and Storage
Chapter 4: System Software
Chapter 5: Application Software
Chapter 6: Telecommunications and Networks
Chapter 7: The Internet and the World Wide Web
Chapter 8: Using Databases to Manage Information
Chapter 9: Understanding Information Systems
Chapter 10: Electronic Commerce
Chapter 11: Programming Concepts and Languages
Chapter 12: Multimedia and Artificial Intelligence
Chapter 13: Security Strategies and Systems
Chapter 14: Computer Ethics
Chapter 15: Information Technology Careers

Special Features

To more precisely meet the needs of the varied introductory computer courses across the country, we have developed eight Special Features that are included in various combinations in the three books. These succinct, well illustrated overviews explain the major concepts within the eight topics:

- Buying and Installing a PC
- Adding Software and Hardware Components to Your PC
- Networks and Telecommunications
- The Internet and the World Wide Web
- Computer Ethics
- Building a Web Site
- Security Issues and Strategies
- Using XML to Share Information

The first five Special Features appear in the Brief book; the Introductory book includes the first two Special Features plus the *Computer Ethics*, *Building a Web Site*, and *Security Issues and Strategies* features. The Comprehensive book includes the two PC features plus the topics of *Building a Web Site* and *Using XML to Share Information*.

Additional Application Exercises: Windows and Internet Tutorials

Recognizing the crucial need for students to be able to use Windows efficiently and effectively, we have developed a set of 15 Windows XP Tutorials that teach the core computer management skills. Students can work through the group of tutorials in one sitting, or they can work through them one at a time as the first activity in the end-of-chapter exercises. The Windows Tutorials appear with the Internet Tutorials at the end of the book.

New Concepts Exercises

New to this edition are three exercises that help expand and reinforce student comprehension of the chapter content. "Knowledge Check" is a set of multiple-choice questions; "Tech Architecture" offers a drawing that students label; and "Ethical Dilemmas" poses an ethical issue that students discuss and debate.

USING THE ENCORE! CD-ROM AND THE INTERNET RESOURCE CENTER

Included with the textbook is a multimedia CD-ROM that adds an experiential and interactive dimension to the learning of fundamental computer concepts. For every chapter, the CD offers

- Tech Tutors: Brief, animated Flash segments that bring key topics to life
- Quizzes: Multiple-choice tests available in both Practice and Test modes with scores reported to the student and instructor by e-mail
- Glossary: Key terms and definitions combined with related illustrations from the text
- Image Bank: Illustrations of concepts and processes accompanied by the related terms and definitions

Additionally, the Encore! CD includes a comprehensive set of computer literacy tutorials called Tech Review, which are accessible at any time and within any chapter.

The CD may be used as a preview or as a sequel to each chapter—or both. That is, you can play each chapter's Flash animations (or videos) to get an overview of what is taught in the book and then study the text chapter before returning to the CD for its enriching content and interactivity. Or, you can complete a chapter and then complete the corresponding chapter on the CD. Either way, you will benefit from working with this integrated multimedia CD-ROM and will find an approach that suits your learning style.

To further address the dynamic and ever-changing nature of computer technology, additional readings, projects, and activities for each chapter are provided on the Internet Resource Center at www.emcp.com. Look for the title of the book under the list of Resource Centers and prepare for some stimulating reading and activities.

ACKNOWLEDGEMENTS AND APPRECIATION

Writing and publishing a book is a complex and expensive task that requires the dedicated efforts of many people. Throughout this project, we authors have had the pleasure and privilege of working closely with the highly skilled and quality-focused professionals at EMC/Paradigm Publishing. From the outset, everyone at EMC/ Paradigm committed to making this new edition a premier computer concepts textbook. We want to express our sincere gratitude to the following individuals.

Tony Galvin, Acquisitions Editor, and Robert Galvin, Vice President and National Sales Manager, leveraged their knowledge of the market and their many associations with college and university instructors to pave the way for a new edition that would reach an ever-broader audience of students taking entry-level computer concepts courses.

Vice President and Publisher George Provol provided us with the all-important financial resources and support needed to complete this project. From the early conception of this work, George was aware of the resources required for such an important project, and he made certain they would be available as needed.

As always, our work with Senior Editor Sonja Brown has been a pleasure and a privilege. From the beginning of this project to the end, Sonja devoted herself completely to making this new edition accurate, attractive, timely, and comprehensive. She was an ever-present source of inspiration as she expertly guided this project from beginning to end. Thank you, Sonja, for your dedication and for your especially valuable contributions to this textbook.

Janice Johnson, Director of Product Development, offered numerous innovative ideas for teaching and presenting material.

Senior Designer Leslie Anderson created the striking covers. David Farr of ImageSmythe updated the page design and crafted the beautiful, easy-to-read page layouts. Photo Researcher Paul Spencer located just the right art to communicate important and difficult-to-understand concepts. Special thanks, also, to Susan Capecchi for her wide-ranging assistance and her commitment to quality with every detail.

We are indebted to technical writer and consultant Deborah Merz, whose careful attention to accuracy and relevancy proved invaluable. Deborah also prepared the chapter readings and exercises for the Internet Resource Center.

Thank you to Denise Seguin, co-author of the *Marquee Office 2003* series, for creating the Internet Tutorials; to Faithe Wempen, author of *PC Maintenance*, for creating the Windows Tutorials; to Carolyn Reser for writing many new thought-provoking and informative sidebars; and to Desiree Faulkner for creating most of the screen captures.

Our families deserve special credit. Our wives, Edith and Alma, and our children, Cindy and Michael, and Amanda and Keith, were constant sources of love, support, and encouragement. Although we can never repay them for their sacrifices on our behalf, we are truly grateful to each, without whose support we could not have written this book.

Consultants and Reviewers

We are indebted to three individuals who served as technical consultants and reviewers for the first edition, which provided the solid foundation for this and future editions:

David Laxton, industry consultant, Cincinnati, Ohio
Deborah Merz, technical writer and consultant, West Bloomfield, Michigan
Mary Kelley Weaver, instructor, St. Johns River Community College

Additionally, we thank the instructors and other professionals who reviewed the content plan early on in the process. As instructors who teach introductory computer courses, and as practicing professionals who are knowledgeable about the latest computer technologies, they brought a real-world perspective to the project:

Roger Anderson
College of Lake County

Elizabeth Bastedo
Central Carolina Community College

Kathy Camarena
Sacramento City College

Sue Chiki
The Hocking College

Barbara Comfort
JS Reynolds Community College

Susan Dozier
Tidewater Community College

Raul Enriquez
Laredo Community College

Pat Feder
Milwaukee Area Technical College

Michael Graves
College of the Sisky

Gail Guarino
Cape Cod Community College

James Kasum
University of Wisconsin - Milwaukee

Dr. Sherry Kersey
Hillsborough Community College

Professor Elizabeth King
Sacramento City College

Dr. Mete Kok
Borough of Manhattan Community College

Conrad Krueger
San Antonio College

Anita Lande
Cabrillo College

Jan Larson
Pikes Peak Community College

Joanne Lazirko
University of Wisconsin - Milwaukee

Dr. Edward Martin
Kingsborough Community College

Anna Mastrolillo
Norwalk Community College

Marilyn Meyer
Fresno City College

Sita Motipara
Skyline College

Toni Murocco
Lincoln Land Community College

Don Read
Bronx Community College

James Reed
San Jacinto College Central

Pat Ryan
North Essex Community College

Marilyn Schmid
Asheville-Buncombe Community College

Jaclyn Winskie
Southeastern Technical College

Robert Wurm
Nassau Community College

Mary Ann Zlotow
College of DuPage

Dedication

Few things, if any, are more precious than one's family, and during recent years my family has grown in size with the addition of younger members. Mere words cannot express the love and joy I feel while in their presence. Perhaps without their knowledge, they bring a greater meaning and sense of purpose to my life, and I treasure their every word and action. That which they bring to my life, and to our family, is immeasurable. For the reasons cited, and for others, I dedicate this book to Jenna, Eli, Will, and Ben.

—Floyd Fuller

For all the times the kids climbed on the computer or poured juice on the keyboard, for all the times she took care of things while I typed, and for all the times she was understanding and thoughtful, I dedicate this book to my wife, Alma Larson.

—Brian Larson

CHAPTER 1

OUR DIGITAL WORLD

UNDERSTANDING TECHNOLOGY

CYBER SCENARIO

It's 10:45 a.m. and Jason Edmiston's flight has just taken off from St. Louis, heading for Chicago's O'Hare International Airport. After the Boeing 747 reaches its cruising altitude, the flight attendant announces that passengers are now permitted to use personal electronic devices, including their computers.

Jason reaches under his seat to retrieve his notebook computer, and plugs it into the telephone slot on the rear of the seat in front of him. With a few keystrokes his computer is activated and he is ready to begin his business day.

His first task is to review his busy schedule. Ramona Ramirez will meet him upon his arrival at 11:50 a.m. Afterward there's lunch with Mirax Corporation's purchasing agents, when he will present his company's marketing suggestions. His busy day will end with dinner at the Lough Bispo Restaurant on Chicago's North Side.

Jason quickly accesses the Internet. He sends an e-mail message to his company, letting his supervisor know he is en route to Chicago. He sends another e-mail to Mark Reminger at Teledex Company in Chicago confirming their meeting at 3 p.m. Four more messages are sent during the next few minutes, each one to a branch office in another part of the country.

He carefully reviews his investment portfolio by accessing his broker's Web site. IBM is down $3.25, Dell Computer is up $2.75, Microsoft Corporation is up $2.25, and Alcoa is up $1.13. All in all, not bad! A graphical summary of his portfolio appears on the screen with the press of a button.

Jason scans the latest headlines by accessing *USA Today*'s Web site. One article grabs his attention. It announces that his company's union has agreed to a settlement. From another brief article, he learns that his company's major competitor is having difficulty with its proposed acquisition of a smaller company.

Returning the laptop to his briefcase, Jason retrieves his Internet-enabled cell phone and calls his wife. When she answers, her image appears in color on the small LCD screen of Jason's phone, as does his image on her Internet-enabled phone. Using his phone's instant messaging feature, the two of them exchange messages almost as if they were talking face-to-face.

Jason's e-mails are among the billions of e-mail messages sent daily throughout North America. The Web sites he accessed are part of the millions of Web sites on the Internet in the year 2003, a stunning expansion from the 130 Web sites available a decade ago. During the one hour it took Jason to fly from St. Louis to Chicago, he accomplished the following tasks:

- communicated with at least six different people at diverse locations
- reviewed the day's trading prices of his stock investments
- read the latest national and regional news
- arranged for a car rental in Chicago
- exchanged visual and audio greetings with his wife

In the not too distant future, Jason and millions of other consumers will be able to accomplish these tasks and more on tiny mobile devices controlled by the human voice.

IMMERSED IN DIGITAL TECHNOLOGY

Computers and other digital devices permeate our daily lives. High-definition televisions (HDTVs) display amazingly clear and colorful images of sports events, reality TV shows, and other popular programs. Electronic coffeemakers, digital alarm clocks, and cell phones quicken and simplify daily routines. Automobile manufacturers use computerized robots to build cars and trucks. Businesses increasingly rely on electronic mail (e-mail) to communicate internally and with vendors and customers. Electronic freeway information signs and traffic monitoring devices help drivers navigate our busy highways and alert drivers to emergencies, such as missing or abducted persons. And some 65 percent of U.S. children ages 2–17 use the Internet from home, school, or some other location, according to a 2003 report from the Corporation for Public Broadcasting. In today's world, living even a day without some type of digital interaction is highly unlikely for most people. What about you? How digital is your life? Complete the survey on the next page to get a sense of the number of digital interactions you have every day. Place a check mark next to each activity you have experienced in the past 24 hours.

- ❏ driving a car
- ❏ tracking appointments on a personal digital assistant (PDA)
- ❏ using a pager
- ❏ calling on a cell phone
- ❏ depositing or withdrawing money at an ATM
- ❏ working on a desktop computer or laptop
- ❏ sending information via a fax machine
- ❏ creating copies with a photocopier
- ❏ riding an elevator
- ❏ playing video games
- ❏ answering a telemarketing call
- ❏ manipulating numbers with a calculator
- ❏ riding on the subway
- ❏ retrieving a voice mail message
- ❏ viewing cable TV via a cable converter box
- ❏ watching a movie on a DVD player
- ❏ cooking with a microwave
- ❏ operating an electronically controlled dishwasher
- ❏ adjusting an electronic thermostat
- ❏ buying food or soda from an electronic vending machine
- ❏ entering a locked building with a security card
- ❏ purchasing an item with a debit card
- ❏ researching airline ticket prices on the Internet
- ❏ selling an item on eBay
- ❏ downloading music from a Web site

Like most people, you are probably aware that you interact with electronic devices every day, but perhaps you were surprised by the large number of your digital experiences. The extent to which computers and digital technology drive daily life has led historians to characterize today's world as a "digital world." You know the term "digital" has something to do with computers. But what does the term mean and why is it important?

Digital Information

Digital refers to a type of electronic signal that is processed, sent, and stored in discrete parts (bits) rather than in a continuous wave, such as a sound wave. These discrete parts are represented by "on" and "off" electrical states, which in turn correspond to the digits 1 (on) and 0 (off). In a computer, all information is represented by this system of 1s and 0s corresponding to on and off electrical currents. Thus, computers use digital information, and computer technology in general is considered digital technology. You will learn more about this fundamental information technology concept in the chapters that follow, but for now, remember that digital refers to information represented by numbers and that all of the interactions listed in the survey above used digital information.

Computerized Devices vs. Computers

Digital processing occurs within miniature electrical circuits etched onto a tiny square of silicon (or another material) called a **chip**, and digital cameras, cell phones, electronic coffeemakers, and computers all contain electronic chips (see Figure 1-1). However, the chips within computerized devices differ considerably from the chips within computers in terms of power and capability, a distinction that separates electronic devices into two broad groups: special-purpose, or embedded computers, and general-purpose computers, or simply computers. The chip within an **embedded computer** has been programmed by the manufacturer to perform a few specific actions. For example, an embedded chip in a digital camera automatically controls the speed of the camera's lens so the right amount of light enters through the lens. An embedded chip in a bar code scanner reads the bar code on clothing tags and identifies the item and its price. A tiny computerized chip in a digital thermometer determines the body temperature of patients at a medical clinic.

The electronic chips within a **general-purpose computer**, on the other hand, contain programs that allow the user to perform a range of complex processes and calculations. For example, a computer containing a word processing program allows a user to create, edit, print, and save various kinds of documents, including letters, memos, and brochures. A **computer**, therefore, is defined as an electronic device that

- operates under the control of a set of instructions, called a **program**, which is stored in its memory
- accepts data supplied by a user
- manipulates the data according to the programmed instructions
- produces the results (information)
- stores the results for future use

FIGURE 1-1: Digital devices operate using electronic chips (right). A device containing a single-purpose chip, such as a digital thermometer (below), is called an embedded computer. A device containing multipurpose electronic chips is classified as a computer (below right).

THE COMPUTER ADVANTAGE

Prior to the early 1980s, computers were unknown to the average person. Many people had never even seen a computer, let alone used one. The few computers that existed were relatively large, bulky devices confined to secure computer centers in corporate or government facilities. Referred to as mainframes, these computers were maintenance intensive, requiring special climate-controlled conditions and several full-time operators for each machine (see Figure 1-2). Because the early mainframes were expensive and difficult to operate, usage was restricted to computer programmers and scientists, who used them to perform complex operations, such as processing payrolls and designing sophisticated military weaponry. Other than a few researchers or technicians having security clearances, most employees were prohibited from entering areas where the computer was housed and operated.

FIGURE 1-2: Early mainframe computers, such as the one shown above, were large, bulky devices that were difficult to operate.

Beginning in the early 1980s, the computer world changed dramatically with the introduction of **microcomputers**, also called **personal computers (PCs)** because they were intended to be operated by an individual user. These relatively small computers were considerably more affordable and much easier to use than their mainframe ancestors. Within a few years, ownership of personal computers became widespread in the workplace, and today, the personal computer is a standard appliance in homes and schools. By 2002, according to research firm Grunwald Associates, 83 percent of U.S. family households owned a computer. In terms of business spending, the information technology (IT) sector now accounts for 60 percent of capital expenditures.

Today's computers come in a variety of shapes and sizes and differ significantly in computing capability, price, and speed. For example, a powerful business computer capable of processing millions of customer records in a few minutes may cost millions of dollars while an office desktop computer used for creating correspondence and budget forecasts may cost less than a thousand dollars. Whatever their size, cost, or power, all computers offer advantages over manual technologies in the following areas:

- speed
- accuracy
- versatility
- storage capabilities
- communications capabilities

Speed

Computers operate with lightning-like speed, and processing speeds are increasing as computer manufacturers introduce new and improved models. Contemporary personal computers are capable of executing billions of program instructions in one second. Some larger computers, such as supercomputers, can execute trillions of instructions per second, a rate important for processing the huge amounts of data involved in forecasting weather, monitoring space shuttle flights, and managing other data-intensive applications.

Accuracy

People sometimes blame human errors and mistakes on a computer. In truth, computers are extremely accurate when accurate programs and data are entered and processed. A popular expression among computer professionals is "garbage in—garbage out" **(GIGO)**, which means that if inaccurate programs and/or data are entered into a computer for processing, the resulting output will also be inaccurate. It is the user's responsibility to make certain that programs and data are entered correctly.

Versatility

Computers are perhaps the most versatile of all machines or devices. They can perform a variety of personal, business, and scientific applications. Families use computers for entertainment, communications, budgeting, online shopping, completing homework assignments, playing games, and listening to music. Banks conduct money transfers, account withdrawals, and the payment of checks via computer. Retailers use computers to process sales transactions and to check on the availability of products. Manufacturers can manage their entire production, warehousing, and selling processes with computerized systems. Schools access computers for keeping records, conducting distance learning classes, scheduling events, and analyzing budgets. Universities, government agencies, hospitals, and scientific organizations

Monitoring space shuttle flights requires an enormous array of computing resources, including ground- and space-based tracking station networks. A single communications satellite, for example, can handle up to 300 million bits of information each second.

Families use computers for entertainment, communications, budgeting, online shopping, completing homework assignments, playing games, and listening to music.

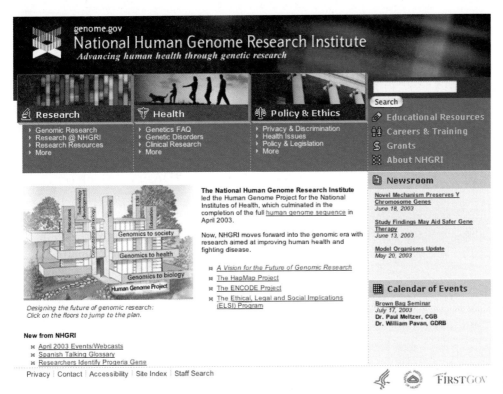

genome.gov
National Human Genome Research Institute
Advancing human health through genetic research

Research | **Health** | **Policy & Ethics**

Research:
▸ Genomic Research
▸ Research @ NHGRI
▸ Research Resources
▸ More

Health:
▸ Genetics FAQ
▸ Genetic Disorders
▸ Clinical Research
▸ More

Policy & Ethics:
▸ Privacy & Discrimination
▸ Health Issues
▸ Policy & Legislation
▸ More

Search

⬦ Educational Resources
⬦ Careers & Training
$ Grants
⬦ About NHGRI

The National Human Genome Research Institute led the Human Genome Project for the National Institutes of Health, which culminated in the completion of the full human genome sequence in April 2003.

Now, NHGRI moves forward into the genomic era with research aimed at improving human health and fighting disease.

⌘ *A Vision for the Future of Genomic Research*
⌘ The HapMap Project
⌘ The ENCODE Project
⌘ The Ethical, Legal and Social Implications (ELSI) Program

Designing the future of genomic research: Click on the floors to jump to the plan.

New from NHGRI
⌘ April 2003 Events/Webcasts
⌘ Spanish Talking Glossary
⌘ Researchers Identify Progeria Gene

Privacy | Contact | Accessibility | Site Index | Staff Search

Newsroom

Novel Mechanism Preserves Y Chromosome Genes
June 18, 2003

Study Findings May Aid Safer Gene Therapy
June 13, 2003

Model Organisms Update
May 20, 2003

Calendar of Events

Brown Bag Seminar
July 17, 2003
Dr. Paul Meltzer, CGB
Dr. William Pavan, GDRB

FIRSTGOV

The National Human Genome Research Institute funds genetic and genomic research, studies the related ethics, and provides education to the public and to health professionals.

conduct life-enhancing research using computers. Perhaps the most ambitious such computer-based scientific research of all time is the Human Genome Project, which was completed in April 2003, more than two years ahead of schedule and at a cost considerably lower than originally forecast. This project represented an international effort to sequence the 3 billion DNA (deoxyribonucleic acid) letters in the human genome, which is the collection of gene types that comprise every person. Scientists from all over the world can now access the genome database and use the information to research ways to improve human health and fight disease.

Storage

Storage is a defining computer characteristic and is one of the features that revolutionized early computing, for it made computers incredibly flexible. A computer is capable of accepting and storing programs and data. Once stored in the computer, a program can be used again and again to process different data. For example, a spreadsheet program such as Microsoft Excel can be used repeatedly to track budget expenditures and to project possible outcomes if income and expenses change. Computers can store huge amounts of data in comparably tiny physical spaces. For example, one compact disc can store about 109,000 pages of magazine text, and the capacities of internal storage devices are many times larger.

Communications

Most modern computers contain special equipment and programs that allow them to communicate with other computers through telephone lines, cable connections, and satellites. Computers having this capability are often linked together so users can share programs, data, information, and equipment such as a printer. The structure in which computers are linked together using special programs and equipment is called a **network**, as shown in Figure 1-3. Newer communications technologies allow users to exchange information over wireless networks using wireless devices such as personal digital assistants (PDAs), notebook computers, cell phones, and pagers.

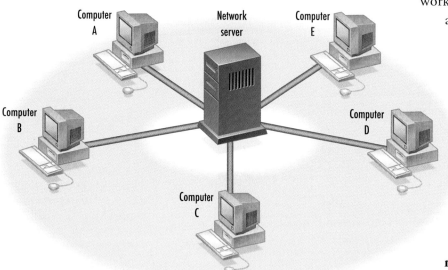

A network can be relatively small or quite large. A **local area network (LAN)** is one confined to a relatively small geographical area, such as a building, factory, or college campus. A **wide area network (WAN)** spans a large geographical area and might connect a company's manufacturing plants dispersed throughout the United States. Constant, quick connections along with other computer technologies have helped boost productivity for manufacturers such as Timken Company, an industrial bearing maker headquartered in Canton, Ohio. All of its tooling machines are networked, and the factory itself is networked to 76 other company locations in the United States and worldwide. Using digital designs and networked machines, the company can produce a customized bearing product in 15 to 30 minutes, which took half a day using older methods.

FIGURE 1-3 : A network is a collection of computers and devices linked together by software and communications devices and media.

The Internet: A Super Network

The network you are most likely familiar with is the Internet, which is the world's largest network. The **Internet** is a worldwide network made up of large and small networks linked together via communications hardware, software, telephone, cable, and satellite systems for the purpose of communicating and sharing information (see Figure 1-4).

Research firms, including Jupitermedia Corporation, estimate that by 2003 nearly 700 million people around the world were using the Internet for various purposes, including

- sending and receiving electronic mail (e-mail)
- researching information, such as weather forecasts, maps, stock quotes, news reports, airline schedules, and newspaper and magazine articles
- buying and selling products and services
- taking online college courses
- accessing entertainment, such as online games and music

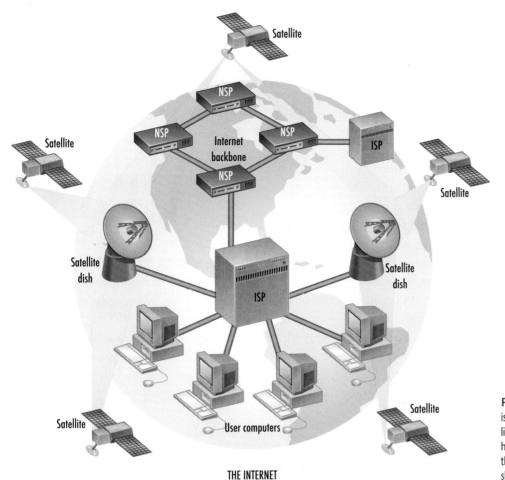

Satellite

NSP

NSP   Internet   NSP   ISP
       backbone

Satellite   Satellite

NSP

Satellite
dish   Satellite
                                              dish

ISP

Satellite   Satellite

Satellite   User computers

THE INTERNET

FIGURE 1-4: The Internet is a worldwide network of networks linked together via communications hardware, software, and media for the purpose of communicating and sharing information.

Figure 1-5 shows the home page of Microsoft Network, one of several online service providers that offer Internet access and provide daily weather reports, stock quotes, and other types of information.

FIGURE 1-5: An online service such as Microsoft Network provides users with Internet access, daily weather reports, stock quotes, and other types of information.

The World Wide Web

The most widely used part of the Internet is the **World Wide Web (the Web)**, a global system of computer networks that allows users to move from one site to another by way of programmed links on Web pages. A **Web page** is an electronic document stored on a computer running the Web site. The document may contain text, images, sound, and video, and may also contain links to other Web pages and other Web sites. Web visitors find information using a **search engine**, which is a software program that locates and retrieves requested information. For example, suppose you entered the topic of "the feeding habits of brown bears" into the program's search box. Within moments, the search engine would display a list of information sources on the Web similar to the list shown in Figure 1-6.

All network and Internet activities begin with individual computers, and it is at the computer level where the information that drives our economy originates. Understanding the broad steps in the processing of information is key to recognizing the significance of computer technology.

FIGURE 1-6: A search engine is a software program that enables a user to search for, locate, and retrieve information available on the World Wide Web.

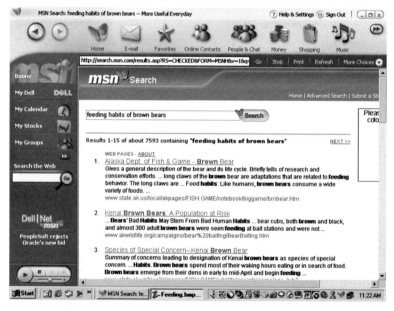

HOW COMPUTERS WORK

Computers are designed to accept data entered by a user, process the data according to program instructions, and then output the processed data in a useful form—as information. Note that data and information are not the same thing. Information is a product of a recurring series of events called the information processing cycle.

Data and Information

Data are raw, unorganized facts and figures. By itself, a piece of data may be meaningless. For example, the fact that an employee has worked 40 hours in one week

TECH VISIONARY

John V. Atanasoff, a brilliant physicist and computer engineer, was born in Hamilton, New York, in 1903. He was a precocious child, demonstrating early on a strong interest in physics and math. At the age of 9, for example, he discovered and repaired some faulty electrical wiring in his family's home. He earned his PhD in physics at the University of Wisconsin–Madison in 1930 at the age of 27. By 1938, he had developed several concepts that became the foundation for the first computers: They should be electronic, binary- based, and use condensers for memory. Working with Clifford Berry at Iowa State University from 1939 to 1942, he built what is regarded as the first electronic digital calculating machine, known as the ABC (Atanasoff-Berry-Computer). Although the ABC was not programmable, it strongly influenced the design of subsequent computers. Atanasoff built computers for the United States Navy and the United States Army from 1942 to 1952 and then went into private business in Rockville, Maryland, where he founded his own research and engineering company called the Ordnance Engineering Corporation.

The ABC device included such innovations as a binary system of arithmetic, parallel processing, regenerative memory, and a separation of memory and computing functions. It was also the first computing machine to use electricity, vacuum tubes, binary numbers, and capacitors. The final product was the size of a desk, weighed 700 pounds, had over 300 vacuum tubes, and contained a mile of wire. It could calculate about one operation every 15 seconds.

Source: Bellis, Mary. "Inventors of the Modern Computer: The Atanasoff-Berry Computer, the first Electronic Computer—John Atanasoff and Clifford Berry." June 6, 2003 <http://inventors.about.com/library/weekly/aa050898.htm>.

may be useless to the payroll department staff. However, by entering additional data, such as the employee's pay rate, number of exemptions and deductions, and then processing the data, department personnel can generate useful information, including paychecks, earnings statements, and payroll reports. Therefore, **information** is defined as data that has been processed (manipulated, organized, or arranged) in a way that converts it into a useful form. Once created, information can be displayed on a computer screen or printed on paper. It can also be stored for future use, such as for processing periodic payroll reports.

Data entered into a computer can be one type or a combination of two or more of the following types:

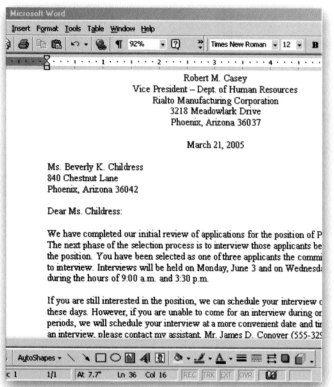

FIGURE 1-7: Letters are an example of text data.

- **Text data** consists of alphabetic letters, numbers, and special characters. These data are typically entered to produce output such as letters, e-mail messages, and reports (see Figure 1-7).
- **Graphics data** consists of still images, including photographs, mathematical charts, and drawings, such as the illustration shown in Figure 1-8.
- **Audio data** refers to sound, such as voice and music. For example, using a microphone a person can enter a voice message that the computer stores in digitized form. Or, a user can download music from a Web site and listen to the songs over speakers connected to the computer (see Figure 1-9).
- **Video data** refers to moving pictures and images, such as a videoconference, film clip, or full-length movie (see Figure 1-10). For example, a user may record a home movie using a digital video camera. The camera is then connected to a computer, which plays the video and displays it on the computer screen.

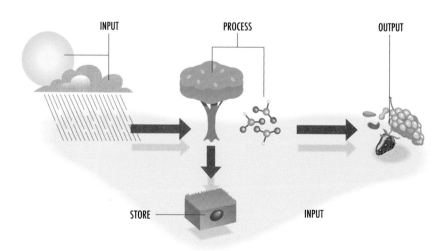

FIGURE 1-8: An illustration is an example of graphics data.

FIGURE 1-9: Speaking program commands into a microphone is a way of entering audio data.

FIGURE 1-10: A movie played on a computer's DVD drive is an example of video data.

The Information Processing Cycle

Using a computer to convert data into useful information is referred to as **information processing** (also called **data processing**). Processing data into information involves four basic functions: input, processing, output, and storage. During processing, these four functions are usually performed sequentially. The stepped actions of input, processing, output, and storage are collectively known as the **information processing cycle**, which is illustrated in Figure 1-11.

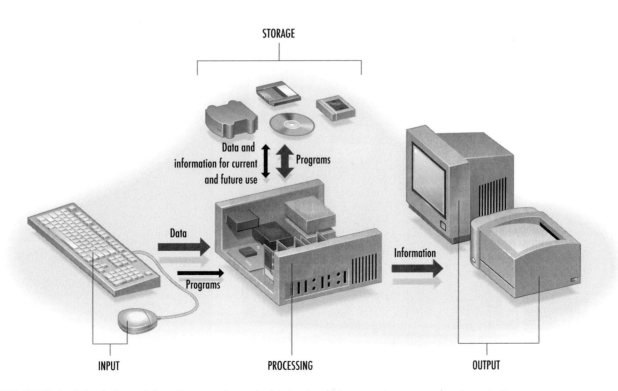

FIGURE 1-11: During an information processing cycle, data is entered into a computer, processed, sent as output, or stored (if required for future use).

Data entered into a computer is called **input**, which also is the name of the first step in the information processing cycle. Once entered through an input device such as a keyboard or mouse, the data is manipulated, or processed, according to the programmed instructions. **Processing** occurs in a computer's electrical circuits. This results in the creation of information called **output**. Output can either be sent to an output device, such as a printer, or kept in **storage** on media such as a floppy disk, compact disc, or hard drive for future use. Information processed by a computer can be output in a variety of forms:

- written, or textual form, as in research reports and letters
- numerical form, as in a spreadsheet analysis of a company's finances
- verbal or audio form, as in recorded voice and music
- visual form, such as photos, drawings, and videos

COMPUTERS AND COMPUTER SYSTEMS

Technically, the term "computer" identifies only the **system unit**, the part of a computer system that processes data and stores the information. A **computer system**, however, includes the system unit along with input devices, output devices, and storage devices. The number and kinds of devices included is a matter of individual need or preference. For example, a buyer shopping for a new personal computer would expect to purchase an entire system, including the system unit, keyboard, mouse, monitor, storage devices, and perhaps a printer. An engineer in a structural design firm might need a more powerful system unit capable of running building design software, along with a larger monitor, a plan printer, and a standard document printer. Figure 1-12 shows a variety of input, processing, output, and storage devices that may be included in a personal computer system.

FIGURE 1-12: A personal computer system typically includes a system unit, monitor, keyboard, mouse, and other devices.

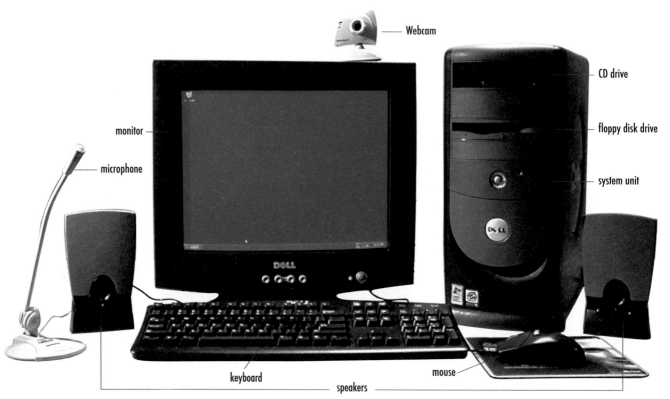

Webcam

CD drive

floppy disk drive

system unit

monitor

microphone

keyboard

speakers

mouse

In the remainder of this book, the term "computer" is used to refer to a computer system that includes all necessary devices that allow a user to input programs and data, process the data, output the results, and store the results for future use.

Some computer systems are single-user computer systems whereas others are multi-user computer systems. A **single-user computer system**, as the name implies, can accommodate a single (one) user at a time and is the type of personal computer system found in homes and in small businesses and offices. A **multi-user computer system** can accommodate many users concurrently. Large businesses typically use these systems to enable several managers and employees to simultaneously access, use, and update information stored in a centrally located system. For example, using computers at their respective workstations, a payroll clerk can access and view an employee's payroll record while a shipping clerk is tracking a customer's shipment at the same time. In addition, the users can interact with each other easily and quickly. The main focus of this book is on general-purpose, single-user computers—personal computers—that enable users to complete a variety of computing tasks. These are the computers you will most likely work with in your home, in your school's computer lab, and on the job.

COMPONENTS OF A COMPUTER SYSTEM

A computer system consists of two broad categories of components: hardware and software. The combination of hardware and software that comprise a particular system depends on the user's requirements, and given the number of hardware devices and software programs available in the marketplace, users can configure all kinds of possible setups. Manufacturers typically offer a system unit, monitor, and keyboard package, leaving the choice of mouse, printer, and other hardware devices up to the buyer. PC system units are usually preloaded with the Microsoft Windows operating system plus some basic programs such as a word processing software.

Computer Hardware: An Overview

Hardware includes all of the physical components that make up the system unit plus the other devices connected to it, such as a keyboard or monitor. These connected devices are referred to as **peripheral devices** because they are outside, or peripheral to, the computer. Examples include a keyboard, mouse, camera, and printer. Some peripheral devices, such as a monitor and hard disk drive, are essential components of a personal computer system. Hardware devices are grouped into the following categories:

- system unit
- input devices
- output devices
- storage devices
- communications devices

The System Unit

The system unit is a relatively small plastic or metal cabinet housing the electronic components that process data into information. Inside the cabinet is the main circuit board, called the **motherboard**, which provides for the installation and connection of other electronic components (see Figure 1-13). Once installed on the motherboard, the components can communicate with each other, thereby allowing data to be processed into information.

The main components of the motherboard are the **central processing unit (CPU)**, also called the **microprocessor** (or simply processor), and internal memory. The **processor** consists of one or more electronic chips that read, interpret, and execute the instructions that operate the computer and perform specific computing tasks. When a program is executed, the processor temporarily stores the program's instructions and the data needed by the instructions into the computer's memory. **Memory**, also called **primary storage**, consists of small electronic chips that provide temporary storage for instructions and data during processing.

FIGURE 1-13: A motherboard holds the main processing and memory chips.

FIGURE 1-14: The microphone, keyboard, and mouse are common types of input devices.

Input Devices

An **input device** is a hardware device that allows users to enter program instructions, data, and commands into a computer. The program or application being used determines the type of input device needed. Common input devices are the keyboard, mouse, and microphone, as shown in Figure 1-14.

Output Devices

An **output device** is a device that makes information available to the user. Popular output devices include display screens (monitors), printers, television screens, and speakers. Some output devices, such as a printer, produce output in **hard copy** (tangible) form, such as on paper or plastic. Other output devices, such as a monitor, produce output in **soft copy** (intangible) form that can be viewed, but not physically handled. Figure 1-15 shows a hard copy output device and a soft copy output device.

FIGURE 1-15: Monitors and printers are the most common output devices for personal computers.

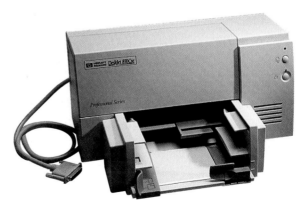

Storage Devices

Unlike memory that stores instructions and data temporarily during processing, **storage devices** and **media**, often called **secondary storage**, provide for the permanent storage of programs, data, and information. Once stored, information can be retrieved, modified, displayed, imported, exported, copied, or printed.

A storage device itself records programs, data, and/or information to a storage medium and retrieves them from the storage medium. Examples of storage devices include floppy disk drives, hard disk drives, Zip® drives, and various kinds of CD drives (see Figure 1-16).

Communications Devices

A **communications device** makes it possible for a user to communicate with another computer and to exchange instructions, data, and information with other computer users. The most popular communications device is a **modem**, an electronic device capable of converting computer-readable information into a form that can be transmitted and received over communications systems, such as standard telephone lines.

FIGURE 1-16: Most new personal computers contain CD (compact disc) drives that can read more than one kind of CD.

Computer Software: An Overview

Software consists of programs containing instructions that direct the operation of the computer system and programs that enable users to perform specific applications, such as word processing. The three main classifications of software are system software, application software, and communications software.

System Software

System software tells the computer how to function and is divided into two categories: operating system software and utility software. The **operating system** is the most important piece of software in a computer system. It contains instructions for starting the computer and coordinates the activities of all hardware devices. Most personal computers use one of the Microsoft Windows operating systems, while Apple Macintosh computers use the Macintosh operating system (see Figure 1-17).

   Utility software consists of programs that perform administrative tasks, such as checking the computer's components to determine whether each is working properly, managing disk drives and printers, and checking for computer viruses.

Application Software

Application software consists of programs that perform specific tasks, such as word processing, spreadsheet preparation, database searching, and slide show presentation. Thousands of commercially prepared application programs are currently available for managing personal and business activities.

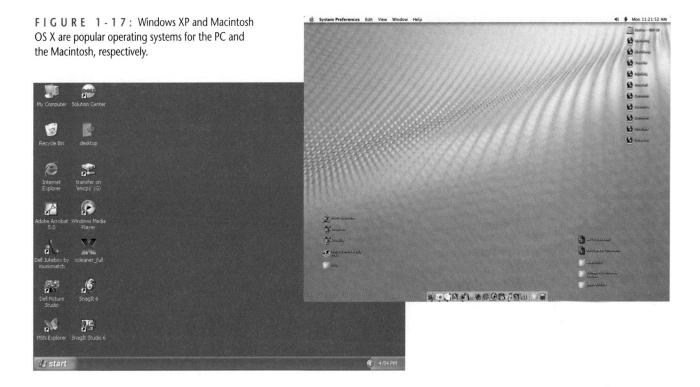

FIGURE 1-17: Windows XP and Macintosh OS X are popular operating systems for the PC and the Macintosh, respectively.

Communications Software

Communications software makes it possible for a computer to transmit and receive information to and from other computers. To communicate over the Internet, a user needs an account with an **Internet service provider (ISP)**, a company that has a permanent connection to the Internet and provides temporary access to individuals and others, usually for a fee. Some ISPs provide communication software that is installed on a subscriber's computer to enable the user to send and receive electronic mail messages to other similarly equipped computers. The software also provides access to the massive storehouse of information on the Internet and the World Wide Web. Other ISPs allow subscribers to simply use standard e-mail software and a **Web browser**, a special program for viewing Web pages, to accomplish the same functions.

CATEGORIES OF COMPUTERS

Rapid advances in computer technology often blur the differences among types of computers, and industry professionals may disagree on how computers should be categorized. Typically, they use criteria based on differences in usage, size, speed, processing capabilities, and price, resulting in the categories named in Table 1-1:

- personal computers
- handheld computers
- workstations
- midrange servers
- mainframe computers
- supercomputers

Category	Size	Instructions Executed Per Second	Number of Accommodated Users	Approximate Price Range
personal computer	fits on a desk, in a briefcase, on a laptop, or is worn	600 million to about 3 billion, or more	a single user, or a part of a network	a few hundred to thousands of dollars
handheld computer	fits in hand(s); some may be carried in a pocket	depending on device, a few hundred	a single user, or a part of a network	depending on the model, $99 to several hundred dollars
workstation	similar to a desktop PC, but larger and more powerful	depending on the type, 3 to 5 billion	a single user, or a part of a network	a few thousand up to several thousands of dollars
midrange server	fits into a large cabinet or a small room	billions of instructions	hundreds of users concurrently	$5,000 to $200,000 based on how it is equipped
large server, or mainframe computer	with needed equipment, occupies a partial or full room	billions of instructions	hundreds or thousands of users concurrently	several thousands up to millions of dollars
supercomputer	with equipment, occupies a full room	trillions of instructions	thousands of users concurrently	several million dollars

TABLE 1-1: Categories of Computers

Note, however, that personal computers and midrange servers both may be used for the same purpose in networking and that the processing capabilities among the different groups may overlap. Handheld computers are given their own category, although technically they are a subset of personal computers. Yet their growing market and importance for business and home users warrants treating them as a separate category.

Personal Computers

A **personal computer** is a self-contained computer capable of input, processing, output, and storage. A personal computer must have at least one input device, one storage device, one output device, a processor, and memory. The processor, or microprocessor, is contained on a single chip. Recall that the chip is a thin piece of silicon containing electrical circuitry. About the size of a postage stamp, the processor chip serves as the computer's central processing unit (CPU), performing calculations and processing data. Think of the CPU as the "brain" of the computer.

The two major groups of PCs are desktop computers and portable computers. A **desktop computer** is a PC designed to allow the system unit, input devices, output devices, and other connected devices to fit on top of, beside, or under, a user's desk or a table (see Figure 1-18).

FIGURE 1-18: A desktop computer, as the name suggests, is designed to fit on top of a user's work area. Tower type system units can be placed on the floor.

A **portable computer** is a personal computer that is small enough to be carried around. Laptop computers and handheld computers are specially designed portable computers. A **laptop computer** can fit comfortably on the lap. As laptop computers have decreased in size, they are now more commonly referred to as **notebook computers** (see Figure 1-19).

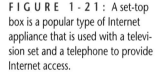

FIGURE 1-19: A notebook computer is a portable computer designed for mobile users, people who frequently move about in their work.

In recent years a variety of wearable computers have been developed. As the name implies, a **wearable computer** is worn somewhere on the body, thereby providing a user with access to mobile computing capabilities and information via the Internet (see Figure 1-20). Futurists predict that wearable computers may be incorporated into clothing items something like the Java Jacket invented in 2000 by Donald Sutherland, a staff engineer at Sun Microsystems. His jacket computer lets him monitor his e-mail, adjust the water temperature in his aquarium, and operate the lights at his home. A six-button keypad is embedded in the cuff.

FIGURE 1-20: This wearable, wireless computer includes a tiny head-mounted monitor and a processor worn around the neck.

The popularity of e-mail and Internet surfing has created a need for small devices collectively called Internet appliances or information appliances. An **Internet appliance** is a limited-function computer capable of connecting to the Internet from the home or another remote location. These appliances are available in a variety of designs, sizes, and colors. Some resemble desktop computers, while others look like cell phones.

FIGURE 1-21: A set-top box is a popular type of Internet appliance that is used with a television set and a telephone to provide Internet access.

Internet appliances typically come ready for use, with software preinstalled by the manufacturer. One type of Internet appliance is a **set-top box** that, as its name implies, is placed on top of or near a television set (see Figure 1-21). Operated with a remote control unit, a set-top box connects to the television and allows Internet access using the TV screen as a display. MSN TV Service, formerly known as WebTV, is the most prevalent set-top box service.

Manufacturers recently began introducing a new type of notebook computer called the tablet PC. A **tablet PC** has a liquid crystal display (LCD) screen on which the user can write using a special-purpose

FIGURE 1-22: A tablet PC is a type of notebook computer that has a liquid crystal display (LCD) screen on which the user can write using a special-purpose pen, or stylus.

pen, or **stylus** (see Figure 1-22). The handwriting is digitized, and the tablet PC can convert it to standard text or it can remain as handwritten text. Tablet PCs also typically have a keyboard and/or a mouse. Tablet PCs rely on **digital ink technology**, where a digitizer (a grid of tiny wires) is laid under or over an LCD screen to create a magnetic field that can capture the movement of the special-purpose pen and record the movement on the LCD screen. The effect is like writing on paper with liquid ink. Once captured, the digitized information can be entered into a computer for processing. Tablet PCs use a special operating system designed for tablet PC technology, such as Microsoft's Tablet PC™ operating system.

Handheld Computers

Even smaller personal computers can fit into the hand (see Figure 1-23). These are known as **handheld computers**, **handhelds**, **pocket PCs**, or **palmtops**. The display and keyboard of these computers are quite small due to space limitations. Some handheld computers contain chips in which both programs and data are stored, eliminating the need for disk drives.

Handheld computers are popular with business travelers. Once back in the office, a user can connect a handheld computer to a larger computer for exchanging information. In recent years a type of handheld computer called a **personal digital assistant (PDA)** has become widely used. With a PDA, a user can perform calculations, keep track of schedules, make appointments, and write memos. Some PDAs use wireless transmitting technology (in the form of radio waves), which allows Internet access from almost any location.

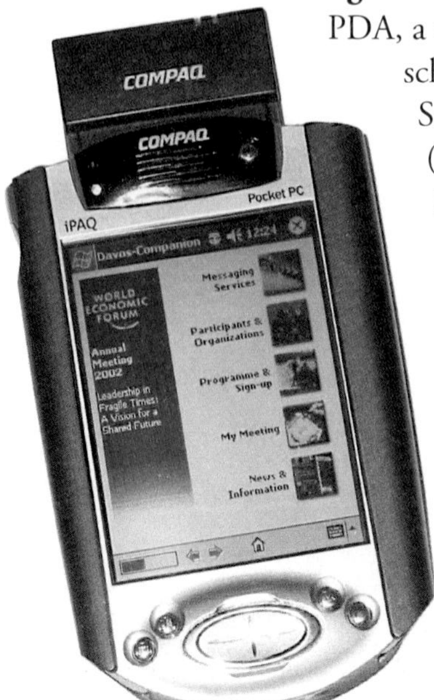

Because of their small keyboards and displays, many PDAs require a pen or stylus for data entry and are known as **pen computers**. Like the tablet PC, a pen computer uses a special kind of software that recognizes human handwriting. Utility meter readers, package delivery persons, and other workers who need to continually move about on their jobs use pen computers to process and store data on the spot.

Some handheld computers are Internet-enabled, meaning they can access the Internet

FIGURE 1-23: A handheld computer is small enough to fit in the palm of a user's hand.

ethics

without wire connections (see Figure 1-24). For example, an **Internet-enabled cell phone**, often called a **smart phone**, allows users to transmit and receive e-mail messages and browse through Web sites designed for display on the phone.

FIGURE 1-24: A variety of Internet-enabled devices allow users to access the Internet, send and receive e-mail messages, and browse the World Wide Web.

Workstations

Workstations resemble desktop personal computers but provide users with more processing power and greater capability (see Figure 1-25). A **workstation** is a high-performance single-user computer with advanced input, output, and storage components that can be networked with other workstations and larger computers.

Workstations are typically used for complex applications that require considerable computing power and high-quality graphics resolution, such as computer-aided design (CAD), computer-assisted manufacturing (CAM), desktop publishing, and software development. Workstations generally come with large high-resolution graphics displays, built-in network capability, and a high-density storage device. Like personal computers, workstations can serve as single-user computers. However, they are typically linked to a network and have access to larger computers, often mainframes.

FIGURE 1-25: A workstation is a high-performance single-user computer with advanced input, output, and storage components that can be networked with other workstations and larger computers.

Midrange Servers

Linked computers are typically connected to a larger and more powerful computer called a **network server**, sometimes referred to as the **host computer**.

FIGURE 1-26: A midrange server is a powerful computer that can accommodate (serve) multiple users in a network. Shown are a variety of midrange servers.

Although the size and capacity of network servers vary considerably, most are midrange rather than large mainframe computers (discussed later). Sun Microsystems, Inc., and Hewlett-Packard Corporation are leading manufacturers of servers.

Midrange servers, formerly known as **minicomputers**, are powerful computers capable of accommodating hundreds of client computers or terminals (users) at the same time. Users can access a server through a terminal or a personal computer. A **terminal** consists of only a monitor and keyboard, with no processing capability of its own. Because it has no processing power and must rely on the processing power of another computer, terminals are often referred to as **dumb terminals**. Midrange servers, such as those shown in Figure 1-26, are widely used in networks to provide users with computing capability and other resources available through the network, such as Internet access, software, data, printers, scanners, and other peripherals.

Mainframe Computers

In a small business environment, a personal computer can be used as a server. Large businesses needing more powerful servers may use mainframe computers. Larger, more powerful, and more expensive than midrange servers, a **mainframe computer** (see Figure 1-27) is capable of accommodating hundreds of network users performing different computing tasks. A mainframe's internal storage can handle hundreds of millions of characters. Mainframe applications are often large and complex. These computers are useful for dealing with large, ever-changing collections of data that can be accessed by many users simultaneously. Like midrange servers, a mainframe computer can also function as a network server.

F I G U R E 1 - 2 7 : A mainframe computer is a large, powerful, and expensive computer system that can accommodate multiple users at the same time. Mainframes and midsize servers are differentiated by their processing capabilities.

Government agencies, banks, universities, and insurance companies use mainframes to handle millions of transactions each day.

Supercomputers

Supercomputers are the Goliaths of the computer industry. A **supercomputer** (see Figure 1-28) is the fastest, most powerful, and most expensive of all computers. Many are capable of performing trillions of calculations in a single second. Performing the same number of calculations on a handheld calculator would take a person two million years.

Supercomputer designers achieve stunning calculation speeds by joining hundreds of separate microprocessors. Many of the machines provide enough disk storage capacity for hundreds of terabytes of data (one **terabyte** is the equivalent of one trillion alphabet letters, numbers, or special characters). In a move to expand supercomputing into the realm of the unimaginable, IBM is working on creating a system called Blue Gene/P that can perform one quadrillion calculations per second, a measure of speed called a **petaflop**. Primary applications include weather forecasting, comparing DNA sequences, creating artificially intelligent robots, and performing financial analyses.

F I G U R E 1 - 2 8 : Super-computers are the world's fastest, most powerful, and most expensive computers, capable of processing huge amounts of data quickly and accommodating thousands of users at the same time.

GLOBE TROTTING

High-tech Solution for a Weighty Issue

For those who have to do heavy lifting on the job, technological help is on the way.

An engineer in Japan has developed a robotic suit that could help ease the burden of moving and shifting hefty items. Called the Power Suit, it's the brainchild of Keijiro Yamamoto. Weighing in at 45 pounds, the Power Suit consists of a backpack computer, airpump, and high-pressure airbags.

Sensors run down the suit's back and limbs, sending muscle movement data to the computer, which then regulates flow from the airpump. The airbags inflate or deflate to assist in the process of lifting and moving heavy objects. In a recent demonstration, a petite woman wearing the suit was able to carry the 150-pound Yamamoto with ease.

The suit would be a boon to workers who risk injury lifting and moving cumbersome objects. And Yamamoto also envisions a streamlined version of the Power Suit that would provide strength and mobility to the disabled.

Source: Kunni, Irene M. "A Muscle Suit You Can Strap Right On," *Business Week*, February 17, 2003.

ALTERNATIVE GROUPING: WIRED VS. WIRELESS

As computers become more powerful and capable of more functions, their differences blur. Some observers already think that the six categories of computers mentioned earlier in this chapter might better be replaced by two categories: wired and wireless.

The first several generations of computers and peripheral devices were connected with wires and cables. Wired environments are still the norm in today's offices, with keyboards, monitors, speakers, printers, and other peripheral devices being connected by wires to the system unit. PCs and workstations, in turn, are linked to each other and to the Internet through a wire telephone line or fiber optic cable.

Although wires and cables are likely to be a feature of the computer world for some time to come, they are increasingly being replaced by newer computing technologies that use infrared signals, radio waves, microwaves, and other signals to communicate wirelessly, without physical connections. The mobility of today's workforce and the need to be able to access the Internet anytime, anywhere have driven the demand for this new generation of computers and communications devices, particularly Internet-enabled cell phones and PDAs. Hybrids also are being developed that combine the most popular features from two or more devices. In May 2003, Japan's J-Phone Co. Ltd. launched the world's first camera-equipped cell phones with a resolution of more than a million pixels, an image clarity offered in low-end digital cameras. A **pixel** is the smallest picture element a monitor can display. Figure 1-29 shows some examples of wireless computers and devices.

Wireless equipment offers more flexibility than wired equipment. As wireless technology improves and as prices come down, we may reach a point where all computers are multifunctional and linked wirelessly, eliminating the need to categorize computers at all.

FIGURE 1-29: Shown are some popular wireless devices for the mobile user.

TECH VISIONARY

Few individuals, if any, have had a greater impact on the computer industry than William Hewlett and David Packard. The business they founded together in Hewlett's garage in 1939 spawned the California high-tech corridor that became known as Silicon Valley. The business was the Hewlett-Packard Corporation, which designs and builds a variety of state-of-the-art computer products, perhaps the best-known being computers and printers. Today, a visitor to almost any computer store will quickly spot Hewlett-Packard products ranging from electronic calculators to Web servers and systems. The "Hewlett" name appears first in the corporate name and on HP products as the result of a coin toss when the two men formed their original partnership.

Hewlett was born May 20, 1913, in Ann Arbor, Michigan. Packard was born September 7, 1912, in Pueblo, Colorado. Both attended Stanford University and were awarded bachelor of arts degrees in 1934. Packard stayed at Stanford to earn a master's degree in electrical engineering, while Hewlett received his master's in electrical engineering at the Massachusetts Institute of Technology.

William Hewlett

HP's first product was a resistance-capacitance audio oscillator based on a design developed by Hewlett when he was a graduate student. This first product was sold to Walt Disney who used eight of them in the production of *Fantasia*. The company's first "plant" was a small garage in Palo Alto, California, with an initial capital investment of $538.

Through the years, both Hewlett and Packard held various corporate offices and government positions and also served as trustees on corporate and college boards. Each received numerous awards both in this country and abroad. In 1993, Packard retired as chairman of the board at Hewlett-Packard Corporation at which time he was named Chairman Emeritus, a title he held until his death in 1996. Hewlett served as company president, vice-chairman of the board, and was named Director Emeritus in 1987. He passed away in July 2000 at the age of 87.

David Packard

Both men leave behind a remarkable legacy of technological innovation and business strategy. Together they built a company known worldwide for innovation and for computer products that, through the years, have been models widely envied among computer engineers.

Source: The Biography Channel.

ON THE HORIZON

Computers, networks, the Internet, and the Web are unquestionably among the most important technological developments in history. Cell phones, wireless personal digital assistants, and the use of the Internet for communications are becoming commonplace. But what about the future? Where is computing technology heading? Social thinkers, futurists, and computer experts may not agree on specific predictions, but their thoughts tend to converge in the area of technology trends we can expect to occur in the first decade of the twenty-first century.

Embedded Computers Everywhere

Expect embedded computers in all areas of personal and work life in the future. Consumers will be able to scan foods and other types of products embedded with special chips to get information on product content, age, and freshness. Before long, every citizen will probably carry a small plastic card housing a tiny microchip that contains complete medical, credit, military, and driving records. "Smart highways" embedded with millions of tiny sensors may alleviate driving worries because they will guide cars speeding along at 120 mph, all the time aware of surrounding traffic.

On-Demand Computing

Some computer industry leaders, including strategists at IBM and American Express, contend that information technology is maturing and entering a phase in which corporations will buy computing resources the way they purchase utilities—paying only for as much as they use. No doubt the downturn in IT spending in the early 2000s helped pave the way for this buy-as-you-go approach, but the ready availability of computing resources over the Internet has also played a role. Called "on-demand computing," the trend means reduced fixed costs and greater flexibility for businesses.

Expanding Use of Wireless Devices

Personal digital assistants (PDAs), Internet-enabled cell phones, combination handheld/cell phones, and a variety of other wireless devices will become the computer devices of choice for an increasingly mobile workforce. Industry researchers IDC and the Gartner Group predict that the worldwide spending in the handheld market is projected to balloon from about $116 billion in 2001 to $265 billion in 2005.

Dubbed "information-in-an-instant," the trend toward the dominance of wireless devices is apparent in moves by prominent companies such as Microsoft

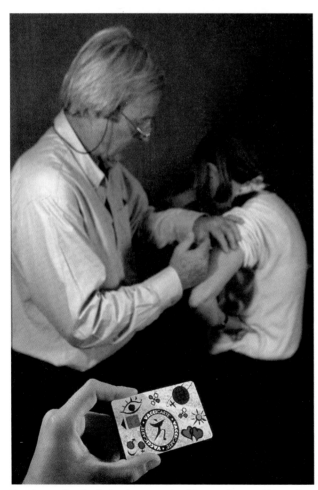

Futurists predict that before long, people will carry a "personal history" card embedded with a microchip that contains one's medical, credit, military, and driving records.

Worldwide spending in the hand-held market is projected to reach $265 billion in 2005.

Corporation and Starbucks Corporation, who have established wireless local area networks that allow workers and customers to browse the Internet from their individual locations. Another wireless technology, called **telematics**, will be incorporated into cars so that drivers can access their corporate networks while commuting. And new telecommunications media will provide Internet access from mobile phones that is six times faster than the access speeds today's systems can achieve. In short, communications and business transactions will be possible anytime, anywhere.

Faster Communication and a Shrinking Global Community

The number of Internet users will grow dramatically, as will the number of ways this information-sharing medium is used. Consider these comparisons:

- Radio took 38 years to reach 50 million listeners.
- Television took 13 years to reach 50 million viewers.
- The Internet took only 5 years to reach 50 million users.

Within the present decade, almost-instant Internet connections will become available throughout the United States, allowing information to be accessed in fractions of a second. Experts predict that by the year 2010, the dollar amount of online shopping will represent more than 40 percent of all sales. Eventually almost everyone in the world will have a personal Web site, and distance learning will become common for people of all ages. For the twenty-first century, it is safe to say that *virtually* anything is possible.

chapter summary

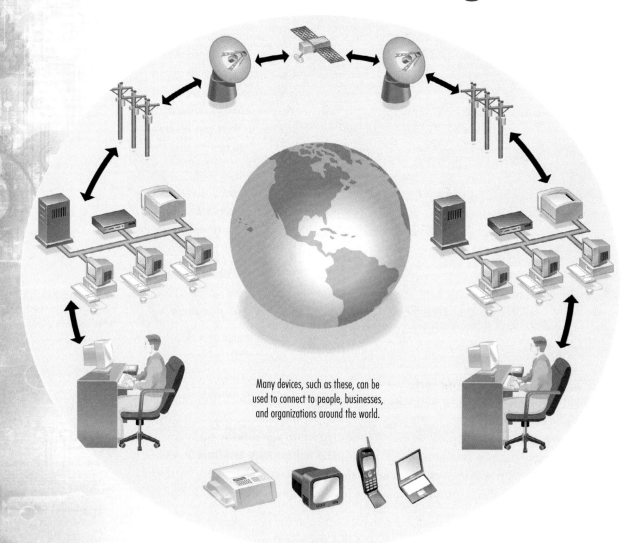

Many devices, such as these, can be used to connect to people, businesses, and organizations around the world.

Immersed in Digital Technology

We are living in a digital world in which computer technology increasingly powers the devices of daily life, including high-definition televisions (HDTVs), VCRs, microwave ovens, watches, cell phones, and automobiles. Embedded chips, computers, networks, and the Internet and World Wide Web enable us to communicate globally. No digital device has exerted a greater impact on our lives than computers. A **computer** is an electronic device that operates under the control of programmed instructions stored in its memory, accepting data (input) that is manipulated (processed) according to the instructions and output as information, which may be stored for future use.

The Computer Advantage

Computers offer advantages in the areas of **accuracy**, **speed**, **versatility**, **storage**, and **communications**. As a result, they are widely used in homes, schools, the workplace, and in society for communicating, managing finances, analyzing data, planning, researching, and for hundreds of other purposes and applications. The Internet and the World Wide Web, in which networks of computers around the world are linked together, continue to play a dominant role in all areas of human activity.

How Computers Work

Data are raw, unorganized facts and figures. Data entered into a computer consists of one or more of the following types: **text**, **graphics**, **audio**, and **video**. **Information** is data that has been processed (manipulated, organized, or arranged) in a way that converts the data into useful forms. Using a computer to convert data into useful information is called **information processing** (also called **data processing**). The **information processing cycle** involves the actions of **input**, **processing**, **output**, and **storage**.

Computers and Computer Systems

The term "computer" identifies only the **system unit**, the part of a computer system that processes data into information. A **computer system** includes the system unit along with input, output, storage, and communications devices.

Components of a Computer System

Computer system components can be divided into two broad groups: hardware and software. **Hardware** includes all of the physical components that comprise the

computer and the **peripheral devices** connected to it. The main hardware components are the s**ystem unit**, **input devices**, **output devices**, **storage devices**, and **communications devices**.

Computer **software** consists of programs containing instructions that direct the operation of the computer system and programs that enable users to perform specific applications. The main types of software are **system software**, consisting of the **operating system** and **utility software**; **application software**; and **communications software**.

Categories of Computers

A **personal computer** is a self-contained computer capable of input, processing, output,

CHAPTER 1

Webcam

monitor

microphone

CD drive

floppy disk d

system unit

keyboard

mouse

speakers

and storage. A **handheld computer** fits comfortably in a user's hand. A **workstation** is a high-performance single-user computer with advanced input, output, and storage components that can be networked with other workstations and larger computers. A **midrange server**, formerly known as a **minicomputer**, is a powerful computer capable of accommodating hundreds of client computers or terminals (users) at the same time. A **mainframe computer** is capable of accommodating hundreds of network users performing different computing tasks.

A **supercomputer** is the fastest, most powerful, and most expensive of all computers.

Alternative Grouping: Wired vs. Wireless

Computers may also be categorized as either wired or wireless. **Wired computers** and devices use wires (cables) to obtain needed power (electricity). **Wireless computers** and devices rely on alternative power sources, such as batteries.

KEY TERMS

application software, 20
audio data, 14
central processing unit (CPU), 18
chip, 6
communications device, 20
communications software, 21
computer, 6
computer system, 16
data, 12
data processing (information processing), 15
desktop computer, 22
digital, 5
digital ink technology, 24
embedded computer (embedded chip), 6
general-purpose computer, 6
GIGO (garbage in—garbage out), 8
graphics data, 14
handheld computer (handheld, pocket PC, or palmtop), 24
hard copy, 19
hardware, 17
information, 14
information processing (data processing), 15
information processing cycle, 15
input, 16
input device, 19
Internet, 10
Internet appliance, 23
Internet-enabled cell phone (smart phone), 25
Internet service provider (ISP), 21
laptop computer (notebook computer), 23
local area network (LAN), 10
mainframe computer, 26
media, 20
memory (primary storage), 18
microcomputer (personal computer, PC), 7
midrange server (minicomputer), 26
modem, 20
motherboard, 18

multi-user computer system, 17
network, 10
network server (host computer), 25
operating system, 20
output, 16
output device, 19
pen computers, 24
peripheral devices, 17
personal computer (PC), 7
personal digital assistant (PDA), 24
petaflop, 27
pixel, 28
portable computer, 23
processing, 16
processor (microprocessor), 18
program, 6
search engine, 12
set-top box, 23
single-user computer system, 17
soft copy, 19
software, 20
storage, 16
storage device (secondary storage), 20
stylus, 24
supercomputer, 27
system software, 20
system unit, 16
tablet PC, 23
telematic, 31
terabyte, 27
terminal (dumb terminal), 26
text data, 14
utility software, 20
video data, 14
wearable computer, 23
Web browser, 21
Web page, 12
wide area network (WAN), 10
workstation , 25
World Wide Web (the Web), 12

Page numbers indicate where terms are first cited in the chapter. A complete list of key terms with definitions can be found in the Glossary at the end of the book.

chapter exercises

The following chapter exercises, along with new activities and information, are also offered in the *Computers: Understanding Technology* Internet Resource Center at www.emcp.com.

EXPLORING WINDOWS

Tutorial 1 demonstrates how to start up a Windows-based PC and log in with a user name, if required. It also explains the proper way to shut down the PC to avoid data loss and file corruption. (See the Exploring Windows tutorials section at the end of the book.)

TERMS CHECK: MATCHING
Write the letter of the correct answer on the line before each numbered item.

a. application software
b. network
c. Web page
d. utility software
e. Internet
f. data
g. World Wide Web
h. software

i. personal computer
j. information
k. computer
l. Internet service provider
m. operating system
n. hardware
o. supercomputer

_____ 1. A collection of raw, unorganized content in the form of words, numbers, sounds, or images.

_____ 2. A global system of linked computer networks that allows users to easily move from one location to another using programmed links.

_____ 3. A worldwide network of computers linked together via communications software and media for the purpose of sharing information.

_____ 4. Data that is organized to be meaningful and potentially useful.

_____ 5. Programs that enable users to perform specific tasks.

_____ 6. The most important piece of software in a personal computer system.

_____ 7. A business that has a permanent connection to the Internet and provides temporary access to individuals and others for free or for a fee.

_____ 8. An electronic document stored at a location on the Web.

_____ 9. A computer designed for use by a single individual and capable of performing its own input, processing, output, and storage.

_____ 10. Programs containing instructions that direct the operation of the computer system and the documentation that explains how to use the programs.

_____ 11. The largest, most powerful, and most expensive category of computers.

_____ 12. Programs that perform administrative tasks, such as checking for computer viruses.

_____ 13. A computer's physical components and devices.

_____ 14. An electronic device that accepts input (programs and data), processes the data into information, stores programs and information, and delivers output (information) to users.

_____ 15. A group of two or more computers, software, and other devices connected by means of one or more communications media.

TECHNOLOGY ILLUSTRATED: IDENTIFY THE PROCESS

What process is illustrated in this drawing? Identify the process and write a paragraph describing it.

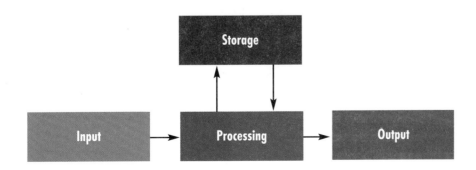

KNOWLEDGE CHECK: MULTIPLE CHOICE
Circle the letter of the best answer from those provided.

1. A small electronic chip programmed by a manufacturer for use in another product, such as a digital camera or microwave oven, is called a(n)

   a. programmed chip.
   b. embedded chip.
   c. component chip.
   d. storage chip.

2. A popular communications device that converts information in computer format into a format that can be carried by communications media, such as a telephone line, is a

   a. laptop computer.
   b. Tablet PC.
   c. modem.
   d. microprocessor.

3. A software program that enables a user to locate and retrieve specific information on the Web, such as the feeding habits of lions, is known as a

   a. utility program.
   b. communications program.
   c. data transfer program.
   d. search engine.

4. The usefulness of computers can be attributed to their speed, accuracy, versatility, reliability, storage, and

   a. communications capabilities.
   b. peripheral components.
   c. decreasing prices.
   d. connectability.

5. Technologies that consist of two or more computers, devices, and software connected by means of one or more communications media, such as telephone lines, are called

   a. computers.
   b. communications.
   c. information processing.
   d. networks.

6. A self-contained computer capable of performing its own input, processing, output, and storage is called a(n)

   a. embedded computer.
   b. digital chip.

c. dual-purpose processor.
d. personal computer.

7. A computer component contained on a single chip, or thin piece of silicon containing electrical circuitry, and serving as the computer's central processing unit is called a

a. wired component.
b. silicon chip.
c. microprocessor.
d. circuit chip.

8. A type of handheld computer that has become widely used in recent years is a

a. personal digital assistant (PDA).
b. cell phone.
c. midrange server.
d. mainframe computer.

9. A type of computer that uses a liquid crystal display screen, stylus, and digital ink technology is called a

a. peripheral device.
b. smart phone.
c. tablet PC.
d. supercomputer.

10. The fastest, most powerful, and most expensive of all computers is the

a. personal computer.
b. supercomputer.
c. mainframe computer.
d. midrange server.

11. Data that has been processed into a useful form is called

a. digital data.
b. input.
c. information.
d. output.

12. Data that consist of still pictures, still photographs, and mathematical models are called

a. image data.
b. visual data.
c. compressed data.
d. graphics data.

13. A computer designed and built to perform multiple functions and tasks that allows users to complete a variety of applications is known as a

   a. versatile computer.
   b. general-purpose computer.
   c. special-purpose computer.
   d. hybrid computer.

14. The main circuit board inside the cabinet of a personal computer that provides for the installation and connection of other electronic components is the

   a. modem.
   b. secondary circuit board.
   c. motherboard.
   d. attachment board.

15. The most important piece of software in a computer system is the

   a. operating system.
   b. application software.
   c. utility software.
   d. communications software.

THINGS THAT THINK: BRAINSTORMING NEW USES
In groups or individually, contemplate the following questions and develop as many answers as you can.

1. Futurists hold that computers will be everywhere. For example, bridges will have computers that will alert city planners when part of a bridge is weakening or too stressed and in need of repair. What other objects can you think of that should have the same type of warning or notice capability built into the device?

2. Many futurists claim that we will be wearing computers in the future. What job problems could be addressed if we start wearing computers that are capable of collecting and analyzing data (tracking inventory, for example)?

KEY PRINCIPLES: COMPLETION
Fill in the blanks with the appropriate words or phrases.

1. The term _____ refers to information represented by the numbers 1 (on) and 0 (off).

2. A(n) _____ is a type of electronic chip found in many of the products we use that performs a specific function or action.

3. In a personal computer, the term "computer" identifies only the _____, the part of a computer system that processes data into information.

4. A collection of computers and devices linked together by software and communications devices and media is called a(n) _____.

5. A(n) _____, also called the host computer, is a computer to which other computers are connected and on which programs, data, and information are stored.

6. A(n) _____ connects computers over a large geographical area.

7. Memory, also called _____, consists of small electronic chips that provide temporary storage for instructions and data during processing.

8. A monitor produces output in _____ form, a type of output that can be viewed, but not physically handled.

9. Software that tells the computer how to operate is called _____.

10. Software that consists of programs that perform administrative tasks, such as checking the computer's components to determine whether each is working properly, is called _____.

11. The most powerful and expensive computers are classified as _____.

12. A type of software program that locates and retrieves requested information from the Web is called a(n) _____.

13. A _____ is a high-end, single-user computer with advanced input, output, and storage components.

14. The processor and memory chips are housed on a computer's _____.

15. CD drives, hard disk drives, and floppy disk drives are examples of _____ devices.

TECH ARCHITECTURE: LABEL THE DRAWING

In this illustration of a computer system, label the devices as input, output, processing, or storage devices.

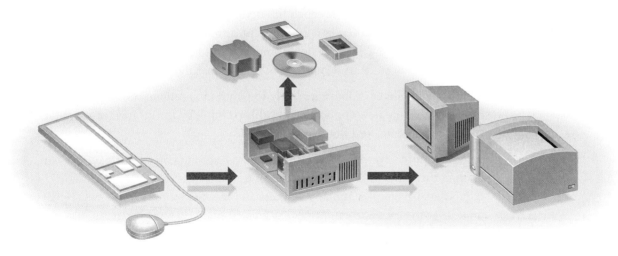

TECHNO LITERACY: RESEARCH AND WRITING
Develop appropriate written responses based on your research for each item.

1. Assume you are offered a free personal computer system of your choice and you are to select the input, output, and storage devices you want. Create a list of uses for your new computer. Then research various computer systems and components advertised in magazines and on the Internet. Choose a computer system that will meet your needs and write a paragraph explaining why you selected a particular personal computer system.

2. Knowing that handheld computers vary in operating system (Palm, PocketPC, etc.), memory, weight, price, and in other ways, create a table or chart that includes the manufacturer's name, handheld model, operating system, weight, and price. Visit a computer store in your area and examine five handhelds being displayed. Using the chart you prepared, record information about each model. Based upon your analysis of the handheld computers you examined, which would you prefer as your own? Are there additional features that affected your decision? Explain the reasons for your decision.

3. The Internet provides easy access to a wealth of information and is considered to be a timesaver for busy people. Prepare a written report explaining what aspects of your life have been simplified or improved by the use of the Internet. Include your predictions for additional Internet capabilities that you expect to use in the next five years.

4. Many projects are underway to expand the use of wearable computers in the workplace, in military applications, and for personal use. Using your school library or other sources of information, research the uses of wearable computers. Based on your findings, write an article describing the application of wearable computers to enhance our daily lives.

TECHNOLOGY ISSUES: TEAM PROBLEM-SOLVING
In groups, brainstorm possible solutions to the issues presented.

1. Today's classrooms are made up of more diverse students and students with a wider range of performance capabilities compared to previous decades. In fact, some theorists claim there is a 200 percent differential in the learning rate in our classrooms today. Imagine how computers will help instructors teach so many different types of students. Consider both traditional and distance learning modes.

2. Artificially intelligent robots are likely to play a large role in our future. What are some possible new applications of this technology in the areas of manufacturing, health care, and home maintenance?

3. Since computers were first introduced, there has been considerable debate concerning their effect on employment. For example, some people argue that computers have replaced many workers and are, therefore, a social evil. Others argue that the computer industry has created many new high-paying jobs in the technology field. In your group, discuss both sides of this issue: Have computers had an overall good effect or bad effect on society?

MINING DATA: INTERNET RESEARCH AND REPORTING

Conduct Internet searches to find information described in the activities below. Write a brief report summarizing your research results. Be sure to document your sources, using the following format, which is recommended by the Modern Language Association (MLA):

- author's name (if known)
- title of document, in quotation marks
- title of Internet page or online periodical, in italics (if not titled, put Home Page or give the name of the organization that created and maintains the page)
- date of publication (for an article) or date site was last updated, if available
- date you accessed the site
- URL, in angle brackets < >

Example: Sanders, Jill M. "The Space Agency Launches a Winner," *NASA News*, January 2004. March 2004 <http://www.mit.edu:000/people/glenn.html>.

1. Using online news sources, select a specific event that occurred in one country (other than the United States) within the past year. Find three separate news reports of the event and describe how each media source perceived the event. What are the similarities? What are the differences? What are the possible reasons for the differences?

2. What kinds of information are available at the Web site of your state government? Your summary should discuss the information available on a particular date.

3. Research the topic of high-tech stock investments as discussed in online news sources. What is the current trend as of the date of your research?

TECHNOLOGY TIMELINE: PREDICTING NEXT STEPS

Look at the timeline below outlining the major benchmarks in the development of computing. Research this topic and fill in as many steps as you can. What do you think the next steps will be? Complete the timeline through the year 2030.

1937   Dr. John Atanasoff and Clifford Berry design and build the first electronic digital computer.

1958   Jack Kilby, an engineer at Texas Instruments, invents the integrated circuit, thereby laying the foundation for fast computers and large-capacity memory.

1981   IBM enters the personal computer field by introducing the IBM-PC.

2004   Wireless computer devices, including keyboards, mice, and wireless home networks, become widely accepted among users.

ETHICAL DILEMMAS: GROUP DISCUSSION AND DEBATE
As a class or within an assigned group, discuss the following ethical dilemma.

The term "plagiarism" refers to the unauthorized and illegal copying of another person's writing or creative work. For example, a student may copy an author's writing from a magazine article or from a Web page and submit the report without giving the original author credit. Also, an individual can illegally retrieve an artist's recordings from Web sites and replay the music again and again, thereby depriving the original artist of royalties.

In your group, discuss the issue of downloading copyrighted music from the Internet for one's personal use. Should such practices be legal or illegal? Should the user be required to pay the copyright owner each and every time the music is replayed? Should there be legal penalties involved?

ANSWERS TO TERMS CHECK AND KEY PRINCIPLES QUESTIONS
Terms Check: 1 – f; 2 – g; 3 – e; 4 – j; 5 – a; 6 – m; 7 – l; 8 – c; 9 – i; 10 – h; 11 – o; 12 – d; 13 – n; 14 – k; 15 – b

Key Principles: 1 – digital; 2 – embedded chip; 3 – system unit; 4 – network; 5 – network server; 6 – wide area network; 7 – primary storage; 8 – soft copy; 9 – system software; 10 – utility software; 11 – supercomputers; 12 – search engine; 13 – workstation; 14 – motherboard; 15 – secondary storage

CHAPTER 2
INPUT AND PROCESSING

UNDERSTANDING TECHNOLOGY

learning objectives

- Define the terms "input" and "processing"

- Categorize input devices for personal computers and explain their functions

- Identify the main components of the system unit and explain their functions

- Explain the four basic operations of a machine cycle

- Describe the different types of computer memory and their functions

- Discuss the importance of expanding a computer's capabilities and explain how it can be accomplished

key concepts

- What Is Input?

- What Is Information Processing?

- How Do Computers Process Data?

- Understanding the System Unit

- Understanding Internal Memory

- Expanding a Computer's Capabilities

CYBER SCENARIO

Jenna Winbon is suddenly awakened by upbeat music coming from the speakers of the computer-controlled sound system in her home. The CD player, along with most of the appliances and electronic devices in her home, is managed by a computer system called a home information infrastructure.

Sitting on her bedside and thinking about the day's priority tasks at the office, she hears the coffeemaker brewing a pot of fresh coffee. In the bathroom the tub begins filling with water heated to a preprogrammed temperature. Leaving her bedroom, Jenna glances at the flat-panel TV screen on the wall and remembers she had recorded the headline news and financial reports from her favorite predawn newscasts. She makes a mental note to watch them later, when she has more time. The more urgent need is to remind her company's purchasing manager to order the new notebook computers for the sales force before the local vendor's special offer expires.

After typing a brief message on her Web phone, she presses the *Send* button and returns to her get-ready-for-work ritual.

Finishing the last bite of her bagel, Jenna gathers her briefcase along with her Web phone and heads for the garage. As she passes the wall clock in the utility room, she is reminded on a digital display that she has an appointment with an advertising copywriter in 35 minutes.

Opening the door from the utility room to the garage automatically starts Jenna's car and opens the garage door simultaneously. As she backs out of the garage, she notices the car's interior temperature is approaching the 74 degrees she had selected on the Preferences menu of the controls system. Feeling a bit thirsty, Jenna asks her built-in navigation system to "find the nearest Starbucks." After noting the location displayed on the retractable screen in the dashboard, she turns her attention to the CD she had selected, enjoying the music and anticipating the taste of a latte.

"Now," she thinks, "if only my appointments and meetings at the office will go as smoothly."

Computer systems similar to the one in Jenna's home may soon become a reality within reach of average consumers. Increasingly, builders are including high-speed cables in the walls of new houses to allow for Internet access and networked media systems throughout the home. Called "structured wiring," this hidden cable system allows flexibility in room design and accommodates state-of-the-art technology such as video and audio monitoring and remotely controlled lighting, cooling, and heating. Future home networks may also offer electronic health checkers that can send a user's health data to a clinic via an Internet-connected blood pressure cuff or thermometer. Refrigerators may be linked to food caterers and doorbells linked to home security services. Home systems such as these will add yet another dimension to the term "cyber space."

INPUT AND PROCESSING TECHNOLOGY

Chapter 1 explained that the process of turning data into useful information is called the *information processing cycle*, and that the four steps of the cycle are input, processing, output, and storage. Performing each step involves the use of specific components and devices, all of which are grouped under the term "hardware." In this chapter you will learn about many of the devices for entering data and programs into the computer and about the computer itself—how it processes data into information and which hardware components are involved in that process.

WHAT IS INPUT?

The term *input* refers to any data or instructions entered into a computer enabling the computer to perform a desired task. Users can input data and instructions using a variety of methods and devices, such as typing on the keyboard or speaking into a microphone connected to a computer. In fast-food restaurants, workers input customers' orders by pressing a key that represents a food item or touching a picture of the item on the computer screen.

INPUT DEVICES

An input device is a hardware device that allows users to enter programs, data, and commands into a computer system. The program or application being used determines the type of input device needed. For example, many computer games require a joystick, whereas writing a letter to another person requires a keyboard. Keyboards, point-and-click devices, and scanners are among the more popular input devices. Every desktop or notebook computer system usually includes at least two input devices.

The Keyboard

The most common input device is the **keyboard**, an electronically controlled hardware component used to enter alphanumeric data (letters, numbers, and special characters). The two main keyboard types are alphanumeric and special-function.

Alphanumeric Keyboards

The keys on most alphanumeric keyboards are arranged as they are on a typewriter, although computer keyboards typically contain additional keys. Keyboards for desktop computers contain from 101 to 105 keys that are pressed to enter data into the computer. Keyboards for smaller computers, such as notebook computers, contain fewer keys. In addition to keys for alphabet letters and symbols, most keyboards contain

- function keys
- special-purpose keys
- cursor-control (arrow) keys
- numeric keys arranged in keypad form

Figure 2-1 shows a typical keyboard with the special key groups and their functions. The placement of the specialty keys varies among hardware manufacturers.

Function keys, labeled F1, F2, F3, and so on, allow a user to quickly access commands and functions.

Numeric keypad, which perfoms the same functions as a calculator, is used for entering numbers quickly.

Special-purpose keys, such as Control, Alternate, and Delete, are used in conjunction with another key to enter commands into the computer.

Cursor-control keys govern the movement of the cursor on the screen and include the Up Arrow, Down Arrow, Right Arrow, and Left Arrow keys on most keyboards.

FIGURE 2-1:
A keyboard, similar to a typewriter keyboard, is used to enter alphanumeric data (words and numbers) and special characters into a computer.

Special-Function Keyboards

Special-function keyboards are designed for specific applications involving simplified, rapid data input. For example, most fast-food restaurant cash registers are equipped with special-function keyboards. Rather than type the name and price of a specific sandwich, the employee need only press the key marked "Fish Sandwich" to record the sale (see Figure 2-2). Special-function keyboards enable fast-food employees, ticket agents, and retail clerks to enter transactions into their computer systems very quickly.

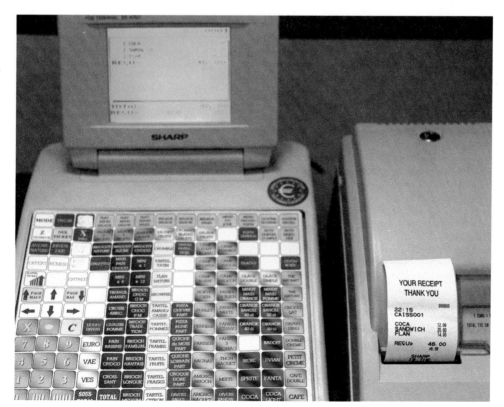

FIGURE 2-2:
Many businesses use special-function keyboards to increase employee efficiency.

CHAPTER 2

The Mouse and Other Point-and-Click Devices

Operating systems such as Windows and Macintosh incorporate a **graphical user interface (GUI)** containing buttons, drop-down menus, and icons to represent program features and commands. The user issues commands by pointing at an icon or menu item with a **mouse**, which after the keyboard is the second most common input device (see Figure 2-3). Moving the mouse causes the **mouse pointer** (cursor) on the computer screen to move in a corresponding way (see Figure 2-4). If you visualize the computer mouse as a small oval with a long cable tail, you can understand how it got its name.

A mouse plugs directly into the computer or keyboard. A mouse used on the Macintosh generally has one button, while a mouse used on a PC generally has two, although three-button models are also available. The button on the left side is used to signal a choice by a single click or a double click, depending on the

FIGURE 2-3: A mouse is an input device that, when moved about on a flat surface, causes a pointer on the screen to move in the same direction.

FIGURE 2-4: A mouse pointer allows users to make selections from a menu and to activate programs represented by icons displayed on the screen.

MOUSE POINTER
When the user moves the mouse (below) on the mouse pad, a pointer on the display screen moves in the same direction.

MOUSE PAD
The user slides the mouse on the smooth surface of the mouse pad.

situation. The button on the right side is used to display special options and menus. On the underside of a mouse is a rubber-coated ball that glides over a rubberized pad with a smooth fabric surface, called a **mouse pad** (refer to Figure 2-4). An **optical mouse** (see Figure 2-5) uses a light sensor instead of a mouse ball to track movement. This type of mouse can be moved around on nearly any smooth surface except glass, so no mouse pad is necessary. A **foot mouse** allows people with carpal tunnel syndrome or other hand or wrist injuries to use a computer.

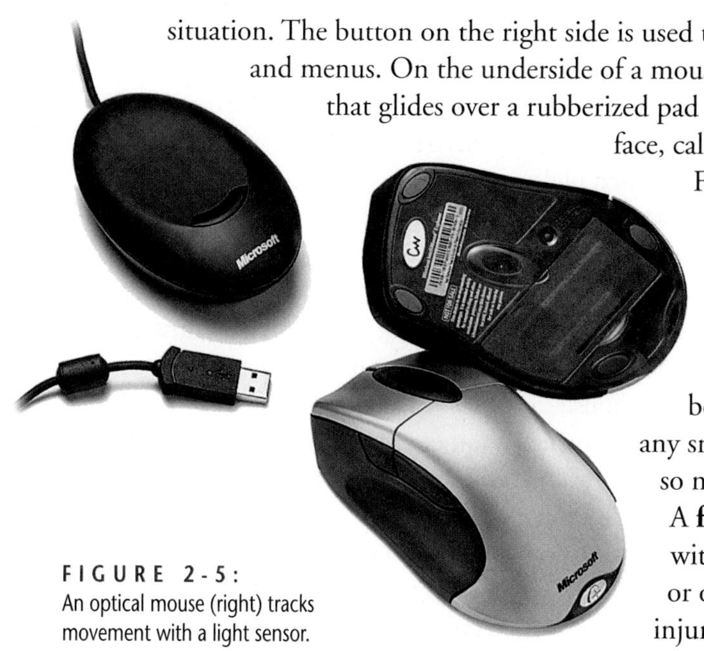

FIGURE 2-5:
An optical mouse (right) tracks movement with a light sensor.

Wireless Keyboard and Mouse

In addition to standard keyboards that connect to the system unit, computer manufacturers also offer wireless keyboards for customers who want to avoid the tangle of telephone and computer device wires that seem to clutter the typical work space. A recently released product called the Microsoft Wireless Optical Desktop for **Bluetooth** (a technology that uses infrared light signals to send information) combines a mouse and a wireless keyboard that includes several extra Windows function keys. Both components require two AA batteries and will operate at distances up to 30 feet from the computer. The keyboard-mouse combination only works with Windows XP, however.

Trackballs

The trackball is an input device similar to a mouse. A **trackball** consists of a plastic sphere resting on rollers, inset in a small external case (see Figure 2-6). The trackball is often described as an upside-down mouse, although unlike the mouse it remains stationary. Users move the ball with their fingers or palm. One or more buttons for choosing options are incorporated into the design of the trackball.

The main advantage of using a trackball is that it requires less desk space than a mouse. A trackball is therefore a good choice for people working in confined areas. Trackballs also require less arm movement, making them useful to those with limited arm mobility. Portable computer packages often include trackballs. Some can be mounted on the side of a laptop or notebook computer so the owner can use the device while sitting in an airplane seat or another confined area. Other portable computers now come with built-in miniature trackballs installed in the same unit as the keyboard. In either case, users can install a regular desktop mouse if they find the trackball inconvenient.

FIGURE 2-6: The ball in a trackball is contained on top of the device or on the side. Rolling the ball moves the pointer on the screen.

Touch Pads and Touch Screens

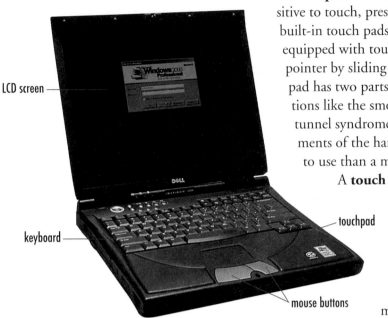

A **touch pad**, also called **track pad**, is a small, flat device that is sensitive to touch, pressure, or motion. Many portable computers have built-in touch pads, as shown in Figure 2-7. Notebook computers equipped with touch pads enable users to move the on-screen pointer by sliding a finger across the surface of the pad. A touch pad has two parts: one part acts as a button, while the other functions like the smooth surface of a mouse pad. People with carpal tunnel syndrome, a painful condition caused by repetitive movements of the hand and wrist, find a touch pad or trackball easier to use than a mouse.

LCD screen

keyboard

touchpad

mouse buttons

A **touch screen** is another example of using sensing technologies. It allows a user to make selections from among a group of options displayed on a screen by pressing a finger against the chosen option. For example, a bank customer can begin making a withdrawal by touching the *Withdraw* option on the ATM (automated teller machine) screen. Touch screens are widely used in ATMs and in kiosks at retail outlets.

FIGURE 2-7: With a touch pad the user traces a finger on the pad, letting the finger function as the mouse. The touch pad also includes a button for clicking commands.

Joysticks

The **joystick** (named after the control lever used to fly fighter planes) is a small box containing a vertical lever that moves the graphics cursor correspondingly on the screen when pushed in a certain direction (see Figure 2-8). It is often used for computer games. Some joysticks have a button in the tip for activation by the user's thumb. Pressing this button performs such actions as firing a game weapon at an object on the screen. Notebook computer users have recently become accustomed to a unique type of joystick, called a "pointing lever," or simply a "pointer." It is about the size of a pencil eraser and fits between the G and H keys of the keyboard (see Figure 2-9). By placing the index finger on top of the lever, users can slightly

FIGURE 2-8: A joystick is an input device used for moving objects about on the computer screen. Many types of computer games require a joystick.

pointing lever

FIGURE 2-9: Some notebook computer keyboards contain a small lever to move a pointer on the screen. Pushing or pulling lightly on the lever adjusts the pointer on the screen.

TECH VISIONARY

In 1965 Gordon Moore predicted that the number of transistors the industry would be able to squeeze onto a computer chip would double every year, while the price per transistor would drop just as dramatically. This prediction, now known as Moore's Law, held true until 1975, when he updated the prediction to a doubling every two years. The performance increase is unprecedented in any other industry in human history, and plays a large part in driving our modern economy. The total number of transistors on a chip has gone from hundreds to millions since 1970, an improvement making today's chips more than 5,000 times more powerful.

Essentially, Moore's Law still holds and will continue to do so for the immediate future. Experts debate how long we can continue to shrink transistors, as some components of the newest transistors (not yet in production) are only three atoms wide. Logically, the smallest possible transistor could be measured in the space of a few atoms, but what will Intel do for an encore after this goal is achieved within the next 10 to 20 years?

Moore was born in San Francisco, California, in 1929. He earned a B.S. in chemistry from the University of California at Berkeley and later a Ph.D. in chemistry and physics from the California

Institute of Technology. He is considered a founding father of Silicon Valley, as he was a cofounder of chip maker Intel Corporation in 1968 and originally served as executive vice president. He became president and CEO in 1975, then chairman and CEO in 1979. Currently, his title is Chairman Emeritus.

Source: <http://www.intel.com>text.

FIGURE 2-10: Some PDAs include a stylus for choosing menu options and writing on the screen.

push or pull it to adjust the pointer on the screen. This type of joystick eliminates a bulky external mouse or joystick and allows the hand to remain close to the keyboard.

Pens and Tablets

Some people complain that drawing with a mouse is like drawing with a bar of soap, although exquisite computer art has been generated using a mouse. Artists, engineers, and others who need precise control over an input device may choose instead to use a **digitizing pen** and a **drawing tablet** to simulate drawing on paper. Owners of personal digital assistants (PDAs) such as the Palm™ handheld and the Handspring™ Visor also may use a stylus, or special pen, to choose menu options and to write information in the screen (see Figure 2-10).

Graphics Tablets

A **graphics tablet** is a flat tablet mapmakers or engineers use to trace precise drawings (see Figure 2-11). Hundreds of tiny intersecting wires forming an electronic matrix are embedded in the tablet surface. The intersection of two wires represents a specific location, or address, each of which has a value of "0." To capture an image, users grasp a stylus or crosshair cursor and trace an image or drawing placed on the tablet surface. As the user draws on the tablet surface with the pen, the values of intersections touched by the pen change to "1s." During the process the exact locations of the 0s and 1s are stored in the computer's memory and can be saved on a storage medium. When the drawing is displayed on the screen or on paper, all "1" bits are displayed as tiny dots, which collectively represent the image. After tracing streets, parks, highways, or other images, users can input location labels with the keyboard.

FIGURE 2-11: Graphics tablets are widely used by engineers, drafters, and others who need to create precise, detailed drawings.

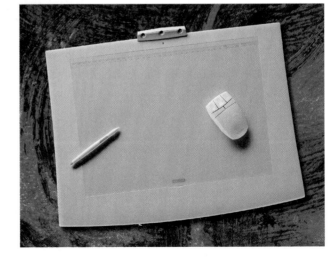

CHAPTER 2

Optical Scanners

An **optical scanner** (or **scanner**) is a light-sensing electronic device that uses lasers to read and capture printed text and images, such as photographs and drawings. The scanned text or image is created and stored as a file rather than as a paper document. Once scanned, the text or image can be displayed, edited, printed, stored on a disk, inserted into another document, or sent as an attachment to an e-mail message. The scanned material is stored as a matrix of rows and columns of dots, called a **bitmap**. Each dot consists of one or more bits of data. The greater the number of bits comprising a dot, the clearer the scanned image. The density of each dot helps determine the quality (resolution) of the captured image. Modern scanners can capture text and images at resolutions ranging from 30 to 48 bits per dot.

Resolution also depends on the number of dots, or **pixels**, per inch (a pixel is the smallest picture element that a monitor can display). The higher the number of dots (pixels), the sharper and clearer the captured image when displayed or printed. Resolution is measured in **dots per inch** (dpi) and expressed as the number of rows and columns. For example, a scanner with a dpi of 600 x 1200 has a capacity of 600 columns and 1,200 rows of dots. Most modern scanners for home or office use a resolution of at least 1,200 dpi. Commercial scanners offer higher resolutions and are more expensive.

Scanners can process information in two different ways. A **dumb scanner** can only capture and input scanned text and images. Once entered into a computer, the text or image cannot be altered. By contrast, an **intelligent scanner** uses **optical character recognition (OCR)** software that allows captured text or images to be edited with a word processor or other application program. Depending on the scanner model, the OCR software may be included in the package, or it may need to be purchased separately.

The two most popular types of scanners are page scanners (flatbed scanners) and handheld scanners. Personal computer users often use page scanners to capture text, graphics, and other data from printed documents. Pages are either laid face down on the scanner's glass surface or fed through the scanner by means of a side-feed device. While the page scanner remains stationary, the scanning device inside moves back and forth to capture an image of the material on the glass surface. With handheld scanners, users manually move the scanner across the material to be scanned. Figure 2-12 contrasts handheld and flatbed scanners. Figure 2-13 illustrates how a scanner works.

FIGURE 2-12: Page scanners (top) and handheld scanners (second and third photos from top) are two popular types of image scanners.

Retailers, wholesalers, shipping companies, banks, hotels, and other businesses use a variety of scanning technologies. **Bar code readers** are the most common commercial scanner application. Almost everything for sale today on the retail level is marked with a bar code, also known as a **Universal Product Code (UPC)**.

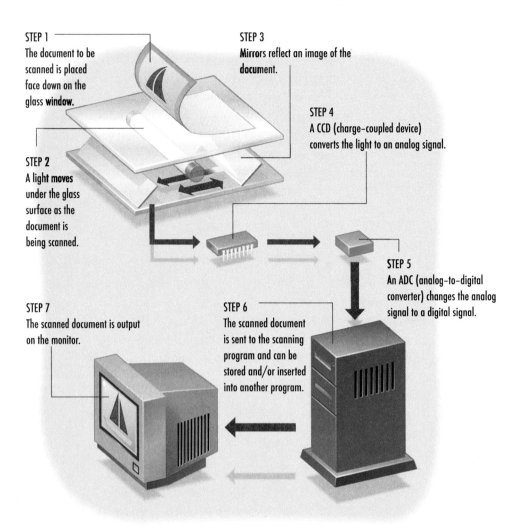

STEP 1
The document to be scanned is placed face down on the glass window.

STEP 2
A light moves under the glass surface as the document is being scanned.

STEP 3
Mirrors reflect an image of the document.

STEP 4
A CCD (charge-coupled device) converts the light to an analog signal.

STEP 5
An ADC (analog-to-digital converter) changes the analog signal to a digital signal.

STEP 6
The scanned document is sent to the scanning program and can be stored and/or inserted into another program.

STEP 7
The scanned document is output on the monitor.

FIGURE 2-13: A scanner captures text and/or images and stores them as a bitmap, a matrix of rows and columns of tiny dots. Each dot represents one or more bits of data. A particular scanner may be either a "dumb" scanner or an "intelligent" scanner.

The lines in a bar code contain symbols that can be read by a bar code reader (see Figure 2-14). Sometimes the reader takes the form of a pen. At other times it is placed below a glass cover at the end of a conveyor belt. Bar code readers translate the lines into a number. The computer then uses this number to find information about the product in a database, such as its name and price. Using bar codes greatly increases accuracy in recording sales and enables retail stores to update inventory files automatically. Overnight shipping services such as Federal Express and United Parcel Service (UPS) often use bar codes to identify packages.

In addition to bar code readers, many retailers have also installed scanners known as **optical readers** at checkout

FIGURE 2-14: A bar code reader uses photo technology to "read" the lines in the bar code. The lines and spaces represent symbols that the computer translates into a number.

stations. Customers can easily pay for purchases by inserting a credit card, cash card, or smart card into a slot on the reader. Cash cards and smart cards are similar in appearance to credit cards, but have different functions. **Cash cards** store cash in digital form. **Smart cards** contain electronic memory and possibly embedded electronic memory. Smart cards can be used for a variety of purposes, including storing cash in digital form, storing a patient's medical records, and identifying an authorized computer network user. The reader scans a card's magnetic strip containing customer and financial data, records the transaction, and transmits the captured information to the retailer's electronic cash register and to the central computer.

Audio Input

The process of entering (recording) speech, music, or sound effects is called **audio input**. Personal computers must contain a sound card to record or play sound. They will also need speakers and a sound-capturing device, such as a microphone, audio CD player, or tape player plugged into a port (slot) on the sound card. Finally, special software is required, such as Windows® Sound Recorder. Figure 2-15 shows a personal computer with a sound system.

Voice input technologies allow users to enter data by talking to the computer. Newer releases of word processing and spreadsheet applications commonly include voice input. Voice recognition and speech recognition are two types of voice input programs.

Voice recognition programs do not understand or process speech. They recognize only preprogrammed words stored in a database. A word database may contain only a few words, or many millions of words. Voice-activated ATM machines, for example, allow customers to conduct financial transactions by speaking into the machine. Voice

FIGURE 2-15: Sound can be entered into a computer with the appropriate software and a microphone. Speakers allow captured or stored sound to be played back.

Cutting Edge

Virtual Input: A Solution for the PDA

An Israeli development company, VKB Inc., has manufactured a virtual keyboard, which was first unveiled at the 2002 CeBIT computer fair in Hanover, Germany.

As shown in the photograph, the virtual keyboard comes to life when the device projects an image of a keyboard onto any flat surface. Then, an infrared system detects user interaction with that surface and sends the signals by wire or by radio waves to the user's mobile phone, PDA, or other computing device.

Siemens Procurement Logistics Services, the European distributor of the new keyboard, says it could usher in a revolution for data input, particularly for PDA and handheld computer users who struggle with the frustration of typing on tiny keyboards. Although its primary application will be for mobile communications and computing devices, it can also be integrated into a variety of other technologies, including medical applications in which the need for a sterile environment is critical. A similar technology being developed as a safety feature for automobiles displays the car's instrument panel on the windshield so the driver's eyes do not leave the road. Many other uses are sure to emerge for this exciting virtual technology.

Sources: www.ananova.com, June 2003; www.siemens.com, June 2003.

CHAPTER 2

recognition capability also is included in Microsoft Office XP and in Office 2003, the most recent release of the application suite. Voice recognition programs are **speaker-independent**, which means they can respond to words spoken by different individuals.

Speech recognition provides another type of voice input in which words spoken by a user are stored in a database. Using a microphone and a type of speech recognition software, such as IBM's Via Voice® or Dragon NaturallySpeaking, words spoken by the user are stored in digital form in the computer. Once words are stored, the user can issue commands and enter data by speaking words that exactly match those recorded previously. A computer with speech recognition capability can continue to learn new vocabulary and commands from user voice input. Speech recognition programs are usually **speaker-dependent**. The computer will recognize words only if they closely match the speech patterns of a previously recorded word. If another person uses the computer, it may not understand verbal commands because of differences in speech patterns.

Video Input

Video input occurs using a special type of video camera attached to the computer and plugged into a **video capture card** in an expansion slot. The video capture card converts the analog video signal into a digital signal (Figure 2-16). It is also possible to connect an ordinary video camera directly to a Macintosh or PC and digitize incoming video by means of a special processing board attached to one of the computer's expansion slots (see Figure 2-17). Incoming video can be live or can come from a previously recorded videocassette. With video-editing software, it is possible to view each frame of the video and edit video sequences.

FIGURE 2-16:
Video input is a technology that allows a video camera to capture and enter motion into a computer.

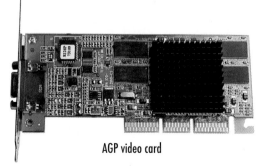
AGP video card

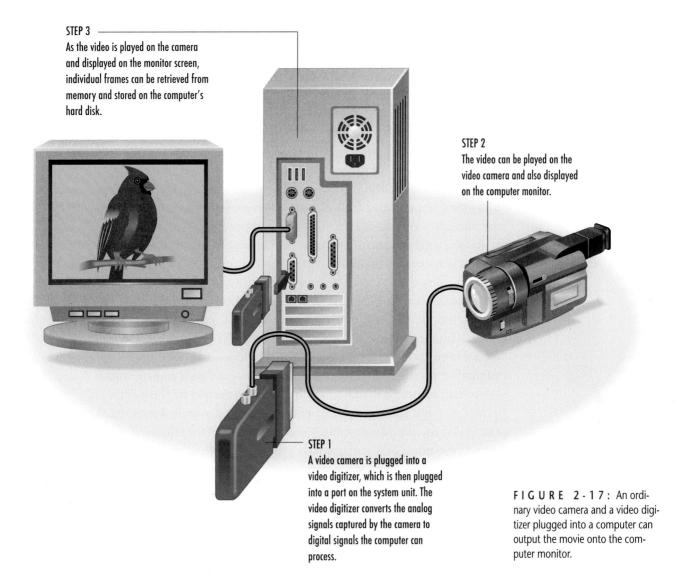

STEP 3
As the video is played on the camera and displayed on the monitor screen, individual frames can be retrieved from memory and stored on the computer's hard disk.

STEP 2
The video can be played on the video camera and also displayed on the computer monitor.

STEP 1
A video camera is plugged into a video digitizer, which is then plugged into a port on the system unit. The video digitizer converts the analog signals captured by the camera to digital signals the computer can process.

FIGURE 2-17: An ordinary video camera and a video digitizer plugged into a computer can output the movie onto the computer monitor.

Applications for Video Input

Businesses, government, and organizations are discovering numerous video-input applications. For example, book publishers can now include a small printed image on a book cover or within a magazine ad allowing an order to be placed when a person holds the image up to a video camera on the computer. The camera captures the printed image, enters it into the computer, and transmits the order over the Internet to the publisher.

Some banks have begun using advanced video-input systems to identify customers. A camera captures an image of a would-be customer and quickly compares the image to those stored in a computer, eliminating the necessity of checking a driver's license or other identification. Similar systems that store an image of a person's eye or fingerprints are used in high-security situations that require quick employee identification, such as military installations and government facilities.

Manufacturers use video technology for quality control. For example, a product moving along an assembly line can be photographed and instantly compared with a stored photograph of the "perfect" product. If a missing or broken part is detected the computer rejects the product before it is packaged for shipment.

Experimental unmanned military vehicles use a vision-input system to avoid obstacles while driving over rough terrain. Similar vision-input technologies may soon be available for civilian vehicles. Vision-input offers great promise for safer driving in the future.

Digital Cameras

While conventional cameras capture images on film, **digital cameras** record and store images in a digitized form that a computer can use. Newer digital cameras can even take short movies. In appearance, digital cameras resemble traditional film-based cameras (see Figure 2-18). Most are portable, although some models are stationary and connect directly to a computer.

Most digital cameras store captured pictures directly in **flash memory** (a type of read-only memory that can be erased all at once) or on a floppy disk. The storage medium is used to transfer the picture into the computer. Users can then adjust the color and size of the image using photo-editing software. They can also print the picture, copy it into another document, post it on a Web site, or e-mail it. Some digital cameras allow users to view and edit pictures in the camera. Many digital cameras can also be connected to a television for viewing or connected to a printer for printing. Figure 2-19 illustrates how a digital camera works.

As with scanners, digital photo quality is measured by the number of bits stored in a dot, and the number of dots (pixels) per inch. The resolution of digital cameras is usually advertised in terms of megapixels (millions of pixels). A camera with a resolution of 4.0 megapixels produces high-quality pictures suitable for most consumers. However, professional photographers would probably gravitate toward a new digital camera, such as the one recently introduced by Eastman Kodak. The camera uses a chip that can capture digital images with a resolution of 4096 x 4096 pixels (about 16 megapixels), which is about twice the resolution of 35-millimeter film and approximately the same clarity achieved by high-end 4 x 5 film cameras made by companies like Hasselblad.

What's even more exciting for computer users is that new digital camera image-sensing technologies are finding their way into cellular telephones. Manufacturers

FIGURE 2-18: A digital camera looks much like a standard camera but captures and stores an image in a digital format that a computer can process.

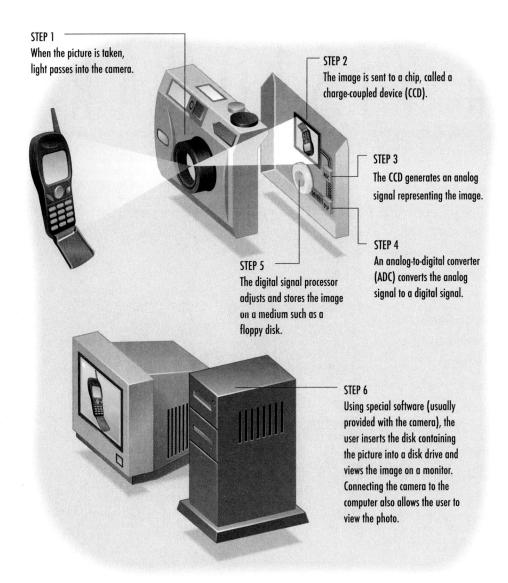

STEP 1
When the picture is taken, light passes into the camera.

STEP 2
The image is sent to a chip, called a charge-coupled device (CCD).

STEP 3
The CCD generates an analog signal representing the image.

STEP 4
An analog-to-digital converter (ADC) converts the analog signal to a digital signal.

STEP 5
The digital signal processor adjusts and stores the image on a medium such as a floppy disk.

STEP 6
Using special software (usually provided with the camera), the user inserts the disk containing the picture into a disk drive and views the image on a monitor. Connecting the camera to the computer also allows the user to view the photo.

FIGURE 2-19: A digital camera captures images by converting them from analog to digital format and storing them on a floppy disk or other storage medium. Once captured and stored, a picture can be printed or inserted into a document such as a sales brochure.

have begun producing inexpensive cell phones that allow users to capture, transmit, and receive pictures and other images. For example, photographs of a newborn child can be instantly transmitted to family and friends, or a biology student on a field trip can take and store photographs of plants and animals for further study. Another new product that represents a combination of technologies is the camcorder/digital camera. In spring 2003, Sony Corporation introduced the world's first camcorders capable of taking two-megapixel photos (1600 by 1200 pixels). The Sony TRV70 and TRV80 offer 2.5-inch and 3.5-inch screens, respectively, and the LCD touch screens serve as input devices. The TRV80 model includes a Bluetooth transmitter that can send photos directly to a Bluetooth-enabled printer or computer. With the addition of a phone jack adapter or Ethernet adapter, the camcorders also can serve as emergency terminals for Internet connections.

All of the hardware devices discussed so far have dealt with input, the first phase of the information processing cycle. The second phase is processing, which involves another set of computer hardware components, most of which reside in the system unit.

TECH VISIONARY

The 2000 Nobel Prize in Physics was awarded to 76-year-old Jack Kilby for his work on the integrated circuit, which paved the way for the technological revolution that became known as the "Information Age." The development of the integrated circuit permitted gigantic gains in computer power.

Kilby's first integrated circuit, about the size of a thumbnail, was built in 1958. His novel idea was to develop the numerous electrical transistors in the chip's circuit from a single block of material, rather than assembling them with wires and other components. Kilby's work led to the integrated circuits of today, shrunk in size and loaded with millions of transistors. Without the integrated circuit, the personal computers of today would not have been possible.

Also credited with coinventing the pocket calculator, Kilby worked for Texas Instruments until 1970 and then became a freelance inventor. He holds more than 60 patents and has been awarded honorary degrees from three universities. Kilby says he had no idea how much his microchip would expand the field of electronics. At home he still listens to music on a turntable and does not own a cell phone.

Kilby received half of the $915,000 prize. The other half was shared by two physicists who invented semiconductor heterostructures. The Nobel Prize is usually awarded for an abstract theoretical insight or an experimental technique. This is the first time the award was given for engineering rather than pure science. As a nod to the worldwide impact of the Internet, the Royal Swedish Academy of Sciences gave the prize to three men whose work enabled the growth of computer technology.

Sources: Johnson, George. "The Nobels: Dazzled by the Digital Light," *The New York Times*, October 15, 2000; Glanz, James. "3 Men Vital to Internet Share Physics Prize," *The New York Times*, October 11, 2000; Crissey, Mike. "Texan's Microchip Speeds Info Age," <http://www.news.excite.com/news/ap/001010/19/nobel-reax>.

WHAT IS INFORMATION PROCESSING?

The purpose of inputting data into a computer system is to process data into a form that is useful. Recall that information processing, also called data processing or simply processing, refers to the manipulation of data according to instructions in a computer program. The program used to manipulate the data may be written by the user or purchased from a software vendor. Data may be manipulated in various ways during processing. For example, a payroll program manipulates data by calculating employee gross pay, taxes to be withheld, deductions, and net pay. The results of those calculations can then be used to print employee paychecks and reports. A commercial word processing program such as Microsoft Word can be used to manipulate text and other data to produce letters, memos, and other documents.

HOW DO COMPUTERS PROCESS DATA?

All computers are electronic devices, which means they operate on electricity, and their programs and data are in electronic form. Programs and data are entered and stored in the computer's memory. When a program is executed, the processing unit retrieves the instructions and data as needed throughout the processing period. When processing is finished, the program and the processed data (information) are stored in the computer's memory until the information is output or saved for future use.

So what happens during processing? Physically, electrical currents representing programs and data are moving about very quickly through electronic circuits between components inside the system unit. The currents are created by tiny switches called transistors, which are either on or off, with "on" represented by the number 1 and "off" represented by the number 0. All data used in computers is represented by combinations of ones and zeros, each of which is considered a **bit** (an abbreviation for **bi**nary digi**t**). As described in Chapter 1, electrical currents or signals within computers are therefore called digital signals, and data is referred to as digital data.

Data Representation: Bits and Bytes

The first large computers made use of the decimal number system, in which numbers are indicated by the symbols 0 through 9. Engineers soon hit upon a much simpler system known as machine language for representing data with numbers. **Machine language** uses **binary numbers** ("bi" means two), which are constructed solely of the symbols 0 and 1. The bit (0 or 1) is the smallest unit of data in the binary system. By itself, a bit is not very meaningful. However, a group of eight bits, or a **byte**, is significant because a byte contains enough possible combinations of 0s and 1s to represent

F I G U R E 2 - 2 0 : In the binary number system, a zero (0) represents an "off" state in which there is no electrical charge, and a one (1) represents an "on" state in which there is an electrical charge. This condition is similar to what happens when an electrical switch is turned on, causing current to flow.

=1

=0

256 (2^8) separate characters. These characters include letters of the alphabet, numbers, and special symbols, such as dollar signs, question marks, and pound signs. To picture the concept of using binary numbers to represent data within the electrical circuits on a computer chip, consider an electric light switch. Flipping the switch to the "on" position causes the current to flow and turns on the light, while flipping the switch to the opposite position turns the light "off" (see Figure 2-20). Various patterns of "on" and "off" could therefore represent alphabet letters and numbers. Two widely used data coding schemes based on the binary system are **ASCII** (American Standard Code for Information Interchange) and **EBCDIC** (Extended Binary Coded Decimal Interchange Code).

ASCII and EBCDIC Coding Schemes

The ASCII data coding scheme is used on many personal computers and various midsize servers. The EBCDIC scheme is used mainly on large servers and mainframe computers. Figure 2-21 illustrates these two coding schemes and the combinations that represent specific characters. Coding schemes such as ASCII and EBCDIC make it possible for users to interact with a computer. For example, pressing a specific key on a keyboard, such as the letter "J," generates an electrical signal. The generated signal is converted into binary form (a byte) and is stored in memory. The computer then processes the digital signal and quickly displays an image (in this case, a "J") on the screen, as shown in Figure 2-22.

Unicode

Although widely adopted as a standard for personal computers, the ASCII system has proved to be too limited because it cannot deal with certain languages, such as Chinese, which

ASCII AND EBCDIC CODING SCHEMES

SYMBOL	ASCII	EBCDIC
0	01100000	11110000
1	01100001	11110001
2	01100010	11110010
3	01100011	11110011
4	01100100	11110100
5	01100101	11110101
6	01100110	11110110
7	01100111	11110111
8	01101000	11111000
9	01101001	11111001
A	01000001	11000001
B	01000010	11000010
C	01000011	11000011
D	01000100	11000100
E	01000101	11000101
F	01000110	11000110
G	01000111	11000111
H	01001000	11001000
I	01001001	11001001
J	01001010	11010001
K	01001011	11010010
L	01001100	11010011
M	01001101	11010100
N	01001110	11010101
O	01001111	11010110
P	01010000	11010111
Q	01010001	11011000
R	01010010	11011001
S	01010011	11100010
T	01010100	11100011
U	01010101	11100100
V	01010110	11100101
W	01010111	11100110
X	01011000	11100111
Y	01011001	11101000
Z	01011010	11101001
!	00100001	01011010
"	00100010	01111111
#	00100011	01111011
$	00100100	01011011
%	00100101	01101100
&	00100110	01010000
(	00101000	01001101
)	00101001	01011101
*	00101010	01011100
+	00101011	01001110

F I G U R E 2 - 2 1 : ASCII is a coding scheme used on many computers, including personal computers. The EBCDIC coding scheme is used mainly on large computers such as IBM mainframe computers.

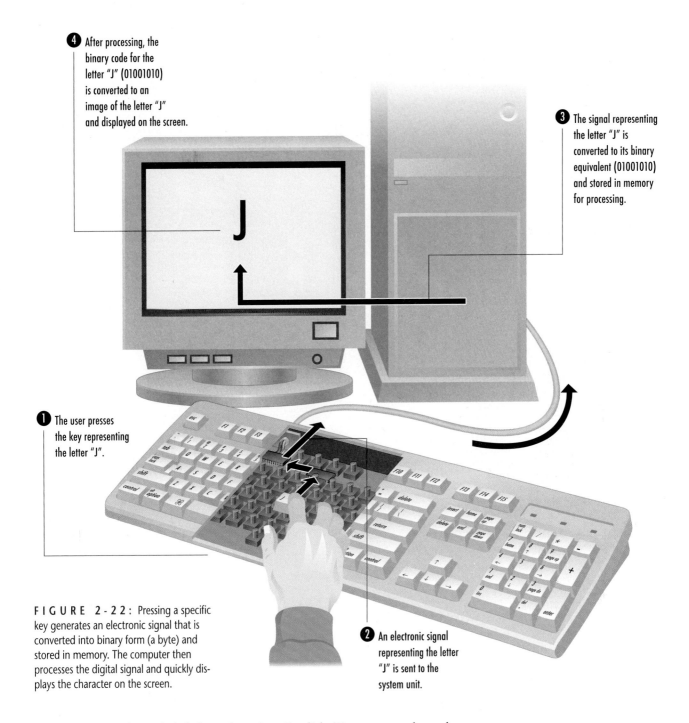

4 After processing, the binary code for the letter "J" (01001010) is converted to an image of the letter "J" and displayed on the screen.

3 The signal representing the letter "J" is converted to its binary equivalent (01001010) and stored in memory for processing.

1 The user presses the key representing the letter "J".

2 An electronic signal representing the letter "J" is sent to the system unit.

FIGURE 2-22: Pressing a specific key generates an electronic signal that is converted into binary form (a byte) and stored in memory. The computer then processes the digital signal and quickly displays the character on the screen.

uses more complicated alphabets than does English. To accommodate a larger array of letters and symbols, computer scientists have developed a system called **Unicode**. Unicode uses two bytes, or 16 binary digits, and can represent 65,536, or 2^{16}, separate characters. Since the first 256 codes are the same in both ASCII and Unicode, existing ASCII coded data is compatible with newer operating systems, including Windows XP and OS/2, that use Unicode.

THE SYSTEM UNIT

The main part of a desktop computer, the system unit, houses the components that process data into information (see Figure 2-23). From the outside, the system unit looks like a metal or plastic cabinet with several button switches and openings in the front and back. The inside is a maze of circuit boards, wires, and cables of

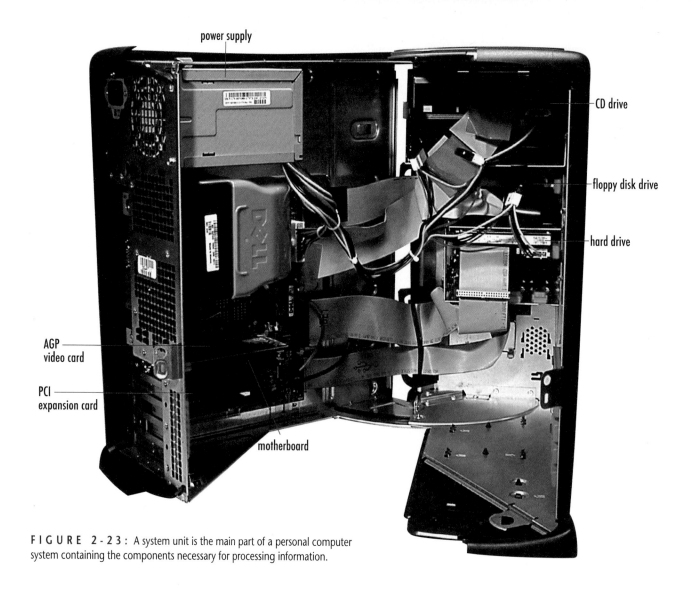

power supply

CD drive

floppy disk drive

hard drive

AGP
video card

PCI
expansion card

motherboard

FIGURE 2-23: A system unit is the main part of a personal computer
system containing the components necessary for processing information.

various colors, a fan for cooling, and empty slots where more circuit boards can be
added. The most important circuit board in the system unit is called the motherboard.

The Motherboard

A **motherboard** is a thin sheet of fiberglass or other material with electrical pathways called **traces** etched onto it. These traces connect components that are sol-
dered to the motherboard or attached to it by various wires or connectors. The
following components are typically found on the motherboard in contemporary
desktop computers (see Figure 2-24):

- central processing unit (microprocessor)
- a system clock (and battery) to synchronize the computer's activities
- sockets for connecting the RAM (random access memory) chips that contain
  the temporary memory where programs and data are stored while the computer is in use
- one or more ROM (read-only memory) chips that contain the computer's
  permanent memory where various instructions are stored

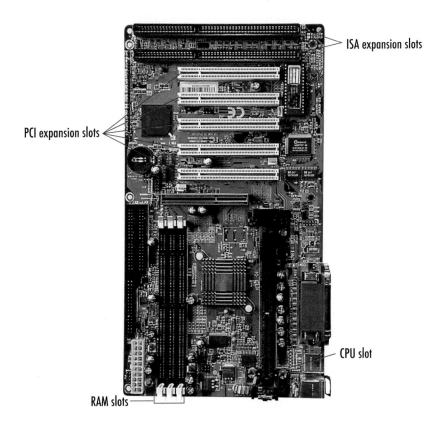

ISA expansion slots

PCI expansion slots

CPU slot

FIGURE 2-24: The motherboard holds the major processing and memory components, including the CPU, RAM, and ROM chips.

RAM slots

- expansion slots for attaching expansion boards (or cards) that add various capabilities to the computer, such as the ability to access files over a network or to digitize sound or video
- ports for connecting devices such as a keyboard, mouse, modem, or printer
- **buses**, electronic connections that allow communication between components in the computer
- a power supply to provide power to the computer

The Central Processing Unit (Microprocessor)

Every computer contains a central processing unit or CPU (refer to Figure 2-24). The CPU of larger computers often spans several separate electronic chips and various circuit boards, whereas in a personal computer the CPU is a single chip. **Electronic chips**, also called **integrated circuits**, are small electronic devices consisting of tiny transistors and other circuit parts on a piece of semiconductor material. This material is known as a **semiconductor** because it is neither a good conductor of electricity (like copper) nor a good insulator (such as rubber). Semiconductor material therefore does not interfere with the flow of electricity in a chip's circuits. The most commonly used semiconductor material is silicon, a type of purified glass.

On a personal computer, all processing functions are contained on a single electronic chip called a microprocessor or processor, as illustrated in Figure 2-25, which shows a drawing of a microprocessor chip along with a photo of a real chip, the Pentium® 4. Because the functions are housed on a single chip, the terms "CPU" and "microprocessor" are used interchangeably. Recall from Chapter 1 that the CPU, or microprocessor, is often referred to as the "brain" of a personal

CHAPTER 2

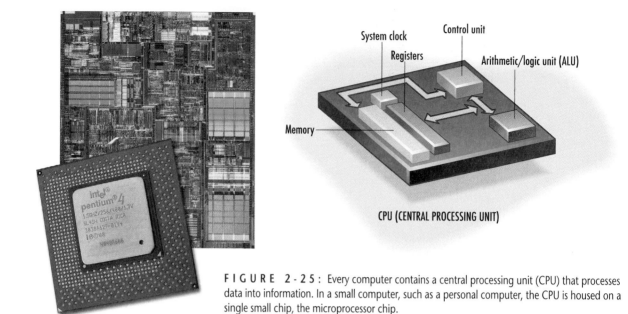

System clock
Registers
Control unit
Arithmetic/logic unit (ALU)
Memory

CPU (CENTRAL PROCESSING UNIT)

FIGURE 2-25: Every computer contains a central processing unit (CPU) that processes data into information. In a small computer, such as a personal computer, the CPU is housed on a single small chip, the microprocessor chip.

computer system because it interprets and executes the instructions for most computer operations (see Figure 2-26). Using a control unit and an arithmetic/logic unit (ALU), the CPU performs five main functions:

- receiving input
- interpreting instructions provided by programs
- executing instructions and processing data
- directing other components of the system to act
- controlling output

Control Unit

FIGURE 2-26: The control unit, ALU, and registers carry out the work of the CPU.

The **control unit** directs and coordinates the overall operation of the computer system (refer to Figure 2-26). It acts as a traffic officer, signaling to other parts of

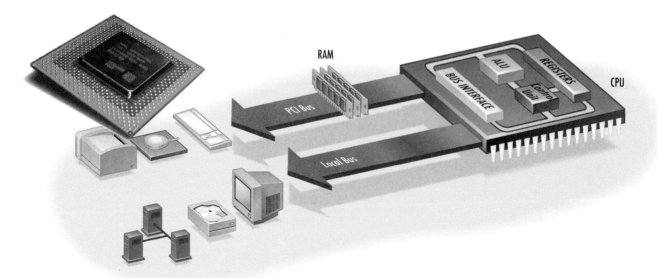

RAM
PCI Bus
Local Bus
BUS INTERFACE
ALU
REGISTERS
Control Unit
CPU

the computer system what they are to do. It interprets program instructions and then initiates the action needed to carry them out. The control unit performs four basic operations for each instruction. These operations, collectively called a **machine cycle**, include *fetching* an instruction, *decoding* the instruction, *executing* the instruction, and *storing* the result (see Figure 2-27). Machine cycles are sometime referred to as **instruction cycles**.

Fetching means retrieving an instruction or data from memory. **Decoding** means interpreting or translating the instruction into strings of binary digits (bytes) the computer understands. **Executing** means carrying out the instruction. **Storing** means writing or recording the result to memory.

The time required to fetch and decode an instruction is called **instruction time**, or **I-time**. The time required to execute and store an instruction is called **execution time**, or **E-time**. These two times are sometimes used together as a measure of processing speed.

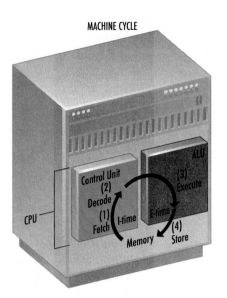

MACHINE CYCLE

FIGURE 2-27: A machine cycle includes the four steps for reading and carrying out an instruction: fetching, decoding, executing, and storing. The machine cycle is the same whether you are using a midrange server, such as the one shown above, or a personal computer.

Arithmetic/Logic Unit

The **arithmetic/logic unit (ALU)** is the part of the CPU that carries out instructions and performs the actual arithmetic and logical operations on the data (refer to Figures 2-25 and 2-26). The arithmetic operations the ALU can perform are addition, subtraction, multiplication, and division. The ALU can also perform logical operations, such as comparing data items. For example, the ALU can determine if one data item, such as the number of hours an employee has worked, is less than, equal to, or exceeds the number of hours in a standard 40-hour work week. If the number of hours worked is less than or equal to 40, the employee's pay is calculated using a particular formula. If the hours worked exceeds 40, a different formula is used for calculating overtime pay.

Registers

To speed up processing, the ALU uses **registers** (temporary storage locations) to hold instructions and data (see Figure 2-28). Registers are accessed much faster than memory locations outside the CPU. Various kinds of registers are used, each serving a specific purpose. Once processing begins, **instruction registers** hold instructions currently being executed. **Data registers** hold the data items being acted upon. **Storage registers** hold the immediate and final results of processing.

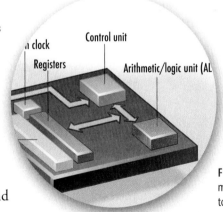

FIGURE 2-28: The arithmetic/logic unit (ALU) uses registers to hold instructions and data.

System Clock

A computer contains a **system clock** in the form of a small electronic chip that synchronizes or controls the timing of all computer operations (refer to Figure 2-25). The clock generates evenly spaced electrical pulses that synchronize the flow of information through the computer's internal communication channels.

Instructions are executed or "triggered" by pulses of the clock. Since an instruction may direct the execution of other events either internal or external to the

CPU, the clock pulse provides a way for these events to occur in harmony. Pulse speed is measured according to the number of clock pulses per second, called **hertz**. One hertz is equal to one pulse per second.

One **clock cycle** is equal to two ticks of the clock. A CPU uses a fixed number of clock cycles to execute each instruction. The faster the clock ticks, the faster the CPU can execute instructions. Personal computers today operate at clock speeds of hundreds of megahertz, and some operate faster than one gigahertz. The speed of the clock affects only the speed of the CPU. It has no effect on the operation of peripheral devices.

Coprocessors

In addition to the main processor, or CPU, a personal computer may also contain one or more coprocessors. A **coprocessor** is a special-purpose chip or board that assists the CPU in performing certain types of operations. For example, a **math coprocessor** performs mathematical computations, particularly *floating-point* operations, which involve numbers in which the decimal point may be in any position (500, 0.511, 34.7, for example). Because math coprocessors greatly increase the speed at which computations are performed, they are especially useful for scientific, engineering, and statistical applications. A **graphics coprocessor**, or **graphics board**, is designed specifically for handling image-intensive applications, such as Web pages and computer-aided design programs.

Factors in Microprocessor Speed and Power

The power and speed of microprocessor (CPU) chips are determined primarily by the number of transistors, the clock speed, and the number of bits that can be handled as a single unit. A variety of microprocessors with varying speeds and capabilities are available. Newer microprocessors are extremely fast and powerful and offer exceptional capabilities. For example, Intel Corporation's Pentium 4 processor, introduced in 2000, contains 42 million transistors and has a clock speed of up to 1.7 GHz (gigahertz). New Pentium 4 versions contain even more transistors and operate at speeds of 4.0 gigahertz or more. Contrast that capability with Intel's 80286 processor introduced in 1982, which had a clock speed of 6–12 MHz (megahertz) and a total of 134,000 transistors. The Celeron™ processor is another popular Intel chip that was revised in 2000 to create three new versions: 600 MHz and 650 MHz chips for full-sized laptop computers and a 500 MHz chip for the ultralight handhelds needing fast processing speed and low power consumption. In 2003, Intel introduced the Pentium M chip for notebook computers. When packaged with an Intel Wi-Fi wireless adapter, the chip is called the Centrino. Notebook manufacturers quickly took advantage of the extended battery life and cooler operating temperatures of the Pentium M by offering several new ultralight notebooks that provide high-performance computing and wireless LAN capabilities. The Pentium M is especially useful for the

CHAPTER 2

Processor	Made By	Year Introduced	Clock Speed	Number of Transistors
80286	Intel	1982	6-12 MHz	134,000
68020	Motorola	1984	16-33 MHz	190,000
80486DX	Intel	1985	16-33 MHz	275,000
68030	Motorola	1987	16-50 MHz	270,000
68040	Motorola	1989	25-40 MHz	1,200,000
Alpha	DEC	1993	150-700 MHz	100,000,000
Pentium	Intel	1993	75-200 MHz	3,300,000
Pentium Pro	Intel	1995	150-200 MHz	5,500,000
Pentium II	Intel	1997	233-450 MHz	7,500,000
Celeron	Intel	1998	266-633 MHz	19,000,000
Athlon	AMD	1999	1.1 GHz	22,000,000
Pentium III	Intel	1999	1.0 GHz	28,000,000
Pentium 4	Intel	2000	up to 5.0 GHz	42,000,000 or more
Athlon XP	AMD	2001	1.5 GHz	37,500,000
Centrino/Pentium M	Intel	2003	1.3-1.7 GHz	77,000,000

TABLE 2-1: Processing Speeds of Popular Microprocessors

Tablet PC, which needs a longer battery life and more processing power to manage handwriting recognition. Table 2-1 shows comparisons of several microprocessors.

A microprocessor's **word size** also affects its power and speed. Related to microprocessors, a **word** is a group of bits or bytes that a computer can manipulate or process as a unit. Some microprocessor chips are 32-bit chips, meaning they can handle 32-bit blocks of data at a time. Newer microprocessors are designed to handle 64-bit blocks of data at a time. For example, Intel's Pentium 4 chip is designed for 64-bit blocks of data, and the chip's main circuitry also accommodates 64-bit words. This means that a 64-bit data path leads from the CPU to RAM, which translates into faster processing.

Techniques for Improving Microprocessor Performance

Since 1971, when Intel Corporation introduced the company's first microprocessor, chip designers have developed many techniques for improving the speed and performance of microprocessors. These techniques center on the raw materials used to make the chips, the density of the circuits on a chip, and changes in the way instructions are executed. Following is a summary of key advances in the development of microprocessors to date:

- **Reduced instruction set computing (RISC).** Many early computers and other devices used processors that contained a lengthy and complex set of instructions for processing data. Most modern computers now use a shortened set of instructions, called RISC, which increases their speed and efficiency.

- **Pipelining.** In older computers the CPU had to completely execute one instruction before starting a second instruction. Modern computers now use a technique called **pipelining**. Pipelining enables the computer to begin executing another instruction as soon as the previous instruction reaches the next phase of the machine cycle. This allows the CPU to execute instructions faster.
- **Closer circuits.** Newer computers contain chips with circuits packed much closer together compared to earlier chips, thereby decreasing the distance that instructions and data must travel. The closer packing makes them much faster and more efficient.
- **New and better materials.** Most chips consist of electrical circuits etched onto a piece of silicon. Some chip manufacturers are designing copper circuits to replace the aluminum circuits used today, because copper is a better conductor of electricity.
- **Parallel processing.** Despite the many performance improvements, most personal computers still use a single processor. This is primarily because a processor is the most expensive computer component, usually costing hundreds of dollars. With a single processor, instructions are executed *serially*, or one at a time. However, scientists have developed ways for two or more processors and memory components to work together simultaneously (in parallel). **Parallel processing** allows two or more processors to work concurrently on segments of a lengthy application, thus dramatically increasing processing capability.
- **Multithreading and hyperthreading.** Some newer microprocessors provide multithreading and hyperthreading capabilities that allow operating systems and applications software, such as Windows, to process applications faster. In programming, a thread is a part of a program that can execute independently of other parts. Multithreading refers to a carefully designed program that enables several threads to execute at the same time without interfering with each other. Intel has developed a technology called hyperthreading, which allows its Pentium series of microprocessors to execute multithreaded software applications simultaneously and in parallel rather than processing threads in linear fashion, thereby greatly increasing processing speed.

Internal Memory

The system unit of a personal computer contains locations called **main memory** or **primary storage** that provide temporary storage for program instructions and data during the processing phase. This memory consists of one or more chips, called RAM (random-access memory), installed on the motherboard or on other circuit boards in the computer. A second type of internal memory is ROM, or read-only memory, which provides permanent storage. Figure 2-29 shows the location of RAM and ROM chips on the motherboard.

Random-Access Memory (RAM)

Random-access memory (RAM) is the temporary memory in which programs and data are stored while the computer is in use. Programs must first be entered, or input, into RAM before they are executed or data is processed. The CPU then moves information from RAM into its registers for processing. RAM performs the following functions:

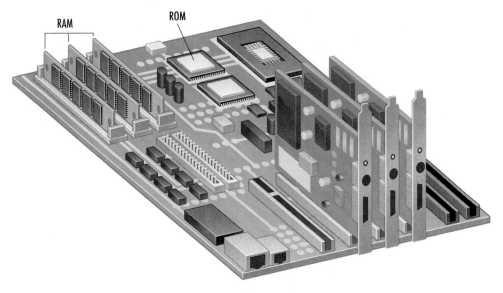

FIGURE 2-29: RAM chips temporarily store programs and data during the processing stage of the information processing cycle. On some small computers, ROM chips contain permanent storage of the operating system and the instructions for managing peripheral devices.

- accepts and holds program instructions and data
- acts as the CPU's source for data and instructions and as a destination for operation results
- holds the final processed information until it can be sent to the desired output or storage devices, such as a printer or disk drive

The CPU must be able to find programs and data once they are stored in RAM. Therefore program instructions and data are placed at specific locations within RAM, known as **addresses**. Each location has its own unique address, just as each person has an individual postal mailing address (see Figure 2-30). When the CPU

FIGURE 2-30: Each memory location has its own unique address, just as each person has a postal mailing address. When the CPU needs an instruction or data from memory, an electronic message is sent to the appropriate address and the instruction or data is transferred to the appropriate register in the CPU.

TECH VISIONARY

CLAUDE SHANNON: DEVELOPER OF INFORMATION THEORY

A computer is basically a machine for processing information. What, then, is information? Claude Shannon, developer of the mathematical science of information known as information theory, described information as a purposeful, organized signal sent from one place to another. When information is sent, it must travel by some medium through some channel. For example, it might travel as an electrical signal sent down a wire or as sound, light, or radio waves sent through the air. Problems in the channel, such as corrosion on a wire or fog in the air, can introduce nonmeaningful elements, or noise, causing the signal to become degraded and information to be lost. Television viewers of the 1960s, who lived before the days of cable with its superb delivery channels, were quite familiar with this phenomenon. Shannon, an engineer for Bell Labs, concerned himself in part with describing mathematically the amount of redundancy, or repetition, that would have to be built into a signal to compensate for noise and thus avoid loss of information.

The signals that contain information can come in one of two forms. They can be continuous, or analog; or they can be discrete, or digital. A sound wave is an analog signal. It can be represented by a continuous, nonbroken line like the one shown at right.

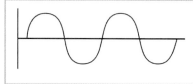

A sound wave

The dots and dashes of Morse code, in contrast, are digital signals because they are broken up into discrete, individual units. (The word digital, by the way, comes from digit, for finger, and refers to the fact that fingers were used for counting discrete, enumerable objects.)

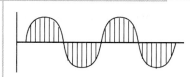

A digitized sound

Information, then, can be analog or digital. Other examples of continuous, or analog, signals include the splashes of paint on a canvas and the height of mercury in a thermometer. Other examples of digital signals include the letters that make up written words and the dots of color that make up the pictures in the Sunday comics.

A digital computer is one that represents information as a series of discrete elements. In most such computers, the discrete elements are binary numbers, base 2 numbers written as strings of 1s and 0s. Interestingly, any analog or continuous signal can be expressed digitally by a technique known as sampling. A sound, for example, can be digitized by taking a sample of the amplitude of the sound wave every few milliseconds.

Continuous color images can be digitized by using a grid of dots and encoding the brightness and hue of the dots, as shown at right.

Of course, digitization of analog signals always involves some loss of information. If the sampling is done frequently enough, however, as in the 2500- or 3600-dot-per-inch advertisements printed on the backs of glossy magazines, no information seems to be lost because of the limited acuity, or sharpness, of our senses. Beyond a certain threshold, or limit, digital signals and analog signals are indistinguishable by humans. In conclusion, a syllogism:

Digitized color image

    a. Just about anything can be digitized by means of sampling.
    b. Computers can represent anything that can be digitized.
    c. Therefore, computers can represent just about anything.

Source: Introduction to Computers and Technology, Paradigm Publishing.

needs an instruction or data from RAM, an electronic message is sent to the instruction's address and the instruction is transferred to the appropriate register in the CPU.

Random-access means that because each RAM location has an individual address, the computer can go directly to the instructions and data it needs, rather than search each individual location one after another (sequentially). RAM memory is both readable and writable, meaning that the contents of any RAM location can be changed and/or read at any time. RAM memory is also **volatile**, meaning that it requires a constant charge to keep its contents intact. If a computer loses power, the contents of its memory are lost. Therefore, it is important to save any valuable work frequently to a permanent storage medium.

The temporary nature of RAM is its most important characteristic. When the computer is finished with one set of instructions and data, it can store another set in the first set's place. RAM is reusable, much like a chalkboard. Instructions and data can be written on the chalkboard (or into RAM) and then erased to make room for new instructions and data to be written in the same space.

Types of RAM

Two types of RAM used with early PCs were Dynamic RAM (DRAM) and Static RAM (SRAM). Some personal computers contained either, or both, types. Without a continuous supply of electrical energy, **DRAM** (pronounced *dee-ram*) chips eventually lose their contents. Because of this, DRAM chips must be constantly refreshed by receiving a fresh supply of energy. **SRAM** (pronounced *ess-ram*) is a static type of RAM that is faster and more reliable (and more expensive) than the more common DRAM. The term "static" refers to the fact that SRAM doesn't need to be refreshed like DRAM and it therefore allows a faster access time.

Over the years, newer computers have been introduced that contain faster microprocessors. To accommodate the increased speed, chip manufacturers have designed and built faster RAM chips. **SDRAM** (Synchronous DRAM) divides RAM into two separate memory banks to increase the processing of memory requests. To overcome the performance limitations of SDRAM, two competing technologies have been developed. **RDRAM** (Rambus DRAM) involves a new memory design that achieves higher data transfer speeds, but it is expensive to manufacture. **DDR SDRAM** (Double Data Rate SDRAM) can transfer data twice as fast as SDRAM because it reads data twice during each clock cycle. DDR SDRAM is more popular in today's market, but even newer technologies such as DDR II and SLDRAM (SyncLink DRAM) are emerging.

The amount of main memory in a computer is important. Large programs, such as desktop publishing and computer-aided design applications, require a lot of main memory. A computer may be unable to use a program if the computer's main memory is insufficient. Additional RAM chips can be installed inside the system unit on most computers.

Measuring RAM Capacities

RAM storage capacities are measured in bytes. Since most personal computers have enough memory to store thousands or millions of bytes, it is common to refer to storage capacity in terms of **kilobytes** (one thousand bytes), **megabytes** (one million bytes), and even **gigabytes** (one billion bytes). Storage capacities of

Abbreviation	Unit of Storage	Equivalent Amount
bit	binary storage	takes value of 0 or 1
byte	8 bits	1 byte usually represents one keystroke
K	kilobyte	1,024 bytes or 2^{10}
MB	megabyte	1,024,000 bytes or about one million bytes
GB	gigabyte	1,024,000,000 bytes or about one thousand MB
TB	terabyte	1,024,000,000,000 bytes or about one million MB
PB	petabyte	about 1,000 TB

TABLE 2-2: Measures of Data Storage

personal computers are typically quoted as 128 megabytes, 256 megabytes, or 512 megabytes. By contrast, today's mainframe computer storage is often measured in terabytes, or trillions of bytes, and the most powerful supercomputers offer storage capacities expressed in petabytes, each of which is approximately 1,000 terabytes. The prefix *tera-* is derived from the Greek word for monster, an apt association to the tremendous size of a terabyte. Table 2-2 displays the various measurements of storage. Table 2-3 shows the amount of memory typically contained in various types of computers.

Cache Memory

A secondary type of processing storage used with RAM is cache memory (pronounced *cash*). **Cache memory** is a holding area in which the data and instructions most recently called by the processor from RAM are stored. When a processor needs an instruction or data from RAM, it first looks for the instruction in cache memory. Because some instructions are called frequently, they are often found in cache memory, shortening processing time. Cache memory may be contained on the CPU in the form of memory chips hardwired onto the motherboard, or as reserved space on a storage device such as a hard disk. Some operating systems also allow users to set aside a portion of RAM to be used as cache memory.

TABLE 2-3: Computer Memory Comparisons

Type of Computer	Number of Processors	Amount of Memory
handheld computer	usually one	64 MB or more
notebook PC	usually one	128 MB or more
desktop PC	usually one	128 MB or more
workstation	one or two	128–1,024 MB or more
midsize server	several	hundreds of GB or more
mainframe	hundreds	hundreds of GB or more
supercomputer	hundreds to thousands	hundreds of TB to several PB (1 petabyte = 1,024 TB)

There are various types of cache memory. **Level 1 cache** is built into the architecture of microprocessor chips, providing faster access to the instructions and data residing in cache memory. **Level 2 cache** may also be built into the architecture of microprocessor chips, as is the norm for current processors. On older computers, it may consist of high-speed SRAM chips placed on the motherboard or on a card that is inserted into a slot in the computer. **Level 3 cache** is available on computers that have level 2 cache, or advanced transfer cache, and is separate from the microprocessor.

Read-Only Memory (ROM) Chips

A computer's system unit has one or more **read-only memory (ROM)** chips that contain instructions or data permanently placed on the chip by the manufacturer (refer to Figure 2-27). The contents of a ROM chip can only be read by the user and cannot be altered or erased. ROM chips are **nonvolatile**, meaning that if power is interrupted, the content of ROM is not lost. A typical PC contains ROM chips on which essential programs have been stored. One such program is the **BIOS (basic input/output system)**, the program that boots (starts) the computer when it is turned on. The BIOS also controls communications with the keyboard, disk drives, and other components. Also activated with the startup of the computer is a **POST (power-on self test)** chip, containing instructions that check the physical components of the system to make certain they are working properly.

A computer also may have ROM chips containing permanent instructions that direct the operation of peripheral devices, including the keyboard, monitor, and disk drives. Without these ROM chips, users would need to enter complex instructions each time the devices are used.

FIGURE 2-31:
Removable flash memory lets users easily transfer data from a handheld device to a personal computer.

Flash Memory

Flash memory, also referred to as flash ROM, is a type of nonvolatile memory that can be erased and reused, or reprogrammed. Flash memory chips are used for storing programs and data on many handheld computers and devices, such as digital cameras, cellular phones, and printers. Removable flash memory cards also are available (see Figure 2-31). With a flash card, users can easily transfer data from a handheld device or a digital camera to a personal computer.

Several different types of removable flash cards are in use today, but they are physically different and incompatible with each other. The manufacturer and type of handheld device purchased will dictate the type of flash card used. CompactFlash™ (CF) cards are used by Hewlett Packard, Epson, and a number of digital camera manufacturers. CF cards weigh less than an ounce and take up about the same amount of space as a matchbook. SmartMedia™ (SM) cards are about the size of a postage stamp and are used by Fuji, Olympus, and Toshiba.

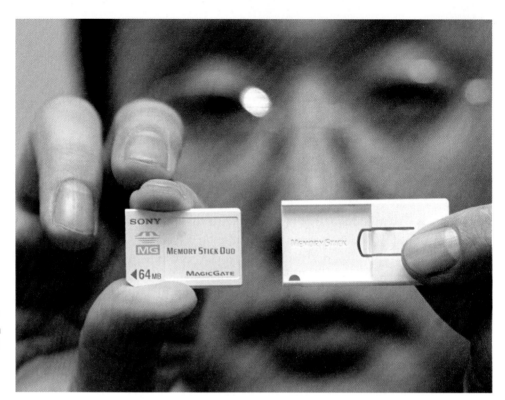

FIGURE 2-32: The Sony MagicGate™ Memory Stick®, shown right, is about one-third the size of the original Memory Stick and is designed for handhelds and other small devices.

Secure Digital™ (SD) and MultiMediaCard™ (MMC) are also about the size of a postage stamp, but SD allows for storage and protection of copyrighted data. The Memory Stick®, made by Sony, is about the size of a piece of chewing gum (see Figure 2-32). The storage capacity of these flash cards can range between 8 MB and 1 GB of data, and capacity is always increasing.

Memory Access Time

Memory access time is the amount of time required for the processor to access (read) data, instructions, and information from memory. This affects the speed at which the computer can process data and therefore the overall performance of the computer. Access time is usually stated in fractions of a second, as shown in Table 2-4. For example, a millisecond (abbreviated as ms) is one–thousandth of a second, and a picosecond (ps) is one–trillionth of a second. A processor with a memory access time of 50 nanoseconds would be twice as fast as one with an access time of 100 nanoseconds. However, computer manufacturers usually describe memory in terms of the amount of memory, not its speed. Thus, a manufacturer may specify a computer as having 64 MB (megabytes) of memory that can be expanded to 512 MB.

Term	Abbreviation	Speed
millisecond	ms	one-thousandth of a second
microsecond	μs	one-millionth of a second
nanosecond	ns	one-billionth of a second
picosecond	ps	one-trillionth of a second

TABLE 2-4: Memory Access Times (expressed in fractions of a second)

EXPANDING A COMPUTER'S CAPABILITIES

Special components, including circuit boards or cards, may be installed to increase a computer's processing capabilities (or to connect new peripheral devices such as modems and disk drives). These components are referred to as expansion boards, and the slots they fit into are called expansion slots.

Expansion Slots and Expansion Boards

An **expansion slot** is an opening allowing the insertion of an expansion board into the motherboard. **Expansion boards** are also referred to as **expansion cards, add-on boards, add-in boards, cards, adapters, adapter boards,** or **interface cards.** Examples of expansion boards include sound boards, video boards, graphics boards, and boards that allow the capture and entering of photos into a computer. Figure 2-33 displays three types of expansion boards.

Although a variety of expansion boards are available, the five main types typically found in today's computers as add-on components are sound boards, video boards, network interface boards, graphics boards, and modem boards. A **sound board** allows sound input, such as voice, by means of a microphone and sound output via speakers. A **video board**, also called a **video adapter**, enhances the quality of pictures and images displayed on the monitor. A **network interface board** allows for communication between the computer and a network. A **graphics board** enables a computer to conform to a particular graphics standard. A **modem board** enables computers to communicate via telephone lines and other communications media. Newly purchased personal computers typically include many of the necessary boards already installed. Examples of expansion boards and their main functions are shown in Table 2-5.

Notebook and other portable computers are often too small to accommodate large motherboards, expansion boards, and other components. As a result, a type of expansion board called a **PCMCIA card**, or **PC card**, has been developed specifically for smaller PCs. The PCMCIA card plugs into the side of a notebook or portable computer. Most are about the size of a credit card, only thicker, and can be unplugged and removed when no longer needed. Type I cards provide additional memory. Type II cards typically

FIGURE 2-33: An expansion board is a circuit board that can be installed inside a system unit, usually on the motherboard. Shown here are a network expansion board, also called a network interface card (NIC); a PCI expansion card; and an AGP video card.

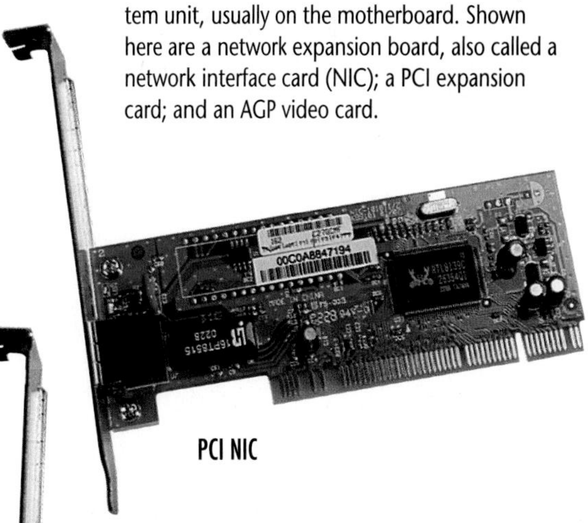

PCI NIC

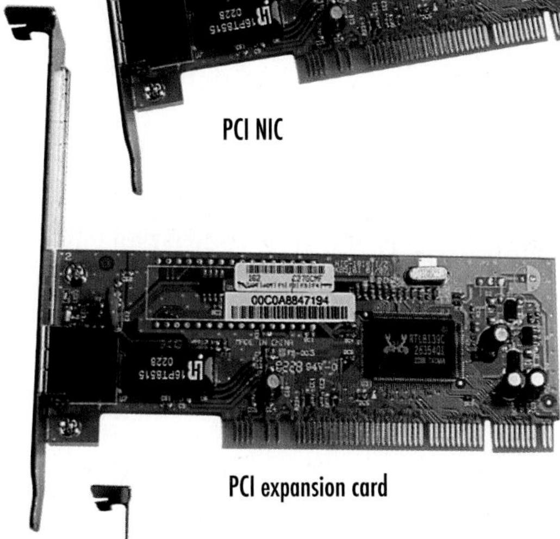

PCI expansion card

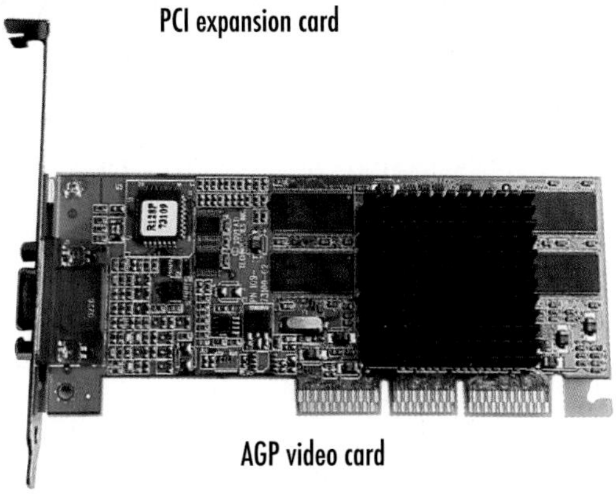

AGP video card

Type of Board	Function
accelerator board	uses specialized chips to speed up overall processing
disk controller board	enables the computer to communicate with a particular disk drive
graphics board	enables a computer system to conform to a particular graphics standard
memory expansion board	allows for additional memory to be installed in a computer
modem board	provides communications between computers
sound board	allows high-quality sound input via a microphone and output via speakers
TV tuner board	allows a PC to pick up television signals
video board	enables the computer to communicate with a computer display

TABLE 2-5: Expansion Boards. Required expansion boards such as disk controller boards and video boards come with computers. Additional expansion boards may be inserted into slots within a computer to add one or more functions.

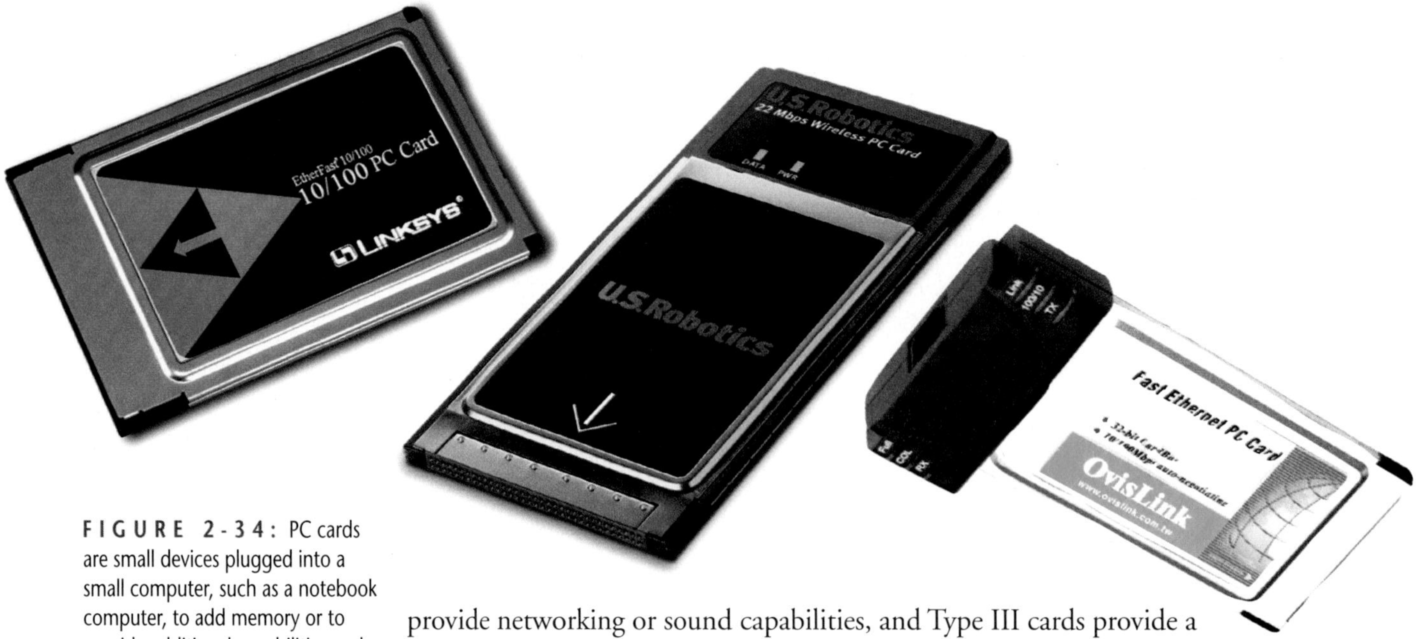

FIGURE 2-34: PC cards are small devices plugged into a small computer, such as a notebook computer, to add memory or to provide additional capabilities such as networking or sound.

provide networking or sound capabilities, and Type III cards provide a removable hard drive. Users can switch back and forth among various types of PCMCIA cards while the computer is running, a capability known as **hot swapping**. See Figure 2-34 for examples of PC cards.

Ports

A **port** (sometimes called an **interface**) is an external plug-in slot on a computer used to connect to a device such as a printer or a telephone line. Personal computers have ports that are "dedicated," meaning they are reserved for connecting a specific device. For example, a personal computer has a dedicated port for connecting a keyboard and another for connecting a mouse. Personal computers may contain one or more of the following types of ports, as shown in Figure 2-35:

- **Serial ports**, also called **communications (COM) ports**, are used for connecting almost any kind of peripheral device such as a keyboard, mouse, or modem. A serial port can transmit data only one bit at a time. Most personal computers have at least one serial port.
- **Parallel ports** are used for connecting peripheral devices to a computer. Most personal computers have at least one parallel port that is usually used for connecting a printer. A parallel port transmits data eight bits at a time. On personal computers, a parallel port uses a 25-pin connector.
- A **video port** connects a monitor and may be built into the computer or provided by a graphics board placed in an expansion slot.
- A **USB (Universal Serial Bus) port** is widely used for high-speed modems, scanners, and digital cameras. Many keyboards and point-and-click devices are now available with USB ports as well. A single USB port can accommodate more than 100 peripheral devices connected together in sequence.
- **SCSI** (an abbreviation for **s**mall **c**omputer **s**ystem **i**nterface and pronounced *scuzzy*) is a parallel interface system used by most Apple Macintosh computers, some PCs, and some UNIX systems for connecting peripheral devices to a computer. SCSI interfaces provide for faster transmission rates than standard serial and parallel ports. Users can attach multiple devices to a single SCSI port.

Due to size constraints, most personal computers have a limited number of ports, restricting the number of devices that can be connected. Some laptop computers can be inserted in a **docking station**, an accessory that provides additional ports plus (typically) a charger for the laptop's battery, extra disk drives, and other peripherals.

Buses

How does data move from one component to another inside a computer? The answer is that every computer contains buses that connect various components and allow the transmission of data. A **bus** is an electronic path within a computer system along which bits are transmitted (see Figure 2-36). The size of a bus, referred to as **bus width**, determines the number of bits the computer can transmit or receive at one time. For example, a 32-bit bus can handle 32 bits at one time, whereas a 64-bit bus can handle 64 bits at one time. The larger the number of bits a bus can handle at one time, the faster the computer can transfer data. One way to visualize a bus is to think of it as a highway allowing data to travel from one location to another, with "bus stops" along the way where data is dropped off or picked up. The more lanes in the highway, the greater the number of "vehicles" ("0s" and "1s") that can travel on the highway at one time.

Computers contain two basic bus types: a system bus and an expansion bus. A **system bus** on the motherboard connects the processor (CPU) to main memory,

power cord plug
mouse
keyboard
USB
network
serial (COM)
parallel (LPT)
video

FIGURE 2-35: Ports are external plug-in slots on a system unit that are used to connect to a device such as a printer or a telephone line.

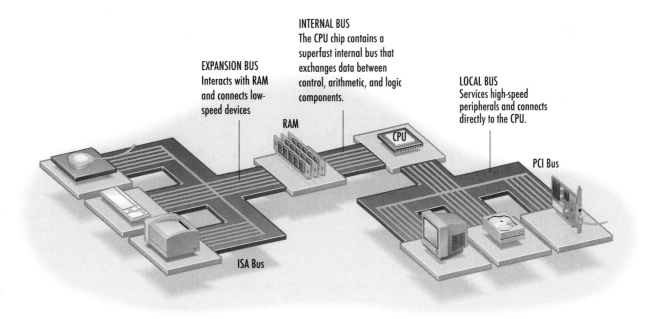

EXPANSION BUS
Interacts with RAM and connects low-speed devices

INTERNAL BUS
The CPU chip contains a superfast internal bus that exchanges data between control, arithmetic, and logic components.

LOCAL BUS
Services high-speed peripherals and connects directly to the CPU.

RAM

CPU

PCI Bus

ISA Bus

FIGURE 2-36: Data in the form of bits travel along a bus to get from one location in a computer system to another, similar to the way vehicles travel along a highway. Bits travel along a bus from memory to the CPU, from input devices to memory, from the CPU to memory, and from memory to storage devices.

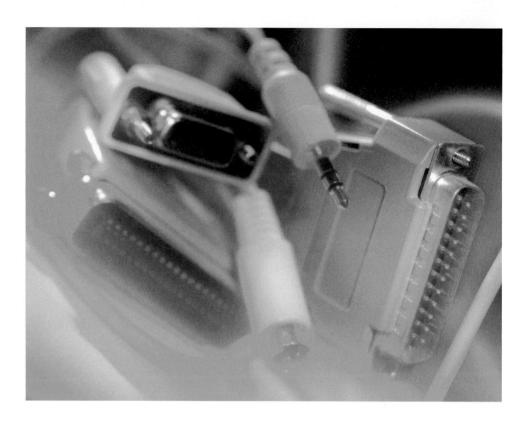

providing the CPU with fast access to data stored in RAM. An **expansion bus** provides for communication between the processor and peripheral devices. For example, data traveling between RAM and a low-speed peripheral device, such as a scanner, travels along an expansion bus.

Expansion Buses

A typical personal computer contains a variety of expansion buses. An **ISA (Industry Standard Architecture) bus**, the most common type of expansion bus, allows devices such as a mouse or modem to communicate with the processor. A **local bus** allows for the connection of high-speed devices such as hard drives. A **PCI (Peripheral Component Interconnect) bus** allows for the connection of sound cards, video cards, and network cards to a computer system. The speed at which data travels along a PCI bus is much faster than the speed at which data travels along an ISA bus. Most personal computers now contain both an ISA and a PCI bus. An **AGP (Accelerated Graphics Port) bus** increases the speed at which graphics (including 3-D graphics) and video can be transmitted and accessed by the computer. Most newer processors, including Intel's Pentium processors, support AGP technology. The **USB (Universal Serial Bus)** eliminates the need to install a board into a slot. This means that multiple external devices can be connected together and then connected to the computer's USB with a single cable. One device may be disconnected and another device connected while the computer is running, a capability known as "**hot plugging**."

Bays and Power Supply

The system unit provides for the installation of additional devices that enhance the functionality of the computer. The devices are installed in system unit locations, called bays. A **bay** is a site where a device, such as a floppy drive, hard drive, or CD-ROM, is installed. The number of bays in a computer determines the number of devices that can be installed, an important factor for buyers to consider when purchasing a PC. Figure 2-37 shows a notebook computer (top) and its various drives and bays (bottom).

PC bays come in different sizes, the most common being a bay for a hard drive or a 3.5-inch floppy drive. A bay may be internal or exposed. An internal bay is not exposed and thus cannot be used for devices such as floppy drives that require access for the manual insertion and removal of floppy disks. An internal bay is concealed entirely within the system unit. A hard disk drive is typically installed in an internal bay.

Like other electronic devices, a computer requires a **power supply** to supply energy to the computer. Many personal computers use a power cord that connects the computer into a standard alternating current (AC) 115–120 volt wall outlet. Because this type of power is unsuitable for use with a computer requiring a direct current (DC) between 5 and 12 volts, the power supply unit in the system unit converts the incoming AC current into DC current.

In addition to plug-in power, portable computers use battery power when plug-in power is unavailable or impractical. Most portable computer batteries are rechargeable, allowing the battery to be recharged for use again and again.

FIGURE 2-37: The notebook computer shown above contains a CD drive bay and a floppy disk drive bay.

cover

memory modules/banks

CD drive

specifications label for hard drive

CD drive bay

cover

floppy disk drive bay

floppy disk drive

battery

ON THE HORIZON

There can be little doubt new and exciting computer technologies will continue to appear on the computing horizon. A variety of new input and processing technologies will increase the speed and capability of computers, making our lives more enjoyable and exciting. The following paragraphs identify some technologies we may expect to be introduced within a few years, if not earlier.

Nanotechnology

Researchers in such fields as physics, chemistry, materials science, and computer science are using nanotechnology, which involves crafting machines from individual atoms, to build microscopic, massively parallel computers that are more powerful than the supercomputers of today. These computers could be programmed to replicate themselves and be injected into a human body to hunt down deadly viruses or cancers and destroy them. Scientists have already used the technology to create carbon nanotubes that are 100 times stronger and 100 times lighter than steel. Using various ways to twist the tubes, computer manufacturers can fashion them into insulators, conductors, or semiconductors.

In late 2001, IBM announced that its scientists had built a computer circuit made of nanotubes, the first logic circuit consisting of a single molecule. Although the circuit can perform only one simple operation (true/false), the development was nevertheless seen as a huge advancement in the field of computer circuitry because it could eventually lead to the creation of processors that hold up to 10,000 times more transistors in the same amount of space. In 2003, a Woburn, Massachusetts, company called Nantero Inc. introduced a nonvolatile random-access memory (NRAM) chip that uses single-walled carbon nanotubules only 20 billionths of a meter wide. The miniscule tubules are arranged in a grid that holds 5 billion bits of data in one square centimeter, which is several times the density of current high-capacity memory chips. Because the NRAM chips are about five times faster than today's speediest memory chips and they are nonvolatile, the chips are considered an exciting development for use as flash memory in digital cameras and cell phones. The federal government predicts that by the year 2015, nanotechnology will be a trillion-dollar-a-year industry and that one in four jobs will be nano-related.

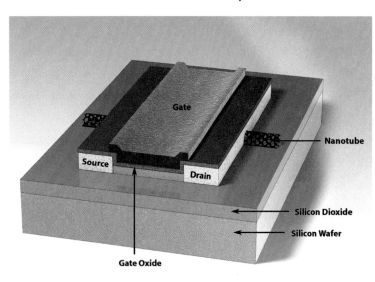

A processor chip using nanotubes might be constructed as shown above.

Cellular Computers

The Internet and Web have created a need for computers capable of handling massive amounts of information. Computers available now are relatively slow in accessing the Internet and downloading information. IBM is creating a new computer structure to better process the massive streams of information the Internet will deliver. The new structure is based on cellular technology that IBM believes will take about five years to perfect. The new technology will allow computers to run on tiny processors that are integrated directly with memory and communications circuits. The company uses the analogy of putting 32 desktop computers on a dime-sized chip. Each of these new chips will contain 32 to 36 cells, each of which will have a 1-gigahertz processor and up to 1 gigabyte of memory. The expected result will be computers with computing capabilities equal to that of today's mainframe computers. Chip manufacturer Intel predicts that future PCs will run at 20 GHz (gigahertz) with a billion transistors. By contrast, Intel's current flagship microprocessor chip, the Pentium 4, has about 42 million transistors and runs at a top speed of 5 GHz.

New and Improved Input Devices

New input devices are regularly showing up in the marketplace. One such device on the drawing board is a small keypad containing special-function buttons representing specific actions to be taken. For example, a keypad might contain buttons that print a file or activate a spell checker when pressed.

San Francisco-based Boost Technology has developed a head-mounted mouse called the Tracer™, which is designed for people who do not have the use of their hands. The user issues commands either by voice or by various head/eye motions, including nodding and blinking. Calling the device "pixel-accurate," its makers predict that Tracer could be highly effective for playing games and even in surgery.

With the mushrooming growth in a mobile workforce, computer manufacturers are researching new ways to input information that overcome the obstacle presented by the small size of handheld devices. An Israeli company called OTM Technologies has created the VPen™, a mobile input device for cell phones and other handhelds, which allows the user to write on any surface and then transmit the writing into streaming digital text onto the display of a PC, a cell phone, a PDA, or another handheld computer. The VPen looks like a regular pen and even comes with an optional ink tip. The device works by using a laser to track the movements of the pen relative to the writing surface; software then converts those movements into text, which is sent to a computer display via infrared signals.

Reconfigurable Chips

Researchers at the University of Texas are developing a processor chip that can change capabilities according to the computing tasks required at any given moment. One of their projects is called Polymorphous TRIPS architecture, in which a chip is partitioned into 100 segments, each of which can be programmed to perform different roles, such as memory or networking. Special software examines the programming instructions and arranges the 100 chip portions in a structure that handles the task most efficiently, thus greatly improving on overall processing speed. For example, if the computer calls up a video, the software would reconfigure the memory circuits as networking circuits, which would then forward the video rather than placing it in memory where it would wait to be acted upon. The project at the University of Texas is a collaborative effort of IBM, Intel, Sun Microsystems, and the Defense Advanced Research Projects Agency (DARPA).

chapter summary

Input and Processing Technology

Hardware devices can be grouped according to how and where they are used in the four steps of the **information processing cycle**. The four steps are *input*, *processing*, *output*, and *storage*.

What Is Input?

The term **input** refers to data and instructions entered into a computer enabling the computer to perform the task desired by the user. **Data** is a collection of raw, unorganized (unprocessed) content in the form of text, numbers, sound, or images. **Information** is data that has been processed in a manner rendering it useful. A **program** is a series of instructions telling a computer how to perform the tasks necessary to process the data and deliver the desired information. The **stored program concept** allows a program to be entered a single time and used again and again. A **command** is an instruction to a program issued by a user. A **user response** tells the program what to do, or the task to perform. A **dialog box** provides options from which a selection can be made.

Input Devices

An **input device** allows programs, data, commands, and responses to be entered into a computer system. Types of input devices include **keyboards**, **mice** (plural for mouse), **trackballs**, **touch pads** and **touch screens**, **joysticks**, **pens and tablets**, **graphics tablets**, **optical scanners**, **bar code** readers, **audio input devices**, **video input devices**, and **digital cameras**.

What Is Information Processing?

Also called **data processing** or simply **processing**, the term **information processing** refers to the manipulation of data according to instructions in a computer program.

How Do Computers Process Data?

All computers are **digital** devices that use the *binary number system*. They are capable of recognizing only "off" and "on" ("0" and "1") states. Each of these "0" and "1" digits is called a bit. A **bit** represents the smallest unit of data in the binary system. A group of eight bits is called a **byte**. Combinations of 0s and 1s are used to represent letters, numbers, and special characters in coding schemes such as **ASCII**, **EBCDIC**, and **Unicode**.

The System Unit

The **system unit** is the component that houses the processing hardware. It consists of the **motherboard**, also called **system board**, to which are attached a **microprocessor (CPU)**, **memory boards and chips**, **storage interfaces**, **ports**, **expansion slots**, and **expansion boards** allowing peripheral devices such as **monitors**, **keyboards**, **mice**, and **disk drives** to function properly. **Buses** allow data to move about inside the system unit.

The Central Processing Unit

The **central processing unit (CPU)** within the system unit is the part of a computer where processing occurs. In a personal computer the CPU consists of a **microprocessor**, or CPU chip, that

processes the data. The CPU contains a control unit and an arithmetic/logic unit. The **control unit** controls activity within the computer. The **arithmetic/logic unit (ALU)** performs processing operations on the data. **Registers** are used for storing instructions and data until they are needed for processing. The system clock synchronizes or controls the timing of all computer operations.

Internal Memory

RAM (random-access memory) chips inside the system unit are used

to store programs while they are being executed, and data while it is being processed. The amount of RAM is measured in bytes. **Cache memory** provides for faster access to instructions and data, speeding up computer applications. **ROM (read-only memory)** refers to chips on which instructions, information, or data has been prerecorded. Once data has been recorded on a ROM chip, it cannot be altered or removed and can only be read by the computer. **Flash memory** is a type of memory that can be erased and reprogrammed.

Computer Expansion

A **port** is a plug-in slot on a computer for connecting a peripheral device. An **expansion slot** is an opening in a computer where a circuit board, called an **expansion board**, can be inserted to add new capabilities to the computer. A **PC card** is a small expansion board that plugs into the side of a notebook or portable computer. The system unit contains areas called **bays** for installing additional devices.

GLOBE TROTTING

Luxury Cruises for Geeks

One perennial truth of working with computers is the never-ending learning curve that requires professionals to retrain themselves periodically throughout their careers. For most IT people this means dull flights to remote cities where one sits in hotel conference rooms and spends hours on end studying the latest electronic widgets. Bucking this grinding approach to retraining is a new trend to make things more fun by holding sessions on a cruise ship instead of in a hotel conference room. The training take a few more days, usually with a weekend included for travel, but surprisingly does not cost much more than training would on dry land. A company called Geek Cruises, based in Palo Alto, California, offers training in Perl, Java, and Database Administration on-board ship. Steaming up to Alaska or down through the Caribbean puts all the IT people in one spot, focused on the subject, and allows for some interesting after-hours relaxation such as dog-sledding or beach-combing.

Source: <http://www.geekcruises.com>

KEYTERMS

Page numbers indicate where terms are first cited in the chapter. A complete list of key terms with definitions can be found in the Glossary at the end of the book.

Accelerated Graphics Port (AGP) bus, 82
address, 73
arithmetic/logic unit (ALU), 69
ASCII, 64
audio input, 57
bar code reader, 55
basic input/output system (BIOS), 77
bay, 83
binary number, 63
bit (binary digit), 63
bitmap, 55
Bluetooth, 52
bus, 67, 81
bus width, 81
byte, 63
cache memory, 76
clock cycle, 70
control unit, 68
coprocessor, 70
data register, 69
decoding, 69
digital camera, 60
digitizing pen, 54
docking station, 81
dots per inch (dpi), 55
Double Data Rate SDRAM (DDR SDRAM), 75
drawing tablet, 54
dumb scanner, 55
Dynamic RAM (DRAM), 75
EBCDIC, 64
electronic chip (integrated circuit), 67
executing, 69
execution time (E-time), 69
expansion board (expansion card, add-on board, add-in board, card, adapter, adapter board, interface card), 79
expansion bus, 82
expansion slot, 79
fetching, 69
flash memory (flash ROM), 60
foot mouse, 51
gigabyte, 75

graphical user interface (GUI), 50
graphics board, 70, 79
graphics coprocessor, 70
graphics tablet, 54
hertz, 70
hot plugging, 82
hot swapping, 80
Industry Standard Architecture (ISA) bus, 82
instruction cycle *See* machine cycle
instruction register, 69
instruction time (I-time), 69
intelligent scanner, 55
interface, 80
joystick, 52
keyboard, 48
kilobyte, 75
Level 1 cache, 77
Level 2 cache, 77
Level 3 cache, 77
local bus, 82
machine cycle, 69
machine language, 63
main memory (primary storage), 72
math coprocessor, 70
megabyte, 75
memory access time, 78
modem board, 79
motherboard, 66
mouse, 50
mouse pad, 51
mouse pointer (cursor), 50
network interface board, 79
nonvolatile, 77
optical character recognition (OCR), 55
optical mouse, 51
optical reader, 56
optical scanner (scanner), 55
parallel port, 80
parallel processing, 72
PCMCIA card (PC card), 79
Peripheral Component Interconnect (PCI) bus, 82
pipelining, 72
pixel, 55

port, 80
power-on self test (POST), 77
power supply, 83
Rambus DRAM (RDRAM), 75
random-access, 75
random-access memory (RAM), 72
read-only memory (ROM), 77
register, 69
resolution, 55
RISC, 71
SCSI, 80
semiconductor, 67
serial port (communications port, COM port), 80
smart card, 57
sound board, 79
speaker-dependent, 58
speaker-independent, 58
special-function keyboard, 49
speech recognition, 58
Static RAM (SRAM), 75
storage register, 69
storing, 69
Synchronous DRAM (SDRAM), 75
system bus, 81
system clock, 69
touch pad (track pad), 52
touch screen, 52
trace, 66
trackball, 51
Unicode, 65
Universal Product Code (UPC), 55
Universal Serial Bus (USB) port, 80
video board (video adapter), 79
video capture card, 58
video input, 58
video port, 80
voice input, 57
voice recognition, 57
volatile, 75
word, 71
word size, 71

chapter exercises

The following chapter exercises, along with new activities and information, are also offered in the *Computers: Understanding Technology* Internet Resource Center at www.emcp.com.

EXPLORING WINDOWS

Tutorial 2 walks you through the steps of taking the Windows XP tour.

TERMS CHECK: MATCHING

Write the letter of the correct answer on the line before each numbered item.

a. motherboard
b. fetching
c. keyboard
d. arithmetic/logic unit
e. bay
f. binary
g. joystick
h. port

i. expansion slot
j. bit
k. ASCII
l. system clock
m. register
n. expansion board
o. mouse

_____ 1. A number system that uses combinations of zeros and ones (0s and 1s) to represent letters, numbers, and special characters.

_____ 2. A circuit board that can be inserted into a computer to give the computer added capability.

_____ 3. Retrieving an instruction or data from memory.

_____ 4. The smallest unit of data a computer can understand and act on.

_____ 5. The main circuit board inside the system unit.

_____ 6. A component of the ALU that temporarily holds instructions and data.

_____ 7. A small electronic chip that synchronizes or controls the timing of all computer operations.

_____ 8. The interface on a computer used for connecting a device.

_____ 9. An opening in the computer allowing a circuit board to be inserted into the motherboard.

_____ 10. A handheld point-and-click input device whose movement across a flat surface causes a corresponding movement of its on-screen pointer.

_____ 11. A small box containing a vertical lever that, when pushed in certain directions, moves the graphics cursor correspondingly on the screen.

_____ 12. The part of the CPU that carries out instructions and performs arithmetic and logical operations on the data.

_____ 13. A site on the system unit where another device, such as a hard drive, can be installed.

_____ 14. A coding scheme used on most computers, including personal computers, to represent data.

_____ 15. The most common input device used to enter alphanumeric characters into a computer.

TECHNOLOGY ILLUSTRATED: IDENTIFY THE PROCESS

What process is illustrated in this drawing? Identify the process and write a paragraph describing the steps.

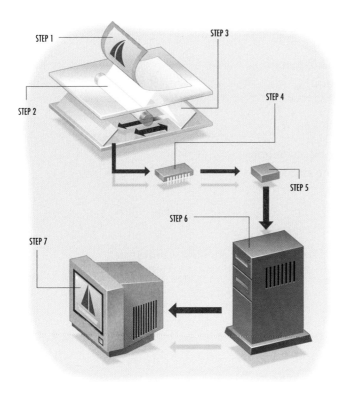

STEP 1

STEP 3

STEP 2

STEP 4

STEP 5

STEP 6

STEP 7

KNOWLEDGE CHECK: MULTIPLE CHOICE
Circle the letter of the best answer from those provided.

1. Data and instructions entered into a computer that enable the computer to perform desired tasks are called

   a. processing.
   b. input.
   c. storage.
   d. controlling.

2. Data that has been processed in a manner that renders it meaningful and useful to the user is called

   a. input.
   b. information.
   c. a program.
   d. fetching.

3. A CPU contains

   a. a card reader and a printing device.
   b. an analytical engine and a control unit.
   c. a control unit and an arithmetic/logic unit.
   d. an arithmetic logic unit and a card reader.

4. The part of a computer that coordinates all of its functions is called its

   a. ROM program.
   b. system board.
   c. arithmetic/logic unit.
   d. control unit.

5. A byte is equal to

   a. four bits, or one nibble.
   b. six bits and one nibble.
   c. two bits.
   d. eight bits.

6. Which of the following does *not* have a processor?

   a. Mainframe
   b. PC
   c. PDA
   d. Terminal

7. The system clock inside a computer ensures that the

    a. computer user will always know the correct time.
    b. computer will run faster than one without a system clock.
    c. activities of the computer will be properly synchronized.
    d. computer will be able to address a 32-bit data bus.

8. An opening on the system unit that allows users to connect other devices to the computer is called a(n)

    a. slot.
    b. opening.
    c. plug-in.
    d. control unit.

9. The parts of the information processing cycle are

    a. fetching, decoding, executing, and storing.
    b. fetching, comparing, interpreting, and outputting.
    c. inputting, interpreting, processing, and outputting.
    d. inputting, processing, outputting, and storing.

10. Processing speed in microprocessors is measured in

    a. megabytes.
    b. hertz.
    c. kilobytes.
    d. bits per second.

11. An input device in which hundreds of tiny wires forming an electronic matrix are embedded in the surface allowing mapmakers and engineers to trace precise drawings is called a(n)

    a. electronic drawing board.
    b. scanner.
    c. graphics tablet.
    d. matrix board.

12. Two widely used data coding schemes based on the binary system are EBCDIC and

    a. BCADIC.
    b. ASCII.
    c. ABCII.
    d. ECRIDA.

13. On a personal computer, all processing functions are contained on a single electronic chip called a

   a. microprocessor.
   b. data processor.
   c. calculation chip.
   d. BIOS chip.

14. The part of the CPU that carries out instructions and performs the actual arithmetic and logical operations on the data is the

   a. control unit.
   b. arithmetic/logic unit.
   c. memory unit.
   d. system clock.

15. A holding area that stores the data and instructions most recently called by the processor from RAM is called

   a. residual memory.
   b. nonvolatile memory.
   c. static memory.
   d. cache memory.

THINGS THAT THINK: BRAINSTORMING NEW USES
In groups or individually, contemplate the following questions and develop as many answers as you can.

1. Scientists have invented the first prototype of a computerized scalpel that can tell a surgeon when to stop cutting during surgery to remove cancerous tumors so that only the diseased tissue is removed. This technology would allow doctors to save healthy tissue, thus potentially improving the patient's odds for survival. What other fields could benefit from this development? Consider possible uses in various industries.

2. Computers can accomplish many tasks today, but there are still some things they cannot do. Think of some of the things you would like the computers of the future to be able to do. Which of the new uses will be the most popular and why?

KEY PRINCIPLES: COMPLETION
Fill in the blanks with the appropriate words or phrases.

1. An input device that uses a light sensor instead of a mouse ball to track movement is called a(n) _____.

2. A type of input device that allows a user to make selections from among a group of options displayed on a screen by pressing a finger against the chosen option is known as a(n) _____.

3. Material captured by a scanner is stored as a matrix of rows and columns of dots, called a _____.

4. Software that allows text or a captured image to be edited or changed with a word processor or other application program is called

_____.

5. Input that occurs using a special type of video camera attached to the computer and plugged into a video capture card is known as

_____.

6. A computer language that uses binary numbers, which are constructed solely of the symbols 0 and 1, is known as _____.

7. A type of code capable of accommodating certain languages having more complicated alphabets than English is called _____.

8. Small electronic devices consisting of tiny transistors and other circuit parts on a piece of semiconductor material are called electronic chips or

_____.

9. The action of retrieving an instruction or data from memory is called

_____.

10. A small electronic chip that synchronizes or controls the timing of all computer operations is a _____.

11. A computer word is _____.

12. Parallel processing allows _____.

13. Random-access memory (RAM) is _____.

14. Cache memory is _____.

15. Four steps or actions in a machine cycle are _____.

TECH ARCHITECTURE: LABEL THE DRAWING

In this illustration of a machine cycle, label the steps as fetching, decoding, executing, or storing.

TECHNO LITERACY: RESEARCH AND WRITING
Develop appropriate written responses based on your research for each item.

1. What is inside the computer case?

   Ask your instructor to allow you to open up a computer in the computer lab and look at the components inside. Using paper and pen, draw the components that you recognize and label each one. At a minimum, include the microprocessor chip, memory chips (RAM and ROM), expansion slots, expansion boards, and ports. Ask your instructor to explain other components you do not recognize. Label each one and write a brief summary of the component's function.

2. How many ways can users input data?

   Page through a computer magazine such as *PC World* or visit a computer store and select a personal computer that interests you. Research and describe all of the different input devices that could be used with that particular computer system.

3. What can you do with an expansion board?

   Describe the various types of expansion boards and their functions. What kind of expansion boards would you like to add to your computer? Why?

4. How do the kinds of computer memory differ?

   Describe the differences between RAM, ROM, flash memory, and cache memory. Is there any relationship between processing speed and the different types of memory? If so, what?

TECHNOLOGY ISSUES: TEAM PROBLEM-SOLVING
In groups, brainstorm possible solutions to the issues presented.

1. As our population ages, the number of Americans with disabilities will increase. Computers and computer technology offer the potential to make life easier for people who are disabled. What are some of the possibilities? What are some of the ways computer technology may be used to improve their lives in the future? Do you foresee any ethical problems with any of these solutions?

2. Even in today's computerized world there are still people who do not like computers and try to avoid them as much as possible. Why do you think people would feel that way? Do you see this attitude increasing or decreasing in the future? What can be done to combat this computer phobia (fear or dislike of computers), or should anything be done at all?

MINING DATA: INTERNET RESEARCH AND REPORTING
Conduct Internet searches to find the information described in the activities below. Write a brief report that summarizes your research results. Be sure to document your sources, using the MLA format (see Chapter 1, page 43, to review MLA style guidelines).

1. Moore's Law is a famous concept in the information technology industry. Developed around a prediction in 1965 by Gordon Moore, cofounder of Intel Corporation, the law holds that the computing capability of integrated circuits, measured by the number of transistors per square inch, doubles every 18 months (originally, Moore said 12 months). Research this topic and explain why Moore's Law continues to be accurate or why it has proved incorrect. What are industry leaders predicting for the future?

2. What is the most powerful supercomputer in the world? Where is it located? Who designed and manufactured the computer? What is it used for?

3. Research the topic of spying technologies that countries use to gather information on each other's activities. What are some of the newest devices and how successful are they?

TECHNOLOGY TIMELINE: PREDICTING NEXT STEPS

Look at the timeline below that outlines the major milestones in the evolution of digital camera technology. Research this topic and predict the next major steps. Complete the timeline through the year 2025.

1982   Sony releases the first commercial electronic still camera, which was a video camera that took video freeze-frames.

1989   The first true digital camera that stored images with digital signals is introduced.

1994   The first digital cameras for the general consumer market are released.

1995   Sony debuts the first digital camcorder.

2002   Cell phones with digital cameras become available in the United States.

ETHICAL DILEMMAS: GROUP DISCUSSION AND DEBATE

As a class or within an assigned group, discuss the following ethical dilemma.

As technology manufacturers look to cut costs, they often consider "outsourcing" production to an offshore company or moving production facilities to countries outside of the United States. Either of these options may result in savings due to lower labor and facilities costs.

In your group, discuss the issues of outsourcing production and moving production facilities to other countries. Are these practices illegal or unethical? Should such cost-cutting measures be considered more important than the employment of U.S. workers? Is it fair for companies to pay workers lower wages in another country? Should there be incentives for companies to maintain their facilities in the United States?

ANSWERS TO TERMS CHECK AND
KEY PRINCIPLES QUESTIONS

Terms Check: 1 – f; 2 – n; 3 – b; 4 – j; 5 – a; 6 – m; 7 – l; 8 – h; 9 – i; 10 – o; 11 – g; 12 – d; 13 – e; 14 – k; 15 – c

Key Principles: 1 – optical mouse; 2 – touch screen; 3 – bitmap; 4 – optical character recognition (OCR); 5 – video input; 6 – machine language; 7 – Unicode; 8 – integrated circuits; 9 – fetching; 10 – system clock; 11 – a group of bits or bytes that a computer can manipulate or process as a unit; 12 – two or more processors to work concurrently on segments of a lengthy application, thus dramatically increasing processing capability; 13 – temporary memory in which programs and data are stored while the computer is in use; 14 – a holding area in which instructions and data most recently called by the processor from RAM are stored; 15 – fetching, decoding, executing, and storing

Buying and Installing a PC

Shopping for a personal computer (PC) can be enjoyable, if you are well informed. Some shoppers think all personal computers are alike so their main objective is to find the cheapest one. Doing so can be a mistake. Many first-time buyers have discovered that the computer they purchased lacked components and features they needed. Avoid making this mistake by arming yourself with information and careful planning. The following sections provide some useful guidelines to help you find the right desktop, notebook, or hand-held PC and then install it.

BUYING A DESKTOP PERSONAL COMPUTER SYSTEM

The decision to buy a PC, such as the one shown in Figure A-1, represents a major investment in both time and money. Chances are that you will use your computer for at least three years, perhaps even longer. Before making the final purchasing decision, complete each step in the process outlined below.

Step One: Identify Your Needs

Before spending your money, prepare a written list of your computing needs and how and where you will be using your new system. Following is a list of questions that will help you identify your needs.

1. **Where will I use my new PC?** If you will be using it only in your home or office, a desktop computer may be suitable. However, if you travel for business or if you need mobility in general, you should consider purchasing a notebook (laptop) computer weighing five pounds or less. See the "Buying a Notebook Computer" section for additional guidelines.

2. **For which purposes will I use my computer?** For example, will you use your PC to prepare letters and reports? Analyze numeric and financial data? Prepare visual presentations? Access the Internet? Listen to music? Create and work with graphics? List all possible uses, since these will determine the software and hardware you need. Generally, if you will use multimedia and/or graphics programs, you will need greater storage and processing capabilities.

3. **How long will I keep this computer?** Try to estimate the number of years you will use your computer before buying the next one. If you expect to use your PC for several years, consider buying one that has expansion slots so you can add new components, such as a modem, printer, or add-on memory boards.

Step Two: Establish a Budget

Ask yourself how much you can realistically afford to pay for a computer. Prices of desktop personal computers range from a few hundred to thousands of dollars. Faster and more feature-rich PCs are usually more expensive. Also, personal computers soon become obsolete. Within a few years you may need a faster and more versatile model.

Step Three: Choose Software to Match Your Needs List

Every computer must have software, including system software and applications software. System software, such as Microsoft Windows or Mac OS, allows a computer to manage its computing resources, including the system unit and input and output devices. Most PCs come with the system software already installed. For general business or academic situations, Windows-based systems are

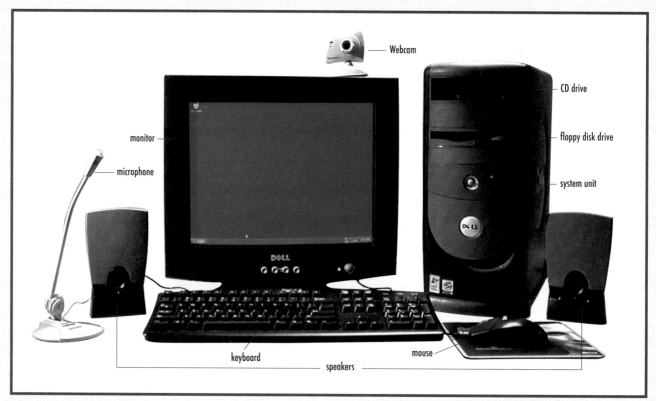

Webcam

CD drive

floppy disk drive

system unit

monitor

microphone

keyboard

mouse

speakers

F I G U R E   A - 1 : A complete personal computer system includes not only the system unit, monitor, keyboard, and mouse, but also a printer and speakers and possibly a webcam.

more widely used, but for graphics applications, a Mac platform is preferable.

Determine the total storage space and processing power you will need for the programs you intend to use. These calculations will drive your hardware choices. Note, too, that some PCs arrive from the factory with a software suite, such as Microsoft Office, already installed. The suite includes word processing, spreadsheet, database management, e-mail, and other applications.

Step Four: Select the Hardware Components

Hardware refers to all of the equipment that makes up a personal computer system: the system unit, input devices, output devices, secondary storage devices, and all peripheral devices, such as printers. Following are some guidelines for selecting PC hardware components.

The System Unit

The system unit is typically a metal cabinet containing the essential components for processing information. Along with other standard components, the system unit contains a microprocessor, main memory (RAM), and slots for installing a graphics board, sound board, modem, or other peripherals. Hard disk drives, CD drives, and DVD drives are also housed in the system unit. Increasingly, PC manufacturers are not including a floppy disk drive in new computers.

- **PC architecture.** PC architecture refers to the design and construction of the PC and its system unit, and not all architectures are the same. For example, the architecture of an Apple Macintosh differs from that of an IBM or IBM-compatible PC. Therefore, software written for an Apple Macintosh PC may not run on an

IBM or IBM-compatible PC. Although some users prefer a Macintosh PC, more software is available for IBM and IBM-compatibles.

- **Microprocessor.** Selecting the right microprocessor is extremely important. Processing speed, typically measured in gigahertz (GHz), is probably the first consideration. The higher the number of GHz, the faster the processor can access and process programs and data. If speed is important, consider choosing a microprocessor with a speed of 2.0 GHz or more. PCs containing microprocessors with speeds up to 3.0 GHz and higher are available.

- **Main memory.** Main memory (RAM) is needed for the temporary storage of programs and data while the data is being processed. Some application software requires a considerable amount of RAM to function properly, and newer software versions usually require more RAM than older versions. Newer desktop PCs typically come with 128 MB of RAM, or more. Make certain the PC has sufficient RAM to run the software you will be using. For example, if you will work with graphics, watch movies, or listen to music, consider buying a PC with 512 MB of RAM.

- **Secondary storage.** What type(s) and amounts of secondary storage are you likely to need? Most computers come with a CD drive and a hard disk drive already installed. A standard compact disc can store up to 750 MB of data, and certain DVDs provide even greater storage capacity. A hard disk drive contains one or more rigid storage platters and provides for the permanent storage of considerably more data. However, the disk itself cannot be removed from the drive. The storage capacity of a hard disk is an important consideration because it is used to store all system and application software, such as Microsoft Word. Typical hard disk capacities are 20, 40, or 60 GB and more.

Other secondary storage devices and media are available. If you will use your PC to play movies, your purchase should include a DVD drive. If you will work with large files, consider purchasing a computer that includes a CD-RW drive. A CD-RW disc is a reusable high-capacity disc that allows you to store huge amounts of data and to erase data no longer needed.

- **Ports.** A port on a personal computer is a connection you can use to connect a device, such as a mouse or printer. A personal computer has internal ports and external ports (see Figure A-2). An internal port allows for the connection of components such as disk drives. External ports allow you to connect peripheral devices such as modems, printers, and mice. The number of available ports determines the number of devices and add-on boards that can be connected to the system unit.

Three basic types of ports are parallel, serial, and USB, and most PCs have at least one of each. A par-

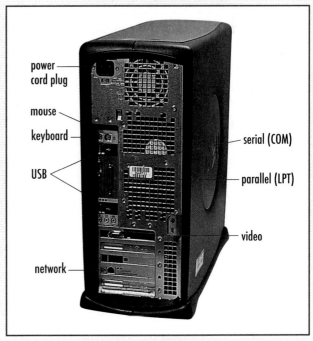

FIGURE A-2: Ports are typically visible on the back of the system unit.

allel port connects an external device, such as a printer. A serial port is a general-purpose port that can be used to connect almost any type of device, including modems, mice, and printers. A USB (Universal Serial Bus) port connects various devices including keyboards, mice, monitors, and printers. USB ports are particularly important if you need to connect a digital camera or connect to the Internet via a cable modem.

Some manufacturers label external ports to make it easy for users to identify ports where devices are to be connected to the system unit. For example, printer, mice, and keyboard ports are often labeled. Many new PCs come with instructions and diagrams that identify the ports to which specific devices are to be connected.

Input Devices

Typical input devices are a keyboard and a mouse, although other kinds of input devices are available. Most keyboards and mice operate similarly. However, there are slight differences in how each "feels" to the user. Before buying a PC, examine the keyboard and mouse for comfort and ease of use. Some sellers will allow you to exchange the keyboard or mouse that comes with the computer for a different one of comparable value.

Output Devices

Output devices produce output in either soft copy or hard copy form. Most PCs come with a monitor (for soft copy output), but you may have to purchase a hard copy device, such as a printer, separately.

- **Monitors.** There are wide differences among PC monitors, with resolution being perhaps the most important variable. Resolution refers to the clarity of the text and images being displayed on the screen. Higher resolutions, such as a resolution of 1,024 by 1,024 pixels, display text and images with exceptional clarity. High-resolution monitors are typically more expensive, but may be worth the extra cost.

Monitor size is another important consideration. Viewing areas range from 15 diagonal inches to 21 inches and higher. Larger monitors are usually more expensive, but may be a priority if you work with graphics or if your vision is weak.

- **Printers.** Two popular types of printers are inkjet and laser, both of which are versatile and capable of producing high-quality output in color. Examine a variety of printers and models and check the price and output quality of each.

Most inkjet printers are quiet, produce high-quality output, and are relatively inexpensive, although the ink cartridges they use can be expensive. Print resolution is an important factor to consider. Some offer impressive resolution and can produce output of amazing color.

Laser printers are fast and can produce high-quality output in both black and color tones. Color laser printers are more expensive than those using only black toner. The cost of color laser printers ranges from a few hundred to thousands of dollars.

BUYING A NOTEBOOK COMPUTER

A notebook (or laptop) computer is a portable personal computer that contains the components and devices people use most often (see Figure A-3). However, various brands and models are available, and you should select the notebook that will match your list of needs, as described in the preceding section. Following are guidelines for buying a notebook computer.

Compatibility

As a buyer, you have a choice between a Windows and Macintosh computer. If you already have a Windows desktop PC and will share programs and data between the two, consider buying a Windows notebook. If, on the other hand, you will be working with graphics applications, you may want to check out Macintosh notebook models.

FIGURE A-3: Notebook computers provide the same basic functionality as a desktop computer and are portable.

Computer Size and Weight

Notebooks vary in weight from about four pounds to more than eight pounds. If you will be carrying it with you, a seven- or eight-pound computer can be quite burdensome.

Keyboard and Pointing Devices

Check out a variety of notebooks and the keyboard and pointing device each offers. Do you prefer a pointing lever or a touchpad? Are you comfortable working on a small keyboard? Select a notebook that has a keyboard and pointing device that feels the most comfortable.

Display Screen

Before you buy, examine the size and clarity of the computer's display screen. Screens range from about 12 inches up to 17 inches, measured diagonally. Larger screens typically offer better viewing but they are heavier and usually more expensive. Also, some

screens must be viewed directly whereas other types can be viewed from various angles.

Disk Type and Capacity

Choose the type and capacity of disk drives. Will you need a floppy disk drive? A hard disk drive? A CD-ROM or CD-RW drive? A notebook hard disk should have a minimum capacity of 30 GB. If you will use the computer to watch movies and/or listen to music, you will need speakers and a DVD drive.

Internal Memory (RAM)

Internal memory capacity is an important consideration. Select a computer with at least 256 MB of RAM. Less RAM will limit the kinds of software you use and the applications you can run on your computer.

Wireless Capability

Consider the option of built-in wireless capabilities. If you will travel and take your notebook with you, having wireless capability is essential. Many hotels, airports, restaurants, and other facilities now provide wireless access.

BUYING A HANDHELD COMPUTER

During recent years, the popularity of handheld computers has ballooned, particularly for mobile workers and people who want computer access anytime, anywhere. Depending on the specific handheld model, these lightweight pocket-sized computers that fit in the palm of one's hand offer a range of features, including an appointment book, notepad, calculator, and calendar. Some are Web-enabled, allowing owners to access information and to send and receive e-mail. Some handhelds also are preloaded with basic application software, including word processing and spreadsheet programs. Data entry and command selection are accomplished with

a pen-like stylus or a small fold-out keyboard (see Figure A-4).

If you are in the market for a handheld, follow these guidelines to narrow the field of choices:

- **Decide how much you are willing to pay.** Prices range from less than $100 to about $1,200, depending on the type of handheld and the features offered. For example, about $250 will buy a handheld with a color 320 by 320-pixel screen, about 25 MB of memory, and a 200 megahertz processor. For about $400, you can get a 400-megahertz chip, 50 MB of free memory, and a screen display of 320 by 480 pixels.
- **Determine which applications you want to run on your computer.** Read available literature and talk with other handheld users to get their opinions and suggestions. For business purposes, you may want programs such as Microsoft Word, Excel, and PowerPoint. For

FIGURE A-4: Handheld computers offer organizer features such as an appointment book, notepad, calculator, and calendar. Additional software, including a word processing program, can be added to some models.

personal use, you may want MP3 capability in addition to the basic organizer functions.

- **Visit a computer retailer and ask a sales associate to demonstrate the various models available.** With the employee's supervision, practice using the computer's touch screen and the device's keyboard and stylus (if available with the computer).
- **Decide whether you want a color or monochrome (black and white) screen.** Most users prefer color, and color-screen resolutions have improved markedly in recent years. A black-and-white display may be acceptable for buyers who will use only the calendar and appointment book features.
- **Check out battery life and accessories.** A long battery life may be a top consideration if your handheld is your only computer or your main work device. Think of the accessories you may need, such as an extra battery, battery charger, and carrying case for your computer. If you travel frequently, you may need a modem, removable storage, and a portable keyboard.
- **Decide whether you need Internet access and wireless capability.** Some handhelds come equipped with a modem and software that provides for wireless connections and Internet access. If you will need these capabilities, make sure the device you are considering offers them.

Before you make a purchase, learn whether the device is upgradeable so you can add additional capability in the future. Memory Sticks, for example, offer a quick and easy way to boost power and performance.

INSTALLING A DESKTOP PERSONAL COMPUTER SYSTEM

Because most notebook computers and handhelds are self-contained, the computer installation process mainly applies to desktop computers. Installing a new desktop PC requires following a few basic steps that should take less than an hour.

Prior to bringing your new PC to your home or office, or having it delivered, you need to decide where to position it. Estimate the total space the system will require. You will want to find a comfortable location near one or more electrical outlets. Avoid placing your PC where it will be exposed to direct sunlight or dampness. If your computer contains a dial-up modem and you will be connecting to an Internet service provider (ISP), your computer should be located near a telephone jack.

Step One: Unpack Your Computer System

While unpacking your new computer and components, locate all items including power cords and cables, manuals, assembly instructions and diagrams, and warranty cards. Keep these items together. Be sure to fill out all warranty cards and mail them to the respective manufacturers to register your purchase in case you need to contact the manufacturer for technical assistance. Store the containers and padding materials in case you need to return the computer or a defective component to the manufacturer. As you continue unpacking, carefully place each component on your desk or table.

Step Two: Connect the Components

After unpacking and placing the system unit at your workplace, look closely at the various ports on the back of the system unit (refer to Figure A-2). Usually, ports are labeled or color-coded to help you match each device with its port. Also, some manufacturers enclose written instructions and illustrations for connecting system devices. Locate these documents and carefully follow the instructions.

Because some system devices and peripherals, including the system unit, monitor, and printer, require electrical power, each uses a power cord. Locate the cord for each device and plug it into the device. Some devices have a permanently attached cord.

You can protect components from damage that can result from power surges by using a surge suppressor (see Figure A-5). Plug the power cords into the device. Later, you will plug the surge suppressor into a wall outlet. (*Caution*: do not plug the surge suppressor into an electric outlet until you are ready to boot up the computer system.)

F I G U R E   A - 5 : A surge suppressor protects computer components from damage during electrical power surges.

Each device that comprises your computer system needs to connect to the system unit by means of a cable. To connect a device, connect one end of the cable into the device itself and the other end into the appropriate port on the system unit (usually located at the back of the system unit). In addition to color coding cables and ports, some manufacturers package a color-coded chart or diagram showing how cables are to be connected. Typically, cable connectors are physically designed to fit a particular port.

Step Three: Boot the Computer

After connecting all devices, plug the surge suppressor into a wall outlet and turn on the computer. Check to make sure all components and devices work properly. If a device does not work, check first to see if the device is properly connected to the system unit, turned on, and plugged into the surge suppressor. If the computer, device, or component still fails to work properly, you can get help from an experienced user or from the seller's or manufacturer's Help Desk.

A FINAL WORD

Although prices are declining, a computer still represents a major expenditure, whether you are buying a desktop, notebook, or handheld PC. Do your homework. Ask for recommendations from friends or colleagues. Carefully examine various computer makes and models and then choose wisely. Chances are, the choice you make is one you will live with for a long time. Making the right decisions results in the purchase of a highly effective and efficient tool you will enjoy using in your home, at the office, in school, or on the road.

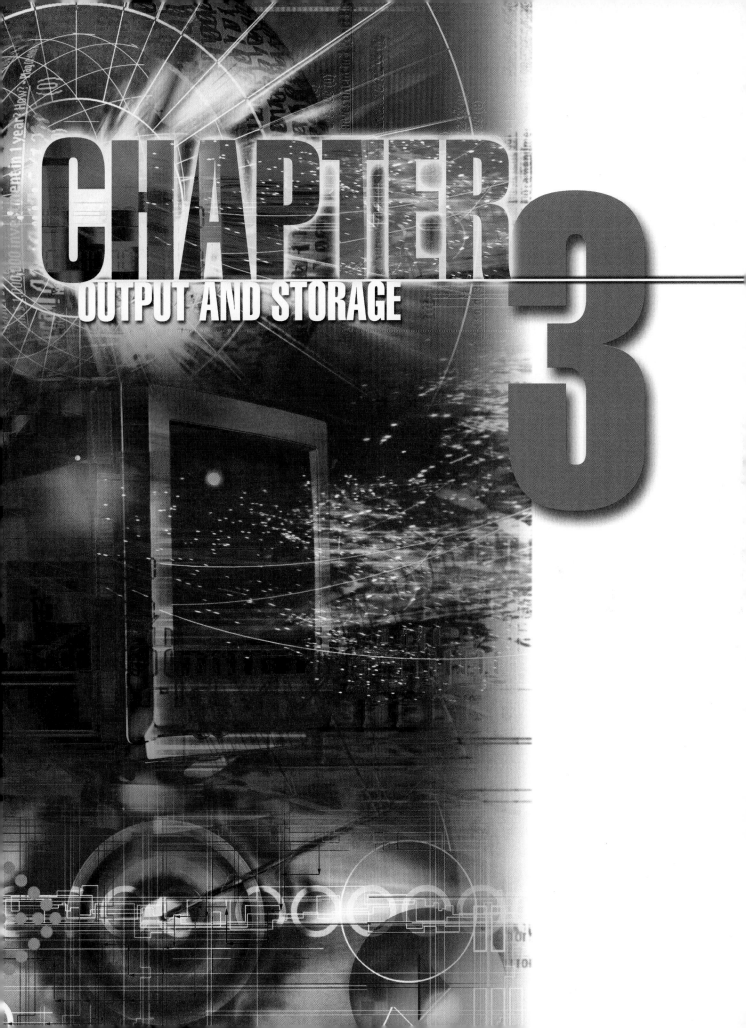

CHAPTER 3

OUTPUT AND STORAGE

UNDERSTANDING TECHNOLOGY

learning objectives

- Define output, and describe hard copy, soft copy, and the different types of output

- Explain the difference between an output device and output media

- Identify the major types of monitor technologies and how they function

- Describe the various types of printers, their printing processes, and the types of printing jobs they are commonly used for

- Identify the less common types of output devices and their uses

- Explain the types of storage media, how they operate, and how data or information is stored on them

key concepts

- What Is Output?

- Types of Display Devices

- Types of Printers

- Speakers and Voice Output

- Storage Devices and Media

CYBER SCENARIO

On the drive to her office, Nell Adams, vice president of marketing at a Miami import company, contemplates her busy day ahead. First, she has a meeting with the company's district marketing managers, after which she will interview a candidate for a vacant district manager position in Denver, Colorado. Although she can't recall her other appointments, she will access her schedule when she arrives at the office. Pulling into her company's downtown parking deck, she parks in her reserved space, grabs her briefcase, locks her car, and takes the elevator to her office on the building's tenth floor.

As she approaches the door of her office suite, she remembers to pause while a security camera quickly photographs the iris of her right eye and compares the image to a previously captured image stored in the company's computer database. Within seconds a digitized voice greets her with the words, "Good morning, Ms. Adams," and the door to her suite is unlocked.

Entering her office, Nell is greeted by her administrative assistant and informed that her morning tea will soon be ready. Nell proceeds to her desk, settles into her chair, and presses a button underneath the desktop. A large screen connected to the information systems database descends from the ceiling as a voice from two hidden speakers says, "Good morning, Ms. Adams. What can I do for you?" Nell responds, "Get me the November sales reports for all marketing districts." Almost immediately, the report for the Southeast district appears on the screen, followed by the remaining district reports, each of which is displayed for 30 seconds. After a brief inspection of the information, Nell issues a voice command to print all the reports. Within minutes, the printer in the mahogany cabinet behind her desk has produced the documents.

Nell then issues a verbal command to display the application form and resume of James Walker, whom she will interview at 10 a.m. for the vacant marketing position. Both documents are immediately displayed in the order they were requested. With Nell's command to print both documents, the laser printer quickly outputs the resume and application, and Nell prepares to examine them more carefully. Finally, Nell issues a request to see her schedule for the day, which is promptly displayed on the drop-down screen above her desk. She spends the next few minutes carefully reviewing the marketing reports and James Walker's employment information.

All in all, it will be a typically fast-paced and productive day for Nell, made possible by modern state-of-the-art computer, storage, and output technologies that provide the information she needs to devise strategies and make decisions. Technologies similar to those Nell uses are rapidly becoming available in the workplace, allowing managers and employees to boost their productivity and enhance their employers' competitive position in the marketplace.

WHAT IS OUTPUT?

Recall from Chapter 1 that output is processed data that can be used immediately or stored in computer-usable form for later use. Output may be produced in either hard copy or soft copy, or in both forms. Hard copy is a permanent version of output, such as a letter printed on paper. Soft copy is a temporary version and includes any output that cannot be physically handled. For example, the information displayed on a bank teller's computer terminal screen during an account balance inquiry is considered soft copy. Voice output such as the telephone company's computerized directory assistance is another form of soft copy. We depend on all sorts of output in our daily lives.

Types of Output

Computer output may consist of a single type of output or a combination of types. A properly equipped computer system is capable of producing four types of output:

- text
- graphics
- audio
- video

Text consists of characters and numbers used to create words, sentences, and paragraphs that comprise various types of text-based documents, including letters, memos, mailing labels, and newsletters. Web pages typically contain text and may also contain other forms of output including graphics, music, voice, and sound.

Graphics, or **graphical images**, are computer-generated pictures produced on a computer screen, paper, or film. Graphics range from simple line or bar charts to detailed and

colorful images and pictures. Graphics are often seen on commercial Web page advertisements.

Audio is any sound, including speech and music. If a computer is equipped with a sound card and speakers, users can insert a CD into its CD-ROM drive and listen to music while relaxing or working on a project. Numerous Web sites provide sound that allows users to listen to a sales pitch describing a product, or to sample selections from an advertised music CD.

Video consists of motion images, similar to those seen on a television or movie screen. Video is often accompanied by audio, making the output even more realistic and lifelike. A popular use of both audio and video is for creating home movies. By attaching a video camera to a computer, anyone can capture and play back movies of family members that record both images and conversation.

Output Devices and Media

An output device is any hardware device that makes information available to a user. A computer produces output using the combination of output devices, media, and software available with a particular system. Popular output devices include displays (monitors), printers, plotters, televisions, and speakers. An **output medium** is any medium or material on which information is recorded. Examples of output media include paper, plastic film, and magnetic tape.

DISPLAY DEVICES (MONITORS)

A **display device**, or **monitor**, is a fundamental component of every single-user computer system and is the most common soft copy output mechanism for displaying text, images, graphics, and video on a screen. Available in a variety of shapes, sizes, costs, and capabilities, monitors allow users to view information temporarily. Figure 3-1 shows examples of some popular types of monitors.

A monitor consists of a plastic case housing a viewing screen and the electronic components that allow information to be displayed on the screen. Most mobile computers contain a monitor housed in the same case as the computer and other components. For example, the monitor of a notebook computer is attached to the case with hinges, allowing it to be viewed when the case is opened. The monitor of a handheld computer is also an integral part of the computer case.

FIGURE 3-1: Shown above are examples of some popular computer monitors.

Monitors are designed to operate smoothly with input devices, such as a keyboard. Information in the form of digital signals is entered into the processor, or CPU, by means of the keyboard or another input device. A **graphics adapter** converts digital signals into text that is immediately displayed on the monitor screen.

While some monitors display information in only one color, called **monochrome**, most are capable of displaying output in vivid color. Some are capable of displaying information in thousands of different colors and shades. Monitors also come in a variety of sizes, from tiny two-inch screens for handhelds and other mobile devices, to large 21-inch screens for PCs (see Figure 3-2). Monitor sizes are measured diagonally, from one corner to the diagonally opposite corner. Common sizes for desktop PC monitors are 15, 17, 19, and 21 inches.

FIGURE 3-2: The two monitors shown represent the typical range of sizes for personal computer displays, from 2 inches to 21 inches.

Cathode Ray Tube (CRT) Monitors

The most common type of monitor for desktop computers is the **cathode ray tube (CRT) monitor**. A CRT is a large, sealed glass tube housed in a plastic case. The front of the tube is the screen. A cable at the rear of the monitor plugs into a graphics adapter board on the motherboard inside the system unit (see Figure 3-3). An electric cord on the monitor plugs into an electrical outlet. CRT monitors use the same cathode ray tube technology used in television sets, so most are fairly large and bulky. Smaller CRTs are used with terminals, such as those found in banks and retail establishments.

The screen of a CRT monitor is coated with tiny dots of phosphor material. Each dot consists of a red, green, and blue phosphor, which is why these displays are called RGB monitors (**R**ed, **G**reen, **B**lue). Red, green, and blue are primary colors and can be combined in various ways to produce a huge range of colors.

FIGURE 3-3: The monitor cable is plugged into the graphics adapter board located on the computer's motherboard.

Three dots make up a pixel. A **pixel** (short for picture element) is a tiny single point in anything being displayed on the screen. An electron beam moves back and forth across the rear of the screen causing the dots on the front of the screen to glow (see Figure 3-4). The glowing dots produce a character or image on the screen composed of pixels. Each pixel can be illuminated, or not illuminated, to produce an image on the screen, as shown in Figure 3-5.

When information is sent to a CRT monitor, it is sent as an analog signal through a **video card**. A video card (also called **graphics card** or **video adapter**) residing on the motherboard inside the system unit converts the digital signals

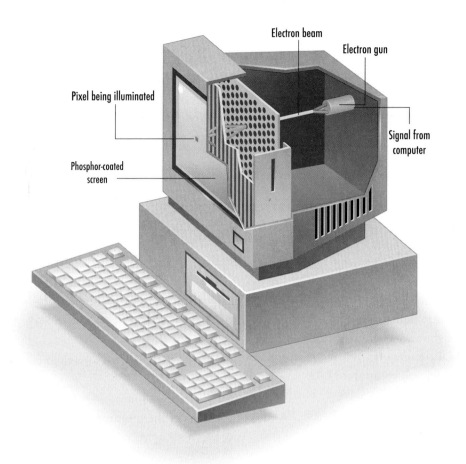

Electron beam

Electron gun

Pixel being illuminated

Signal from computer

Phosphor-coated screen

FIGURE 3-4: In cathode ray tube (CRT) monitors, an electron beam moves back and forth across a phosphor-coated screen, causing pixels to be illuminated.

produced by the computer into analog signals and sends them through a cable to the monitor (refer to Figure 3-3). The type of display determines how the images appear on the screen.

YOUR WORLD-WIDE SOURCE

FIGURE 3-5: Images are displayed using pixels on the monitor screen. The greater the number of pixels, the sharper the image.

Flat-Panel Displays

Flat-panel displays use a technology that allows them to be smaller, thinner, and lighter than CRT monitors. An additional benefit of these lightweight compact screens is that they consume less power compared to CRT monitors. These features make them desirable among users of mobile devices, and they are increasingly found on desktop computers as well. Figure 3-6 shows a notebook computer with a flat-panel display.

The majority of flat-panel displays use liquid crystals to produce information on the screen. In a **liquid crystal display (LCD)**, liquid crystals are sandwiched between two sheets of material. Electric current passing through the crystals causes them to twist. This twisting effect blocks some light waves and allows other light waves to pass through, creating images on the screen.

LCD monitors use digital signals, unlike CRT monitors that employ analog signals. Electronic circuitry converts analog signals coming from the video card back into digital signals. LCD monitors are typically more expensive than standard CRT monitors because of this digital circuitry.

FIGURE 3-6: Notebook (laptop) computers use flat-panel displays because they are smaller, thinner, and lighter than CRT monitors.

Notebook computer LCD units feature either passive-matrix or active-matrix color displays. In a **passive-matrix display**, also called a **dual-scan display**, a single transistor controls an entire column or row of the display's tiny electrodes. Viewing the screen requires the user to look directly at it. In an **active-matrix display**, also known as a **thin-film transistor (TFT)** display, separate transistors control each color pixel, allowing viewing from any angle. Active-matrix displays typically provide higher resolutions than passive-matrix displays, but they are usually more expensive and use more power (see Figure 3-7). Although active-matrix displays are most commonly found on portable computers, the technology has matured to the point that they are now used for desktop and other larger computers. Large-size LCD monitors are now available that can be mounted on a wall in a video conferencing room.

FIGURE 3-7: Active-matrix displays produce clearer, sharper images compared to passive-matrix displays.

Monitor Performance and Quality Factors

The quality and performance of monitors depend on three main factors:

- amount of RAM in the graphics adapter
- resolution
- refresh rate

TECH VISIONARY

STEVEN JOBS: CEO, APPLE COMPUTER

Steven Jobs could serve as the prototype of America's computer industry entrepreneur. A college dropout fascinated with the counterculture and Eastern thought, Jobs transformed himself into a millionaire by the age of 30. Additionally, he is credited with changing the way people think about technology and helping to ignite the personal computer revolution.

Jobs started his career as a video game designer at Atari. After spending time in college and traveling in the Middle East, Jobs returned to the United States and reconnected with friend and fellow technology enthusiast Steve Wozniac, who was work-

ing at Hewlett-Packard and building computers in his spare time. Jobs became convinced that Wozniak's latest computer, which became the Apple I, had market potential. Each sold a few prized possessions to raise $1,300, and together Jobs and Wozniac started their computer business in Jobs' garage in 1976, naming the company Apple Computer based on Jobs' fond memories of a summer job in an Oregon orchard.

The Apple I was the first personal computer that appealed to a broad market of businesses, schools, and the public, and Apple Computer quickly became a $335 million company. But by 1981, IBM had joined the race for market dominance with the launching of the IBM PC, and Apple began losing ground. Meanwhile, Jobs was leading a development team that would soon change the face of personal computing. In December 1979, Jobs and his team visited the elite Xerox PARC research center, where they saw the Alto computer, a prototype that featured a graphical user interface and a mouse. Jobs' team rushed back to the office and modified specifications for the Lisa (a computer named after Jobs' daughter). Both the Lisa and its successor, the Macintosh, were launched with a mouse and a point-and-click interface.

Although the graphic user interface radically changed the way people use computers, the Macintosh fell short of its early sales predictions. In 1985, Jobs left the company. In 1986, he founded NeXT Software and purchased Pixar Animation Studios from filmmaker George Lucas. Under Jobs, Pixar produced *Toy Story* (the first wholly computer-generated film), *A Bug's Life*, *Toy Story 2*, and *Monsters Inc.*, all highly successful ventures.

In a strange twist, Jobs was invited back to Apple in 1996 when Apple bought NeXT for $400 million. Jobs became interim CEO, and helped turn around the company's dwindling market share with the introduction of the tremendously popular iMac and iBook computer lines in the summer of 1998.

In January 2000, Jobs was appointed permanent CEO of Apple Computers Inc. That same month, Apple also announced a $200 million investment in EarthLink, an Internet service provider that works with Apple to bring new online features to computer users. Under Jobs' direction, Apple continues to produced a variety of popular, innovative products.

Sources: A&E Television. "Steve Paul Jobs," May 2003 http://search.biography.com/print_record.pl?id=23331.

CHAPTER 3

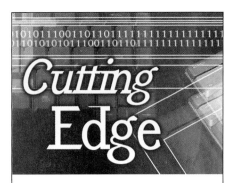

Wear Your Screen on Your Sleeve

Ultra-thin, bendable computer displays may soon be a reality for PC manufacturers. A Cambridge, Massachusetts, company called E Ink Corporation has teamed with mobile display manufacturer Royal Phillips Electronics of Amsterdam to create a prototype of an ultra-thin flexible screen with a thickness of only three human hairs. The device is so flexible it can be bent, twisted, and rolled into a half-inch cylinder without affecting the clarity of the text or images. Black text is displayed on a whitish-gray background with a resolution comparable to that of a typical laptop computer screen.

Research scientist Yu Chen headed the team that developed the 3-inch wide flexible screen consisting of a stainless steel foil covered with a thin layer of circuits and topped with a film of electronic ink. The ink is a liquid of miniscule capsules of black and white particles with opposing electrical charges. Sending a negative voltage through circuits behind the capsules moves the positive white particles to the capsule's top. A positive current does the same to the negative black particles. The human eye blends the resulting patterns of black- or white-topped capsules into text displayed in a traditional column. Information and power is fed to the screen through a wired hookup. However, Chen's team is working on a self-contained system that could receive data through a wireless connection.

Companies are expected to use the ultra-thin flexible screen to develop electronic newspapers and books plus wearable computers made of clothing with the computer screen sewn into the garment.

Sources: E Ink press release, May 12, 2003. <http://www.eink.com>. *Technology Research News,* May 13, 2003.

Amount of RAM

Graphics adapters usually have their own built-in video memory. Different types of video memory used with video cards include VRAM, WRAM, SGRAM, and SDRAM. The amount of video memory on a video card determines the number of colors and the resolution of the display. It also dictates the speed at which signals are sent to the monitor. The amount of video memory ranges from 128 MB to 512 MB.

The number of colors a video card can display is determined by the number of bits used by the card to store information about each pixel (called **bit depth**). An 8-bit video card, often referred to as 8-bit color, uses 8 bits to store information about each pixel, whereas a 16-bit video card uses 16 bits. For example, an 8-bit video card can display 256 colors (2^8). A 16-bit video card can display 131,072 colors.

The greater the number of bits, the better and more clearly the image will be displayed on the screen. A 24-bit video card can display images more clearly than an 8-bit or 16-bit video card, and in true color. The term **true color** refers to any graphics device using at least 24 bits to represent each pixel. True color means that more than 16 million unique colors can be represented, a range that accommodates the complex shades and hues of our natural world (hence the term "true"). Since humans can only distinguish a few million colors, this is more than enough to accurately represent any color image.

Resolution

As with scanners and digital cameras, the number of pixels in the display determines the monitor's quality, or **resolution**. The greater the number of pixels, the higher the resolution and the more detailed the image. However, higher resolutions result in smaller displayed characters and images, which can be an advantage (more elements can be displayed) or a disadvantage (smaller images and text may be difficult to see). Higher-resolution settings also consume more processing power because additional power is required to continually refresh a larger number of pixels. The increase in power consumption slows down the amount of processing power immediately available for other processing activities.

Screen resolutions typically range from 640 x 480 to 1600 x 1200 pixels or more. Lower resolutions are suitable for displaying draft-quality text and images. Higher resolution allows more accurate images to be displayed on the screen, and may be desirable for users such as artists or Web page designers, who regularly work with higher-quality text, graphics, and other detailed images. For a comparison, look at Figure 3-8, which shows a photo displayed in a low-resolution and a high-resolution format. Most monitors sold today offer a range of resolution settings, which can be adjusted using the Control Panel/Display option in Windows.

Another factor influencing image resolution is dot pitch. **Dot pitch** refers to the distance between the centers of pixels on a display. Less distance between pixels increases the quality of the displayed image. A smaller dot pitch makes text and graphics easier to read. Monitor dot

FIGURE 3-8: In the 800 x 600 pixels screen resolution (left), the desktop icons and the photo are larger than in the 1280 x 1024 pixels screen resolution (below).

pitch can range from 0.25 mm (millimeters) to 0.31 mm. A monitor having a dot pitch of 0.26 mm will display high-quality text and graphics and is suitable for most applications.

Refresh Rate

Refresh rate is yet another factor affecting monitor quality. Just as light from a flashlight becomes dimmer as the batteries run down, images displayed on a monitor screen become weaker as the current used to produce them diminishes. This causes the screen to flicker. To avoid this problem, power is continually being sent to the monitor to refresh the display. **Refresh rate** refers to the number of times per second the screen is refreshed (redrawn). To avoid flickering, the refresh rate should be at least 72 Hz (Hertz). High-quality displays have a fast refresh rate that produces a constant, flicker-free image that causes less eyestrain for the user.

Monitor controls are typically located on the front of the monitor and allow adjustment of the brightness, contrast, positioning, height, and width of images displayed on the screen. Monitors usually come with screen settings preset by the manufacturer. The Windows operating system allows users to change monitor settings by clicking on the *My Computer* icon, the *Control Panel* icon, and then clicking on the *Display* icon. Users can change the settings to meet their needs, or easily change back to the preset (default) settings.

Monitor Ergonomics

Ergonomics is the study of the interaction between humans and the equipment they use. Extensive research has shown that the correct use of a monitor can greatly reduce eyestrain, fatigue, and other potential problems.

Many monitors have built-in features that address ergonomics issues. These features allow adjustment of the monitor to make viewing more comfortable, to minimize eye and neck strain, and to reduce glare from overhead lighting. Some have controls that allow adjusting the monitor for the brightness, contrast, height, and

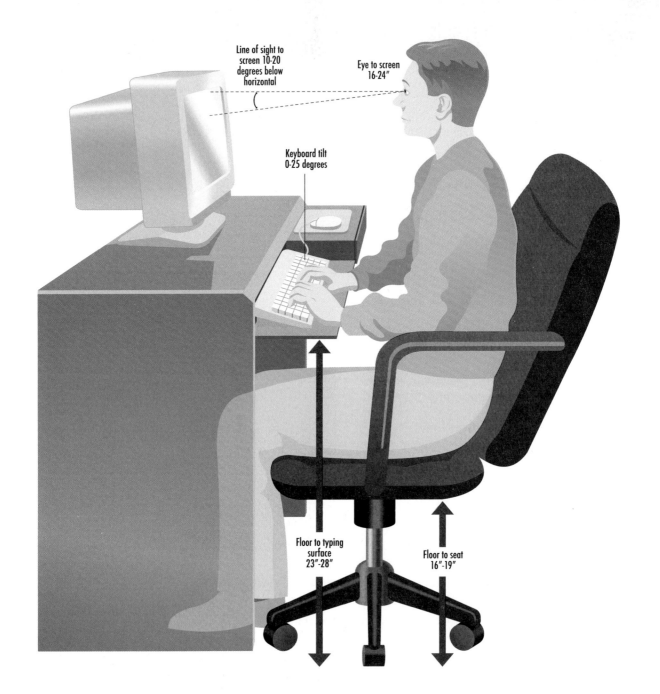

Line of sight to
screen 10-20
degrees below
horizontal

Eye to screen
16-24"

Keyboard tilt
0-25 degrees

Floor to typing
surface
23"-28"

Floor to seat
16"-19"

FIGURE 3-9: Correct positioning when using a monitor can reduce physical fatigue and discomfort.

width of displayed images. Monitor brightness is a matter of individual preference. Some ergonomic specialists recommend the use of an antiglare screen to reduce glare from the screen. It is important for both users and monitors to be positioned correctly. Figure 3-9 illustrates the correct positioning to provide maximum comfort and ease of use.

Wearable Displays

Some mobile workers need and use hands-free wearable computers that allow them to perform their work without having to stop what they are doing to use a computer. Xybernaut Corporation's MA4-TC allows users immediate access to information essential to their activities. For example, a work crew can wirelessly connect to the corporate network to send and receive work-related data and information, such as a wiring diagram needed to locate a faulty electric outlet. Data and information are displayed on a headset-mounted full-color video console comparable to a 15-inch monitor when viewed at a distance of 15 inches.

The use of wearable computers and displays is becoming widespread due to their cost-effectiveness and ability to eliminate work delays. Future improvements to wearable displays will render them even more effective and adaptable to a greater variety of work-related applications. Figure 3-10 shows some examples of wearable computers.

Television Displays

Many home computer users take advantage of their television sets for displaying computer output. Televisions use CRT tubes, and a TV can become a display device when connected to a computer by means of an electronic device called an **NTSC converter**. An NTSC converter device converts the computer's digital signal into an analog signal that can be displayed on the television screen (see Figure 3-11).

A newer type of television technology, **high-definition television (HDTV)**, does not require an NTSC converter. Because HDTV uses digital signals instead of analog signals, computers can be connected directly to the television set. HDTV sets typically include a wider screen and provide higher resolution than standard television sets. These features make HDTV attractive for presenting information to large groups.

The Federal Communications Commission (FCC) has mandated that all television stations transmit program signals in both analog format and digital format by 2006. As the manufacture of high-definition televisions becomes more competitive, the cost of HDTV sets will almost certainly decline and their overall quality will improve.

FIGURE 3-11: A television set can be used as a computer monitor.

PRINTERS

A **printer** is the most common type of device for producing hard-copy output on a physical medium, such as paper or transparency film. Almost all printers are capable of printing in either portrait or landscape format. In **portrait format**, a printed page is taller than it is wide. Portrait format is usually used for letters, memos, reports, and newsletters. In **landscape format**, a printed page is wider than it is tall. Landscape format is best suited for financial spreadsheets and other types of tabular reports. These types of reports typically include many columns of data, and trying to print them in portrait format would not leave enough space.

Printers are separated into two broad categories, based on how they interact with the print medium: impact and nonimpact. **Impact printers** print much like a typewriter, by physically striking an inked ribbon against the paper. **Nonimpact printers** form characters and images without actually striking the output medium, using electricity, heat, laser technology, or photographic techniques.

Within these two broad categories of printers there are three types of printers popular among personal computer users: dot-matrix printers, ink-jet printers, and laser printers. Each type includes a range of printers that vary in quality of output and in printing speed. Table 3-1 compares printer types and their characteristics.

In order to be able to print, a computer must have a printer board installed on the motherboard inside the computer. The printer board contains a port extending to the rear of the system unit. A printer connects to the computer by means of a cable attached to the rear of the printer. The other end plugs into the port on the printer board. An electric cord at the rear of the printer plugs into an electric outlet.

Dot-Matrix Printers

A **dot-matrix printer** forms and prints characters in a manner similar to the way numbers appear on a football scoreboard. A close look at a scoreboard will reveal that each number consists of a pattern of lighted bulbs. For a dot-matrix printer, the "lighted bulbs" are tiny dots forming characters and images on the paper (the "scoreboard").

Type of Printer	Uses	Quality of Output	Resolution	Speed	Price Range
dot-matrix	printing draft-quality material and multipart forms	fair	240 - 720 dpi	50 - 1120 cps (characters per second)	$200 - $1,000
ink-jet	various high-quality printing needs and color printing	good to excellent	600 x 600 - 4800 x 1200 dpi	1 - 6 ppm (pages per minute)	$69 - $350
photographic ink-jet	printing high-quality photographs and other graphics	excellent	600 x 600 - 5760 x 720 dpi	1 - 3 photos per minute	$200 - $1,000
laser: monochrome	high-quality printing needs	good to excellent	600 x 600 - 1200 x 1200 dpi	6 - 30 ppm (BW)	$200 - $500
laser: color	high-quality printing needs	good to excellent	600 x 600 - 2400 x 2400 dpi	6 ppm (color)	$500 - $5,000
plotter	printing drawings and designs	good to excellent	360 - 1200 dpi	varies considerably according to print size and quality	$1,500 - $15,500

T A B L E   3 - 1 : Comparison of Printers

In dot-matrix printing, a print head strikes an inked ribbon and deposits ink on the page, which is why dot-matrix printers are classified as impact printers. Inside the print head are thin wires, and their impact produces tiny dots of ink arranged to represent text, symbols, or images, as shown in Figure 3-12. The number of dots in a linear inch (dpi) is a measure of the resolution, or print quality.

The print head of a dot-matrix printer may contain from 9 to 24 pins, depending on the printer model and manufacturer. The number of pins determines the number of dots the print head can print during one impact. More pins produce more dots in each character, resulting in higher-quality print. Dot-matrix printers print one character at a time. Their speed is measured by the number of characters per second (cps) the printer is capable of printing. These printers range in speed from a few characters to several hundred characters per second, with 450 cps being a typical rate.

The print quality of most dot-matrix printers is often inferior to higher-quality printers. The clarity of the printing may be described as **draft quality** (approximately 300 dpi), which is acceptable for some printing. For important business letters and documents, most users prefer **letter quality** clarity (approximately 1200 dpi).

Because dot-matrix printers are impact printers, they are capable of printing multipart forms containing an original and carbon copies. For this reason they are more commonly found in businesses and schools. For example, colleges and universities typically use dot-matrix printers for printing class rolls and grade reports. Individuals seldom use dot-matrix printers since they rarely need to print multipart forms and they usually prefer higher-quality print output.

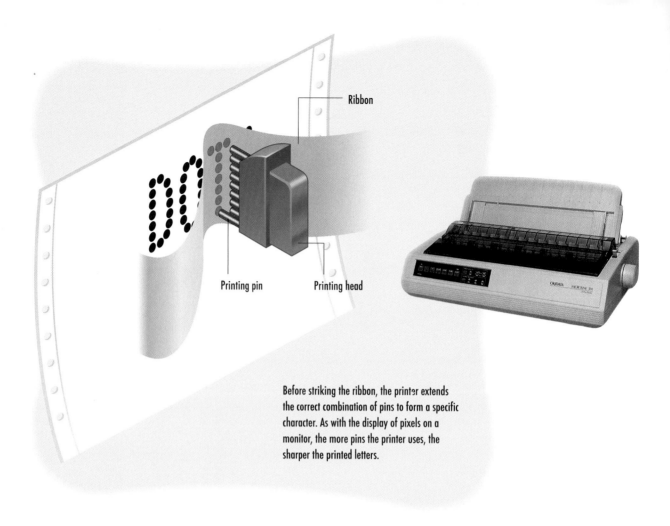

Ribbon

Printing pin   Printing head

Before striking the ribbon, the printer extends
the correct combination of pins to form a specific
character. As with the display of pixels on a
monitor, the more pins the printer uses, the
sharper the printed letters.

FIGURE 3-12: A dot-matrix printer prints characters in matrix format similar to the way numbers are
displayed on a football scoreboard.

Ink-Jet Printers

For applications requiring letter-quality print, most people choose nonimpact
printers, such as ink-jet and laser printers. Technological improvements and
declining prices have made these two types the preferred printers among personal
computer users. An **ink-jet printer** is a nonimpact printer that forms characters
and images by spraying thousands of tiny droplets of electrically charged ink onto
a sheet of paper as the sheet passes through the printer (see Figure 3-13). The
printed images are in dot-matrix format, but of a higher resolution than images
printed by dot-matrix printers. This is because the tiny dots produced by high-end
printers are much closer together. In fact, the dots are so dense the printed characters and images may appear as letter-quality characters and images, rather than as a
group of dots.

Typical resolutions are 600 dpi for black-and-white printing and 2400 dpi for
color printing on high-quality paper. Higher resolution means higher-quality characters and images. Some high-end ink-jet printers are capable of producing photo-
graphic-quality output almost as detailed and colorful as photos processed using
traditional darkroom methods.

Most ink-jet printers use two or more ink cartridges, one for black print and
one or more for color printing. Each cartridge has multiple holes, called nozzles.

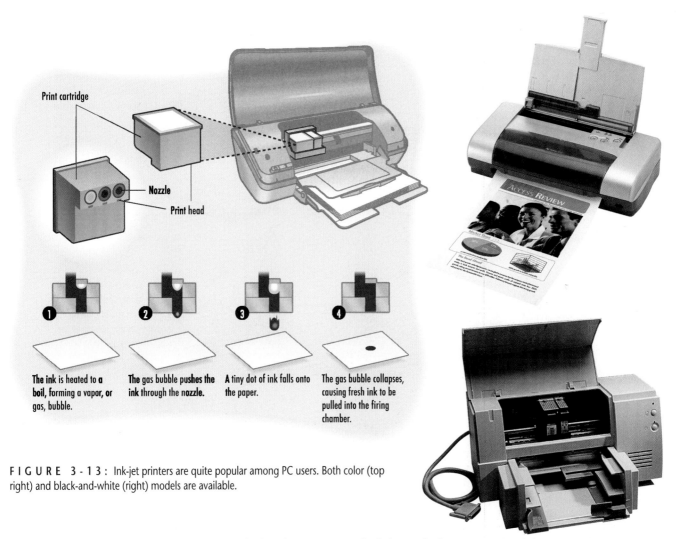

Print cartridge

Nozzle

Print head

1 The ink is heated to a boil, forming a vapor, or gas, bubble.

2 The gas bubble pushes the ink through the nozzle.

3 A tiny dot of ink falls onto the paper.

4 The gas bubble collapses, causing fresh ink to be pulled into the firing chamber.

FIGURE 3-13: Ink-jet printers are quite popular among PC users. Both color (top right) and black-and-white (right) models are available.

During printing, combinations of tiny ink droplets are propelled through the nozzles by heat and pressure onto the paper, forming characters and images.

The number of pages per minute (ppm) a printer can produce determines an ink-jet printer's speed. Speeds currently range from 1 to 16 pages per minute for draft-quality output. Printing color photos and other graphical images may slow the printing speed to as few as one or two pages per minute.

The cost of operating an ink-jet printer can vary greatly. A typical single page text document using only black ink may cost from $.02 to $.06 per page. By comparison, the cost of printing a combination of black and color characters and images may range from $.08 to $.20 per page. Printing a full-color photograph may cost $.90 or more.

Unlike dot-matrix printers, most ink-jet printers are relatively inexpensive. Prices of ink-jet printers range from less than $100 to $350. Their inexpensive price and versatility make them popular among personal computer users. They can be used for printing letters, memos, reports, spreadsheets, brochures, and a variety of other printing applications. Some computer manufacturers now bundle an ink-jet printer with each computer they sell.

Photograph Printers

A **photograph printer** is a unique high-quality ink-jet printer designed to print high-quality color photographs in addition to other types of print output (see Figure 3-14). Most photograph printers can print photographs after they have

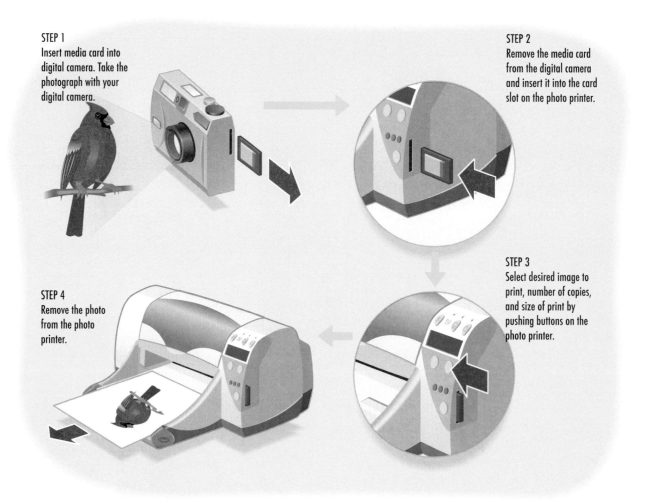

STEP 1
Insert media card into digital camera. Take the photograph with your digital camera.

STEP 2
Remove the media card from the digital camera and insert it into the card slot on the photo printer.

STEP 3
Select desired image to print, number of copies, and size of print by pushing buttons on the photo printer.

STEP 4
Remove the photo from the photo printer.

FIGURE 3-14: A photograph printer is a unique type of ink-jet printer used for printing high-quality photographs and other printing needs.

been loaded (entered) from a digital camera into the computer and displayed on the screen. Some allow sending a photograph directly from a floppy disk to a printer. Still others contain a slot for inserting a medium containing photographs, such as a **SIM card** used with some digital cameras. Once the medium is inserted, the controls on the printer can be used to select a particular photograph, change its size, and choose the number of copies to print. Sizes for printed photographs range from 3 x 3 inches to 14 x 17 inches. The versatility of photograph printers makes them suitable for home and business use as they can be used for almost every printing need.

Laser Printers

A **laser printer** is a nonimpact printer that produces output of exceptional quality using a technology similar to that of a photocopy machine. Laser printers are used for any printing application, including those requiring output of printing-press quality material. Their speed and ability to produce clear, crisp text and images have made them the fastest growing segment of the printer market. Prices range from a few hundred dollars for a black-ink laser printer (monochrome) to a thousand dollars and up for a color laser printer.

A laser printer creates text and graphics on a rotating metal drum using a laser beam. During printing, components inside the printer read characters and relay them to a printer device called a laser mechanism. A laser beam produces characters

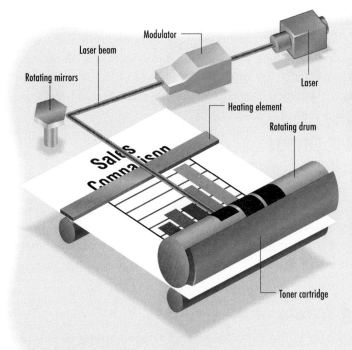

Modulator

Laser beam

Rotating mirrors

Laser

Heating element

Rotating drum

Sales Comparison

Toner cartridge

A mechanism inside the printer reads the characters and sends the information to the laser device. Then the laser sends light signals through a series of mirrors in the drum, creating tiny dots of light. The dots create magnetic fields on the drum matching the shape of the characters (or images), which attract the toner powder. As the drum rotates, toner is pressed onto the paper.

FIGURE 3-15: Laser printers produce output of exceptional quality and are among the most popular printers.

and images on a rotating drum inside the printer by altering the electrical charge wherever the beam strikes the drum. The charges produce tiny magnetic fields (dots) on the drum, forming characters. As the drum rotates, it picks up an ink-like powder called **toner**, similar to copy machine toner. The sensitive dots on the drum are then deposited onto the paper. Using heat and pressure, a set of rollers fuses the toner onto the paper, forming the printed image. The circumference of the drum is approximately the same as the length of a standard sheet of paper. With one revolution of the drum an entire page is printed. The printing process is illustrated in Figure 3-15. Laser printers produce text and images of exceptional quality.

Plotters

A **plotter** is a type of printer used to produce specialized kinds of large-sized high-quality documents, including architectural drawings, charts, maps, diagrams, and other images. Plotters are also used to create engineering drawings for machinery parts and equipment. Figure 3-16 shows an example of a plotter.

FIGURE 3-16: Engineers often use plotters for producing high-quality, detailed prints of building, process, and machine designs.

On a plotter, the printed image consists of a series of tiny dots tightly packed to produce a high-quality printed image. The printing mechanism consists of a row of tiny electrically charged wires. When the wires come into contact with the specially coated paper, an electrostatic pattern is produced that causes the toner to be fused onto the paper. Most plotters are expensive, ranging in cost from hundreds to thousands of dollars.

SPEAKERS AND VOICE OUTPUT

Computer users want to be able to record sounds as well as hear the sounds included in Web sites, videos, and computer games. With sound capability it is now possible to listen to Web pages or watch television over the Internet. Certain software applications can read e-mail or Web pages out loud, which is of particular benefit to people who are visually impaired. The importance of sound capability is growing rapidly, and it is increasingly being seen as a required feature for personal computer systems.

Speakers and Sound Systems

Most personal computers have built-in **speakers** that produce warning sounds to alert users to errors or other matters that require attention. A computer equipped with a powerful sound card like Creative Labs' Sound Blaster® Pro can produce high-quality sound through attached speakers using CD-ROMs, MIDI (Musical Instrument Digital Interface) keyboards, or the Internet (see Figure 3-17). Applications for which speakers are particularly important include computer games, multimedia distance learning programs, audio e-mail, and videoconferencing.

A **speaker headset** is a miniature version of larger speakers. Speaker headsets are already quite familiar because they are frequently used with portable devices, including music CD players. As the name suggests, a speaker headset consists of two or more small speakers mounted at the tips of a flexible wire band that fits

FIGURE 3-17:
Computer speakers allow users to hear sound effects from a computer game or an instructor's voice in a multimedia educational course.

FIGURE 3-18: Wearing a speaker headset reduces the noise and helps the user focus.

comfortably on the head, with the speakers positioned over the ears. Some computer users working in close proximity to other workers often use a speaker headset to minimize sound distractions (see Figure 3-18).

Voice Output Systems

Modern hardware and software technologies make it possible to produce synthesized human speech in the digital form a computer can understand and use. Most people have already experienced this technology when they have dialed a telephone number and heard a computerized voice say, "The number you have dialed is no longer in service," or, "The number you dialed has been changed." This same technology (**voice output**) is now available for use with all computers, and is becoming increasingly popular. Voice output can be used to listen to talk shows, news reports, athletic events, political speeches, interviews, and more.

OTHER TYPES OF OUTPUT

In addition to the types of output already described, there are a number of other output devices available. Two of the most frequently encountered examples are facsimile (FAX) machines and multifunction devices (MFDs).

Facsimile (Fax) Machines

A **facsimile machine**, also called a **fax machine**, is an electronic device that can send and receive copies (facsimiles, or **faxes**) of documents through a telephone line. A fax device may be a stand-alone machine or a circuit board inserted into a slot inside a computer (see Figure 3-19). The technology of faxing involves scanning the page(s), converting the text and images into digitized data, and transmitting them. A fax device at the receiving end converts the digitized data into the document's original form that can be printed or stored.

Many personal computers come equipped with a **fax/modem board** that fits into an expansion slot. In addition to serving as a modem, the board provides many of the features of a stand-alone fax machine at a lower cost. A type of software called a **fax program** is needed to send and receive a fax. With fax programs, users can compose, send, receive, print, and store faxes. Some of the better fax programs use optical character recognition (OCR) technology to convert a faxed transmission back into text so the document can be edited using any of the popular word processing programs.

FIGURE 3-19: Fax machines and fax circuit boards can send and receive copies of documents sent over communications media, such as telephone lines.

Multifunction Devices

FIGURE 3-20: A multifunction device is a device that provides multiple capabilities, such as scanning, copying, printing, and faxing.

A **multifunction device (MFD)** is a piece of equipment that looks like a printer or copy machine, but which provides a variety of capabilities, including scanning, copying, printing, and sometimes faxing (see Figure 3-20). The capabilities of multifunction devices vary according to the manufacturer and device model. Some print in black only, while others offer color printing. The X83 by Lexmark, for example, offers 2400 x 1200 dpi printing, 48-bit flatbed scanning, PC free color and black copying, and direct scan-to-PC fax capabilities.

Multifunction devices offer several advantages over a combination of separate devices. They occupy less desktop space and they are usually less expensive than the combined cost of purchasing several devices. The main disadvantage is that all functions are lost if the device breaks down or becomes inoperable.

STORAGE DEVICES AND MEDIA

Information created and output on the devices discussed above can be stored for future use. Storage is the final phase of the information processing cycle. Earlier you learned that RAM memory provides temporary storage of programs and data during processing, and that this temporary storage is lost when the computer is turned off. To avoid losing programs and data every time the computer is turned off, all computers provide for permanent storage. **Permanent storage**, also known as **secondary storage**, **auxiliary storage**, or **external storage**, consists of devices and media used for permanent recording. Stored information can later be retrieved, edited, modified, displayed, imported, exported, copied, or printed. Some secondary storage systems also allow users to make changes to the stored information and to permanently save the altered information.

File Types

Almost all information stored in a computer must be in a **file**. There are many different types of files, including data, text, program, and graphics files. To distinguish among various files, the user gives each one a unique file name. A computer's operating system (operating systems are explained in Chapter 4) may impose restrictions on the format of file names. For example, earlier versions of Windows restricted the length of a file name to eight characters. Newer versions allow longer file names, but there are some characters that cannot be used in a file name.

A file name is followed by a period (.) and a set of characters called a **file extension**, which identifies the type of file. For example, the characters Payroll.xls identify a file named Payroll. The "xls" identifies the Payroll file as a Microsoft Excel spreadsheet file. File names and file extensions must be separated by a period.

File extensions identify specific file types. Some are automatically added to a file by the operating system or program when a file is saved. However, in some situations a user can add an extension to a file to avoid confusion between similar files. Table 3-2 shows some examples of commonly used file extensions and the type of files they identify.

Secondary Storage Systems

A secondary storage system consists of two main parts, a storage device and a storage medium. A storage device is a hardware component that houses a storage medium on which data is recorded (stored), similar to the way in which a VCR (the device) is used for recording a television program on the tape (the medium)

TECH VISIONARY

Jeff Hawkins is credited with developing and reinventing the handheld device that became the PalmPilot. Hawkins is the founder, chairman, and chief product officer of Handspring and former cofounder of Palm Computing. A technologist with some 20 years of expertise, Hawkins holds nine patents for various handheld devices and features. The secrets to his success, he says, are past failures, a combination of optimism and realism, his shirt pocket, and a pen.

Hawkins founded Palm Computing in 1994 with Donna Dubinsky, believing that they could build a better handheld. Hawkins had achieved notoriety as the "architect of pen-computing technologies" and expanding on this technology, he and Dubinsky successfully led Palm Computing as it brought handheld computing into the mainstream. The failures of their initial inventions, namely, Apple's Newton, the Sharp Wizard, and the Zoomer, were what propelled Hawkins back to the drawing board and to the eventual development of the PalmPilot.

His problem-solving strategy was to find and interview as many owners of the failed handhelds as he could find and to ask them two very important questions: "Why were you disappointed in the product? And what were you hoping it would do?" Responses led him to measure his shirt pocket and design a handheld to fit it. In addition, the handheld had to sync with a desktop, perform instantly, and remain relatively inexpensive. His design began with a piece of wood that he whittled down to size. Then, as he walked around with it in his pocket, he whittled a chopstick to model the pen and pretended to write on the wood block. Next, he mocked up a screen, taped it to the block, and interacted with it. In an "Aha!" moment, Hawkins saw his error in trying to make computers read the way people write; the answer was in getting people to learn to write so that computers could read. "Graffiti," a recognition solution that works like a keyboard, was added to his handhelds, which inspired the launch of the Pilot in 1998, the Visor in 1999, and later the Palm.

In 1998, Hawkins founded his second company, Handspring, which makes a Palm-compatible handheld. Eventually, he predicts, the handheld will become the center of all personal computing and the way most people will get to the Internet. He foresees a wireless future that will "transform the world" and an always-on Internet connection "that will change the way people think." He also sees wireless technology offering connections for the underprivileged nations, giving them "equal footing" in creating businesses and improving their quality of life.

Noting that he was always interested in engineering and alternative energy "because that is what my family did," he recalls his father's advice to " 'look into this microelectronics stuff; that looks interesting.' " His next venture? Neurobiology and brain research.

Sources: Schwartz, Ephraim. "Jeff Hawkins, Handhelds," *InfoWorld*, October 6, 2001; Barnett, Shawn. "Jeff Hawkins: The man who almost single-handedly revived the handheld computer industry," Pen Computing Home Page.

File Extension	Full Name	Type of File
.bmp	bitmap graphic	bit-mapped format for graphics
.bak	backup	backup file
.bat	batch file	DOS file created in batch form
.com	command	executable command file (DOS)
.exe	executable file	executable file (DOS and Windows)
.eps	Encapsulated PostScript Vector graphic	graphics file format used by the PostScript language
.pcx	PC Paintbrush	graphics file format
.jpg	Joint Photography Experts Group	compression format for graphical images
.pif	program information file	instructs Windows how to run non-Windows programs
.tif	Tagged Image File format	type of bit-mapped image
.doc	document	Microsoft Word (document) file
.xls	Excel spreadsheet	Microsoft Excel spreadsheet file
.mdb	Microsoft database	Microsoft Access database file
.ppt	PowerPoint®	Microsoft PowerPoint® file
.wbm	wireless bit-mapped	wireless bit-mapped graphic format for mobile computing devices

TABLE 3-2: Examples of Commonly Used File Extensions

inside a cassette. Some type of secondary storage device is usually built into a PC system, but is not visible unless the case housing the CPU and related components is removed. There are two main types of storage systems: magnetic and optical.

MAGNETIC STORAGE DEVICES AND MEDIA

Magnetic storage devices are the most commonly used types of secondary storage. They are broadly classified into two categories: those using a permanent storage medium and those using a removable storage medium. A **permanent storage medium**, such as a hard disk, is permanently attached to the system unit. A **removable storage medium**, such as a floppy disk, can be removed by the user and replaced by another medium.

Magnetic storage devices are also categorized by the way the data stored in them is accessed: *sequentially* (in the order in which data was stored) or *directly* (in any order, randomly). **Sequential access** can be compared to the way musical selections on a cassette tape are recorded and accessed one after the other. **Direct access** is comparable to the way songs are stored and selected on a CD player. Although the songs are stored one after another, any song can be played by selecting its number.

The speed of a disk storage device is measured by **access time**, the time a storage device spends locating a particular file. Recall that information in a computer's memory can be accessed quickly, in millionths of a second. However, accessing a file stored on a disk is slower. The access times of storage devices are measured in thousandths of a second. The speed at which data is transferred from memory or from a storage device is called the **data transfer rate**. As with access time, data transfer rates of storage devices are much slower than data transfer rates from memory.

A magnetic storage device works by applying electrical charges to iron filings on the surface medium. Specific particles are either magnetized (representing a 1-bit) or not magnetized (representing a 0-bit). Recall from Chapter 1 that a combination of 0 and 1 bits represents a byte, that is, a letter, number, or special character.

Magnetic storage devices are popular because they provide an inexpensive means for recording large amounts of information. The media used by magnetic storage devices can be read, erased, or rewritten, and can therefore be used over and over. The three most common types of magnetic storage devices for personal computers are

- floppy disks
- hard disks
- tape cartridges

Among these three types of storage devices, floppy and hard disks far outnumber tape cartridges. Both hard disks and floppy disks provide direct-access storage, but hard disks provide greater storage capacity and allow data to be accessed much faster. However, because hard disk systems are usually permanently installed (non-removable) and floppy disks are removable, most computers come equipped with both types for greater flexibility and convenience. Tape cartridges are removable, provide sequential-access storage, and are often used for backing up data.

Floppy Disks and Disk Drives

A **floppy disk**, also called a **diskette** or simply a **disk**, is a thin, circular Mylar® (polyester film) wafer sandwiched between two sheets of special cleaning tissue inside a rigid plastic case (see Figure 3-21). Floppy disks are widely used for saving (backing up) copies of files and programs. Because they are removable, they can be used to share files with other computer users. They can also be used to install and load commercial software, although because programs typically require a large amount of disk

FIGURE 3-21: Nearly all personal computers sold today come with a floppy disk drive.

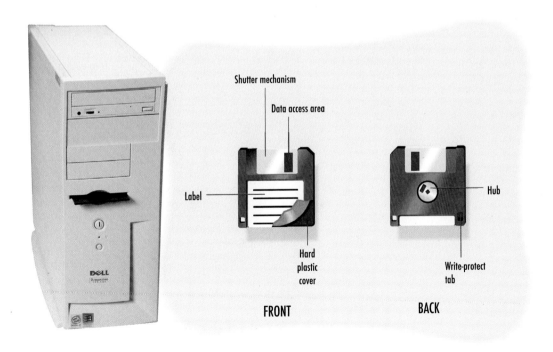

Shutter mechanism

Data access area

Label

Hard plastic cover

FRONT

Hub

Write-protect tab

BACK

space, most are now shipped on CD-ROMs. Computer manufacturers build a floppy disk drive into most models of desktop or laptop/notebook computers. The user accesses the drive by inserting a floppy disk into a slot on the outside of the system unit case. In recent years, PC manufacturers have begun moving customers away from the floppy disk because of the extensive range of alternative storage options. Apple Computer, for example, eliminated the floppy in its release of the iMac in 1998, and in 2003 both Dell Computer and Hewlett-Packard began offering certain models without a floppy drive. Some analysts, however, predict that the floppy disk will remain a fixture in the PC world for some years to come.

Data is stored along the tracks and sectors of both hard and floppy disks. A **track** is a numbered concentric circle. A **sector** is a numbered section or portion of a disk similar to a slice of pie. A group of sectors is called a **cluster**, which is the smallest unit of storage space that is assigned a memory address. As programs or data are stored along the tracks on the disk, the computer automatically maintains a file directory, called a **file allocation table** or **FAT file**. FAT files on the disk keep track of the disk's contents. This directory shows the name of each file stored on the disk, its size, and the sector in which the file begins.

When in use, the disk spins and exposes its recording surfaces to the disk drive's read/write heads. As the disk rotates, the read/write heads move back and forth across the disk surface. When the user wants to access a particular file, the computer searches the file allocation table to find the requested file and its location on the disk. After learning the requested file's location, the computer locates and retrieves the requested file. Figure 3-22 illustrates how this works in a floppy disk drive.

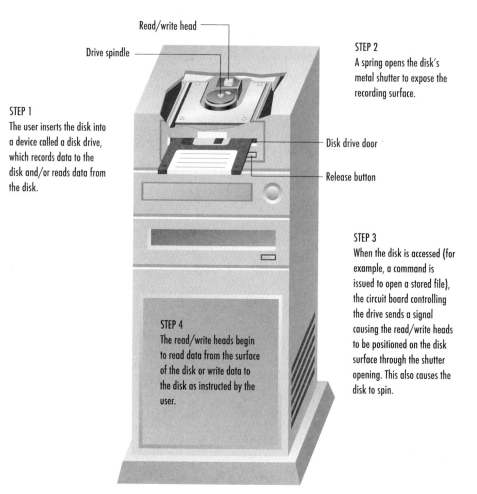

FIGURE 3-22: Once the floppy disk is inserted into the drive, data is recorded onto the disk or retrieved by means of read/write heads inside the drive.

Read/write head

Drive spindle

STEP 2
A spring opens the disk's metal shutter to expose the recording surface.

STEP 1
The user inserts the disk into a device called a disk drive, which records data to the disk and/or reads data from the disk.

Disk drive door

Release button

STEP 3
When the disk is accessed (for example, a command is issued to open a stored file), the circuit board controlling the drive sends a signal causing the read/write heads to be positioned on the disk surface through the shutter opening. This also causes the disk to spin.

STEP 4
The read/write heads begin to read data from the surface of the disk or write data to the disk as instructed by the user.

Disk Type	Storage Capacity	Storage Device
high-density (HD)	1.44 MB	floppy disk drive
double high-density (DHD)	2.88 MB	floppy disk drive
SuperDisk (Imation Corp.)	120 MB	SuperDisk drive
Zip® disk (Iomega Corp.)	100-250 MB	Zip® drive
HiFD (Sony Corp.)	200 MB	HiFD drive

TABLE 3-3 Floppy Disk Storage Capacities

Floppy disks for early personal computers provided only 360 KB of storage. As hardware capabilities increased, floppy disk capacity increased to 720 KB. Today's PCs typically use floppy disks with storage capacities of 1.44 MB. Physically, the disks measure 3.5 inches in diameter, although other less commonly used sizes are also available. Table 3-3 lists the main types of floppy disks along with their storage capacities and related storage devices.

Higher-Capacity Floppy Disks

Until recently, a storage capacity of 1.44 megabytes was sufficient to handle most files. However, the increasing popularity of multimedia programs that include video files and desktop publishing applications requiring graphics files has created a need for ever-greater storage capacities. To accommodate these needs, manufacturers have developed higher-capacity storage devices such as the SuperDisk drive, the Zip® drive, and the HiFD (High-Capacity FD) disk drive. The SuperDisk uses both floppy and hard-disk technology and requires specially formatted floppy disks. Figure 3-23 shows a Zip disk and an external Zip drive. Note that high-capacity drives can also read and write to standard 3.5-inch floppy disks.

FIGURE 3-23: Higher-capacity floppy disks such as the SuperDisk, the HiFD disk, and the Zip® disk (shown here) provide large secondary storage capacities.

Formatting and Handling a Floppy Disk

Before data can be stored on a disk, the manufacturer or the user must format the disk based on the type of disk drive and operating system with which it is intended to be used. During the **formatting** process, the disk surface is arranged into tracks, sectors, and clusters ready for the storage of data (see Figure 3-24). It is important that floppy disks be cared for properly to prevent damaging the contents. Figure 3-25 illustrates guidelines for handling and storing floppy disks.

Hard Disks and Hard Drives

Hard disks provide permanent storage for system software, application programs, and user files. A **hard drive** system consists of one or more rigid metal platters (disks) mounted on a metal shaft in a container that contains an access mechanism (see Figure 3-26). The container is sealed to prevent contamination from dust, moisture, and other airborne particles, allowing the system to operate more efficiently.

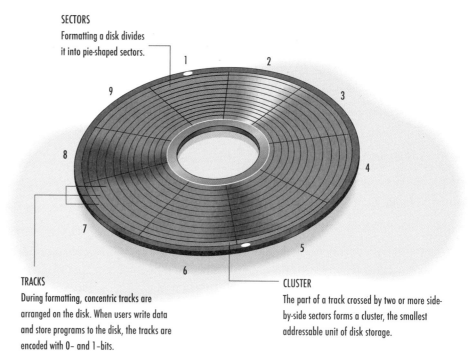

SECTORS
Formatting a disk divides it into pie-shaped sectors.

TRACKS
During formatting, concentric tracks are arranged on the disk. When users write data and store programs to the disk, the tracks are encoded with 0- and 1-bits.

CLUSTER
The part of a track crossed by two or more side-by-side sectors forms a cluster, the smallest addressable unit of disk storage.

FIGURE 3-24: The process of formatting a floppy disk results in the disk being arranged into tracks and sectors. Data is stored in sectors along the tracks.

Hard drives range in size from 1 to 5.25 inches in diameter. Storage capacity ranges from 4 GB to more than 30 GB.

People frequently use the terms *hard disk* and *hard drive* to mean the same thing, even though in technical terms the hard drive is the storage device and the

FIGURE 3-25: The hard plastic cases of floppy disks do not totally protect the circular wafers inside. Improper handling of disks can damage stored data.

DO:
1. Do insert the disk into the drive carefully.
2. Do store the disk in a safe place when not in use.

DO NOT:
1. Do not open the disk's shutter or touch the recording surface on the disk.
2. Do not place heavy objects on the disk.
3. Do not eat, drink, or smoke near a disk.
4. Do not expose the disk to heat, sunlight, or cold.
5. Do not place the disk near magnetic fields, such as TVs, radios, monitors, or calculators.

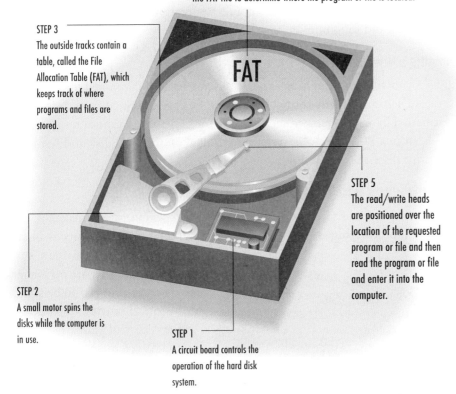

STEP 4
When a program or file is requested, the read/write heads move to the FAT file to determine where the program or file is located.

STEP 3
The outside tracks contain a table, called the File Allocation Table (FAT), which keeps track of where programs and files are stored.

STEP 5
The read/write heads are positioned over the location of the requested program or file and then read the program or file and enter it into the computer.

STEP 2
A small motor spins the disks while the computer is in use.

STEP 1
A circuit board controls the operation of the hard disk system.

FIGURE 3-26: A hard drive contains one or more hard disks on which data is stored. When activated, read/write heads move in and out between the disks to record and/or read data.

hard disk is the magnetic storage medium. A hard drive unit may be either nonremovable (fixed) or removable (interchangeable). Most personal computers arrive from the factory with a fixed hard drive installed within the system unit housing. Some also include an interchangeable hard drive that functions like a floppy disk drive. Iomega Corporation's Jaz® cartridge, for example, is a removable hard drive offering 1 GB of storage; recently available from Iomega is an external hard drive offering 30 GB of storage (see Figure 3-27).

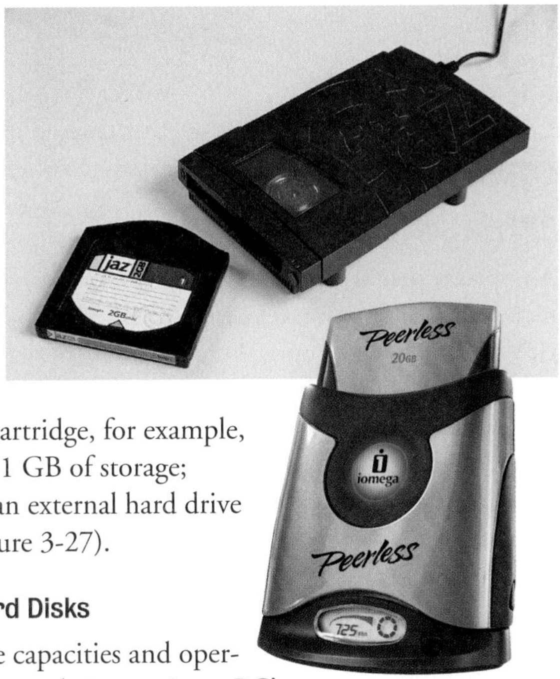

FIGURE 3-27:
Shown are the Jaz® cartridge (1 GB storage) and the Peerless External Hard Drive (30 GB storage) from Iomega.

Comparing Floppy Disks and Hard Disks

Hard disks offer far greater storage capacities and operate much faster than floppy disks, greatly improving a PC's efficiency. Hard disk storage capacities are stated in terms of gigabytes (billions of bytes), whereas floppy disk capacities are stated in megabytes (millions of bytes). Computers sold today often contain hard drives with 30 or more gigabytes of storage capacity. A hard disk rotates faster than a floppy disk. It continues spinning while the computer is in operation, whereas a floppy disk spins only when data is being stored or accessed. Continuous spinning of a hard disk provides faster access because it enables the disk surface(s) to move past the read/write heads faster (refer to Figure 3-26). This speeds up the computer's operation because important system commands and functions are accessed and executed more quickly.

Formatting a Hard Disk

Hard disks contain many more tracks and sectors than are contained on floppy disks. Manufacturers usually format hard disks, but preformatted hard disks can be reformatted by users. Inexperienced users should never attempt to reformat a hard disk, since a PC's operating system is installed on the hard disk and reformatting destroys all of the previous contents.

Tape Cartridges and Tape Drives

One of the first types of secondary storage media for computers was magnetic tape. Today **tape cartridges** are used mainly for backing up the contents of a hard drive, and for archiving large amounts of data that are no longer actively used but need to be saved for historical purposes. A tape cartridge is a small plastic housing containing a magnetically coated ribbon of thin plastic. Similar to a pocket-size tape recorder, a **tape drive** is used to read and write data to and from the tape (see Figure 3-28). Administrators of local area networks (LANs) often use magnetic tape cartridges to back up company data on a daily basis. Tape cartridges provide a relatively inexpensive, sequential-access type of storage.

FIGURE 3-28: Tape cartridges are used with personal computers mainly for backing up the contents of a hard drive. The tape is housed in a small plastic container that also contains a tape reel and a take-up reel.

OPTICAL STORAGE DEVICES

An **optical disc** is a plastic disk 4.75 inches in diameter and about 1/20th of an inch thick. Both **compact discs (CDs)** and **digital versatile (or video) discs (DVDs)** are types of optical discs that are available in a variety of formats (see Table 3-4). Optical disc systems are widely used on computer systems of all sizes, and almost every new PC comes equipped with a **CD drive** (see Figure 3-29). The drive can read nearly any kind of data recorded on an optical disc, including text, graphics, video clips, and sound. Increasingly, DVD drives also are standard equipment on new PCs, particularly those designed to handle high-end multimedia applications.

Laser technologies are used to store information and data on compact discs. A high-intensity laser records data by burning tiny indentations called **pits** onto the disc surface. Flat, unburned areas on the disc are called **lands**. A low-intensity laser reads stored data from the disc into the computer by reflecting light through the bottom of the disc. Each pit absorbs the light, causing the computer to read the pit as a binary digit 0. Each land reflects the light, causing the computer to read the land as a binary digit 1. The arrangement of 0s and 1s can thus represent data (see Figure 3-30).

Optical Disc	Storage Capacity	Features
Compact Disc	650 MB–700 MB	
CD-ROM		can be written to only once; used for distributing digital data such as computer software and for storing large data and graphics files
CD-R		used mainly in small businesses for creating one-of-a-kind CDs
CD-RW		allows rewriting; used mainly for backing up important files
Digital Versatile Disc	4.7 GB–17 GB	
DVD-ROM		can be written to only once; typically used to create master copies of movies
DVD-R		can be written to only once
DVD-RW		recordable and rewritable
DVD+R		recordable one time only
DVD+RW		recordable, rewritable up to 1,000 times; cannot be read by set-top players and many computer DVD drives
DVD-RAM		recordable and rewritable up to 100,000 times
DVD-Video		used in the entertainment industry for recording movies that are sold or rented

T A B L E 3 - 4 : Types and Storage Capacities of Optical Discs

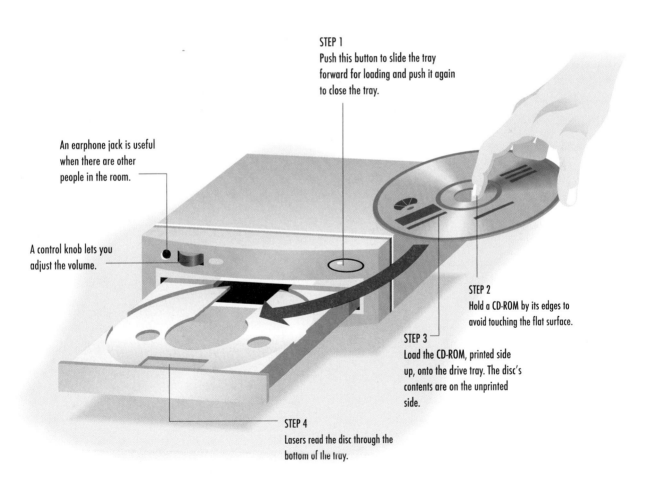

F I G U R E 3 - 2 9 : Optical disc systems are used for very large storage needs. Various types of optical discs are available in addition to the standard CD-ROM.

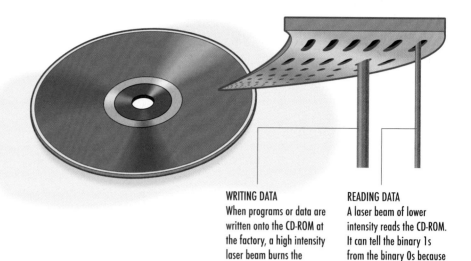

WRITING DATA
When programs or data are written onto the CD-ROM at the factory, a high intensity laser beam burns the surface to inscribe them.

READING DATA
A laser beam of lower intensity reads the CD-ROM. It can tell the binary 1s from the binary 0s because the light is reflected from the nonburned surface but not from the darkened pits.

Optical disc data is typically stored along a single track that spirals outward from the center of the disc to the outer edge, in the same way music is stored on a phonograph record. Data is stored on the disc in sectors, similar to the sectors on a hard disk or floppy disk (see Figure 3-31).

Optical disc technologies are not necessarily compatible with one another, and some require a different type of disc drive and disc. Within each category there are varying storage formats, although the **CD-ROM** (pronounced *see-dee-rom*) is relatively standard for computer data storage. (Refer to Table 3-4 for a comparison of optical disc storage capacities). Bit for bit, optical disc systems offer less expensive storage and greater durability than floppy disks, hard disks, and tape cartridges.

FIGURE 3-31: On an optical disc, information is stored in sectors along a single track that spirals outward from the center of the disc to its outer edge.

Single track spirals to edge of disc

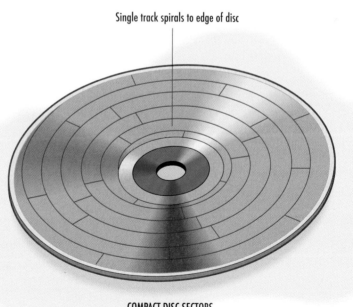

COMPACT DISC SECTORS

CD-ROM Discs

Most optical disc systems are of the CD-ROM type. Like an audio CD found in the home or automobile, a CD-ROM comes with data already encoded. The data is permanent and can be read many times, but it cannot be changed. A CD-ROM drive is needed to access the stored data. Since CD-ROMs conform to a standard size and format, any CD-ROM can be used with any CD-ROM drive. Computer CD-ROM drives are also capable of playing audio CDs. CD-ROMs are well suited for storing large computer applications containing graphics, sound, and video. A typical CD-ROM can hold about 650–700 megabytes (MB) of information, or about 450 times as much as a high-density floppy disk. An example of this capacity in real terms is the fact that the entire 32-volume set of the *Encyclopaedia Britannica 2004* plus the *Merriam-Webster's® Collegiate Dictionary and Thesaurus*, an atlas, and timelines can be stored on just two CD-ROMs.

Data transfer rates vary among different CD-ROM drives—a factor that can be very important depending on the application being used. For example, a slow transfer rate can result in poor image quality or garbled sounds. CD-ROM speeds are expressed as a multiple of the speed of the first CD-ROM drives (150 KB per second). For example, the data transfer rate of a 20X CD-ROM drive is 3,000 KB per second (150 KB x 20 = 3,000 KB) and a 40X CD-ROM drive is 6,000 KB per second (150 KB x 40 = 6,000 KB). The higher the number, the faster the data transfer rate of the CD-ROM drive. Faster speeds result in clearer images and better sounds. Newer CD-ROM drives have data transfer rates ranging from 40X to 75X.

CD-R Discs

Many manufacturers now include a CD-R drive with the computers they sell. A **CD-R (compact disc, recordable) drive** allows a PC user to record, or "burn," information on a **CD-R disc** using a device called a **CD-burner**, also known as a **CD-writer**. This device writes once to the disc, and the resulting CD or CD-ROM can be read by a standard CD-ROM drive. Figure 3-32 shows CD-R discs ready for recording.

FIGURE 3-32: CD-R discs offer an inexpensive way for individuals and businesses to create their own CDs.

Most CD-R drives can write data at speeds up to 8X and read at speeds up to 24X. In describing the speed of a CD-R, the device's writing speed is listed first. For example, a speed of 8 X 24 means the drive writes at a speed of 8X and reads at a speed of 24X. The main disadvantage of a CD-R is that it can be written on only one time. CD-RW technology overcomes this limitation.

CD-RW Discs

A newer type of optical disc storage technology is called **CD-RW (compact disc, rewritable)**. CD-RW uses an erasable disc that can be rewritten multiple times, similar to a floppy disk or hard disk. To use a CD-RW system, a CD-RW drive and special software are required. CD-RW discs are often used in the movie industry for making original copies of movies. Once perfected, the movie is copied to other optical discs that cannot be changed.

A typical CD-RW drive has a write speed up to 12X, a rewrite speed up to 4X, and a read speed up to 32X. These speeds are usually shown on a CD-RW drive package as 12X/4X/32X. Rewrite speeds are typically slower than write speeds because the drive must first locate the file containing the information to be rewritten and then make the required changes.

With storage capacities of up to 700 MB or more, CD-RW discs are ideal for storing and backing up large or important files, such as the contents of a hard disk. In addition, they allow the creation of large files, such as those containing music, that can be shared with other users who have CD-ROM drives. Newer CD-RW burners can write an entire CD in 4 minutes and copy a 3-minute song to the user's hard drive in 5 seconds. Because of their flexibility, CD-RW disks are rapidly replacing the more limited CD-R discs.

DVD-ROM Discs

Many of today's complex applications demand huge amounts of storage capacity, often requiring several standard CD-ROMs. DVD-ROM technology was developed to overcome this limitation. **DVD-ROM (digital versatile disc-read only memory)** is an extremely high-capacity disc capable of holding many gigabytes of data, currently ranging from 4.7 gigabytes (GB) to 17 gigabytes. In appearance, a DVD looks just like a CD (see Figure 3-33). The basic technology for storing data on these two types of optical discs also is the same, although minor differences in DVD technology allow for higher storage capacities. For one, packing the pits more closely means a denser disc. Manufacturers can also create two layers of pits, approximately doubling the storage capacity, and they can create double-sided discs. These variations in techniques account for the range of storage capacities from 4.7 GB for a single-sided, single-layered disc to 17 GB for a double-sided, double-layered disc. A 17 GB disc can hold the entire contents (text and color images) of a large retailer's catalog.

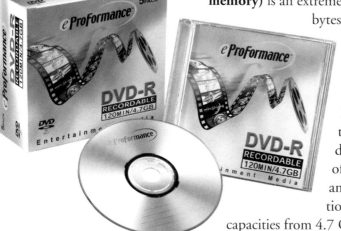

FIGURE 3-33: A DVD disc looks like its relative, the compact disc.

DVD-ROM technology was initially developed to store full-size movies. However, a DVD can also store text, graphics, images, and sound. This technology requires the use of a DVD-ROM drive or player. Because DVD-ROM drives and DVD players are backward-compatible, most can also read CD-ROMs, CD-Rs, CD-RWs, and audio CDs. Newer DVD-ROM drives are capable of reading from the disc at speeds up to 40X. DVD-ROMs are available in a variety of versions, including versions that are both recordable and rewritable. Two of the more widely used formats are DVD-R and DVD-RW.

DVD-R Discs

As with CD-R discs, a **DVD-R (digital versatile disc-recordable)**, can be recorded on only one time. Once data, video, or sound is recorded on the disc, the information is permanently stored. DVD-R discs created by a DVD-R device can be read by most commercial DVD-ROM players.

DVD-R discs are used extensively by the music and movie industries for creating commercial copies of music and movies. Several thousand or even millions of copies can be made from the original DVD-R.

A typical DVD-R disc can hold up to 4.7 gigabytes of data, enough capacity to hold a full-length movie or hundreds of music pieces. Using a two-layer standard, manufacturers can increase the storage volume to 8.5 GB, and adding a second side means boosting the total capacity to 17 GB. A new format called the Blu-ray Disc will store 27 GB, which represents more than 13 hours of movies compared to the standard DVD capacity of 133 minutes. Nine electronics companies, including Sony, have collaborated in developing the Blu-ray Disc, and industry observers predict that this disc may soon become the standard recording format. Manufacturers are continually researching new techniques for creating discs with even greater storage capacities.

DVD-RW Discs

Another type of digital versatile disc, called **DVD-RW (digital versatile disc-rewritable)**, allows recorded data to be erased and recorded over numerous times without damaging the disc. The rewriting capability makes DVD-RW discs more versatile and therefore more popular among users needing inexpensive, reusable storage media with large storage capacities. A single-layered, single-sided DVD-RW disc can store up to 4.7 gigabytes of data.

DVD-RW discs and players are becoming increasing popular. They can be used for routine storage of programs, files, and data, making a back-up copy of the contents of a hard disk, and for archiving important files. Like DVD-R discs, data recorded on a DVD-RW disc by a DVD-RW device can be read by most commercial DVD-ROM players. Figure 3-34 lists guidelines for the handling and care of compact discs and DVDs.

DO:

1. Store each disc in a jewel case or a CD holder.
2. Use a felt-tip permanent marker to write a contents name on the disc (the side with the manufacturer's name imprinted).
3. Hold the disc by its edges.

DO NOT:

1. Do not touch the bottom surface of the disc.
2. Do not stack discs unless they are in a jewel case or holder, as stacking can warp them.
3. Do not place objects on the disc.
4. Do not expose disc to direct sunlight or excessive heat.
5. Do not place food or beverages near a disc.
6. Do not allow under-surface of the disc to rub against desktop or any solid object.

FIGURE 3-34: CDs and DVDs must be handled carefully and protected from excessive heat.

Large System Computer Storage

Large computer systems, such as mainframe and server systems, typically use storage devices and media similar to those used with smaller computers. However, large computer storage devices provide much higher capacities than smaller computers because of the huge amounts of data they deal with. For example, a large business may need multiple hard disks for storing thousands of employee records. Similarly, imagine the capacities needed for storing all domestic airline flight schedules for a year.

Magnetic Storage Devices for Large Computer Systems

Large computer systems typically use magnetic disk and magnetic tape secondary storage devices and media. For large computers, **magnetic disk storage** consists of a disk drive housing multiple hard disks contained in a rigid plastic container called a **disk pack**. A disk pack is mounted inside a disk drive. A metal shaft extends through the center of the vertically aligned disks. When activated, electromagnetic read/write heads record information and/or read stored data by moving inward and outward between the disks, as shown in Figure 3-35.

Disk storage provides users with direct, or random, access to stored data. Disk storage is preferred when users need to access stored information quickly. For example, disk storage allows bank and utility company employees to quickly access and update thousands of customer accounts.

Another type of secondary storage for large computer systems is **magnetic tape storage**, which uses removable reels of magnetic tape (see Figure 3-36). The tape contains tracks that extend the full length of the tape. Each track contains metallic particles representing potential 0 and 1 bits. As is true of magnetic disks, combinations of bits are magnetized, or not magnetized, to represent bytes of data (see Figure 3-37).

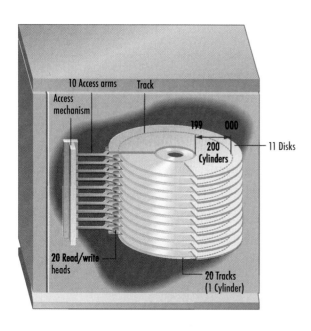

FIGURE 3-35: A disk pack houses multiple vertically aligned disks in a rigid plastic container placed inside a disk drive. When activated, read/write heads read or record on the disks by moving inward and outward between them.

Because magnetic tape is a sequential storage technology, information is accessed or updated in sequential order, that is, in numerical order. For example, if the user wants to access the twentieth record on the tape, the previous 19 records must first move past the read/write heads before the twentieth record can be accessed. Magnetic tape storage is typically used in situations where large amounts of information, such as all employee payroll records, are to be updated. In this case, all records are to be updated and the order in which individual records are processed is not important.

Magnetic tape storage may be used for other kinds of applications. Information stored on magnetic disk is often backed up onto tape and stored in a safe place in case it is needed. For example, a serious fire could damage or destroy a company's disk drives, tape drives, and other equipment. Having a backup copy of the data can eliminate the need to reconstruct important information.

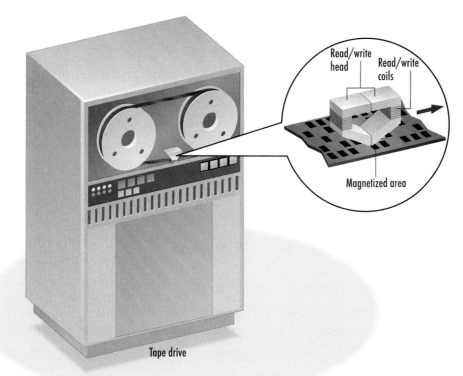

Tape drive

FIGURE 3-36: A tape drive records and reads data from a reel of magnetic tape. Many large businesses and organizations use this sequential-access storage medium for backing up important programs and data.

Optical Storage Devices for Large Systems

WORM (write once, read many) disks are a type of optical laser disk used for very high-capacity storage. They are mainly found in mainframe applications. WORM disks can only be written once and cannot be overwritten. This safety feature, combined with their high capacity, makes them ideal for storing archival-type material such as records or images. One of the drawbacks to WORM disks is that they are usually readable only by the drive on which they were written. The rapid advances in optical disk technology mean that newer optical disk formats such as CD-R are gradually supplanting WORM disks.

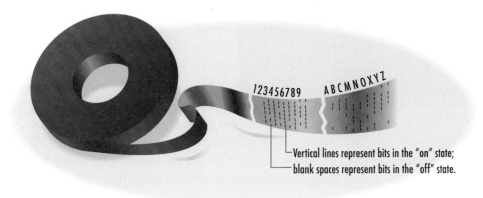

FIGURE 3-37: Data is stored as magnetic particles along tracks extending the full length of the tape.

ON THE HORIZON

Scientists, computer engineers, and entrepreneurs of all kinds are working feverishly to develop new and improved hardware devices that will make information access faster and easier. After all, much is at stake—the millions and billions of dollars in revenue to be shared by successful individuals and companies. Inventors are also motivated by the great satisfaction that comes with creating something new and better. Several trends are worth watching.

Increased Optical Disc Storage Capacity

Computer users needing huge storage capacities may be pleased with a new type of optical disc storage called FMD-ROM. Introduced by Constellation 3D Inc., a Fluorescent Multi-Layer Disc (FMD) holds up to 140 gigabytes (GB) of data. This capacity is currently 215 times greater than a CD-ROM (.65 GB) and 23 times greater than a DVD-ROM (6 GB).

FMD-ROM discs contain fluorescent materials embedded in the pits and grooves of all 10 or more layers. The fluorescent materials are stimulated to produce coherent and incoherent light when in contact with a laser. Data is stored in the incoherent light. Because the technology is not based on reflection, multiple layers are read at the same time.

FMD-ROM discs are compatible with existing CD-ROM and DVD-ROM drives. FMD-ROM drives are also backward-compatible, meaning they will accept and read CDs and DVDs.

Improved Monitors

Computer monitors will become even thinner and more flexible. New materials will enable manufacturers to create monitors that can be rolled up like a piece of paper. At the same time, monitor resolution will continue to increase, and within a decade we may be able to see multiple Web documents simultaneously on the screen, eliminating the current problem of having to scroll while reading documents at Web sites.

Holographic Storage

Storage needs are ballooning because of the increasing use of multimedia files. Indeed, some experts estimate that storage needs are doubling every 100 days and that the answer is holographic storage. Its multidimensional images allow the layering of digitized information throughout the holograph, thereby outpacing by far the capacity of today's magnetic and optical discs. By 2010, according to estimates by IBM scientists at the company's Almaden Research Laboratory, we will see CD-size holographic storage media with a storage capacity of a terabyte of data (1,000 GB).

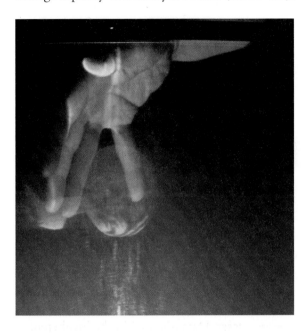

PC Magazine translates that capacity into the following comparison: one holographic CD could store the entire archive of the Library of Congress, whereas today, this data would require billions of CDs.

Electronic Paper

Instead of scrolling through the pages of *The New York Times* on your monitor, one day soon you will read the news on a tablet of electronic paper that instantly displays stories as the news happens. Xerox Corporation and E-ink are developing the new technology, which uses "ink" consisting of a clear liquid of microcapsules. These miniscule containers hold white titanium dioxide and black carbon particles that are treated to have alternating positive and negative electrical charges. When stimulated with a negative electric field through a display driver, the white particles move to the front. When a positive field is applied, the black particles move to the front. The combination of white and black create characters and images. Experts predict the technology will appear in handheld devices by about 2006.

High-Tech Tracking

The San Bushmen of the Kalahari in South Africa have an uncanny tracking ability. Just by looking at an animal's spoor, they can determine the animal's sex and age, its health, what it ate recently, and whether it was slowly meandering, grazing, or fleeing an enemy. This amazing knowledge, passed down orally over a thousand years, faces extinction as the Bushmen's primitive hunter-gatherer society is threatened by encroaching political and social forces.

Louis Liebenberg is a physicist and researcher who years ago realized the importance of preserving the Bushmen's wisdom for future generations. He spent more than a decade hunting with the Bushmen, learning their skills and becoming one of the best trackers in South Africa. He then developed a handheld computer which the illiterate Bushmen can use to compile the information they so effortlessly glean from animal tracks. The device uses CyberTracker software and a GPS system to relay the data to a central database.

This combination of new-age technology with age-old ways of the Kalahari has revolutionized wildlife management and research. It has proved an effective tool in the fight against poaching and the drive to save rare species, plus it brings in more tourists. And by providing job opportunities, it may also help save the Bushmen culture. More than 120 San Bushmen trackers have been taught to use the computerized animal-tracking device, and CyberTracker teams are working in eight national parks in South Africa.

Sources: Kwinter, Sanford. "Trailblazer," *Wired*, June 2003. Barron, Chris. "Quest for the Last Readers of the Spoor," *The Sunday Times*, October 25, 1998. "The CyberTraker: Combining Indigenous Knowledge and Computer Technology for Improved Wildlife Management."

chapter summary

Output Devices and Media

Output is processed data, usually text, graphics, or sound that may be produced as hard copy or soft copy. An **output device** is a hardware device that makes information available to a user. An **output medium** is material on which information is recorded. Computer systems can produce four types of output: **text**, **graphics**, **audio**, and **video**.

A **display device**, or **monitor**, is the most common soft-copy output device. Some monitors display information only in **monochrome**, while most can display output in color. The most common type of monitor is the **CRT (cathode ray tube) monitor**.

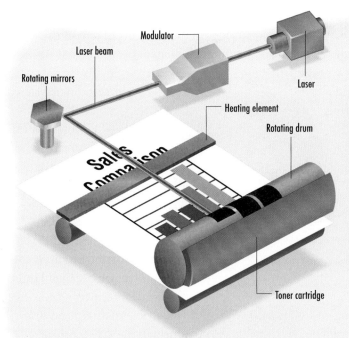

Modulator

Laser beam

Rotating mirrors

Laser

Heating element

Rotating drum

Sales Comparison

Toner cartridge

A mechanism inside the printer reads the characters and sends the information to the laser device. Then the laser sends light signals through a series of mirrors in the drum, creating tiny dots of light. The dots create magnetic fields on the drum matching the shape of the characters (or images), which attract the toner powder. As the drum rotates, toner is pressed onto the paper.

Television sets and **flat-panel displays** are also popular. Factors that influence a monitor's **resolution** include the number of **pixels** and the **dot pitch**. Factors in monitor performance and quality include the amount of RAM in the graphics adapter, the monitor resolution, and the **refresh rate**.

Considered the most common hard-copy output devices, **printers** are classified as **impact printers** that print by physically striking an inked ribbon against the paper or **nonimpact printers** that form characters and images using electricity, heat, laser technology, or photographic techniques to produce output. The three main types of printers are **dot-matrix printers**, **ink-jet printers**, and **laser printers**.

Most personal computers have built-in **speakers**, and newer models often include a **speaker headset**.

Voice output is available with all new computers and is becoming increasingly popular.

A **facsimile (fax) machine** is a device that can send and receive copies or duplicates of documents through a telephone line. A **multifunction device** is a single piece of equipment that provides multiple capabilities, including scanning, copying, printing, and sometimes faxing.

Files

Data or information created and saved using a computer is called a **file**. A file name is typically followed by a period (.) and a set of characters called a **file extension**, which identifies the type of file. Similar files are often stored in a **directory**, a special kind of file that allows other files to be grouped together logically. A file's extension is usually created by the software program.

Storage Devices and Media

Also called **auxiliary storage** or **external storage**, **secondary storage** devices and media provide the capability of reentering and reusing stored information. A **storage device** is a component that houses a **storage medium** on which data is recorded (stored). Two main types of storage systems are magnetic and optical.

A **magnetic storage device** works by applying electrical charges to iron filings on revolving media, orienting each filing in one direction or another to represent a "0" or a "1." Data is stored and retrieved, or accessed, either sequentially (in linear order) or directly (in any order, randomly). Three main types of magnetic storage media are floppy disks, hard disks, and tape cartridges. A **floppy disk** (or **diskette**) is a thin, circular Mylar® wafer, sandwiched between two sheets of special cleaning tissue inside a rigid plastic case. Data is stored along the **tracks** and in the **sectors** of a floppy disk. A **hard disk** system consists of one or more rigid metal platters (disks) mounted on a metal shaft and sealed in a container that contains an access mechanism. **Tape cartridges**, consisting of a small plastic housing containing a magnetically coated ribbon of thin plastic, are used mainly for backing up the contents of a hard drive and for archiving large amounts of data.

Optical disc systems are widely used on computer systems of all sizes. Most new PCs come equipped with an **optical disc drive** that can read data recorded on an **optical disc**, which is a flat, round, plastic disk. Data is stored as tiny indentations, called **pits**, and flat areas, called **lands**. Two lasers record and read the data. The main optical disc formats are **CD (compact disc)** and **DVD (digital versatile disc)**. Each disc type has various versions, including recordable one time only and both recordable and rewritable.

Mainframe systems typically use storage devices and media similar to those used with smaller computers. For large computers **magnetic disk storage** consists of a disk drive housing multiple hard disks contained in a rigid plastic container called a **disk pack**. Another type of secondary storage for large computer systems is **magnetic tape storage** using removable reels of magnetic tape. **WORM (write once, read many) disks** are a type of optical laser disk used for very high-capacity storage such as images.

KEYTERMS

Page numbers indicate where terms are first cited in the chapter. A complete list of key terms with definitions can be found in the Glossary at the end of the book.

access time, 122
active-matrix display (thin-film transistor (TFT) display), 106
audio, 103
bit depth, 108
cathode ray tube (CRT) monitor, 104
CD (compact disc), 128
CD-burner (CD-writer), 131
CD drive, 128
CD-R (compact disc, recordable) drive, 131
CD-ROM (compact disc, read-only memory), 130
CD-RW (compact disc, rewritable), 131
cluster, 124
data transfer rate, 122
direct access, 122
disk pack, 134
display device (monitor), 103
dot-matrix printer, 112
dot pitch, 108
draft quality, 113
DVD (digital versatile disc), 128
DVD-R (digital versatile disc-recordable), 132
DVD-ROM (digital versatile disc, read-only memory), 132
DVD-RW (digital versatile disc-rewritable),133
ergonomics, 109
facsimile (fax) machine, 119

fax, 119
fax/modem board, 119
fax program,119
file, 120
file allocation table (FAT file), 124
file extension, 120
flat-panel display, 106
floppy disk (diskette, disk), 123
formatting, 125
graphic (graphical image), 102
graphics adapter, 103
hard disk, 127
hard drive, 125
high-definition television (HDTV), 111
impact printer, 112
ink-jet printer, 114
land, 128
landscape format, 112
laser printer, 116
letter quality, 113
liquid crystal display (LCD), 106
magnetic disk storage, 134
magnetic storage device, 122
magnetic tape storage, 134
monochrome, 104
multifunction device (MFD), 120
nonimpact printer, 112
NTSC converter, 111
optical disc, 128
output medium, 103
passive-matrix display (dual-scan

display), 106
permanent storage (secondary storage, auxiliary storage, external storage), 120
permanent storage medium, 122
photograph printer, 115
pit, 128
pixel, 104
plotter, 117
portrait format, 112
printer, 112
refresh rate, 109
removable storage medium, 122
resolution, 108
sector, 124
sequential access, 122
SIM card, 116
speaker headset, 118
speakers, 118
tape cartridge, 128
tape drive, 128
text, 102
toner, 117
track, 124
true color, 108
video, 103
video card (graphics card, video adapter), 104
voice output, 119
WORM (write once, read many) disk, 135

chapter exercises

The following chapter exercises, along with new activities and information, are also offered in the *Computers: Understanding Technology* Internet Resource Center at www.emcp.com.

EXPLORING WINDOWS

Tutorial 3 teaches the four methods for running an application: from the Start menu, using the desktop icons, using the Run command, and from a file management window. You will learn to choose a method based on the situation.

TERMS CHECK: MATCHING
Write the letter of the correct answer on the line before each numbered item.

a. plotter
b. pixel
c. tape cartridge
d. optical disc
e. formatting
f. ergonomics

g. laser printer
h. sector
i. diskette
j. monitor
k. facsimile machine
l. dot-matrix printer

_____ 1. A type of printer used for large-sized high-quality printing, including architectural drawings, charts, maps, diagrams, and other images.

_____ 2. A hard-copy output device that produces characters in a manner similar to the way numbers appear on a football scoreboard.

_____ 3. An electronic device that can send and receive documents through a telephone line.

_____ 4. A tiny single point in an alphabetic letter, number, graphic, or picture displayed on the screen.

_____ 5. A numbered section of a disk similar to a slice of pie.

_____ 6. A flat, round, plastic disc measuring approximately 4.75 inches in diameter on which data is stored in the form of pits and lands.

_____ 7. The study of the interaction between humans and the equipment they use.

_____ 8. The most common soft-copy output device.

_____ 9. A hardware device that produces high-quality hard-copy output using a technology similar to that of photocopy machines.

_____ 10. The procedure for preparing a floppy disk for use.

_____ 11. Another name for a floppy disk.

_____ 12. A storage medium, contained in a small plastic housing, capable of holding large amounts of data, and used mainly for backing up the contents of a hard drive.

TECHNOLOGY ILLUSTRATED: IDENTIFY THE PROCESS

What process is this? Identify the process illustrated in the drawing below and write a paragraph explaining it.

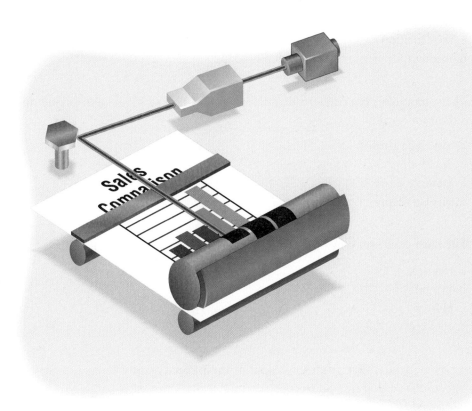

KNOWLEDGE CHECK: MULTIPLE CHOICE
Circle the letter of the best answer from those provided.

1. Processed data that can be used immediately or stored in computer-usable form for later use is called

   a. input.
   b. output.
   c. data retrieval.
   d. manipulated data.

2. A tiny single point in anything being displayed on a screen is called a

   a. dot.
   b. screen point.
   c. pixel.
   d. microsync.

3. A term that describes the number of pixels in the display, or the quality of the text and graphics being displayed, is

   a. resolution.
   b. density.
   c. coordination.
   d. element filtering.

4. The component that converts digital signals into text so it can be displayed on a monitor is called a(n)

   a. hypertext card.
   b. RAM chip.
   c. graphics adapter.
   d. analog adapter.

5. The most common type of device for producing hard-copy output is the

   a. monitor.
   b. printer.
   c. plotter.
   d. speaker.

6. A type of printer that produces output of exceptional quality using a technology similar to that of a photocopy machine is the

   a. inkjet printer.
   b. dot-matrix printer.
   c. impact printer.
   d. laser printer.

7. A piece of equipment that looks like a printer or copy machine, but which provides a variety of capabilities, including scanning and copying, is known as a

    a. scanner.
    b. duplicator.
    c. multifunction device.
    d. special-purpose device.

8. A type of printer used to produce specialized kinds of large-sized high-quality printing, including architectural drawings and other images is a(n)

    a. dot-matrix printer.
    b. inkjet printer.
    c. photographic printer.
    d. plotter.

9. A type of printer that prints characters in a manner similar to the way numbers appear on a football scoreboard is the

    a. dot-matrix printer.
    b. inkjet printer.
    c. laser printer.
    d. photograph printer.

10. Permanent storage is also known as all of the following except

    a. secondary storage.
    b. auxiliary storage.
    c. primary storage.
    d. external storage.

11. The time a disk storage device spends locating a particular file is called

    a. data transfer rate.
    b. access time.
    c. file search time.
    d. disk spin rate.

12. A personal computer storage device that allows a user to record information on a compact disc is called a

    a. CD-recorder.
    b. floppy drive.
    c. CD-etcher.
    d. CD-burner.

13. On a floppy disk, a numbered concentric circle is called a

    a. sector.
    b. cluster.
    c. track.
    d. ring.

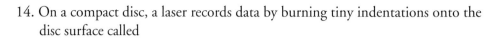

14. On a compact disc, a laser records data by burning tiny indentations onto the disc surface called

    a. lands.
    b. pits.
    c. tracks.
    d. sectors.

15. Which one of the following is not an optical disc format?

    a. hard disk.
    b. CD-ROM.
    c. CD-RW.
    d. DVD.

THINGS THAT THINK: BRAINSTORMING NEW USES
In groups or individually, contemplate the following questions and develop as many answers as you can.

1. Car washes and parking garages currently use digital license plate readers to identify customers' vehicles and to ensure that correct fees are paid for the companies' services. A camera in the license plate reader takes a picture of the front or rear of the vehicle. Optical character recognition software then converts the number in the photo to text, which is sent to a database of license numbers for verification. Although the digital license plate readers have some limitations, including problems reading curvy letters or unusual typefaces, security experts think this technology could be valuable in tracking the movement of vehicles around airports or other high-security areas. What other uses can you think of for digital license plate readers? What kinds of problems might be associated with the technology?

2. Smart cards are plastic cards the size of credit cards with tiny chips embedded in them. They are growing in popularity with major U.S. corporations because of their ability to protect personal information, such as account numbers, during Internet business transactions. With a Web-enabled cell phone, a user could access a company Web site, order a product, and then pay for it by inserting a smart card into a slot in the phone. Can you think of other ways in which this intelligent plastic could be used? Brainstorm applications in business and beyond.

KEY PRINCIPLES: COMPLETION
Fill in the blanks with the appropriate words or phrases.

1. A(n) _____ is a computer-generated picture produced on a computer screen, paper, or film.

2. A(n) _____ display is used for portable computers and other applications where weight and space considerations are critical.

3. The most common type of monitor for desktop computers is the _____.

4. The term _____ refers to the speed at which a monitor redraws images on the screen.

5. The distance between pixels on a display is called _____.

6. Processed data that can be used immediately or stored in computer-usable form for later use is called _____.

7. _____ is a term that refers to the permanent storage of computer programs, files, and data.

8. A thin, circular Mylar® wafer, sandwiched between two sheets of cleaning tissue inside a rigid plastic case is a(n) _____.

9. A(n) _____ system consists of one or more rigid metal platters (disks) mounted on a metal shaft and sealed in a container containing an access mechanism.

10. A(n) _____ is a secondary storage medium on which data is typically recorded by means of a high-intensity laser.

11. A small plastic housing containing a magnetically coated ribbon of thin plastic that is used mainly for backing up the contents of a hard drive and for archiving large amounts of data is a(n) _____.

12. Printers that form characters and images using electricity, heat, laser technology, or photographic techniques to produce output are called _____ printers.

13. Three main types of magnetic storage media for personal computers are _____, _____, and _____.

14. A file name is typically followed by a(n) _____, which identifies the type of file.

15. On a floppy disk, data is stored along the _____ and in the _____.

TECH ARCHITECTURE: LABEL THE DRAWING

In this illustration of a floppy disk, identify the pie-shaped sections and the two types of data storage areas.

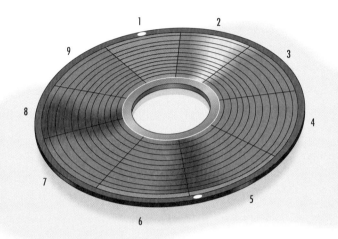

TECHNO LITERACY: RESEARCH AND WRITING

Develop appropriate written responses based on your research for each item.

1. What is inside the printer?

   Ask your instructor to allow you to open up a printer in the computer lab and look at the components inside. Using paper and pen, draw the components that you recognize and label each of them. At a minimum, include the printing mechanism, the ribbon, ink or toner container, and paper tray or container. Ask your instructor to explain other components you do not recognize. Write a brief summary of each component's function.

2. How many ways can a user output data?

   Page through a computer magazine such as *PC World*, or visit a computer store and select a personal computer that interests you. Research and describe all the different output devices that could be used with that particular computer system.

3. Which features should be considered when you purchase a printer?

   Hewlett-Packard is a major manufacturer of printers for personal computers. Visit the company's Web site at www.hp.com to learn about the various kinds of printers HP produces. Select one printer and write a brief report describing the following features of the printer:

   a. type of printer (ink-jet, laser, etc.)
   b. model number
   c. printing speed

d. color printing capability

e. amount (if any) of storage capacity inside the printer

f. graphics printing capability

4. Which storage device meets my needs?

Numerous secondary storage devices are available for personal computers. Research the major brands and models. Create a table that compares the various storage devices and media. Identify the one that would best meet your needs, and explain why. How would you use it?

TECHNOLOGY ISSUES: TEAM PROBLEM-SOLVING
In groups, brainstorm possible solutions to the issues presented.

1. Computers currently offer both visual and audio communication. Under development are devices and technologies that will incorporate olfactory communication, allowing users to smell various types of products while looking at them on the computer screen. What are some new applications of this technology for the food industry? Can you think of other industries that could use this capability?

2. Picture yourself working in the Information Technology department of a mid-sized company. Your responsibilities include evaluating employees' computer system needs and recommending equipment purchases. Recently, the company president hired a new employee and you must evaluate her computer system needs. The new employee is Marsha Wellington, a graphics designer, who will be responsible for designing sales and promotional pieces for the company.

    Considering you have a budget of $8,500 for equipping the computer system (or systems) she needs, research possible configurations and prepare a report outlining your recommendations, including costs. Assume that she needs a complete computer system, including graphics software, high-resolution color monitor, and high-resolution printing capability. (*Hint: Check computer magazines, retail stores, and Internet sites such as* www.gateway.com, www.dell.com, *and* www.apple.com.)

MINING DATA: INTERNET RESEARCH AND REPORTING
Conduct Internet searches to find the information described in the activities below. Write a brief report that summarizes your research results. Be sure to document your sources, using the MLA format (see Chapter 1, page 43, to review MLA style guidelines).

1. Renting data storage is becoming widely used among large companies that generate huge amounts of data. Using the Internet, locate information that explains data storage hosting and discusses the benefits, costs, and potential growth rate for this service.

2. Using an Internet search engine, find out how "geographic information systems" (also called GIS) are used. Find three companies or government agencies that use GIS and summarize how they use this technology.

TECHNOLOGY TIMELINE: PREDICTING NEXT STEPS

Look at the timeline below that outlines the major milestones in the development of storage devices and media. Research this topic and think of what the next steps will be. Complete the timeline through the year 2010 or later, if the research warrants it.

1956   IBM unveils the 350 Disk Storage Unit, the first random-access (direct-access) hard disk.

1973   IBM releases the 3340, the first Winchester hard disk with a capacity of 70 megabytes (MB) spread over four disk platters.

1985   The first CD-ROM drives make their debut on personal computers.

1998   The DVD-ROM drive debuts with 5.2 gigabytes (GB) of rewritable capacity on a double-sided cartridge—enough to hold a two-hour movie.

2001   Constellation 3D Inc. introduces a new type of optical disc storage called FMD-ROM, which holds up to 140 GB of data.

2003   USB flash drives (also called keychain drives because they are about the size of a key fob) hit the consumer market.

ETHICAL DILEMMAS: GROUP DISCUSSION AND DEBATE

As a class or within an assigned group, discuss the following ethical dilemma.

Many companies today have the ability to monitor employees' Internet usage as well as their inbound and outbound e-mail messages. Employees may consider this an invasion of privacy, but employers contend that they have the right to track usage of company property and ensure employees are doing their jobs efficiently. Is it legal for companies to monitor employee Internet and e-mail usage? Is it ethical for them to do so? Should employers be required to tell employees when they are being monitored? How much personal use of workplace computers should employees be allowed?

ANSWERS TO TERMS CHECK AND KEY PRINCIPLES QUESTIONS

Terms Check: 1 – a; 2 – l; 3 – k; 4 – b; 5 – h; 6 – d; 7 – f; 8 – j; 9 – g; 10 – e; 11 – i; 12 – c

Key Principles: 1 – graphic; 2 – flat-panel; 3 – CRT monitor; 4 – refresh rate; 5 – dot pitch; 6 – output; 7 – secondary storage; 8 – floppy disk; 9 – hard disk; 10 – optical disc; 11 – tape cartridge; 12 – nonimpact; 13 – floppy disks, hard disks, tape cartridges; 14 – file extension; 15 – along the tracks and in the sectors

special feature

Adding Software and Hardware Components to Your PC

Installing system software, application programs, and hardware components with early PCs was difficult and cumbersome compared to the installation process with modern computers. In the past, users had to enter complex instructions. Thus, an experienced computer technician or other professional was needed to install the software or hardware properly. Today's computer manufacturers have made these activities easier by including installation instructions and diagrams with their products. Additionally, Microsoft Windows includes features that enable users to install software and hardware more easily and quickly. For example, the Windows Install and Uninstall features contain instructions for installing or removing application programs and hardware devices. In the following sections you will learn how to install software programs and add hardware devices to your personal computer system.

Manufacturers such as Dell Computer preload most of their new PCs with the Windows operating system, some application programs, and basic hardware devices. Because most PCs use Windows, it is assumed in the following sections that you are using a Windows-based computer.

INSTALLING OR UPGRADING THE OPERATING SYSTEM

Sometimes situations occur that require you to re-install the operating system and application programs. An operating system (OS) contains programs that direct a computer's operations and programs that manage the computer's internal and

external components. If Windows was not preinstalled on your computer, a CD-ROM containing the OS may have been included in the package, or you can purchase one at a computer store or at another retail outlet.

Installing the OS on your hard disk is relatively simple. With your computer turned off, insert the CD-ROM containing the OS into the CD drive at the front of the system unit. Turn the computer on. A small ROM chip on the motherboard will search for an operating system and find it on the CD, along with a file of instructions for installing the OS. Installation instructions will be displayed on the screen. Follow the instructions to complete the process.

When a new version of the OS becomes available, you may want to install it on your computer, a procedure known as **upgrading**. To install the upgraded version, insert the CD-ROM containing the new version in the CD drive. Follow the instructions on

your screen to install the new version. The installation should be completed in a few minutes.

INSTALLING APPLICATION SOFTWARE

Application software enables users to perform specific types of activities and tasks for which computers were designed. The type of software purchased depends on the user's intended purpose, and there are application programs available for almost every need. The most widely sold type is productivity software that enables users to improve their efficiency at home and on the job. Examples of productivity software include word processing, spreadsheet, database, desktop publishing, presentation graphics, project management, and computer-aided design.

> • • • • • TIP • • • • •
>
> **System requirements for installing the software are usually printed on the software package or box. Among the requirements is the minimum amount of hard disk space (capacity) needed to house the software. Be sure your hard disk has enough unused capacity to store the software. If there is insufficient capacity on your hard disk, you will be alerted to this problem.**

To install Microsoft Word, or another productivity program, find the user's manual packaged with the software and read the section that explains the installation procedure. Follow the instructions carefully.

In the unlikely event the software came without installation instructions, you can install the software by completing the following steps:

1. Insert the CD-ROM or floppy disk that contains the software in the appropriate drive. (If the medium is a CD-ROM, insert the disc by holding the edges and insert the disc with the printed side facing up.)
2. Using the mouse, double-click the My Computer icon on the desktop.

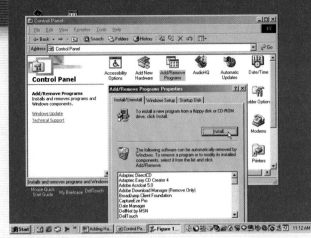

FIGURE B-1: Add/Remove Programs Properties Window

3. With the My Computer window displayed, double-click the Control Panel icon.

4. With the Control Panel window displayed, click the Add/Remove Programs icon (see Figure B-1).

5. Click the Install button.

6. A series of easy-to-follow instructions will be displayed on the screen. Follow the directions and sit back while the software is being installed on the computer's hard disk in the Programs directory.

7. After the software has been installed, you can access the program by clicking the Start button, the Programs option, and then selecting the program you installed, such as Word. (***Note:*** the installation process is the same for almost all application programs.)

> • • • • • **TIP** • • • • •
>
> **If a previous (older) version of the software is already installed on your hard disk and you are installing an upgrade (a newer version), only the needed parts of the newer version will be installed. Also, files you created using the older version will remain intact, allowing you to continue using those files.**

CONNECTING SYSTEM COMPONENTS

Your PC probably came with basic components such as the system unit, monitor, keyboard, mouse, and maybe a printer. Other than the system unit, the other components are referred to as peripherals, because they are external (or peripheral) to the system unit. In the following sections, you will learn about device drivers and plug-and-play features and how to connect add-on peripheral devices to the system unit so that, collectively, all devices and components function smoothly as a computer system.

Device Drivers and Plug-and-Play Features

Every device, whether it is a printer, disk drive, or keyboard, must have an associated driver program. A **driver** controls the device, translating commands between the device and programs that use the device, so that it functions as intended. Each device has its own set of specialized commands that only the driver knows. Most programs access devices by using generic commands. A driver accepts generic commands and translates them into specialized commands for the device.

Some drivers, such as the keyboard driver, are included with the computer's operating system, because the manufacturer assumes you will use the keyboard that came with the computer. Other special devices, such as a scanner or joystick, may come with the device's driver program on a floppy disk or CD-ROM that you will need to load. Beginning with Windows 95, the operating system includes drivers for a variety of devices, allowing the user to choose the needed ones. A driver designed for use in a Windows environment often has a .DRV file extension.

Some computer systems will automatically configure devices and expansion boards, a feature known as **plug-and-play**. With plug-and-play, a user should be able to plug in a device and use it immediately. Newer Apple Macintosh computers are plug-and-play systems, and both Microsoft and Intel use a technology called PnP (short for plug and play) that supports plug-and-play installation.

If you purchased your PC in the past two or three years, it probably has the plug-and-play capability. Adding new components is a matter of plugging the devices into the appropriate ports on the back of the system unit.

Adding Hardware and Software Components to Your PC

Locating System Unit Ports

The back of the system unit contains several ports (see Figure B-2). Many manufacturers label the ports, and some companies include an installation diagram with their computers. Additionally, cables that come with a computer usually will fit into only one port. These aids assist users in setting up a computer system.

Connecting a New Printer

Most printers purchased for home or office use are either inkjet or laser. Both types require a container of ink called a toner cartridge. If your printer came without a toner cartridge or a printer cable, you'll need to purchase these items.

   Installing a printer is a simple task. To connect the printer to the system unit and to a power source, complete the following steps:

1. With the power turned off, plug one end of the printer cable to the printer and the other end to the port located at the back of the system unit.

(*Note:* Make sure both ends are securely fastened. The cable attaches to the printer by a wire or screws). Plug the other end into the port at the back of the system unit. (There is only one port into which the cable connector will fit.)

2. Plug the power cord into the remaining connector on the printer and the other end into the surge protector.

3. With the computer turned on and the desktop displayed on the screen, click the My Computer icon and then click the Control Panel icon to display the Control Panel window.

4. Click the Printers icon to display the Printers window.

5. Click the Add Printer icon to display the Add Printer wizard (see Figure B-3). Follow the on-screen instructions to complete the installation process.

INSTALLING EXPANSION BOARDS AND DEVICES INSIDE THE SYSTEM UNIT

Most computers are shipped with printed instructions for installing internal components, expansion

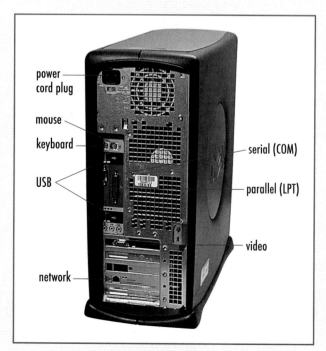

F I G U R E   B - 2 :   Back Panel of a System Unit

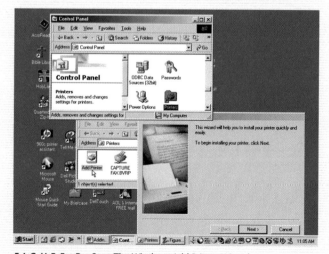

F I G U R E   B - 3 :   The Windows Add Printer Wizard

boards, and other devices inside the system unit. At some time you may want to add one or more of these components to increase your computer's capabilities. For example, you may want to install additional RAM capacity, a modem, an extra disk drive, or a DVD drive. The instructions most likely include a section explaining the procedure for gaining internal access to the motherboard, expansion slots, and other components. Follow the steps carefully.

> ● ● ● ● ● **TIP** ● ● ● ● ●
> Computer prices have declined significantly during recent years. If your computer is more than two or three years old, you may find it more cost-effective to purchase a new computer system with more capabilities and greater capacity than to upgrade your present computer.

Precautionary Measures

Before attempting to install any device or circuit board inside the system unit, you should perform the following steps in sequence:

1. Turn off your computer and all other devices.
2. Ground yourself by touching an unpainted metal surface at the back of the computer (system unit) before touching anything inside the computer. While you work, periodically touch an unpainted metal surface to dissipate any static electricity that might cause damage to the computer.
3. Unplug the power cable to your computer, and then press the power button to ground the system board.
4. Disconnect all devices connected to the computer, including the monitor, from electrical outlets or the surge protector to reduce the potential for personal injury or shock. Also, be sure to disconnect any telephone or communication lines from the computer.

An extensive variety of devices and circuit boards can be installed inside the system unit to render the computer more useful, including CD drives, floppy disk drives, DVD drives, graphics boards, sound boards, modems, and memory (RAM) boards. Unless you have training and experience in the installation of internal devices and circuit boards, you may want to have the work done by a certified PC technician who can perform and guarantee the installation. In such cases, ask questions and make sure the technician or company is one supported by the manufacturer of your computer. Additionally, some components should be installed or replaced only by a certified technician. For example, to replace a microprocessor in some computers you need a special tool designed for this purpose. Installing or replacing storage drives involves a series of complex steps that are probably better left to an experienced technician.

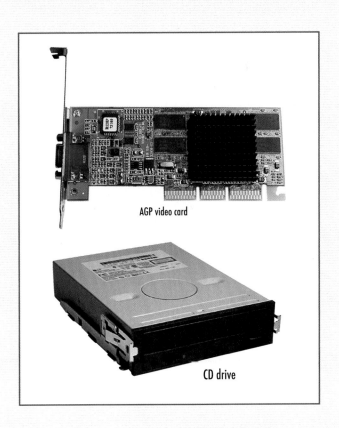

AGP video card

CD drive

Adding Hardware and Software Components to Your PC

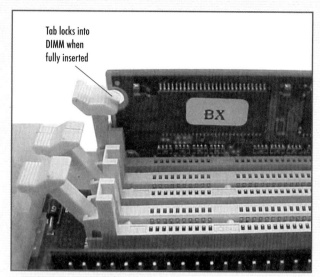

Tab locks into DIMM when fully inserted

FIGURE B-4: Installation of a DIMM Module

Unlike the installation of microprocessors, storage drives, and other components that may require the services of a service technician and typically involve a series of complex steps and special tools, installing expansion boards is considerably easier. Many users prefer to install one or more expansion boards, such as a RAM board, to enhance the computer's capabilities. The user's manual that came with your computer may contain instructions for installing various types of boards, such as RAM boards. Also, manufacturers of expansion boards usually include printed installation instructions and illustrations in the package along with the board.

The installation procedures for various types of boards are quite similar. Chances are that after you have installed one kind of expansion board, such as a RAM board, you will find the installation of other kinds of boards quite similar as well as easier.

Installing a RAM Board

Older PCs came with a type of RAM called SIMM (short for single inline memory module). Newer Pentium PCs contain a type of RAM called DIMM (short for dual inline memory module). The user's manual supplied with your computer will specify the type in your system. The main difference in the

way the two modules are installed is that SIMM modules are inserted into an expansion board at an angle and a DIMM module is inserted vertically. Assuming your computer uses DIMM modules, you can easily install an additional DIMM module by completing the following steps:

1. Study carefully the printed instructions and illustrations(s) that came in the package along with the DIMM module. The illustrations or diagrams identify the slot where you will insert the module.
2. With the system unit panel removed to expose the motherboard, locate the slot where you will insert the module. (**Note:** Your computer should already contain at least one RAM module and may provide multiple slots for adding more RAM. Select an empty slot, perhaps the one closest to the already installed RAM module, although any available slot may be used.)
3. Match the orientation of the DIMM module with the slot. The module will fit only one way because of notches in the slot.
4. Firmly press the DIMM module (board) straight down into the slot, until the clips on both ends fit over the notch in the DIMM module (see Figure B-4). The DIMM module fits properly if the clip snaps into place. (**Caution:** Do not exert too much pressure on the DIMM module. The module should easily snap into place when inserted properly.)

A Final Word

A variety of software and hardware products are available to expand the capacity and functionality of your computer. However, you must decide whether to upgrade your old PC or purchase a new one with greater capabilities. Additionally, you need to decide whether you should perform the installation of new software or hardware or use the services of a trained professional. Consider the cost of an upgrade, the reputation of the prospective technician, and whether or not you feel competent in performing an upgrade.

CHAPTER
SYSTEM SOFTWARE

4

UNDERSTANDING TECHNOLOGY

learning objectives

- Define software and identify the three principal types of system software

- Explain the concept of an operating system and identify its main functions

- Identify the differences between command-line interfaces and graphical user interfaces (GUIs)

- Differentiate PC, server, and wireless device operating systems

- Describe the different types of utility programs and their functions

- Explain language translators, and describe the primary difference between compilers and interpreters

key concepts

- What Is Computer Software?

- System Software

- Operating Systems

- Software User Interfaces

- PC Operating Systems

- Server Operating Systems

- Wireless Device Operating Systems

- Utilities and Language Translators

CYBER SCENARIO

Shortly after sunrise, Vincente Chamarro boards the high-speed train that will take him to his biweekly staff meeting at InterMed. The company designs and manufactures pacemakers and other medical devices that can be monitored over the Internet. Vincente is a product manager for InterMed's Cardiac Devices division. For more than three years he has worked from his mountain home and communicated with the InterMed office by computer and telephone (telecommuting), but he meets face-to-face with the marketing team every two weeks to maintain personal contact and to resolve any issues that cannot be handled well through remote communication.

Arriving in the city at 7:30 a.m., Vincente gets off the train and heads for the company headquarters two blocks away. As he walks to work he pulls a cell phone from his pocket and says a Web address, "www.ananova.com," into the mouthpiece. In a few seconds the face of a virtual newsreader named Ananova appears on the high-resolution screen of the cell phone. Vincente says, "News," and Ananova begins reading the latest headlines from around the world.

As he walks into his office on the ninth floor of the InterMed building, Vincente remembers that he needs to check his bank balance. He issues a command to his computer with the words, "Turn on and go to the Web site for Fidelity National Bank." He continues with, "This is Vincente Chamarro. What's the balance in my checking account?" The bank's automated teller system recognizes his voice and promptly reports that he has $1,956 in his account. "Good," he thinks, "no need to transfer any funds from savings."

The marketing team will meet to discuss plans for exhibiting at the upcoming international trade show for cardiac surgeons to be held in Zurich, Switzerland. Reflecting on his communication needs for the show, Vincente decides to buy a new handheld that will let him track all the materials his company ships to Zurich. A handheld would also provide access to current cultural events and street locations for Zurich and other European cities.

Vincente accesses a Web site where he can purchase the most powerful handheld on the market. A webcam enabled with advanced pattern recognition software captures his image and quickly compares it with others in a database of images. "Hello, Vincente," says a human-sounding voice. "Would you like to place an order?" Vincente tells the automated ordering system what he wants. The order is repeated for confirmation and the purchase is deducted from his bank account. He can expect to receive his new "toy" in two days.

Vincente's meeting with his marketing manager and team members proceeds without a hitch. They approve his plan to use the company's Ananova-like synthetic character, Jillian, to pitch their new devices over computer monitors at the international trade show. Vincente stays late to finish a rough draft of the script for Jillian, dictating to his computer until 8 p.m. He then directs the computer to send copies to team members and leaves to catch the 8:50 train home.

Vincente Chamarro's job is made easier through advances in speech recognition, natural language processing, and artificial intelligence technologies. Driving these changes is an intricate interaction among computer hardware manufacturers, scientists, and software developers.

WHAT IS COMPUTER SOFTWARE?

Software is the term for the programs that tell a computer what to do and how to do it. Software manages the computer's resources, including all hardware devices. Software programs work by issuing instructions to computers to perform actions in a certain order, allowing them to process data into information. Hardware is the term for the physical components of any computer system, such as the motherboard, circuitry, and peripheral devices. A popular expression in computer circles is that "software drives hardware," meaning that without software a computer can do little more than search for essential program files that direct the computer to load additional software. It is the software that launches information processing and puts the hardware to work. Software is divided into two main categories:

- application software programs that perform a single task such as word processing, spreadsheet analysis, or database management (discussed in Chapter 5)
- system software programs that manage basic operations such as starting and shutting down the computer and saving and printing files

SYSTEM SOFTWARE

System software includes those programs that control the operations of a computer system, meaning the system unit as well as all components and devices that comprise the computer system. System software performs a number of essential functions, including starting the computer, formatting disks, copying files, and enabling applications to work smoothly with a computer. It thus serves as the gateway between the user, the user's application software, and the user's computer hardware (see Figure 4-1). The three major categories of system software are operating systems, utility programs, and language translators.

OPERATING SYSTEMS

An operating system (OS) is the most important piece of software on a personal computer. It is typically installed on the computer's hard disk and loaded into RAM (random access memory) when the computer is started. Once started, the operating system manages the computer system and performs a variety of interdependent functions related to the input, processing, output, and storage of information, including

- managing main memory, or RAM
- configuring and controlling peripheral devices
- managing essential file operations, including formatting or copying disks, and renaming or deleting files
- monitoring system performance
- providing a user interface

Table 4-1 lists the operating systems commonly found on today's personal computers, which are the machines that predominate in the workplace and home environments.

Not all operating systems will run on every computer. For example, an operating system designed and written for the Apple Macintosh computer usually will not run on an IBM-compatible computer. The computers are said to have

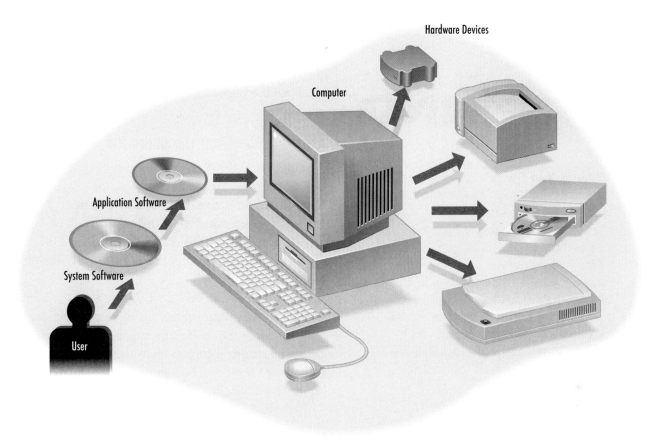

Hardware Devices

Computer

Application Software

System Software

User

FIGURE 4-1: System software serves as the gateway (interface) between the user, the user's application, and the computer's hardware.

different platforms. A **platform** is a foundation or standard around which software is developed.

The two determinants of a platform are the operating system and the processor type. For example, early versions of Windows were called 16-bit operating systems because they supported microprocessors that could process 16 bits of data at a time. Later Windows versions, including Windows 95 and 98, supported 32-bit processors, and Windows XP has both 32- and 64-bit versions.

Operating System	Developer	Computer Designed for	Type of Interface
Macintosh OS 9	Apple Computer	Macintosh	graphical user interface
Macintosh OS X	Apple Computer	Macintosh	graphical user interface
Windows 98	Microsoft Corporation	IBM PC and compatibles	graphical user interface
Windows NT® Workstation	Microsoft Corporation	IBM PC and compatibles	graphical user interface
Windows 2000 Professional	Microsoft Corporation	IBM PC and compatibles	graphical user interface
Windows Me	Microsoft Corporation	IBM PC and compatibles	graphical user interface
Windows XP Professional	Microsoft Corporation	IBM PC and compatibles	graphical user interface
OS/2	IBM	IBM PC and compatibles	graphical user interface

TABLE 4-1: Commonly Used Operating Systems for Personal Computers

GLOBE TROTTING

Operating systems and other software that run on a specific personal computer platform are referred to as native to that platform. Thus there is software native to the PC platform and to the Macintosh platform.

Booting (Starting) the Computer

The procedure for starting or restarting a computer is called **booting**. Starting a computer after power has been turned off is referred to as a **cold boot**. Restarting a computer while the power is still on is called a **warm boot**. Most computer systems allow users to perform a warm boot by pressing a combination of keyboard keys.

When a computer is booted, an electrical current from the power supply sends signals to the motherboard and its components, including the processor chip. The electrical current resets the processor, which then looks for the ROM chip containing the basic input/output system (BIOS).

The BIOS chip contains instructions that start the computer. The BIOS chip(s) also performs a series of tests, called power-on self test (POST). POST instructions check the computer's components and peripheral devices, including RAM, the system clock, keyboard, mouse, and disk drives. The POST checks determine whether the components and devices are connected and functioning properly. If problems are identified, many operating systems will notify the user to take corrective action. If components and devices are working properly, the BIOS searches the **boot drive** (the drive that houses the operating system) for operating system files.

The operating system then takes control of the computer and loads the system configuration and other necessary operating system files into memory. Portions of the operating system are automatically loaded from the hard disk into the computer's main memory, including the kernel and frequently used operating system instructions. The **kernel** is an operating system program that manages computer components, peripheral devices, and memory. It also maintains the system clock and loads other operating system and application programs as they are required. The kernel is **memory resident**, remaining in memory while the computer is in operation. Other operating system parts are **nonresident** and remain on the hard disk until they are needed. The loaded portion (memory resident) contains the most essential instructions for operating the computer, controlling the monitor display, and managing RAM efficiently to increase the computer's overall performance.

With Microsoft Windows, the operating system displays the Windows desktop and executes programs in the StartUp folder once loading is complete. Users can

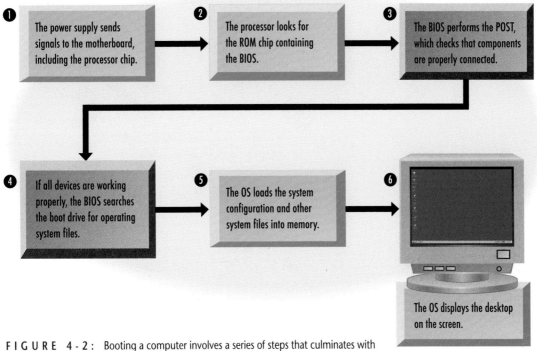

1. The power supply sends signals to the motherboard, including the processor chip.

2. The processor looks for the ROM chip containing the BIOS.

3. The BIOS performs the POST, which checks that components are properly connected.

4. If all devices are working properly, the BIOS searches the boot drive for operating system files.

5. The OS loads the system configuration and other system files into memory.

6. The OS displays the desktop on the screen.

FIGURE 4-2: Booting a computer involves a series of steps that culminates with the display of the OS desktop on the screen.

then click on the Windows *Start* button, the *Programs* button, and activate an application program such as Microsoft Word or Excel. The process of booting a computer is illustrated in Figure 4-2.

Managing Memory

An important operating system function is optimizing RAM so that processing occurs more quickly, an activity referred to as throughput. **Throughput** is a measure of the computer's overall performance. Loading programs and data from secondary storage into RAM speeds up processing because it takes significantly less time for the processor to access the programs from RAM than from secondary storage. Processing cannot occur until the programs and data are moved from RAM to the processor. Users can add RAM chips or upgrade the processor if programs, such as downloads from e-mail or Web pages, execute slowly.

To speed up the transfer of programs and data to the processor even further, some computers contain cache memory. Recall from Chapter 2 that cache memory may be contained on the CPU in the form of memory chips hardwired onto the motherboard or as reserved space on a storage device such as a hard disk. Some operating systems also allow users to set aside a portion of RAM to be used as cache memory.

As information is being processed, the operating system assigns application programs and data to selected areas of RAM called buffers. **Buffers** hold information and data waiting to be transferred to or from an input or output device. When the information or data residing in the buffers is no longer needed, it is erased (cleared) by the operating system. When a document is placed in a buffer, the CPU is free to begin executing the next computer instruction or carry out the user's next command.

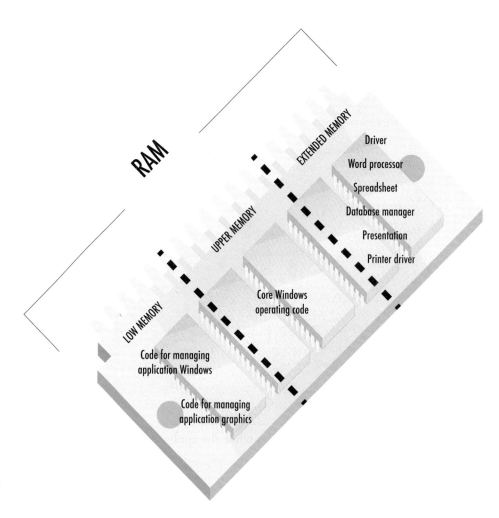

RAM

EXTENDED MEMORY

Driver

Word processor

Spreadsheet

Database manager

Presentation

Printer driver

UPPER MEMORY

Core Windows
operating code

LOW MEMORY

Code for managing
application Windows

Code for managing
application graphics

FIGURE 4-3: Windows
loads portions of code into all three
areas of RAM on startup.

Some output devices, such as printers, may contain their own buffer memory chips. A computer typically sends a document to a printer much faster than the printer can print it. With **print spooling**, a document is held in a buffer until the printer is ready. Once printed, the buffer is cleared and ready to accept other printing jobs.

An important part of managing RAM is allowing an individual user to work on two or more applications at the same time. This capability is called **multitasking**. When using a multitasking operating system, such as Microsoft Windows, it is not necessary to quit one application before working in another. For example, if a Microsoft Word document and a Microsoft Excel spreadsheet are both loaded into RAM, users can switch back and forth between the two applications as often as they wish. Figure 4-3 illustrates how Windows uses RAM.

Configuring and Controlling Devices

Configuring and controlling computer components and attached devices is a major function of the operating system. Included with a computer's operating system are small programs called **drivers**. Drivers enable the operating system to communicate with peripheral devices, including the keyboard, monitor, mouse, modem, printer, and disk drives. A keyboard driver recognizes input, while a monitor driver directs the display of text and images. If a user decides to add other devices, a driver will need to be installed for each new device. A driver program usually accompanies the device, and is contained on a disk with easy-to-follow instructions to guide users through the installation process. Many driver programs are also available on the device manufacturer's Web site.

Managing Essential File Operations

An operating system contains a program called a **file manager** to maintain a record of all stored files and their locations, allowing users to quickly locate and retrieve files. File managers also perform basic file management functions, such as keeping track of disk storage space; formatting and copying disks; and renaming, deleting, sorting, or viewing stored files. Figure 4-4 shows the Microsoft Windows XP desktop with the All Programs submenu selected and Windows Explorer highlighted. File management functions can be accomplished using Windows Explorer.

Monitoring System Performance

An operating system typically includes a **performance monitor** for checking the computer system's speed and efficiency, as well as the performance of the CPU, memory, and storage disks. In Microsoft Windows, clicking the command sequence of *Start, Programs, Accessories, System Tools,* and *System Monitor* accomplishes this function. A user can also participate in monitoring the system's performance. For example, if a user makes a mistake or issues an incorrect command, the operating system may display a warning message asking the user to respond. (In Windows, for example, an onscreen message displays telling a user to close an application if the user attempts to shut down the computer while the application is still running.)

Providing Basic Security Functions

An operating system can protect against unauthorized users gaining access to the computer and stored information. Many operating systems require users to enter a valid name and password before they can access a computer or network. A **user**

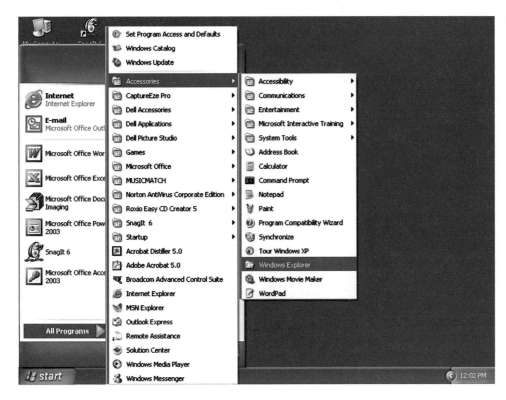

FIGURE 4-4: Users can copy, delete, and move files with Windows Explorer.

name, also called a **user ID**, is a unique combination of characters (letters and numbers) identifying an individual user.

A **password** is a unique combination of characters that allows a user to gain access to computer resources, such as data and files. When a password is keyed in, most operating systems display a series of characters (such as asterisks) that differ from those entered. This is to prevent other people from seeing the entered characters. The user ID and password combinations are compared with a list of authorized users. If the combination of user ID and password is on the list, the operating system allows access. The operating system denies access if the user ID and password combination does not match any of those on the list.

Computer network operating systems provide additional security measures, such as maintaining a record of attempts to access the network and its resources. The network administrator can determine which computer made the attempt and the time the attempt was made, allowing suspicious activity to be traced.

SOFTWARE USER INTERFACES

All software, including operating systems, contains a **user interface** that allows communication between the software and the user. The interface controls the manner in which data and commands are entered as well as the way information and processing options are presented on the screen. Application programs are written for use with specific operating systems. The operating system and application software user interfaces must be able to work together (be compatible). Two types of user interfaces have been developed for personal computers:

- command-line interfaces
- graphical user interfaces (GUIs)

Command-Line Interfaces

Early personal computer operating systems, including CP/M (Control Program for Microcomputers) and DOS (Disk Operating System), used what is known as a **command-line interface**. This interface presented the user with a symbol called a **prompt** (for example, C:\>), indicating the computer was ready to receive a command. Users would respond by typing in a line of code telling the computer what to do. For example, the command COPY A:\INCOME.STM C:\ would instruct the computer to copy the file named INCOME.STM, located on drive A, to drive C. Command-line interfaces were ideal for early personal computers, which had limited graphical display capabilities, but they could also be complicated and difficult to learn. The commands often involved long sequences of code. A mistyped letter would lead to an error message, forcing the user to type the command again. Figure 4-5 illustrates the use of the DIR (directory) command in DOS.

Graphical User Interfaces

In 1983, Apple Computer introduced its Lisa computer. Lisa featured an entirely new kind of operating system with a screen display known as a **graphical user interface**, or **GUI**. Based on the Alto computer operating system developed at the Xerox Corporation's Palo Alto Research Center, this new type of interface was graphics-based rather than command-based, making it more intuitive and user-friendly. Unfortunately, the Apple Lisa was a commercial failure because of its high

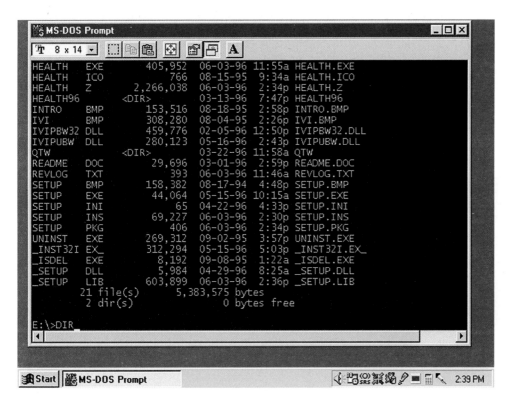

```
MS-DOS Prompt                                          _ □ ✕

T  8 x 14  ⌄   ☐ ☖ ☐  ⊞  ☞☐  A

HEALTH   EXE      405,952  06-03-96 11:55a HEALTH.EXE
HEALTH   ICO          766  08-15-95  9:34a HEALTH.ICO
HEALTH   Z      2,266,038  06-03-96  2:34p HEALTH.Z
HEALTH96     <DIR>         03-13-96  7:47p HEALTH96
INTRO    BMP      153,516  08-18-95  2:58p INTRO.BMP
IVI      BMP      308,280  08-04-95  2:26p IVI.BMP
IVIPBW32 DLL      459,776  02-05-96 12:50p IVIPBW32.DLL
IVIPUBW  DLL      280,123  05-16-96  2:43p IVIPUBW.DLL
QTW          <DIR>         03-22-96 11:58a QTW
README   DOC       29,696  03-01-96  2:59p README.DOC
REVLOG   TXT          393  06-03-96 11:46a REVLOG.TXT
SETUP    BMP      158,382  08-17-94  4:48p SETUP.BMP
SETUP    EXE       44,064  05-15-96 10:15a SETUP.EXE
SETUP    INI           65  04-22-96  4:33p SETUP.INI
SETUP    INS       69,227  06-03-96  2:30p SETUP.INS
SETUP    PKG          406  06-03-96  2:34p SETUP.PKG
UNINST   EXE      269,312  09-02-95  3:57p UNINST.EXE
_INST32I EX_      312,294  05-15-96  5:03p _INST32I.EX_
_ISDEL   EXE        8,192  09-08-95  1:22a _ISDEL.EXE
_SETUP   DLL        5,984  04-29-96  8:25a _SETUP.DLL
_SETUP   LIB      603,899  06-03-96  2:36p _SETUP.LIB
        21 file(s)     5,383,575 bytes
         2 dir(s)              0 bytes free

E:\>DIR_
◀                                                          ▶
```

Start | MS-DOS Prompt   2:39 PM

FIGURE 4-5: The DOS command DIR shows a directory, or list of files, stored on a medium such as a hard or floppy disk.

price and the limited availability of software applications. The following year Apple introduced the Macintosh, another computer incorporating a GUI. This time Apple scored a success (see Figure 4-6). The Macintosh operating system revolutionized personal computing.

GUIs are now the most popular type of personal computer interface. They are easier to use than command-line interfaces because they enable users to interact with on-screen simulations of familiar objects. Remembering long strings of commands is no longer necessary, since the screen itself becomes a virtual desktop on which the user's work (programs and documents) is spread out (see Figure 4-7). **Icons**, or thumbnail pictures, appear on the desktop and represent such familiar items as a trash can or recycle bin (for deleting or throwing away files) and file folders (for storing groups of files).

In addition to representing common commands, icons are used to symbolize programs and files. For example, a calculating program may be represented by a tiny calculator on the screen, or a time management program might be represented by a clock. To use an analogy, GUIs are to operating systems what special keyboards are to cash registers in fast-food restaurants. Both use pictures or text symbols to stand for complex commands, simplifying and streamlining actions for the user.

GUIs were made possible with the development of mouse technology and the introduction of more powerful computers and high-resolution monitors. Almost all PCs arrive from the factory with a GUI operating system preinstalled, and most application software is designed to work with them smoothly. Once a user knows the features of a GUI such as Windows, she will already know how to execute the fundamental operations of any Windows-based application because both the operating system and the application use the same icons and commands. A typical GUI offers many features to make tasks easier, including

FIGURE 4-6: Apple's Macintosh quickly became popular after it was introduced in 1984.

CHAPTER 4

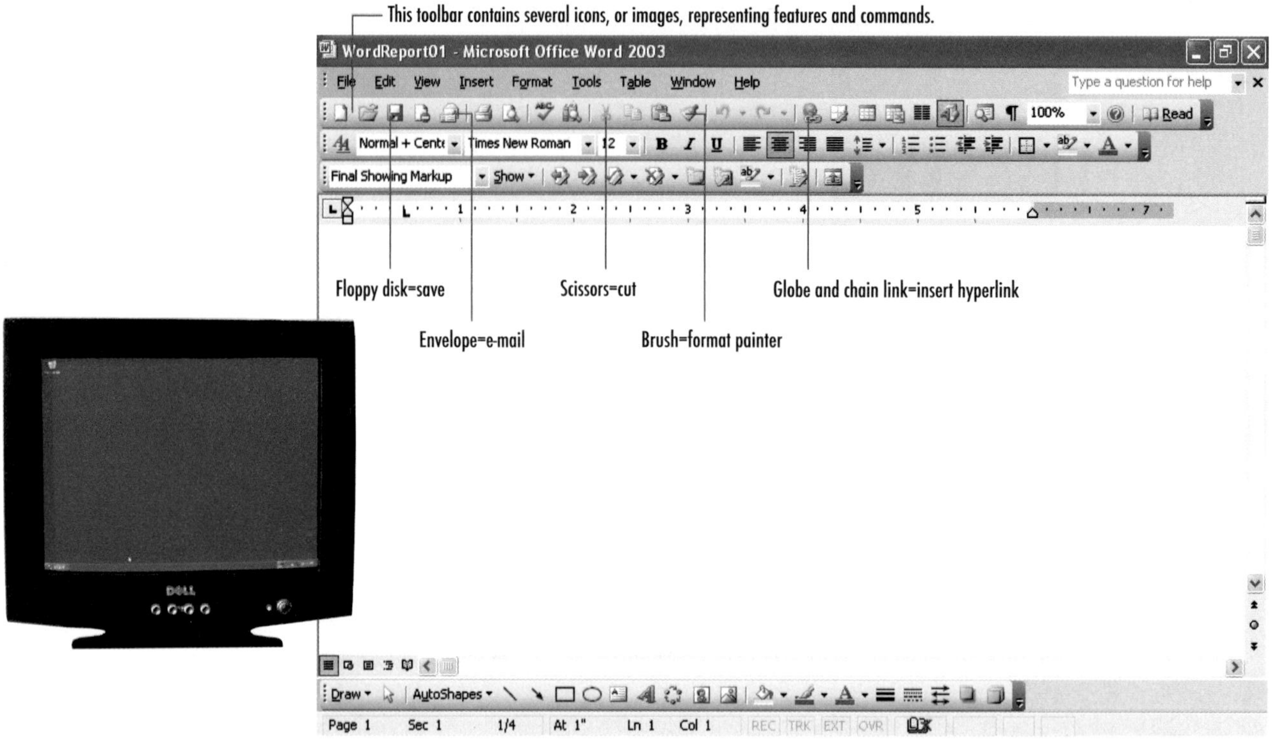

This toolbar contains several icons, or images, representing features and commands.

Floppy disk=save

Envelope=e-mail

Scissors=cut

Brush=format painter

Globe and chain link=insert hyperlink

F I G U R E 4 - 7 : A graphical user interface (GUI) allows a user to interact with icons (familiar objects) on the screen.

- key feature option menus
- common command icons
- on-screen desktop
- display windows
- dialog boxes
- online help

Key Feature Option Menus

A **menu** provides a set of options. Users can select options they want by highlighting the option and clicking on it with the mouse, or by typing one or more keystrokes. Making a selection launches an action, such as saving a document.

When activated, many software programs display a menu bar (also called a **main menu**) at the top or side of the screen. A **menu bar** is a horizontal or vertical bar listing the highest-level command options by name, usually composed of one or two words. Each high-level option may be accompanied by another menu, called a **drop-down menu** (or **pull-down menu**), containing various lower-level options (see Figure 4-8). These menus may in turn include submenus offering more precise choices.

Software programs usually contain predetermined default options. A **default option** is one that has been preprogrammed by the software publisher under the assumption that this option is the choice favored by most users. For example, newer versions of Microsoft Word include 10-point Times New Roman as the default font. Users can choose a different font by clicking the Format option on the menu bar, and then the Font option from the drop-down menu that appears. Depending on the action being taken, some drop-down menu options may be unavailable to users at certain times. Options that are available

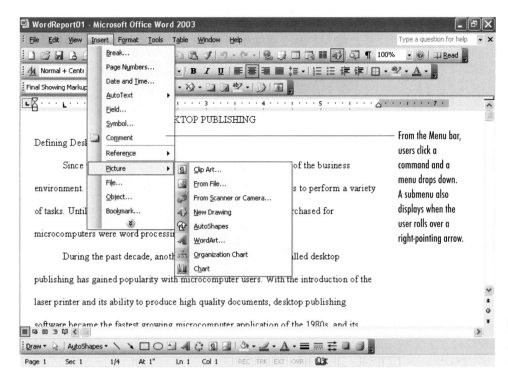

From the Menu bar, users click a command and a menu drops down. A submenu also displays when the user rolls over a right-pointing arrow.

FIGURE 4-8: Almost all programs provide a main menu. When users select a menu item, a drop-down menu is displayed, providing additional choices.

typically appear in darker type. Unavailable options usually appear grayed out, or dimmed, letting the user know the option cannot be chosen. Figure 4-9 shows a drop-down menu containing choices that are available and some that are not.

On drop-down menus, a small triangular pointer to the right of an option indicates that additional options are available. Clicking on the pointer displays the associated menu. A check mark at the left of an option indicates the option has

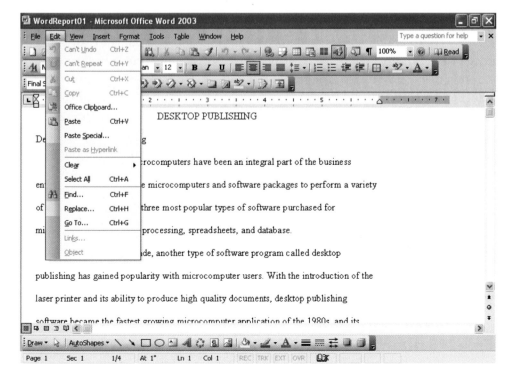

FIGURE 4-9: Options available on a menu appear in darker print. Options that are unavailable appear in grayed-out print.

CHAPTER 4

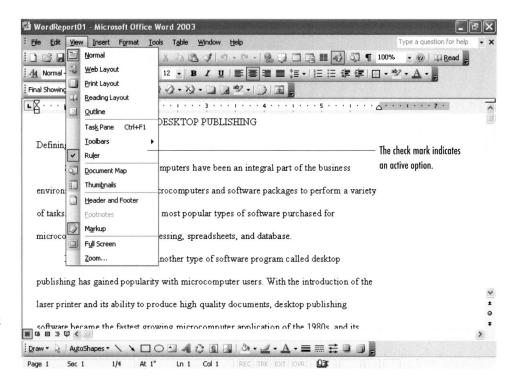

FIGURE 4-10: A check mark to the left of an option indicates that the option has been selected and is therefore active.

The check mark indicates an active option.

been selected and is therefore active. Figure 4-10 shows a drop-down menu associated with the View option in Microsoft Word.

In Figure 4-10, notice the check mark at the left of the Ruler option. This means the Ruler option is selected and that the ruler is displayed at the top of the page or document. The pointer to the right of the Toolbars option indicates an associated drop-down menu containing various toolbar options. Among the toolbars users can select to be displayed are Standard, Formatting, AutoText, and Drawing.

Common Command Icons

GUIs use icons to represent common actions such as opening, saving, or printing files. These icons may be displayed in a row near the top of the screen, called a **toolbar**. When the mouse pointer is positioned on an icon, a one- or two-word identification label (often called a Screen Tip) displays immediately below it. Clicking the icon launches the associated action. For example, in Microsoft Word a document can be printed by clicking on a small printer icon in the toolbar (Figure 4-11). For many users, clicking on an icon is easier than having to remember and enter a series of keystrokes.

As with menus, some icons may be unavailable and appear in grayed-out or dimmed form. These icons usually represent actions that depend on a related, previous action. For example, Microsoft Word will not allow a user to select the

Print

FIGURE 4-11: A graphical user interface (GUI) uses pictures and symbols (icons) to represent commands. For example, clicking the printer icon prints a file.

TECH VISIONARY

William H. (Bill) Gates III is a cofounder and, at present, chairman of the board of directors of Microsoft Corporation, the world's leading provider of software for personal computers. Born on October 28, 1955, Gates grew up in Seattle, Washington, where he attended public elementary school before moving on to the private Lakeside School in North Seattle. He began programming computers at the early age of 13.

In 1973, Gates entered Harvard University. While at Harvard, Gates developed a version of the BASIC programming language for the first microcomputer, called the MITS Altair. He dropped out of Harvard in his junior year to devote his full time to building Microsoft Corporation, a company he had started in 1975 with his boyhood friend Paul Allen. Guided by a belief that the personal computer would be a valuable tool on every office desktop and in every home, Gates and Allen began developing software for personal computers.

Twenty-five years later, Microsoft and Bill Gates (along with Allen and other early players) are worth billions. Under Gates's leadership, Microsoft has forged a mission to advance and improve software technology to make it easier, more cost-effective, and more enjoyable for people to use computers. The company is committed to a long-term view, which is reflected in its annual investments of millions of dollars for research and development. Gates and his wife, Melinda, have endowed a foundation with more than $21 billion to support philanthropic causes dedicated to worldwide health and education, such as providing vaccines for children in developing countries and scholarship programs for low-income high-achievers.

Microsoft has been quick to take advantage of opportunities created by the Internet. Gates has a substantial investment, along with cellular telephone pioneer Craig McCaw, in the Teledesic project, an ambitious plan to launch low-orbit satellites around the earth to provide a worldwide two-way broadband telecommunications service.

Source: <http://www.microsoft.com/billgates/bio.asp>.

scissors icon (for "cutting" or removing text) until the word or paragraph to be deleted has been highlighted (selected) with the mouse.

On-Screen Desktop

GUIs for personal computers incorporate the concept of an on-screen **desktop**. A desktop is a screen on which graphical elements such as icons, buttons, windows, links, and dialog boxes are displayed, much as manila folders, pens, scissors, and paper might be arranged on a desk. Using a desktop containing these elements is easier for many users because it allows them to interact quickly and accurately with the computer. During the installation of a software application, an icon representing the program may be automatically added to the desktop. Figure 4-12 shows an example of a desktop displaying a variety of icons and buttons.

A **button** is a graphical element that causes a particular action to occur when selected. For example, clicking the Windows Start button in the lower left corner of the screen displays a menu of options related to starting and operating the computer (see Figure 4-13). When a button is selected, the button changes color or appears in depressed form, as though it has been pressed by a user's finger.

Display Windows

The main feature of a graphical user interface is the display window. A **display window** is a rectangular area of the screen used to display a program or various kinds of data, such as text and numbers. At the top of each window is a horizontal bar called the **title bar**, displaying the window's name, as shown in Figure 4-14. Windows are useful in multitasking environments, which allow multiple programs and applications to be open at the same time (concurrently). By dividing the screen into different windows, users can see and work with the output produced

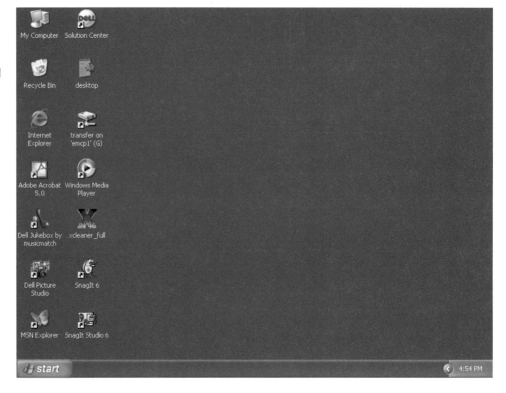

FIGURE 4-12: Most PCs are preloaded with a GUI with an onscreen desktop. A desktop is a work area displaying graphical elements such as icons, windows, and buttons. Graphical elements allow faster, easier access to programs and commands.

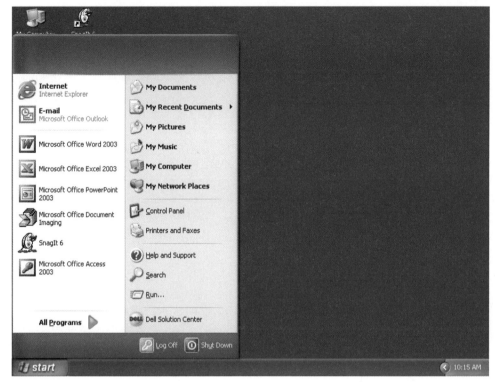

FIGURE 4-13: Clicking the Start button in Windows XP displays a menu of options, including My Documents, My Recent Documents, My Computer, My Network Places, Help and Support, Search, Run, Log Off, and Shut Down.

by each program. To work within a particular program—to enter data, for example—clicking on the program's window brings it to the forefront. Figure 4-15 shows multiple windows, each representing a different program.

Documents are sometimes too large to be displayed in their entirety in a window. To overcome this problem, **scroll bars** at a window's side or bottom enable

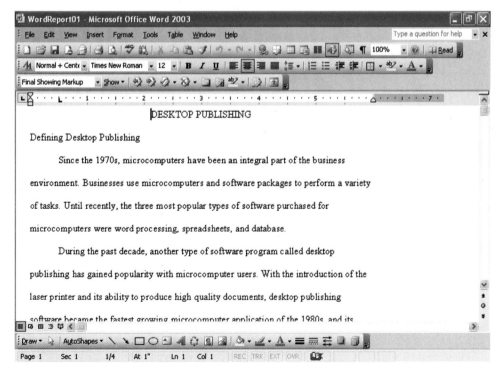

FIGURE 4-14: A display window, the main feature of a GUI, is a rectangular area used to display a program, data, or communications. A title bar at the top of the window contains the name of the item and the program in the display window.

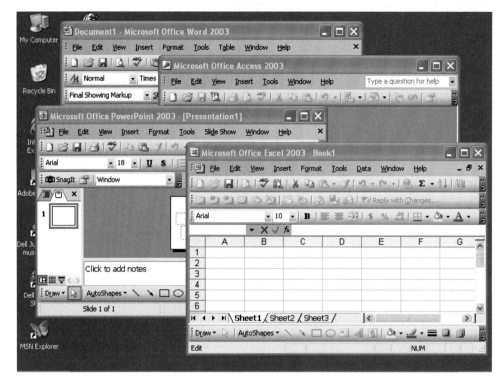

FIGURE 4-15: Most GUIs allow users to work with multiple applications at the same time. Each application appears in its own window. A user can switch back and forth among applications by clicking on a window's title bar.

users to see and work with the portions of a document that are beyond the edge of the screen. Small arrows at the tips of a scroll bar can be used to move documents horizontally or vertically. A small box between the two arrows can also be used to scroll through a document page by page.

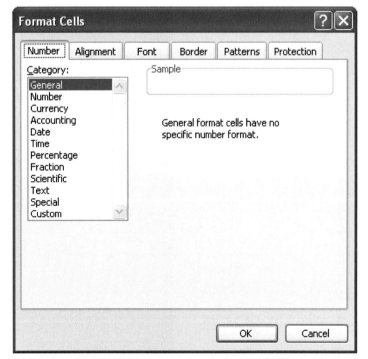

FIGURE 4-16: Dialog boxes, such as the Format Cells dialog box in Microsoft Excel 2003, provide information to a user and also offer choices or prompt responses so commands can be executed.

Dialog Boxes

GUIs use **dialog boxes** to provide information and to prompt responses (see Figure 4-16). A dialog box is a window that displays temporarily and disappears once the user has entered requested information. Interactions between the user and the software are carried out through various elements that allow choices. Some of the more common elements are tabs, option buttons, check boxes, and text boxes.

- **Tabs**. Many dialog boxes offer several option subsets, each labeled as if it were a manila folder within a file drawer. The name of a subset of options is displayed in a **tab** at the top of the folder. Clicking the tab brings the selected group of options to the front of the dialog box (the file drawer). Figure 4-17 shows a dialog box with tabs.

- **Option Buttons**. Another standard dialog box element is an outlined box containing a set of buttons called **option buttons** (also called **radio buttons**). Named for their resemblance to the push buttons on car radios, these buttons offer different choices. Just as with a standard car radio, only one button at a time can be activated. For example, clicking the Print icon in Microsoft Word 2003 displays a dialog box containing a section of option buttons for Page range (see Figure 4-18). Only one of these options can be selected at a time.

- **Check Boxes**. A **check box** contains multiple options that can be turned on or off. An option in the box can be turned on by clicking it. When an option is activated, a check mark appears beside it. Unlike buttons that limit users to selecting a single option, check boxes allow users to choose multiple options at one time. Figure 4-19 shows a check box with multiple options activated (checked).

- **Text Boxes**. Information is entered into a **text box** to allow the computer to continue or complete a task. For example, to save a document in Microsoft Word, users must first click on the File menu,

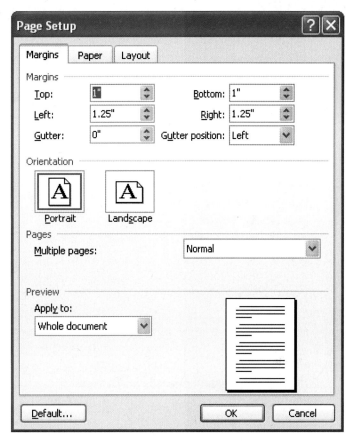

FIGURE 4-17: Tabs at the top of a dialog box indicate separate option subsets. Clicking on a tab brings that group of options to the front of the dialog box. Tabs in this Microsoft Word 2003 Page Setup dialog box are Margins, Paper, and Layout.

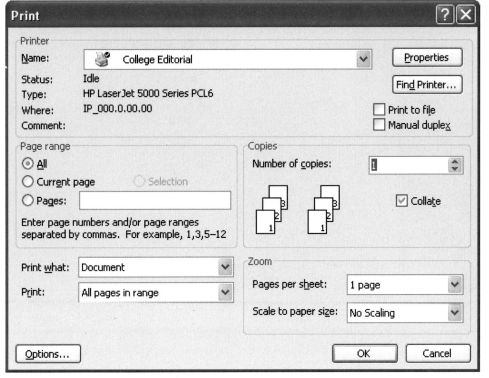

FIGURE 4-18: Option buttons within a dialog box provide choices. The buttons in the Page range section of the Word 2003 Print dialog box allow users to print all document pages, only the current page, or selected pages.

FIGURE 4-19: A check box contains multiple options that can be turned on or off by users. When an option is selected, a check mark appears beside it, indicating it is turned on.

and then click Save or Save As to display the desired dialog box. Once the dialog box appears, a drive where the document will be saved needs to be indicated, and a file name for the document typed in a text box (see Figure 4-20). Most dialog boxes also contain *OK* and *Cancel* buttons that allow users to submit or re-enter the information entered into a text box or a check box.

Online Help

Computer users will occasionally encounter problems or think of questions while they are working with an operating system or application. Answers can be found by clicking the Help option or by pressing a designated key. Clicking the Help option causes a dialog box to appear that asks the user to specify the kind of help needed. The program then searches its online documentation and displays a menu of topics to choose from. Selecting a topic causes a set of helpful instructions to display on the screen, as shown in Figure 4-21.

FIGURE 4-20: A text box is used for entering information that will allow the computer to complete a task. At the Save As dialog box, the user must indicate the drive to be saved to and the file name.

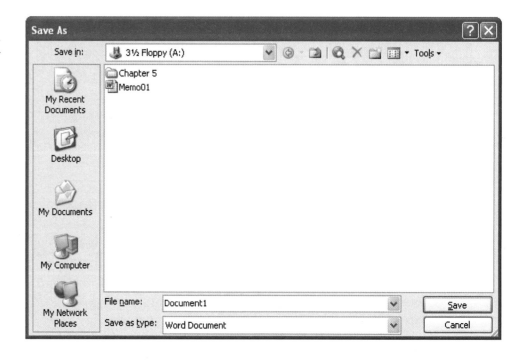

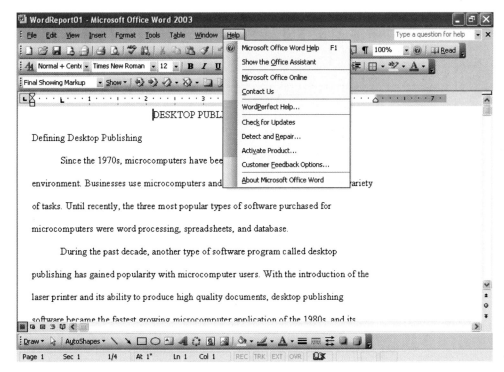

FIGURE 4-21: Clicking on the Help option on the menu bar displays a list of topics from which a selection can be made.

Some programs display Help messages based on either the user's location in the program or the activity the user is performing. This kind of Help system is referred to as being **context sensitive**, as the system can sense needs based on what the user is doing.

PC OPERATING SYSTEMS

Microsoft Windows is currently the dominant operating system for personal computers. Over a period of about fifteen years, Windows has evolved from a GUI/DOS combination (Windows 3.0 through 3.11) to a true GUI with versions for all types of personal computers (Windows XP). According to some estimates, Windows is used on about 90 percent of all PCs. The remaining 10 percent are primarily Apple Macintosh personal computers using the Apple Mac OS operating system.

Windows 3.X

Microsoft embraced the term "windows" to describe the graphical user interface it developed for use on PCs. Version 3.0 was the first, introduced in 1985. It was quickly followed by versions 3.1 and 3.11, which contained significant improvements (see Figure 4-22). Strictly speaking, the three versions were not actually operating systems. They were **operating environments**, meaning they were graphical interfaces on top of an underlying DOS kernel. Apple Computer unsuccessfully sued Microsoft, claiming the company had copied the "look and feel" of the Mac OS. The failure of Apple's suit opened the door for the development of successive versions of Windows and other graphical user interfaces. Examples include UNIX X-Windows from the Massachusetts Institute of Technology (MIT), and IBM's OS/2, a GUI for PCs that made its debut in 1988. Though considered an

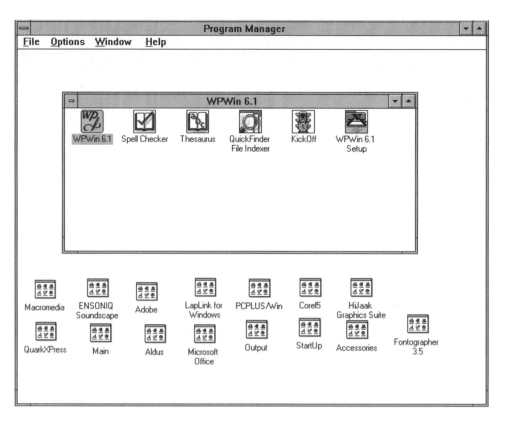

FIGURE 4-22: Loading Windows 3.1 caused the Program Manager screen to display, allowing users to click on icons to launch programs.

excellent program, IBM's OS/2 has had little success in the marketplace. Various versions of Windows now dominate the home and business PC market.

Windows 95

Windows 95 was an important Windows operating system released in August 1995. It was a significant improvement over its precursor, Windows 3.11. Windows 95 offered a new user interface as well as Internet access. It supported 32-bit applications, which ran faster than the 16-bit versions supported by previous editions of Windows. Many of the older DOS limitations were removed, including the recognition of only 640K of memory and a file name limitation of eight characters. However, Windows 95 still included some DOS programs and could run DOS-based applications. Windows 95 enjoyed immediate acceptance by users with its improved GUI, increased speed, and ease of use (see Figure 4-23). Minimum system requirements for running Windows 95 are

- 486/25 MHz-based processor
- 8 MB of RAM
- 40 MB of available hard disk space
- VGA (video graphics adapter) or higher-resolution display
- Microsoft mouse or compatible pointing device

Windows 98

An upgraded version of Windows 95, **Windows 98** contained several new and improved features. Basic operations such as startup, the launching of applications, and shutdown were faster compared to Windows 95. Windows 98 offered improved access to the Internet and World Wide Web through its Web browser,

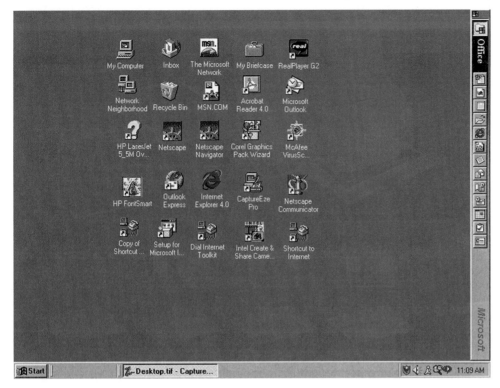

FIGURE 4-23: The Windows 95 desktop offered an improved graphical interface.

Internet Explorer. It allowed users to set up an **active desktop** with icons linked to the Internet and the Web (see Figure 4-24). A Web Publishing Wizard enabled users to publish pages on intranets or the Internet. Equally important, Windows 98 provided support for multimedia peripherals, including DVD-ROM drives and

FIGURE 4-24: The Windows 98 desktop allowed users to set up an active desktop with icons linked to the Internet and the Web.

USB devices. It ran faster and capitalized on several new and improved features available with newer and more powerful computers. Minimum system requirements for running Windows 98 Second Edition are

- 486DX/66 MHz or higher processor
- 24 MB of RAM
- 205 MB of available hard disk space (more for additional options)
- CD-ROM or DVD-ROM drive
- VGA or higher-resolution monitor
- Microsoft mouse or compatible pointing device

Windows NT (Workstation)

Windows NT is a powerful GUI operating system designed for executing large applications in networked environments. First released in 1993, Windows NT was available in a server version for network server computers, and as a workstation version for networked computers (see Figure 4-25). Windows NT used the Windows 95 GUI, but not its DOS features. It offered more powerful multitasking and memory management capabilities than Windows 95, and it could run programs written for both DOS and Windows. It was designed to take advantage of 32-bit processors and could be used with other processors as well. Windows NT accommodated multiple-networked computers processing applications concurrently. Minimum system requirements for running NT on Intel-based systems are

- 486/25 MHz or higher Pentium-compatible processor
- 12 MB of RAM; 16 MB recommended
- 110 MB of available hard disk space
- CD-ROM drive or access to a CD-ROM over a computer network
- VGA or higher-resolution monitor
- Microsoft mouse or compatible pointing device

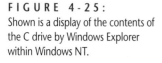

FIGURE 4-25:
Shown is a display of the contents of the C drive by Windows Explorer within Windows NT.

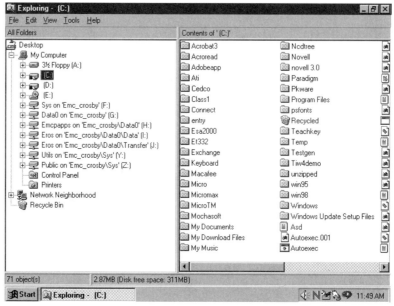

TECH VISIONARY

In 1978, Tim Paterson graduated from college with a degree in computer science and landed a job with Seattle Computer Products (SCP), a memory board manufacturer, as the company's only full-time engineer. One of Paterson's first assignments was to design a general-purpose operating system for a microcomputer the company was developing. Over a period of four months, Paterson created a system he named QDOS (Quick and Dirty Operating System), an operating system that evolved into DOS (Disk Operating System) and eventually became synonymous with the early PCs.

According to Paterson, Microsoft initially paid SCP $10,000 for the right to market DOS, along with a $15,000 per-customer fee. Not being in the software business, SCP didn't realize the full potential for its product and was unaware that Microsoft's customer was IBM.

Shortly before IBM's first personal computer (the IBM-PC) was introduced in 1981, Microsoft purchased DOS from SCP for $50,000. Since then, millions of DOS operating systems have been installed on PCs, a deal that earned SCP more than $1 million from Microsoft and that helped make Microsoft the world's leading software manufacturer.

Source: *InfoWorld*, August 6, 2001.

CHAPTER 4

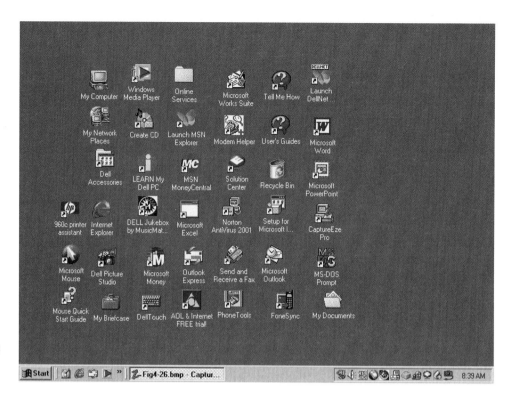

FIGURE 4-26: Windows Me is a popular operating system for home PCs.

Windows Millennium Edition

Windows Millennium Edition (Me), introduced in 1999, is designed for users of the less powerful PCs found in homes and small offices (see Figure 4-26). Although less expensive than the more powerful, feature-rich versions of Windows 2000, Windows Me supports the use of CD-ROM and DVD-ROM drives and is thus an ideal platform for games and other multimedia applications that incorporate videos, graphics, and music. It offers home networking capabilities, and provides Internet access through Microsoft's Web browser, Internet Explorer.

Windows 2000 Professional

Windows 2000 Professional, introduced in late 1999, was designed for use with business computers and was the successor to Windows 98 for office environments. Incorporating the power of Windows NT, Windows 2000 Professional can link computers in a network environment. This more advanced operating system is particularly well suited for newer, faster, and more powerful PCs. Because it requires more disk space for storage, it runs better on computers equipped with newer microprocessors. Figure 4-27 shows the Windows 2000 Professional desktop. Minimum system requirements for Windows 2000 Professional are

- 133 MHz or higher Pentium-compatible processor
- 64 MB of RAM
- 2 GB hard disk with a minimum of 650 MB of available space
- CD-ROM, CD-R, CD-RW, or DVD-ROM drive
- VGA or higher-resolution monitor
- Microsoft mouse or compatible pointing device

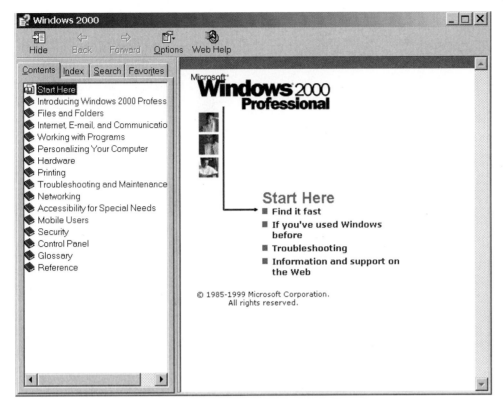

FIGURE 4-27: Shown is the Windows 2000 Professional Help screen with the Contents tab selected.

Windows XP Professional

Microsoft's newest operating system, **Windows XP**, is designed for the latest computers that are fast, powerful, and have lots of memory and hard disk space. It requires two gigabytes of hard drive space to install. The XP operating system combines the more powerful features of Windows 2000 and Windows NT. Microsoft Corporation touts XP as virtually crash-proof, offering greater stability and reduced computer downtimes for large corporate users.

New features built into Windows XP are impressive. Unlike earlier Windows versions that were incompatible with many hardware and software add-ons, XP is designed to work smoothly with more than 12,000 hardware devices. This system is designed to keep files and settings separate for every PC user. Users must log on with a name and password so the operating system will know which desktop to bring up. This makes XP ideal for school computer labs and for businesses where multiple users share the same PC.

Users of earlier Windows versions will quickly notice the many cosmetic changes in Windows XP. The XP taskbar and window borders appear as shimmering light blue, and icons have a three-dimensional look. Design changes are evident throughout the XP's GUI. A click on the Start button displays two columns—one to the left that lists recently used programs, and one to the right listing everything else, including My Documents, My Computer, and the Control Panel. The desktop sports a refreshingly clean look filled with a photo of a gentle hillside. Users who do not like the cosmetic changes can turn them off to make the desktop look like an older version of Windows. Figure 4-28 shows the desktop of Windows XP Professional.

Windows XP is extremely user-friendly. For example, a new CD can be burned simply by dragging folders and files onto the CD burner icon. A new "E-mail this

file" button shrinks digital photos to a usable size as they are sent, to avoid tying up a recipient's phone line for long periods. Built-in automatic firewall software helps block hacker invasions from the Internet. A new Windows Messenger program allows the exchange of instant messages over the Internet with other users on MSN, Hotmail, or Windows Messenger "Buddy Lists."

Older PCs may not support Windows XP's increased needs. Minimum system requirements for installing and effectively using Windows XP include

- 300 MHz or faster Pentium-compatible or Celeron-compatible processor
- 2 GB of hard disk space for installation
- minimum of 64 MB of memory (128 MB is recommended)
- CD-ROM or DVD drive
- Microsoft mouse or compatible pointing device

Young enthusiastic users may find Windows XP especially useful as it provides impressive features for managing photo and music files. Just plugging a digital camera into the computer displays a dialog box that enables photos to be copied to the computer, printed, or displayed as a slide show. Music files can easily be downloaded and the user can enjoy a concert right from the desktop using Windows Media® Player.

Many other new and improved features that users will find useful are built into Windows XP. Its impressive design is a welcome departure from older Windows versions. However, some users may not appreciate all the new XP features. For example, it is the first Windows version to be copy-protected. Users wanting to reinstall XP or install it on a newly purchased computer may find they are locked out, requiring the purchase of another copy.

Macintosh Operating System

The **Macintosh OS** was the first commercial GUI, released in 1984 and updated many times since the initial release. It included a virtual desktop, drop-down menus, dialog boxes, and icons representing common commands and programs. With its impressive graphics and ease of use, it quickly became the model for other GUIs. Soon after its introduction, manufacturers and users of IBM-PCs and compatibles wanted a comparable GUI for their computers. Within a short time Microsoft introduced its first Windows product for IBM-PCs and compatibles.

The Mac OS only runs on Apple Macintosh computers. It contains many impressive and useful features, including both the Netscape Navigator™ and Internet Explorer Web browsers. Its extraordinary graphics capabilities help make the Apple Macintosh the computer of choice among graphic designers, desktop production specialists, printing companies, and publishers.

Mac OS 9, the version widely available in 2000, contained several new and improved features. It offered better speech recognition, supported files up to two terabytes (two trillion bytes), provided for multiple users, allowed for file encryption, and supported voice-entered passwords.

Mac OS X (see Figure 4-29) was introduced in spring 2001. Particularly noteworthy is the new interface, called Aqua®, and its UNIX operating system foundation, which is considered a stable and powerful system. With the debut of Mac OS X, more than 200 developers, including Microsoft, Adobe, IBM, Sun Microsystems, and Hewlett-Packard, agreed to create software for the new system. Mac OS X provides greater stability and true multitasking capability.

The bottom of the startup screen is similar to the Windows taskbar. MAC OS X also provides a terminal window that reveals the file system tree, enabling users to quickly locate programs and files. MAC OS X includes versions of popular

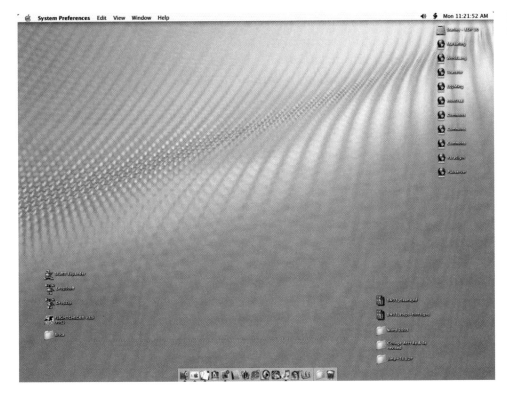

FIGURE 4-29: The Mac OS X Interface is called Aqua.

CHAPTER 4

programs, including the QuickTime® player and Stuffit™, a file compression program. It comes with Microsoft's Internet Explorer 5 and FTP capability, allowing users to easily send and receive large files. Its backward compatibility supports applications from previous versions, such as OS 9.

OS/2

IBM's **OS/2** GUI operating system was the company's response to the popularity of Microsoft Windows and the Apple Mac OS. The latest version of OS/2 is called OS/2 Warp. In addition to running native application programs, OS/2 can run programs written for DOS and Windows systems. The OS/2 operating system is designed mainly for business PC users running business applications. A network server version also has been developed.

SERVER OPERATING SYSTEMS

Some operating systems are designed specifically for use with local area networks, allowing multiple users to connect to the server and to share network resources such as files and peripheral devices such as printers. The kind of operating system selected for use with a network depends on network architecture and processing requirements.

Novell NetWare

NetWare®, developed by Novell, Inc. during the 1980s, is a popular and widely used operating system for microcomputer-based local area networks. Network users have the option of working with or without network resources. When a user logs on to a NetWare-equipped network, NetWare provides a shell around the user's personal desktop operating system (such as Windows), allowing the retrieval or saving of files on the server's shared hard disk. Users can also print using the network's shared printer. The NetWare operating system resides on the network's shared hard disk, allowing network users to communicate with the operating system.

Those who prefer not to work on the network do not have to log in. Instead, they work just as they would with their own stand-alone personal computer. However, users must log on to the network if they wish to use the network's resources. See Chapter 6 for more information on network operating systems.

Windows NT Server

Microsoft's **Windows NT Server** was one of Microsoft's earlier entries into the client/server market. It supports the connection of various peripheral devices (including hard drives and printers) and multitasking operations in which networked computers can process applications at the same time. Windows NT Server was designed to take advantage of Intel-compatible microprocessors and to keep track of usage by each computer on the network. It was quickly adopted by many local area networks immediately after it was introduced.

Windows 2000 Server

Microsoft's **Windows 2000 Server** is designed for network servers. It supports multitasking operations and allows for the connection of various peripheral devices. Installed on a properly equipped server computer, Windows 2000 Server provides for Internet access and the development of Web pages. Some former Windows NT users have upgraded their operating systems with Windows 2000 Server because of its added features. Windows 2000 Advanced Server and Datacenter Server are editions created for the largest network environments. Advanced Server supports up to nine processors and can handle up to 8 gigabytes of data, while Datacenter Server can support up to 32 processors and 64 gigabytes of data. Figure 4-30 shows the Windows 2000 Advanced Server interface.

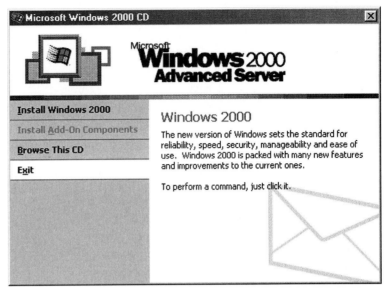

FIGURE 4-30: The Windows 2000 Advanced Server interface allows easy installation of add-ons.

Windows Server 2003

Windows Server 2003 is Microsoft's latest release of its server operating system. It comes in four editions: Standard Edition, Enterprise Edition, Datacenter Edition, and Web Edition The Standard Edition is intended to support small-to-medium sized businesses. The Enterprise Edition supports large businesses that cluster multiple servers together for increased power. The Datacenter Edition is also meant for large organizations, as it offers the ability to cluster even more servers together for mission-critical application support. The Web Edition is a scaled-down version of the software that allows companies to choose a more economical solution for servers that host only Web applications.

UNIX

Developed in the early 1970s by programmers at Bell Laboratories, the **UNIX** operating system was originally designed for servers and large computer systems (see Figure 4-31). It uses a complex command-line interface and offers some superb capabilities, including simultaneous access by many users to a single powerful computer. From its inception, UNIX has been a **multi-user operating system**, an operating system that allows many people to use one CPU from remote stations. It is also a **cross-platform operating system**, one that runs on computers of all kinds, from PCs to supercomputers.

FIGURE 4-31: UNIX is the operating system of choice for many computers, from PCs to supercomputers.

UNIX was the first language of the Internet because of its dominance in universities and laboratories, and many Internet service providers continue to use it to maintain their networks.

Linux

Linux (pronounced LIN-UKS) is one of the fastest-growing operating systems. Based on the UNIX operating system, it was created by a Finnish programmer named Linus Torvalds, who began developing the operating system as part of a research project. Torvalds is now part of the Open Source Development Labs, which is dedicated to the acceleration of the adoption of Linux in enterprise computing. He continues to devote much of his time to refining his namesake operating system, as do thousands of developers around the world.

Torvalds designed Linux as an **open-source software program**, which means that the developer retains ownership but makes the programming code available free to users, who are encouraged to experiment with the software, make improvements, and share the improvements with the entire user community. Open-source software contrasts with another category called **proprietary software**, which includes the majority of programs in widespread use. A company or an individual owns proprietary software programs and requires a fee for using the software.

Like UNIX, Linux was designed mainly for use with servers and large computer systems, including midrange servers and mainframes. However, versions are available for smaller computers such as PCs and handheld computers. Linux can be downloaded via the Internet for free, and numerous utilities are also available.

In addition to downloading Linux from the Internet, there are other ways Linux can be obtained. Some vendors will install Linux on new computers, or provide a CD-ROM containing the software. Some books about the software include a CD-ROM that can be used to install it. A copy of the software may also be obtained from other users. Various versions of Linux are available, including command-line versions and GUI versions. Two popular GUI versions are called GNOME and KDE.

Linus Torvalds, top, began developing the Linux operating system as part of a research project. Richard Stallman, bottom, a professor of computer engineering at Massachusetts Institute of Technology and founder of the Free Software Foundation, contributed to the development of Linux.

Linux software has quickly gained widespread acceptance and usage. One reason is that it can accommodate both Windows and Macintosh programs, and is thus cross-platform compatible. Some companies market their own versions of the software, such as Red Hat, Corel, and Oracle (see Figure 4-32). Many computer professionals believe Linux is a strong competitor with other, more established operating systems. IBM and Hewlett-Packard have created internal Linux business units to support their customers' ventures into the Linux environment.

The future for Linux is promising. In addition to its growing popularity as a general-purpose operating system, several companies are testing and refining Linux for use with the embedded chips found in a variety of mobile devices, including Internet appliances and handheld devices.

WIRELESS DEVICE OPERATING SYSTEMS

In recent years a great variety of wireless devices and supporting operating systems have been developed. Three popular systems for wireless devices are Palm OS®, Windows CE, and Pocket PC.

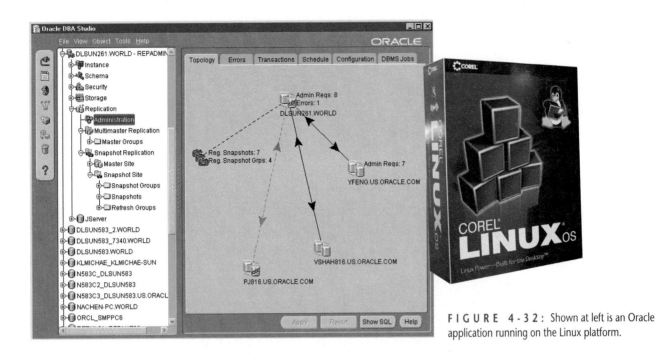

FIGURE 4-32: Shown at left is an Oracle application running on the Linux platform.

Palm OS

Palm Inc., manufacturer of one of the earliest calendar and time management devices on the market, has developed its own operating system for its handheld personal digital assistants. Called **Palm OS**, this system provides a simpler but less powerful graphical user interface than the one included with Windows CE. Palm OS is used in the various versions of the PalmPilot, in the Sony Clié®, and in the Handspring™ Visor (see Figure 4-33).

Windows CE

The **Windows CE** operating system is a scaled-down version of the Windows 95 operating system used in wireless devices and other systems with embedded processors, such as cellular telephones, pagers, and medical devices (see Figure 4-34). It is a 32-bit, multitasking, GUI operating system with special built-in power management, Internet, and e-mail capabilities. Windows CE allows the interchange of information with desktop and networked Windows-based PCs. (Note: Unlike the name Windows Me, where Me stands for a term—Millennium Edition—the CE in Windows is not an abbreviation and has no significance.)

Pocket PC

The **Pocket PC** operating system (Pocket PC OS) is a custom version of Windows CE. Pocket PC is software that is a combination of an operating system (Windows CE) and application components (such as Pocket Word and Pocket Excel) for use on small handheld computers or PDAs. Dell, Toshiba, and Hewlett-Packard's PDAs use Pocket PC software. The latest version of the software, Pocket PC 2003, was released in June 2003.

Windows Mobile 2003

Windows Mobile 2003 is an upgrade from Pocket PC 2002. The changes to this latest version are minor, but are considered significant improvements. Windows

FIGURE 4-33: The Palm Tungsten C handheld computer uses the Palm OS.

FIGURE 4-34: Windows CE is used in the Web-enabled telephone shown in the far left in this figure. Many Nokia cell phones use the Symbian OS, which was developed by Nokia, Motorola, Sony/Ericcson, Siemans, Panasonic, and Psion.

Mobile 2003 makes it easier to set up a Wi-Fi (wireless) connection and allows a user to access more Web content. On handheld LCD screens, data and images appear more legible. Other improvements over the earlier version include greater data security, improved search and time-zone handling, and minor improvements in the datebook and calendar.

MICROSOFT'S .NET INITIATIVE

Historically, operating systems and applications programs were packaged and sold in stores or downloaded by users from the manufacturer. Recently, Microsoft Corporation has developed a new product called the .NET Initiative, which incorporates applications and a suite of tools and services that operate over the Internet. According to company officials, users will be able to integrate fax, e-mail, and phone services; centralize data storage; and automatically synchronize and update all of their computing devices. From the user's perspective, four main principles of Microsoft .NET are

- Boundaries between applications and the Internet will be erased. Instead of a user interacting with a single application or a single Web site, .NET will connect the user to an array of computers and services that will combine data and objects.
- Software will be rented over the Internet instead of purchased at a store. Essentially, the Internet will be housing all of a user's applications and data.
- Users will have access to their information on the Internet from any device, anytime, and anywhere.
- There will be new ways for users to interact with application data, such as speech and handwriting recognition.

Microsoft .NET consists of an Internet programming infrastructure, a user environment, and services that support multiple devices, all of which are built around the Extensible Markup Language (XML). It includes server and client software and services built around familiar products such as Windows, Office, and MSN that will be linked by the Internet. Microsoft is developing .NET operating systems for a variety of devices, including servers, PCs, and wireless devices. Windows CE .NET, for instance, was developed for wireless devices as part of the .NET initiative. An updated version, Windows CE .NET 4.2, takes the Windows .NET platform to the next level by providing faster performance, better integration and operation with other Windows technologies and products, and increased compatibility across various Windows CE-based devices.

Windows CE .NET 4.2 contains some new features that provide developers of embedded devices, such as handheld computers, with greater functionality and flexibility when designing embedded systems. Prominent new features include

- faster performance
- improved browsing and multimedia capabilities
- improved real-time support
- improved driver support for devices such as printers

UTILITIES AND LANGUAGE TRANSLATORS

System software may contain other special software, or allow for the use of specialized programs. Two important examples of this kind of system software are utility programs and language translators.

Does Information Want to Be Free?

Do software developers deserve a return on their investments? Aren't software users morally and ethically compelled to respect the developer's property rights? On the other hand, isn't the Internet Age all about using and sharing information? Doesn't restricting the use of software infringe on free speech?

Researchers report that a large core of Internet users espouse the idea that "information wants to be free." The nonprofit Free Software Foundation considers free software "a matter of liberty, not price." It has defined four essential freedoms: the freedom to use a software program for any purpose; the freedom to study how it works and adapt it to one's needs; the freedom to redistribute copies; and the freedom to improve the program. These freedoms—contingent upon access to the source code of software programs—benefit everyone, the foundation argues.

The opposing view is championed by the Business Software Alliance, which maintains that curbing software piracy results in expanded employment opportunities and economic growth. It claims that even a 10 percent reduction in software piracy would grow the economy by $400 billion, create 1.5 million jobs, and generate $64 billion in taxes. The Alliance also points out that the piracy is a global concern. The opportunities for the greatest economic growth from software development are in Asia, where, ironically, software piracy is rampant.

It may be a moot question. Upcoming generations of college students familiar with the issue of downloading copyrighted music are entering the workforce. Could the widespread acceptance of this practice possibly become a gateway activity to workplace software piracy? Observers concede that it will take an enormous effort from the business sector to educate the public, enact legislation, and enforce the protection of software piracy laws in an environment of consumers who may have spent their formative years swapping music files.

Source: Dean, Katie. "Focus on Software Piracy Problem," *Wired News*, April 9, 2003. July 2003 <http://www.wired.com/news>.

Utility Programs

Recall from Chapter 1 that a **utility program** performs a single maintenance or repair task, such as checking for viruses, uninstalling programs, or deleting data no longer needed. An operating system typically includes several utility programs that are preinstalled at the factory. Several companies, including Symantec and McAfee, produce software suites containing a variety of utility programs. Symantec's Norton SystemWorks™ includes programs that allow users to check for and erase viruses, diagnose and repair hard disk problems, optimize hard drive performance, restore deleted files, erase deleted files permanently, perform file management, and rescue and restore files from a crashed hard drive (see Figure 4-35). Users can also purchase and install additional utilities programs of their choice. Table 4-2 lists some popular kinds of utility programs. Utility programs are usually stored on a hard disk along with the basic operating system and activated when needed by the user.

Utility programs are useful for correcting many of the problems that computer users are likely to encounter. Some of the most popular kinds of utility software are antivirus software, diagnostic utilities, uninstallers, disk scanners, disk defragmenters, file compression utilities, backup utilities, and disk toolkits.

Antivirus Software

Virus checkers such as Norton AntiVirus™ or McAfee VirusScan® are one of the most important types of utility programs (see Figure 4-36). A **virus** is programming code buried within a computer program, data, or e-mail message and transferred to a computer system without the user's knowledge. Virus contamination of a computer system can have consequences varying in severity from the mildly annoying to the disastrous. Antivirus utilities perform many functions to keep a computer's software healthy. They scan new disks or downloaded material for known viruses, and diagnose storage media for viral infection. They can also monitor system operations for

FIGURE 4-35:
Symantec's Norton SystemWorks™ can perform a variety of maintenance and repair tasks, including defragmenting a disk and checking for viruses and erasing them.

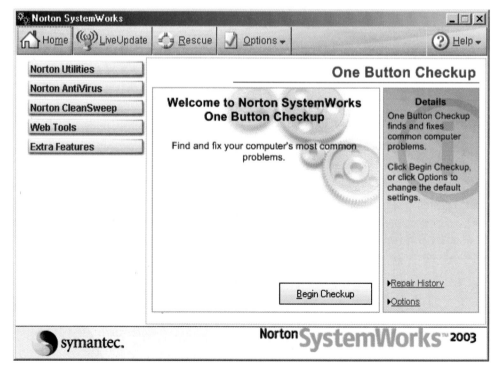

Utility Program	What the Utility Does
antivirus software	protects the computer system from a virus attack
backup utility	makes a backup copy of files on a separate disk
file compression utility	reduces the size of files so they take up less disk space
device driver	allows hardware devices, such as disk drives and printers, to work with the computer system
diagnostic utility	examines the computer system and corrects problems that are identified
disk optimizer	identifies disk problems, such as separated files, and rearranges files so they run faster (includes disk scanners and disk defragmenters)
disk toolkit	recovers lost files and repairs any that may be damaged
extender utility	adds new programs and fonts to the computer system
file viewer	displays quickly the contents of a file
screen capture program	captures as a file the contents shown on the monitor
uninstaller utility	removes programs, along with related system files

T A B L E   4 - 2 : Kinds of Utility Programs

suspicious activities, such as the rewriting of system resource files, and alert users when such activities are occurring. Most businesses use antivirus utilities as a daily startup routine. Home users find them valuable as well, as their computer systems are no less vulnerable to damaging viruses. The spread of viruses across the Internet represents the major source of virus transmission, principally through attachments to e-mail messages. See Chapter 14 for a further discussion of this topic.

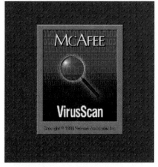

F I G U R E   4 - 3 6 : McAfee VirusScan is a popular virus-checking utility.

Diagnostic Utilities

A **diagnostic utility** diagnoses a computer's components and system software programs and creates a report identifying problems. The utility provides suggestions to correct any problems encountered, and in some situations can repair problems automatically. The Windows operating system contains a diagnostic utility. More advanced diagnostic utilities software can be purchased separately from software vendors.

Uninstallers

An **uninstaller** is a utility program for removing (deleting) software programs and any associated entries in the system files. When an application program is installed, the operating system stores additional files related to the program. Associated files may remain on the hard disk and waste valuable space if a user attempts to remove a program without using an uninstaller utility. An uninstaller utility solves this problem and frees up disk space by automatically removing both programs and related files.

Disk Scanners

Disk scanners examine hard or floppy disks and their contents to identify potential problems, such as bad sectors. During the scanning process a disk scanner program checks for both physical and logical problems. For example, it detects and notifies users if a disk contains clusters or sectors that are damaged and therefore unusable. Scan Disk is the disk scanner utility included with the Microsoft Windows operating system.

Disk Defragmenters

Disk defragmenter utilities scan hard or floppy disks and reorganize files and unused space, allowing operating systems to locate and access files and data more quickly. Operating systems store a file in the first available sector on a disk. However, there may not be enough space in one sector to store the entire file. If a portion of the sector already contains data, the remaining portions of the file are stored in other available sectors. This may result in files stored in noncontiguous (separated) sectors, known as fragmented files. This causes operating systems to take more time locating and retrieving all segments of a particular file.

This problem can be solved by **defragmenting** the disk so files are stored in contiguous sectors. Microsoft's Windows operating system includes a disk defragmenting utility called Disk Defragmenter. If a system does not come equipped with a disk defragmenter, utilities packages containing one can be purchased.

File Compression Utilities

A **file compression** utility compresses (shrinks) the size of a file so it occupies less disk space. Examples of compression utilities are WinZip®, PKZIP®, and StuffIt®. Files are compressed by reducing redundancies, such as the binary descriptions of rows of identically colored pixels in graphics files. The ability to compress and decompress files is especially helpful when sending or receiving large files on network systems or over the Internet.

Compressed files, often called zipped files, typically have a .zip file extension. Users must compress (zip) the file. When a compressed (zipped) file is received, it must be uncompressed (unzipped) to restore its original form. Both senders and recipients of compressed files must have compression software installed on their computers.

Backup Utilities

Backup utilities allow users to make copies of the contents of disks or tapes. The entire contents can be backed up, or only selected files. Some backup utilities will compress files so they take up less space than the original files. Because compressed files are unusable until they are uncompressed, many backup utilities include a restore program for uncompressing files.

Disk Toolkits

Disk toolkits, such as Norton Utilities Disk Doctor™, contain utility programs that let users identify and correct a variety of problems they may have with a hard or floppy disk. Disk toolkits can diagnose and repair problems with files on the disk as well as physical damage to the disk.

Spam Blockers

The proliferation of unwanted e-mail messages, called **spam**, is a serious concern among Internet users. According to Brightmail, a company that blocks spam for some of the nation's top Internet service providers, spam messages that advertise products and services ranging from automobiles to dating services now account for nearly 40 percent of all Internet e-mail traffic.

Utility programs called **spam blockers** are available that allow users to block incoming spam messages. Popular spam blockers include iHateSpam™, Matador™, SpamCatcher™, and SpamSubtract PRO.

Language Translators

A computer cannot understand programming code written in a human language, such as English or Spanish. Instead, it can only understand machine language: binary code written in zeros (0s) and ones (1s). Operating systems and other programs may be written using machine language, which enables them to execute very quickly.

Machine language is difficult to learn and programmers find that writing machine language programs is time-consuming. To avoid this, application programs are usually written using more English-like programming languages, called **high-level languages**. Examples of high-level languages are COBOL, Java™, and BASIC, which has several versions. Figure 4-37 shows a sample of programming code in DOS BASIC.

High-level languages must be translated into machine-language format before the CPU can execute them. To accomplish this task, special programs called **language translators** are used to translate (convert) high-level language into machine language so it can be run by the computer. Microsoft Windows includes a version of BASIC.

The two major types of language-translating software are interpreters and compilers. Each programming language generates code that needs to be either compiled or interpreted for execution. A **compiler** translates an entire program into machine language before the program will run. Each language has its own unique compiler. After reading and translating the program, the compiler displays a list of program errors that may be present. Once the errors are corrected, a compiled program will usually execute more quickly than an interpreted program.

Interpreters differ from compilers by reading, translating, and executing one instruction at a time. Since an interpreter acts on just one line of instruction at a time, it identifies errors as they are encountered, including the line containing the error, making it somewhat more user-friendly.

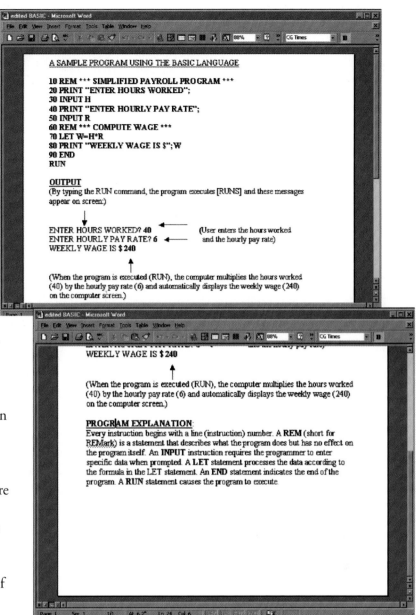

FIGURE 4-37: Shown is a simple payroll program written in DOS BASIC.

ON THE HORIZON

Inspired by breakthroughs in processing technology as well as changing market needs, developers of system and utilities software are continually brainstorming new programs and improvements to existing software. Although trying to divine the path of software development is risky, some of today's leading-edge technologies provide clues to the future.

User-Friendly System Software

Understanding and using system software and operating systems has long perplexed many users, especially those with little or no training. Recognizing this problem, software manufacturers strive to make new system software more user-friendly. Very soon these programs may include wizards similar to the wizards currently built into many application programs. Wizards are small programs designed to assist users by automating tasks. In the future, system software users may be able to click on wizard icons to automatically perform tasks such as formatting disks or copying files.

Improved Utilities Software

Many software products now available are segmented, meaning users must buy several products to have all the utilities they need. Although some manufacturers currently offer products that include a variety of programs, users soon may be able to more easily purchase a suite containing all needed utilities, including antivirus programs, a firewall that automatically blocks hackers using the Internet to gain access to the user's computer, and even programs that can identify hacker locations.

New User Interface Design for Operating Systems

Like other types of software, operating systems for the PC are evolving in an "all-in-one" direction. New designs are likely to incorporate speech and handwriting recognition, multimedia elements in the display, a Web browser, and even gesture recognition. The integration of these technologies into a single interface will meet the classic market needs of faster, easier interactions with the user. Watch for these new developments by the end of the decade.

Linux: An Open-Source Challenge to Windows?

For PC users, Windows has reigned as king of the operating systems market for several years. However, some industry analysts predict that Linux will steal market share from Windows as the open-source software model continues to gain new followers and as more productivity applications are designed for Linux. Currently, Linux is primarily known as a player in the server world. The Google search engine, for example, runs Red Hat Linux on more than 8,000 PC servers.

Linux and Embedded Linux appear in a variety of applications and products without users being aware of their presence. TiVO®, a popular digital video recorder, contains a Linux kernel on its PowerPC processor. And in late 2001,

Toyota Corporation, headquartered in Torrance, California, adopted the Linux operating system for a network that connects its automobile dealerships across the United States.

Toyota selected the Linux operating system for a new network that connects 1,200 U.S. Toyota dealerships. A new information-management program called Ximian Evolution™ runs on Linux and Unix for the PC. Created by Ximian of Boston, the program integrates e-mail, task and contact lists, scheduling, and calendars and can be downloaded free from Ximian's Web site. The company also sells an office suite for Linux that includes word processing, spreadsheet, and graphics editing programs.

Fans of Linux praise its stability, flexibility, and generally low cost (vendors usually package it with various tools; hence there is a charge). Linux also appears to be less vulnerable to security break-ins. Linux customers will concede, however, that using Linux requires a higher level of competence than does using Windows.

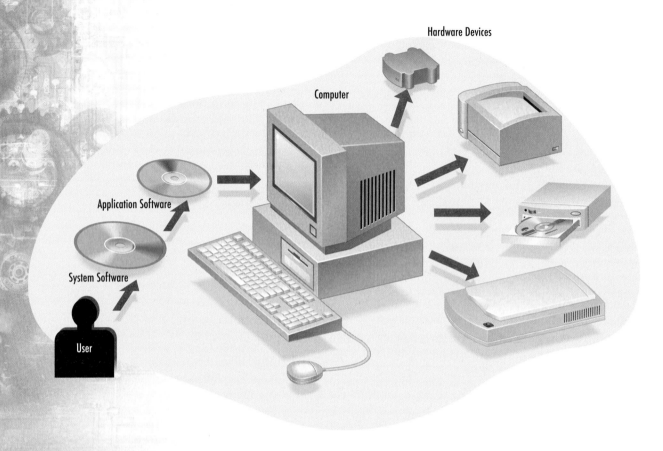

Hardware Devices

Computer

Application Software

System Software

User

What Is Computer Software?

Software is the broad term for the programs that tell a computer what to do and how to do it. **Programs** are sets of instructions telling computers to perform actions in a certain order. The two main categories of software are **application software** and **system software**. Application software includes programs that perform a single task such as spreadsheet analysis. System software includes programs that manage the basic operations of a computer such as starting up and saving and printing files.

The **operating system** is the most important piece of software on a personal computer. It manages main memory, or RAM; controls and configures peripheral devices; formats and copies disks; manages essential file operations; monitors system performance; and provides a user interface. Operating systems are designed for a particular **platform**, which is determined by the type of computer and processor.

Software User Interfaces

All software, including operating systems, must have a **user interface** to

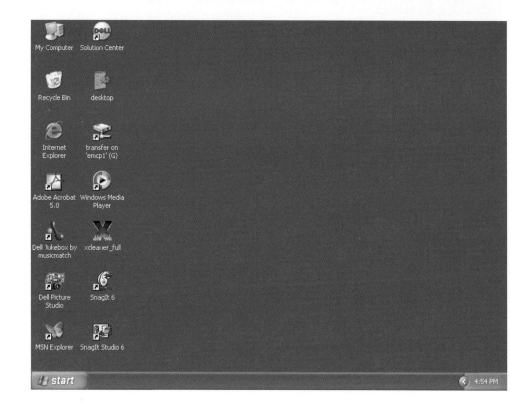

allow communication between the software and the user. The interface controls the manner in which data and commands are entered and the way information and processing options are presented on the screen. Two types of user interfaces have been developed for personal computers: command-line interfaces and graphical user interfaces (GUIs). **Command-line interfaces** are, as the name suggests, designed to accept commands from the user in the form of lines of text code. The DOS operating system has a command-line interface. **Graphical user interfaces (GUIs)** accept user commands in the form of mouse clicks on icons or menu items. Windows is the most commonly used GUI for personal computers, and it uses the same icons and basic file commands as Windows-based applications, which makes learning the new applications much easier. The major GUI features with which users interact include key feature option menus, common command icons, an on-screen desktop, display windows, dialog boxes, and online help.

PC Operating Systems

Since its development in 1985, **Windows** has increasingly dominated the PC market with each new version, beginning with Windows 3.1, and continuing with versions 3.11, 95, 98, NT, Me, 2000, and XP, the most recent release. Besides adding features with each version, the Windows releases have required increasingly more powerful microprocessors and more disk space for installation. Windows XP requires a processor speed of at least 300 MHz and hard disk space of 2 GB.

Macintosh, UNIX, and OS/2 Operating Systems

The **Mac OS** was the first commercial GUI, serving as a model for the Windows GUI that followed. Long a favorite of graphic artists and designers, the Mac OS only runs on Apple Macintosh computers. Its newest version, Mac OS X, includes a new interface called Aqua and is based on the **UNIX** operating system. IBM's **OS/2** GUI operating system was developed to compete with Microsoft Windows and the Apple Mac OS. The latest version, OS/2Warp, can run programs written for both DOS and Windows systems. A network server version also has been developed.

Server Operating Systems

Server operating systems are designed for local area networks, allowing multiple users to connect to the server computer and to share data files, programs, and peripheral devices. **Novell NetWare** is a popular and widely used operating system for microcomputer-based local area networks. Other major server operating systems include **Windows NT Server**, **Windows 2000 Server**, **Windows Server 2003**, **UNIX**, and **Linux**.

Wireless Device Operating Systems

The development of wireless devices has created a need for operating systems designed exclusively for them. Three popular systems for wireless devices are **Palm OS**, **Windows CE**, and **Pocket PC**.

Microsoft's .NET Initiative

The .NET Initiative incorporates applications and a suite of tools and services that operate over the Internet using XML. Users likely will rent applications over the Internet and will be able to integrate fax, e-mail, and phone services. The Internet will house all of a user's data.

Utilities and Language Translators

A **utility program** performs a single maintenance or repair task. Common utility programs include virus checkers, diagnostic utilities, uninstallers, disk scanners, disk defragmenters, file compression utilities, backup utilities, disk toolkits, and spam blockers. A **language translator** is a special program that converts a high-level program language into machine language so the computer can run the program. Two major types of language translators are **compilers** and **interpreters**. Compilers translate an entire program at once, whereas interpreters act on just one line of instruction at a time.

KEYTERMS

active desktop, 173
backup utility, 188
boot drive, 156
booting, 156
buffer, 157
button, 166
check box, 169
cold boot, 156
command-line interface, 160
compiler, 189
context sensitive, 171
cross-platform operating system, 181
default option, 162
defragmenting, 188
desktop, 166
diagnostic utility, 187
dialog box, 168
disk defragmenter, 188
disk scanner, 187
disk toolkit, 188
display window, 166
driver, 158
drop-down menu (pull-down menu), 162
file compression, 188
file manager, 159
graphical user interface (GUI), 160
high-level language, 189
icon, 161
interpreter, 189
kernel, 156
language translator, 189
Linux, 182
Macintosh OS, 179
memory resident, 156
menu, 162
menu bar (main menu), 162
multitasking, 158
multi-user operating system, 181
NetWare, 180

nonresident, 156
open-source software program, 183
operating environment, 171
option button (radio button), 169
OS/2, 180
Palm OS, 183
password, 160
performance monitor, 159
platform, 155
Pocket PC, 183
print spooling, 158
prompt, 160
proprietary software, 182
scroll bar, 167
spam, 188
spam blocker, 189
tab, 168
text box, 169
throughput, 157
title bar, 166
toolbar, 164
uninstaller, 187
UNIX, 183
user interface, 160
user name (user ID), 159–160
utility program, 186
virus, 186
warm boot, 156
Windows 95, 172
Windows 98, 172
Windows 2000 Professional, 176
Windows 2000 Server, 181
Windows CE, 183
Windows Millennium Edition (Me), 176
Windows NT, 174
Windows NT Server, 180
Windows Server 2003, 181
Windows XP, 177

Page numbers indicate where terms are first cited in the chapter. A complete list of key terms with definitions can be found in the Glossary at the end of the book.

CHAPTER 4

chapter exercises

The following chapter exercises, along with new activities and information, are also offered in the *Computers: Understanding Technology* Internet Resource Center at www.emcp.com.

EXPLORING WINDOWS

Tutorial 4 focuses on maximizing, minimizing, and restoring application and file management windows. You also will learn how to move and resize a window.

TERMS CHECK: MATCHING
Write the letter of the correct answer on the line before each numbered item.

a. on-screen desktop
b. window
c. interpreter
d. utility
e. software
f. booting

g. check box
h. system software
i. graphical user interface (GUI)
j. icon
k. menu bar
l. platform

_____ 1. Programs that tell a computer what to do and how to do it.

_____ 2. An interface that uses menus, buttons, and symbols, making it easier to work with text, graphics, and other elements.

_____ 3. A horizontal or vertical row display that shows the highest-level command options.

_____ 4. An on-screen work area displaying graphical elements such as icons, buttons, windows, links, and dialog boxes.

_____ 5. A picture or symbol representing an action such as opening, saving, or printing a file.

_____ 6. A rectangular area of the screen used to display a program, data, or information.

_____ 7. The element in a dialog box that allows an option to be turned on or off.

_____ 8. Translation software that reads and executes one program line at a time.

_____ 9. A type of program that performs a maintenance or repair task, such as formatting a disk.

_____ 10. A term that refers to the starting of a computer.

_____ 11. The foundation or standard around which software is developed.

_____ 12. A set of programs controlling the operation of a computer system, including all components and devices connected to it.

TECHNOLOGY ILLUSTRATED: IDENTIFY THE PROCESS

What process is illustrated in this drawing? Identify the process and write a paragraph describing it.

A:\word\mydocs\stories

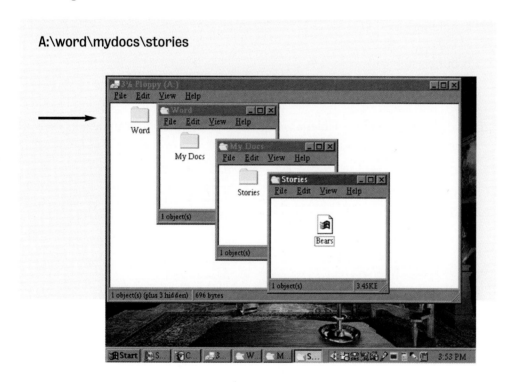

KNOWLEDGE CHECK: MULTIPLE CHOICE

Circle the letter of the best answer from those provided.

1. An option that has been built into a software program under the assumption that it is the one most likely to be chosen is called a(n)

   a. default.
   b. driver.
   c. buffer.
   d. algorithm.

CHAPTER 4

2. A rectangular area of the screen used to display a program, data, or information is a

    a. pane.
    b. menu.
    c. toolbar.
    d. window.

3. A box that provides information or requests a response is called a(n)

    a. query box.
    b. dialog box.
    c. answer box.
    d. data box.

4. A section of memory used to hold information and data waiting to be transferred to or from an output device is a

    a. holding area.
    b. cell.
    c. buffer.
    d. floppy disk.

5. A small program that enables a computer to communicate with devices such as printers and monitors is a

    a. driver.
    b. graphical user interface (GUI).
    c. speaker.
    d. compiler.

6. DOS stands for

    a. driver operating software.
    b. disk ordering system.
    c. density of software.
    d. disk operating system.

7. A program that converts a high-level programming language into machine language is called a

    a. coprocessor.
    b. binary operator.
    c. utility program.
    d. language translator.

8. Which of the following is not a function of an operating system?

   a. providing a user interface
   b. processing data
   c. managing RAM
   d. configuring and controlling peripheral devices

9. A foundation or standard around which software is developed is called a

   a. system program.
   b. platform.
   c. utility.
   d. PC model.

10. Which of the following features is not typically found in a GUI?

    a. pull-down menu
    b. dialog box
    c. icon
    d. command line

11. A term that refers to the measure of the computer's overall performance is

    a. operating speed.
    b. throughput.
    c. progression.
    d. hertz.

12. A screen on which graphical elements such as icons, buttons, windows, links, and dialog boxes are displayed is called the

    a. desktop.
    b. menu bar.
    c. icon interface.
    d. title bar.

13. A program that performs a single maintenance or repair task, such as checking for viruses, is called a(n)

    a. repair program.
    b. maintenance program.
    c. utility program.
    d. operating system.

14. A computer can understand only

    a. the COBOL language.
    b. utility programs.
    c. language translators.
    d. machine language.

15. The most important piece of software on a personal computer is the

    a. operating system.
    b. utility program.
    c. application program.
    d. defragmenting program.

THINGS THAT THINK: BRAINSTORMING NEW USES
In groups or individually, contemplate the following questions and develop as many answers as you can.

1. One of the new features introduced in Windows XP is the "remote assistance" feature. This allows someone with Windows XP to access (via the Internet) another user's Windows XP computer as if they were there in person. The primary intent is for software vendors or ISPs to provide technical support to their customers from distant locations. What other uses of this remote assistance technology can you imagine? What problems can you see this technology causing?

2. One of the new features introduced in Windows XP is a copy-protection feature called "product activation" that Microsoft included to reduce software piracy. When Windows XP is installed on a PC, the installer must use an activation wizard to register the product key. This product key is then permanently tied to the internal address of that computer. If someone tries to install the same copy of Windows XP on another computer, the activation process will not work. Can you think of legitimate needs that consumers might have to reinstall or copy the software that would not be considered piracy? Can you think of any nonsoftware industries that might have a use for this copy-protection technology?

3. Many antivirus utility programs use "heuristics" to discover new viruses. The use of heuristics means that the antivirus program assesses programming code against a set of rules to determine if the programming code exhibits any suspicious behavior. For example, if the programming logic appears to modify system files, send out hundreds of e-mails at a time, or performs an action that could be dangerous to a computer system, the file (or e-mail) message will be quarantined for the user's protection. This behavior-based approach to identifying viruses has proved to be more effective than traditional virus discovery techniques. Can you think of other uses for behavior-based problem-solving software?

KEY PRINCIPLES: COMPLETION
Fill in the blanks with the appropriate words or phrases.

1. A collection of programs that manage basic operations such as starting and shutting down the computer and saving and printing files is known as
_____.

2. A foundation or standard around which software is developed is called a(n)
_____.

3. An operating system program that manages computer components, peripheral devices, and memory is the _____.

4. A _____ is a software program that enables the operating system to communicate with a peripheral device such as the keyboard, monitor, mouse, or printer.

5. A _____ is a unique combination of characters that allows a user to gain access to computer resources, such as programs, data, and files.

6. A _____ option is one that has been programmed by the software publisher under the assumption that this option is the choice favored by most users.

7. A _____ is a graphical element that causes a particular action to occur when selected.

8. A _____ contains multiple options that can be turned on or off.

9. GUIs use _____ boxes to provide information and prompt responses to the user.

10. The _____ was the first commercial GUI, released in 1984 and updated many times since the initial release.

11. One of the fastest growing operating systems, called _____, was developed by Linus Torvalds, and is based on the UNIX operating system.

12. Microsoft released the _____ operating system for users of less powerful PCs found in homes and small offices.

13. A _____ is programming code buried within a computer program or an electronic mail message and transferred to a computer system without the user's knowledge.

14. A utility program that scans hard or floppy disks and reorganizes files and unused space, allowing operating systems to locate and access files and data more quickly is called a disk _____.

15. A language translator that reads, translates, and executes one instruction at a time is known as a(n) _____.

TECH ARCHITECTURE: LABEL THE DRAWING

In this illustration of an on-screen desktop, label the four graphical elements called out with arrows.

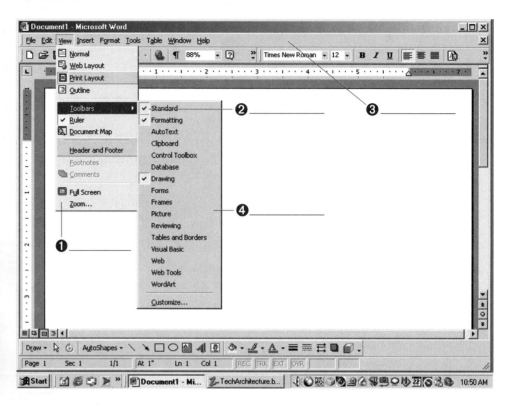

TECHNO LITERACY: RESEARCH AND WRITING

Develop appropriate written responses based on your research for each item.

1. How do the Windows 2000 Professional and Windows XP Professional desktops stack up?

   Find a personal computer that uses Windows 2000 Professional, and another PC that uses the new Windows XP Professional. Start each computer so you can see and examine the desktop. Identify and compare the elements visible on each system's desktop. Which elements do you like best on each of the two desktops? Why? If you could choose either operating system for your own PC, which would you prefer, and why?

2. Is there a vaccine for this virus?

   With team members assigned by your instructor, investigate a computer virus that has infected large numbers of computers in recent years. Discuss and answer these questions:

   - What does the virus do?
   - Where did it originate, and how does it spread?
   - What were the costs of the damage?
   - How widespread was the outbreak?
   - How was the virus stopped?

TECHNOLOGY ISSUES: TEAM PROBLEM-SOLVING
In groups, brainstorm possible solutions to the issues presented.

1. User expectations for operating systems are complex. Some users want more robust technical features and programming utilities, and others want them to become more user-friendly and "intelligent," so the OS can predict what the user wants or needs to do. Brainstorm ways these conflicting expectations can be resolved, addressed, or reconciled by the developers of operating systems.

2. Researchers and developers claim that one of the most important goals for operating systems is to become self-healing. Discuss what this characteristic means and list the types of problems "self-healing" computers will be designed to solve.

3. Microsoft claims it will soon break the mold and create a new generation OS interface that is touch- and voice-driven. If the company is right, what adaptors or utilities will be required to accommodate physically disabled customers and others with special needs?

MINING DATA: INTERNET RESEARCH AND REPORTING
Conduct Internet searches to find the information described in the activities below. Write a brief report that summarizes your research results. Be sure to document your sources, using the MLA format (See Chapter 1, page 43, to review MLA style guidelines).

1. Research the advantages and disadvantages of open-source software programs such as Linux. Is there evidence to suggest that providing source code to developers results in better programs over a shorter development time?

2. Several companies are dreaming up designs for the PC of the future. Research the design ideas of companies such as Anderson Design and the Fun-Kshun or the Ikebana computers, Sozo Design and the Ottoman computer, Stratos and the Titan computer, and Palo Alto Products and its Unimod computer. Discuss these questions as you study their computer designs for the future:

   - What design objectives are guiding the design decisions?
   - What markets are being targeted?
   - How might the market respond?
   - Will these products win acceptance?
   - What advice could you offer designers to ensure a positive market response?

3. A variety of utility programs are currently available, and new ones are being developed on an ongoing basis. Research the topic of utility programs to answer the following questions:

   - What are the most popular utilities? (Which are used most often, according to industry research?)
   - What utilities are included in Windows 2000 and Windows XP?
   - What are some new utilities under development?
   - What is the most effective way to "package" utilities for consumers? Individually? In groups of those most commonly used? What are other options?

CHAPTER 4

TECHNOLOGY TIMELINE: PREDICTING NEXT STEPS

Many improvements have been made to the Windows operating system since it was first introduced by Microsoft. Below is a timeline showing versions of Microsoft Windows and the year each was introduced. Visit Microsoft's Web site at www.microsoft.com and other sites to learn more about Windows and its features. Predict when the next version is likely to be introduced, and prepare a list of features you believe the next version will, or should, include.

1992 Windows 3.1

1995 Windows 95

1998 Windows 98

1999 Windows 2000

2001 Windows XP

ETHICAL DILEMMAS: GROUP DISCUSSION AND DEBATE

As a class or within an assigned group, discuss the following ethical dilemma.

The illegal copying of commercial software is a major concern among software publishers, including Microsoft, Corel, and others. According to publishers, thousands of copies are made and distributed to other users in violation of copyright laws.

Software publishers may spend thousands and even millions of dollars developing new software products. Illegal copies distributed to other users rob publishers of profits they would have gained from the sale of these products. Additionally, publishers say they must charge legitimate customers higher prices to make up for lost sales.

Many users believe that purchasing a legal copy makes the buyer the product's owner, which should entitle them to make extra copies. Additionally, they point out that because software publishers have the option of making their products "copy protected," publishers must not consider copying a serious problem.

What is your position on this issue? Are there situations that justify copying copyrighted software? Why or why not? What are your ethical obligations, if any, concerning this matter?

ANSWERS TO TERMS CHECK AND KEY PRINCIPLES QUESTIONS

Terms Check: 1 – e; 2 – i; 3 – k; 4 – a; 5 – j; 6 – b; 7 – g; 8 – c; 9 – d; 10 – f; 11 – l; 12 – h

Key Principles: 1 – system software; 2 – platform; 3 – kernel; 4 – driver; 5 – password; 6 – default; 7 – button; 8 – check box; 9 – dialog; 10 – Macintosh OS; 11 – Linux; 12 – Windows Me; 13 – virus; 14 – defragmenter; 15 – interpreter

CHAPTER
APPLICATION SOFTWARE
5

UNDERSTANDING TECHNOLOGY

learning objectives

- Define application software and provide examples of the different kinds of tasks it can be used for

- Identify the four major categories of application software

- Explain the difference between commercial and custom software programs

- Describe the various types of software ownership

- Define communications software and explain its potential uses

key concepts

- What Is Application Software?

- Productivity Software

- Software for Home and Personal Use

- Educational and Reference Software

- Communications Software

CYBER SCENARIO

Erik Townsend is a sophomore at Mountain View College in the central Appalachian Mountains, working toward completing a B.A. in Spanish. During the day Erik grooms dogs and cats for a living. At night and in his spare time he works on completing his degree through the school's distance learning program.

Erik needs to focus on a term paper he has been putting off. Grabbing a bottle of spring water and a handful of crackers, he seats himself comfortably at his PC and turns it on. He hears a familiar voice from the computer ask, "Erik, what would you like to do?" Erik responds, "Write a term paper for my Contemporary Spain class." "The topic?" asks the computer. Erik thinks for a moment and replies, "Spanish Cultural Life."

Within a few seconds a list of articles appears on Erik's monitor, thanks to the work of a know-bot. **Knowbots** are intelligent software agents that filter and retrieve information found on the Internet. Erik clicks on an article titled "History of Dance in Spain," and then clicks the *Summary* button. Special software summarizes the article, documents the source, pastes the information into a file called "Term Paper Notes," and stores it on the hard drive.

"What next?" asks the computer. Erik answers that he wants to learn more about bullfighting. Soon a list of articles describing Spain's traditional national sport appears on Erik's screen, but the articles are written in Spanish, which Erik does not understand. No problem! After selecting four articles, Eric clicks the *Download* button and special software translates the articles in real time before they are placed into his Term Paper Notes file.

After additional research and some careful planning, Erik is ready to write a draft of his term paper. He uses a word processing program for the text, occasionally inserting photos from Spain that he found on the Web. Four hours later, he only has to edit the text and lay out the photos using a desktop publishing program. With a little luck, he figures he will complete the final product and e-mail it to his instructor by 2 a.m., leaving time for a few hours of sleep before reporting to work the next morning.

Software available now, or in the near future, helps Erik Townsend make effective use of his most valuable resource—time. He is able to schedule his class work at his convenience, direct the computer to find information meeting his criteria, instantly translate information from one language into another, and prepare documents that look as though they were created by a commercial publisher. Erik is using software programs to greatly improve his productivity, which is the major purpose of application software for individual use.

WHAT IS APPLICATION SOFTWARE?

Application software enables users to perform the types of activities and work that computers were designed for. The specific type of application used depends on the intended purpose, and there are application programs available for almost every need.

Three broad types of application software are available for business users: individual, workgroup, and vertical programs.

Individual application software refers to programs individuals use at work or at home. Examples include word processing, spreadsheet, database management, and desktop publishing programs. Table 5-1 displays the different application software categories and their uses.

Vertical application software is a complete package of programs that work together to perform core business functions for a large organization. For example, a bank might have a mainframe computer at its corporate headquarters connected to conventional terminals in branch offices, where they are used by managers, tellers, loan officers, and other employees. All financial transactions are fed to the central computer for processing. The system then generates managers' reports, account statements, and other essential documents. This type of software is usually custom-built and is frequently found in the banking, insurance, and retailing industries.

Workgroup application software enables people at separate PC workstations to collaborate on a single document or project, such as designing a new automobile engine. This type of software is also called **groupware**, which is discussed later in the chapter.

Software Type	Uses
individual application software	create letters, spreadsheets, slide shows, and database reports; design and develop publications; design Web pages
vertical application software	perform core business processes for a particular type of industry; software is typically custom-designed
workgroup application software (groupware)	collaborate on the development of documents; communicate online through instant messaging and e-mail; conduct virtual meetings; share calendars, image banks, and databases of information; track and manage projects; generate Web pages

TABLE 5-1: Types of Application Software

APPLICATION SOFTWARE: COMMERCIAL AND CUSTOM PROGRAMS

Application software is also categorized by its market availability. Commercial application software is available for purchase or lease, whereas custom software is usually developed to meet the special needs of a single company. Because commercial programs have a huge market, they cost much less than a custom program built for one customer. Shareware and freeware are two additional types of application software that are available in today's market.

Commercial Programs

Commercial software includes programs created and sold to the public on a retail basis by software development companies such as Microsoft, Adobe, or Corel (see Figure 5-1). Both individuals and companies buy commercial software, although businesses typically purchase network versions that can be installed on servers for access by more than one employee.

These products are considered proprietary software, meaning that a company or an individual owns the copyright (see Figure 5-2). A license packaged with the software grants the customer or user permission to make a backup copy, but prohibits the distributing of copies to other people. The illegal copying or unauthorized use of copyrighted software is called **software piracy**. By completing and submitting the product registration information, purchasers receive a license from the manufacturer granting them the right to use, but not own, the software. In a network environment, a **site license** provides multiple-user rights. Registering the software provides the benefits of technical assistance and notification of software upgrades.

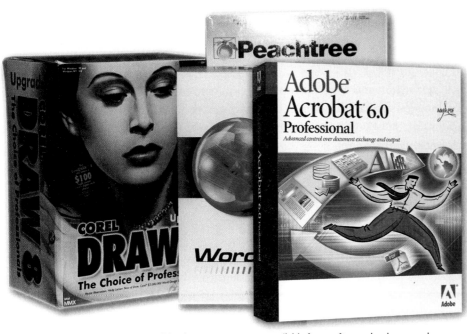

F I G U R E 5 - 1 : Many commercial software programs are available from software developers such as Microsoft, Adobe, Peachtree, and Corel.

> Warning: This computer program is protected by copyright law and international treaties. Unauthorized reproduction or distribution of this program, or any portion of it, may result in severe civil and criminal penalties, and will be prosecuted to the maximum extent possible under the law.

[OK]
[System Info...]
[Tech Support...]
[Disabled Items...]

Commercial application software can be obtained from many sources, including manufacturers, computer stores, bookstores, mail-order houses, and the Internet. Programs purchased through a retail source are usually contained on one or more CD-ROMs and come packaged with documentation and a registration card. Programs purchased and downloaded from a Web site typically include online documentation and an electronic registration form that can be e-mailed to the vendor. Many application programs are commercially successful and are periodically upgraded, while others enjoy only brief marketplace popularity and soon disappear.

Custom Programs

Businesses often have needs that commercial software cannot meet. For example, since payroll data and processing requirements vary among companies, commercial payroll programs may lack certain specialized features. The alternative to purchasing commercial software is to hire programmers to develop software to meet the company's requirements. The resulting software is called a **custom program**, or **customized software**, and is usually owned by the customer. Because of their unique processing requirements, large businesses often maintain a substantial inventory of customized application software programs.

ethics

New Nations Under the Internet

What makes a nation? In early history, societies covered small geographic ranges, slowly expanding to areas defined by natural borders such as rivers, mountains, or oceans. Typically, nations were forged by groups of people united to defend and protect themselves and to work toward the health and betterment of their members.

What forces and needs will create the nations of tomorrow? Futurists say we could soon see the emergence of a new world order consisting of *virtual* nations. Using the freedom and openness of the Internet to transcend the usual geographic borders, individuals united by a common interest—be it economic, social, political, or religious—will be able to form their own societies. A catalytic event or a charismatic leader could be the trigger that brings a "v-nation" into existence. For example, a v-nation could emerge that confers degrees or prescribes medicine without deferring to the existing education and medical establishments. A v-nation could even take on all of the attributes of a nation: a government, a monetary and trading system, citizenship, and armed forces. They could even aspire to ownership of land to fortify their power.

V-nations have the potential to be malevolent, but by breaking down the traditional barriers of distance or national divisions, the Internet could foster a new level of communication and cultivate v-nations where resources are shared to provide for global education, medical care, food, or employment opportunities. The looming question is: Should traditional nations develop guidelines for creating v-nations? Or is it unethical and impractical to try to control, even minimally, the creation of societies over the Internet?

Source: Dillard, Mike and Hennard, Janet. "The Approaching Age of Virtual Nations," *The Futurist,* July-August 2002.

Shareware and Freeware

Relatively few software programs were available for purchase when PCs were still in their infancy in the early 1980s. Some programmers began writing software to meet their own needs and made the programs available for free, or for a small fee, usually over the Internet. Others wanted computer users to test their programs and offer suggestions for improvement. This type of software program distribution can be divided into two categories: shareware and freeware.

Shareware is software developed by an individual or software publisher who retains ownership of the product and makes it available for a small "contribution" fee. The fee is typically $5 to $50, and is payable only after a user has tried the product and decided to continue using it. The voluntary fee normally entitles users to receive online or written product documentation, new software updates,

and technical help. Most shareware developers even encourage users to share the product with others in the hope that they will end up paying for product support, which is how the developers make their money.

Freeware is software that is provided free of charge to anyone wanting to use it. Hundreds of freeware programs are available, many written by college students and professors who create programs as class projects or as part of their research. Their motive is altruistic—they want to share their creation with others and are not interested in making a profit. Some freeware programs have become quite widely used, including Mosaic, a popular Web browser; PC Suite, a collection of programs that includes a word processor and spreadsheet; and WebCT, one of the most popular distance-learning platforms. Some freeware programs—for example, WebCT— begin as free software but eventually become viable commercial products.

Freeware does have some drawbacks compared to commercial software. Because freeware developers do not charge for their products, they are not obligated to guarantee that the products are error-free. They also may not provide users with documentation or technical help.

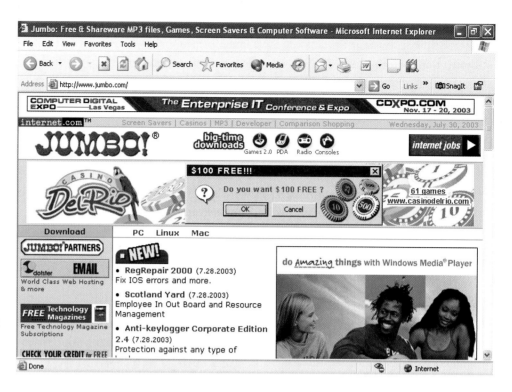

FIGURE 5-3: The Jumbo! Web site is one of several Web sites with freeware programs for downloading.

Early freeware programs were distributed over electronic bulletin boards and at computer users' club meetings. Now, the Internet provides an almost unlimited market for both shareware and freeware. Figure 5-3 identifies a Web site with a variety of freeware programs that can be downloaded.

APPLICATION SOFTWARE FOR INDIVIDUAL USE

The thousands of application programs that individuals use to perform computing tasks at work and at home can be grouped into four types:

- productivity software
- software for home and personal use
- educational and reference software
- communications software

PRODUCTIVITY SOFTWARE

Productivity software is designed to improve efficiency and performance on the job and at home, and is the largest category of application software for individual use. Employment notices appearing in newspapers and magazines often identify required computer skills, such as word processing or spreadsheet expertise. Some employment notices even specify that an applicant must be certified in a particular application, such as Word, Excel, or WordPerfect. Certified applicants often receive priority consideration over those without such qualifications.

In-depth knowledge and skill in using productivity software applications can make a potential employee more valuable to a business, organization, or agency. Table 5-2 lists productivity software categories and examples of each group.

Category	Software Example	Common Uses
word processing	Microsoft Word, Corel® WordPerfect®	write, format, and print letters, memos, reports, and other documents
desktop publishing	PageMaker®, QuarkXPress™	produce newsletters, advertisements, and other high-quality documents
spreadsheet	Microsoft Excel™, Lotus® 1-2-3, Corel Quattro Pro®	produce spreadsheets and manipulate financial and other numerical data
database management	Microsoft Access, Corel Paradox®	organize and manipulate textual, financial, and statistical records and data
presentation graphics	Microsoft PowerPoint®, Lotus Freelance Graphics	create and display slide shows
project management	Microsoft Project	schedule and manage projects
computer-aided design	AutoDesk AutoCAD®, Microsoft Visio®	create and edit detailed designs of products

T A B L E 5 - 2 : Examples of Productivity Software

Word Processing

Word processors can be used to create almost any kind of printed document. They are the most widely used of all software applications because they are central to communication. Communicating is a skill essential to nearly every business

endeavor. At one time computers appealed only to scientists and programmers. Their utility for everyone became evident when they advanced enough to allow the easy creation, editing, saving, and printing of documents. Computers would not play the central role that they do in our society today without their word processing capabilities.

Almost all computers can run word processing software applications, and word processing is probably the easiest application to learn and use. Figure 5-4 shows a sample business letter created using Microsoft Word, the most widely used word processor. Word processing programs are often available for more than one platform. For example, Microsoft Word and Corel WordPerfect are available for DOS, Windows, and Macintosh computers. Another popular word processor is Lotus Development's Word Pro.

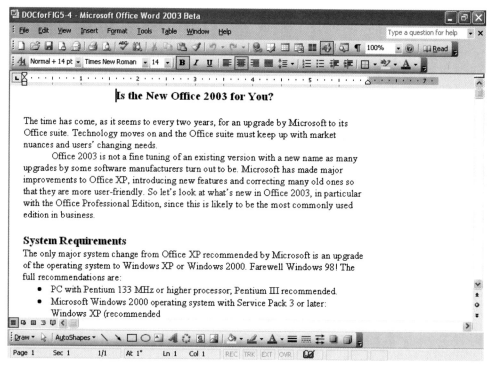

FIGURE 5-4: Word processing programs can be used to create, edit, and print a variety of documents, including memos, letters, and reports.

Whatever the type of document created with a **word processing** program, the essential parts of the procedure remain the same:

- create (enter) text
- edit the text
- format the document
- save and print the file

Creating Text

Creating text refers to the development of a document by entering text, numbers, and graphics using one or more input devices, such as a keyboard or mouse. Documents can be created starting from a blank page, or by using a previously created and stored form called a **template**. With the wizard feature, a user creates template-type documents incorporating specific information about the user, such as company name and address. Both templates and wizards are used extensively in the Microsoft Office and Corel WordPerfect suites.

Editing Text

The process of altering the content of an existing document is called editing. Editing occurs anytime something is inserted, deleted, or modified within a document. Editing features allow users to make changes until they are satisfied with the content. Perhaps the most valued word processor editing feature is a **spelling checker**, which matches each word in a document to a word list or dictionary. A spelling checker is not context-sensitive. It will not flag words that have been spelled correctly, but used incorrectly—for example, "their" when "there" would have been correct. A **grammar checker** checks a document for common errors in grammar, usage, and mechanics. Grammar checkers are no substitute for careful review by a knowledgeable editor, but they can be useful for identifying such problems as run-on sentences, sentence fragments, double negatives, and misused apostrophes.

Formatting Text

Word processing programs allow many different types of formatting, or the manipulation of text to change its appearance at the word, paragraph, or document level. The following features are found in many word processors:

- **Text formatting.** Text formatting features include the ability to change font type, size, color, and style (such as bold, italic, or underlined). Users can also adjust leading (the space between lines) and kerning (the amount of space that appears between letters). Figure 5-5 shows a page of text with special formatting features applied.
- **Paragraph formatting.** Paragraph formatting changes the way a body of text flows on the page. Features related to the appearance of a paragraph include placing the text in columns or tables, aligning the text left, right, center, or justified within the margins; and double- or single-spacing lines. As an example, in Figure 5-5 the paragraphs are left aligned with the first line indented, the title is centered, and the text is double-spaced.
- **Document formatting.** Document formatting lets users specify the form of a document as a whole, defining page numbers, headers, footers, paper size, and margin width. A **style** is a special shortcut feature that allows text to be

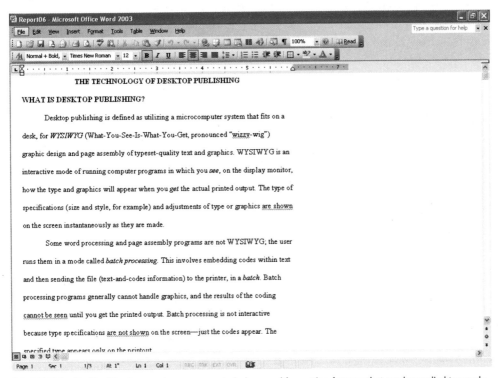

F I G U R E 5 - 5 : Word processing programs include several formatting features that can be applied to words, lines, paragraphs, pages, or entire documents.

CHAPTER 5

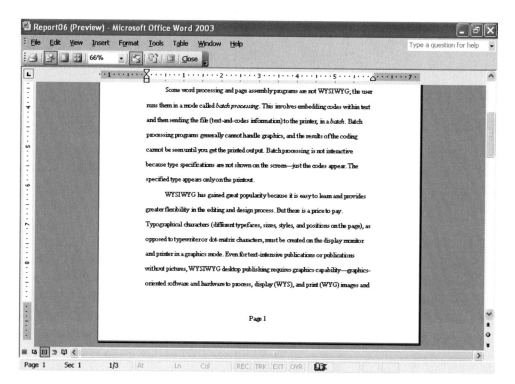

Some word processing and page assembly programs are not WYSIWYG; the user runs them in a mode called *batch processing*. This involves embedding codes within text and then sending the file (text-and-codes information) to the printer, in a *batch*. Batch processing programs generally cannot handle graphics, and the results of the coding cannot be seen until you get the printed output. Batch processing is not interactive because type specifications are not shown on the screen—just the codes appear. The specified type appears only on the printout.

WYSIWYG has gained great popularity because it is easy to learn and provides greater flexibility in the editing and design process. But there is a price to pay. Typographical characters (different typefaces, sizes, styles, and positions on the page), as opposed to typewriter or dot-matrix characters, must be created on the display monitor and printer in a graphics mode. Even for text-intensive publications or publications without pictures, WYSIWYG desktop publishing requires graphics capability—graphics-oriented software and hardware to process, display (WYS), and print (WYG) images and

Page 1

FIGURE 5-6: Formatting features such as footers automatically add page numbers and other information.

formatted in a single step. Styles allow users to apply text and paragraph formatting to a page, and then automatically apply those same attributes to other sections of text. Figure 5-6 displays pages of a report with a special footer.

Saving and Printing

Storing a copy of the displayed document to a secondary storage medium such as a floppy or hard disk is called saving. A saved document (or portion of a document) can be retrieved and reused. Saving a document requires specifying the drive and assigning a file name to the document. The three-character extension following the file name is generally added automatically by the application.

Printing means producing a hard copy of a document on paper or another physical medium, such as transparency film. Although most documents are eventually printed, a document may first be sent electronically over a network to another computer, where the receiver may choose to print the document.

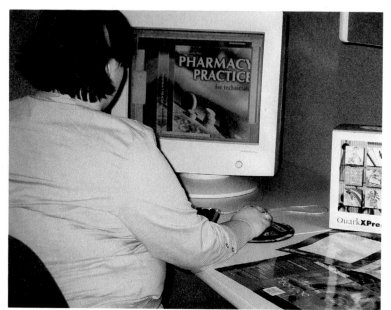

Desktop Publishing

Desktop publishing (DTP) software allows users to create impressive documents that include text, drawings, photographs, and various graphics elements in full color (see Figure 5-7). Professional-

FIGURE 5-7: Desktop publishing software can be used to produce print shop quality documents, such as banners, brochures, and newsletters.

CHAPTER 5

TECH VISIONARY

BILL ATKINSON, MACPAINT, AND HYPERCARD

Rarely does a computer programmer achieve the status of a hero, but many computer users have reason to grant heroic status to Bill Atkinson, the legendary programmer who created the first painting program for personal computers, MacPaint. Atkinson's concept for the program, which helped to popularize the first personal computer graphical user interface, was simple and clever: the user was presented with a white screen (a sketchpad) and a set of painting tools, including a paintbrush and a paint bucket. Selecting the paintbrush with the mouse cursor changed the cursor into a brush tip. When the brush tip was moved across the white screen with the mouse button depressed, it turned the pixels beneath it from white to black. By this means, shapes were formed on the screen. Selecting the paint

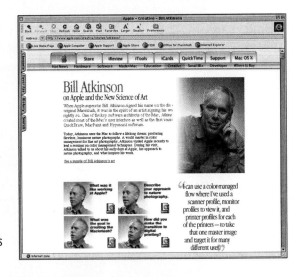

bucket enabled the user to fill an area with a predefined pattern. Later, Atkinson and others developed color versions of painting programs based on the same concept.

Not content to rest with this significant accomplishment, Atkinson initiated a second software revolution by creating Hypercard, a program that enabled users to build customized programs, called stacks, without learning a complex programming language. To develop a program in Hypercard, a user first created a stack of cards, like the cards in an old-fashioned library card catalog, employing painting and text tools to design these cards. The user could then add buttons, icons, and text fields to the cards. The user could apply simple scripts in the HyperTalk scripting language to these objects. These scripts caused the buttons, icons, and text fields to perform such tasks as moving to another card, making mathematical calculations, importing text, animating graphics, and bringing up dialog boxes. Using Hypercard, nonprogrammers were able to create their own programs. Hundreds of thousands of Hypercard programs were created, including tutorials, gradebooks, statistical analysis applications, and slide shows.

Hypercard is not widely used today, but it was the program that first introduced many personal computer users to the concept of hypertext—pages containing text and graphics that are linked to one another in an associative rather than linear fashion. The same concept is today the basis of the World Wide Web. Hypercard was also ahead of its time because it gave ordinary computer users—people who were not programmers—the ability to assemble their own programs using object-oriented programming, in which user-definable objects, containing both instructions and data, were combined in erector set fashion to produce full-scale applications. In the future, it is likely that successors to Hypercard—programs that enable users to create individualized applications—will be widely used on corporate intranets, on the Internet, and on the network user interfaces that will replace older operating systems. For these reasons, many people consider Atkinson a visionary, one of those rare programmers whose work takes a quantum leap into the future.

Source: Introduction to Computers and Technology, Paradigm Publishing.

quality publications can be produced with DTP software. Textbooks such as this one may be designed and laid out with a desktop publishing application such as PageMaker or QuarkXPress. The completed files are sent to a commercial printer for printing on high-quality paper. The pages are then collated and bound into finished books. Using a page layout program requires extensive training and a background in graphics design.

Major word processors offer a limited selection of desktop publishing features, usually the capability of drawing graphics, importing images, formatting text in special fonts and sizes, and laying out text in columns and tables. These features are sufficient for creating simple newsletters, fliers, and brochures. Microsoft Publisher, included in some editions of the Microsoft Office suite, provides more sophisticated desktop publishing elements, including predefined layouts, pull quotes, picture captions, and picture frames.

PageMaker, a feature-rich program from Adobe Systems, Inc., allows users to create a master page that establishes the format of repeating elements on all pages of a publication, such as page numbers and the chapter number and title. The program includes page description features that allow users to determine how each page will look. Graphics can be cropped and placed precisely where they are wanted.

FIGURE 5-8:
High-quality color documents like these can be produced using desktop publishing software.

When an image is inserted into a publication, PageMaker inserts tiny rectangles at the edges, allowing it to be resized by dragging the rectangles to the desired position. Figure 5-8 shows documents created with desktop publishing software.

Spreadsheets

Electronic spreadsheets are software versions of the ruled worksheets accountants used in the past. They provide a means of organizing, calculating, and presenting financial, statistical, and other numerical information. Figure 5-9 shows a sample student grade calculation spreadsheet produced using Microsoft's Excel spreadsheet program. Other well known spreadsheet programs include Lotus 1-2-3 and Corel Quattro Pro.

Businesses find spreadsheets particularly useful for evaluating alternative scenarios when making financial decisions. The spreadsheet uses "what if" calculations to evaluate possibilities. For example, company management might ask, "What happens to our profit if our sales increase by 50 percent, or our labor costs decrease by 10 percent?" These types of questions can be answered quickly and accurately by entering **values** (data, such as numbers) and mathematical **formulas** into a spreadsheet. Calculations are made immediately (see Figure 5-10).

"What if" calculations are used in school and home scenarios as well. A college instructor could show a worried student the test score needed in order to

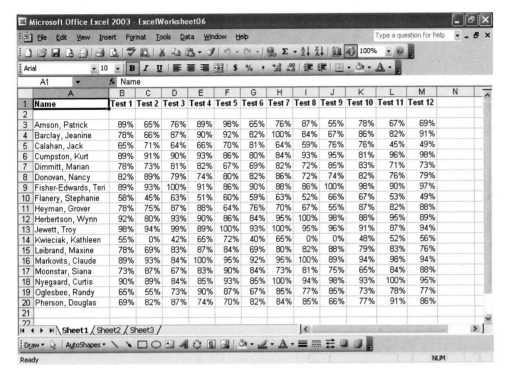

FIGURE 5-9: Many instructors use spreadsheets to record and calculate student grades.

achieve a certain grade. Or, a young couple could determine the effects of various income and savings strategies on their retirement plans. Since the computer does all of the tedious calculations, users can experiment with many different data combinations.

Other common business uses of the spreadsheet include calculating the present value of future assets, analyzing market trends, making projections, and manipulating customer and company statistics.

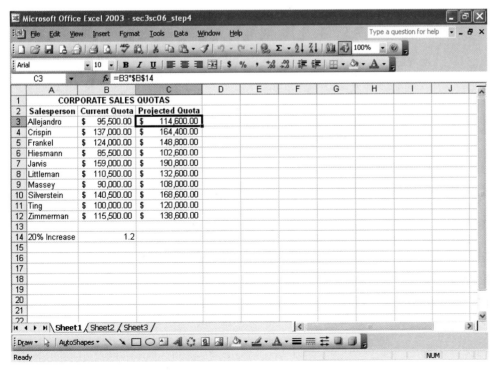

FIGURE 5-10: "What if" calculations can be used to evaluate different possibilities. For example, if salesperson Allejandro increases sales by 20 percent, the new quota becomes $114,600. To calculate what happens if Allejandro increases sales by 40 percent, one could simply change the formula in Row 14.

GLOBE TROTTING

Pandora's Box in Paradise

The king calls his country "a paradise on earth." The few travelers who have made it there have dubbed it "the last Shangri-La." It is Bhutan, a tiny Buddhist nation nestled in the snow-capped mountains between India and China.

Bhutan has a population of fewer than 700,000. More than 165 species of animals, including the endangered snow leopard, roam its virgin forests, and one-fourth of the land is set aside as national parks. The benevolent monarchy spends a generous 18 percent of its national budget on education and health care. At the same time, it also takes great care to preserve Bhutan's culture and heritage, as illustrated in the edict that all Bhutanese wear the national dress. Bhutan has such a utopian appeal that 95 percent of its exchange students eventually return home.

This storybook land has managed to stay almost completely isolated from the outside world. For one thing, it is physically difficult to reach. Fewer than 8,000 tourists trek to Bhutan each year. The only road that traverses the country is often obstructed by winter snow and summer landslides. The country's lone airline operates with two planes, which are frequently grounded due to poor weather. Bhutan claims the highest unclimbed peak in the world because no one is allowed to disturb the spirits of its mountains. But probably the biggest factor in insulating Bhutan's identity and culture is that it remained free of television and the Internet—until 1999, that is, when Bhutan Broadcasting Service began offering one hour per night of programming produced inside the country. But cable TV, first from illegal satellite dishes, and eventually from sanctioned local cable companies, has since intruded onto the scene.

At the same time, Druknet, Bhutan's only ISP, was launched as part of the celebration commemorating the Silver Jubilee of the king's coronation. Although the original idea was for only intracountry e-mail service, the king decided at the last minute to open the door to the World Wide Web. Now, a handful of cyber-cafes and six private IT training institutes operate in the capital city of Thimphu.

The advantages to opening this door are obvious. For one thing, Bhutan's lone college will be able to access a far bigger library than it could ever offer in its tiny collection. And the growing unemployment among Bhutan's very young population may be stemmed by the development of an indigenous software industry or Internet commerce opportunities.

But this is a country where the king has proclaimed that "happiness takes precedence over economic prosperity." Will Bhutan be able to protect its culture from the corrupting influences of the outside world? How will the powerful forces of information technology be kept from eroding a happiness rooted in a strong national identity? Bhutan faces a tremendous challenge as it struggles to achieve opposing goals: to open its people to the endless amount of information and influence from outside, while attempting to protect itself from the negative influences of the outside world.

Source: Schell, Orville. "Gross National Happiness," *Red Herring*, February 2002.

For the individual user, spreadsheets fulfill many purposes, including

- preparing and analyzing personal or business budgets
- reconciling checkbooks
- analyzing financial situations
- tracking and analyzing investments
- preparing personal financial statements
- estimating taxes

Common Spreadsheet Features

Although spreadsheet programs differ, most offer the following features:

- **Grid.** Spreadsheets display numbers and text in a matrix (**grid**) formed of columns and rows. Each intersection, or **cell**, has a unique address consisting of the column and row designations. Columns are usually identified alphabetically, while rows are numbered. For example, cell address A1 refers to the cell located at the intersection of column A and row number 1 (refer to Figure 5-10).
- **Number formatting.** Numbers may be formatted in a variety of ways, including decimal point placement (1.00, .001), currency ($, £, ¥), or whether they are positive or negative (1.00, -1.00).
- **Formulas.** Mathematical formulas ranging from addition to standard deviation can be entered into cells, and they can process information derived from other cells. Formulas use cell addresses, not their contents. For example, a formula might direct a program to multiply cell F1 by cell A4. The formula would then multiply the numerical contents of the two cells. The use of cell addresses means that a spreadsheet can automatically update the result if the value in a cell changes.
- **Macros.** Most spreadsheets allow users to create a **macro**, a set of commands that automates complex or repetitive actions. For example, a macro could check sales figures to see if they meet

quotas, and then compile a separate chart for those figures that do not. The macro would automatically perform all the steps required.

- **Charting.** A **chart** is a visual representation of data that often makes the data easier to read and understand. Spreadsheet programs allow users to display selected data in line, bar, pie, or other chart forms. Figure 5-11 shows selected spreadsheet data displayed in bar chart form.

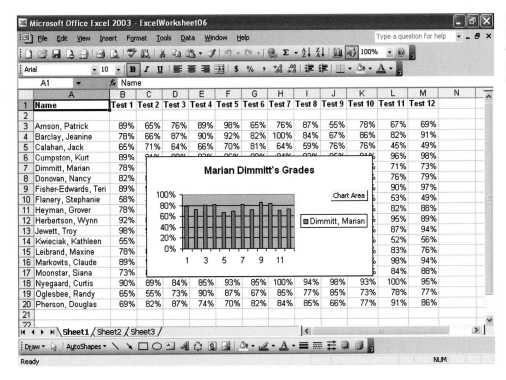

FIGURE 5-11: Microsoft Excel 2003 includes several charting options. A bar chart is useful for presenting a visual comparison of a student's test scores over time.

Database Management

Prior to computers, employee, voter, or customer records were typically placed in file folders and stored in metal cabinets, along with thousands of other folders. Locating a particular folder could prove time-consuming and frustrating, even if the records were stored in an organized manner.

Many of these manual systems have been replaced by electronic databases that use appropriate software to manage data more efficiently. Although the first electronic databases were developed for large computer sys-tems, today's database software is also available for PCs. Microsoft's Access, Lotus Development's Approach®, and Corel's Paradox are among the more popular and best-selling database programs for personal computers.

In a computerized database system, data is stored in electronic form on a storage medium, such as hard or floppy disks or CDs. A **database** is a collection of data organized in one or more tables consisting of **fields** (individual pieces of information) and **records** (a collection of related fields).

Client ID	First Name	Last Name	Street Address	City	State	Zip Code	Telephone
110	Margaret	Kasper	40210 42nd Avenue	Auburn	WA	98001	(253) 555-9003
116	Kevin	Stein	12034 South 22nd Avenue	Kent	WA	98035	(253) 555-2980
125	Maddie	Singh	450 Mill Avenue	Renton	WA	98228	(253) 555-6673
130	Abigail	Jefferson	1204 Meridain Road	Auburn	WA	98001	(253) 555-5665
141	Consuelo	Day	13321 North Lake Drive	Kent	WA	98036	(253) 555-0998
144	Carlina	McFadden	7809 52nd Street East	Auburn	WA	98001	(253) 555-2939
157	Arthur	Jefferson	23110 North 33rd Street	Renton	WA	98230	(253) 555-4889
164	Jean	Briggs	2110 West Valley Avenue	Kent	WA	98036	(253) 555-8992
187	Chris	Cervantez	8722 Riverside Road	Renton	WA	98228	(425) 555-7263
217	Arthur	Norheim	10533 Ashton Boulevard	Kent	WA	98036	(253) 555-8996
225	Jennifer	Czubek	8790 34th Avenue	Renton	WA	98228	(425) 555-3441
298	Mindy	Garvison	68 Queens Avenue	Kent	WA	98033	(253) 555-1195
321	Jeffrey	Day	317 Meridian Street	Kent	WA	98033	(253) 555-3129

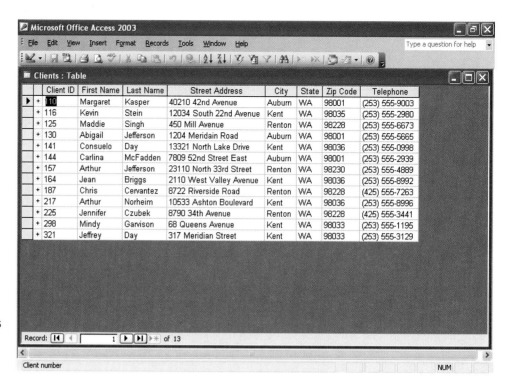

FIGURE 5-12: Within a database program, data is organized into one or more tables, each with its own name. A table consists of columns and rows. A complete row of information is called a record.

Figure 5-12 shows an example of a table created in a database program. A commercial database program typically allows users to create a form for entering data. Figure 5-13 shows an electronic form used for entering information that will become a record in the table shown in Figure 5-12. Users can add, remove, or change the stored data.

Database management systems (DBMSs) allow users to create and manage a computerized database, and to produce reports from stored data. Almost all

FIGURE 5-13: Forms provide an efficient way to enter data into a table.

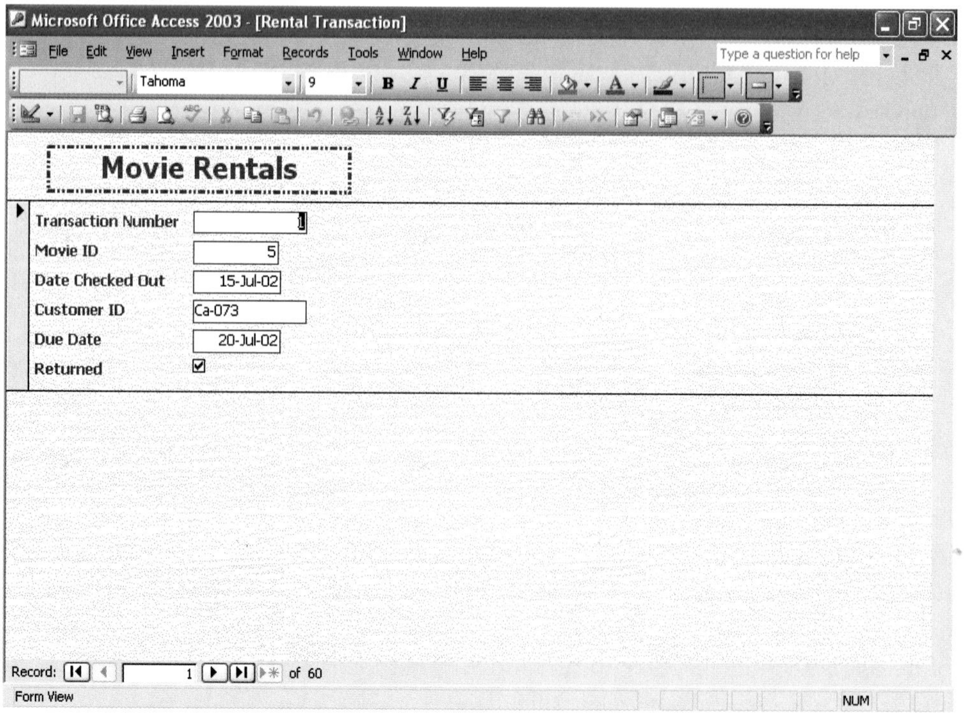

businesses and organizations use database management systems to manage inventory records, scientific or marketing research data, and customer information. For example, a university collects the data that students supply during the course registration process and stores that data in a database. To produce a roll for each class, the DBMS is instructed to locate and retrieve the names of students registered for each course, and to insert (in a specified order) the names in a report. The printed report is sent to the instructor.

Businesses use database software in much the same way. For example, a business storing customer data in a database can use a DBMS to create and print reports containing the names of customers in specific areas or territories. Sales representatives can use the reports to contact the listed customers. Figure 5-14 shows an example of a report.

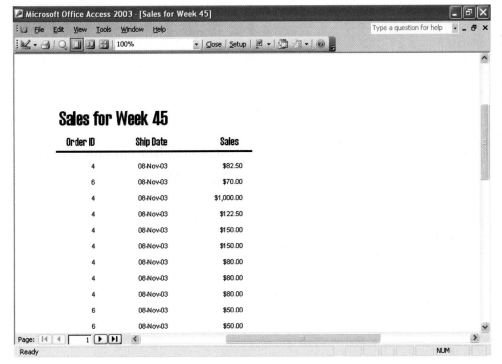

FIGURE 5-14: A report is a selection of data in a database. The user chooses which types of information should be included in the report, and the database automatically finds and organizes the data.

Although various DBMS programs are available, the most popular type is the relational database model. In a **relational database**, tables can be linked (or related) in a way that allows data to be retrieved from more than one table. Tables are linked through a common data field, such as a product number. Accessing a product number lets users retrieve different kinds of information associated with that number, even though the information may be stored in several different tables in the database.

For example, suppose a potential customer visits an automobile dealer and expresses an interest in buying a blue Chevrolet Corsica. The dealer may have several Chevrolets in stock, but may not know if there is a blue Corsica among them. Using a computerized relational database, the dealer can quickly find the answer by querying (asking) the database, which would then search all linked tables for blue Corsicas. Figure 5-15 illustrates the manner in which separate tables are linked to provide a response to a query.

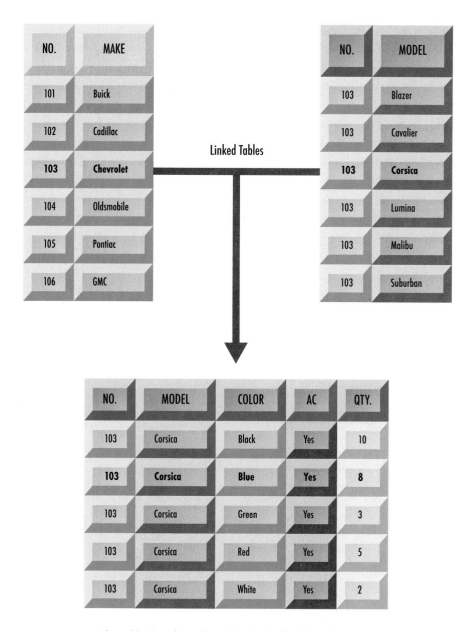

FIGURE 5-15: A relational database allows multiple tables to be linked so that users can retrieve related data from more than one table.

Linked Tables

Relational databases frequently include multiple tables of data. This simplified illustration shows how tables may be linked. For example, suppose you visit an automobile dealer's showroom and inquire about Chevrolet Corsica automobiles. Using a computerized database, the salesperson can quickly access information from the three database tables shown in the illustration. A linkage of the tables shows that the dealership currently has eight blue Chevrolet Corsica automobiles in stock.

Common Database Features

Features commonly found in database programs include

- **Sort.** Records can be **sorted** (arranged) in many different ways. For example, the records included in the table shown in Figure 5-16 could be sorted by city, or ZIP Code.
- **Find.** Information in a table can be located by using **Find** to look up a number or a particular type of text, such as a name or an address.

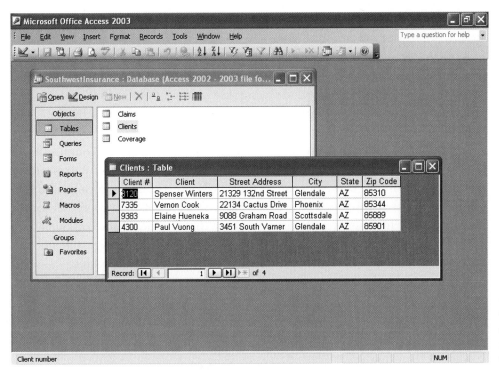

FIGURE 5-16: Records in the Clients table can be sorted in different ways and used to create a report that answers a specific query, or question.

- **Query.** Searches much more advanced than the Find command can be conducted by using a **query**, or method of asking the database for results. The database can be queried using **SQL (Structured Query Language)** or **QBE (Query by Example)**. One of these query methods could be used to search the table in Figure 5-16 for contacts in ZIP Code 85889.
- **Links.** Tables can be linked in meaningful ways that make sense for a particular business. For example, the Clients table in Figure 5-16 could be linked to Claims and Policy List tables.
- **Reports. Reports** can be created by combining information from linked tables. For example, Client and Policy List tables could be combined to produce invoices for clients.

Presentation Graphics

Anyone who has attended group lectures or presentations knows how boring they can be. One way to make a presentation more interesting is to use presentation graphics software. **Presentation graphics software** allows users to create computerized slide shows that combine text, numbers, graphics, sounds, and videos. Sales representatives use **slide shows** to promote products to customers, trainers and instructors use them to accompany lectures, and businesspeople use them for delivering information and

CHAPTER 5

presenting strategies at meetings. Microsoft PowerPoint and Corel Presentations™ are two popular presentation software programs.

Another advantage of presentation software is that it allows users to easily repurpose information, meaning that the information can be modified to suit different audiences. Other capabilities include being able to import files created in other programs, such as word processors or spreadsheets. This material can then be incorporated within one presentation.

In addition to presenting a slide show via computer, users can also output the presentation as 35mm **slides**, transparencies, or hard-copy handouts. A presentation run on a portable computer can be projected onto a screen using a multimedia projector (a self-contained projection unit with a plug-in for a computer) or an LCD panel (a semitransparent projection device that attaches to the computer and sits on top of an overhead projector). Figure 5-17 shows the opening slide and lists the text for following slides in a presentation on the history of computers.

FIGURE 5-17: Microsoft PowerPoint allows users to check slide content and format by displaying the text of several slides at a time (note slide text in the left pane).

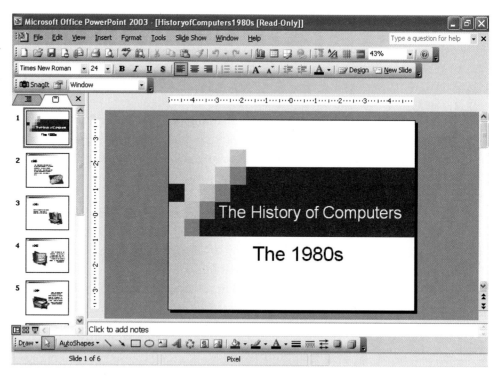

Common Features of Presentation Software

Presentation applications typically include

- **Wizards.** Most presentation programs offer users a choice of presentation types. After a particular type is chosen the program provides a **wizard**, or miniprogram, to guide the user step by step through the creation of the slide show.
- **Templates.** Predesigned style formats, called templates, save time because they contain background colors, patterns, and other elements that work well together. Users can also create their own personalized templates.
- **Handouts.** Creating handouts with Microsoft PowerPoint is as easy as selecting an option from the Print dialog box. Handouts can be in outline or note

format. It is also possible to create handouts containing graphic reproductions of the slides.

- **Clip art.** Powerful, attention-grabbing graphics enliven presentations and can sometimes convey messages more effectively than text alone. Presentation programs generally include collections of **clip art** (simple line drawings) that can be inserted into slides. Additional images can be located and imported from other sources, including the Internet and clip art software packages.

Software Suites

Some commercial software vendors bundle and sell a group of software programs as a single package called a **software suite**, also known as **integrated software** (see Figure 5-18). Software suites typically include the four most widely used applications: word processing, database management, spreadsheet, and presentation programs. Some, such as Microsoft Office, also include Web page authoring programs

FIGURE 5-18: A software suite is a collection of applications bundled and sold as a single product.

since the development of personal Web sites is becoming increasingly important to consumers. Suites are popular because buying one is cheaper than purchasing the component programs separately.

Software suites offer other advantages. Because the programs were developed using the same user interface, all programs in the suite work in a similar manner. Once someone has become familiar with one program, learning to use the others is easier because of the similarity of screen layouts, menus, buttons, icons, and toolbars.

Another strong feature of suites is their ability to seamlessly integrate files from other programs. For example, information produced using a spreadsheet can be placed into a word processing document, or a database table can be imported into a slide show presentation.

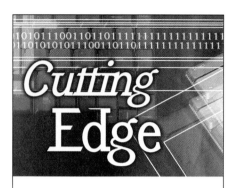

One method of moving information from one suite program to another is by copying and pasting. Although quite easy, this method has some disadvantages. For example, if a user created a PowerPoint slide show containing a copied Excel spreadsheet file, the Excel file would need to be recopied each time it is updated with new calculations.

A second method called **object linking and embedding (OLE)** addresses the problem of changing or updating information. It involves creating an object (a table, chart, picture, or text) in one program and then sharing it with another program. Two types of sharing are possible: embedding and linking. Embedding is a type of copying, allowing the embedded file to be changed using the original program's editing features. However, the changes are not reflected in the original file. Using the example in the previous paragraph, a spreadsheet file embedded in the PowerPoint presentation could be edited, but the changes would appear only in the PowerPoint presentation. However, linking the file ensures that any changes made in the original spreadsheet will also be reflected in the PowerPoint presentation.

Project Management

Many businesses regularly engage in planning and designing projects, as well as scheduling and controlling the various activities that occur throughout the life of the project. For example, before a construction firm begins erecting a building, it needs to develop a comprehensive plan for completing the structure. During planning, an architect prepares a detailed building design, or set of blueprints. Schedules are then prepared so that workers, building materials, and other resources are available when needed. Once construction begins, all activities are monitored and controlled to ensure that they are initiated and completed on schedule.

Prior to computers, projects like this were planned, designed, scheduled, and controlled manually. Today these tasks are performed using **project management software**. This type of software facilitates the effective and efficient management of complex projects. It can be used for just about any project, including those involving construction, software development, and manufacturing. Microsoft Project is one example of project management software that can be used to optimize the planning of projects and to track schedules and budgets (see Figure 5-19).

Computer-aided Design

Computer-aided design (CAD) software is a sophisticated kind of productivity software, providing tools that enable professionals to create architectural, engineering, product, and scientific designs (see Figure 5-20). Engineers can use the software to design buildings or bridges, and scientists can create graphical designs of plant, animal, and chemical structures. Some software programs display designs in three-dimensional form so they can be viewed from various angles. Once a design has been created, changes can easily be made until it is finalized.

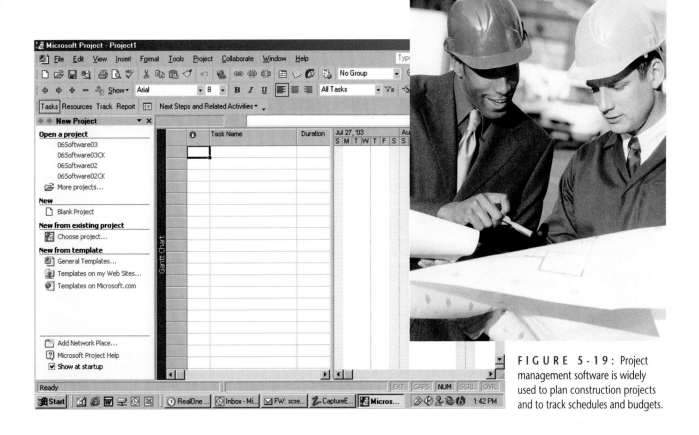

FIGURE 5-19: Project management software is widely used to plan construction projects and to track schedules and budgets.

An aircraft engineer designing a new type of aircraft can use CAD to test many design versions before the first prototype is built. This process can save companies considerable time and money by eliminating defective designs before beginning production.

Full-feature CAD programs are very expensive. Some producers of CAD software offer scaled-down versions of their more expensive software for use by small businesses, and for individual and home use.

SOFTWARE FOR HOME AND PERSONAL USE

When browsing computer stores, shoppers are likely to see numerous software applications designed for home and personal use. Among the many products available are applications for writing letters, making out wills, designing a new home, landscaping a lawn, preparing and filing tax returns, and managing finances. Software suites are also available for home and personal use, although sometimes the suites available for home use do not contain all the features found in business versions.

FIGURE 5-20: Computer-aided design software is used to create designs for buildings, bridges, and commercial products.

More than one-half of U.S. homes now include a personal computer on which a variety of software applications have been installed. Most application software programs are relatively inexpensive. Some vendors advertise popular word processing programs for as little as $99.

Personal Finance

Personal finance software assists users with paying bills, balancing checkbooks, keeping track of income and expenses, maintaining investment records, and other

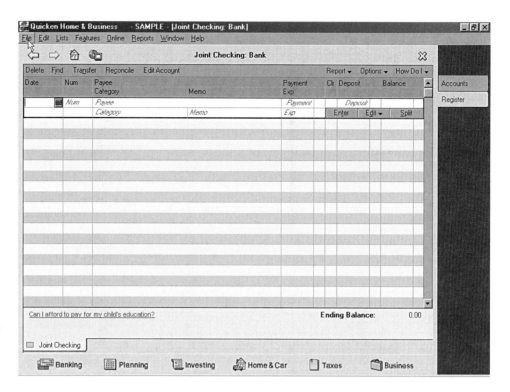

FIGURE 5-21: Personal finance software enables users to manage personal finances by helping them pay bills, balance checkbooks, keep track of income and expenses, maintain investment records, and other financial activities.

financial activities (see Figure 5-21). The software also enables users to readily view how their money is being spent.

Some personal finance software provides online services available over the Internet and Web. These services allow users to go online to learn the status of their investments and insurance coverage. They can also conduct normal banking transactions, including accessing and printing bank statements showing monthly transaction summaries. These programs can perform most of the financial activities previously requiring mail or telephone contact.

Tax Preparation

Tax preparation software is designed to aid in analyzing federal and state tax status, as well as to prepare and transmit tax returns. Most of the programs provide tips for preparing tax documents that can help identify deductions, possibly resulting in great savings. Some programs include actual state and federal tax forms for entering tax data. Programs that do not include forms provide instructions for downloading them from the software publisher's Web site. Finished tax returns can be printed for mailing or filed electronically. Because federal and state tax laws change frequently, as do tax forms, users will probably need to obtain the software version for the appropriate taxable years or period.

Legal Documents

Legal software is designed to help analyze, plan, and prepare a variety of legal documents, including wills and trusts. It can also be used to prepare other legal documents, such as the forms required for real estate purchases or sales, rental contracts, and estate planning. Included in most packages are standard templates for various legal documents, along with suggestions for preparing them.

The program will begin by asking users to select the type of document they want to prepare. In order to complete a document, a series of questions will need to be answered, or a form will appear for users to enter

needed information. Once this activity is complete, the software adapts the final document to meet individual needs.

After a document is prepared, it can be sent to the appropriate department, agency, or court for processing and registration. It is always a good idea to have an attorney review documents to make certain they are correct and legal in the intended state or local jurisdiction.

Games And Entertainment

Entertainment software refers to programs that provide fun as well as challenges. Included in this group are interactive computer games, videos, and music. Several popular entertainment programs come with versions of Microsoft's Windows

FIGURE 5-22: Entertainment software allows users to enjoy a variety of entertainment experiences, including music and games.

operating system, including Backgammon, Checkers, Pinball, Solitaire, and Minesweeper (see Figure 5-22).

If a PC is equipped with a CD-ROM drive, music CDs can be played just as they would on a standard or automobile CD player. Music can also be downloaded from commercial and personal Web sites. If a PC is equipped with a DVD drive, users can purchase or rent movies and play them on their computers.

GRAPHICS SOFTWARE

Users can choose from a variety of software applications designed for creating and modifying images. Programs available in computer stores and other retail outlets typically are designed for painting and drawing images or for editing various kinds of graphics. Two main types of graphics software are painting and drawing programs and image-editing programs.

Painting and Drawing Software

Painting and drawing programs are available for both professional and home users. The more expensive professional versions typically include more features and greater capabilities than do the less expensive personal versions.

With a **painting program**, a user can create images in bit-map form and also color and edit an image one bit at a time (see Figure 5-23). Windows Paint is an example of a popular painting program. A **drawing program** enables a user to create images that can be easily modified. The size of a drawn image can be decreased without a reduction in image resolution. However, increasing the size may result in a loss of resolution quality. Popular drawing programs include CorelDRAW®, Adobe Illustrator™, and Macromedia FreeHand.

Both painting programs and drawing programs provide an intuitive interface through which users can draw pictures, make sketches create various shapes, and edit images. Programs typically include a variety of templates that simplify painting or drawing procedures. Once finished, a painting or drawing can be imported into other documents, such as personal letters, signs, business cards, greeting cards, and calendars.

Image-Editing Software

The market demand for image-editing programs has increased concurrently with the popularity of digital cameras. An **image-editing program** allows a user to touch up, modify, and enhance image quality (see Figure 5-24). Editing features include changing color, cropping, resizing, applying special features, and eliminating red-eye effects from photographs. Once edited, images can be stored in a variety of formats and inserted into other files, such as letters and advertisements. Adobe Photoshop® and Windows Imaging are popular image-editing programs.

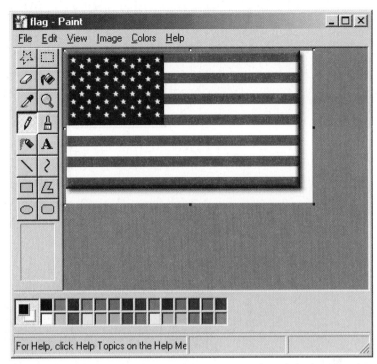

F I G U R E 5 - 2 3 : The Windows Paint program provides tools for drawing and painting a variety of objects.

F I G U R E 5 - 2 4 : The Windows Imaging program provides numerous tools for editing an image.

EDUCATIONAL AND REFERENCE SOFTWARE

The widespread use of home computers has brought about an increase in the availability of educational and reference software, making computers a popular learning and reference tool. Examples of **educational and reference software** include encyclopedias, dictionaries, and learning tutorials.

Encyclopedias and Dictionaries

Almost everyone has used an encyclopedia or dictionary at one time or another. An **encyclopedia** is a comprehensive reference work containing detailed articles on a broad range of subjects. Before computers, encyclopedias were only available in book form. They are now available electronically, usually in CD-ROM format. Many new PCs include a CD-ROM–based encyclopedia, such as *Encyclopaedia Britannica* or Microsoft Encarta® (see Figure 5-25).

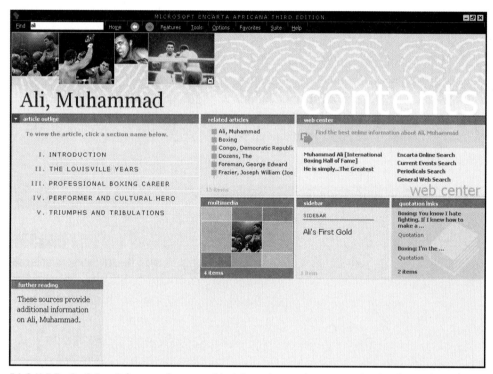

FIGURE 5-25: Reference software provides information on a huge range of topics. Shown above is an entry from Microsoft Encarta.

A variety of dictionaries are available on CD-ROM. A standard **dictionary** is a reference work containing an alphabetical listing of words, with definitions that provide the word's meaning, pronunciation, and usage. Examples include *Webster's Dictionary* and *Webster's New World Dictionary of Computer Terms*. Other specialized dictionaries, such as multilanguage dictionaries, contain words along with their equivalent in another language for use in translation.

Learning Tutorials

Many people learn new skills by using CD- or Internet-based tutorials. A **tutorial** is a form of instruction in which students are guided step-by-step through the learning

TECH VISIONARY

Dan Bricklin is a respected and honored technology visionary. In 1969 he enrolled at MIT and became friends with fellow student Bob Frankston, who was to play a major role in his career some years later. After receiving a degree in computer science, Bricklin worked as a programmer at Digital Equipment Corporation (DEC) for a brief period before beginning his studies toward a master's degree in business administration at the Harvard Business School.

Having worked on programming for an online calculator and a word processing program for DEC, Bricklin understood how useful computers could be in business, but his classroom experience also showed him their limitations and inefficiencies. Students had to learn to perform calculations for business spreadsheets manually, inserting new figures for everything from labor costs to shipping, then recalculating the effect of each change on the bottom line. The process was tedious and every new calculation was an opportunity for mistakes that could lead to serious business errors.

Out of his frustration with the tasks and his certainty that there must be a better way to do it, Bricklin began to develop a software program that would do for numbers what word processing did for words—enable the user to insert and delete data and to see an immediate change in the results.

Bricklin joined up with Bob Frankston, his friend from MIT, and together they began to turn Bricklin's basic ideas into a commercially viable product. Founding a company called Software Arts in 1978, Bricklin worked on the functional design and documentation of the new software while Frankston wrote the programming. By the fall of 1979 a version of their program was ready. The program was called VisiCalc, short for Visual Calculation. Almost immediately, VisiCalc became a huge commercial success and the foundation for the development of a long line of spreadsheet programs that followed.

VisiCalc had a major impact in two ways. First, it allowed businesses to redistribute costs and revenues on a trial basis to see immediately how the changes would affect the bottom line. The second impact was on the computer industry itself. For the fledgling Apple Computer Company, VisiCalc was a tremendous boost because the first version was written to run on the Apple II, and people bought the computer just so they could run VisiCalc. The reputation of VisiCalc as a serious business application did much to establish the PC as a legitimate business computer. In 1985, Lotus Software purchased Software Arts.

Bricklin continues making contributions in the computing field. With his present venture, called Trelix, Bricklin helps individuals and businesses create and edit Internet projects.

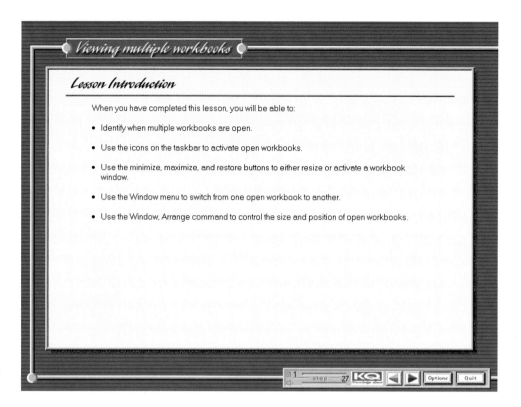

Viewing multiple workbooks

Lesson Introduction

When you have completed this lesson, you will be able to:

- Identify when multiple workbooks are open.

- Use the icons on the taskbar to activate open workbooks.

- Use the minimize, maximize, and restore buttons to either resize or activate a workbook window.

- Use the Window menu to switch from one open workbook to another.

- Use the Window, Arrange command to control the size and position of open workbooks.

FIGURE 5-26: Tutorials guide users step-by-step through the learning process using graphics, text, and audio media. Some applications include tutorials with the software.

process (see Figure 5-26). Tutorials are available for almost any subject, including learning how to assemble a bicycle, use a word processor, or write a letter. Once an electronic tutorial is accessed, students need only follow the instructions displayed on the screen. Many tutorials include graphics to help guide students during the learning process. Software manufacturers often provide tutorials for training users in the application of software products, such as their word processors, spreadsheets, and databases. The goal is to help users acquire skill in using the manufacturer's product, in the hope that this will entice users to make a purchase.

COMMUNICATIONS SOFTWARE

One of the major reasons people use computers is to communicate with others and to retrieve and share information. Software that enables communication over the Internet and the Web is available for individual, home, and business use. This software allows users to send and receive e-mail, browse and search the Web, engage in group communications and discussions, and participate in videoconferencing activities.

Internet Service Providers

When users subscribe to an Internet service provider (ISP), the ISP provides them with a CD-ROM or disk containing communications software that can be installed on their computer's hard drive. This software includes the programs needed for sending and receiving e-mail, and for browsing and searching for information available on the Web. Some software also enables users to participate in group communications and discussions. The kinds of programs provided vary among Internet service providers. (Chapter 6 discusses e-mail applications, and Chapter 7 includes a detailed discussion of Internet service providers.)

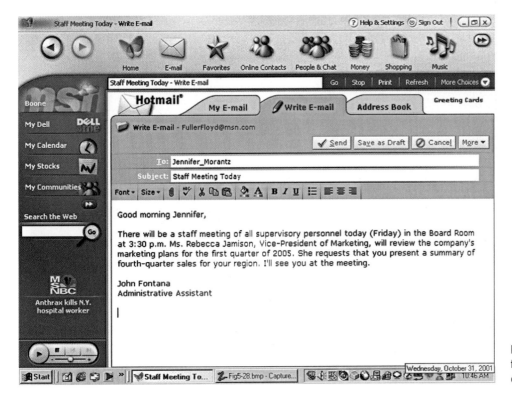

FIGURE 5-27: E-mail is a fast and efficient way of communicating with other computer users.

Electronic Mail

Electronic mail (e-mail) is rapidly becoming the main method of communication for many individual, home, and business users. **E-mail** is the transmission and receipt of messages over a worldwide system of communications networks. The real value of e-mail lies in its speed and low cost. Messages can be sent and received within seconds or minutes, and transmission costs are minimal.

Preparing an e-mail message is similar to preparing a word processing document. Users can create, edit, send, receive, forward, print, store, and delete e-mail messages. Most e-mail software will notify users when a message has been received. Figure 5-27 shows an e-mail message displayed in the Inbox of MSN, a popular ISP that provides an e-mail program.

Web Browsers and Search Engines

Recall that Web browsers, also called browsers, allow users to move from one location to another on the Web, and to access and retrieve Web pages. Web browsers use a GUI that can retrieve and display Web pages containing graphics, pictures, and other high-resolution text and images.

Most browsers provide for sending and receiving e-mail messages, participation in chat groups, and the ability to maintain a listing of favorite Web sites and pages. The two most popular browsers are Microsoft's Internet Explorer and

FIGURE 5-28: A Web browser allows users to move from one location to another on the Web, and to locate and retrieve information.

Netscape's Navigator. Figure 5-28 shows the opening screen of Microsoft's Internet Explorer.

Search engines are used to search, locate, and retrieve information from various Web sites. Among the more popular search engines are Yahoo!, WebCrawler, AltaVista, Lycos, Google, and HotBot. These programs can be accessed by typing the search engine Internet address in the browser address box. Figure 5-29 shows the home page of HotBot (www.hotbot.com).

FIGURE 5-29: A search engine is a software program for finding information on a desired topic.

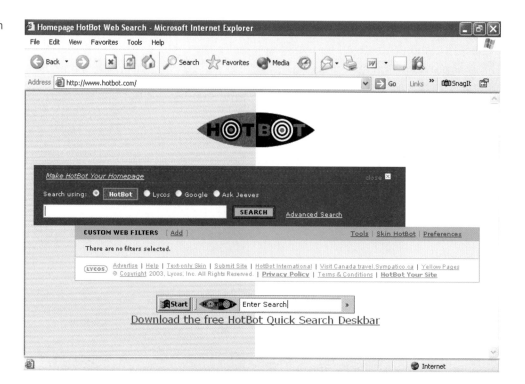

Instant Messaging Software

Instant messaging (IM) is a technology that enables people to communicate with other users over the Internet in real time. Subscribers to instant messaging services must have instant messaging software installed on their computers. Because there are no established IM standards, people wishing to communicate need to use the same or compatible IM software. Instant messaging can be used on all types of devices, including PCs, handheld computers, notebook computers, and Web-enabled cell phones.

Once members are signed up with an instant messaging service, they can exchange messages or files and use the service to participate in chat groups. Some IM services will notify members of an incoming message and also provide financial news, stock quotes, appointments, weather updates, and other practical information.

Groupware

Groupware allows people to share information and collaborate on various projects, such as designing a new product or preparing employee manuals. Groupware can be used over a local area network (LAN), wide area network (WAN), or the Internet. All group members must be using the same groupware programs to collaborate on projects.

Most groupware includes an address book of members' contact information and an appointment calendar. One of the most desirable features of groupware is a scheduling calendar that allows each member to track the schedules of the other members. This makes it possible to coordinate activities and to arrange meetings to discuss project activities and other matters.

Videoconferencing

A **videoconference** is a virtual meeting between two or more participants at different locations using computer networks and **videoconferencing software** to transmit audio and video data. Participants communicate as though they were in the same room. Two types of videoconference systems are point-to-point (two participants) and multipoint (multiple participants).

A **point-to-point videoconferencing system** works like a video telephone. Each party's computer has a video camera, microphone, and speakers. During a conference, their voices and images are carried over the network, appearing in a window on the other participant's monitor.

A **multipoint videoconferencing system** allows three or more people to sit in a virtual conference room and communicate as though they were seated next to each other. The system also allows individuals or groups at multiple sites to communicate with each other (see Figure 5-30). Multipoint videoconferencing is especially effective for businesses with branches or plants separated by long distances.

Videoconferencing is growing rapidly in the medical field. Physicians and other health professionals often conduct seminars and share medical advice and related information via videoconferences. The technology experienced a significant increase in use shortly after the terrorist attacks on the World Trade Center in New York on September 11, 2001. Many people felt reluctant to travel, and the ability to communicate by video allowed business to continue normally.

FIGURE 5-30:
Videoconferencing software enables conference participants to communicate over long distances as though the participants are in the same room.

ON THE HORIZON

Inspired by breakthroughs in processing technology and changing market needs, software developers are continually brainstorming new programs or improvements to existing software. Some of today's leading-edge technologies allow us to make educated guesses about digital applications that soon may be standard-issue.

Z-learning: Dreaming Your Way to a Degree

The Lucidity Institute in Palo Alto, California, is exploring a phenomenon known as lucid dreaming to see if it can be used for learning. Research at Stanford University has demonstrated that the physical activity in a dream exhibits the same neural impulses in the brain as occur during waking states. A Lucidity Institute researcher, Stephen LeBerge, predicts that this knowledge may lead to the possibility of tutoring individuals while they sleep.

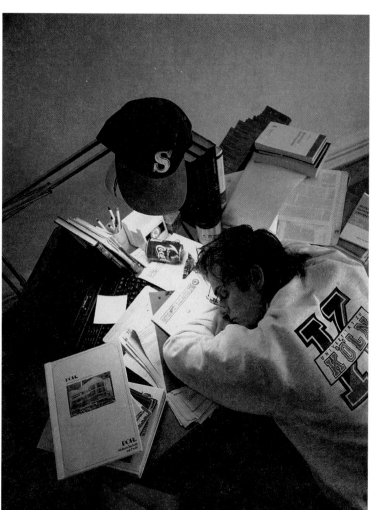

Imagine learning Spanish or chemistry while sleeping! Although still in the research and development stages, the basic knowledge and technology is already in place that may someday allow individuals to be tutored or trained while asleep. Sleeping students would awaken refreshed, with new knowledge and information that can be recalled as though it was learned in the classroom.

Advances in Speech Recognition Software

Several hardware devices and productivity applications currently incorporate speech recognition software. Although much improved compared to earlier attempts, the present speech recognition technologies have yet to meet the high accuracy transcription demanded by industries such as medicine. The proliferation of Web-enabled handheld computers indicates a trend of continuing improvements in speech recognition, simply because of rising market demand.

IBM has developed a technology called **conversation speech biometrics**, which may provide one of the significant advances. It is particularly suited for identification and verification needs, such as those required during Internet purchases. The technology works by comparing voices to a database of known speakers. The software is able to recognize voices even though the database may not include the exact words spoken.

A related technology called **natural-language processing (NLP)** has advanced to the stage where systems can understand the conversations of a five-year-old child. If NLP software can live up to its potential and eventually recognize adult speech, it could revolutionize personal and business communications.

Pattern Recognition Software

Pattern recognition software translates images into digital information, filters out any unnecessary data, and then compares the result against a reference model. This type of software can be used for facial identification and verification. One version, IBM DB2 Intelligent Miner for Data, is currently used to evaluate customers' responses and choices at Web sites, looking for buying patterns and using that information to try to sell new products.

Distributed Computing

Software designers are picturing a future in which software programs consist of groups of services available through the Internet, rather than from CD-ROMs. The first generation of companies offering these programs were called application service providers (ASPs), and though their vision held great promise, market enthusiasm for the idea cooled in 2000.

The next generation of software as services will be offered in the **distributed computing model**, and the quest is being led by computer industry giants IBM, Microsoft, and Sun Microsystems. Based on an open set of standards and protocols, the distributed computing model combines the power of an almost limitless number of computers over the Internet. Distributed computing is often called **grid computing**, as well, particularly in reference to some of the huge, scientific research projects that have been launched in recent years. SETI@Home, for example, is a project in which home computer users donate overnight usage of their systems to search for signs of intelligent life beyond our planet. Special software recognizes times when the computer is idle and uses that time toward the project. Industry experts estimate that the SETI@Home project has amassed the effect of thousands of years of computing power, simply by harnessing idle PC processing time.

Recently, computer industry leaders have adapted the distributed computing technology for the business world by developing distributed computing software that allows the pooling and sharing of resources over the Net. Possible applications are limitless, but the more pragmatic ones include energy management and traffic control systems for large urban areas. In effect, companies create virtual organizations to share data and computing, as well as human brainpower and resources. The end result is enormous cost savings and skyrocketing productivity.

chapter summary

Application Software

Application software performs the types of activities and work that computers were designed for. **Individual application software** refers to programs used by individuals. **Vertical application software** is a complete package of programs for performing core business functions. **Workgroup application software** enables people at separate PC workstations to work together.

Commercial and Custom Programs

Commercial software refers to programs available for retail sale. **Proprietary software** is copyrighted software owned by a company or an individual. **Software piracy** involves the illegal copying or unauthorized use of copyrighted software. A **site license** provides multiple-user rights in a network environment. Software developed to meet special business needs is called **custom software**. **Shareware** is software available for a small "contribution" fee. **Freeware** is software provided for free.

Productivity Software

Productivity software is designed to improve efficiency and performance on the job. **Word processors** can be used to create almost any kind of printed document. **Desktop publishing (DTP) software** allows the creation of professional-looking printed documents. **Electronic spreadsheets** are programs that provide a means of organizing, calculating, and presenting financial, statistical, and other numeric information. A **database** is a collection of data organized in one or more tables containing **records**. A commercial database program usually allows users to create forms for entering data into a database. A **database management system (DBMS)** allows users to create and manage a computerized database and to create reports. A **relational database** allows tables to be linked in a way that allows data to be retrieved from more than one table. **Presentation graphics software** lets users create computerized **slide shows**. **Software suites** are software programs bundled and sold as a single package. **Project management software** assists with the management of various kinds of complex projects. **Computer-aided design (CAD) software** provides tools that enable professionals to create architectural, engineering, product, and scientific designs.

Software for Home and Personal Use

Many of the productivity programs used on the job are also used by individuals on their home computers. **Personal finance software** can help manage personal finances. **Tax preparation software** helps users prepare and transmit tax returns. **Legal software** is designed to analyze, plan, and prepare a variety of legal documents. **Entertainment software** refers to a large group of software programs that provide fun and often challenge users' thinking abilities as well.

Graphics Software

Graphics software consists of programs that allow users to create and modify graphical elements such as drawings and photos. Two types are **painting**

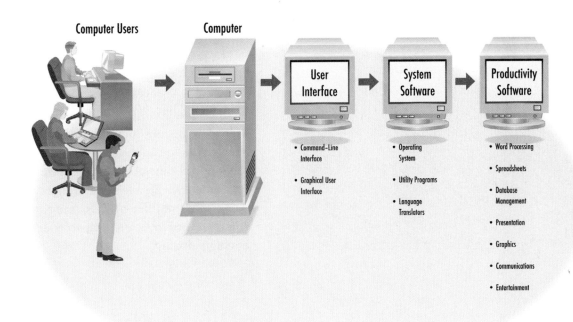

CHAPTER 5

programs and **image-editing programs**.

Educational and Reference Software

The widespread use of home computers has brought about an increase in the availability of educational and reference software. An **encyclopedia** is a comprehensive reference work containing articles on a broad range of subjects. A **dictionary** is a reference work containing an alphabetical listing of words, with information given for each word. A **tutorial** is a form of computerized instruction in which the student is guided step-by-step through the learning process.

Communications Software

One of the main purposes for which people use computers is to communicate with others and to retrieve and share information. **Electronic mail (e-mail)** is the transmission and receipt of messages over a worldwide system of communications networks. Web browsers allow users to move from one location to another on the Web, and to access and retrieve Web pages. **Search engines** find information located on Web sites. **Instant messaging (IM)** allows users to communicate with each other in real time. A **videoconference** is a conference between two or more participants at different sites, using computer networks and **videoconferencing software**.

KEYTERMS

cell, 220
chart, 221
clip art, 227
commercial software, 209
computer-aided design (CAD) software, 228
conversation speech biometrics, 240
custom program (customized software), 210
database, 221
database management system (DBMS), 222
desktop publishing (DTP) software, 216
dictionary, 234
distributed computing (grid computing) model, 241
drawing program, 232
educational and reference software, 234
electronic mail (e-mail), 237
electronic spreadsheet, 218
encyclopedia, 234
entertainment software, 231
field, 221
find, 224
formula, 218
freeware, 211
grammar checker, 215
grid, 220
groupware, 208
image-editing program, 233
individual application software, 208
instant messaging (IM), 239
knowbots, 207
legal software, 231
macro, 220
multipoint videoconferencing system, 239
natural-language processing (NLP), 241

object linking and embedding (OLE), 228
painting program, 232
personal finance software, 229
point-to-point videoconferencing system, 239
presentation graphics software, 225
productivity software, 212
project management software, 228
QBE (Query by Example), 225
query, 225
record, 221
relational database, 223
report, 225
shareware, 211
site license, 209
slide, 226
slide show, 225
software piracy, 209
software suite (integrated software), 227
sort, 224
spelling checker, 214
Structured Query Language (SQL), 225
style, 215
tax preparation software, 230
template, 214
tutorial, 234
value, 218
vertical application software, 208
videoconference, 239
videoconferencing software, 239
wizard, 226
word processing, 214
workgroup application software, 208

Page numbers indicate where terms are first cited in the chapter. A complete list of key terms with definitions can be found in the Glossary at the end of the book.

CHAPTER 5

chapter exercises

The following chapter exercises, along with new activities and information, are also offered in the *Computers: Understanding Technology* Internet Resource Center at www.emcp.com.

EXPLORING WINDOWS

Tutorial 5 focuses on using the My Computer feature of Windows to browse the contents of your computer drives.

TERMS CHECK: MATCHING

Write the letter of the correct answer on the line before each numbered item.

a. software piracy
b. database
c. software suite
d. legal software
e. word processors
f. proprietary software

g. presentation graphics software
h. tutorial
i. encyclopedia
j. productivity software
k. values
l. application software

_____ 1. A collection of data organized in one or more tables consisting of fields and records.

_____ 2. Software produced and owned by a business and offered for purchase or lease.

_____ 3. Data entered into cells in an electronic spreadsheet.

_____ 4. Software designed to enhance efficiency and performance in the workplace.

_____ 5. The illegal copying or unauthorized use of copyrighted software.

_____ 6. Software used to create documents such as wills, trusts, or rental contracts.

_____ 7. A software program used to create slide shows.

_____ 8. A broad category of software that allows users to perform tasks such as creating documents or preparing income tax returns.

_____ 9. The most widely used of all software applications.

_____ 10. A group of productivity programs bundled and sold as a single package.

_____ 11. A form of instruction in which students are guided step-by-step through the learning process.

_____ 12. A comprehensive reference work containing articles on a broad range of subjects.

TECHNOLOGY ILLUSTRATED: IDENTIFY THE PROCESS

What process is illustrated in this drawing? Identify the process and write a paragraph describing it.

No.	Make
101	Chevrolet
102	Ford
103	Buick
104	Chrysler

No.	Model
102	Taurus
102	Mustang
102	Thunderbird
102	F-150

No.	Color
102	Beige
102	Red
102	Green
102	Silver

KNOWLEDGE CHECK: MULTIPLE CHOICE

Circle the letter of the best answer from those provided.

1. Software that enables users to perform the types of activities and work computers were designed for is called

   a. working software.
   b. tutorial.
   c. system software.
   d. application software.

2. A group of software programs bundled into a single package is called

   a. combination software.
   b. a software suite.
   c. a special package.
   d. a software collection.

3. A method for incorporating files from one program into another within a suite of applications is called

    a. program assembling (PA).
    b. program linking (PL).
    c. incorporation.
    d. object linking and embedding (OLE).

4. Software available for a small "contribution fee" once the user tries the product and decides to continue using it is known as

    a. shareware.
    b. contribution ware.
    c. system software.
    d. developer ware.

5. Software designed to improve efficiency and performance at work is called

    a. system software.
    b. worker software.
    c. productivity software.
    d. user software.

6. Software used to create professional-quality publications is called

    a. a desktop publishing (DTP) program.
    b. a word processor.
    c. application software.
    d. print software.

7. A previously created and stored form is called a(n)

    a. user form.
    b. program form.
    c. electronic form.
    d. template.

8. A word processor editing feature that checks a document for common errors in grammar, usage, and mechanics is called a(n)

    a. spelling checker.
    b. grammar checker.
    c. English checker.
    d. syntax checker.

9. A visual representation of data that often makes it easier to read and understand is a

   a. monitor screen.
   b. document.
   c. spreadsheet.
   d. chart.

10. The transmission and receipt of messages over a worldwide system of communications networks is called

    a. e-mail (electronic mail).
    b. file transfer.
    c. telnet.
    d. electronic communication.

11. Software versions of the ruled worksheets accountants used in the past are called

    a. accounting software.
    b. worksheet software.
    c. electronic spreadsheets.
    d. financial software.

12. A collection of data organized in one or more tables consisting of fields and records is known as a(n)

    a. electronic spreadsheet.
    b. raw data.
    c. composite information.
    d. database.

13. A comprehensive reference work containing detailed articles covering a broad range of subjects is a(n)

    a. encyclopedia.
    b. dictionary.
    c. reference manual.
    d. database.

14. A communication method that enables people to communicate over the Internet with other users in real time is called

    a. real time processing.
    b. electronic telephoning.
    c. instant messaging.
    d. electronic messaging.

15. Software that allows people to share information and collaborate on various projects, such as developing a new product, is called

    a. collaboration software.
    b. groupware.
    c. shareware.
    d. developmental software.

THINGS THAT THINK: BRAINSTORMING NEW USES

In groups or individually, contemplate the following questions and develop as many answers as you can.

1. Many application software programs feature wizards. Wizards assist with tasks by prompting users to enter data and then automatically performing the needed functions. Microsoft PowerPoint is one example of a program featuring wizards that guide users through the process of creating a slideshow. Discuss some of the software programs you are familiar with and come up with ideas for wizards that might make the software even more user-friendly. Are there any types of situations where you would not want a wizard to assist you? If so, describe them.

2. Encyclopedias have moved from the printed page to the electronic age in the space of less than ten years. Electronic encyclopedias offer extra features that the printed versions could not. Users can learn about subjects by watching videos, by viewing three-dimensional images, or by listening to sound or music. Another convenience is the ability to instantly view related material using hyperlinks. The same features can and are being used to develop electronic textbooks, and some industry observers predict that these features could someday make textbooks such as the one you are reading obsolete. Do you agree, or do you feel that textbooks still offer advantages that an electronic version might not? Support your answer with examples.

KEY PRINCIPLES: COMPLETION

Fill in the blanks with the appropriate words or phrases.

1. Programs created and sold to the public on a retail basis by software development companies such as Microsoft or Corel are known as

    _____.

2. The term _____ refers to the illegal copying or unauthorized use of copyrighted software.

3. The process of altering content of an existing document is called
   _____.

4. A set of commands that automates complex or repetitive actions is known as
   a(n) _____.

5. A program that allows the user to create and manage a computerized database,
   and to produce reports from stored data is a(n) _____.

6. _____ software makes it possible to create slide shows that
   combine text, numbers, graphics, sounds, and video.

7. _____ software is a sophisticated kind of software providing
   tools that enable professionals to create architectural, engineering, product,
   and scientific designs.

8. A _____ is a form of instruction in which students are guided
   step-by-step through the learning process.

9. _____ allows people on a network to share information and
   collaborate on various projects, such as designing a new product or preparing
   employee manuals.

10. A standard _____ is a reference work containing an alphabet-
    ical listing of words, with definitions that provide the word's meaning, pro-
    nunciation, and usage.

11. _____ software enables users to readily view how their money
    is being spent.

12. A _____ database allows tables to be linked in a way that
    allows data to be retrieved from more than one table.

13. Spreadsheets display numbers and text in columns and rows known as a matrix
    or _____.

14. Software provided without charge to anyone wanting to use it is called
    _____.

15. Two types of videoconference systems are _____ and
    _____.

TECH ARCHITECTURE: LABEL THE DRAWING

The figure below is a spreadsheet into which text and numerical data can be entered and calculations performed. Label each of the spreadsheet components as indicated.

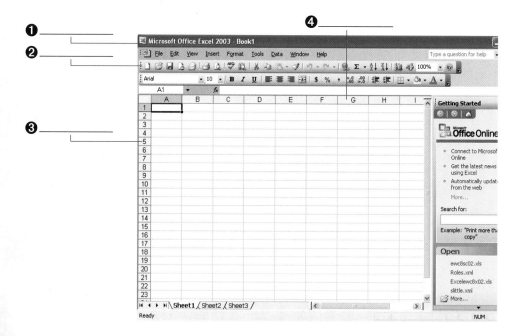

TECHNO LITERACY: RESEARCH AND WRITING

Develop appropriate written responses based on your research for each item.

1. Which program can improve my productivity?

   Visit a computer store in your area. Select a particular productivity program on display and read the product description on the package. What platform is the program written for? What is the price? Will the program run on your computer? For what purpose(s) might you be able to use the program?

2. What's hot in applications software?

   Visit your school library and look through computer magazines to find an article describing a new and innovative productivity software program. Write a summary describing the program's purpose, main features, and specifications. Include information about the user interface, the amount of internal memory needed to run the program, and the amount of disk space required to store the program. Why do you think this program is innovative? What needs does this product fulfill? Are there competing products on the market? Do you think the product will be a commercial success? Why or why not?

3. Is a picture worth a thousand words?

   Ask your instructor (or another person) for the name of a business or organization in your area that regularly uses presentation graphics software to train sales representatives or to provide information. Find out if you can obtain a copy of a presentation. Watch the slide show and then write an evaluation of its effectiveness. List the technologies used (hardware and software), and describe the features that impressed you most.

TECHNOLOGY ISSUES: TEAM PROBLEM-SOLVING
In groups, brainstorm possible solutions to the issues presented.

1. Instant messaging (IM) has become a popular communication tool in social situations and in the workplace. However, the IM software offered by AOL, Yahoo!, and MSN only allows people with the same software to communicate. For example, AOL IM users can only communicate with other AOL IM users. What would be the benefits to each of these companies if they opened up their software to allow communication with anyone using instant messaging? How might this change come about?

2. Thinking about the different types of application software discussed in this chapter, determine how you might use some of these programs to organize activities in your life. Identify three software programs you might use if you were planning a vacation. Why did you pick these programs? What aspects of vacation planning do each of the three application software programs support?

MINING DATA: INTERNET RESEARCH AND REPORTING
Conduct Internet searches to find the information described in the activities below. Write a brief report that summarizes your research results. Be sure to document your sources using the MLA format (see Chapter 1, page 43, to review MLA style guidelines).

1. The first "killer app" in the history of software development was Visicalc, an early calculation program that is credited with founding the electronic spreadsheet software industry and launching widespread sales of the personal computer. Research the meaning of the term "killer app" and propose some possibilities for the next one. Explain the reasons for your choice.

2. Explore the topic of grid computing. What kinds of applications are being planned by IBM, Microsoft, and Sun Microsystems? Are some types of industries better suited than others for using grid computing? Does the size of a company make a difference?

TECHNOLOGY TIMELINE: PREDICTING NEXT STEPS
The timeline below features some of the key milestones in the evolution of encyclopedias from printed books to digital content. Thinking about the increase in information available and the rapid growth in computing technologies, predict two additional milestones in the encyclopedia marketplace that are likely to occur within the next 20 years.

1771   The first *Encyclopaedia Britannica* was printed

1917   The first *World Book Encyclopedia* was published

1981   The first digital version of *Encyclopaedia Britannica* was created for the Lexis-Nexis service

1993   Microsoft announces the availability of the first release of the *Encarta* online encyclopedia on CD-ROM

1994   *Encyclopaedia Britannica* is made available on the Internet on CD-ROM

1998   The complete *World Book Online* Web site is launched

2001   A multilingual encyclopedia called *Wikipedia* is launched and supported in an "open source" model

ETHICAL DILEMMAS: GROUP DISCUSSION AND DEBATE
As a class or within an assigned group, discuss the following ethical dilemma.

When software is downloaded from the Internet and installed on a personal computer, there is a possibility that it contains spyware. Spyware is software that gathers information through an Internet connection without a user's knowledge. Some of the information commonly gathered includes a user's keystrokes, hardware configuration, Internet configuration, data from the user's hard drive, and data from cookies. Typically, this information is gathered and sent to the spyware author, who then uses it for advertising purposes or sells the information to another party.

Do you consider this to be an invasion of privacy? Should it be illegal to include spyware inside another software program? What if the software license agreement includes a disclaimer that says that spyware may be installed? Is it harmless if the information is just being gathered for market research? What other problems do you see with this technology? Can you think of any ways to protect Internet users from spyware?

ANSWERS TO TERMS CHECK AND KEY PRINCIPLES QUESTIONS

Terms Check: 1 – b; 2 – f; 3 – k; 4 – j; 5 – a; 6 – d; 7 – g; 8 – l; 9 – e; 10 – c; 11 – h; 12 – i

Key Principles: 1 – commercial software; 2 – software piracy; 3 – editing; 4 – macro; 5 – database management system (DBMS); 6 – presentation graphics; 7 – computer-aided design (CAD); 8 – tutorial; 9 – groupware; 10 – dictionary; 11 – personal finance; 12 – relational; 13 – grid; 14 – freeware; 15 – point-to-point, multipoint

Computer Ethics

Ethics are the rules we use to determine the right and wrong things to do in our lives. Most ethical beliefs are learned during childhood and are derived from our family, society, or religious tradition. Ethics are not the same as laws or regulations. Ethics are internalized principles that influence the decisions we make, whereas laws are external rules, the violation of which is punishable by society.

The Origin of Ethics

In many societies, ethics are based on what is thought to be God's, or a Supreme Being's, will. Another view alleges that ethics are based on eternal laws of unknown origin that do not change. Both of these ethical viewpoints fall under the **moral realism** school of ethical thought, which holds that ethical principles have objective foundations; that is, they are not based on subjective human reasoning.

Still other philosophers claim that ethics differ from society to society, from person to person, and from situation to situation. This school of ethical thought is known as **moral relativism**, also referred to as **situational ethics**. Most ethical belief systems are based on one of these two schools of thought, or sometimes a mixture of these beliefs.

In many societies, ethics derive from religious beliefs and traditions.

Normative and Applied Ethics

The study of ethics can be divided into two main categories: normative ethics and applied ethics. **Normative ethics** involves determining a standard or "norm" of ethical rule that underlies ethical behavior. **Applied ethics** refers to the application of normative ethical beliefs to controversial real-life issues. For example, while most cultures believe it is wrong to steal, some people may believe that the stealing of food by a starving person is ethically acceptable.

What Are Computer Ethics?

New technologies always create ethical dilemmas because they allow humans to act in new and unforeseen ways. Computer technology poses numerous ethical dilemmas. The adapting of traditional ethical thought and behavior to these issues has resulted in new interpretations of the old rules and has led to the formation of a new branch of applied ethics called **computer ethics**.

COMPUTER ETHICS: ISSUES

Early computers were large mainframe devices maintained by a team of engineers and programmers. Ethical decision-making regarding these large computers and their capabilities was limited to the few people involved in designing and using the machines.

Computer technology has advanced rapidly. Today, more than half of all U.S. households have at least one personal computer. The widespread availability of personal computers and the Internet means that millions of people are now faced with the ethical responsibilities inherent in controlling a powerful technology.

Three categories of ethical issues that have emerged with the evolution of computer technology are privacy protection issues, property protection issues, and personal and social issues. **Privacy protection** issues are issues involving the use and abuse of personal information. **Property protection** issues are those involving the use and abuse of property. **Personal and social issues** are those involving issues of personal morality or beliefs.

PRIVACY PROTECTION ISSUES

Individuals want to keep certain personal and financial information private. In our society, we realize there are times when we need to reveal personal information, such as when we apply for a job, a loan, or a credit card. Most people are willing to reveal information if it is absolutely necessary, but they expect that this information will remain confidential.

Unfortunately, the privacy that many people traditionally have taken for granted is being eroded as computer technology facilitates the gathering and transfer of information. In fact, any communication over the Internet makes us increasingly vulnerable to monitoring and data-gathering activities that can compromise our privacy. The cumulative effect of many different methods of gathering, processing, and sharing personal information can be disastrous, especially if the data it falls into the wrong hands.

A controversial privacy issue concerns the use of publicly available data. A wide range of personal information has always been available through pub-

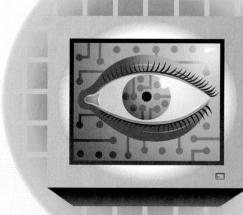

Sending information over the Internet is fast and easy, but it also makes users vulnerable to monitoring and data-gathering activities that compromise individual privacy.

lic records, such as birth records, drivers' licenses, and more. This information was scattered across a wide range of jurisdictions and often stored in dusty record books. Now, database companies have created electronic databases that can provide this information to anyone with access to the Web. Many people are worried this information may be misused.

Commercial Threats To Privacy

One of the key threats to privacy comes from electronic commerce activities. Since the earliest days of e-commerce, users have expressed serious concern about the potential abuse of personal data entered at Web sites. Buyers must provide certain information to pay for the goods or services purchased over the Internet. Many commercial sites also seek information about consumer preferences or buying habits. Once entered on the Internet, personal information can be used to create **consumer profiles** containing information about lifestyle and buying habits that marketers use to target potential customers and to sell their goods. New tracking technologies allow organizations to gather personal data without the permission or knowledge of consumers.

Cookies

One of the most controversial of tracking technologies is the cookie. **Cookies** are small programs placed on a user's computer hard drive by Web sites possessing this technology. Persistent cookies can remember passwords, User IDs, and user preferences and can automatically customize a site to those preferences during repeat visits. To accomplish this, cookies record information about the user's IP address, browser, computer operating system, and URLs visited.

Global Unique Identifiers

Another tracking technology with potential for misuse is the Global Unique Identifier (GUID). **GUIDs** are identification numbers that can be coded into both hardware and software, thereby eliminating any anonymity now enjoyed by Internet users. If GUID use becomes widespread, it will always be possible to track down the originators of unpopular or controversial messages or ideas, which will deal a severe blow to Internet privacy.

Cell Phones and Handheld Computers

A third type of technology that threatens personal privacy and can be used for tracking an individual's transactions or location is the cell phone and the handheld computer. Experts predict that in the near future, most people will conduct routine activities such as banking, paying bills, and shopping on the Web from a tiny chip embedded in a cell phone, or other portable device. Ever more powerful devices may be able to contain a person's credit card numbers, social security information, health records, and more. Wireless devices are extremely vulnerable to interception by others, partly because they transmit data into the air where anyone may intercept it.

Protection from Commercial Threats to Privacy

Consumer demands for privacy protection have led to several different kinds of responses in both the public and private sectors. Three types of responses are industry self-regulation, government regulation, and consumer self-protection.

Industry Self-Regulation

Seeking to allay consumer privacy concerns, many commercial Web sites have adopted privacy state-ments. A **privacy statement** promises that an e-tailer will protect the confidentiality of any information revealed by a customer. However, some privacy advocates claim that industry self-regulation is insufficient, and incidents such as online retailer ToySmart's attempt in 2000 to sell its customer database in violation of its privacy statement demonstrate that privacy statement promises cannot always be trusted.

Government Regulation

Passing new laws that protect consumer privacy has increasingly been viewed as the answer to the alleged failure of the Internet commerce industry to safeguard users. A number of bills to protect consumer privacy have been proposed at both the state and federal levels, but only one major piece of federal legislation has yet been passed. The Children's Online Privacy Protection Act (COPPA) of 1998 became effective on April 21, 2000. This act prohibits the gathering and sharing of personal data about children without parental permission.

Much of the debate over privacy legislation concerns whether or not consumers should have the right to choose to receive cookies or to not receive cookies. Industry advocates prefer the opt-out (not-to-receive) feature, while privacy advocates worry that many consumers may not possess the computer skills to select that option.

Consumer Self-Protection

You can take a number of steps to reduce the likelihood of your personal privacy being violated. *First,* make sure you conduct e-commerce transactions only on sites protected by encryption programs, such as Secure Sockets Layer (SSL). *Second,* look for sites with privacy statements and read them carefully to see what protection the site offers. Sites that pledge compliance to third-party privacy programs offer a higher level of security. *Third,* set your browser to either warn you when cookies are going to be placed on the hard drive or to reject them altogether. You can install a soft-

Protect your privacy by shopping online only on secure sites and never provide more information than is absolutely necessary.

ware program that allows you to accept or reject them as you see fit. *Finally,* never volunteer more information than is absolutely necessary to complete an e-commerce transaction. Providing details about your lifestyle, habits, interests, or shopping preferences only increases the chance that this information will be passed on to third parties for marketing purposes.

Government Threats to Privacy

Organized crime groups routinely use the Internet to conduct their activities. The FBI believes interception of these transmissions is essential. In order to monitor e-mail messages, the FBI developed an Internet wiretap program called **Carnivore**, later renamed DCS1000. According to the FBI, Carnivore has the ability to intercept communications while ignoring messages it is not authorized to intercept. While many people understand the FBI's concerns, some critics believe government agencies themselves need careful policing to ensure that they do not invade the privacy of innocent citizens.

Workplace Threats to Privacy

Some employers use special software programs that monitor workers' behavior and read messages sent and received by employees. Many employees find this kind of monitoring demeaning, and they question their employer's right to do it, yet there are no laws preventing electronic surveillance of employees in the workplace.

While at work, employees are using company property, and the company has the right to monitor the use of that property. Employers insist they are justified in such snooping in order to prevent employees from engaging in activities that could result in liability for the company. However, if a company has pledged to respect employee privacy, it must keep that pledge.

PROPERTY PROTECTION ISSUES

The convenience provided by linking computers through the Internet also creates some drawbacks. Computer viruses can travel around the world in seconds, damaging programs and files. Hackers can enter into systems without authorization and steal, alter, and even destroy data. In addition, the wealth of information on the Web and the increased ease with which it can be copied have made it simple for people to plagiarize. **Plagiarism** is using others' ideas and creations (their **intellectual property**) without permission.

Intellectual Property

Intellectual property includes just about anything that can be created by the human mind. To encourage innovation and thus benefit society as a whole, our legal system awards patents to those who invent new and better ways of doing things. A **patent** assigns ownership of an idea or invention to its creator for a fixed number of years. To encourage and protect artistic and literary endeavors, authors and artists are granted **copyrights** to the material they create, allowing them the right to control the use of their works. Patent and copyright violation is punishable by law, and prosecutions and convictions are frequent. A recent and major threat to intellectual property rights posed by the Internet is the downloading of music, which was pioneered by the Napster Web site. Napster allowed computer users to share MP3 files, a digital file format for musical recordings. In a 2001 court ruling, the company's actions were ruled illegal. The issue remains alive, however, as lawmakers and the recording industry struggle to define a fair, enforceable policy.

The Internet makes it easy to access and copy written works, photos, and artwork that may be copyrighted, and wholesale copying is illegal. However, it is legal to use a limited amount of another person's written material without permission as long as this use is acknowledged (cited), is for noncommercial purposes, and involves excerpts of no more than 300 words of prose or one line of poetry. This right is called **fair use** and is dealt with under the U.S. Copyright Act, Section 107.

Damage Due to Hacking and Viruses

Hackers who break into computer networks and Web sites have a direct effect on personal computer users. A major danger associated with hacking is **identity theft**, which is the theft of personal credit card information and other private data. The hacker then uses the victim's personal data to apply for additional credit cards, a driver's license, and so on. Then comes the spending spree, and the victim ends up with a long list of unexpected bills.

Viruses can damage a user's computer or the software running on it. A virus must enter a computer disguised in another file (usually an e-mail attachment), which may be downloaded from the Internet. Viruses may also reside on disks or CDs and even on legitimate copies of software programs direct from manufacturers.

Protection from Hacking and Viruses

The best way to avoid viruses is to never open an e-mail attachment from an unknown source. The second strategy is to install an antivirus program, which, when activated, seeks out and destroys any known viruses found on a computer. To keep up with the proliferation of new viruses, you need to continually update the antivirus software by downloading new program versions from the software company's Web site.

FREEDOM OF SPEECH AND OTHER PERSONAL AND SOCIAL ISSUES

The Internet contains material that would not be allowed in many jurisdictions if it were received by more traditional means, such as paper mail or TV. Examples of these types of materials are sites featuring pornography or hate speech.

Pornography Sites

Pornography is material containing sexually explicit images or language deemed unacceptable by society. Because people differ in their feelings toward sexuality, no universal agreement exists as to material that is acceptable and material that constitutes pornography.

Adult pornography on the Internet is available with few if any restrictions and is unwelcome in

To avoid viruses, never open an e-mail attachment from an unknown source and install an antivirus program.

many homes. Even those who do not find pornography disturbing generally agree that it should not be viewed by children or certain vulnerable adults.

Hate Speech Sites

The freedom of speech guaranteed by the Constitution of the United States allows great latitude in what a person can say. Consequently, a great number of Web sites contain written material that many find offensive. This includes material inciting hatred against people of certain races, religions, or beliefs, and material calling for the overthrow of the government. Some hate speech sites use foul or inappropriate language, and some even post material that may be dangerous, such as information on making drugs or explosives.

Legislation against Internet Pornography

Although to date few if any real restrictions on adult pornography on the Internet have been put in place, strict legislation does forbid the use of children in pornography on the Internet. A series of federal laws, the most recent being the Child Pornographic Prevention Act of 1996, enact harsh penalties for that distributing or possessing child pornography. Despite tougher enforcement, however, the anonymous nature of the Internet makes the legal battle against pornography on the Internet exceedingly difficult.

Self-Protection From Unwanted Material

The freedom of speech guaranteed by the United States Constitution has been interpreted as protecting both acceptable and unacceptable expressions. Unless a Web site contains material that overtly and directly threatens the livelihood or well-being of an individual, a group, or the government, it enjoys protection as free speech.

For computer users, the best protection against offensive or unwanted material on the Internet is just to avoid it. If you happen to stumble across material that is pornographic or disturbing in any way, merely click the Back button on your browser

and leave the offending site. One way parents and guardians can protect themselves and their dependents from pornographic or hate speech Web sites is by the use of filtering software. **Filtering programs** can perform a number of helpful functions. They can prevent access to sites, keep track of sites visited, limit connection time, and preventing downloading. In 2000, Congress passed the Children's Internet Protection Act (CIPA), which requires public schools and libraries to install Internet filtering software. Many schools also adopt Acceptable Use Policies to guide users and administrators about Internet use.

The Digital Divide

Not everyone in the world enjoys the privileges made possible by modern digital technologies. Even within developed nations, access to digital technology is not evenly distributed. The gap between those who have access to computers and the Internet and those who do not has been called the **digital divide**.

In the United States and around the world, Internet access varies widely among communities. Wide disparities in Internet access and usage exist between Caucasian Americans, Hispanic Americans, and African Americans and between lower-income and more affluent families, men and women, rural and urban communities, and the disabled and nondisabled populations.

When viewed globally, the digital divide is striking. According to a 2001 United Nations Human Development Report, people in industrialized countries constitute only 15 percent of the world's population, but comprise 80 percent of all Internet users. In South Asia, a mere 1 percent of the population has Internet access.

Software Producers' Responsibilities

Software makers are protected by copyright legislation. But what rights do software makers themselves owe to the people who use their software programs? Bad software costs United States businesses an estimated $100 billion in lost productivity annually.

Every day computer users around the world experience problems attributed to poor software design.

In their defense, software programmers point out that their software must interact with a number of other software programs and hardware systems, any one of which may cause problems due to incompatibility. While they try to ensure that their programs work well and are compatible with connecting software and hardware, it is impossible to guarantee 100 percent reliability. Critics, however, respond that many companies simply refuse to do enough to eliminate programming errors.

Protection from Poorly Designed Software

If software does not perform according to the manufacturer's promise, a simple protection is to ask for a refund. Many stores have generous refund policies, and a consumer's right to return goods is protected by the Uniform Commercial Code. This code contains language covering buyers' rights and allowing buyers to reject any product, "if the goods or the tender of delivery fail in any respect to conform to the contract." But this protection covers only the right to return the product for a refund. In cases where actual damages are suffered due to the software, victims must pursue redress through the legal system by filing suit. Legal measures only address the unfortunate results of poor software design. In reality, the best protection against software problems is for software manufacturers and designers to produce better software programs in the first place.

Accessibility

An estimated 30 million Americans suffer from some sort of disability. As the American population ages, this number will certainly increase. People with certain disabilities may be unable to use computers and the Internet.

Some problems faced by many handicapped persons involve the use of computer hardware. Individuals with motor impairment or missing limbs, for example, cannot use a mouse or a conventional keyboard. Persons with visual impairments may experience difficulty viewing their monitors unless their screen is capable of enlarged displays.

Improving Accessibility

Disabled Americans have been active in asserting their right to improved accessibility to computer

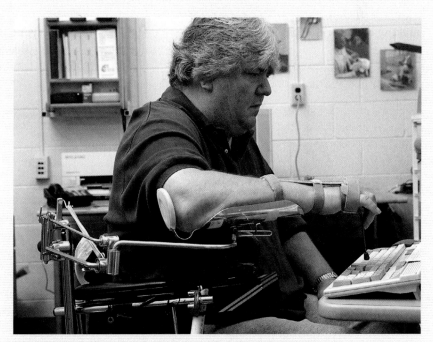

A key pusher attached to an arm brace enables this user to type on a computer.

technology and efforts are underway to make computing devices and software more accessible for physically impaired individuals.

The disabled and their supporters point out that incorporating features making computers and the Internet accessible to the disabled makes sense financially. Improving access to computers and the Internet will increase the number of potential customers for these goods and services.

NBEA Computer Education Task Force Code of Ethics for Information Systems

1. Intellectual Property:

Users must respect intellectual property. This includes not copying copyrighted materials belonging to a business, educational institution, or another individual.

Users may not copy their own software or another user's copyrighted materials to the institution's computers nor give the copyrighted software to others to copy.

Users may not without proper authorization modify or reconfigure software on the institutions' computers.

2. Computers and Computer Labs in Educational Institutions:

Users with proper authorization may use computer labs and may access only the areas granted in the authorization. For example, if one is granted access to certain software applications but decides to access some other area, such as the Internet, he or she is in violation of the stated policy.

Users may not use another person's password to gain access to areas not authorized for that individual nor disclose a password belonging to someone else.

Users will not intentionally modify individual computer hard drives or networks without the stated permission of the institution's proper authority.

Users will respect the security of the institution's computers or computer networks. Users will not:

• Download materials onto the institution's hard drives or network drives without permission from the designated authority.
• Create their own special areas on any computer or network without permission from the designated authority.
• Read, alter, or delete another person's computer and electronic files.
• Copy another individual's work and pass it on as his/her own.
• Create, install, or knowingly distribute a computer virus.
• Violate the institution's policies or willfully treat the computer in such a manner that would cause the computer to crash.

Users will take full responsibility for all messages they transmit and will in no way transmit communications on the institution's computer that are considered fraudulent, defamatory, harassing, obscene, or threatening.

System administrators will perform their duties fairly, in cooperation with the user community, respecting the privacy of users as far as possible, and will refer to proper authorities those who are in violation of the institution's policies.

This code of ethics was developed by the NBEA Computer Education Task Force. Although it targets computer use in educational institutions, it may easily be applied to personal and business computer use as well.

THE NEED FOR PERSONAL ETHICAL GUIDELINES

Computers and the Internet are very powerful tools. With a few taps on a keyboard, users have the ability to do good or to create great damage. A doctor can use the Internet to diagnose a patient many miles away. Companies can use the Internet to sell products and services around the world. Every day, users benefit by being able to use e-mail to contact friends and relatives and conduct business. On the other hand, computer technology can be used to spread damaging viruses, to break into computer networks in order to steal or damage material, to use copyrighted material unlawfully, to spread hatred and promote violence, and to create numerous other problems for society.

What can be done to prevent unethical behavior on computers and the Internet? Certainly, laws can be passed to punish the most egregious violations.

But legislation is never the only, or even an adequate, answer to ethical dilemmas. Rather, sound ethical principles must begin with the individual. For starters, all computer users should be aware of the power of a computer. They should understand its capacity for good or harm, and they should realize the societal and personal consequences of perpetrating illegal or harmful behaviors with computers. Moreover, they should read, think about, and consider adapting for their own use one of several computer codes of ethics or acceptable use policies put forward by computer professional organizations, libraries, and schools. One such code is displayed above.

In the rapidly evolving world of computer technology, it is unlikely that a consensus will ever be reached on a single ethical code for the computer industry. Still, all users should consider it a point of personal integrity to use computers and the Internet ethically at all times.

CHAPTER

TELECOMMUNICATIONS
AND NETWORKS

6

UNDERSTANDING TECHNOLOGY

learning objectives

- Explain the role of telecommunications in the operations of networks and the Internet

- Describe the characteristics of data transmission

- Identify the kinds of wired and wireless media and explain how they are used

- Compare the major network classifications and discuss their functions

- Define network topology and discuss the four principal types

- Describe communications protocols and explain their functions in data communications

key concepts

- Using Telecommunications Systems to Connect to the Internet

- Communications Media

- Network Classifications

- Network Topologies

- Network and Communications Hardware and Software

- Communications Software and Protocols

CYBER SCENARIO

Standing in front of his partially completed new home, Steve Rodriguez pictures the day it is finished and imagines the excitement of moving in. His dream house is halfway to becoming a reality—on time, and better yet, at a cost nearly 30 percent less than he originally estimated. What accounts for the extraordinary savings?

The remarkable cost savings in constructing Steve's new home are a direct result of using a collaborative project management software application accessed over the Internet. This Web tool links the builder, the contractors, the materials manufacturers, and all vendors—plus the customer—at a central information site where the progress and vision of the project are apparent at all times.

Significant savings are achieved using collaborative project management software because builders can order materials and have them delivered on the day they are needed, a concept called "just in time." They also can assign contractors to jobs in the most time-effective manner, as related phases of the work are completed. For example, the heating and air conditioning systems installer is scheduled and called immediately after the carpenter finishes framing the house—not too soon, and not a day too late.

According to a report by Bank of America Securities, 33 percent of the money spent on residential construction is lost because of backlogs, delays, and scheduling errors. A contractor might show up to complete a plumbing or heating project, only to find that the site is not ready. Time lost is money lost.

Another efficiency collaborative project management software affords is the capability of ordering construction materials online, directly from manufacturers, a factor further lowering expenses. Instant messaging among all project partners means problems can be addressed in real-time. Team members confer with each other using a variety of Web-enabled hardware, including desktop PCs, cell phones, and handheld Palm Pilots or Handspring Visors. Even vendors not officially part of the project can be granted access to the site on an as-needed basis.

NETWORKING OVER THE WEB

In Chapter 1 you learned that sharing information among computers is made possible by linking computers together in a network, and that the Internet is a worldwide network of networks. Additionally, you learned that the World Wide Web is a global system of computer networks that allows users to move (jump) from one Web site to another Web site. This worldwide linkage of computers enables users to communicate and work together efficiently and effectively.

Working together over the Web highlights the value of networks, especially the power and promise of the largest network in the world—the Internet. For years companies have managed projects by communicating over their internal networks. Expanding the process to include all of the companies involved in a project is a major new direction, prompted by the increased outsourcing of projects and enabled by the growth of the Internet.

Different types of online collaborative project management software offering many of the features mentioned above are available, such as eRoom® 5.0 by Documentum. A more futuristic version of the technology is called CAVE (computer automatic virtual environment), a product that lets participants at different locations inhabit the same virtual space on the Internet. Rather than requiring user input, the software tracks each participant's actions and automatically and continually updates them on-screen. Moving this networking technology from leading-edge to mainstream status will require continuing improvements in hardware, in software, and in the speed of today's telecommunications systems.

TELECOMMUNICATIONS: CONNECTING NETWORKS TO THE INTERNET

Computers were originally stand-alone devices, incapable of communicating with other computers. This situation changed with the development of special telecommunications hardware and software in the 1970s and 1980s that led to the creation of the first private networks, allowing connected computers to exchange data. Data could take the form of a request for information, a reply to a request from another computer, or an instruction to run a program stored on the network.

Telecommunications originally referred to the sending and receiving of information over telephone lines. As telecommunications systems evolved, the term was broadened to include other types of media used to transmit data, including satellite systems, microwave towers, and wireless devices such as cell phones. Figure 6-1 illustrates the basic concept of telecommunications.

NETWORKING COMPONENTS

Recall that a network consists of two or more computers, devices, and software connected by means of one or more communications media, such as wires or telephone lines. These wires and telephone lines form the fundamental part of a network—the channel or medium through which data bits and bytes are transmitted. Because communications media are basic to networking, it is helpful to begin the study of networks by exploring the process of data transmission and the different types of media used to send data across networks.

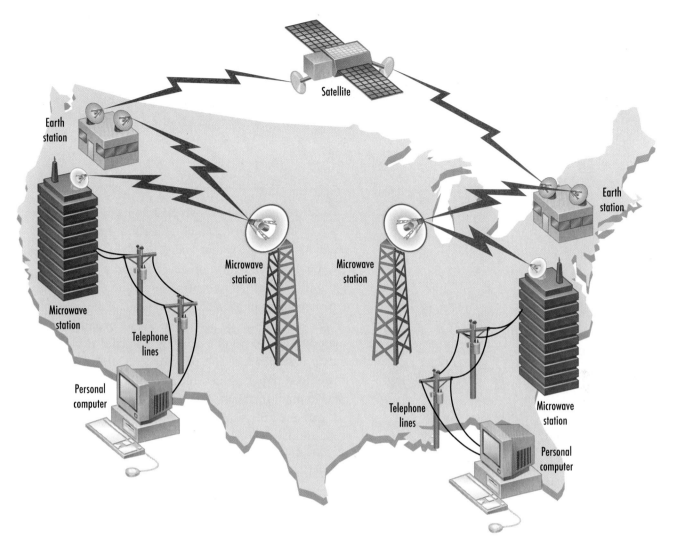

F I G U R E   6 - 1 : Telecommunications, the combined use of computer hardware and communications software for sending and receiving information over communications media, makes it possible for computer users throughout the world to communicate.

DATA TRANSMISSION CHARACTERISTICS

The transmission of data over computer networks is characterized by

- bandwidth (rate of transmission)
- analog or digital (type of signal)
- parallel or serial (order of bits)

Bandwidth

Data is transferred from one computer to another in digital form (1s and 0s), known as bits. In a network, the number of bits that can be transferred per second over a given medium is known as **bandwidth**. The basic measurement of bandwidth is **bits per second (bps)**. Table 6-1 lists common incremental measurements of bandwidth.

Bandwidth varies among different types of communications media. To understand bandwidth, consider the difference in the amount of traffic that can be

Abbreviation	Term	Meaning
1 Kbps	1 kilobit per second	1 thousand bits per second
1 Mbps	1 megabit per second	1 million bits per second
1 Gbps	1 gigabit per second	1 billion bits per second
1 Tbps	1 terabit per second	1 trillion bits per second

T A B L E 6 - 1 : Measurement of Bandwidth

handled per hour by a two-lane highway compared to a four-lane highway. The broader four-lane highway can handle more traffic than a two-lane highway, just as broader bandwidth media can handle greater volumes of data than narrower bandwidths. A communications medium capable of carrying a large amount of data at faster speeds is referred to as a **broadband medium**, whereas one carrying a smaller amount of data at slower speeds is referred to as a **narrowband medium**. Fiber-optic cable is an example of a broadband medium; twisted-pair cable, commonly used in telephone lines, is an example of a narrowband medium.

Bandwidth can be an important factor in choosing a communications medium. Broadband media are more suitable when large amounts of data need to be transmitted quickly, such as with high-quality sound and video transmission. When only small amounts of data need to be transmitted and transmission time is less important, such as for simple text transmission, narrowband media may be suitable. Price is always a consideration, as more bandwidth is costly.

Analog and Digital Transmission

Telephone systems were established to carry voice transmissions using analog signals. **Analog signals** are composed of continuous waves transmitted over a medium at a certain **frequency range**, which is the number of complete fluctuations in energy per sound wave. Changes in the wave transmissions reflect changes in voice and sound **pitch**, or tone, as shown in Figure 6-2. In addition to telephone lines, most cellular networks, cable television systems, and satellite dishes use analog communications media for carrying voice and sound transmissions.

Computers cannot understand data in analog form. Instead, computers use the binary number system to transform data into digital signals. Newer communications technologies generally employ digital signals.

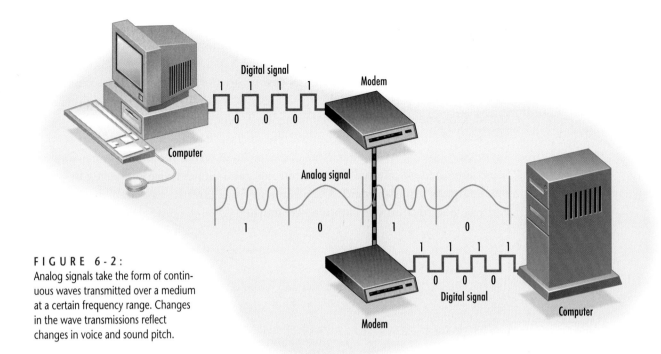

FIGURE 6-2:
Analog signals take the form of continuous waves transmitted over a medium at a certain frequency range. Changes in the wave transmissions reflect changes in voice and sound pitch.

Modems

Whenever digital data is sent from one computing device to another over an analog communications medium, such as a telephone line, both the sending and receiving devices must be equipped with a modem.

Modems convert digital signals into analog form so an analog communications medium can send those signals. Modems also convert incoming analog signals back to their digital equivalents so computers can receive those signals (see Figure 6-3). Some newer modems are able to transmit and receive digital data without analog conversion, provided they are connected to the right communications media.

The term "modem" is derived from the words **mo**dulate and **dem**odulate. Modulation refers to the process of changing a digital signal into an analog signal, while demodulation refers to the process of changing an analog signal into a digital

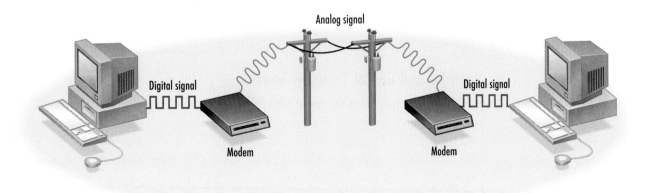

FIGURE 6-3: Modems convert digital signals into analog form so that an analog communications medium, such as a telephone line, can send those signals. Modems also convert incoming analog signals back to their digital equivalents so computers can receive those signals.

signal. Most personal computers use a type of modem called a **dial-up modem**, which can dial a telephone number, establish a connection, and close the connection when it is no longer needed.

Modems can be internal or external (see Figure 6-4). An **internal modem** is an electronic board (card) inserted into an expansion slot on a computer's motherboard. One end of a standard telephone line is plugged into the modem port and the other end into a telephone outlet. The advantage of an internal modem is that it does not take up space on a user's desktop. An **external modem** operates in the same fashion as an internal modem, but is a stand-alone device connected by cable to a computer's motherboard. The advantage of an external modem is that it can easily be moved from one computer to another.

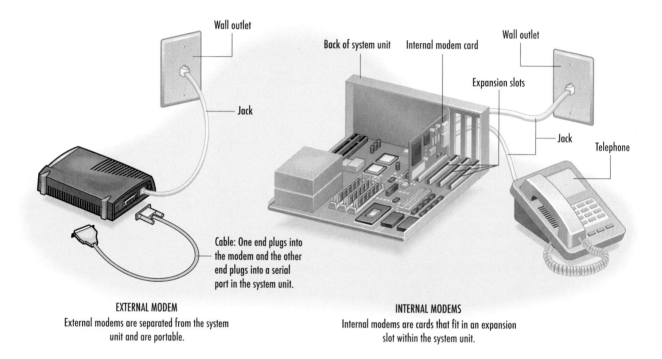

EXTERNAL MODEM
External modems are separated from the system
unit and are portable.

INTERNAL MODEMS
Internal modems are cards that fit in an expansion
slot within the system unit.

F I G U R E   6 - 4 :   An internal modem is an electronic board plugged into a slot on a computer's motherboard. An external modem is a stand-alone device connected by cable to a computer.

Notebook and other portable computers use **PCMCIA modems** (**P**ersonal **C**omputer **M**emory **C**ard **I**nternational **A**ssociation) that insert into a PCMCIA slot. The modem is connected to a telephone outlet using a standard telephone line. Mobile users without access to standard telephone outlets can use a special cable to connect the PCMCIA modem to a cellular phone.

Parallel and Serial Transmission

Recall that peripheral devices are typically connected to the system unit of a personal computer by means of a cable, one end of which is plugged into the device and the other end plugged into a port, or interface, on the system unit. Also, recall that an add-on board, such as an internal modem, contains a port that allows a computer to be connected to a medium, such as a telephone line.

Most computers are equipped with two types of ports: parallel and serial. A parallel cable is needed to connect a device to a parallel port, whereas a serial cable is needed to connect a device to a serial port. Many peripheral devices, including printers and mice, may be either parallel or serial.

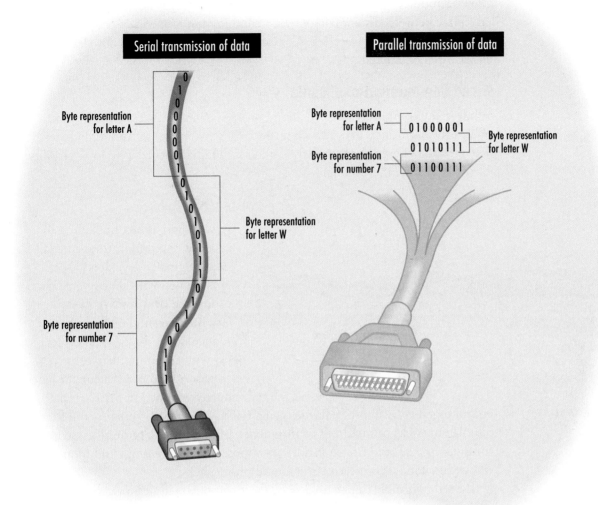

Serial transmission of data	Parallel transmission of data

Byte representation for letter A

Byte representation for letter W

Byte representation for number 7

Byte representation for letter A — 0 1 0 0 0 0 0 1

0 1 0 1 0 1 1 1 — Byte representation for letter W

Byte representation for number 7 — 0 1 1 0 0 1 1 1

Data travels within a computer system and over long distances in either parallel or serial form. During transmission, 8 bits (representing a single byte) plus 1 bit called a parity bit are transmitted. A **parity bit** is an extra bit added to a byte, character, or word to ensure there is always either a predetermined even or odd number of bits and therefore an accurate transmission. The parity bit also indicates the end of the 8-bit byte. In **parallel transmission**, 8 bits (a byte) plus a parity bit are transmitted at the same time over 9 separate paths. In **serial transmission**, the byte plus the parity bit are transmitted one bit after another in a continuous line. Thus, parallel transmission is generally faster than serial transmission. Serial and parallel transmissions are compared in Figure 6-5. A modem that connects the system unit to a telephone line contains a serial port because the telephone line expects the data being transmitted to be in serial form. Serial ports are designed and built according to either the RS-232 or RS-422 standard, which specifies the number of pins required for the port's connector. Two common connectors for serial ports are a 9-pin connector and a 25-pin connector.

FIGURE 6-5: In serial transmission, all the data bits are transmitted one bit after another in a continuous line. In parallel transmission, a group of 8 bits (1 byte) plus a parity bit are transmitted at the same time over nine separate paths.

COMMUNICATIONS MEDIA

Users must have access to communications media to communicate between computing devices. A **communications medium** is a physical link (a connection) that allows computers in different locations to be connected. When communications take place between distant computers, a combination of media may be used, some of which the user may never see. Communications media are broadly classified as either wired or wireless.

Wired Communications Media

While many computers, devices, and networks now use wireless technologies, many others continue to use wired technologies as a means of communicating. The medium chosen depends mainly on user requirements relating to availability, cost, speed, and other factors.

Twisted-Pair Cable

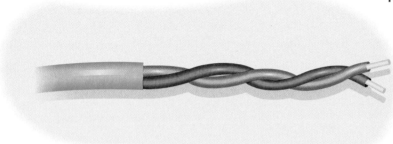

FIGURE 6-6:
Twisted-Pair Cable

Twisted-pair cable, one of the older types of communications media, was originally developed for telephone networks. Early versions consisted of wires wrapped (twisted) around one another to reduce noise. Today such cables used with computer networks typically consist of two parallel copper wires, each individually wrapped in plastic and bound together by another plastic casing (see Figure 6-6). The pairs are often bundled in packs of hundreds or thousands, buried in underground electrical conduits (pipes), and run to various locations, such as buildings and rooms, where they can be connected to standard phone jacks.

Twisted-pair cable can be used to connect computers in networks for transmitting data over relatively short distances. Millions of home computer owners use this medium with a modem because the cable is already in place. The advantages of twisted-pair cable are its availability and low price. To ensure more accurate transmissions over long distances, repeater stations may be positioned along the way to refresh (strengthen) the communication signals.

Coaxial Cable

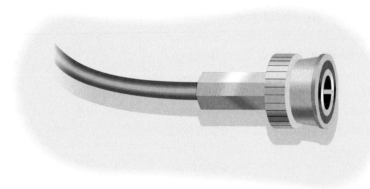

FIGURE 6-7:
Coaxial Cable

Coaxial cable is commonly used for VCR and cable television connections, in telephone networks, and in some computer networks. The cable consists of an insulated center wire grounded by a shield of braided wire (see Figure 6-7). Coaxial cable is more expensive than twisted-pair, but is less susceptible to interference and can carry much more data. **Baseband** coaxial cable, often used in computer networks, is about 3/8 inch thick and has a single channel for transmitting digital signals at about 10 Mbps. Broadband coaxial cable has several channels, each of which can carry about 10 Mbps. Broadband is used for cable television transmissions.

TECH VISIONARY

ROBERT METCALFE: INVENTOR OF ETHERNET

Born in Brooklyn, raised on Long Island, and educated at MIT and at Harvard (where he received a PhD in computer science), Robert M. Metcalfe earned fame and fortune as the inventor of the world's most widely used LAN communication protocol, Ethernet. Over one hundred million computers are linked with Ethernet LANs, and many of them are connected to the Internet.

Metcalfe conceived of Ethernet in 1973 while working at the Xerox Palo Alto Research Center (Xerox PARC), which was also the birthplace of the graphical user interface, of WYSIWYG computing, and of the pointing device known as the mouse. For a while, Metcalfe taught at Stanford University, but in 1979 he left to found 3Com Corporation, of Santa Clara, California, the leading manufacturer of Ethernet adapter cards and other equipment. Metcalfe's invention has made him a billionaire.

In the 1980s Metcalfe taught at Stanford University and in the early 1990s he was a visiting fellow at the University of Cambridge, England. During this time he became known for his writing in addition to his previous technical and business accomplishments. Metcalfe became CEO of InfoWorld Publishing in 1992, and vice president of IDG Technology in 1993. In one of his "From the Ethernet" columns for *InfoWorld* magazine, he predicted a collapse of the Internet due to excessive traffic. While such a collapse has not yet occurred, many people do experience excessive delays when using the Internet, and most observers agree that network backbone upgrades are necessary. Metcalf is also widely known for what is called Metcalfe's Law, which states that the value of a network increases exponentially with the number of machines (and users) connected to it.

Source: Introduction to Computers and Technology, published by EMC/Paradigm Publishing.

Millions of cable television subscribers already have cable installed in their homes and offices. By adding a special type of modem called a **cable modem** (sometimes called a **broadband modem**), they can take advantage of this communications medium to receive much faster data transmission speeds than twisted-pair cable can offer. According to a March 2003 survey conducted by the Pew Internet and American Life Project, cable modems are the preferred medium for broadband connections to the Internet, with 67 percent of broadband users connecting via cable modems. To use a cable modem, a device called a **splitter** must be installed. One part of the splitter connects to the television cable, and the other part connects to the cable modem.

Fiber-Optic Cable

Twisted-pair and coaxial cable both contain copper conductors and transmit electrical signals—streams of electrons. Instead of copper, fiber-optic cable uses a string of glass to transmit photons—beams of light. A **fiber-optic cable** typically consists of hundreds of clear fiberglass or plastic fibers (threads), each approximately the same thickness as a human hair. Data is converted into beams of light by a laser device and transmitted as light pulses (see Figure 6-8). Billions of bits can be transmitted per second. At the receiving end, optical detectors convert the transmitted light pulses into electrical pulses that computing devices can read. The advantages of using fiber-optic cables include

- faster transmission speeds (up to 1 trillion bps)
- higher data transmission volumes
- minimal interference
- greater security
- longer cable life

Fiber-optic cable is expensive and difficult to work with, but the advantages of using the technology outweigh the disadvantages. The most important advantage of fiber-optic cables is that they are a very high bandwidth (broadband) media, and therefore they have become the medium of choice for many local area networks. However, when data must be sent to distant computers, or to networks using analog

FIGURE 6-8:
Fiber-Optic Cable

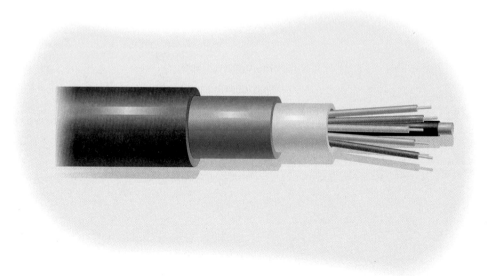

media, the sending computer or the network's host computer uses a modem to convert the data into analog form.

Integrated Services Digital Network (ISDN) Lines

In some locations special digital telephone lines, called **ISDN lines**, are available. They can be used to dial into the Internet and transmit and receive information at very high speeds, ranging from 64 Kbps to 128 Kbps. Using an ISDN line requires a special ISDN modem. Monthly fees for ISDN lines are higher than for regular phone lines, adding to a user's communications costs. With the widespread adoption of high-speed cable modems and DSL lines at a relatively low cost, the growth of ISDN line usage remains flat.

Digital Subscriber Line (DSL)

Digital Subscriber Line (DSL) technology uses existing copper phone lines and new optimized switched connections to achieve faster telecommunications speeds than traditional dial-up phone access. DSL separates voice and data into discrete channels so that users can still make phone calls while connected to the Internet via a DSL modem. DSL is considered a broadband technology, as connection speeds range from 144 Kbps to 1.56 Mbps.

Currently cable modems provide the strongest competition to DSL lines. According to a March 2003 survey by the Pew Internet and American Life Project, 28 percent of households with broadband connections to the Internet used DSL. However, DSL technology is not available in all locations because there is a physical limitation on how far away from a telephone company office a DSL line can reach.

T Lines

T line is a term coined by AT&T for a type of extremely high-speed telephone connection. **T1 lines** allow for both voice and data transmission and can carry data at a speed of 1.544 Mbps. **T3 lines** are even faster, capable of carrying data at speeds of up to 44.7 Mbps. There are no T2 lines. Businesses often lease T1 lines to connect to the Internet. Only the 50 largest U.S. corporations and major research labs use T3 lines. The Internet itself also uses T3 lines for its main communications media (backbone). Probe Research reports that 298 million T1 connections were in place by late 2001, compared to only 2.8 million T3 lines. The firm predicts that by 2005, T3 installations will increase to 57 million, while T1 installations will fall to 150 million.

Wireless Communications Media

Wireless media transmit information as electromagnetic signals through the air in much the same way as a battery-operated radio sends radio waves. Individual users, businesses, and organizations are rapidly embracing wireless technologies as workers become more mobile and wireless devices become more powerful. Wireless technologies include

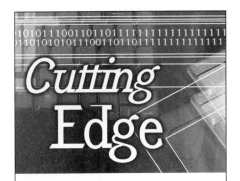

Networking Ants

Observe the lowly ants. Without any central plan, they magically assemble an efficient network for themselves. They do this by responding to the chemical trails that each ant secretes. Interacting with the individual chemical trails, the ants slowly establish a well organized and adaptive community without any commands from above.

Now researchers at Humboldt University in Germany think that what works for insects, bacteria, and slime molds may also work for autonomous fragments of computer code. They set up a computer simulation of electronic agents running randomly across a grid of unconnected nodes. Just like the ants, the electronic agents eventually established an effective network. As an agent crossed a node, it produced a chemical trail. The amount and strength of the chemical trail decreased with time and distance from the node. What resulted was a network that had been established from the bottom up, rather than in a hierarchical fashion.

The beauty of this type of network is that it immediately responds to unexpected failures or upheavals. Adjustments are made as the network builds, and if a connection is broken, it can be instantaneously restored.

Self-assembly is already at work in the Internet, which is constantly being reassembled and updated based on the interactions of millions of users. The Humboldt researchers predict that the ants' model offers promise for future networking technologies, including self-assembly circuits and groups of robots that coordinate actions among themselves. The workings of the model may even be applied to create adaptive cancer treatments.

Source: Patch, Kimberly. "On the Back of Ants," *Technology Review*, March 19, 2003.

- microwave systems
- satellite systems
- cellular technology
- infrared technology

Microwave Systems

Microwave transmission involves the sending and receiving of information in the form of high-frequency radio signals. A **microwave system** transmits data through the atmosphere from one microwave station to another, or from a microwave station to a satellite and then back to earth to another microwave station, as shown in Figure 6-9. When data is sent between microwave stations, the stations must be

FIGURE 6-9: A microwave system transmits data through the atmosphere from one microwave station to another, or from a station to a satellite and then back to earth. The stations must be positioned at relatively short line-of-sight intervals because radio signals cannot bend around objects, such as mountains.

positioned at relatively short line-of-sight intervals because radio signals cannot bend around mountains and other obstacles. Therefore, there must be no visible obstructions between the sending and receiving microwave stations. The terrain determines the distance between microwave stations; it is rarely more than 25 miles. Microwave stations are often placed on top of hills, mountains, or buildings to ensure unobstructed transmission routes.

Satellite Systems

A **communications satellite** is a solar-powered electronic device containing several small, specialized radios called transponders. **Transponders** receive signals from transmission stations on the ground, called **earth stations**. Communications satellites are positioned thousands of miles above the earth. A satellite receives transmitted signals, amplifies them, and then retransmits them to the appropriate locations on earth (see Figure 6-10). Satellites orbit the earth at the same speed as the earth's rotation, making them appear stationary when viewed from the ground. This is called a **geosynchronous orbit**. One of the benefits of satellite systems is

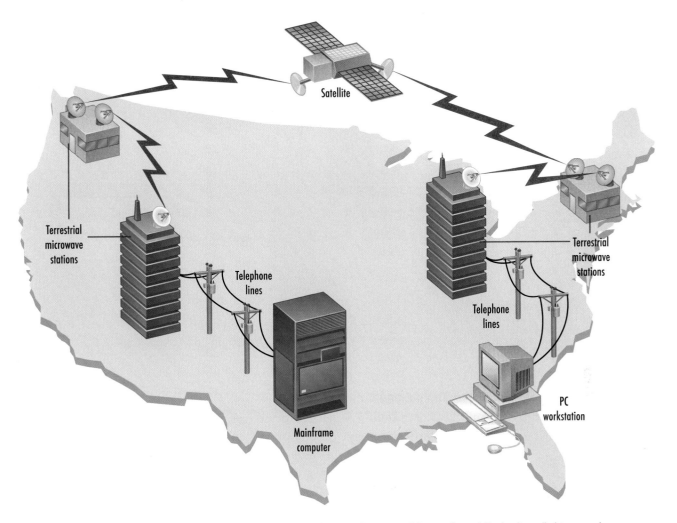

F I G U R E   6 - 1 0 : A communications satellite is a solar-powered electronic device containing small, specialized radios called transponders for receiving signals from transmission stations on the ground. A satellite receives the transmitted signals, amplifies them, and then retransmits them to the appropriate locations on earth. Satellites orbit the earth at the same speed as the earth's rotation, making them appear stationary when viewed from the ground.

the small number of satellites needed to transmit data over long distances. In fact, a small number of satellites properly positioned can receive and transmit information to any location on earth.

Communications satellites are capable of transmitting billions of bits per second, making them ideal for transmitting very large amounts of data. Because of the time it takes to send and receive data across such long distances, satellites are more appropriate for one-way communications such as television and radio applications, rather than for interactive applications such as telephone conversations or computer conferencing. The expense involved in building a satellite, sending it into orbit, and maintaining it is very high. Because of this, companies often share satellite technology as they are unable to bear the full cost of operating their own system.

Several satellites now in orbit handle domestic and international data, video, and voice communications for owners and subscribers. For instance, banks use satellites to transmit thousands of customer transactions to other banks. Money can be transferred from an account in New York to an account in London within seconds.

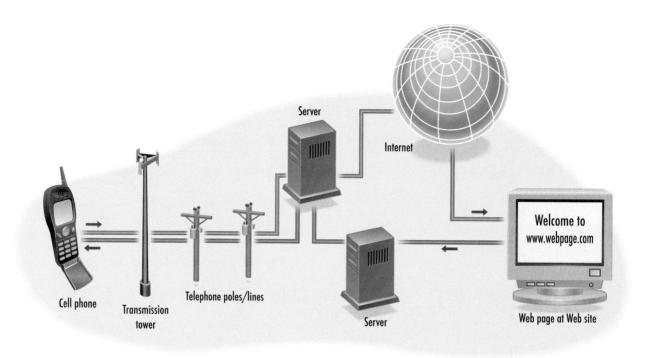

FIGURE 6-11: Signals
sent by cell phones are transmitted
and received from cell to cell until
they reach their intended destination.

Cellular Technology

People can communicate wirelessly to and from nearly anywhere in the world
using **cellular technology**. Cellular phones and devices work by maintaining contact with cellular antennae that resemble metal telephone poles positioned
throughout a cellular calling area. Each area, called a **cell**, has its own antenna
encompassing an area approximately 10 to 12 square miles in diameter. As users
move from cell to cell, the closest antenna picks up the signal and relays it to the
appropriate destination, as shown in Figure 6-11.

Communications networks that support cellular communications also work
well for handling business data. Using a portable computer with a cellular modem,
a person can access Internet resources as well as information stored on a company's
intranet databases. This can be especially important for users in areas where communications facilities are crude or nonexistent. Wireless modems may be used with
a variety of mobile devices, including notebook and handheld computers, personal
digital assistants (PDAs), and cellular telephones. Using a device with a wireless
modem requires the services of a **wireless service provider (WSP)** to provide
wireless Internet access.

Infrared Technology

In recent years infrared technology has become increasingly popular for providing
wireless communication links between computers and peripheral devices (see Figure
6-12). **Infrared technology** transmits data as light waves instead of radio waves.
Television remote control units use the same technology. One drawback to infrared
technology is that objects placed between sending and receiving devices can interrupt transmissions because the light waves must follow a line-of-sight path.

Wireless keyboards, also called cordless keyboards, are a recent application of
infrared technology. The battery-powered keyboards communicate with computers
by transmitting data to a receiver connected to a port on the computer's system
unit. A wireless mouse is another popular infrared device that works in the same

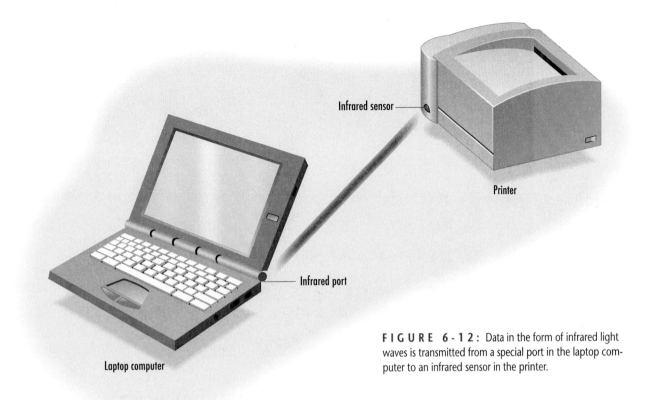

Infrared sensor

Printer

Infrared port

Laptop computer

FIGURE 6-12: Data in the form of infrared light waves is transmitted from a special port in the laptop computer to an infrared sensor in the printer.

way as a wireless keyboard, requiring less desktop space because there is no need for a cable.

NETWORK CLASSIFICATIONS

Networks vary enormously, from simple interoffice systems connecting a few personal computers and a printer, to complex global systems connecting thousands of computers and computer devices. Networks can be classified by their architecture, by the relative distances they cover, and by the users they are designed to support.

Networks Classified by Architecture

The term **network architecture** refers to the way a network is designed and built, just as the architecture of a building refers to its design and construction. Client/server and peer-to-peer are the two major architectural designs for networks.

Client/Server Architecture

In **client/server architecture** (see Figure 6-13), networked personal computers, workstations, or terminals (**clients**) can send requests to, and receive services from, another typically more powerful computer called a **server**. The server can store programs, files, and data that are available to authorized users. For example, suppose that someone wants to use a PC in the school's computer lab to write a letter to a friend. After starting the client computer, the user issues a request to use Microsoft Word, perhaps by simply clicking on the Word icon displayed on the computer screen. The request goes to the network's server, where Microsoft Word is stored. The server prepares a copy of Microsoft Word and sends it to the client computer. Once the software is loaded, it can be used to type and print the letter.

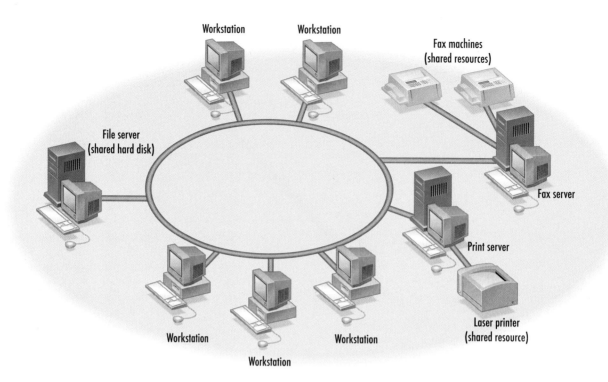

FIGURE 6-13: In a client/server architecture, a networked client computer sends information to a server, which then relays the information back to the client computer, or to another client on the same network.

A major advantage of the client/server model is that application programs, such as Microsoft Office, can be stored on the server and accessed by multiple users. This eliminates the need to install individual copies of programs on each computer within the network.

Peer-to-Peer Architecture

Peer-to-peer architecture (see Figure 6-14) is a network design in which computers comprising the network have equivalent capabilities and responsibilities, each acting as both client and server. Peer-to-peer networks are usually simpler to install and maintain and are less expensive. However, they may not perform as well as client/server networks when operating under heavy workloads. Windows 2000 Professional and Windows XP Professional contain software to set up a peer-to-peer network.

Networks Classified by Coverage

Small networks confined to a limited geographical area are called local area networks (LANs), while wide area networks (WANs) are extensive and may span hundreds of miles.

Local Area Networks (LANs)

Local area networks (LANs) are private networks serving the needs of businesses, organizations, or schools with computers located in the same building or area, such as those found on a college campus. LANs make it convenient for multiple users to share programs, data, information, hardware, software, and other computing resources. LANs use a special computer, called a **file server**, to house all of the

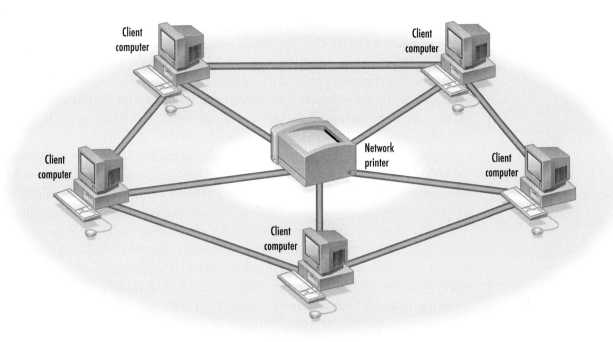

FIGURE 6-14: In peer-to-peer architecture, computers act as both client and server.

network resources. Users can easily access programs and data from the file server and a high-capacity disk system internal to or attached to the file server. A **print server** allows multiple users to share the same printer. Using networks to share resources such as applications programs, hard disk capacity, and high-quality printers saves companies money in hardware, software, and related costs. Figure 6-15 shows the arrangement of a LAN.

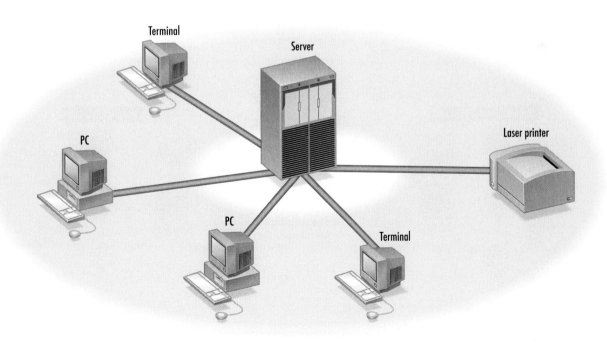

FIGURE 6-15: Local area networks (LANs) are private networks that serve the needs of businesses or organizations with computers located in the same building or area.

Wide Area Networks (WANs)

Wide area networks (WANs) span large geographical areas, connecting two or more LANs (see Figure 6-16). A business might use a WAN to communicate between a manufacturing facility in one state and corporate headquarters in another. Governments, universities, and large corporations use WANs to share data between separate networks. WANs typically make use of high-speed leased telephone lines, wireless satellite connections, or both.

There are several types of wide area networks. A **metropolitan area network (MAN)** is a wide area network limited to a specific site, such as a city or town. A **public access network (PAN)** is a wide area network operated and maintained by a large company, such as AT&T, MCI, or Sprint, which provides voice and data communications capabilities to customers for a fee. Businesses that use the facilities of large communications companies to provide subscribers with additional services are called **value added networks (VANs)**. Typical services offered include access to various network databases, electronic mail, and online advertising and shopping. America Online is a well known VAN.

In recent years a special type of Internet-based WAN has become increasingly popular among large businesses that need a cost-effective way to expand their networking options. This specialized WAN is called a **virtual private network (VPN)**. Instead of leasing T1 lines to connect distant offices across the country, a company establishes a VPN by having each branch office set up a local Internet connection. Additional software and security procedures overlay these public Internet connections to create a secure private network that allows offices to communicate as if they were within the same corporate network—even though they

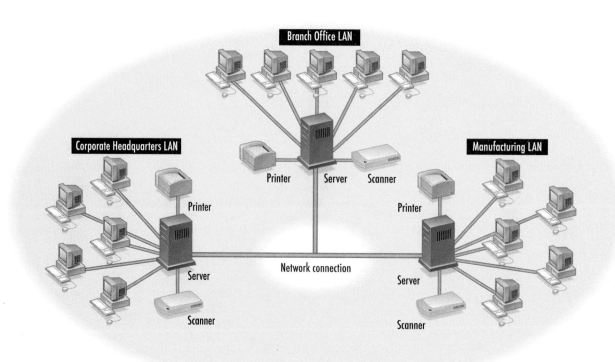

FIGURE 6-16: A wide area network (WAN) connects two or more LANs over a large geographical area.

are actually using the Internet. Factors that make a VPN an attractive option are the cost savings (about $200 to $300 per month for an Internet connection versus $1,200 or more per month for a T1 line), and the reliability, wide availability, and nearly unlimited bandwidth capacity of the Internet.

Networks Classified by Users

Networks can also be classified by the groups of users they were designed to accommodate. This classification includes intranets and extranets.

Intranets

A network that is housed within an organization to serve internal users is called an **intranet**. Access to an intranet's Web site is typically protected by a **firewall**, which consists of special hardware and/or software that prevents or restricts access to and from the network (see Figure 6-17). All inquiries and messages entering or leaving the intranet pass through the firewall, which examines them and blocks those that do not meet the firewall's specified security criteria.

An intranet functions in the same way as a LAN that is not connected to other networks outside the organization. Stored information is available only to authorized

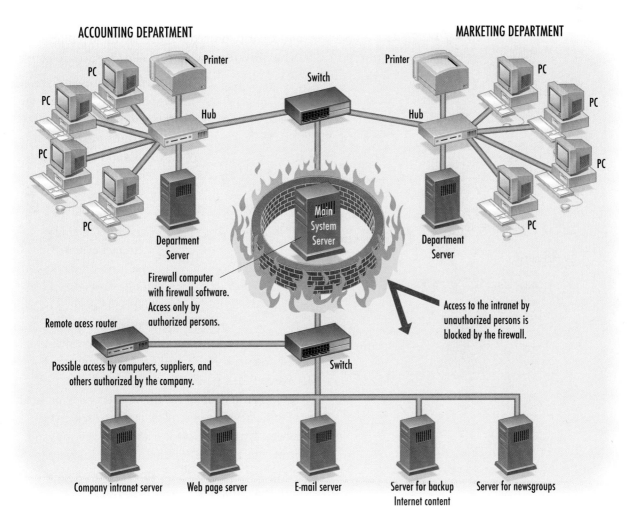

FIGURE 6-17: An intranet is contained within an organization's network. Access to an intranet's Web site is typically protected by a firewall consisting of special hardware and/or software that limits usage to authorized users.

users, and certain kinds of information may be available only to specific persons, groups, or departments within the organization. For example, access to a company's new product designs may be restricted to employees in the research and design department who have special passwords.

One of the largest intranets in the world is under development for the U.S. Navy and the Marine Corps. The awarding of the $7 billion contract to Electronic DataSystems Corporation in late fall 2000 marks the first time a branch of the military has hired an outside company to set up and manage its network, which will link sailors and marines in the continental United States; Hawaii; Alaska; Puerto Rico; Guantanamo Bay, Cuba; and Iceland. Satellites will connect ships at sea. The system is anticipated to be fully operational by late 2003.

Extranets

An **extranet** (illustrated in Figure 6-18) is an extension of an intranet that allows specified external users, including customers and business partners, access to internal applications and data via the Internet. The organization must provide user IDs and passwords to these authorized outside users.

A properly designed and implemented extranet can provide many useful services. Mobile workers can connect their notebooks or handheld computers to a company extranet via a communications medium such as a telephone line. Once connected, workers can send and receive e-mail messages. Managers can contact mobile workers carrying small pagers. Some newer pagers allow users to exchange e-mail messages. Extranets may also allow fax transmission.

Like intranets, extranets can be used for a variety of business activities. For example, an automobile manufacturer can post a request for bids for raw materials, such as engine parts, seat covers, and tires. An accompanying electronic bid form allows potential suppliers to submit a bid to supply these materials.

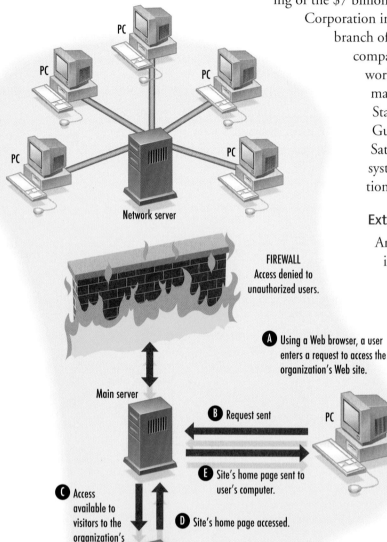

Organization's network

PC PC PC PC PC

Network server

FIREWALL
Access denied to unauthorized users.

Main server

A Using a Web browser, a user enters a request to access the organization's Web site.

B Request sent

PC

C Access available to visitors to the organization's Web site.

D Site's home page accessed.

E Site's home page sent to user's computer.

Web server

FIGURE 6-18: An extranet allows customers and business partners access to a company's internal computerized applications and data via the Internet.

CHAPTER 6

NETWORK TOPOLOGIES

Network topology, or layout, is the pattern by which the network is organized. Topology should not be confused with the actual wiring path of a network, which is determined by the physical layout of walls and floors and other environmental factors.

One way to think of topology is to picture a map showing roads, rivers, railroads, cities, mountains, and other features. The relationship between the various locations can be understood by looking at the map. A diagram of a network's topology functions in much the same way. This allows a viewer to locate each network component, or **node**. The common network topologies are bus, star, and ring.

Bus Topologies

In a **bus topology**, all computers (nodes) are linked by means of a single line of cable with two endpoints. The cable connection is called a bus. All communications travel the length of the bus. Each computer has a network card with a **transceiver**, a device that sends messages along the bus in either direction. Messages contain data, error-checking code, the address of the node sending the message, and the address of the node that is to receive the message. As the communication passes, each computer's network card checks to see if it is the assigned destination point. If the computer finds its address in the message, it then reads the data, checks for errors in the transmission, and sends a message to the sender of the data acknowledging that the data was received. If the computer's network card does not find its address, it ignores the message. Figure 6-19 shows the layout of a bus topology.

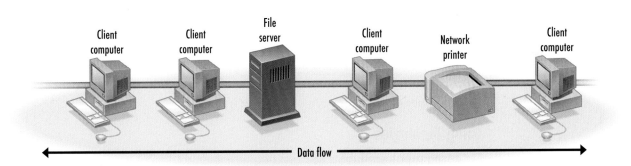

Problems can occur if two or more computers send messages at the same time. This creates an interference pattern, and when one of the computers detects this pattern it jams the network, stopping all transmissions. Computers that are sending messages then wait and resend, a process that is repeated until a message gets through without being blocked. Another problem with linear bus topology is that a broken connection along the bus can bring down the whole network. Bus topologies commonly use coaxial or fiber-optic cables. They are less expensive than some other network layouts, but may be less efficient.

FIGURE 6-19: In a bus topology, all computers are linked by one cable, the bus. All communications travel the full length of the bus, with each computer's networking transceiver checking the message for its intended destination.

Star Topologies

In a **star topology** (also referred to as a **hub-and-spoke topology**), multiple computers and peripheral devices are linked to a central computer called a **host**, in a

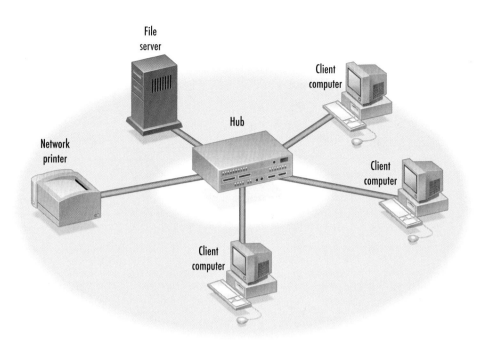

F I G U R E 6 - 2 0 : In a star topology, all computers are linked to a central host computer, through which all communications travel.

point-to-point configuration resembling a star (see Figure 6-20). The host computer is usually a more powerful midrange server or mainframe computer. It acts as a switching station, reading message addresses sent by the nodes and routing the messages accordingly. Companies with multiple departments needing centralized access to databases and files often prefer this topology.

The chief disadvantage of star topology is its dependence on the host computer. Because all communications must go through the host, the network becomes inoperable if it fails to function properly. On the other hand, the hub can prevent the data collisions that may occur with bus topologies, and the rest of the network can remain operational if a node's connection is broken.

Ring Topologies

In a **ring topology** there is no host computer, and each computer is connected to two other computers in a circular path (see Figure 6-21). A type of ring technology called token ring uses a single electronic signal, or token, to pass information from the source computer to the destination. A computer is bypassed if it isn't working. As with bus topologies, a potential drawback to ring topologies is that if two computers try to send communications at the same time, one or both messages may become garbled.

Hybrid Topologies

Some businesses prefer using one kind of topology throughout the organization, while others prefer to use several different kinds. Indeed, the more common practice is for companies to combine network layout types to suit their particular situation. Systems that mix topologies in a network are called **hybrid topologies**. For example, a company's plant in Ohio may use a ring topology, while another plant in North Carolina may set up a bus topology.

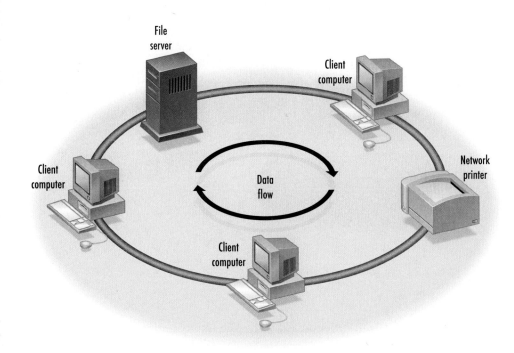

FIGURE 6-21: In a ring topology, each computer is connected to two other computers in a circular path.

Physical versus Logical Topologies

One of the elements that makes networking potentially confusing to beginners is that the term "topology" has two levels of meaning. On the one hand, it refers to the physical arrangement of LAN components, including PCs, peripherals, and cables as discussed in the preceding section. On the other hand, it refers to the way the data travels through the physical connections, which is called its logical arrangement. For example, workstations might be physically connected to a central hub, forming a star, but might pass data from PC to PC in a circular fashion, forming a logical ring.

There are two primary logical topologies: bus and ring. The main difference between them is in the way they avoid collisions in network traffic. In a logical bus topology, the network is like a telephone party line. A computer that wants to send some data listens to make sure no other PC is sending data, and then it sends. In a logical ring topology, the token system is used to prevent collisions. There is only one token in the ring, and only the PC in possession of it may send data. PCs do not monitor the network to see whether the line is free; instead they wait until they receive the token.

NETWORK AND COMMUNICATIONS HARDWARE

Setting up a computer network generally requires special hardware to link all of the computers and to facilitate communications. LANs and WANs may require different hardware devices.

Hubs

A **hub** is an electronic device used in a LAN to link computers and allow them to communicate with one another (see Figure 6-22). The hub may be a separate

FIGURE 6-22: Hub, Router, and Gateway

device, or a server that can function as a hub. The hub coordinates the message traffic being sent and received by computers connected to the network.

Repeaters

Information often travels long distances. However, the wires and cables used may not be designed to carry messages the full distance. **Repeaters**, also called **amplifiers**, are designed to rectify this problem. Repeaters are specially designed electronic devices that receive signals along a network, increase the strength of the signals, and then send the amplified signals along the network's communications path. They function much like an amplifier in a home stereo system. A network spread over wide distances may use several repeaters along the way. Figure 6-23 shows an example of a repeater.

Routers

A **router** is an electronic device usually found in large networks, including the Internet. Routers are used to ensure that messages are sent to their intended destinations (refer to Figure 6-22). As is true with repeaters, a large network covering many miles may use several routers. When a router receives a message, it sends

FIGURE 6-23:
Network Repeaters

(routes) it along the path to the next router, and so on, until the message reaches its final destination.

Routers are designed and programmed to work together. If a part of the network is not working properly, a router can choose an alternate path so the message will still arrive at its final destination.

Gateways

Gateways (see Figure 6-24) are hardware and/or software that allow communication between dissimilar networks. For example, a gateway is needed if an investment broker using a ring topology network wants to retrieve information stored on a star topology network.

Bridges

A **bridge** consists of hardware and/or software allowing communication between two similar networks. If the investment broker in the previous example wants to retrieve information stored on the same kind of network another broker is using, a bridge between the two networks allows mutual communication. Figure 6-24 illustrates the difference between a bridge and a gateway.

FIGURE 6-24: A bridge (A) is a combination of hardware and software that enables devices on one LAN to communicate with devices on another similar LAN. A gateway (B) is a combination of hardware and software that allows dissimilar networks to communicate.

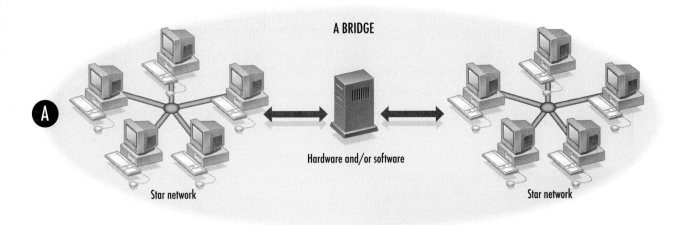

A BRIDGE

A

Star network — Hardware and/or software — Star network

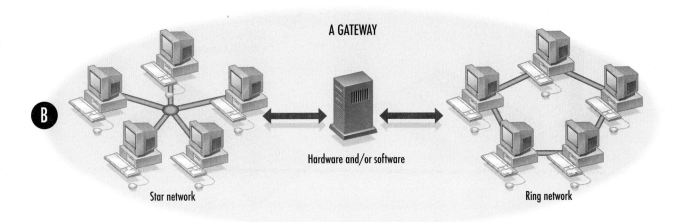

A GATEWAY

B

Star network — Hardware and/or software — Ring network

FIGURE 6-25: Network Multiplexer

Multiplexers

A **multiplexer** is an electronic device that increases the efficiency of a network system by allowing low-speed devices to simultaneously share a single high-speed communications medium in multiples of 8, 16, 32, or more. When used to connect devices with the host computer, the multiplexer accepts data from several devices, combines or multiplexes it, and immediately sends it across a single high-speed medium to a second multiplexer. The second device divides, or demultiplexes, the data and then transmits it to the host computer. Figure 6-25 shows an example of a multiplexer.

Concentrators

Concentrators transmit data from only one device at a time over the channel. The data is then multiplexed with other data and stored until there is enough data to make transferring it over an expensive communications medium more cost effective. Using a concentrator assumes that not all terminals will be ready to send or receive data at the same time. A mid-size server with memory functions that allow for the storage and forwarding of transmissions can function as a concentrator.

Network Interface Cards

The most common LAN architecture is the client/server model, although a variety of LAN architectures are used. Recall that in a client/server LAN a personal computer, workstation, or terminal (a client) is used to send information or a request to another computer (a server). This computer then relays the information back to the original client computer, or to another client computer. In order for a client computer to communicate with a server or another computer it must

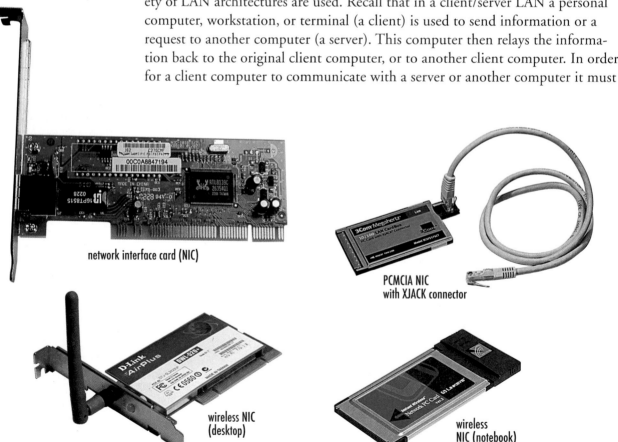

network interface card (NIC)

PCMCIA NIC
with XJACK connector

wireless NIC
(desktop)

wireless
NIC (notebook)

FIGURE 6-26: Shown above are various types of network interface cards.

be connected to a network. Each networked client computer must contain a network interface card (NIC), examples of which are shown in Figure 6-26. Most NICs are designed for a particular kind of network, protocol, and media, although some can work with more than one type of network.

NETWORK SOFTWARE

Many different kinds of software are required to make a network operational. A network's architecture determines the kind of software needed. For example, a client/ server network requires a different kind of software than a peer-to-peer network.

The most important type of networking software is a network operating system. A **network operating system (NOS)** includes special functions for connecting computers and devices. Some network operating systems, such as UNIX and the Mac OS, have networking functions built in. Popular network operating systems for DOS and Windows systems include Novell's Netware™, and Microsoft's LAN Manager®, Windows NT, Windows 2000, and Windows XP, each of which is designed to enhance a system's basic operating system by adding networking features.

NetWare is a popular LAN operating system developed by Novell Corporation. It runs on a variety of different types of LANs. NetWare provides users with a consistent interface that is independent of the actual hardware used to transmit and receive messages. Novell's newest version, called NetWare 6, includes new functions that make it even more versatile than previous versions. The software works smoothly with the network operating system, making it into a vehicle for accessing services over the Internet. Users can now access NetWare software from any browser via a single URL.

While earlier versions required the removal of all NetWare components before installing an updated version, NetWare 6 allows a network manager to install the new software over an existing version. It includes a new feature, called iFolder®, which provides users access to stored data from any location. Another feature, called Internet Printing, lets users access network printers via the Internet. NetWare 6 provides for the transfer of information in virtually any file format, and can be installed on networks of all sizes and complexities.

COMMUNICATIONS SOFTWARE AND PROTOCOLS

Recall from Chapter 5 that communications software is a type of utility software that allows computers to "talk" with each other. Combined with the appropriate hardware, communications utilities allow users to connect their computers to other computers, such as network servers, and to access and use resources on a LAN or WAN. Communications software also allows modem dial-up for sending e-mail messages, accessing the Internet, surfing the Web, and more. The software must adhere to a particular network protocol for network communications.

Newer PCs containing a modem often come equipped with communications software. If not, it can be purchased from a variety of

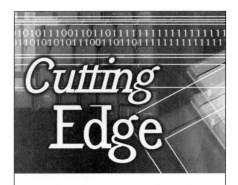

Superfast Fiber-Optic Lines for Homes

After years of debate, the nation's largest telecommunications companies have agreed on a set of standards that in the future will enable users to have superfast fiber-optic lines installed directly into their homes. When fully implemented, these lines would carry data 100 times faster than standard telephone lines. Regional phone giants, including SBC Communications, Verizon Communica-tions, and BellSouth have also agreed on standards for the needed communications equipment, currently being referred to as fiber-to-the-premises (FTTP) equipment. By acting in concert, the phone companies can place massive orders and demand lower prices for communications and other kinds of equipment. Because the three companies have so much clout, the rest of the industry will probably adopt the same standards, creating even greater economies of scale.

Analysts consider FTTP the most significant addition to telecommunications technology since the introduction of wireless networks. Although broadband access is increasing and is capturing the attention of consumers, fiber-optic lines are expected to be a strong competitor, delivering lightning-speed Internet access, interactive games, movies on demand, phone calls, and high-definition TV. As the cost drops, telecommunications companies will put fiber optics rather than traditional copper lines into new homes. But because millions of homeowners may want the new technology, fiber-optic cable to new homes won't become common until 2007 or 2008. The promise of dramatically faster telecommunications access may make the wait seem worthwhile.

Source: Maney, Kevin, *USA Today*, May 29, 2003.

sources. Users who subscribe to an Internet service provider are typically provided with communications software that can be installed.

Communications Utilities Features

Communications software programs contain many useful features. Most programs can be used to

- access and use the services of an ISP (Internet service provider), such as e-mail and use of Web browsers
- send and receive information to and from other computers through LAN and WAN networks
- send and receive faxes

Communications Protocols

A **protocol** is a set of rules and procedures for exchanging information among computers on a network. To avoid transmission errors, the computers involved must have the same settings and follow the same standards. Numerous protocols have been developed over the years. Table 6-2 shows a sample of communications protocols now being used.

Efforts are currently under way to simplify protocols by establishing standards that all computer and communications equipment manufacturers will adopt and follow. The International Organization for Standardization, based in Geneva, Switzerland, has defined a set of communications protocols called the **Open Systems Interconnection (OSI) model**. The United Nations has adopted the OSI model. However, a variety of protocols likely will remain in use unless users universally accept the OSI model.

Directional Protocols

Almost all communications use directional protocols to determine the flow of transmissions among devices. The three possible directions are simplex, half-duplex, and full-duplex, as illustrated in Figure 6-27.

Type of Protocol	Purpose/Use
Hypertext Transfer Protocol (HTTP)	defines how Web pages are transmitted
Simple Mail Transfer Protocol (SMTP)	sends e-mail messages between servers
Post Office Protocol (POP)	retrieves e-mail from a mail server; newest version is POP3
Internet Message Access Protocol (IMAP)	retrieves e-mail from a mail server; newer than POP and has replaced POP on some e-mail servers; newest version is IMAP4
Transmission Control Protocol/Internet Protocol (TCP/IP)	connects host computers on the Internet
File Transfer Protocol (FTP)	allows large files to be transmitted and received over the Internet

T A B L E 6 - 2 : Examples of Communications Protocols

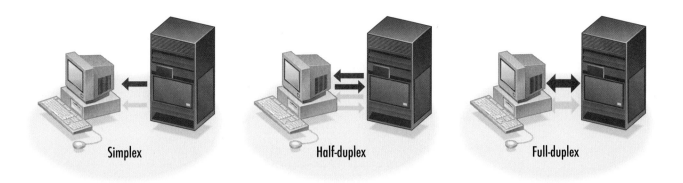

Simplex   Half-duplex   Full-duplex

F I G U R E 6 - 2 7 : With simplex transmission, communications flow in only one direction. With half-duplex transmission, communications can flow in either direction, but in only one direction at a time. With full-duplex transmission, communications can flow in both directions at the same time.

- **Simplex Transmission.** Communications flow in only one direction with **simplex transmission**. This can be compared to a public announcement system at a football game. The announcer can speak to the audience, but cannot receive messages from the audience. Likewise, a computer that transmits data via a simplex channel can either send or receive data, but cannot do both.
- **Half-Duplex Transmission.** With **half-duplex transmission** communications can flow in both directions, but not at the same time. A walkie-talkie system is an example of half-duplex transmission. Two-way communication is possible, but only one person can speak at a time. When used over long distances, half-duplex transmission often results in delays. Thus, half-duplex transmission is typically used with a central computer system and the terminals connected to it. Users usually need to wait for a response from the main computer before continuing.
- **Full-Duplex Transmission.** Simultaneous transmission in both directions is achieved through **full-duplex transmission**, which can be compared to two people communicating via telephone. Both can speak and hear at the same time. Full-duplex transmission eliminates delays due to response time, which can be an important advantage when large amounts of data are transmitted between mid-size servers, mainframe computers, and supercomputers.

Asynchronous and Synchronous Transmission Protocols

Earlier you learned that data is sent over communications media in serial form, that is, one bit after another bit until the complete message is transmitted. Since the bits in serial transmission are sent out one at a time, transmission protocols have been developed to alert the receiving device as to where characters (bytes) begin and end. These protocols, called asynchronous and synchronous transmission, are illustrated in Figure 6-28.

When communications are sent by **asynchronous transmission**, each byte of data is surrounded by control bits. The front bit, called a **start bit**, signals the beginning of a character. The bit at the end, called a **stop bit**, signals the end of that character. There is also an error-checking bit called a parity bit. Data sent by asynchronous transmission is transmitted at irregular intervals, and a modem is usually involved.

Synchronous transmission provides a faster and more efficient way of sending data. With **synchronous transmission**, blocks of bytes are wrapped in start and stop bytes

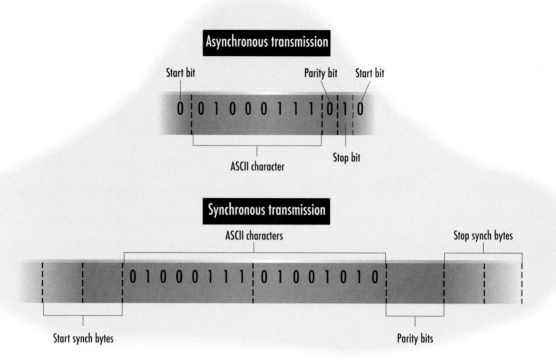

FIGURE 6-28: With asynchronous transmission, control bits surround each byte of data. An extra bit is added at the beginning and end of each character to signal its beginning (start) and ending (stop). A parity bit checks for errors. Synchronous transmission provides a fast and efficient way of sending data. Blocks of bytes are wrapped in start and stop bytes called synch bytes.

called **synch bytes**. Large computer systems often use synchronous transmission due to the faster transmission speed. PC users wanting to retrieve data from large computer systems can buy add-in boards that provide synchronous transmission.

Computers communicating with each other must use the same transmission method. If a computer uses the asynchronous method to send data, a computer using the synchronous method will not be able to receive the data.

Local Area Network (LAN) Protocols

Protocols that govern data transmissions vary among LANs using different topologies or different PCs and workstations. Many LANs of the bus topology type are set up using **Ethernet** protocols. These protocols specify how the network is to be set up, how network devices communicate with each other, how problems are identified and corrected, and how components are connected. Ethernet provides for fast and efficient communications.

Ring and star topology networks use a **token ring protocol** that sends an electronic signal (token) around the ring quickly. The token is capable of carrying both an address and a message. As a token passes by a workstation, the workstation checks to see if the token is addressed. If the token has no address, the workstation can latch onto the token, thereby changing the token's status from free to busy. The workstation then adds an address and message to the token. The receiving station receives the message and changes the token status back to free. The token then continues around the ring.

Wide Area Network (WAN) Protocols

Protocols have been developed for use with WANs. A widely used networking program called **Systems Network Architecture (SNA)** uses a **polling protocol** for transmitting data. Workstations are individually asked if they have a message to transmit. If a polled workstation replies "yes," the protocol transmits the message and then questions (polls) the next device.

A newer type of network software for ring networks dispersed over a large area and connected by fiber-optic cables is called **Fiber Distributed Data Interface (FDDI)**. The software links the dispersed networks together using a protocol that passes a token over long distances. FDDI may be used to connect various university campuses wanting to share information.

Internet and Web Protocols

The Internet and the Web require specific protocols to communicate with computers around the world. The Internet uses a transmission technique called packet switching, in which data is divided into small blocks, or packets, which are sent along the Internet to their destinations. A protocol called Transmission Control Protocol/Internet Protocol (TCP/IP) governs how packets are constructed and sent to their destinations.

The World Wide Web uses the **Hypertext Transfer Protocol (HTTP)** to transfer Web pages to computers. Most Web addresses, or URLs, begin with the letters "http" to indicate the protocol is being used. Millions of files are available to Web users. Large files can be transmitted and received using **File Transfer Protocol (FTP)**. For example, a company accountant can send a multipage employee report to the U.S. Department of Labor, or receive a complete copy of the newest tax laws from the IRS over the Internet.

Electronic Mail Protocols

Most ISPs provide an electronic mail service to facilitate the sending and receiving of e-mail messages. Messages are transmitted according to a communications protocol called **Simple Mail Transfer Protocol (SMTP)**. SMTP, installed on the ISP's or online service's **mail server**, determines how each message will be routed through the Internet, and then sends the message.

Upon arrival at a receiving mail server, messages are transferred to another server, called a **Post Office Protocol (POP)** server. POP allows the recipient to retrieve the message. Figure 6-29 illustrates how electronic mail is sent and received with SMTP and POP.

Wireless Application Protocols

The market for wireless communications has enjoyed tremendous growth, with wireless technology now available in virtually every location on earth. Every day, millions of users exchange information using a variety of devices, including notebook computers, cellular telephones, pagers, messaging services, and other wireless communications products.

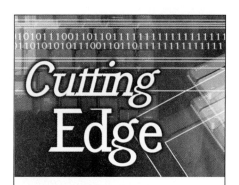

Cutting Edge

Wi-Fi with Your Burger

In late 2003, the McDonald's fast-food restaurant chain launched a major wireless Internet rollout in several hundred restaurants in three major markets. At participating McDonald's restaurants in the Manhattan test market, customers with a wireless-enabled portable computer received one hour of free high-speed Internet access. Customers also were able to purchase a single session of up to 60 minutes for $3. The network is open to all wireless users, so customers and its employees do not have to set up an account.

Internet access on the Wi-Fi network initially is being provided by Cometa, a partnership between IBM, AT&T, and Intel. Another Internet service provider, T-Mobile, has its own Wi-Fi initiative set up in selected Starbucks sites.

Wireless Internet access locations, called hot spots, are on the rise. Many also include hardwired access. A McDonald's in Media, Ohio, has claimed to be the first Golden Arches in the nation to offer both 802.11b Wi-Fi Internet access and regular hardwired access. And overseas, McDonald's of Japan is looking to install some 4,000 hot spots in the restaurant's Japanese outlets.

Source: <http://www.boston.internet.com/news/article.php/2107771> March 2003.

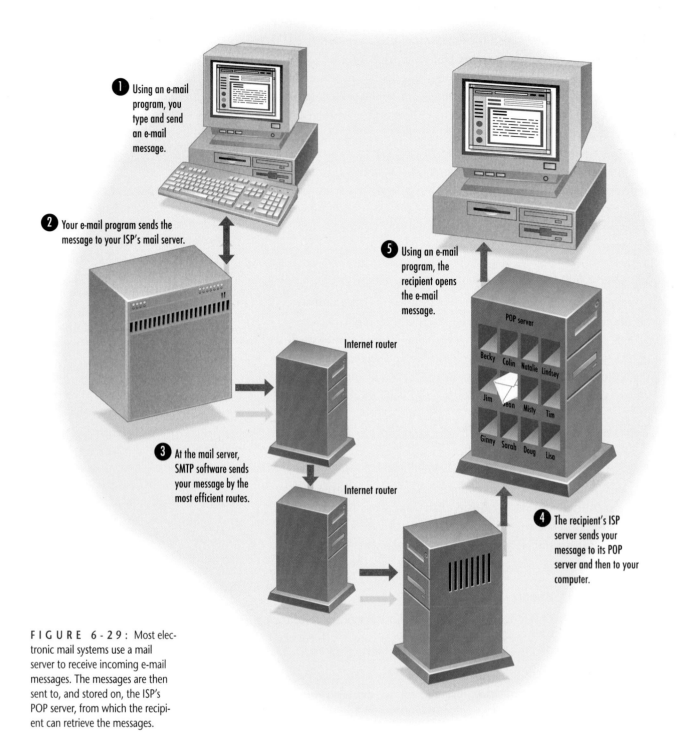

① Using an e-mail program, you type and send an e-mail message.

② Your e-mail program sends the message to your ISP's mail server.

③ At the mail server, SMTP software sends your message by the most efficient routes.

Internet router

Internet router

④ The recipient's ISP server sends your message to its POP server and then to your computer.

⑤ Using an e-mail program, the recipient opens the e-mail message.

POP server

Becky Colin Natalie Lindsey

Jim Jean Misty Tim

Ginny Sarah Doug Lisa

FIGURE 6-29: Most electronic mail systems use a mail server to receive incoming e-mail messages. The messages are then sent to, and stored on, the ISP's POP server, from which the recipient can retrieve the messages.

Until recently, LANs were limited to the physical hard-wired infrastructure of the building in which they were located. Wireless technologies break down these physical communications barriers by eliminating the need for the expensive hard wiring. The **Wireless Application Protocol (WAP)** enables wireless devices to access and use the Internet using a client/server network.

The major motivation and benefit of wireless LANs is increased mobility. Users can access LANs and the Internet without regard to location and distance, almost without restriction. Technological advances in wireless hardware, software, and application protocols make all this possible.

An early WAP still in use is called **Internet Protocol**, or simply **IP**. With version 4 of this protocol, the Internet provider address of the mobile device does not change when the device is moved from a home network to a different (foreign) network. A connection is maintained by implementing a forwarding routine. A major disadvantage of IP is that the device may not be used while it is being moved between locations. A newer version of IP (version 6) allows a mobile device user to inform the local provider where to forward data packets if a new provider is being used.

In 1997 the Institute of Electrical and Electronic Engineers (IEEE), an organization that develops standards for computers and the electronics industry, approved the 802.11 protocol for wireless LAN technology. Commonly called **Wi-Fi**, the **802.11 protocol** specifies an over-the-air interface between a wireless client device and a server, or between two wireless client devices. Based on a transfer rate of 1 Mbps to 2 Mbps, the protocol includes specifications that provide for the transmission of data and graphics, and that allow information to be downloaded from Web sites to wireless devices, such as Web-enabled notebook computers and cell phones. Wi-Fi is an industry standard and is the basis on which most new wireless devices are being designed and built. The new Centrino computer chips from Intel were developed for Wi-Fi, and Windows XP also was designed to handle Wi-Fi.

Three variations of the 802.11 protocol are widely used. The first major revision, **802.11b**, was approved in 1999 by IEEE. Offering a relatively low cost and a faster transfer rate of 5.5 Mbps to 11 Mbps at a range of up to 250 feet (76 meters), 802.11b is popular in home and small office wireless networks.

In 2001, IEEE approved the **802.11a** standard, which offers transfer rates of up to 54 Mbps when devices are at a range within 60 feet of the primary access point, or hub. Transfer rates are approximately 22 Mbps at longer distances. The 802.11a standard operates in a different frequency range, which results in less interference from other devices. One potential drawback is that 802.11a networks are costly to implement in comparison to 802.11b networks.

In June 2003, IEEE approved the **802.11g** standard, which operates in the same frequency range as 802.11b but offers transfer rates similar to 802.11a—up to 54 Mbps. Also called **wireless 3G**, this technology is compatible with 802.11b devices, thus offering business and home customers a fairly inexpensive option to upgrade their networks.

Outside of self-contained home or office wireless networks, Wi-Fi technology is being used in a number of free-standing public networks called "hot spots." McDonald's Corp. and Starbucks Corp. are two of the companies introducing Wi-Fi access for a fee, and numerous free hot spots have been launched around the world.

Wireless data transmission technologies have been popular with some businesses that need to contact agents or representatives in the field, such as the insurance industry. However, some businesses have found wireless transmission technologies unattractive, because they require too much bandwidth. Wireless 3G is a communication technology offering exceptional data transfer speeds. The bandwidth for devices using 3G ranges from 384 Kbps for mobile device users up to 2 Mbps for stationary users. Financial institutions will likely be among the principal beneficiaries of wireless 3G technologies.

ON THE HORIZON

The future holds tremendous promise for computer network users. New hardware, software, and media are appearing that will make telecommunications and networks more efficient, reliable, and useful. Some of these technologies already exist, and are in the process of further development to unleash their full potential. A number of new developments in fiber-optic technology and infrared transmission hold promise in solving existing obstacles to high-speed communication over networks, including the Internet.

Increased Bandwidth Availability

Some small businesses and organizations are unable to obtain access to the fiber-optic communications medium since carriers and service providers are often

unwilling to extend connectivity to areas that do not offer a sufficient customer base. One possible solution is free-space optics, a nascent technology that uses lasers to send optical signals through the air. Two optics providers, LightPointe Communications of San Diego and Lucent Technologies, are developing and perfecting optics technologies meant to ease the problem.

Another technology that may help improve fiber optic access is DWDM (dense wave division multiplexing). DWDM allows several data streams to be transmitted over a single fiber. XO communications in Reston, Virginia, has developed a new DWDM-based service that provides users with sole use of a single wavelength of light on a single strand of fiber-optic cable.

Higher-speed Optical Fibers

The backbone of modern networks is fiber optic-based, but expanding the optical medium nationwide—and eventually worldwide—will increase transmission speed and capacity by what will seem like light-years compared to today's capabilities. This stunning potential will be realized by recent developments in optical technology that allow a single strand of fiber thinner than a human hair to carry every phone call and e-mail used by every person in the world.

Hollow fiber is another development that some believe represents the next wave in fiber-optic cable. If hollow fiber can be perfected, researchers believe data in the form of infrared light could be transmitted virtually unimpeded down tiny corridors inside glass strands stretching thousands of miles. Manufacturing costs would be lower and there would be a strong demand by users needing higher bandwidth transmission.

While there are a number of different applications for these new fiber-optic technologies, companies are expected to utilize them in four significant ways:

- Long-distance carriers will spend billions on the latest optical equipment, upping network capacity by 80 to 160 times.
- Telephone companies will update the optical "rings" that carry voice traffic around a region of cities. Data transmission will jump to 10 GB per second, 10 times faster than current capabilities.
- Telephone companies will also upgrade phone network electrical switches to optical switches, which in some situations are thousands of times faster.
- Businesses will replace their Ethernet connections with optical connections supplied by large communications firms at a relatively low cost. Downloads will take seconds instead of hours.

Beaming Data

Drs. Moshen Kavehrad and Svetla Jivkova, researchers at Pennsylvania State University, are now working to develop faster infrared transmission technologies over networks, replacing the radio waves now used with some networking systems, including Apple's AirPort system. Infrared transmission represents tremendous potential for the future. Data traveling through space in the form of infrared light can move faster than radio waves, and with potentially less interruption. The goal of the research is a technology that would allow the transmission of data using beams of infrared light that would connect computers to one another, and to a central transmitter and receiver connected to a larger network. Using infrared light would allow computing devices to be pointed in any direction.

This infrared technology could transmit 2 GB a second, approximately a thousand times as much data as a cable modem, and with few transmission errors. Infrared offers an advantage for activities that require huge bandwidths for transmitting graphic and voice data, such as videoconferencing.

chapter summary

Telecommunications

Telecommunications refers to the use of computer hardware and software for sending and receiving information over communications media, making it possible for computer users throughout the world to communicate with each other.

Analog signals take the form of continuous waves transmitted over a medium at a certain **frequency range**. **Digital signals** send data in the form of bits. In **parallel transmission**, the data bits are sent at the same time along multiple paths. In **serial transmission**, all of the data bits are transmitted one bit after another in a continuous line.

Communications Media

A **communications medium** is a physical link that allows computers to be connected to other computers in different locations. Communications media are broadly classified as either wire or wireless. **Twisted-pair cable** consists of two independently insulated wires twisted around each other. **Coaxial cable** consists of an insulated center wire grounded by a shield of braided wire. A **fiber-optic cable** contains hundreds of clear fiberglass or plastic fibers (threads). An **ISDN line** is a special digital telephone line that transmits and receives information at very high speeds. **T lines** are extremely high-speed dedicated connections between two points. A **microwave system** transmits data via high-frequency radio signals through

the atmosphere. **Satellite systems** receive transmitted signals, amplify them, and then transmit the signals to the appropriate locations. **Cellular technology** uses antennae resembling telephone towers to pick up signals within a specific area (cell). **Infrared technology** transmits data as infrared light waves from one device to another, providing wireless links between PCs and peripherals.

Networks

Network architecture refers to the way a network is designed and built. **Client/ server architecture** sends

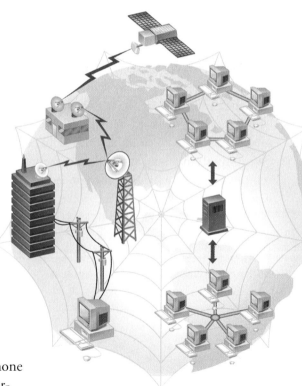

information from a client computer to a server, which then relays the information back to the client computer, or to other computers on the network. In

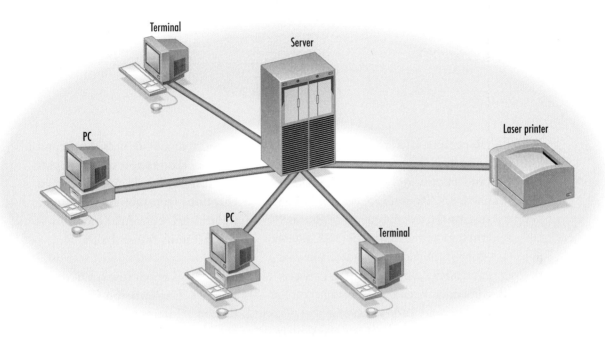

Terminal

Server

Laser printer

PC

PC

Terminal

peer-to-peer architecture, each PC or workstation has equivalent capabilities and responsibilities.

Local Area Networks (LANs) are private networks that connect PCs or workstations located in close proximity, storing software applications and other resources on a special computer called a file server. A print server allows multiple users to share the same printer. A wide area network (WAN) spans a large geographical area. There are various types, including metropolitan area networks, public access networks, value added networks, and virtual private networks. An intranet is a network that is accessible only by a business or organization's members, employees, or other authorized users. Access to an intranet's Web site is restricted by a firewall. An extranet is a network that makes certain kinds of information available to users within

the organization, and other kinds of information available to outsiders, such as companies doing business with the organization.

Network topology, or layout, refers to the way computers and peripherals are configured to form networks. In a bus topology, all computers are linked by a single line of cable. In a star topology, multiple computers and peripheral devices are linked to a central computer, called a host. In a ring topology, each computer or workstation is connected to two other computers, with the entire network forming a circle. Hybrid topologies combine different kinds of network layouts into one.

Network and Communications Hardware and Software

A hub is an electronic device used in a LAN to link groups of computers.

CHAPTER 6

Repeaters, also called **amplifiers**, are electronic devices that receive signals and amplify and send them along the network. **Routers** are electronic devices used to ensure messages are sent to their intended destinations. A **gateway** consists of hardware and/or software that allows communication between dissimilar networks. A **bridge** consists of hardware and/or software that allows communication between two similar networks. A **multiplexer** is an electronic device that increases the efficiency of a network system by allowing low-speed devices to simultaneously share a single high-speed communications medium. With a **concentrator**, data is transmitted from only one device at a time over the channel.

Communications Software and Protocols

Communications software allows computers to connect to other computers and to access and use network resources. A **protocol** is a set of rules and procedures for exchanging information between network devices and computers. **Directional protocols** determine the directional flow of transmissions among devices. Three possible directions are **simplex**, **half-duplex**, and **full-duplex**. Data sent by **asynchronous transmission** protocols is transmitted at irregular intervals. With **synchronous transmission**, blocks of bytes are wrapped in start and stop bytes called **synch bytes**. On the Internet, **Transmission Control Protocol/Internet Protocol (TCP/IP)** governs how packets are constructed and sent to their destinations. The World Wide Web uses the **Hypertext Transfer Protocol (HTTP)** to transfer Web pages to computers. Large files can be transmitted and received using **File Transfer Protocol (FTP)**. Messages are transmitted using **Simple Mail Transfer Protocol (SMTP)**. **Post Office Protocol (POP)** allows the recipient to retrieve messages. **Wireless Application Protocol (WAP)** enables wireless devices to access and use the Internet using a client/server network. In 1997, the Institute of Electrical and Electronic Engineers (IEEE) approved a new protocol for wireless LAN technology, called **802.11**. Since then, three versions have been approved: **802.11b**, **802.11a**, and **802.11g**.

KEYTERMS

Page numbers indicate where terms are first cited in the chapter. A complete list of key terms with definitions can be found in the Glossary at the end of the book.

802.11 protocol, 289
802.11a, 289
802.11b, 289
802.11g, 289
analog signals, 260
asynchronous transmission, 285
bandwidth, 259
baseband, 264
bits per second (bps), 259
bridge, 281
broadband medium, 260
bus topology, 277
cable modem (broadband modem), 266
cell, 270
cellular technology, 270
client, 271
client/server architecture, 271
coaxial cable, 264
communications medium, 263
communications satellite, 268
concentrator, 282
dial-up modem, 262
Digital Subscriber Line (DSL), 267
earth stations, 268
Ethernet, 286
external modem, 262
extranet, 276
Fiber Distributed Data Interface (FDDI), 287
fiber-optic cable, 266
file server, 272
File Transfer Protocol (FTP), 287
firewall, 275
frequency range, 260
full-duplex transmission, 285

gateway, 281
geosynchronous orbit, 268
half-duplex transmission, 285
host, 277
hub, 279
hybrid topology, 278
Hypertext Transfer Protocol (HTTP), 287
infrared technology, 270
internal modem, 262
Internet Protocol (IP), 289
intranet, 275
ISDN line, 267
local area network (LAN), 272
mail server, 287
metropolitan area network (MAN), 274
microwave system, 268
multiplexer, 282
narrowband medium, 260
network architecture, 271
network operating system (NOS), 283
network topology, 277
node, 277
Open Systems Interconnection (OSI) model, 284
parallel transmission, 263
parity bit, 263
PCMCIA modem, 262
peer-to-peer architecture, 272
pitch, 260
polling protocol, 287
Post Office Protocol (POP) server, 287
print server, 272

protocol, 284
public access network (PAN), 274
repeater (amplifier), 280
ring topology, 278
router, 280
serial transmission, 263
server, 271
Simple Mail Transfer Protocol (SMTP), 287
simplex transmission, 285
splitter, 266
start bit, 285
star topology (hub-and-spoke topology), 277
stop bit, 285
synch byte, 286
synchronous transmission, 285
Systems Network Architecture (SNA), 287
T line, 267
T1 line, 267
T3 line, 267
telecommunications, 258
token ring protocol, 286
transceiver, 277
transponder, 268
twisted-pair cable, 264
value added network (VAN), 274
virtual private network (VPN), 274
wide area network (WAN), 274
Wi-Fi (802.11 protocol), 289
wireless 3G, 289
Wireless Application Protocol (WAP), 288
wireless service provider (WSP), 270

chapter exercises

The following chapter exercises, along with new activities and information, are also offered in the *Computers: Understanding Technology* Internet Resource Center at www.emcp.com.

EXPLORING WINDOWS
Tutorial 6 focuses on the steps and strategies for creating and renaming folders on your hard drive.

TERMS CHECK: MATCHING
Write the letter of the correct answer on the line before each numbered item.

a. router
b. protocol
c. broadband medium
d. electronic mail
e. star network
f. simplex
g. intranet
h. gateway

i. LAN
j. bandwidth
k. communications satellite
l. twisted-pair cable
m. communications medium
n. telecommunications
o. network topology

_____ 1. A solar-powered electronic device containing a number of small, specialized radios, called transponders, that receives signals from transmission stations on the ground.

_____ 2. A communications medium capable of carrying a large amount of data at fast speeds.

_____ 3. The way computers and peripherals are configured to form networks.

_____ 4. One of the older types of media originally developed for telephone networks.

_____ 5. A set of rules and procedures for exchanging information between network devices and computers.

_____ 6. An electronic device typically used with large networks, including the Internet, to ensure that messages are sent to their intended destinations.

_____ 7. Hardware and/or software that allows communication between two dissimilar networks.

_____ 8. A physical link that allows a computer in one location to be connected to a computer in another location.

_____ 9. A transmission method in which information can flow in only one direction.

_____ 10. A term that refers to the number of bits that can be transferred per second over a given medium.

_____ 11. A private network that serves the needs of businesses and schools with computers located in close proximity.

_____ 12. An internal network that is accessible only by a business's employees.

_____ 13. The combined use of computer hardware and communications software for sending and receiving information over communications media.

_____ 14. The process of sending, receiving, storing, and forwarding messages in electronic form over communications facilities.

_____ 15. A network in which multiple computers and peripheral devices are linked to a central, or host, computer.

TECHNOLOGY ILLUSTRATED: IDENTIFY THE PROCESS

What process is illustrated in the drawing below? Identify the three types of transmission and explain the main difference among them.

CHAPTER 6

KNOWLEDGE CHECK: MULTIPLE CHOICE

Circle the letter of the best answer from those provided.

1. A(n)_____ signal is a transmission signal in which information is sent in the form of continuous waves over a medium at a certain frequency range.
   a. analog
   b. digital
   c. serial
   d. bandwidth

2. The term _____ refers to the amount of data that can travel over an analog medium.
   a. synchronous
   b. digital
   c. serial
   d. bandwidth

3. _____ is an older type of communications medium originally developed for use by telephone networks.
   a. Fiber-optic cable
   b. Satellite system
   c. Twisted-pair cable
   d. Coaxial cable

4. _____ is a type of wire that consists of an insulated center wire grounded by a shield of braided wire.
   a. Fiber-optic cable
   b. Satellite system
   c. Twisted-pair cable
   d. Coaxial cable

5. _____ is an increasingly popular communications medium that requires no phone lines or cables.
   a. Coaxial cable
   b. Cellular technology
   c. Twisted-pair cable
   d. Fiber-optic cable

6. A _____ is an electronic device used in a local area network that links computers and allows them to communicate.
   a. gateway
   b. router
   c. repeater
   d. hub

7. Standards (rules) that govern the transfer of information among computers on a network and those using telecommunications are called
   a. parallel transmissions.
   b. serial transmissions.
   c. communications protocols.
   d. Web languages.

8. _____ is a type of directional protocol that allows information to be sent in both directions, but in only one direction at a time.
   a. Half-duplex
   b. Hypertext transfer protocol
   c. Operating system protocol
   d. Transponder

9. The method of transmission in which blocks of bytes are wrapped in start and stop bytes is called
   a. asynchronous transmission.
   b. synchronous transmission.
   c. parallel transmission.
   d. security transmission.

10. A network architecture that uses a central, or host, computer through which all transmissions pass is called
    a. client/server architecture.
    b. peer-to-peer architecture.
    c. computer architecture.
    d. layout architecture.

11. In a _____ topology, multiple computers and devices are linked to a central computer, called a host.
    a. bus
    b. star
    c. ring
    d. hybrid

12. A _____ consists of hardware and/or software that allows communication between dissimilar networks.
    a. bridge
    b. repeater
    c. multiplexer
    d. gateway

13. A _____ is a private network that connects PCs and workstations located in close proximity, storing software applications and other resources on a special computer called a file server.
    a. local area network
    b. wide area network
    c. value added network
    d. metropolitan area network

14. An electronic device used in a local area network to link groups of computers is called a
    a. repeater.
    b. router.
    c. hub.
    d. gateway.

15. In _____ , all of the data bits are transmitted one bit after another in a continuous line.
    a. parallel transmission
    b. serial transmission
    c. unilateral transmission
    d. digital transmission

THINGS THAT THINK: BRAINSTORMING NEW USES
In groups or individually, contemplate the following questions and develop as many answers as you can.

1. Currently, connectivity to the Internet is achieved through utility providers such as telephone, cable, and wireless providers. What other utilities or service providers do you think might be used to provide additional ways to access the Internet? What benefits do these alternatives provide as compared to today's alternatives? What obstacles need to be overcome in order to make these alternatives appealing to the market?

2. Retailer Best Buy is teaming up with home builders to install sophisticated networks in new homes. Additional features above and beyond standard home wiring include high-speed Internet access; sharing of files, printers, and games; and home theater wiring with Surround Sound. How could this type of network wiring benefit institutions such as schools, libraries, and hospitals?

3. Infrared technology has been implemented in computer peripherals such as the keyboard and the mouse, and it can also be used to synchronize data between handheld computers and desktop computers. Because infrared signals are easily interrupted, this technology is most useful for devices that will be in close proximity to the desktop computer. Keeping that in mind, what other peripheral devices could take advantage of infrared technology? What devices should probably remain connected in other ways to maintain a constant connection?

KEY PRINCIPLES: COMPLETION
Fill in the blanks with the appropriate words or phrases.

1. _____ refers to the use of computer hardware and software for sending and receiving information over communications media, making it possible for computer users throughout the world to communicate with each other.

2. A physical link that allows computers to be connected to other computers in difference locations is called a _____.

3. An _____ line is a special digital telephone line that transmits and receives information at very high speeds.

4. _____ refers to the way a network is designed and built.

5. With _____ transmission, information is transmitted in both directions, but in only one direction at a time.

6. A _____ topology combines different kinds of network layouts into one.

7. In a _____ topology, all computers are linked by a single line of cable.

8. In a _____ topology, each computer is connected to two other computers, with the entire network forming a circle.

9. An _____ is a network that makes certain kinds of information available to users within the organization, and other kinds of information available to outsiders, such as companies doing business with the organization.

10. A _____ is an electronic device used to ensure messages are sent to their intended destinations.

11. Hardware and/or software that allows communication between two similar networks is called a _____.

12. Notebook and other portable computers use _____ modems.

13. Three possible directional protocols that determine the directional flow of transmissions among devices are _____, _____, and _____.

14. With _____, blocks of bytes are wrapped in start and stop bytes called synch bytes.

15. The World Wide Web uses the _____ to transfer Web pages to computers.

TECH ARCHITECTURE: LABEL THE DRAWING

In this illustration of a network, identify the type of topology. Then label each component and use arrows to show the path of communication on the network.

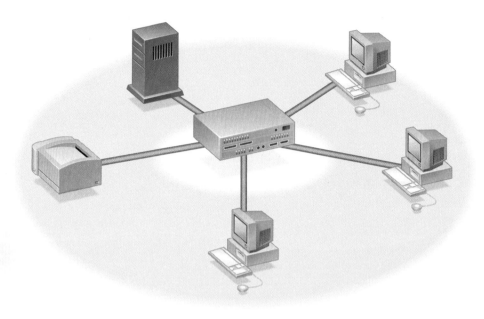

TECHNO LITERACY: RESEARCH AND WRITING

Develop appropriate written responses based on your research for each item.

1. What kinds of networks are used in your local area?

   Investigate the types of networks that local organizations are using. Begin your research with your school, then call or visit three businesses. Ask all parties for the same information: type of network, network topology, number of computers on the network, and the communications media used, including whether wire or wireless. Write a summary explaining why each organization established its particular setup. What were their primary needs, and how does the network meet those needs?

2. How can networks improve efficiency?

   Choose a few situations in which people use personal computers. Possibilities include homes, businesses, school media centers, and college dormitories. Then create a two-column list that identifies in column one the functions people in such situations carry out using computers. In column two, write a brief one or two sentences explaining how these functions might be performed more efficiently by means of networking.

TECHNOLOGY ISSUES: TEAM PROBLEM-SOLVING

In groups, brainstorm possible solutions to the issues presented.

1. Intranets typically provide individuals within an organization with access to relevant information, applications, and other resources, and an extranet typically

extends access to a subset of these items that are relevant to specified external users. Prepare a list of subjects or areas that your school's intranet contains (or should contain). Now identify which of these areas might be relevant to provide to your family via an extranet.

2. Some companies and individuals find it difficult to obtain high-speed Internet access because they are located in remote areas, or in places with a customer base too small to interest an ISP. What do you think can be done to help these businesses and individuals? Do you think people have a right to high-speed Internet access? Should the government play a role in solving this problem?

MINING DATA: INTERNET RESEARCH AND REPORTING

Conduct Internet searches to find the information described in the activities below. Write a brief report summarizing your research results. Be sure to document your sources, using the MLA format.

1. Data mining is a technology that businesses use to glean new information from the data stored in their databases. The technology uses relational tables similarly to the way they are used in relational databases. For example, an auto dealership could use data mining to identify past customers who paid their car loans on time and then send those customers new product offerings. A comparable tool called text mining is being developed by large companies such as IBM and SAS. Text mining will facilitate the analysis of thousands of textual documents that may be stored on a company's file server. Locate information explaining text mining; then write a summary of what it is and how it could be used. Try IBM's Web site as a first source: www.ibm.com.

2. Using the Web for scientific communication offers great potential, but technical problems still remain. Research the ways people are trying to solve presentation issues using non-HTML formats, browser-native HTML, HTML with components, and server-side programming. What solutions are emerging?

TECHNOLOGY TIMELINE: PREDICTING NEXT STEPS

Review the timeline below that summarizes major benchmarks in the development of the Internet. Based on your knowledge and any research you might conduct, think of three changes that may occur over the next ten years and add them to the timeline.

1957   With the Soviet Union's launch of Sputnik, the United States forms the Advanced Research Projects Agency (ARPA)

1966   ARPA introduces its plan for a national network

1973   First international connections are made to the ARPAnet

1986   NSFNET is created

1991   World Wide Web is launched

1999   First full-service, Internet-only bank is opened

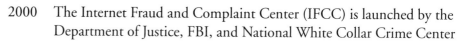

2000   The Internet Fraud and Complaint Center (IFCC) is launched by the Department of Justice, FBI, and National White Collar Crime Center

2002   Online retail sales reach $45 billion in the United States

2003   Nielsen-Netratings estimates there are 580 million Internet users worldwide

ETHICAL DILEMMAS: GROUP DISCUSSION AND DEBATE
As a class or within an assigned group, discuss the following ethical dilemma.

As companies realize the consequences of security breaches in their systems, they are looking for experienced computer security specialists to help protect their systems from intrusions. Some companies hire former hackers, many of whom are convicted criminals, because they believe that their experience finding security holes is extremely valuable. Other companies would not even consider hiring them because of the security threats they pose to their employers.

   If you were responsible for the security of a large company's network and systems, would you hire a consultant who was an experienced hacker or stick to a security consultant without a record of hacking? How would you convince management that you made the right decision? What safeguards would you put in place with the consultant to make sure that he was being thorough in the security assessment without taking advantage of his position?

ANSWERS TO TERMS CHECK AND KEY PRINCIPLES QUESTIONS
Terms Check: 1 – k; 2 – c; 3 – o; 4 – l; 5 – b; 6 – a; 7 – h; 8 – m; 9 – f; 10 – j; 11 – i; 12 – g; 13 – n; 14 – d; 15 – e

Key Principles: 1 – telecommunications; 2 – communications medium; 3 – ISDN; 4 – network architecture; 5 – half-duplex; 6 – hybrid; 7 – bus; 8 – ring; 9 – extranet; 10 – router; 11 – bridge; 12 – PCMCIA; 13 – simplex, half-duplex, full-duplex; 14 – synchronous transmission; 15 – hypertext transfer protocol

CHAPTER 7

THE INTERNET AND THE WORLD WIDE WEB

UNDERSTANDING TECHNOLOGY

learning objectives

- Describe the range of activities made possible by the Internet

- Explain how to connect to the Internet

- Discuss the different elements that make up a Web site

- Describe how information travels across the Internet

- Discuss some of the newer Internet applications

- Analyze the major Internet policy and development issues

key concepts

- The Internet: A Global Network

- Required Hardware, Software, and Services for Connecting to the Internet

- Navigating the Internet

- Viewing Web Pages

- Searching for Information on the Internet

- Newer Internet Applications

- Internet Community, Policy, and Development Issues

CYBER SCENARIO

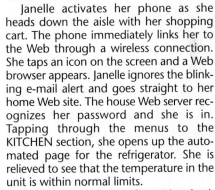

Janelle Mendoza pulls into the supermarket parking lot and parks in a spot near the entrance. As she prepares to leave her car, she realizes that she forgot to bring her shopping list. Mulling over her options, she shrugs, takes her cell phone out of her purse, and walks into the store.

Janelle activates her phone as she heads down the aisle with her shopping cart. The phone immediately links her to the Web through a wireless connection. She taps an icon on the screen and a Web browser appears. Janelle ignores the blinking e-mail alert and goes straight to her home Web site. The house Web server recognizes her password and she is in. Tapping through the menus to the KITCHEN section, she opens up the automated page for the refrigerator. She is relieved to see that the temperature in the unit is within normal limits.

Janelle then selects a live video feed, and from miles away a Web cam begins transmitting images of the refrigerator contents. She smiles, recalling the day she purchased the refrigerator with all its ultra-modern connectivity features. Janelle remembers telling her husband that the options were great, but that she could not picture herself ever using them. But here she is, viewing a full-color display of the inside of her refrigerator.

Janelle examines what is in the refrigerator, and sees that she needs to buy chicken, milk, and some more fruit. Scrolling back to the menu, she chooses PANTRY to check the supply of cereal and bread. With a satisfied smile, she snaps the phone shut and pushes her cart down the aisle to begin selecting the items she needs.

Only a few short years ago, live video on a cell phone seemed like science fiction, but today the technology is becoming commonplace. By 2007, according to industry projections, sales of cell phones containing digital cameras will surpass the sales of all other digital cameras combined. Forecasters also envision the two products eventually merging into one.

THE INTERNET: A GLOBAL NETWORK

The Internet is the largest computer network in the world. Its design closely resembles a client/server model, with network groups acting as clients and ISPs acting as servers (see Figure 7-1). Since the inception of the Internet in the early 1970s, this enormous invisible structure has expanded to connect more than 500 million users worldwide. Many knowledgeable observers consider this vast system of networked computers and telecommunications systems the most significant technical development of the twentieth century, potentially connecting every person on earth to vast resources of information and services.

Individuals, organizations, businesses, and governments use the Internet to accomplish a number of different activities, which can be subdivided into categories:

- communications
- research
- distance learning
- entertainment
- e-commerce

Communications

One of the chief functions of the Internet is its ability to allow people to quickly and easily communicate with one another. Internet users have a number of different communications applications that they can take advantage of, including e-mail, chat rooms, instant messaging, blogs, mailing lists, electronic bulletin boards, newsgroups, telecommuting, and file transfer.

Electronic Mail

Electronic mail (e-mail) is the most widely used Internet application. It allows users to create, send, receive, save, and forward messages in electronic form. It is a fast, convenient, and inexpensive way to communicate. Computer industry research firm IDC estimates that the number of e-mail mailboxes worldwide will increase from 505 million in 2000 to 1.2 billion in 2005. Further, IDC predicts that the number of e-mails sent on an average day will exceed 36 billion.

Each e-mail user has a unique electronic address, which is supplied by his Internet service provider (ISP). Sending an e-mail message is simple. A message writer only has to specify the recipient's e-mail address, type a subject in the subject bar, create a message, and click the *Send* button.

Files can be attached to an e-mail message. In Microsoft Outlook® and Outlook Express, the attachment feature is called Insert File (see Figure 7-2). Virtually any kind of electronic document can be attached and sent with an e-mail message, including reports, spreadsheets, photos, and video files. Recipients can then open the attached files for viewing or storing on their computer.

Large file attachments are often compressed as zip files. A **zip file** is usually half the size of the original file, meaning that it takes half the time to **download** (copy from the host computer). To view a zipped file it must be **unzipped**, a process that reverses the compression process and creates a new file that is full sized again.

Spam: Unwanted Communication

Although recipients welcome most e-mail messages, a significant and growing number are considered junk e-mail, or spam. The term spam refers to any type

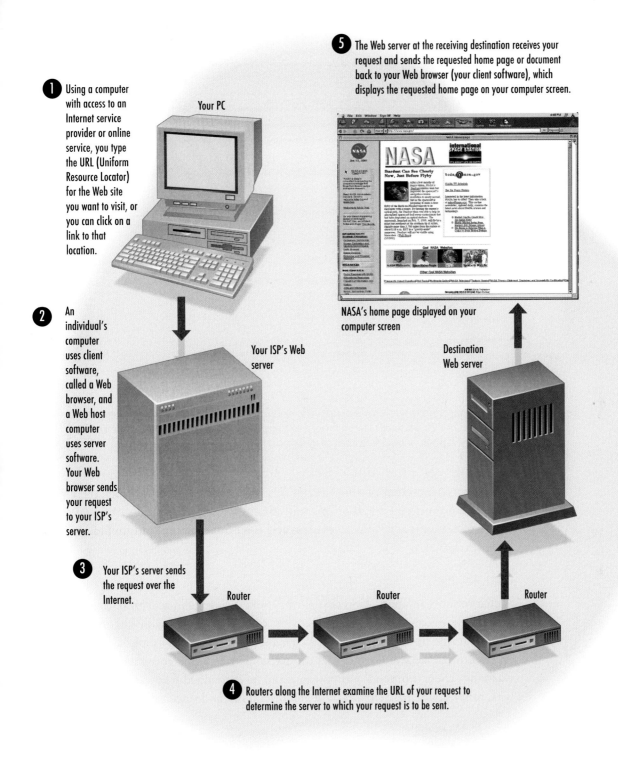

1 Using a computer with access to an Internet service provider or online service, you type the URL (Uniform Resource Locator) for the Web site you want to visit, or you can click on a link to that location.

Your PC

5 The Web server at the receiving destination receives your request and sends the requested home page or document back to your Web browser (your client software), which displays the requested home page on your computer screen.

NASA's home page displayed on your computer screen

2 An individual's computer uses client software, called a Web browser, and a Web host computer uses server software. Your Web browser sends your request to your ISP's server.

Your ISP's Web server

Destination Web server

3 Your ISP's server sends the request over the Internet.

Router   Router   Router

4 Routers along the Internet examine the URL of your request to determine the server to which your request is to be sent.

FIGURE 7-1: The Internet functions like a global client/server network.

of unwanted message sent in mass numbers and/or repeatedly over the Net. Spam has become a major and growing problem that threatens the very useful-ness of the Internet itself. In 2003, America Online (AOL) blocked approxi-mately 3 billion spam e-mails every day. Considering that an additional segment of junk messages managed to skirt the spam-blocker software and reach some-one's mailbox, and that AOL is only one of a group of e-mail service providers, the total number of spam messages sent daily is considerably larger than 3 billion.

Paper clip icon (click to attach a file)

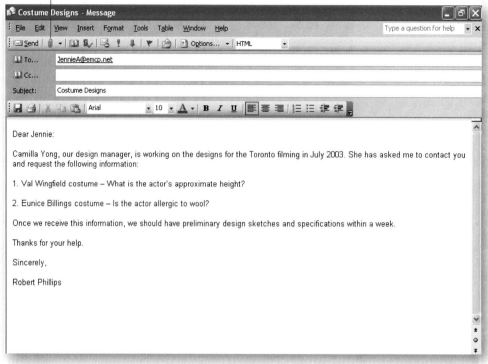

FIGURE 7-2: Microsoft Outlook includes e-mail capabilities. Users attach files to e-mail messages by clicking the paper clip icon, or by clicking Insert on the Menu bar.

Lawmakers are contemplating further measures to control spam, since the e-mail servers that must receive all of this unwanted mail require billions of dollars worth of extra capacity just to process and screen the spam floods, which grow larger each year.

Chat Rooms

A chat room is an application that allows users to engage in **real-time** (live) dialogue with one or more participants. Most online services provide chat rooms. Users can sign up to participate in a chat room on almost any topic. For example, an environmentally conscious user can participate in a chat room discussing global warming. User comments and opinions can be exchanged freely and anonymously with other online participants, and are often frank and uncensored.

Instant Messaging

Instant messaging (IM) works like a chat room, but usually with only two participants in a connection. IM also allows for conversations to take place in real time, using a chat room-like environment. The process is similar to a telephone conversation, but all the communication is done via typing. People who know one another's handle (user name) can open connections and engage in one-on-one conversations. What makes this system different from normal chatting is that it constantly runs in the background while users are working on their PCs. The program automatically notifies users when someone wants to contact them for a chat. Because of this feature IM systems demand a person's attention, making them more interruptive than e-mail.

Signing up for an instant messaging service is similar to signing up for a free e-mail account, such as is offered by hotmail.com. Usually, there is no fee for the service. AOL Instant Messenger™, Yahoo® Messenger, and IRC (Internet relay chat) are popular IM systems (see Figure 7-3). It is important for users to remember when talking to strangers through any form of chat that the system is essentially anonymous, and it can be difficult to determine with whom one is really communicating—and whether or not that person can be trusted.

The main use of IM has been social, but the corporate world has gradually accepted it as a business communications tool. Some corporate Web sites offer users the option of having interactive conversations with customer service representatives via instant messaging. Employees accustomed to instant messaging in their personal lives also find it convenient to communicate with coworkers and clients using this medium. As more organizations have realized the benefits of instant messaging, the vendors of instant messaging software have added business features and robust security to support this growing trend. Figure 7-4 shows a comparison of user numbers for e-mail, cell phones, and instant messaging based on statistics from Forrester Research.

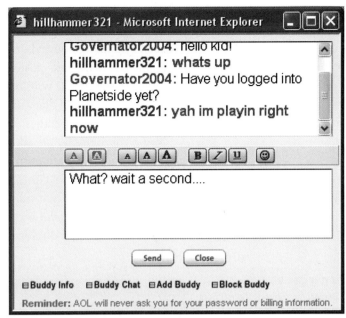

FIGURE 7-3: AOL Instant Messenger

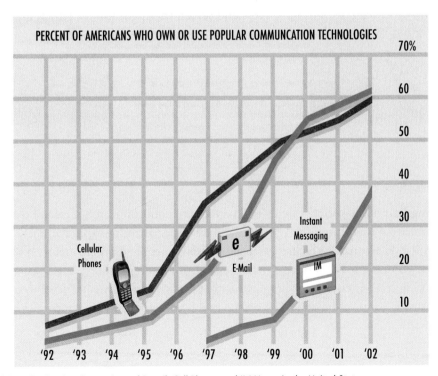

FIGURE 7-4: Comparison of E-mail, Cell Phone, and IM Usage in the United States.

Source: Forrester Research

Blogs

Originally called *weblogs* (a combination of the words "web" and "logs"), **blogs** are frequently updated journals, or logs, containing chronological entries of personal thoughts and Web links posted on a Web page. The content and style of blogs vary as widely as the people who maintain them (called "bloggers"), but in general they function as a personal diary or guide to others with similar interests. Blogger.com is a Web site specifically dedicated to supporting thousands of blogs (see Figure 7-5).

In the corporate world, blogs provide a unique opportunity for businesses to communicate with their employees, customers, and partners. Bloggers add a personal, informal tone to company communications, achieving a realism that sometimes is absent from the traditional glossy marketing brochures. This growing trend is under the careful watch of company attorneys, who are responsible for the company's image and disclosure of sensitive information.

FIGURE 7-5:
Blogger.com supports thousands of blogs.

Mailing Lists

Mailing lists allow people interested in a topic to communicate via e-mail with others sharing their interests. Users can e-mail a special address that will relay their message to everyone on the list, often hundreds of people. Participants then receive a digest containing all the list's e-mail messages for a certain time period, usually daily. One convenience of mailing lists is that groups can discuss topics they are interested in without having to be online at the same time, which they must be in the case of a chat room.

Electronic Bulletin Boards

Electronic bulletin board systems (BBS), often called simply **message boards**, are electronically stored lists of messages that anyone with access to the board can read. As with a classroom or dormitory bulletin board, users can post messages, read

TECH VISIONARY

Tim Berners-Lee, the father of the World Wide Web, graduated from Queen's College, Oxford, in 1976. While working as an independent consultant for the Centre Européen pour la Recherche Nucléaire (CERN) in Geneva, Switzerland, he conceived of a program for storing information based on the associations between ideas. This program, which Berners-Lee called Enquire, later became the basis for the World Wide Web. In 1984, Berners-Lee began a fellowship at CERN, where he worked on computer systems for scientific data acquisition. While a fellow at CERN, he proposed a hypertext system, based on his Enquire program, to be known as the World Wide Web. This system would allow computer users around the world to exchange information using linked hypertext documents. Berners-Lee introduced URLs, HTTP, and HTML; wrote the first World Wide Web server-and-client software; and created a WYSIWYG ("what you see is what you get") hypertext browser for the NeXT Step operating system.

The World Wide Web made its debut on the Internet in the summer of 1991. Since then, the Web has grown to become one of the primary modes of communication in the contemporary world. In 1994, Berners-Lee took a staff position at the Laboratory for Computer Science at the Massachusetts Institute of Technology, where he works as director of the W3 Consortium, an organization that sets standards and helps to bring coherence to global Web development.

Berners-Lee's efforts have earned him numerous awards. In 1995, he received the Kilby Foundation's Young Innovator of the Year award and was co-recipient of the ACM Software Systems award. He has honorary degrees from the Parsons School of Design, New York, and Southampton University and is a Distinguished Fellow of the British Computer Society.

Source: <http://www.w3.org/People/Berners-Lee>.

existing messages, or delete messages. The Internet provides a channel to hundreds of boards around the world. Figure 7-6 shows an example of a message board.

Like chat rooms, most bulletin boards are centered on topics. Many people prefer them to mailing lists because they are not as intrusive. Instead of receiving e-mail messages that eventually fill up their mailboxes, users have the option of checking the bulletin board at their convenience. Boards soon build up a body of information that can be used for future reference or research.

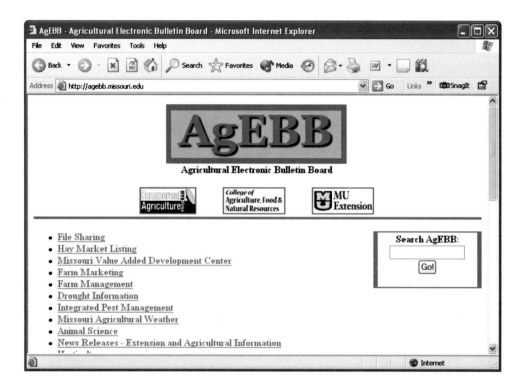

Newsgroups

Newsgroups are collections of posted articles organized by subject. There are thousands of possible subjects, and many servers that support newsgroups. Each collection focuses on different issues, ranging from politics to Windows technical support. They are useful as repositories of in-depth information. Most newsgroups are free, although some require a subscription fee.

Telecommuting

Millions of workers are now performing their work activities at home by using a computer, a modem, and a telephone line. This activity is known as **telecommuting** or **telework**. Some employers have discovered that allowing employees to telecommute offers important advantages, including increased employee productivity, an opportunity to employ highly productive but disabled workers, and savings on travel costs to and from the workplace. According to *BizReport*, a survey conducted for AT&T in 2003 reported that by 2005, 80 percent of companies around the world will have telecommuters.

File Transfer Protocol

File Transfer Protocol (FTP) allows users to communicate by transferring files to and from remote computer systems. FTP was the original method used for transferring files on the Internet. Although Hypertext Transfer Protocol (HTTP) is now the standard means for accomplishing file transfers, FTP is still extensively used. Users often need authorization before they can access any files available on the remote system (FTP site), but some site operators allow users to log on anonymously. An FTP site displays files that users can click on to download to their computers (see Figure 7-7). FTP allows any kind of file to be retrieved. For example, students can download workbook chapters made available on their school's FTP site, or an engineer can download and view blueprints placed on an architect's FTP site.

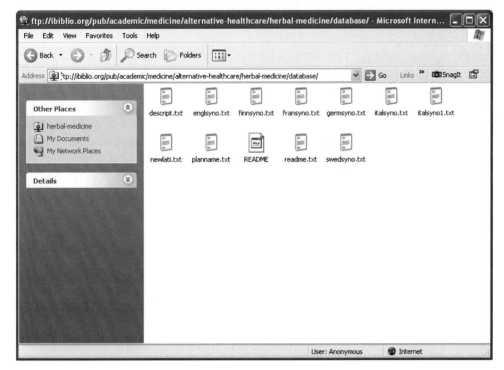

FIGURE 7-7: This FTP site shows files available for downloading.

Research

The Web has opened up thousands of opportunities for people interested in research. Aided by increasingly sophisticated software, users can explore any topic, from anacondas to Zen Buddhism. Information retrieval has become an important application for students, writers, historians, scientists, and the curious.

In addition to the information available on millions of Web sites, material from libraries and databases from around the world also is available for viewing at the touch of a keyboard. Researchers can access books, periodicals, photos, videos, and sound files from the comfort of their own homes. Information can be read online or downloaded for later use.

A search engine is a good starting place to find practically anything on the Internet. **Search engines** are software programs available at Web sites that store searchable snapshots of the information found on millions of other Web sites. Most college research projects today begin on the Web rather than in the library, and the first tool used is the student's favorite search engine.

Distance Learning

Some colleges and textbook publishers offer online courses and study programs over the Internet. This relatively new Internet application is referred to as distance learning. **Distance learning** may be defined as the back and forth electronic transfer of information and course materials between learning institutions and students. A course presented in this manner is called an **online course**. WebCT and Blackboard are two popular online course platforms used on college campuses. Instructors can provide their own content within the platform, or they can access content developed by publishers. Figure 7-8 displays a typical opening screen for an online course.

Distance learning is becoming increasingly popular with students of all ages, and with people whose interests may not be included in a standard college curriculum or at a nearby school. It has also proved an attractive learning alternative for students whose schedules or careers make it difficult for them to attend regular classes. Distance learning offers them an opportunity to pursue

F I G U R E 7 - 8 : Both WebCT and Blackboard include course management and communication tools, such as e-mail.

or continue their education while maintaining their jobs. An early and well-known college provider of online courses is the University of Phoenix, whose home page is shown in Figure 7-9.

Entertainment

Using computers for entertainment purposes is a common activity among Internet users of all ages, particularly younger people. Computers are capable of emulating almost all entertainment devices, and they can be used to play games, listen to music, or even to watch movies or video programs.

Online Games

An enormous number of free games are available online, including traditional games such as backgammon, checkers, and bridge. Some retail games, for example, *StarCraft®*, *Age of Empires II®*, and *Quake®*, require users to buy the software. Users can play by themselves or compete with two or more players. To attract new players, some Web sites offer prizes to the winners of multiplayer games. Virtual reality games are also on the rise. **Virtual reality** involves a computer simulation of an environment or set of surroundings that does not exist, but is reasonably convincing to the user. Games attempt to create a virtual reality by giving a people a virtual body, called an **avatar**, which serves as their point of view in the game world. Some 400,000 players pay monthly fees to play *EverQuest®*, the most popular online game in the United States.

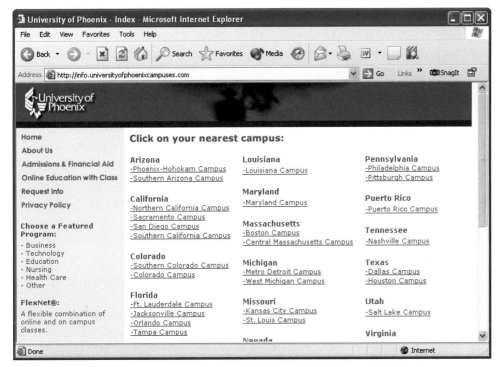

FIGURE 7-9: The University of Phoenix was one of the first providers of online college courses.

Online Gambling

Online casinos are a novel and controversial entertainment feature. Users can log on and gamble in a virtual casino online. Although they may be prohibited by law in many areas, online casinos are difficult to police as they may be located in any part of the world. It may seem like playing a game, but any losses are real and will be billed to the user's credit card.

Music and Video

Music from various Internet sources can be downloaded and played on computers. Some Web sites charge a small fee for this service, but most are free and depend on advertising for funding. Copyright considerations are clouding the issue, and the availability of music free for downloading is rapidly diminishing. The section on peer-to-peer file sharing later in this chapter covers this issue in more depth.

MP3 (Moving Pictures Expert Group Layer III) is the most widely used music file format. **MP3** is a compression format capable of reducing the size of CD-ROM music files by a factor of 10 to 14. This is done by removing recorded sound that cannot be perceived by the human ear. Because the MP3 format results in much smaller files, they are easily downloaded. Once a file is on a computer's hard disk, it can be transferred to a portable MP3 player, where it resides on the player's solid state memory (see Figure 7-10). An MP3 player has no moving parts, so there are no skips in the music, and the device is very reliable.

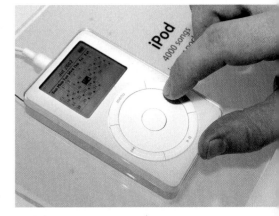

FIGURE 7-10: Portable MP3 players offer a convenient way to listen to music downloaded from the Internet.

It is also possible to view video over the Internet, including television shows, music videos, and even movies. Many news networks and newspapers offer video on their Web sites. Users can click on a story and then view a short video newscast filling them in on all the details.

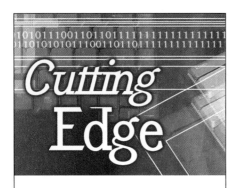

Cutting Edge

I Vote by E-Vote

Americans residing overseas account for at least six million votes. That's a significant number, but it can take weeks for absentee ballots to be received and counted. Delayed absentee ballots caused a minor furor in the much-debated 2000 election. In an ideal world, voters away from home could have their vote counted in seconds using the Internet. That is exactly the goal of the Secure Electronic Registration and Voting Experiment (SERVE). SERVE plans to have 100,000 overseas voters use the Internet in the 2004 Presidential primaries and election.

The Pentagon is managing this $22 million experiment. South Carolina, Hawaii, and selected counties in eight other states will be set up to process voter registration applications, send ballots, and accept votes instantly from eligible voters overseas who can get to a PC with Internet access.

SERVE could be a useful tool in turning out the vote, as long as the integrity of the system can be maintained. But that's the rub. Voter coercion and tampering are a concern in any election. Adding the Internet into the mix opens entirely new avenues for fraud. Many doubt that an Internet voting system would be immune to damage from hackers.

The Pentagon's Federal Voting Assistance Program claims that all necessary steps have been taken to protect the voting system. The system uses state-of-the-art encryption technology, intrusion detection, and firewalls, and has been subjected to tests by the Pentagon's own hackers. Its proponents claim that Internet votes will be safer than any absentee ballot sent by mail.

Source: "Troops, Expats 2004 Vote Online," *Wired News,* July 13, 2003; <http://www. Wired.com.

Internet users can view video files using an application such as Microsoft Window's Media® Player. There are many formats used for digital movies, such as MPEG, or the newer MP4 and WMV formats. Unlike music, there is no single standard that dominates digital movies the way MP3 files dominate music. Because video files are very large, downloading movies or long clips is a slow process unless a user has a high-speed Internet connection.

Obtaining and viewing illegal digital copies of movies is a common occurrence on many college and university campuses because these institutions are often equipped with the high-speed Internet connections that speed up the downloading process. As is the case with many music files, some video files are placed on the Internet in violation of their copyright terms, and are the subject of law enforcement efforts.

Electronic Commerce

Electronic commerce (e-commerce) refers to the Internet exchange of business information, products, services, and payments. E-commerce is commonly divided into two categories defined by target audience: business-to-consumer (B2C), and business-to-business (B2B).

Online shopping expenditures make up the bulk of B2C e-commerce, with the top category being apparel, followed by books, music, videos, auction items, toys, and computer hardware. And although the U.S. economy suffered a downturn at the turn of the century, retail e-commerce sales continue to grow as a segment of overall spending. According to the Commerce Department, for example, retail e-commerce sales for the first quarter of 2003 increased 25.9 percent from the first quarter of 2002. Online purchasing represents only about 1.5 percent of total retail sales, but the percentage has grown steadily since 2000 (see Table 7-1).

Many retailers post online catalogs that potential buyers can browse before making a purchase. Selected items are added to a virtual "shopping cart." The shopping cart functions just like a real shopping cart, allowing customers to place purchases in the cart or remove them later if they change their minds. Once shopping is finished the next stop is a virtual "Checkout Counter," where the customer pays for the purchase by entering a credit card number or by another electronic payment method. Within a few days, the items will arrive at the purchaser's address.

In addition to selling products and services, businesses are using the Internet to advertise products, order inventories from manufacturers and wholesalers, order raw materials, recruit employees, file government reports, and many other activities. These categories constitute the B2B segment of e-commerce. New business uses for the Internet are being discovered every day, and current uses are continually being improved to make them even more successful. Chapter 10 discusses e-commerce in detail.

| Period | Retail Sales in Millions of Dollars* | | E-Commerce Percent of Total Sales |
	Total	E-Commerce	
2000 1st Quarter	715,102	5,722	0.8
2000 2nd Quarter	775,364	6,250	0.8
2000 3rd Quarter	768,559	7,079	0.9
2000 4th Quarter	812,667	9,248	1.1
2001 1st Quarter	723,710	8,009	1.1
2001 2nd Quarter	801,115	7,904	1.0
2001 3rd Quarter	777,882	7,894	1.0
2001 4th Quarter	850,608	10,788	1.3
2002 1st Quarter	740,020	9,470	1.3
2002 2nd Quarter	818,609	9,761	1.2
2002 3rd Quarter	822,125	10,465	1.3
2002 4th Quarter	864,653	13,770	1.6

Source: U.S. Census Bureau, Department of Commerce

* Figures do not include online travel services and ticket sales.

TABLE 7-1: Estimated Retail Sales: Total and Online from 2000 through 2002

CONNECTING TO THE INTERNET

Millions of people throughout the world are able to connect to the Internet. Although the United States has the largest number of Internet users, some areas in Asia and Europe are showing strong growth. Figure 7-11 shows the top 15 countries in Internet usage as of the end of 2002, according to Computer Industry Almanac. The organization estimates that by 2005, the worldwide number of Internet users will reach more than 1 billion.

Hardware and Software Requirements

The following equipment and software are required to connect to the Internet:

- computer, WebTV, personal digital assistant (PDA), or Web phone
- dial-up modem, digital subscriber line (DSL) modem, or cable modem
- telephone line or cable connection
- telecommunications software
- Web browser
- an account with an Internet service provider (ISP) or value added network (VAN)

An ISP is a company that provides Internet access for a fee, or sometimes for free. Firms that provide free access usually require subscribers to view advertisements when viewing Web pages. Value added networks (VANs) are large ISP companies that provide a connection to the Internet as well as additional content such as online news, weather forecasts, financial reports, and sports news. Some popular VANs are America Online (AOL) and the Microsoft Network (MSN). It should

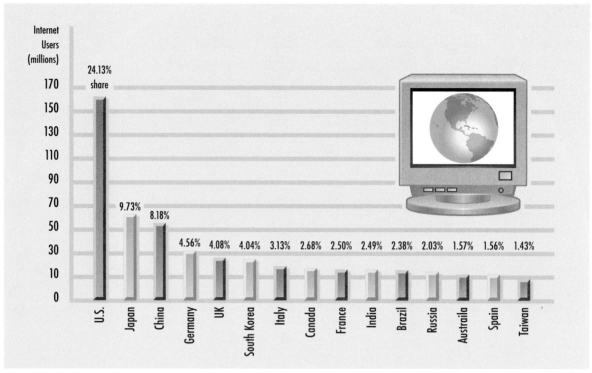

Source: Computer Industry Almanac Inc.

FIGURE 7-11: Top 15 Countries in Internet Use

be noted that all ISPs and online services are equal in terms of the number of e-mail users and Web sites they can reach.

ISPs are available on the local, regional, and national level. In the United States, local ISPs typically operate within a state, regional ISPs serve one or more states, and national ISPs provide connections from anywhere in the country. Larger ISPs provide local telephone numbers in several cities so that connections can be made without paying for long-distance calls. National ISPs are convenient for people who travel a great deal, but their monthly charges are usually considerably higher than local ISPs.

Dial-Up Access and LAN Connections

There are two main ways for users to connect to the Internet: through dial-up access or by using a LAN connection. **Dial-up access** allows access to the Internet over a standard telephone line by using a computer and a modem to dial into an ISP or VAN connection. Dial-up access is a feature typically included with the software provided by an ISP or VAN. Once the software is installed (see Figure 7-12), a dial-up access icon can be placed on the user's computer desktop. Clicking on the icon initiates a connection to the Internet.

LAN connections provide faster and more direct Internet access by connecting users to an ISP on a direct wire at speeds 20 or more times faster than can be achieved through a dial-up modem. Because they are more expensive than dial-up access, LAN connections are more commonly found in the workplace. Despite the increased cost ($50 per month and up), there are approximately 6 million LAN users in the United States using cable and DSL connections to connect from their homes.

ISP setup icons

FIGURE 7-12: Windows Desktop with ISP Setup Icons

Installing the Hardware and Connecting to an ISP

Several steps are required to connect a computer to the Internet through an ISP. These steps can be difficult for beginners, but fortunately they usually only need to be done once.

- The computer needs to be turned off so that a modem or LAN card can be installed.
- The modem or LAN card needs to be connected by phone line to a phone jack or LAN connection.
- The computer must be booted up (started) so the computer will recognize that new hardware has been installed. It will then ask for any software disks that came with the hardware, and these must be installed according to the instructions provided by the computer.
- The computer must be rebooted (started up again) and any software provided by the ISP or VAN must be installed. When installation is complete, the computer must be shut down and started up one more time.

Once the hardware and software are installed, the computer is ready to be connected to the Internet. Immediate errors in the connection steps probably indicate that the installation was done improperly, meaning that it must be repeated to correct the problem. The process may require some troubleshooting, so patience is required.

Connecting to the Internet is a straightforward process once the necessary hardware and software have been installed.

- The computer must be turned on.
- The software that connects the computer to the ISP (only required for home connections through dial-up modems) must be activated. Sometimes simply running the Web browser will do this. LAN connections are always online.
- A program will ask for a user name and password for dial-up connections. Microsoft Internet Explorer® offers an option that automatically saves this information so that it does not need to be entered every time.
- Once the user is logged on, the Web browser needs to be activated so users can begin surfing the Web.

Alternatives to Telephone Connections

Using a regular telephone line is usually the slowest telecommunications medium for setting up an individual Internet account through a dial-up ISP. Table 7-2 provides a comparison of the alternatives to connecting by telephone line. Faster options include the following systems:

- cable
- DSL (Digital Subscriber Line)
- wireless service providers and wireless portals
- satellite

Cable Modem

Cable television offers the advantage of simultaneous Web access and telephone calls, but the service is not available everywhere. In addition, the service slows down as more subscribers sign up in a neighborhood or location. Nationwide, as of 2003, there were 2.3 times as many subscribers to cable modem service (16 million) as compared to DSL (7 million). Cable TV companies provide a special modem and software for high-speed Internet access. The cost is about $50 monthly, plus a possible installation fee.

Digital Subscriber Line

Digital Subscriber Line (DSL) service is as fast as cable modem and provides simultaneous Web access and telephone use, but the service is usually available

Hardware	Download Speed*	Upload Speed*	Millions of Users in USA
56K modem	28Kbps	28Kbps	70
cable modem	1Mbps	500Kbps	16
DSL	1Mbps	500Kbps	7
Wi-Fi	varies widely	varies widely	<1
satellite	500Kbps	56Kbps	3

*Upload speed means how fast you can send a file from your computer to another computer out on the Internet. Download speed measures how fast you can receive a file from another computer. In most cases, download speed is more important.

Note: The speeds actually attained may vary greatly depending on quality of service and equipment.

T A B L E   7 - 2 : Connection Speeds for Telecommunications Media

only to users within three miles of the telephone carrier's central switching office. The line is dedicated to one household, and is not shared with neighbors. A DSL provides access to the Internet through the user's existing phone lines, with the phone carrier or Internet service provider providing the DSL modem and the network card. DSL service costs about $50 monthly, plus an installation fee. Some carriers include the Internet service account in the monthly fee for the line.

Wi-Fi

The fastest growing segment of Internet service involves wireless connections to the Internet. Thousands of Wi-Fi "hotspot" portals are springing up, allowing access in public places and even aboard airplanes. Wi-Fi portals support the IEEE 802.11 standard for radio-wave connections to the Internet. Wireless connections to the Internet are typically slower and more expensive than wired connections, but provide a great deal of portability. Both the price and the relative speed of these connections are improving.

Satellite

Downloading Web files is quick via satellite, but users cannot talk on the phone and surf the Web at the same time. Uploading is not as fast as downloading. To use a satellite connection, a person needs a satellite dish, a modem built into the PC or handheld, and an Internet account. Costs are about $50 per month for the service, plus about $350 for the dish, modem, and installation charges. Forrester Research reported in 2003 that approximately one-third of all households in the United States had digital cable or satellite service.

NAVIGATING THE INTERNET

Once connected and online, the next step for users is to start up a Web browser to begin surfing the Web. To access and move about the Web they need to know how to navigate using the browser, an activity called **browsing** or **surfing**. It is also helpful to know something about Internet protocol (IP) addresses and Uniform (or Universal) Resource Locators (URLs), and to know how these are used to identify and locate all the resources available on the Internet.

Web Browsers

A Web browser is an application that finds Web pages and displays them on the computer screen. The two most popular browsers are Microsoft's Internet Explorer

and Netscape Navigator, which was developed by Netscape Communications (now owned by AOL/Time Warner). Internet Explorer currently holds about 90 percent of the browser market. Both offer the following capabilities:

- automatic identification and connection to any local port providing a connection to the Internet
- POP3 mail service, for reading and sending e-mail
- HTML code viewing (the language of Web pages)
- Java™ applet support (special programs written for the Web)
- easy-to-use interfaces that allow for control commands such as a favorites list, a stop access button, and a go-back button

A new Web technology called a metabrowser has been developed to provide even more efficient Internet surfing than conventional Web browsers. **Metabrowsers** allow users to put all their favorite sites onto one page, reducing the number of clicks it takes to check favorite Web pages. Users can create "views" that organize favorite sites by category, such as finance, news, or entertainment. Scrolling down allows one site to be viewed after another. Firms offering metabrowsers include Octopus, Quickbrowse, OnePage, and Hodlee.

Internet Protocol Addresses and Universal Resource Locators

Web browsers locate material on the Internet using **Internet Protocol (IP) addresses**. An IP address works like an Internet phone number. It is a four-group series of numbers separated by periods, such as 207.171.181.16, representing a server on the Internet. Every server connected to the Web can be located using its IP address.

Since remembering IP numbers would be difficult, every computer also has a corresponding Web address called a **Uniform Resource Locator**, or **URL**. For example, the IP address above is represented by the URL http://www.amazon.com, home page of the pioneering online bookseller Amazon.com.

A URL contains several parts separated by a colon (:), slashes (/), and dots (.). The first part of a URL identifies the communications protocol to be used. In the case of the Amazon home page above, it is hypertext transfer protocol (HTTP). The material immediately following the protocol is format information, such as *www* for World Wide Web pages. Following the format information is the **domain name**, identifying the person, organization, server, or topic (such as Amazon) responsible for the Web page. The **domain suffix** comes last, identifying the type of organization.

Boot-Up Camp

In the far mountains of North Korea, a military academy has been training more than a thousand computer professionals a year in the art of cyberwarfare. Hacking, entering systems, creating viruses, and programming weapons guidance have been taught to soldiers since the 1980s at the "Automated War Institute."

That's what South Korea claims. The U.S. Pentagon and State Department have never confirmed that such a training school exists. But North Korea is considered one of the most militarily bent nations on earth, spending a great part of its national budget on defense. Although its people are lacking some basic necessities, the government has never scrimped on keeping up with state-of-the-art military technologies. For this reason, many experts believe a North Korean hacker academy does exist. Isolation from the Internet due to trade sanctions and the lack of a reliable electrical grid may make it difficult for North Korea to keep its computer training up-to-date, but the country has managed to build a comprehensive network that links all government offices. Although the network is limited in size and reach, North Korea conceivably could launch cyberattacks from other locations. In the event of a war in the Koreas, North Korea's ability to attack or disrupt U.S. military computer programs could certainly complicate matters.

Allaying some of those worries is the widely accepted assessment that South Korea is one of the world's most computer literate nations. It has 177 military computer training facilities that have already trained more than 200,000 soldiers in its own cyber tactics.

Source: McWilliams, Brian. "North Korea's School for Hackers," *Wired News*, June 2, 2003, <http://www.wired.com/news>.

	Institutions and Organizations	
Suffix	**Institution or Organization**	**Example**
.com	company or commercial institution	Ford, Intel
.edu	educational institution	Harvard, Washington University
.gov	governmental site	NASA, IRS
.int	international treaty organization, Internet database	NATO
.mil	military site	U.S. Department of Defense
.net	administrative site for the Internet or ISPs	EarthLink, Qwest
.org	nonprofit or private organization or society	Red Cross

	Countries		
.af Afghanistan	**.fr** France	**.nz** New Zealand	**.ch** Switzerland
.au Australia	**.de** Germany	**.no** Norway	**.tw** Taiwan
.at Austria	**.il** Israel	**.pl** Poland	**.uk** United Kingdom
.be Belgium	**.it** Italy	**.pt** Portugal	**.us** United States
.br Brazil	**.jp** Japan	**.ru** Russia	**.yu** Yugoslavia
.ca Canada	**.kr** Korea	**.za** South Africa	**.zw** Zimbabwe
.dk Denmark	**.mx** Mexico	**.es** Spain	
.fi Finland	**.nl** Netherlands	**.se** Sweden	

T A B L E 7 - 3 : Common Domain Suffixes Used in URLs

In the Amazon example, *com* stands for company. Table 7-3 lists other domain suffixes in common use. The entire URL constitutes a **pathname** describing where the information can be found.

In 1998, the U.S. Commerce Department created the Internet Corporation for Assigned Names and Numbers (ICANN) and assigned it the task of expanding the list of existing domain suffixes. In late 2000, ICANN acted on this authority to approve a number of new suffixes (see Table 7-4).

.aero	airline groups
.biz	general use
.coop	business cooperatives
.info	general use
.museum	museums
.name	personal Web sites
.pro	professionals

T A B L E 7 - 4 : New Domain Suffixes

Experienced Web surfers may notice that some URLs include a forward slash (/) and a name after the domain suffix, such as http://www.nasa.gov/mars. This element is an optional addition called a **file specification**, and indicates the name of a file or file folder. At some Web sites a vast amount of information is available on the server. Typing the file specification after the domain suffix will allow easier and faster access to the information, if a user knows the name of the file, page, or folder she is seeking.

The Path of a URL

After a URL is typed into a browser window, it is sent to the Internet. Routers then identify it and forward the request to the appropriate Web server. The Web server uses the HTTP communications protocol to determine which page, file, or object is being requested. Upon finding the item, the server sends it back to the originating computer, where it is displayed on the screen.

Packets

A file sent over the Internet is not sent as a single file. Instead, messaging software breaks each file into packets and sends them over separate routes. The path a packet takes depends on which servers are available. This process is called **packet-switching**. At the destination, a computer receives the data and reassembles the file. If any pieces are missing, the receiving computer requests that they be sent again. This is why Web pages sometimes appear incomplete, and some portions may take longer than others to fully load. The journey a packet takes is outlined in Figure 7-13.

FIGURE 7-13: Files are split up into packets and sent along different routes, then reassembled at their destination.

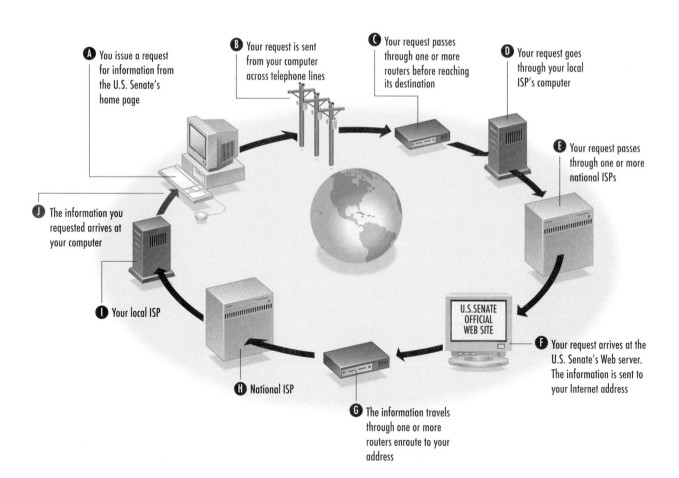

A You issue a request for information from the U.S. Senate's home page

B Your request is sent from your computer across telephone lines

C Your request passes through one or more routers before reaching its destination

D Your request goes through your local ISP's computer

E Your request passes through one or more national ISPs

F Your request arrives at the U.S. Senate's Web server. The information is sent to your Internet address

U.S. SENATE OFFICIAL WEB SITE

G The information travels through one or more routers enroute to your address

H National ISP

I Your local ISP

J The information you requested arrives at your computer

The concept of dividing files into packets has its origins in the Cold War, when the Internet was originally conceived as a system to maintain communication among the military and other government agencies in the event of a nuclear war. To prevent breakdowns, the system is designed to keep working even if part of it is destroyed or inoperable. A packet sent from New York to Los Angeles, for example, might travel through Denver or Dallas, but if those systems are busy (or destroyed) the packet could go up to Toronto before returning to Los Angeles. This design feature, called **dynamic routing**, is part of what makes the Internet work so well even with heavy traffic loads.

VIEWING WEB PAGES

A Web page is the term for a single document viewable on the World Wide Web. A **Web site** includes all of the Web pages comprising the site. The pages may be located on the host computer, while other pages may be located on remote servers that could be anywhere in the world. For example, the majority of the material on the CNN site (www.cnn.com) is located on CNN servers, but there are often links to materials contained in other Web sites that are not owned or controlled by

CNN. The first page displayed when a Web site is accessed is usually the site's **home page**. Like the table of contents in a book, the home page is an introduction to the site and lists the types of information or features available.

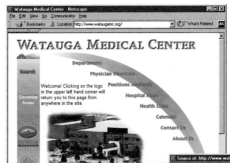

HTML

Web pages are created using **Hypertext Markup Language (HTML)**, a sample of which is shown in Figure 7-14. A

FIGURE 7-14: This Web page is created from the HTML coding shown below.

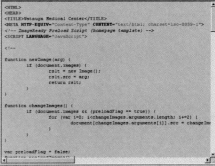

markup language is a set of specifications describing the characteristics of elements that appear on a page, including headings, paragraphs, backgrounds, lists, and so on. A **hypertext** document presents information enhanced with links to other documents. This presentation method allows users to read only the basic information or click the links to access additional information on another Web page. Technically called a **hyperlink**, a **Web link** is any element on the screen that is coded in HTML to transport viewers to another page or site. Links are often underlined text. However, they can also take the form of buttons, photos, or drawings. HTML gives developers wide latitude in determining the appearance and design of Web pages. Most Web browsers, including Microsoft's Internet Explorer and Netscape's Navigator, can display Web pages in HTML format.

XML

A new and improved Web language called **Extensible Markup Language (XML)** is becoming increasingly popular. Whereas HTML only defines the format of a Web page, XML organizes and standardizes the structure of data so that computers can communicate with each other directly. XML is more flexible than HTML, as it is really a **metalanguage** (a language for describing other languages). It allows developers to design their own custom languages that work with limitless types of

documents and file formats. Using an XML application, for example, suppliers and manufacturers could turn their computers loose in the Internet market, letting them find, purchase, and sell products and services through XML-coded sites. Medical researchers could allow their computers to search the databases of other research centers to identify possible treatments based on new scientific breakthroughs. Several software producers, including Microsoft, are now using XML in developing some of their applications. Microsoft's .NET technology and the Office 2003 suite both incorporate XML to manage data and to connect directly with other XML-enabled applications over the Internet.

Audio, Video, and Animation Elements

Most computer users are accustomed to the basic elements of a Web page that attract and hold the interest of those viewing the page, such as text, photos, and links. As the Web grows more sophisticated, elements such as sounds and movies are being incorporated into pages to increase attention and expand the range of activities a Web page can perform. Various miniprograms make these additions possible, including Java applets, and plug-ins such as Shockwave®, Apple QuickTime, Adobe Acrobat® Reader™, and Macromedia Flash™ Player.

Java Applets

Java is a programming language Web site designers frequently use. It was created for use on the Internet, and is similar in nature to the C or C++ programming languages (see Chapter 11 for more information on Java). Java applets (**applet** is the term for a miniature program) are small Java programs that are run by Web browsers. Like macros, they provide the ability to program online games and highly interactive interfaces.

Cookies

Cookies are very small files stored on your hard drive by Web sites that you visit. Often, these files are harmless and are used to store preference information, such as your user ID and password at a chat site. Sometimes, however, these files can be used to track the surfing habits of users without their knowledge. By placing a file on your computer that indicates what sites you have visited, other related sites can read this information and track your actions. Security settings on your browser can be adjusted to warn you when cookie files are being accessed or to prevent their operation altogether.

Plug-Ins

Sometimes a Web site will ask for approval to add a plug-in to the viewer's Web browser. A **plug-in** is a miniprogram that extends the capabilities of Web browsers in a variety of ways, usually by improving graphic, sound, and video elements. Most plug-ins are harmless, without any hidden features that may cause problems. However, as a general rule it is a good idea to view a site before giving permission to load any plug-ins. If there are viewing errors, they are probably caused by missing plug-ins. If a user thinks the site is trustworthy, she can hit the *Refresh* button on the browser, which automatically reloads the site and causes the plug-in dialog box to reappear. The "Yes" box granting permission to install plug-ins can be selected, allowing improved Web page performance.

One of the most widely known plug-ins is Shockwave by Macromedia. Sites using Shockwave normally take longer to load, but are graphically superior, with higher-resolution graphics, interactive features, and streaming audio. Flash Player and Apple's QuickTime are two other popular plug-ins that let users experience animation, audio, and video.

Advertisements

Advertising is a necessary commercial Web page element, producing income for the companies that own and maintain Web sites. With the economic downturn experienced by the technology industry in 2001, Web-based enterprises (often referred to as **dot-com companies**) came under increasing pressure from investors to earn more revenue from hits (visits) at their Web sites. As a result, many of these companies have experimented with forms of advertising that vary from being interesting to downright annoying.

Banners

A **banner** is a graphic that invites viewers to click it so that they will be directed to a new Web site selling a product or service. Banners are usually rectangular shapes appearing across the top or bottom of a Web page. This is a common ad form that can provide helpful information for those interested in the product being advertised. However, some Web masters place so many banners on their Web pages that visitors find them annoying; sometimes to the point that they will leave a site and go elsewhere (see Figure 7-15).

FIGURE 7-15: A Web Page with Banners and Pop-up Advertisements

CHAPTER 7

Blind Links

Some links misrepresent their true function. A frequently encountered example is a link with wording such as "Next Page," that actually directs viewers to an advertising Web page. This deception is called a **blind link**, and is considered bad form by reputable Web page designers (see Figure 7-16). Blind links are often encountered on free-host Web sites. These

FIGURE 7-16: This banner is not a Microsoft dialog box. If viewers click it, they will be directed to a Web page selling a product or service.

sites do not charge a fee for hosting Web pages, but do require that the pages display banners and other forms of advertising chosen by the company hosting the Web pages.

Pop-Up Windows

Another common and only slightly less intrusive form of advertisement is the **pop-up window** (see Figure 7-17). Named for their tendency to "pop" unexpectedly into the middle of the screen, these windows can be closed or minimized so the viewer can see the Web page. Minimizing a pop-up will sometimes cause it to cease functioning, while closing it may make it pop up again later. In extreme cases, pop-ups may be designed to resist any attempt to remove them. They may have no readily apparent closing "X" in the upper corner, or they might just fire back onto the screen as fast as they can be clicked off. On Windows machines, pop-ups without Close buttons can often be removed by pressing Alt-F4.

Elements that Track Surfing

Many Web sites are connected to databases that allow retailers and other types of companies to gather information on visitors. When users click a *Purchase* button

FIGURE 7-17: A Pop-up Window Advertising a Product

FIGURE 7-18: Banner Ad with CGI Click Counter

or an advertisement, a **Common Gateway Interface (CGI)** script (a program written in a special **script language**) makes an entry into the database. Users will know that they are being tracked if they move their mouse over a possible advertisement and notice that a long URL appears on the browser status bar at the bottom of the screen. These URLs usually end with a string of letters and numbers (see Figure 7-18). The issue of tracking Web site visitors is a hot topic among people concerned about protecting individual privacy.

Escaping Web Page Traps

Some Web sites can actually change browser settings permanently, or may attempt to prevent viewers from leaving by continually popping up more windows and disabling the *Back* button. These **Web page traps** can be avoided. One way is to alter Web browser settings to increase the level of security (see Figure 7-19). This will cause the browser to prompt users whenever it encounters suspicious behavior. Unfortunately, these higher security settings may cause the browser to prompt users constantly, even when they are visiting legitimate sites. If users do fall into one of these traps, they can press the Control-Alt-Delete key sequence, which will open the Task Scheduler. The computer can be rebooted, or the affected program can be selected and closed.

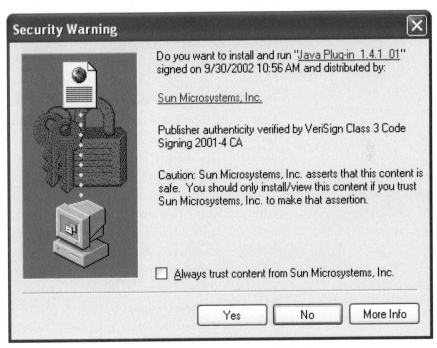

FIGURE 7-19: The Microsoft Internet Explorer Security Dialog Box

WebRings

One relatively safe way to move from site to site on the Internet is by using a WebRing (see Figure 7-20). Each site on a **WebRing** maintains a link to the next site, forming a ring, hence the name WebRing. WebRings link sites devoted to a similar theme or topic. Sites dedicated to hobbies or special interests typically include this navigation feature. WebRings are generally moderated by someone

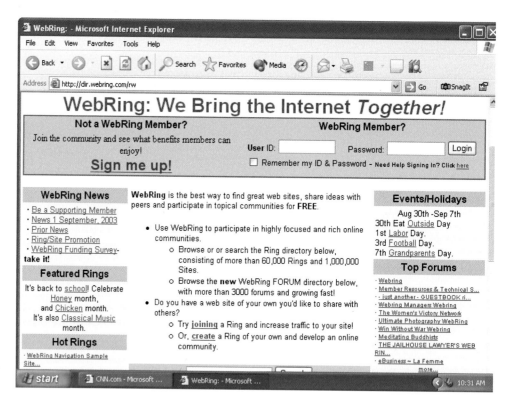

FIGURE 7-20: The Yahoo! WebRing home page has listings for hundreds of different WebRings organized around different topics.

who wants to help people find Web sites that would not otherwise be easily accessible. Webrings are an excellent way for hobbyists to find soul mates who share their passion for falconry, old cars, nineteenth-century tea sets, or hundreds of other interests.

SEARCHING FOR INFORMATION ON THE INTERNET

One of the most useful capacities of the Internet is its ability to act like a global library of limitless data on practically any topic. Better still, it doesn't even require a library card or a trip to a university to use it. At present, more than a billion pages of information are available on the Web.

Users can search for and retrieve information from Web pages by using a search engine. Recall that a search engine is a software program that can find and retrieve information located on the World Wide Web. Unlike a browser, in which an address is entered to access a Web site, a search engine allows users to locate information by entering search criteria in the engine's search box. For example, suppose a student wants to find information about the Battle of Vicksburg for a history class report. Typing the search criteria—in this case the words "Battle of Vicksburg"—in the search box, and clicking the Search button causes a list of articles, hyperlinked to their respective Web sites, to appear on the student's screen. They can be selected and read by clicking the article title. Some of the most frequently used search engines are listed in Table 7-5. Figure 7-21 shows the Google home page.

Picking the Right Search Engine

Beginning Web users quickly discover that finding the information they need is not always easy. The first task is to locate a good search engine. Not all search engines offer the same features, and some perform certain types of searches better

Search Engine	URL
Yahoo!	www.yahoo.com
Google	www.google.com
AltaVista	www.altavista.com
Lycos	www.lycos.com
Excite	www.excite.com
HotBot	www.hotbot.com

TABLE 7-5: Popular Search Engines

than others. Differences in capabilities are related to the number of Web pages cataloged by an engine, the search methodology used, and the number of different search tools available to refine searches.

Another factor to consider in selecting a search engine is that some now accept fees from Web sites so that they will be placed at the top of a search results list. This means that the first few entries on a search results list from that type of search engine may not necessarily contain information most relevant to the search criteria.

Search Techniques

One of the primary considerations in any Internet search is selecting the right **keywords** (**search terms**). Using too many keywords will result in users having to wade through hundreds or even thousands of search results to find what they are looking for. Using vague, obsolete, or incorrectly spelled terms further reduces the

FIGURE 7-21: The Home Page for the Google Search Engine

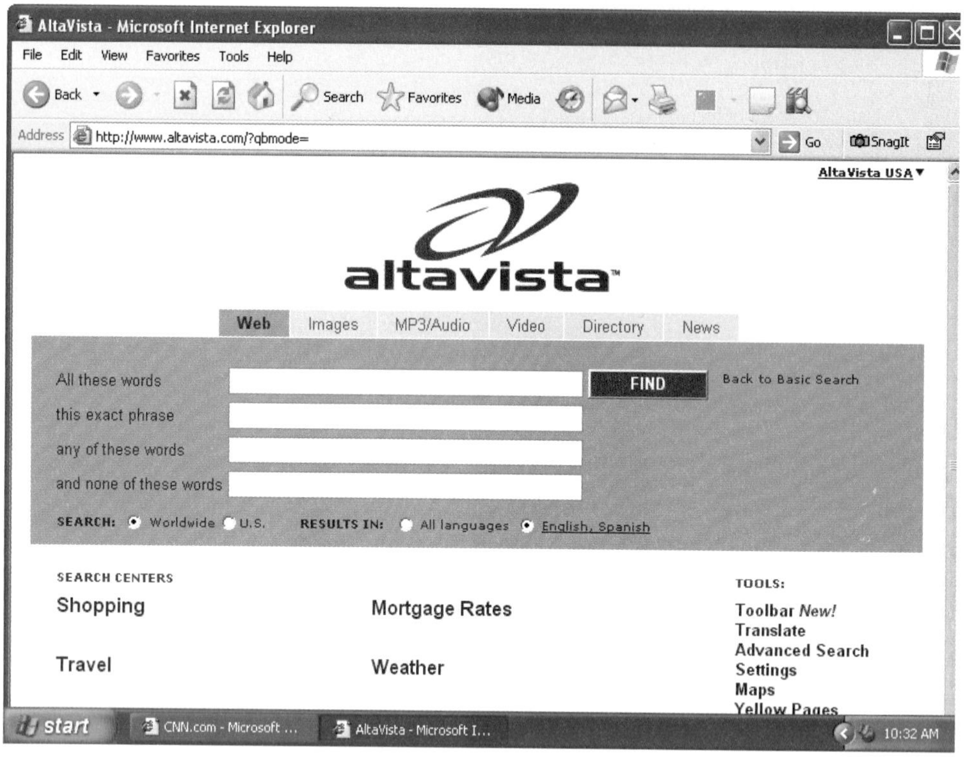

FIGURE 7-22: The AltaVista Advanced Search Page

chances of a successful search. Users need to think of what combinations of words are likely to be found in the material they are looking for. To get the most out of a search, a user needs to know how a search engine's advanced search options work. Figure 7-22 shows AltaVista's advanced search page.

Advanced searching employs logic statements known as **search operators** to refine searches. Three of the most common search operators are AND, OR, and NOT.

AND connects search terms and returns search results containing references to all the terms used. For example, asking the search engine to search for dogs AND cats would return only those sites containing references to both dogs and cats. Using OR returns results containing references to any of the search terms. Asking a search engine for dogs OR cats would result in sites that have references to either dogs or cats, or both. OR is usually the default logic option on search engines. NOT is used to exclude a keyword. Asking for dogs NOT cats would result in only sites that referred to dogs, but had no mention of cats.

Using logical statements and other advanced search features will greatly speed up the search process and increase the likelihood of success. There are almost a billion documents available on the Web, and as their numbers increase the likelihood of finding an individual document diminishes.

NEWER INTERNET APPLICATIONS

The Internet is far from static. Not only does the content change daily, but the very way in which the Internet is used and understood as a communication medium is constantly evolving. Thousands of innovative applications are introduced each year, but only a few survive the tough demands of the marketplace.

Peer-to-Peer File Sharing

Peer-to-peer (P2P) file sharing is a relatively recent player among popular ways to use the Internet. P2P allows people to download material directly from other users' hard drives, rather than from files located on Web servers. Napster, the famous pioneer of peer-to-peer file sharing, functioned by maintaining a list of files made available for sharing by subscribers to the system. For example, someone would let Napster know that he had 50 music files on his hard disk that he would be willing to share. Other users could then use Napster to locate these files and request that they be sent to their computers. Peer-to-peer is a powerful idea that allows every computer to function as a server as well as a client. Figure 7-23 shows how peer-to-peer file sharing works.

At its peak, Napster was being used to download music files by almost 70 percent of U.S. college students and had more than 70 million users worldwide. Unfortunately, many of the files being shared in this way were copyrighted material. Napster eventually lost a series of lawsuits filed by copyright holders and was forced to shut down. It is currently trying to remake itself into a profit-making corporation that will charge for copyrighted material and pass the fees collected on to the copyright holders. Whether its popularity will continue once it is a fee-based system remains unknown.

While Napster restricted file downloading to MP3 music files, many similar peer-to-peer systems allow the downloading of nonmusic files, including video. The movie industry estimates applications such as KaZaA are being used to download millions of songs and full-length movies on a daily basis. The volume of free downloads can only increase as connection speeds improve and make each movie download faster. This has caused a significant loss of sales for the music industry in particular, with sharply declining sales of an estimated of 5 percent to 10 percent each year since Napster's debut in 1999. Figure 7-24 shows the home page of KaZaA, a Napster-like Web site.

Using peer-to-peer applications to harness the individual efforts of millions of computers around the world represents a vast potential for communications that has not yet been realized. Where this technology is taking us and whether it will redefine the definition of copyrighted material remains to be seen. What is clear is that prohibiting these systems will be difficult. Unlike Napster, most peer-to-peer applications are freeware and have no owner. There is, therefore, no one to sue to force the systems to shut down.

FIGURE 7-23: Peer-to-peer file sharing allows every computer to function as a server as well as a client.

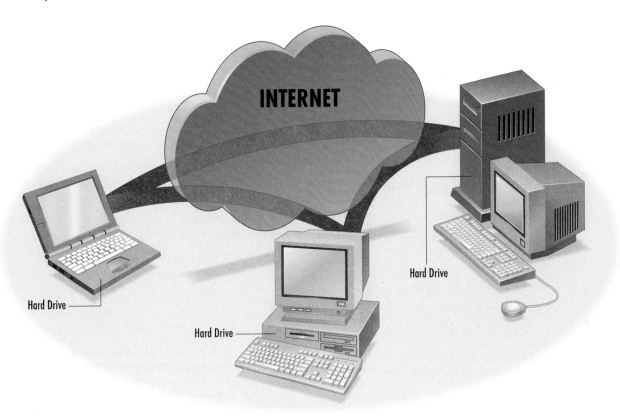

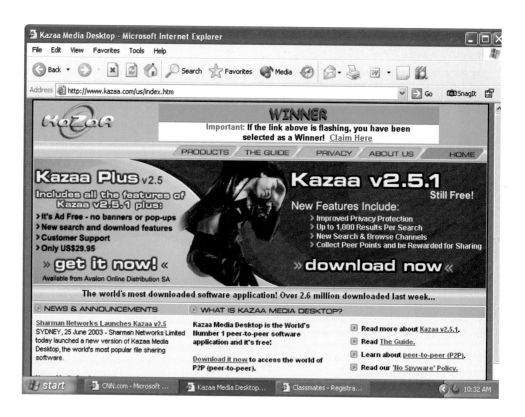

FIGURE 7-24: The Home Page for KaZaA, a Popular Napster Clone

Internet Telephone Service

Internet telephone services, also called **Voice over IP**, are another increasingly popular way to use the Internet. By accessing one these services, two or more people with sufficiently good connections can use the Internet to make telephone calls around the world. Once the voices are digitized and broken down into packets, they can be transmitted anywhere, just like any other form of data. There are no long-distance telephone charges, and users only pay their normal ISP connection fees. Connecting to these services only requires that users at each end of the connection download a shareware program and install it. Users are required to select a password, and are required to log on when they establish a connection, just as might be done with an instant messaging system. Internet-ready phones can now be purchased for use by entire organizations, completely bypassing the traditional phone service, including long-distance charges.

Webcasting, Streaming Audio, and Video

An alternative to downloading a piece of music or a video is to access it using **streaming techniques** (also known as **webcasting**). Streaming sends a continuous stream of data to the receiving computer where it is immediately displayed. Old data is erased as new data arrives. This protects the owner of copyrighted material to some degree, as a complete copy of the material is not downloaded, and therefore cannot be copied and shared. High-quality video streaming normally requires a fast (LAN-based) connection.

Webcams

Tiny video cameras called **webcams** allow conversations over the Web through live video transmission. Often mounted on top of a computer monitor, the cameras automatically create and transmit video to the PC. Despite the fact that the images are a bit grainy and jerky, millions are in use. As the technology improves, their popularity is sure to increase even further.

Free E-Mail

Free e-mail services work by using a Web browser as an e-mail interface. After logging on to a free e-mail Web site, a computer user can send and receive e-mail messages. Providers can offer this service for free because their income is derived from the advertising that users must endure as they use a free e-mail account (see Figure 7-25).

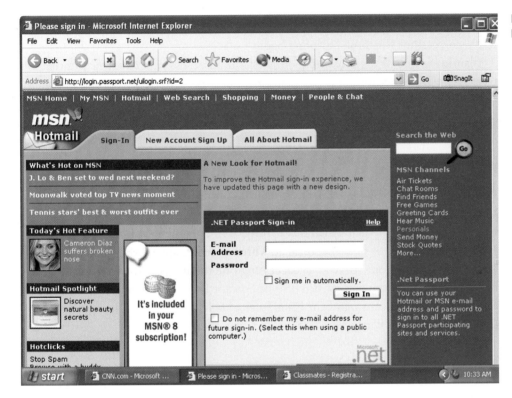

FIGURE 7-25: The Hotmail Home Page

These services have several advantages over the mail service provided by an ISP. The chief advantage, of course, is that they are free. Another advantage is that they can be accessed from any Internet connection because users are not tied to the connections offered by their ISP. Users can also establish several free e-mail accounts to use for different purposes. Another convenience of free e-mail is that if users ever experience a problem, such as harassment, they can shut down their old free e-mail account and open a new one.

Audio Mail

Audio mail is a fledgling type of electronic mail that allows people to transmit messages by voice. As with e-mail, attachments can be included. The technology can be compared to voice mail, without telephone charges.

Free ISP Connections

Many users opt for free ISP connections. These connections work well, but are always dial-up only. They also come with banner ads that take up a significant portion of the screen and are nearly impossible to avoid. Free services may insist that users occasionally click on ads or they will be disconnected. Anyone willing to put up with this inconvenience can surf for free.

INTERNET COMMUNITY ISSUES

Internet users around the world form a community and, like any social organization, the community exhibits the entire range of behavior, from considerate and creative to insulting and damaging. Unfortunately, the anonymous nature of Internet interaction tends to bring out the worst in some people. The fear of embarrassment or shame that governs behavior in face-to-face encounters is lessened when people meet on the Internet. This means that some individuals act very differently than they would if they were in a public forum, ruining the Internet experience for many people. The problem is exacerbated by the fact that there are few repercussions for those behaving badly.

Flaming is one of the most frequently encountered examples of rude Internet behavior. Guidelines for good Net behavior, called **netiquette**, have been developed to encourage people to interact productively. Moderated environments are another solution to inappropriate behavior. They allow a moderator to police behavior in certain settings such as chat rooms, mailing lists, and message boards.

Flaming

Flaming is the Internet equivalent of insulting someone in a face-to-face setting. Flaming often occurs in public forums, such as e-mail, message boards, or chat rooms. Taking advantage of their anonymity, some people seem to take a perverse joy in being as rude as possible, to the point that they drive people away. Flame wars are flames that are traded back and forth, often among multiple parties. The best policy is to ignore flames. It is also important for anyone using a public Internet forum to be aware of the basic rules of behavior to avoid doing anything that might provoke flaming.

E-Mail Pointers

The ease with which e-mail can be composed and sent makes it very easy to make mistakes that might be regretted later. There are several very important points to remember when writing and sending e-mail messages:

- Once sent, they cannot be retrieved.
- A permanent copy of an e-mail message probably remains somewhere on the Internet.
- E-mail is easily forwarded or copied.

For these reasons it is always a good idea to avoid sending any e-mail messages that have been written in anger or haste. It is better to save the e-mail, and then look at it again later when emotions have cooled. If the writer still feels that the e-mail should be sent, she still has that option. However, in most cases she will realize that sending the e-mail would not be a good idea, and may be something she would later regret. Once the *Send* button is clicked, it is too late to do anything.

Another factor to bear in mind is the ease with which e-mail can be copied or forwarded. An e-mail message criticizing someone could easily end up in that person's mailbox minutes after it is sent, after the original recipient forwards it.

Netiquette

The term *netiquette* is a result of combining the words *Net* and *etiquette*. Netiquette exists to address behavior problems such as flaming and sending rude or hurtful e-mail messages. Most netiquette is based on the Golden Rule, which stipulates that people should treat others as they would like others to treat them. Some netiquette deals with certain Internet conventions that need to be learned in order not to inadvertently offend other users. For example, newcomers commonly type messages in all capital letters without realizing that by convention, this is commonly understood to mean that the writer is shouting. Without intending it, an e-mail writer using the all-caps style will be making people uncomfortable or even angry. Knowing the common rules of netiquette can help avoid this problem and other unintentional offenses (see Table 7-6).

Rule 1:	Remember the Human.
Rule 2:	Adhere to the same standards of behavior online that you follow in real life.
Rule 3:	Know where you are in cyberspace.
Rule 4:	Respect other people's time and bandwidth.
Rule 5:	Make yourself look good online.
Rule 6:	Share expert knowledge.
Rule 7:	Help keep flame wars under control.
Rule 8:	Respect other people's privacy.
Rule 9:	Don't abuse your power.
Rule 10:	Be forgiving of other people's mistakes.

Excerpted from the book Netiquette, *by Virginia Shea* (Albion Books, 1994)

TABLE 7-6: Core Rules of Netiquette

Moderated Environments

Moderated environments are the answer for many people who want to avoid the seedy side of the Net. Many chat rooms, message boards, and mailing lists have a **moderator**, an individual with the power to filter messages and ban people who break the rules. Rules violations can be anything from hurling insults to simply straying off-topic. A moderator running a chat room on travel, for example, might ban people for excessively discussing their favorite movies. Usually, a moderator has complete power over the situation and can ban people in any way he sees fit. If a moderator is too harsh, people might switch to another group.

INTERNET POLICY AND DEVELOPMENT ISSUES

A number of technical and legal issues are influencing the direction and development of the Internet. Companies and individuals are clamoring for standard protocols and increased transmission bandwidths. Consumers worry about the privacy and security of their Internet communications and transactions. Copyright holders are looking for stronger protection for their intellectual property. And for every Internet user, the threat of viruses being transmitted over the Internet is a daily worry.

Privacy Issues

Privacy is a major concern for many users, particularly with e-mail communications and e-commerce transactions. Almost everyone is aware that e-mail messages can be intercepted and read by others. There is the real possibility that an employee's e-mail messages may be read by her supervisor, and under current law employers have a right to do just that. This practice is becoming more common as businesses discover employees spending time surfing the Web for personal reasons instead of performing their work. For more on employee monitoring and similar topics, see Chapter 13.

Security Protection

Security is a major concern, especially in electronic commerce transactions. Businesses selling products and services over the Internet have discovered that many potential customers are reluctant to use a credit card for payment. Stories abound about hackers penetrating computer systems and using stolen credit card numbers. To allay these fears, major retail companies have instituted sophisticated encryption systems that protect customers' financial information.

Another worry for many people is protecting their children from Web sites with harmful or inappropriate material. A proxy, for example, can be set up to make a URL check, which will disallow packets to and from Web sites that are off-limits. This is how Internet connections at elementary schools protect children from adult sites. A number of commercial software packages incorporate this feature. Some of them also allow tracking of Internet usage so that parents can monitor which Web sites their children have visited.

Viruses

Computer viruses represent a significant threat to all computer systems. A **virus** is a computer code that can damage or destroy valuable programs and data. Some viruses clog and choke storage devices by making innumerable copies of themselves, while others erase everything on a storage device. A virus will often display messages or graphics, sometimes corrupting programs or operating systems and causing them to crash. To date, tens of thousands of viruses have infiltrated the PC world at one time or another. New viruses appear regularly, and are frequently sent over the Internet via e-mail, causing frustration, and sometimes serious losses of data and money. The "I Love You" virus that appeared in 2000, for example, cost U.S. businesses an estimated $11 billion (see Figure 7-26).

The possibility of virus transmission over wireless devices and the Internet is a recent concern, since the technology is quite new and evolving rapidly. Industry observers note that as the operating

FIGURE 7-26: The "I Love You" virus spread rapidly through e-mail systems.

systems of handhelds climb in power—some models now have the computing capability of a desktop—so will the potential for virus invasions.

To eliminate the threat, virus scanning software is widely available. However, virus scanners can only detect known viruses. New technology is needed that can detect viruses when they are first created and launched. Computer users need to be fully aware of how viruses are transmitted and be on guard for unusual e-mail attachments from unfamiliar or anonymous senders.

Copyright Infringement

Copyright law violations are frequent occurrences on the Internet. Much of the material found on the Web is copyrighted. Copying and using copyrighted items without permission is illegal, and most Web sites include a copyright notice that spells out general guidelines for how the site's content may be used (see Figure 7-27). Nevertheless, copyright laws are frequently ignored, and violators sometimes end up in court.

Because existing copyright laws were written with printed materials in mind, Congress passed a new law in 1998 that addressed the major issues related to protecting digital content on the Internet, which can include text, videos, music, and many other file formats. Called the **Digital Millennium Copyright Act of 1998**, the law generally prohibits people from defeating software encryption programs and other safeguards that copyright holders have established to control access to their works. Entertainment companies have tried to protect their movies on DVD by including security codes, but hackers have already developed programs capable of cracking them. A key provision of the Digital Millennium Copyright Act of 1998 makes the use and distribution of the security-cracking codes illegal, and imposes civil damages ranging from $200 to $2,500. Repeat offenders face criminal penalties of up to $1 million in fines, or 10 years in jail.

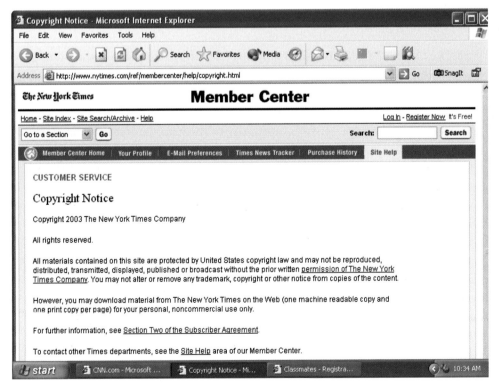

FIGURE 7-27: A Copyright Notice on *The New York Times* Home Page

ON THE HORIZON

The Internet is having trouble keeping up with the rapid increase in users and the increased workload created by the popularity of bandwidth-intensive applications such as music and video files. The broadband connections needed to enjoy these new applications are not evenly distributed. Several ongoing projects promise to provide solutions for these problems in the future. Once these connectivity problems are dealt with, people around the world will be able to enjoy the new Web services that are only a few short years away. These new services are only the beginning, and there are exciting possibilities even further down the line.

Satellite Internet Connections

Many people living in remote or sparsely populated areas are not served by broadband Internet connections. Cable or optical fiber networks are very expensive to install and maintain, and ISPs are not interested in providing service to areas or individuals unless they think it will be profitable. One hope for people without broadband connections is provided by satellite TV networks. Remote ISPs connect to the satellite network using antennae attached to their servers. Data is relayed to and from ISP servers to satellites, which are in turn connected to an Internet backbone access point. While the connection speeds might not be as fast as those offered by regular land-based broadband access, they are faster than the service twisted-pair cable can offer and much better than no access at all.

Another Internet?

A remedy for the traffic clogging the information highway is **Internet2**, a revolutionary new type of Internet currently under development. When fully operational, Internet2 will enable large research universities in the United States to collaborate and share huge amounts of complex scientific information at amazing speeds. Led by over 170 universities working in partnership with industry and government, the Internet2 consortium is developing and deploying advanced network technologies and applications. The primary goals of Internet2 are to

- create a leading-edge network capability for the national research community
- enable revolutionary Internet applications
- ensure the rapid transfer of new network services and applications to the broader Internet community

Internet2 is a testing ground for universities to work together and develop advanced Internet technologies such as telemedicine, digital libraries, and virtual laboratories. An example of such collaboration is the Informedia Digital Video Library (IDVL) project. Once implemented, IDVL will offer a combination of speech recognition, image understanding, and natural language processing technology to automatically transcribe, partition, and index video segments, enabling intelligent searching and navigation, along with selective retrieval of information.

Internet2 universities will be connected to an ultrahigh-speed network called the Abilene backbone. Each university will use state-of-the-art equipment to take

FIGURE 7-28: The Internet2 Home Page

advantage of transfer speeds provided by the network. More can be learned about Internet2 by visiting the project's Web site at www.internet2.edu. Figure 7-28 shows the home page for Internet2.

Bring Your Own Access: Internet Services for a Fee

Industry observers, including the research firm Forrester, predict that large portals such as AOL, MSN, and Yahoo! will soon determine effective structures and marketing strategies to get consumers to pay for Internet services. This new market, called **bring-your-own-access (BYOA)**, will combine essential *content*, for example, news and weather, with *services*, such as search, directory, e-mail, IM, and online shopping, into a new product with monthly access charges. But to entice current and potential customers into the BYOA market, ISP and telecom companies must offer improvements in the areas of security, privacy, and ease-of-use. Additionally, they are expected to develop new ways to personalize content and add value to the current range of Internet services.

The Web in 2030

Ray Kurzweil, a computer futurist, has looked ahead to the year 2030 and visualized a Web that offers no clear distinctions between real and simulated environments and people. Among the applications he sees as very possible are computerized displays in eyeglasses that could offer simultaneous translations of foreign language conversations, **nanobots** (microscopic robots) that would work with our brains to extend our mental capabilities, and more sophisticated avatars (simulated persons on-screen) that people will interact with online. Technologies that allow people to project their feelings as well as their images and voices may usher in a period when people could "be" with another person even though they are physically hundreds or even thousands of miles apart.

chapter summary

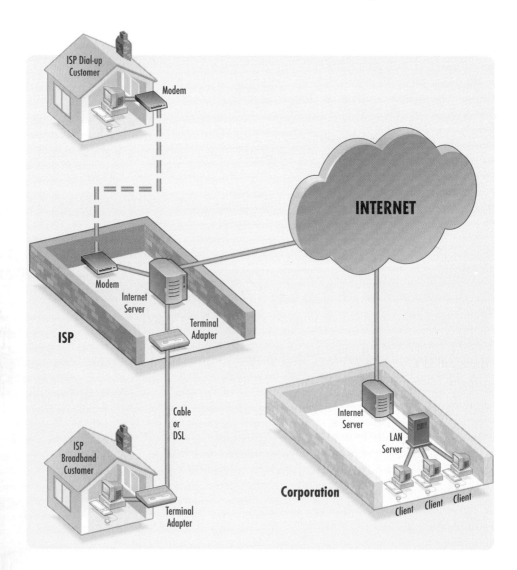

The Internet: A Global Network

Besides communications, the Internet can also be used for research, distance learning, entertainment, and e-commerce. Search engines can be used to conduct research. Computers can be used for entertainment purposes, including playing games, listening to music, and even viewing movies and videos. **Electronic commerce (e-commerce)** refers to the Internet exchange of business information, products, services, and payments. E-commerce is commonly divided into two categories defined by target audience: business-to-consumer (B2C) and business-to-business (B2B).

Connecting to the Internet

An Internet service provider (ISP) is a company that provides Internet access. Value added networks (VANs) are large ISP companies that provide a connection to the Internet as well as additional content. There are two main ways for users to connect to the

Internet: through **dial-up access** or by using a **LAN connection**. High-speed options include **cable**, **Digital Subscriber Line (DSL)**, **Wireless**, and satellite connections.

Navigating the Internet

To access and move about the Web, users need to know how to navigate using a **browser**. **Metabrowsers** allow users to put all their favorite sites onto one page. Web browsers locate material on the Internet using **Internet Protocol (IP) addresses**. Every IP also has a corresponding Web address called a **Uniform Resource Locator (URL)**, which is a **pathname** describing where the information can be found. The Internet breaks files into many pieces of data, called **packets**, and sends them out over separate routes, a process called **packet-switching**.

Viewing Web Pages

A Web page is the term for a single document viewable on the World Wide Web. A **Web site** includes all of the Web pages comprising the site. The first page displayed after a Web site is accessed is usually the site's **home page**. A **hyperlink** (also **Web link**, or **link**) is any element on the

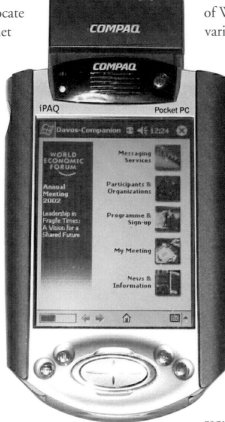

screen that is coded to transport viewers to another page or site. Web pages are usually created using **Hypertext Markup Language (HTML)**. **Extensible Markup Language (XML)** is a new and improved Web language that allows computers to communicate with each other directly. Web site designers frequently program using **Java** and **Java applets**. A **plug-in** is a miniprogram that extends the capabilities of Web browsers in a variety of ways.

Companies advertise on Web sites using **banners**, **blind links**, and **pop-up windows**. **WebRings** link sites devoted to a similar theme or topic.

Searching for Information on the Internet

Searches are conducted using **keywords (search terms)**. Advanced searching requires the use of logic statements known as **search operators** to refine searches and improve results.

Newer Internet Applications

Peer-to-peer (P2P) file sharing allows people to download material directly from other users' hard drives. **Internet telephone services** provide free long-distance service. An alternative to

CHAPTER 7

downloading a piece of music or a video is to access it using **streaming techniques** (also known as **webcasting**). Tiny video cameras called **webcams** allow conversations over the Web through live video transmission. Free e-mail services work by using a Web browser as an e-mail interface. **Audio mail** allows people to transmit not only text and pictures but also a recording of their voice.

Internet Community Issues

Flaming is one of the most frequently encountered examples of rude Internet behavior. Guidelines for good behavior, called **netiquette**, have been developed to encourage people to interact productively. **Moderated** environments are another solution to inappropriate behavior.

Internet Policy and Development Issues

Developers have not reached an agreement on a common **communications standard**. Incompatible standards mean that businesses and consumers are inconvenienced, and the full potential of the application is not realized. Limited **bandwidth** in many areas slows down transmissions speeds, especially with the huge **multimedia** files that are increasingly common. **Privacy** and **security** are major concerns, particularly with e-mail communications and e-commerce transactions. **Encryption systems** can protect customers' financial information. Computer **viruses** represent a significant threat to all computer systems. To eliminate the threat, **virus scanning** software is widely available. Copyright law violations are frequent occurrences on the Internet. The **Digital Millennium Copyright Act of 1998** generally prohibits people from defeating software encryption programs and other safeguards that copyright holders have established to control access to their works.

KEY TERMS

Page numbers indicate where terms are first cited in the chapter. A complete list of key terms with definitions can be found in the Glossary at the end of the book.

chapter
exercises

The following chapter exercises, along with new activities and information, are also offered in the *Computers: Understanding Technology* Internet Resource Center at www.emcp.com.

EXPLORING WINDOWS

Tutorial 7 teaches different methods for copying and moving files and folders on your computer.

TERMS CHECK: MATCHING

Write the letter of the correct answer on the line before each numbered item.

a. packet
b. HTML
c. netiquette
d. spam
e. flaming
f. keyword
g. electronic commerce (e-commerce)
h. electronic mail (e-mail)
i. search engine
j. plug-in
k. Web browser
l. banner
m. zip file
n. dynamic routing
o. virus

_____ 1. A common type of compressed data file.

_____ 2. Term used to find information using a search engine.

_____ 3. A small software program that can be downloaded to extend a browser's capabilities.

_____ 4. Business conducted using the Internet.

_____ 5. Unwanted messages sent in mass numbers and/or repeatedly over the Internet.

_____ 6. Engaging in insulting or rude personal attacks over the Internet.

_____ 7. A program that allows users to search for and retrieve information on the World Wide Web.

_____ 8. Small rectangular advertisements used to promote products and services on Web pages.

_____ 9. The method used to send packets by a variety of different routes to their final destination.

_____ 10. A code prescribing civilized behavior for Internet users.

_____ 11. A program allowing Web pages to be displayed on a user's computer screen.

_____ 12. The programming language used to create most Web pages.

_____ 13. A fragment of data sent across the Internet.

_____ 14. A computer code that can damage or destroy programs and data.

_____ 15. Electronic messages sent across the Internet.

TECHNOLOGY ILLUSTRATED: IDENTIFY THE PROCESS
What concepts are portrayed in the drawing below? Write a paragraph explaining the process or processes this illustration represents.

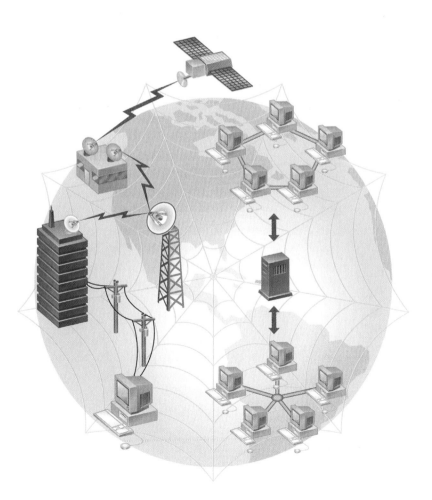

KNOWLEDGE CHECK: MULTIPLE CHOICE
Circle the letter of the best answer from those provided.

1. The first screen visible when entering a Web site is called the

   a. Webmaster.
   b. home page.
   c. banner.
   d. hyperlink.

2. A deceptive link that transports users to advertisements on other Web sites is a(n)

   a. hyperlink.
   b. TCP packet.
   c. blind link.
   d. HTML.

3. Of the following types of Internet connections, which generally provides the fastest speed?

   a. dial-up modem
   b. DSL
   c. ISDN
   d. They are all about the same.

4. Logic rules used when conducting advanced searches using a search engine are called

   a. packets.
   b. operators.
   c. search terms.
   d. search objects.

5. Files contained in e-mail messages are known as

   a. attachments.
   b. clip-ons.
   c. plug-ins.
   d. packets.

6. A type of ISP connection that provides high-speed access that might have to be shared with other users is a

   a. dial-up modem.
   b. cable modem.
   c. DSL.
   d. None of the above

7. An element on a Web page that is coded to transport viewers to another page or site is called a

    a. blink link.
    b. hyperlink.
    c. blog.
    d. home page.

8. HTML stands for

    a. high-tech marketing language.
    b. high-tech markup language.
    c. hypertext markup language.
    d. hypertext marketing language.

9. A file can be transported from a Web page to a PC by

    a. uploading.
    b. hacking.
    c. piracy.
    d. downloading.

10. ISP stands for

    a. international satellite phone.
    b. Internet satellite protocol.
    c. Internet service provider.
    d. international satellite provider.

11. Instant messaging is different than e-mail because

    a. you have to pay for the service.
    b. instant messaging is interruptive, like a phone call.
    c. there is only one provider of instant messaging services.
    d. All of the above

12. Message boards on Web sites are sometimes called

    a. system boards.
    b. chat rooms.
    c. mailing lists.
    d. bulletin board systems.

13. Telecommuting or telework involves

    a. avoiding the effort of commuting in a car to work every day.
    b. working online from home rather than in an office.
    c. a new and growing way for companies to reduce operating costs.
    d. All of the above

14. Why should users of chat rooms and instant messaging environments be wary of online strangers?

    a. Cyberspace is full of dangerous criminals.
    b. Users don't need to worry about it; people they meet online can't possibly harm them.
    c. The anonymous nature of online conversations mean that you don't really know with whom you are conversing.
    d. Police are everywhere online, listening for criminal intent.

15. If you wanted to set up a video phone system in your house so that you could see the person whom you were talking to as well as hear them, what would you need?

    a. A webcam
    b. An Internet-ready telephone
    c. A normal video camera and an adapter cable
    d. Two phone lines, one for the video and one for the voice

THINGS THAT THINK: BRAINSTORMING NEW USES

In groups or individually, contemplate the following questions and develop as many answers as you can.

1. Cell phones, household appliances, vending machines, road systems, and buildings are just a few of the things that can be wired to the Internet for control and monitoring purposes. How will this change the definition of the Internet and how we think about it? What new applications might be possible, if roads can tell us what the traffic situation is, cars can tell how much fuel they have left, and VCRs can tell how much recording capacity remains?

2. Instant messaging (IM) technology has grown from a social medium to a business communications tool. Financial services and retail Web sites offer customers live "chat" with customer service representatives, and colleagues within an organization can informally meet whenever the need arises. How is this likely to evolve as video instant messaging becomes more popular? What additional benefits will businesses gain internally and externally with this technology?

KEY PRINCIPLES: COMPLETION

Fill in the blanks with the appropriate words or phrases.

1. The graphic persona of a player in a virtual reality game is called a(n) _____.

2. _____ is an example of a metalanguage.

3. A small file stored on a Web surfer's hard drive that might be used to track behavior is called a(n) _____.

4. _____ supports the new IEEE 802.11 wireless communications standard.

5. A new peer-to-peer file-sharing system that follows in the footsteps of the now defunct Napster is called _____.

6. The part of a URL that comes last and identifies the type of organization is called the _____.

7. Another term used for telecommuting is _____.

8. A four-group series of numbers separated by periods represents a(n) _____.

9. An advertisement that occupies a rectangular portion of the screen is called a(n) _____.

10. Unwanted, repeated messages that are transmitted over the Internet are called _____.

11. The design feature that describes how packets are moved around the Internet by the best available route is called _____.

12. Web sites often ask for the user's approval before downloading and installing a _____ to provide additional functionality on a Web site.

13. A(n) _____ is a group of related Web sites that are linked together.

14. The use of streaming techniques to access audio and video is called _____.

15. The most widely used Internet application is _____.

TECH ARCHITECTURE: LABEL THE DRAWING

The illustration below shows the path of a packet across the Internet. Label each step in the process.

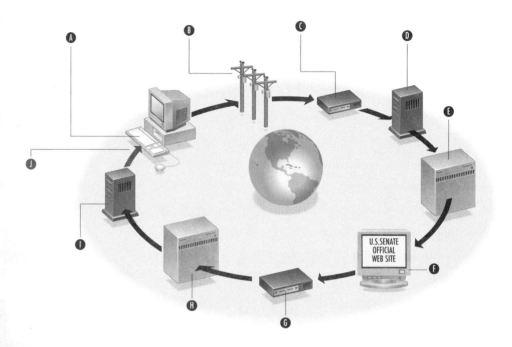

TECHNO LITERACY: RESEARCH AND WRITING

Develop appropriate written responses based on your research for each item.

1. Find at least four free-hosted Web site providers, such as www.geocities.com or www.homestead.com. Compare the features they support. Which ones have wizards that automatically build Web sites? Which allow form-based uploading? Which allow FTP client connections? Do any come with downloadable Web page editors? Visit some sites developed using these free hosts. Do they load quickly? Are there an excessive number of advertisements? Write a report comparing and contrasting free-host providers and decide which one you think is the best.

2. Use a free-hosted Web site provider to create and post a Web page that presents your resume to the world. The purpose of this site is to impress potential employers. At least one scanned-in image should be on the Web page. Make sure your resume page has a title and subtitles for any sections. Add at least three hyperlinks that lead to other Web pages, such as links to the school you are attending or to one of your favorite Web sites.

3. Find out which ISPs are available in your area. Which one would best meet your needs? If you do not have access to a computer at home, assume you are researching this information for your school. For each ISP identify the services offered, including the equipment, type of server(s), and software used. Find out information on the cost for the service as well. Then create a chart in Excel or Word comparing the ISPs in terms of services offered and the cost. Present the information to your class using a PowerPoint slide show.

TECHNOLOGY ISSUES: TEAM PROBLEM-SOLVING
In groups, brainstorm possible solutions to the issues presented.

1. Do you believe that federal and state governments should invest heavily in the provision of Internet hookups for schools and libraries? Why or why not? If the government pays for Internet hookups, should it have a say in how schools and libraries use the Internet? Should high schools and colleges require that students use electronic versions of textbooks downloaded from the Internet once the technology is perfected? What are the advantages and disadvantages?

2. Many people use the Web to become self-employed or to telecommute. If you were to consider working from your home, what problems/advantages do you foresee? Is there more risk involved? More freedom? Less work or more work? What would be your greatest concern? Back up your answers by conducting research on this topic using the Web.

3. Experts claim that the shelf life of knowledge is only two to three years in many fields, including areas as diverse as medicine, technology, engineering, and history. How can distance learning and Web-based tools help address this issue? Given this problem, do you think diplomas should be stamped with an expiration date?

MINING DATA: INTERNET RESEARCH AND REPORTING
Conduct Internet searches to find the information described in the activities below. Write a brief report summarizing your research results. Be sure to document your sources using the MLA format.

1. Research the pros and cons of using a wireless system to connect several home or office computers to the Internet. Include the approximate costs of cabling, hubs, installation, system speeds, convenience, and security. Research your answers and use supporting data from the Web. A good place to start looking for information about this equipment is www.shopper.com.

2. Research the availability and cost of cable modems and DSL services in your area. Could your home system benefit from these services today? How much more expensive is the connection when compared to dial-up modem systems? How much would it cost to install the service? How much faster and more reliable would it be? When comparing the costs, include the cost of a second phone line for a dial-up system, since the faster systems have the advantage of not tying up the phone.

3. Find a page with Flash animation on the Internet. Game advertisements from companies such as Disney, Sony, and Microsoft tend to use these frequently. Did the Web page ask you to download a plug-in? Are the resulting graphics superior? How much longer does it take to load a page with Shockwave graphics compared to one with simple HTML?

TECHNOLOGY TIMELINE: PREDICTING NEXT STEPS
Listed below is a timeline of some of the major events in the history of cybercrime, particularly dealing with the creation of viruses. As you review the list, think of what

major steps may occur next, both in terms of hacker actions and the government's response. Complete the timeline through 2010 with your predictions.

1984   The press gets wind of several high-profile incidences of criminal security system breaking and uses the term "hacker" to describe such criminals.

1986   The Electronic Communications Privacy Act and the Computer Fraud and Abuse Act pass Congress.

1988   Robert Morris releases a worm that brings much of the Internet to a halt.

1990   On January 15, 1990, AT&T's long-distance telephone switching system crashes. During that time, 70 million phone calls went uncompleted.

1990   In May, Operation Sundevil commences. Sundevil was the code name for a sweeping crackdown by the government upon cybercrime.

2000   In January, Yahoo.com, Amazon.com, CNN.com, and eBay.com, among others, are shut down for one hour each by hackers.

2000   In March, a 13-year-old hacker breaks into a government security system that tracks U.S. Air Force planes worldwide, damaging a "secret" system. The youth faces incarceration until age 21.

2001   A cyberwar flares up between Chinese and American hackers after a U.S. Navy plane collides with a Chinese fighter aircraft, killing the Chinese pilot. Each side attacks thousands of sites in the other nation.

2002   In November, the FBI arrests three men who gained unauthorized access to credit reports and caused consumer losses of over $2.7 million.

2003   In May, the Department of Justice, FBI, and Federal Trade Commission conduct a major cybercrime sweep called "Operation E-Con" that results in 130 arrests and $17 million in property seizures related to Internet auction scams, bogus investment, credit card fraud, and identity theft.

ETHICAL DILEMMAS: GROUP DISCUSSION AND DEBATE
As a class or within an assigned group, discuss the following ethical dilemma.

The appeal of Internet chat rooms is often the anonymity that the medium provides. In minutes, you can create a user name, log in to a chat room, and discuss a variety of topics with relative strangers without others knowing your true identity. However, what are the consequences if the chat room sponsor shares your account information with your family, employer, or law enforcement authorities? What prevents the chat room sponsor from doing this? Would you have any recourse against the sponsor? Does this change your perspective on what you would say or not say in a chat room?

ANSWERS TO TERMS CHECK AND KEY PRINCIPLES QUESTIONS
Terms Check: 1 – m; 2 – f; 3 – j; 4 – g; 5 – d; 6 – e; 7 – i; 8 – l; 9 – n; 10 – c; 11 – k; 12 – b; 13 – a; 14 – o; 15 – h

Key Principles: 1 – avatar; 2 – XML; 3 – cookie; 4 – Wi-Fi; 5 – KaZaA; 6 – domain name; 7 – telework; 8 – IP address; 9 – banner; 10 – spam; 11 – dynamic routing; 12 – plug-in; 13 – WebRing; 14 – webcasting; 15 – e-mail

Building a Web Site

Web site construction can be as simple as creating a personal home page or as complex as creating a site for disseminating the accumulated records and documents of a department of the federal government. The complexities of constructing a state-of-the-art site are far beyond the scope of this Special Feature, but a few pointers will enable just about anyone to get a simple site up and running.

A Web site consists of pages that may contain text, graphics, animation, audio clips, movies, links to other pages and sites, forms for entering information into databases, and other materials. Pages are created using the Hypertext Markup Language (HTML), a script language that also allows many "embedded" languages such as Java or Visual Basic to run within it. You can view the HTML behind any Web page by saving the Web page file on your local computer (click File/Save As in your Web browser and save the file as a Web page). Then start up Notepad, the simple editor that comes with all versions of Windows, and use Notepad to open the saved Web page file. What you will see will be something like the HTML displayed in Figure F-1. If you use a Web browser to view the same file, you will see the page shown in Figure F-2.

Using HTML script, or code, to create Web pages offers some special advantages. Unlike the code in software that people buy at a retail outlet, the source code of Web pages is actually transmitted to users' computers when they navigate to a URL. Web pages are therefore easy to examine and learn from. In fact, it is perfectly legal to download the HTML source code for an existing page and copy the format of the page—as long as you change its content. However, it is considered "bad form" to copy the work of others without crediting the original developer. A second advantage of using a script language such as HTML is that it greatly reduces the size of file that needs to be transmitted, and thereby decreases the amount of time required for the Web browser to display the page on the user's screen.

```
<html>

<head>
<meta http-equiv="Content-Type" content="text/html; charset=windows-1252">
<meta http-equiv="Content-Language" content="en-us">
<meta name="GENERATOR" content="Microsoft FrontPage 4.0">
<meta name="ProgId" content="FrontPage.Editor.Document">
<title>CS 261 Homepage</title>
</head>

<body>

<div align="center">
  <center>
  <table border="0" cellpadding="0" cellspacing="8" width="638">
    <tr>
      <td align="right" valign="top" width="231">
        <p align="left"><font size="4"><strong><a href="index.htp">Prof's Home
        Page</a><br>
        <a href="mailto:">Send E-Mail</a></strong></p>
        </font>
      </td>
      <td width="8"></td>
      <td valign="bottom" width="361"><font size="5">Homepage for CMPSC 261</font>
        <p><font size="5">Programming and Problem-Solving II</font></p>
      </td>
    </tr>
    <tr>
      <td valign="top" width="231">
        <b>Course Links:</b>
        <p><b>HAVE A GOOD SUMMER!</b></p>
          <ul>
            <li>
          <b><a href="CS261_Schedule.htm">Scheduled Assignments</a></b></li>
            <li>
          <a href="CS261_Syllabus.htm"><b>Course Syllabus</b></a>

ETC.....
```

FIGURE F-1: HTML is the language of a Web page.

FIGURE: F-2: This is the same file as in Figure F-1, viewed with a Web browser.

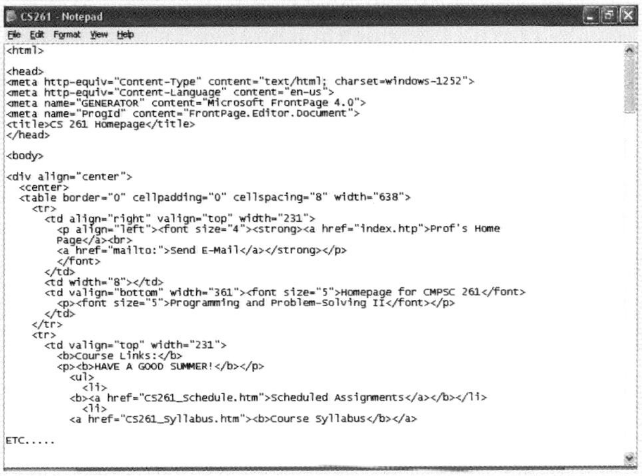

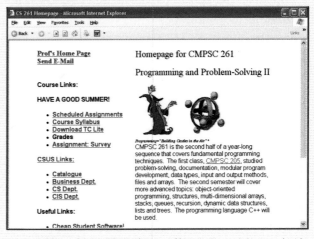

PLANNING A WEB SITE

Once you have decided to create a Web site, you need to center your planning around the following questions:

- Who will host the site?
- How will the site be organized?
- What software will be used to create the Web pages?
- Which links should be added to the site?
- Where can I register the site?
- To which search engines should I submit the URL?

Choosing a Host

One of the first tasks in Web site development is finding a good host for the site. Essentially, a **Web host** lets you store a copy of your Web pages on the hard drive of a powerful computer connected to the Internet with a fast connection that can handle thousands of users. It is possible to host a Web site on your own computer, but this is only feasible if you own an extra computer that can be dedicated to the role of a Web server, have a high-speed Internet connection, and feel confident about handling the job of network security and routing. Most people's situations do not fit those criteria. Fortunately, several free and fee-based Web hosting services are available.

Free Web-Hosting Services

Most beginners opt for free Web hosting. Free hosting services allow users to post very small Web sites that are paid for by advertisements the hosting system automatically adds to the HTML of the user's Web pages. They charge you no money, but often the service is slow with many annoying pop-ups and banner ads. Still, it is recommended that a beginner start here, both because it is an inexpensive way to get started and because free Web hosts tend to provide simple, easy-to-use interfaces designed for novices. Figure F-3 displays the URLs and logos of three widely used free Web hosts.

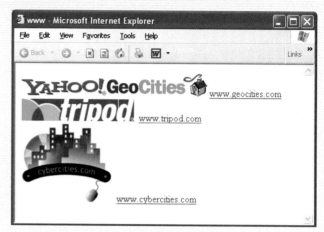

FIGURE F-3: Popular Free Web Hosting Sites

Free Hosting from ISPs

Users should always check into the availability of free hosting from their own ISPs. Often, as part of a package deal, ISPs will offer several megabytes of free Web hosting that is included in the monthly Internet access fees. Although subscribers tend to ignore the opportunity, this option often means good service with fewer advertisements than may appear through the better-known free hosting services.

Fee-Based Hosting Services

Many excellent fee-based Web hosts exist on the Internet, but try the free hosting first, as this experience will enable you to judge more accurately the services of paid hosts before you spend any money. Web hosting services usually offer at least two or three levels of hosting plans, which typically specify data storage amounts, data transfer rates, FTP access options, telephone support, and available Web authoring programs and other developer aids. Read current reviews from users and independent publications and also examine the size, number, and quality of other Web sites hosted by that service. Do they display quickly and smoothly? Are the sites available 24 hours a day with minimal downtime?

Organizing the Site

As you plan a Web site, decide what types of content you will include and then think about how all of the

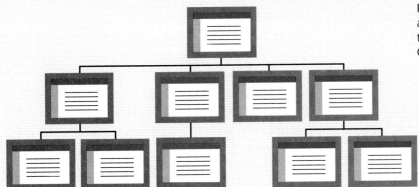

pages should link together. Most Web sites consist of a home page that provides the starting point for users entering the site. Like the top of a pyramid or the table of contents of a book, that home page leads to other Web pages via hyperlinks. Figure F-4 illustrates the relationship between the home page and other pages on a Web site.

Most home pages have the default name of index.html (or sometimes index.htm). Browsers look for pages with these names first when a specific file at a Web site is requested, and index pages display by default if no other page is specified. For a demonstration of this feature, try typing in the following URLs: www.google.com and www.google.com/index.html. Note that both addresses bring up the same home page. When developing a Web site, remember to name your most important page (your home page) index.html. This will allow users to get to your home page without specifying a file name. They only need to remember your Web site URL.

Choosing Software to Build Web Pages

After having selected a hosting service, signing up for an account, and planning the structure of your site, your next step is to decide whether to write scripts in HTML or to make use of software known as page-building programs or Web authoring programs. Most hosts offer a simplified program in the form of a Web page wizard, or template, which asks a series of questions and provides several commonly

desired features to generate a "generic" Web page with a minimum of user effort. It is a good idea to start with a wizard-generated Web page. For most users, their first Web page is similar to their first painting: the value of the end result is that it teaches the process. And for many users, the simple generic pages meet their needs.

Web-Authoring Programs

For those who get "the bug" and really enjoy the process of crafting Web pages, there are several **page-building software** programs that the major Web hosts provide to help build interesting pages of the user's design. Programs include Microsoft FrontPage, Macromedia Dreamweaver, NetObjects Fusion, Symantec Visual Page, Allaire HomeSite, and Adobe PageMill. Some of these programs are large Java applications, and it is important to note that they tend not to run well over a dial-up connection. For this kind of work, it is recommended that you use the computers in your school's labs where high-speed LAN connections are usually available.

Web Pages from Microsoft Office Programs

In addition to specialized page-builders, many Microsoft Office programs, including Word, offer users the ability to simply save a given file as a Web page. The program converts the file from a .doc or other document format to an .html file type. This is one of the easier ways to make Web pages, as it allows the user to avoid the learning curve that must be overcome when starting with an unfamiliar development tool.

Writing HTML Scripts

Web authoring programs were developed so that users could create Web pages without having to learn HTML. Learning HTML, however, is not difficult, and creating pages directly in HTML gives a Web author considerable flexibility because he or she is not limited to the tools provided by an authoring program. More information on this topic is available on the Encore CD packaged with this text. Access the "Tech Review" element. Then select one or more of the eight interactive tutorials on using HTML to build Web pages.

Adding Images to Web Pages

Most Web authoring programs include a body of clipart images, which are essentially low-quality generic graphics such as images of construction signs or mailboxes, and so on. In addition to these standard images, you can upload any image file from your computer to the host computer for use on Web pages. Note, though, that images often will not show up on a Web page that was built locally and uploaded because the image files need to be transmitted to the host separately.

Adding Links

Most Web pages are pretty dull without hyperlinks. A hyperlink can be almost anything on the screen, but most are either strips of text (normally highlighted in blue) or an image. To make a hyperlink, most Web authoring programs include a button that resembles a chain link or a globe. The process typically involves selecting a bit of text or an image and then clicking on the link button. A dialog box displays asking the developer to type in a URL or select a local page on the same computer as the Web page. Normally, links to other sites require a full URL that begins with the familiar prefix http://. Figure F-5 shows a link to another site created with Microsoft FrontPage. Creating a local link does not require a full URL. Figure F-6 shows a link being created to a local file.

Uploading Files

With your files complete, you can either post them on your local computer or network, or you can transmit them to a Web host computer so that they can be seen on a Web site and accessible to the world at large. Typically, the Web host site displays a button or menu item labeled "Upload" or "Import," which allows image files, HTML files developed in a productivity program such as

FIGURE F-5: Microsoft FrontPage creates a hyperlink to an off-site page.

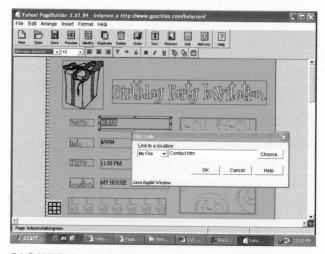

FIGURE F-6: GeoCities PageBuilder creates a local link.

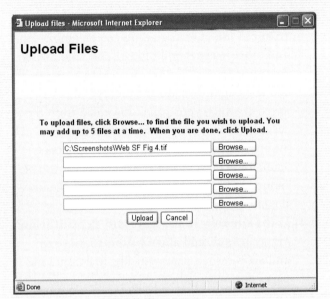

FIGURE F-7: The Upload Files Screen in GeoCities PageBuilder

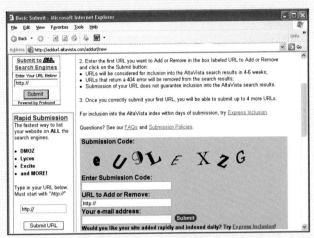

FIGURE F-8: AltaVista's Site Submission Screen

Microsoft Word, and other Web pages to be copied from your computer to the fast server computer at the host site. Figure F-7 shows GeoCities Page-Builder's Upload Files screen.

Getting Your Own URL

If you have built your own Web site and will host it, you need to obtain a URL. The process is relatively simple and inexpensive. The major challenge is finding a Web address that is catchy and has not already been bought and registered by someone else. As with user IDs, most new dot-commers discover that their first ten URL ideas have already been registered. Even if you type a Web URL into your browser and it finds no answering Web site, you cannot be assured that the name is open and free. Often, companies buy lists of Web addresses with plans to use them in the future. One way around this obstacle is to use one of the other domain extensions, such as .net or .biz.

You also can work with Internic, the core service that maintains the Internet's primary list of domain name registries, and for a nominal fee buy a new, unused Web address. Other registration services also are available to simplify the process, which may

include a package deal covering registration, a free search for conflicting addresses, and some level of Web hosting.

Submitting a URL to Search Engines

Hundreds of search engines populate the Net, but the top ten get most of the traffic. Many hosting services advertise that they will submit your Web site to several hundred search engines for a fee. While these services might save time, they may not adequately describe your site to these engines and might not garner the results you are hoping for. Often, simply going to the top search engine sites and taking the time to do it yourself is worth it and will get your site listed more effectively. Figure F-8 shows a site submission screen for AltaVista, one of the most popular search engines, and Table F-1 displays a list of other widely used search engines. Bear in mind that most search engines require six weeks to three months to list your site, so don't expect immediate results.

EVALUATING YOUR WEB SITE

Whether you are advertising a business or establishing a personal presence, your Web site should offer information quickly and in a visually pleasing manner. Take time to evaluate the site after you have posted it and periodically thereafter to ensure that it

Search Engine	URL
Yahoo!	www.yahoo.com
Google	www.google.com
AltaVista	www.altavista.com
Lycos	www.lycos.com
Excite	www.excite.com
HotBot	www.hotbot.com

TABLE F-1: Popular Search Engines

meets your original goals. Consider these key points in your objective review:

- **Are the pages readable?** Is important information featured prominently so users automatically focus on it? The typeface should be attractive; the language should be simple and accurate. Strive for a clean look, using ample margins and white space.

- **Are the pages interesting?** An impressive and balanced use of text, graphics, color, animation, and other features will capture and hold a visitor's interest.

- **Do the pages download quickly?** Check the speed at which your pages download from the server. A visitor to your site may abandon it and move to other sites if downloading takes more than a few seconds. Avoid the overuse of frames and animation that can cause pages to download slowly.

- **Is the site easy to navigate and to print from?** Hyperlinks should allow visitors to move to and view desired pages quickly. Make sure the pages print correctly.

Regular reviews of your Web site will reveal any design and function issues, which you can then address. An equally important element in managing the site is to keep its content fresh and current.

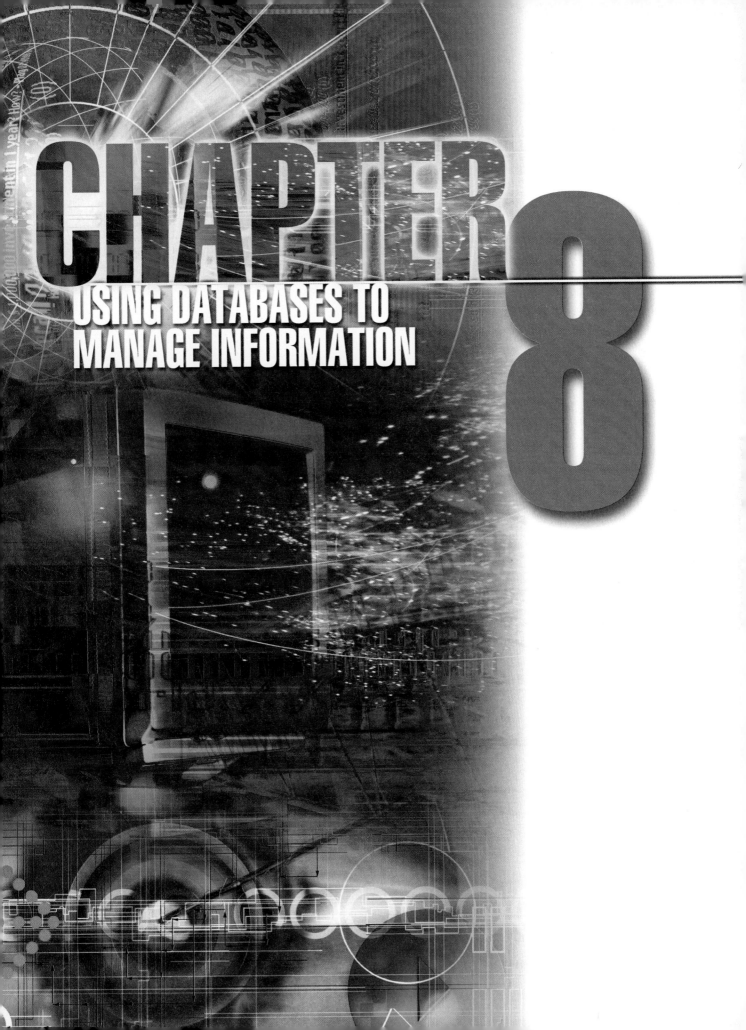

CHAPTER

USING DATABASES TO MANAGE INFORMATION

8

UNDERSTANDING TECHNOLOGY

learning objectives

- Explain how databases work and identify their basic structural elements

- Discuss the different database classifications

- Describe the elements of a database management system (DBMS) and their functions

- Explain how query languages are used to find information in a database

- Describe how databases are designed and administered

- Identify the different methods that can be used to validate data

key concepts

- Levels of Data within a Database

- Managing Information

- Database Management System Software

- Database Classifications

- Planning and Designing Database Systems

- Administering and Using Databases

CYBER SCENARIO

Father's Day was fast approaching and Lenora still couldn't decide what kind of gift to buy her father-in-law. She was never really sure if he appreciated the cologne, neckties, or fishing gear she usually ended up buying. Vowing that this year was going to be different, Lenora decided to try one of the new Internet consumer-profiling services she had seen advertised on TV. All she had to do was answer a short questionnaire describing her father-in-law. The service would provide a complete profile of her father-in-law's gift likes and dislikes, using her answers as well as information gathered from e-commerce sites.

The profile generated by the service showed that Lenora's father-in-law wasn't interested in new ties; there was no record of his purchasing a necktie for years. The same was true for fishing gear; no sign of any past purchases. With a sigh, she delved into the shaving category. It seemed that he did his shopping by smartcard at a local discount house, and she found information on his favorite brands of aftershave, razors, and shaving cream. Lenora smiled to herself as she thought of how old-fashioned her father-in-law was. He didn't use an electric razor, and the brands he liked were not popular with younger men. He hadn't purchased any shaving articles for almost 45 days, so he could certainly use these items.

She ordered a few packages of his favorite brands, checked the Gift Wrap box, and clicked the Buy button. The Web site informed Lenora of the total cost, and confirmed that the gifts would arrive on time. The entire shopping experience had taken a mere 12 minutes. Lenora breathed a sigh of relief, knowing that this time she had bought her father-in-law gifts he was sure to like.

Lenora's search illustrates how e-commerce transactions involve a series of online database interactions. The initial search for a product queries (asks) a database for information. A sales record is created in the company's database when a payment is made. That database then uses the customer's credit card number to access a bank database and electronically transfer funds to the retailer. Finally, the e-commerce site's database interacts with a shipping company's database to ensure that the purchase reaches the customer without delay.

WHAT IS A DATABASE?

A database is a computerized system for storing information in an organized manner so that it can be searched for and retrieved when needed. Businesses, government groups, private organizations, and academic institutions all use databases, and they represent the dominant use of computing power in the business world today. Without databases the Internal Revenue Service could not collect income taxes, the American Red Cross could not allocate funds, and colleges across the country could not operate efficiently. Schools use databases to store and handle grades, class schedules, tuition payments, library fines, and other records relevant to education. Colleges typically use enrollment trend reports to plan for new courses and to branch out into new academic areas. In these cases they might use not only their own database information, but also reports from national college associations and the federal government.

Databases are used for more than routine operations. Executives commonly consult company databases to aid in their decision-making. If a company is considering opening a new branch office, managers and other strategic planners can carefully examine databases describing the purchasing habits of local consumers in order to choose the best location.

Data vs. Information

The terms *data* and *information* are key concepts in understanding the importance of computerized databases. Recall from Chapter 1 that data is a collection of raw, unorganized (unprocessed) content in the form of words, numbers, sounds, or images. Data associated with other useful data on the same topic becomes information. The ability to associate or organize stored data in a variety of meaningful ways represents the power of database software. For example, an insurance company might store ZIP Code information in its database, but a ZIP Code alone is not particularly useful. However, when the ZIP Code is associated with other data such as a name, address, or phone number, this set of organized data becomes information that can be used to locate and identify a customer.

Historical Database Forms

Databases as storage systems existed long before computers came into being. Important records such as birth certificates, medical histories, income tax files, payroll records, and car license data were stored on paper before the first database software was developed in the 1950s and 1960s. These printed documents were usually collected and organized in filing cabinets. Locating information and structuring it for various purposes was possible, but it involved sifting through stacks of paper, identifying the desired data, and then writing or typing selected items on more paper so that people could analyze the information. For example, if a health department wanted to determine if a flu outbreak had resulted in a significant

increase in deaths within a certain age group, workers had to read mounds of death records and manually note the causes of death and the ages of the victims. Today the same task could be executed in minutes using a computerized database.

Computerized databases have become so useful in all areas of public life that paper-based storage systems are rarely encountered. The few exceptions are small independent medical offices and some small retail shops, but even these businesses are rapidly moving to electronic systems.

The Importance of Accurate Data

Databases are records of events or situations, so they must be continually updated to ensure that the data they contain is accurate. Consider, for example, the situation of an insurance company that maintains a database containing names, addresses, birth dates, and policy information. Several different departments in the company may share the database. Marketing sends out information whenever policy benefits change. They also send mailings to people who may be interested in new benefits. The accounting department uses the database for mailing billing notices. Company managers regularly generate reports, or information combined from linked database tables, to forecast new directions for the firm. If a policyholder moves to a new address, the database must be updated to reflect the change, or the information the company uses will be incorrect. Any inaccuracy will create an avalanche of problems throughout the different company departments.

This constant requirement for altering and amending masses of data is called **database maintenance**, and it is the focus of many jobs in the marketplace. Every retail clerk, for example, helps tally store sales. Each entry is stored in a database that constantly tracks a store's current status. From the company's viewpoint this task is of vital importance. Sales information entered into the database allows managers to decide what supplies need to be ordered, and provides a constantly updated snapshot of revenue.

LEVELS OF DATA WITHIN A DATABASE

The ability to organize and reorganize data for different purposes is due to two database characteristics: their vast storage potential and the way they organize data. Traditional databases organize data in a hierarchical fashion, containing information about entities in the form of fields, records, and files. Files are then arranged in directory trees. Figure 8-1 illustrates this hierarchy.

FIGURE 8-1: A traditional database, as shown above, organizes data in a hierarchy of fields, records, and files.

Entities

An **entity** is a person, place, thing, or event. Database files record information about different entities using fields, records, and files. A typical entity might be a sale transaction that describes products removed from inventory and the amount of money received for those products. Other examples of entities include student grades, traffic violations, and telephone records.

Fields

The smallest element of data in a database is a field. A field is a single value, such as a name, address, or dollar amount. A field generally has three attributes:

- data type: usually numeric or text (numbers and text)
- name: assigned by the person developing the database
- size: the number of characters that can be entered

A field called *FirstName* might have a size of 20 characters. Any name longer than 20 characters would be automatically truncated (shortened) by the database to fit into the field. The most common data types are **numeric** (numbers only) and text, also called **alphanumeric** (letters, numbers, or special characters). Other types exist, such as logical yes/no fields, time and date fields, and memo fields, which allow unlimited character input. The more unusual data types include pictures, movies, and sound. Table 8-1 shows various field data types.

Records

A collection of related fields describing an event or situation is called a record. If a record covers mailing information, it would likely include fields for *name, address, city, state,* and *postal code.* Figure 8-2 shows a Microsoft Access design screen laying out the record structure.

Data Type	Description of Data
text (alphanumeric)	textual information such as a person's name
number	numeric data such as a count of inventoried products
yes/no (logical)	yes/no states such as "married" or "retired"
currency	dollar amounts such as a bank account balance
memo	lengthy text information, notes, or history
object	nontextual information such as pictures
hyperlink	connects a record to a Web address
date/time	allows only valid times/dates, such as November 12, 2002
autonumber	integer that automatically increases whenever used; generally is used to make a primary key that automatically changes in order to be unique

TABLE 8-1: Common Field Data Types

Different fields may use different data types.

CHAPTER 8

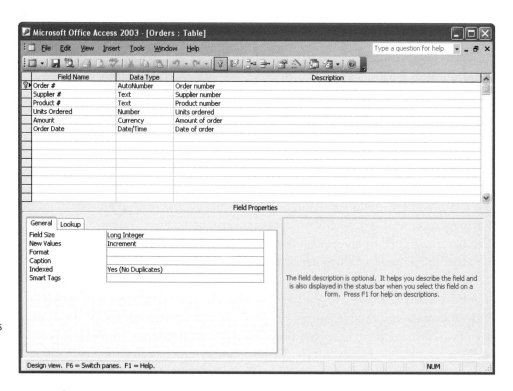

Files

A **database file** is a collection of records of the same type. When a database is designed and built, the designer must decide what records will be used, which fields will be in those records, and which data type and size each field will have. The record layout is used as the basis for each record in the table. For example, if a company's database has a record type called CUSTOMER, then there would be a record of CUSTOMER type for each customer. All the records would use the same set of fields. When all the records of the same type are combined, they become a database file.

Understanding Files: File Directory Trees

All files, including database files, are stored in directory trees. In Windows-based programs a **directory tree** is represented as a hierarchal system of icons called directories, sometimes referred to as folders. On a single hard drive there might be many directories and subdirectories, and some of the subdirectories may in turn have their own subdirectories. Files may be associated with any of these directories. The tree analogy derives from viewing the hard drive "root" directory as the root or trunk of the tree, the subdirectories as branches from that trunk, and the files as leaves sprouting from the branches. A more familiar analogy for personal computers is that of a filing cabinet, with folders that hold other folders or files. Understanding the hierarchy of files and folders established by the operating system is necessary for anyone who sets up a database and/or maintains it.

MANAGING INFORMATION

Networked databases allow businesses to save time and money by coordinating their operations. If each department in a business kept its own customer records, there would be duplicate entries, wasting time and causing confusion. If the different departments share a single networked database, information only has to be entered once, and it can then be accessed freely by anyone needing it.

The most common database application is an **information system**, which is a system of computer hardware, software, and operating procedures. Information systems are designed to meet the information needs of a company, such as tracking income and expenditures, recording transactions, sharing resources, and planning for future growth. A variety of information systems have evolved as software capabilities and market needs have changed over the years. Chapter 9 discusses information systems in depth, so this chapter provides only a brief overview of the topic as it relates to databases.

Management Information Systems

A **management information systems (MIS)** is used to track and control every transaction through a database. The term **transaction** means a business activity central to the nature of an enterprise. A transaction can be the sale of a product, the flight of an airliner, or the recording of a college course grade. A database stores the information that is at the core of any MIS system.

An MIS for an airline flight information display would need to handle flight numbers, gate numbers, and expected arrival and departure times. This information is available for viewing by the public and by the company employees. The data comes directly from a computer running an MIS. Every attendant at the ticket counter who enters data using a keyboard is communicating with the MIS. When a flight finally does depart, another MIS run by the Federal Aviation Administration (FAA) uses radar systems to track its progress toward its destination.

Office Information Systems

First popularized in the 1960s, the **office information system (OIS)** concept was billed as a replacement for paper-based information systems. An OIS is sometimes known as an **electronic office**. Many people thought that the advent of electronic offices would lead to "paperless offices." Unfortunately, computer systems tend to generate more paperwork than their noncomputerized counterparts. This is in large part due to the ease with which printers can churn out documents, as compared to the precomputer era when documents would have been typed manually.

The electronic office today is the norm rather than the exception. Most organizations of any size use a computerized OIS to manage their operations. For example, a shipping company OIS may hold records for every customer and corporate account and may use them to identify key clients. When an important client calls in, the receptionist can look him up in the database and immediately direct his call to the right agent. Clerks can also quickly access company work orders and check the status of any client orders.

Decision Support Systems

A **decision support system (DSS)** is another common form of information system. Rather than simply tracking the day-to-day operations of a business, a DSS is designed to help management make decisions about an operation. A DSS might include a predictive model of the business that allows managers to work with "what-if" scenarios. If a business is considering expansion or the release of a new product, a DSS can help determine if the change would be likely to succeed or fail. The database could provide information on past performance, which the business owners could use to judge the cost of the expansion and any changes to revenue that might result.

Factory Automation Systems

Computer-aided manufacturing (CAM) and **computer-integrated manufacturing (CIM)** are information systems that support factory automation. Generally, CAM refers to systems that run an assembly line directly, controlling the manufacturing process from the shop-floor level of conveyor belts and robots. CAM systems form a portion of a complete CIM system, a higher-level concept indicating a system that controls a manufacturing process from beginning to end. The database at the core of these systems stores information about factory operations, including counters that automatically add each item manufactured to inventory as it is made. Figure 8-3 shows a CIM system operating a plant.

FIGURE 8-3: CIM and CAM systems are used to automate manufacturing.

TECH VISIONARY

Larry Ellison, cofounder and CEO of Oracle Corporation, is one of the most flamboyant and outspoken entrepreneurs of this century. Ellison is one of the richest as well. With a net worth of $50 billion and a financially successful company, he has reached the pinnacle of corporate success.

Among some of his friends and peers, Ellison may be considered an eccentric. It has been rumored that he once tried to purchase a Russian MIG fighter plane, but U.S. customs would not allow the plane into the country. In another incident, Ellison reportedly upset San Jose airport officials by landing his private jet after an 11 p.m. curfew, an action resulting in a $10,000 fine. To many of his fellow business associates, however, he is a business genius, a marketing whiz, and an avid promoter of simplified computing machines and network computers.

Oracle is the world's leading supplier of information management software, and the world's second-largest independent software company, boasting annual revenues of more than $9.7 billion. The company's diverse product line includes database software products, applications servers, software information management tools, and software suites for electronic commerce applications. Oracle's database software is the most widely used corporate database worldwide, and the company's product line continues to expand at a rapid pace.

Source: Oracle Corporation home page and other Web sources.

DATABASE MANAGEMENT SYSTEM SOFTWARE

Databases are controlled by database management system (DBMS) software. A DBMS is a set of tools that database designers and administrators use to structure the database system a company needs. IBM's DB2® and Oracle® from Oracle Corporation dominate the DBMS market on midrange computers such as AS/400s and Sun servers. In the PC market, Microsoft Access is a widely used DBMS. In addition to maintaining the overall structure of the data, a DBMS has many other functions. Database keys, query tools, security elements, metadata, and backup and recovery utilities allow users to manipulate database data into information.

Database Keys

Keys are attributes that can be used to identify a set of information and therefore provide a means to search a database. Within a database, fields are used as keys, and the designer designates the most important field in a record as the **primary key**. The primary key must also be unique, so it can be used to locate a record quickly. First names are poor keys because many people have the same first name. In a database that tracks traffic and parking violations, car license plate numbers could be used as a primary key because no two cars have the same license number. Phone, bank account, credit card, airline reservation confirmation, and work order numbers are commonly used as primary keys because they are unique. Primary keys are usually large numbers, but they may also be alphanumeric, like most drivers' license numbers. Figure 8-4 shows the keys used in a record.

It is possible to search a database without using the primary key, but it will be more difficult as other keys may not be unique and therefore may return a confusing array of results. This is why customers are usually asked to provide some form of unique identification when they call a company to inquire about a billing error

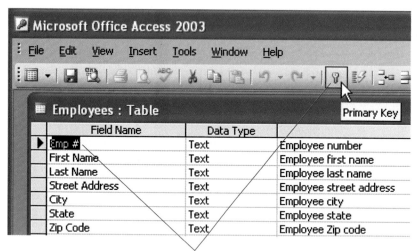

Clicking the Primary Key button on the Table Design toolbar in Microsoft Access 2003 designates a field in each table as a primary key.

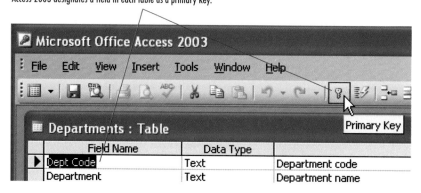

FIGURE 8-4: Primary keys are used to find records.

or a product order. The requested information acts as a primary key, enabling the person assisting them to locate records quickly. If a service representative asked for a name, he would have to sort through records of everyone with the same name. This would waste time, as there could be thousands of duplicate names in a large

ethics

database. Managing the enormous amounts of information in a database would be nearly impossible without primary keys.

Users may need to browse records to find the desired information when a record's primary key is unknown. **Data browsing** is the process of moving through a database file, examining each record and looking for information. This strategy is also used when a search on a secondary key returns many results that must be sifted. Hunting through the best results returned by a search engine is a form of data browsing.

Query Tools

Databases are stored in the form of data files until the system needs to perform **file processing** on the information. At that point, it is copied into RAM. Databases are sometimes too large to fit into RAM all at once, so only portions of the total data can be manipulated at any one time. To work with large amounts of data, database management systems come equipped with **query tools** that help users narrow down the amount of information that needs to be searched. Queries allow users to ask questions designed to retrieve needed information. For example, a query combined with a report can be used to ask a grades database to list all students in the top 10 percent of academic achievement. The results could be used to print a report that would be the dean's list for that semester.

Requesting information involves the use of a query language. **Structured Query Language (SQL)** is the most popular database query language. It is simple when compared to a programming language, but it is also "structured," meaning that it is not as freeform as natural programming languages that mimic human speech. SQL is a very commonly supported query format and works with most databases in use today. Since it is standardized and so widely supported, SQL is often used to bridge communications gaps between database systems running on computers employing different operating systems.

The basic query command supported by SQL is the **SELECT command**, which asks a database to return records that match specified criteria. The command uses the keywords SELECT [fields] FROM [table] and specifies the table and fields from which the information is to be selected (see Figure 8-5).

```
SELECT      Student.FName, Student.LName, Student.StuID
FROM        StudentData
WHERE       Student.GPA>3.49
AND         Student.Enrolled="YES"
```

F I G U R E 8 - 5 : This SQL statement could be used to search for the top students in a college, with top defined as those students with a grade point average (GPA) above 3.49.

Information from one query can be used to pull up data from more than one record source through a process called **joining**, which matches data from fields in various record files. This is usually done by matching up primary keys used as fields in one record to specify a relationship to another record. For example, if student names and grades were entered as separate records, "out of state" could be used as the primary key to find the grades of out-of-state students (see Figure 8-6).

Security Measures

A DBMS also provides **security measures** to protect and safeguard data. Payroll, accounts receivable, and e-mail storage systems all contain sensitive information that must be protected against theft, alteration, or deletion. Competitors, hackers, crackers, or disgruntled employees can do a great deal of harm if they are allowed access to critical company databases.

Maintaining data security is a critical issue for database administrators. Security methods include restricting access by requiring user identification and passwords. Usually only users with higher access levels can change data in a database, and only those with the highest level of access can change the format of the data itself.

Metadata (Data Dictionary)

Metadata is information about data. **Data dictionary** is the term for a body of metadata. Metadata can be used for many things, but often describes the significance of various elements of a database. If a record field was called FNAME, metadata might describe this as being a text field with a maximum length of 20 characters, used for holding a person's first name. These characteristics might not be immediately obvious from the name FNAME. Designers, users, and

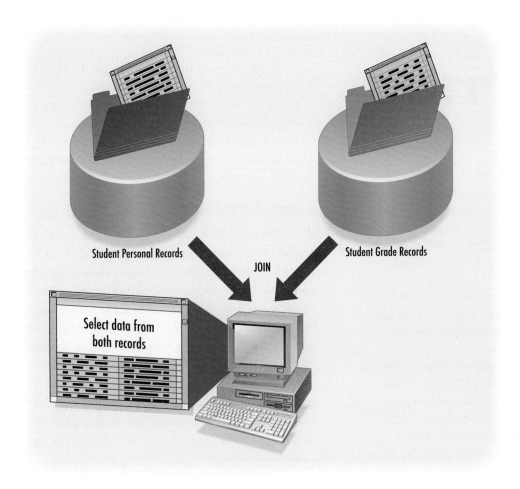

FIGURE 8-6: Joining matches data from fields in various record files. Using "out of state" as the primary key in the Student Personal Records and the Student Grade Records would find the grades of out-of-state students.

administrators use metadata to manage databases. In a DBMS, this function is performed by the **system catalog**.

Backup and Recovery Utilities

Another major element that DBMS systems provide is a method for backing up and restoring lost data. Almost all companies keep sales, marketing, customer, payroll, and tax records on a database. To lose this data would be disastrous, so regular backups are made and stored safely. Important backup information is often stored in safes (see Figure 8-7) or off-site.

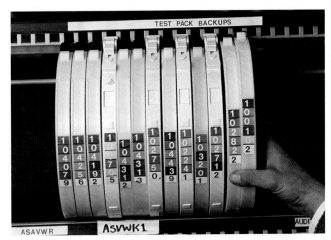

FIGURE 8-7: Critical software backups are often stored in a safe.

DATABASE CLASSIFICATIONS

Databases are often categorized by the way they organize data (data models), or by their function (storing information for ongoing processes versus storing information for historical purposes). **Data models** define the structure of information to be contained in a database, how the database will use the information, and how the different items in the database relate to each other. The goal of a database

GLOBE TROTTING

Bio-pirates Beware

When the Spanish were colonizing what is now Central America, one of the problems they encountered in high-altitude areas was a lowered birth rate among their domesticated animals. The Incan people knew the solution: feed the animals the maca plant, legendary for its fertility powers. Patents on the maca plant are now in the hands of U.S. drug manufacturers.

The yacon, a plant similar to the sunflower that can be used to produce nonmetabolized sugar, has been grown in the Andes for centuries. Today it is grown and patented in Japan, and the windfall from sales of the nonfattening sweetener will go to Japanese companies.

The yellow Enola bean is indigenous to Mexico and has been grown there for hundreds of years. But now Mexican bean exporters are being sued by a U.S. company for infringing on their yellow bean product.

Each of these situations is considered a case of bio-piracy, in which the knowledge and resources of indigenous peoples are appropriated by outsiders. A new database may help give credit to the traditional knowledge holders and at the same time open up valuable information to the public. Called TEKPAD (Traditional Ecological Knowledge Prior Art Database), the database was established by the American Association for the Advancement of Science (AAAS). Anthropologists, tribal healers, or farmers can list their remedies and plants in the database, which can then be used by patent offices to determine whether a drug is original or has already been in use. Currently, there are more than 30,000 entries in TEKPAD, and the AAAS, along with other groups dedicated to helping preserve the cultures of indigenous peoples, is working to add new discoveries from local communities.

The seas may be getting rougher for bio-pirates. Case in point: For centuries, the South African Kung Bushmen have chewed the leaves of the Hoodia cactus to stave off hunger on long hunting trips. Two years ago they discovered that a Western pharmaceutical company had developed a weight-loss product containing an active ingredient stemming from the Hoodia. After a legal battle, the Bushmen have won the right to receive a royalty from all sales of the company's anti-obesity drug.

Sources: "Healing Powers Go Online," *BBC News,* March 18, 2003 <http://news.bbc.co.uk/2/hi/technology/2858253.stm>; TEKPAD Homepage, <http://ip.aas.org/tekindex.nsf>.

model is to identify and organize the database contents in a logical way.

In terms of broad functional categories, **operational databases** are used to store information for ongoing processes, such as tracking store inventory and sales, while **data warehouses** are information repositories that can be mined and used for statistical purposes, reports, and other forms of analysis.

Databases Classified by Data Model

The data model employed by a database is so central to the way it works that most databases are named after them. The data model chosen matters primarily to the database developer, as most data models can provide any kind of data or interface. Advanced data models tend to be more reliable and consistent, allowing for greater connectivity with outside systems. They also tend to be easier to work with and less expensive to develop and maintain. Common data models include flat file, relational, object-oriented, distributed, multimedia, and hybrids.

Flat File Databases

Traditional data file storage systems that lack the ability to interrelate data in an organizational structure are known as **flat file** systems—flat because they contain only one table or file. These systems are simple and easy to use, but in general flat file systems are slower to respond because the records must be searched sequentially. They also consume more disk space than other types of databases. Flat files can be useful for finding information, but relational database systems offer faster, more comprehensive reporting capabilities.

Relational Databases

Most modern databases use a **relational database** model in which fields can be shared among all the files in the database, making it possible to connect them. In a relational database, files are called **tables** (consisting of rows and columns), the records are called **tuples**, and the fields are called **attributes**. Although many of the element definitions are the same as with a traditional flat file system, the primary difference concerns the organization of the tuples and their relationship to the table they are in.

Compared with flat file models, the most important advantage relational database models have is that information can be shared, extracted, and combined more easily among different tables. In a traditional system, an entity's address might be stored in several different records. If the entity's address information ever changes, address records would have to be updated in every location. If any record was overlooked, it would contain outdated information, meaning that any output using that record would be inaccurate. In relational databases, rather than having an attribute (field) called *address* repeated in many records, it would be stored once and shared among multiple tables. In a relational database, a single change to an attribute would change that attribute in all the tables at once. Figure 8-8 illustrates a relational database model.

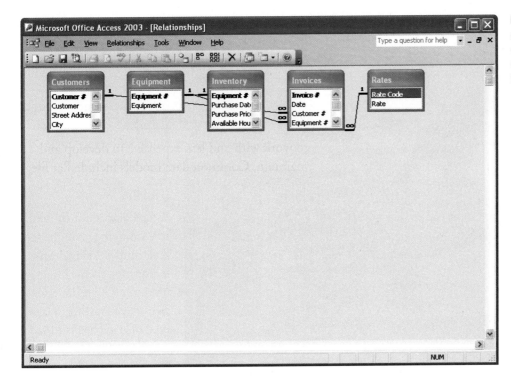

FIGURE 8-8: Relational databases are easy to update, since changing an attribute in one table changes that attribute in all of the tables simultaneously.

Object-oriented Databases

Object-oriented databases are relatively new and there is no widely accepted standard for defining them. In general, object-oriented databases store data in the form of objects. Each object contains both the data related to the object (such as the fields of a record) and the actions that the user might want to perform on that object. A record object created for a payroll department might contain the salary of an individual, along with the calculations required to withhold taxes and print out a paycheck. Object-oriented databases allow for faster development and access times, speeding up database functions and making their development easier.

Distributed Databases

Distributed databases are a relatively new type of database model. These databases function in a networked environment, with each computer storing a portion of the total amount of data in the network. The Internet functions something like a distributed database, with millions of computers around the world holding all of the different pieces of information that can be accessed.

Many smaller forms of distributed databases exist as well. They may use the Internet, or an isolated LAN that is not accessible from the outside world. These databases are valued for their ability to hold more information than any one computer can contain, and they are cheaply and easily expanded. Distributed databases offer advantages in cost, expandability, and storage capability. A major disadvantage is that they do not operate as quickly as mainframe or supercomputer databases, where all information is contained on one computer.

Multimedia Databases

As computer storage and processing speeds continue to increase, so do the number of multimedia databases. In addition to the text and numbers handled by a typical database model, **multimedia databases** allow the storage of pictures, movies,

sounds, and hyperlinked fields. A multimedia employee database file, for example, may include snapshots of employees, along with recordings of their voices.

Hybrids

A database is not limited to employing a single data model. Several different models may be used to allow more effective data handling. This type of database is called a **hybrid**. Combining relational and object-oriented database models is

a popular form of hybrid database. Relational databases can only handle simple mathematical calculations, such as addition or subtraction, so users may have to use separate applications to perform complex functions. Combining relational and object-oriented data models allows for more sophisticated analysis within the framework of the relational database. The advent of the Web and the increasing availability of multimedia files is another factor increasing the popularity of this type of hybrid.

Databases Classified by Function

The two major functional classifications for databases are operational databases and data warehouses. Operational databases are working systems that are continually being updated. For example, a large supermarket may use an operational database that is updated every time a shopper purchases an item. In contrast, a data warehouse is a system from which data is extracted and analyzed by a company's staff in order to make strategic decisions. A data warehouse typically is not modified or updated with new information.

FIGURE 8-9: Supermarket cashiers update an operational database each time they scan an item at the checkout counter.

It is possible for a database system to perform more than one function at the same time. Also, these classifications are not generally associated with a specific data model. Operational databases, for example, might use flat-file or relational structures. The list of database types is still evolving, and new classes may emerge in the future. Web databases are one example of a function classification that has evolved in recent years.

Operational Databases

An operational database works by offering a snapshot of a fluid situation. These systems are called operational databases because they are usually used to track an operation or situation, such as the inventory of a store. Examples of operational databases include inventory tracking systems, such as that used at a supermarket or at a large retail chain such as K-mart. The store has products in stock and on the shelves for customers to purchase. As cashiers scan the bar codes on merchandise, the transactions automatically update a database that tracks the amount and location of each item in the store. When pasta or canned tomatoes are running low, the database automatically orders more. Figure 8-9 shows a supermarket worker interacting with an operational database.

Data Warehouses

Data warehouses are used to store data gathered from one or more databases. Unlike operational databases, data warehouses do not change, delete, or manipulate the information they store. As their name implies, data warehouses function as vast storage places for holding information that can later be used in a variety of ways.

Law enforcement records are one example of a data warehouse, with vast collections of photographs and arrest records on file for reference or for statistical use (see Figure 8-10). Companies also maintain data warehouses to test new ideas against past results. Many of the largest company databases contain information dating back to the 1950s. Companies are increasingly experimenting with these databases, using data mining techniques to sift through information and identify previously unnoticed trends. The strategy resembles survey work, but produces

FIGURE 8-10: Criminal records are stored in data warehouses. Records include photos such as this one of Al Capone.

real results rather than estimating future behavior. Data mining systems often include elements of artificial intelligence. For more on data mining techniques, see Chapter 12.

Web Databases: A Special Class

Web pages often have associated databases of their own. Online shopping sites allow users to type in credit card and shipping information without ever talking to a person (see Figure 8-11). This data is entered into a database, which is later used to track orders and payments. Most **Web databases** are considered operational databases because they process information on a regular, continuous basis as their primary function. Some Web databases are structured on a distributed database model, depending on the amount of traffic they receive. Databases are increasingly being attached to the Internet. This makes the data available on a global scale. A database may have a fantastic fund of information, but its usefulness is limited to the number of users who can access the data. With the trend toward Web-based databases, people can search databases that would have been inaccessible a few short years ago, such as the Vatican Library.

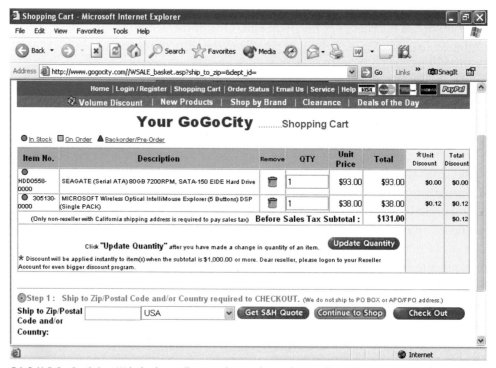

FIGURE 8-11: Web databases allow people to make purchases online.

PLANNING AND DESIGNING DATABASE SYSTEMS

Planning and designing a database system requires a combination of knowledge, skills, and creativity. This job is usually handled by a **systems analyst**. A systems analyst may also become responsible for administering the database after it is built. Like a structural engineer who designs buildings and draws blueprints, a systems analyst is an experienced specialist who can identify project needs and then design a structure or system to fulfill them.

The Database Management Approach

The development and maintenance of database structures and applications employs a methodology called the **database management approach**, sometimes shortened to the **database approach**. Using the software tools of a database management system (DBMS), a systems analyst or database designer follows three broad steps in the planning process:

1. **Create an organizational structure for the data.** A designer first focuses on creating an abstract structure that imitates a real-life situation, drawing on an analysis of the information needs and the purpose(s) of the database. Decisions are made as to the kinds of records needed, the number of fields needed in each record, and how fields should be associated to form records. Choosing the data type and formatting for each field is another basic decision. With the field-record-file structure established, the database is ready to accept data.
2. **Design an interface that makes the database user-friendly.** Users do not need to understand a database's internal structure. Their most important consideration is that they are able to easily enter data and request information. An **interface program** called a **front end** makes this possible. It interacts with the DBMS, the software that manipulates and manages the database. The DBMS, therefore, is referred to as the **back end**. One of the primary functions of the interface is to prevent erroneous data from entering the database. Figure 8-12 shows the relationship of the DBMS, the interface, and the database.

FIGURE 8-12: Through the interface program, a user can interact with the database management system, the software that controls the database.

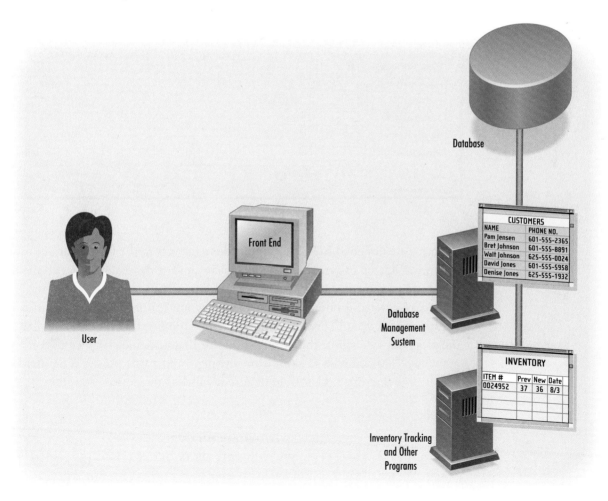

3. Set up reporting capabilities to allow for inquiry and response. Because these functions represent the main database information analysis tools, they are a major focus of the designer's work. A DBMS typically includes reporting features, and the designer chooses how and where in the system the features can be used.

Database Objects: Tools in the DBMS

Database management systems provide reporting tools called **database objects** that are used by database designers to build the system interface and the reporting features. Major database objects include forms, reports, and data filters.

Forms

A **form** is a template that allows users to enter data into the database. Forms perform the important jobs of detecting and preventing erroneous or incomplete data input. A form can be configured to allow the input and display of data in any fashion that the system designer sees fit. Forms can allow users to search through data, move to other forms, print reports, and make changes. Many jobs involve working with forms in a database, such as airline ticketing and hotel front desk work. Figure 8-13 shows a Microsoft Access form ready to accept data input.

FIGURE 8-13: A Microsoft Access Database Form Ready for Input

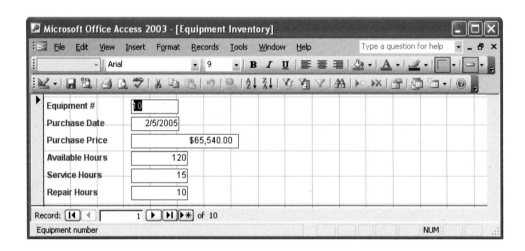

Forms are designed to let users input their answers to the form's questions or prompts. Default answers are included to ensure that the database has all the data required for its fields. Defaults are assumed input that will be utilized in the absence of entered input. Many software programs feature dialog boxes containing questions with default answers. If a user simply presses the Enter key, or clicks OK, the program will assume the default input for that question. For example, if a program asks "Do you wish to save before exiting?" and a user presses the Enter key, it will assume that the work should be saved, which is the default option.

Reports

A report is a formatted body of output from a database. Most reports are designed to be printed out for later review. Monthly phone bills, report cards, and grade transcripts are all examples of database reports. Figure 8-14 shows a database report.

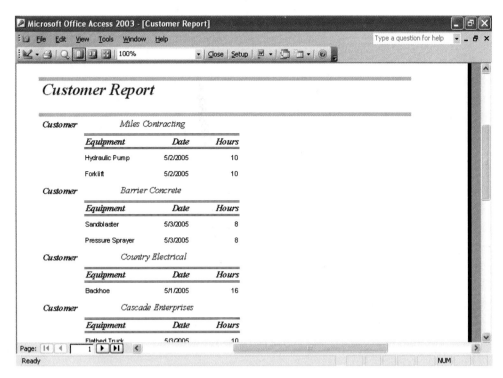

FIGURE 8-14: Reports are one of the most important database outputs.

A report can be generated by request or automatically. For example, credit checks are a type of database report that is not issued on a regular basis. Instead, they are usually issued at the request of commercial firms or consumers. Other types of reports, such as paychecks, are generated automatically on regularly scheduled dates.

Data Filters

Some reports can be requested using filtering criteria, called **data filters**, so that only a subset of the data is presented. For example, if a user wishes to view only accounts receivable overdue by 90 days, a report can be run filtering all accounts except for those overdue by that amount of time. Search engines on the World Wide Web are really data-filtering systems. Search engines maintain massive databases of Web pages. The page contents can be searched using keywords. If a user searches for "cat and dog" for example, a search engine would bring back pages containing the words "cat" and "dog." The report generated in this instance is the HTML Web page transmitted to the user, with the listed Web pages highlighted as blue hyperlinks.

In general, the more specific the data filter, the more limited and focused the result, and the greater the likelihood that the report offers the desired content. Creating good, effective data filters is an important goal of database designers.

ADMINISTERING DATABASES TO ENSURE HIGH-QUALITY INFORMATION

Many factors affect database performance, and thus the quality of the information generated. Database designers must consider each factor, and then ensure that corrections for possible problems arc built into the system. Once problems occur, it is the job of the database administrator to solve them. A **database administrator** is responsible for maintaining and updating the database and the DBMS software.

Larger systems require a team, or perhaps even an entire database and a department of people dedicated to the task.

A database administrator's duties are varied. Any changes in company policy often result in changes to the company database. If billing information sent to customers is supposed to have additional information, the appropriate report must be edited and tested. If a stand-alone system were changed to a networked system, the database must be set up to handle multiple users, and issues such as security and reliability must be thoroughly worked out.

Database administrators are critical players in the success of any organization, since they are largely responsible for preventing computer **downtime**, or time in which the system is unavailable (see Figure 8-15). Consider an airline reservation system. If the computer system is down, the company cannot function, and the employees are getting paid for doing nothing. Customers do not like to be kept waiting, or to be told, "The computer system is down." Hearing that phrase usually means that a database administrator is working feverishly to solve a problem. Major factors that database administrators must be aware of include the corruption or loss of data; backup and recovery operations; database response times; record locking; and data integrity, contamination, and validation.

Data Loss or Corruption

Data loss and data corruption are the most serious failures that can occur in a DBMS. Data loss occurs when data input can no longer be retrieved. **Data corruption** occurs when data is unreadable, incomplete, or damaged. Strategies for backing up data are the major method for recovering lost or corrupted data.

F I G U R E 8 - 1 5 : Database administrators keep databases running.

FIGURE 8-16: Banks and other financial institutions commonly store critical data on backup tapes.

Backup and Recovery Operations

A key part of any DBMS is a **backup and recovery** scheme. Data can always be lost through power interruptions or equipment failure, so ensuring that data is backed up and recoverable is an important task for database administrators. To lessen the chance of accidental data loss, it is important that backup files are stored separately from original material.

Tape backups are a commonly used backup method, as tapes are cheap mass storage media that can be placed in a company safe for protection. They are common in the financial field because bank databases contain valuable and irreplaceable data. A bank cannot operate if it loses information related to customer accounts. In essence, a bank is a gigantic database, and all of its employees service that database. Since modern banks keep few account records on paper, any database failure would be a catastrophic event. Figure 8-16 shows a room filled with shelves of computer backup tapes.

Database Response Time

The length of time a database operation takes is largely dependent on the speed of the hard disk being used. The lag time between a user issuing a command and the

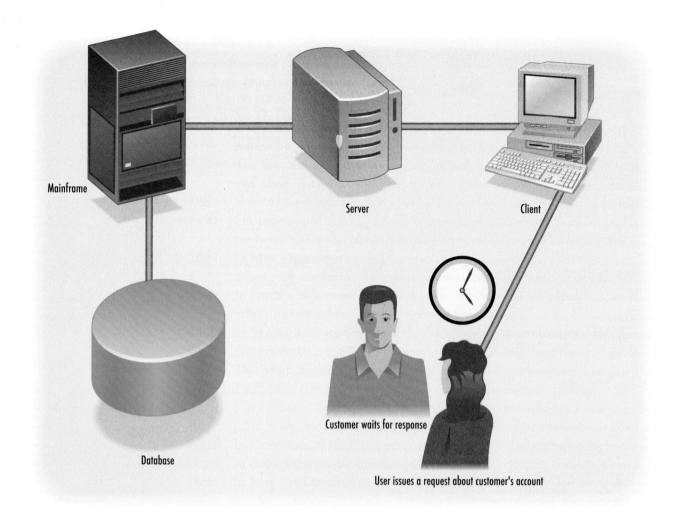

Mainframe

Server

Client

Database

Customer waits for response

User issues a request about customer's account

FIGURE 8-17: Database response time is the lag time between a user issuing a command and the database system taking action.

database system taking action is called the **database response time**. Network conditions may also affect response time if someone is using a remote access to perform database operations. This type of delay is magnified in the case of a distributed database, as several computers may have to work together to perform the entire operation. Figure 8-17 illustrates the lag that is often experienced in a distributed database.

Record Locking

Many databases are designed to be used by more than one user at a time. This is usually achieved by networking computers so that information can be shared. Although there is no conflict when two users are viewing the same record, simultaneous attempts to update a record can cause a problem. **Record locking** is an automatic protection process that occurs when users attempt to edit existing records in a multi-user system. The system automatically checks to see if anyone else is working on the same record, and only allows one user at a time to edit or delete the record. During the process of changing a record, it is considered "locked," and the DBMS will generate an error message for any other users attempting to alter it at the same time.

Data Integrity

The term **data integrity** is used to describe the accuracy of the information provided to database users. A system with high data integrity is obviously more valuable to users than a system containing a large percentage of errors. For example, a sales database with high data integrity will produce mailing lists with fewer incorrect addresses, increasing the percentage of sales material that reaches the intended targets and ultimately increasing sales.

Redundancy, or the duplication of data in several fields, is an enemy of data integrity. Having the same value in multiple places creates opportunities for error when changes are made. For example, if an address is entered in several database locations, any changes to that address would have to be entered in all the locations. Another example of this problem might occur if a person signs up more than once for the same account. Unless there were preventive measures in place, this could cause two separate records to be created. For example, a customer may get partway through an online purchase only to be disconnected. If the customer returns and repeats the process, two copies of the transaction may have been created, leading to duplicate products being delivered, and the customer charged for both.

Redundancy errors are difficult to weed out, and database administrators spend a good deal of time using up-front checks and data validation strategies to locate them. One technique used is called **normalization**, a process intended to eliminate redundancy among fields in relational databases. Normalization works to prevent duplicate data storage, reducing the chance that some data will not be updated when changes are made.

Data Contamination

Once in the system, an error can cause a ripple effect known as data contamination. **Data contamination** is the spread of incorrect information. In many situations data contamination can have serious consequences, such as in credit rating checks. If a company database erroneously shows that a customer has defaulted on a credit purchase, it will eventually be reported to a credit agency. The customer could then receive a poor credit rating, and the company could be liable for any damages resulting from their mistake. Preventing data contamination is one of the goals of data validation.

Data Validation

Among database administrators, the concept of data validation is summed up by the phrase **garbage in—garbage out (GIGO)**. GIGO means that bad input will result in bad output, which is why administrators use data validation methods to prevent bad data (garbage) from entering a system.

Data validation is the process of making certain that data entered into the system is both correct and complete. A database is only a reflection of reality, and it is not self-correcting. It is dependent on

Cutting Edge

Stretching the Surgeon's Reach

It was just a standard gall bladder operation, lasting only 54 minutes. But this procedure, conducted on September 7, 2001, was anything but routine.

The million-dollar surgery took place in Strasbourg, France. The surgeons were operating via computer from New York, 4,300 miles away. This was "Operation Lindburgh," the first complete telesurgery. Here's how it worked. In New York, the surgeons used a video screen and controls connected via a high-speed fiber-optic line to direct the arms of a Zeus laparoscopic surgical robot in the operating room at the European Institute of Telesurgery in Strasbourg. Flesh-and-blood surgeons were standing by to take over if a problem arose.

The key obstacle in telesurgery has always been the time delay involved in video coding/decoding and the signal transmission time. Experiments on pigs had shown that keeping the delay under 200 milliseconds was critical. For Operation Lindburgh, France Telecomm was able to reduce the average delay during the surgery to 150 milliseconds.

Telesurgery is the third revolution in surgery within last decade. The first revolution was the advent of minimally invasive surgery using camera guidance. Next came computer-assisted surgery, allowing surgeons to use software and computer images to increase their accuracy. Now, with telesurgery, doctors will be able to operate in the most remote locations: third-world countries that lack trained specialists, war zones, the Antarctic, and even outer space.

Sources: "The Telesurgery Revolution," *The Futurist*, January-February, 2002; "Doctors Claim World First in Telesurgery," BBC News, September 19, 2001; "World's First Telesurgery a Success," June 2003 <http://www.mad.scientist.org>.

accurate input to maintain its validity, and therefore its usefulness. Because errors are far more difficult to detect and remove once they are in a system, the best way to ensure that a database is error-free is to prevent errors from being entered in the first place. Anyone who has ever tried to rectify a billing error will appreciate the difficulties involved in straightening things out once they go wrong.

There are a variety of techniques that designers or administrators can use to prevent false data from entering a system. Data validation checks are methods of restricting input so that false data cannot be as easily entered into the system. Validation methods include range, alphanumeric, consistency, and completeness checks. Figure 8-18 shows a warning about incomplete data entry.

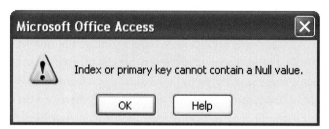

FIGURE 8-18: Data validation requires complete and accurate input. This Access screen displays if the user tries to enter a Null (zero) value in a database field.

Range Checks

Range checks are simple error-checking systems usually performed on numeric data entries. For example, to reduce errors in birth date entries, a range check could be created specifying that no birth dates prior to 1890 be accepted, since it is very unlikely that anyone born before that date is still alive.

Alphanumeric Checks

When entering a value for a field, only certain characters may be allowed. **Alphanumeric checks** allow only letters of the alphabet and digits to be entered. This would prevent users from entering incorrect characters, such as dollar signs ($), in a "customer home address" field.

Consistency Checks

Consistency checks may be made against previously entered data that has already been validated. For example, a validation system will indicate an error if a user attempts to enter phone numbers or social security numbers that do not match previously validated information for these items.

Completeness Checks

Completeness checks ensure that every required field is filled out. One of the greatest threats to data integrity is the natural human tendency to tire of entering data. This leads users to submit input before every field has been completely filled out. To prevent this, one of the first checks performed on any data entry is a check for completeness, meaning that valid entries were provided for every field marked "required." Incomplete records cannot be allowed into the system, such as credit card numbers without expiration date information.

USING DATABASES

A database is ready for data entry and manipulation once it is designed and set up. The activities performed with a database are referred to as **data processing**, which is a broad term describing the handling of various types of interactions or events. The processing of database interactions can be set up using batch or transaction processing, or a combination of both of these methods.

Batch Processing

With **batch processing**, data processing occurs at a scheduled time, or when a critical point has been reached. Batch processing saves redundant effort by rearranging data all at once, rather than continuously. A database may only incorporate changed records at midnight each day, rather than whenever the new data was entered. Massive databases may take anywhere from several minutes to several hours to update. Batch processing streamlines the process by carrying out the work during off-hours. However, it can introduce some lag into the system, and users are sometimes informed that data will not appear until the day after it was entered. When this occurs, it is usually due to batch processing.

Transactional Processing

Transactional processing is more continuous and tends to be done with smaller databases or with operational databases that require all information to be very current. **Real-time systems**, such as factory automation or air traffic control systems, can't afford to wait until midnight to update. The data must be kept accurate down to the second in systems that provide data for these types of critical functions. In transactional processing, records of "events" such as the purchase of an item, the construction of an automobile part, or the departure of a flight are sent to the database for processing one at a time.

Online transactions are a form of transactional processing (called **OLTP** for **online transactional processing**) used at e-commerce Web sites that require fast, always-on processing. One of the great benefits of such systems is that they are effectively in business 24 hours a day. Credit cards are involved in most online sales transactions, and customers expect a quick response so that their orders can be processed.

Mixed Forms of Processing

Transactional and batch processing techniques are often mixed in the same system. For example, in situations involving online orders, a transactional process may be used to handle credit card verifications, while batch processing may be used to handle work orders requesting that items be taken from inventory and delivered to customers.

DATABASE USERS

Most people use databases only while performing their jobs, and are not involved in database design or management. This does not mean that these employees do not have very important jobs. A great deal of effort goes into keeping a database accurate, and this requires constant maintenance. A database must be updated every time a bill is paid, an address is changed, or an order is placed. **Data entry operators** type data into databases and make sure that it is accurate. Many others work with databases regularly as part of their jobs, including the accountants, executives, and salespeople of any organization.

Many operations are regularly performed on a database as a daily routine. For a situational model, consider a school's grades database. The system controls and maintains student transcripts for all the students of the institution, so records are constantly being added, modified, deleted, and sorted.

Adding Records

Adding records to the system is a common operation. If a student completes a course, a grade record is added to that student's transcript, listing the course taken, the date of completion, and the final grade received.

Modifying Records

If a correction is needed to any prior entry, the record in question could be brought up and the change made on a form, such as a letter grade B being changed to an A. Personal information concerning students might also require changes, such as home and school addresses.

Deleting Records

In the example of a college database, grade records are rarely deleted. Since a grade transcript database is really a data warehouse rather than an operational database, deleting a record does not make sense unless the grades were entered in error and need to be corrected.

Sorting Records

Sorting is a critical function for any database, and involves arranging records in a particular order, such as alphabetically or numerically. When a record is added to a file, for example, the file must be sorted so that the results can be more easily searched. A phone book is an example of a set of printed data that is sorted alphabetically. It is easy to imagine how difficult it would be to find a specific phone number if the listing was not alphabetized. Sorting data in a database (based on the ordering of a key field) greatly reduces the amount of time it takes to find any one record.

Most database systems sort records automatically on the basis of their primary key. Social security numbers are used in many colleges as primary keys, as they are unique and don't require a student to learn a new number. However, sorting records by primary key isn't helpful if the primary key for a student is unknown. If a professor wished to change a grade for a student, but didn't know that student's social security number, it could take a long search to find that one record. In that case the database could be sorted by name, and the results searched to isolate the correct student.

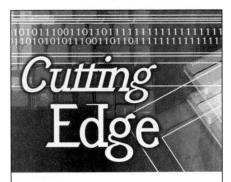

The Entire Human Genome as a Database

After having successfully mapped out the entire human genome years ahead of schedule, Celera Genomics is now busy making use of the database it has created. Putting up $75 million for the project with a few partner companies, Celera is investing in the future benefits of the information it can mine from the database that describes the blueprints of humanity. As is true for many of the companies with which Celera shared the data, a primary value of the massive data is in isolating specific genes and associating them with human diseases. This effort takes a great deal of research, as only 1 percent of the DNA strand is useful for study. The work now is focusing on isolating SNPs, which are the portions of DNA strands that differ from one individual to the next.

Celera is a pioneering company in the wide-open field of genetic biology, and they invite partner companies to join in unlocking the secrets of human life. "With six billion people on the planet, predicting all the diseases—we're talking about a century or more of work," says Craig Venter, Celera's president and chief scientific officer.

Source: <www.cnn.com>

ON THE HORIZON

Industry observers point to some new trends that could mean more data for the dollar, less work for database administrators, and more efficient systems. These improvements will streamline operations and reduce costs, resulting in savings for customers and clients.

Access to Legacy Databases

Legacy databases are databases that run using languages, platforms, or models that are no longer supported by an organization's current database system. In order to be able to continue to access the information stored on these databases, their programming code must be made compatible with the newer system. An effective way to do this is to migrate legacy applications to operating systems that follow open or standard programming interfaces, which will allow a company to use its legacy applications on most operating systems.

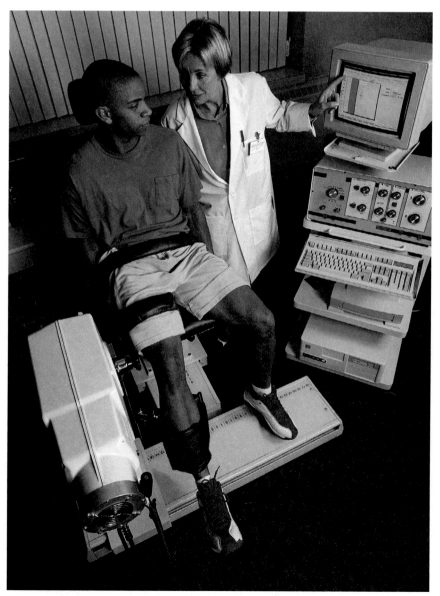

Another option for accessing legacy databases is to use software tools that allow the data to be read directly by newer database systems. This avoids the need to convert the existing code to newer code, saving time and money.

Database Interconnectivity

There is increasing pressure on database vendors to produce products that work together smoothly. Newer databases interrelate better than previous versions by reducing the number of different file formats and routines needed to move information from one database system to another. Although few universal standards exist, information workers will likely see increased interconnectivity in the future.

Improved File Organization Systems

Efforts are underway to create a new file organization system that bans the simple but tedious file folder directory tree. Newer systems will allow for easier file

management with a more intuitive interface. As hard disks bloat into sizes of 100 gigabytes or larger, it is more important than ever to have a system that can locate every file simply and reliably. These newer designs will allow people to search files with queries and to organize files using search engine-type features such as bookmarks or "favorites."

Nationwide Medical Databases

The medical community looks forward to the day when medical records change from manila folders full of dusty documents to a nationwide registry of electronic medical records available to medical personnel anywhere. With these new medical database systems, doctors located anywhere in the world could pull up charts immediately with a few clicks of the mouse. Full color 3-D X-rays could be included in electronic patient records. People receiving care away from home would no longer have to worry that their doctor did not have all their medical records. There are obstacles to this wonderful new application of technology. Cost is one. Medical systems tend to cost much more than other systems due to legalities and the need for complicated approval processes. Everyone involved must have medical training, raising costs even further. Data validation is critical, as lives may be lost if data is faulty. Privacy issues are another roadblock. Medical records are as private and closely guarded as financial ones. Security must be maintained. Should any doctor be able to see a record, or should only the doctors who are given the password be given full access? Can patients access their own records? What about incapacitated patients unable to grant permission? Some medical providers are embracing such databases with a more limited scope, only sharing information about patients in the same HMO plan, for example. So far, no nationwide system exists, but it is very likely that such systems will appear soon.

chapter summary

What Is a Database?

A **database** is a computerized system for storing information in an organized manner so that it can be searched for and retrieved when needed. **Data** associated with other useful data becomes **information**. The constant need to alter and amend masses of data is called **database maintenance**. Databases organize data in a hierarchical fashion, storing information about **entities** in the form of **fields**, **records**, and **files**.

The most common database application is an **information system**, which is a system of computer hardware, software, and operating procedures. **Management information systems (MIS)** are used to track and control every transaction through a database. **Decision support systems (DSS)** are another common form of information system. **Computer-aided manufacturing (CAM)** and **computer-integrated manufacturing (CIM)** are information systems that support factory automation.

Database Management System (DBMS) Software

Databases are controlled by **database management system (DBMS)** software. **Keys** are attributes that can be used to identify a set of information, and the designer designates the most important field in a record as the **primary key**. **Data browsing** is the process of moving through a database file, examining each record and looking for information. **Queries** allow users to ask questions designed to retrieve needed information. **Structured Query Language (SQL)** is the most popular database query language. A DBMS also provides **security measures** to protect and safeguard data. **Metadata** is information about data, and a **data dictionary** is the term for a body of metadata. **Backup and recovery utilities** provide a method for backing up and restoring lost data.

Database Classifications

Databases are often categorized by the way they organize data (**data models**), or by their function (**operational databases**, **data warehouses**, and **Web databases**). Common data models include **flat file**, **relational**, **object-oriented**, **distributed**, **multimedia**, and **hybrids**.

Planning and Designing Database Systems

The job of planning and designing a database system is usually handled by a **systems analyst**. The development and maintenance of database structures and applications employs a methodology called the **database management approach**. Database designers use **database objects** to build the **front end** and the reporting features. A **form** is a template that allows users to enter data into the database. **Defaults** are assumed input that will be utilized in the absence of entered input. A **report** is a formatted body of output from a database. Some reports can be requested using filtering criteria, called **data filters,** so that only a subset of the data is presented.

Database Administration

A **database administrator** is responsible for maintaining and updating the DBMS software. Files are stored in **directory trees**. A key part of any DBMS is a **backup and recovery scheme**, to recover data in the event of **data loss** or **data corruption**. **Tape backups** are a commonly used backup method. The **lag time** between a user issuing a command and the database system taking action is called **database**

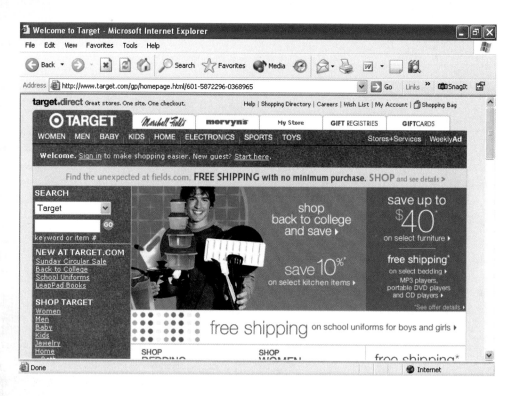

response time. **Record-locking** is an automatic protection process that occurs when users attempt to edit existing records in a multi-user system. **Garbage in—garbage out (GIGO)** means that bad input will result in bad output. **Data validation** is the process of making certain that data entered into the system is both correct and complete. Validation ensures **data integrity** and protects against **redundancy**. Other validation methods include **range**, **alphanumeric**, **consistency**, and **completeness** checks.

Using Databases

The activities performed with a database are referred to as **data processing**.

With **batch processing**, data processing occurs at a scheduled time, or when a critical point has been reached. **Transactional processing** is more continuous, and tends to be done with smaller databases or with operational databases that require all information to be current. **Online transactions** are a form of transactional processing used at e-commerce Web sites requiring fast, always-on processing.

Database Users

Various employees in an organization are involved in maintaining databases as part of their daily tasks. Routine operations performed on database systems include adding, modifying, deleting, and sorting records.

KEYTERMS

alphanumeric, 363
alphanumeric check, 384
attribute, 372
back end, 377
backup and recovery, 381
batch processing, 385
completeness check, 384
computer-aided manufacturing (CAM), 366
computer-integrated manufacturing (CIM), 366
consistency check, 384
data browsing, 369
data contamination, 383
data corruption, 380
data dictionary, 370
data entry operator, 386
data filter, 379
data integrity, 383
data model, 371
data processing, 385
data validation, 383
data warehouse, 372
database administrator, 379
database file, 364
database maintenance, 361
database management approach (database approach), 377
database object, 378
database response time, 382
decision support system (DSS), 366
directory tree, 364
distributed database, 373
downtime, 380
electronic office, 365
entity, 363
file processing, 369
flat file, 372

form, 378
front end, 377
garbage in—garbage out (GIGO), 383
hybrid, 374
information system, 365
interface program, 377
joining, 370
key, 368
legacy database, 388
management information systems (MIS), 365
metadata, 370
multimedia database, 374
normalization, 383
numeric, 363
object-oriented database, 373
office information system (OIS), 365
online transactional processing (OLTP), 386
operational database, 372
primary key, 368
query tools, 369
range check, 384
real-time system, 385
record locking, 382
redundancy, 383
relational database, 372
security measures, 370
SELECT command, 370
Structured Query Language (SQL), 370
system catalog, 371
systems analyst, 376
table, 372
transaction, 365
transactional processing, 385
tuples, 372
Web databases, 376

Page numbers indicate where terms are first cited in the chapter. A complete list of key terms with definitions can be found in the Glossary at the end of the book.

chapter exercises

The following chapter exercises, along with new activities and information, are also offered in the *Computers: Understanding Technology* Internet Resource Center at www.emcp.com.

EXPLORING WINDOWS
Tutorial 8 teaches you how to delete and restore files in the Recycle Bin and how to empty the Recycle Bin to maintain plenty of free hard disk space.

TERMS CHECK: MATCHING
Write the letter of the correct answer on the line before each numbered item.

a. data contamination
b. primary key
c. table
d. multimedia database
e. data validation
f. alphanumeric

g. database objects
h. record locking
i. data integrity
j. query
k. field
l. redundancy

_____ 1. The smallest element of data in a database.

_____ 2. A type of data validation requiring that data be in text or numeric form.

_____ 3. A question posed to a database.

_____ 4. In a relational database, the term used to describe what is called a file in other database models.

_____ 5. This feature allows only one person to use or modify a record at a time.

_____ 6. Errors that are multiplied and carried to other parts of a database, and possibly to other databases.

_____ 7. This type of database is used to handle video, graphic, and music files.

_____ 8. The field used to uniquely identify each record.

_____ 9. Two records containing identical information would be found using this type of check.

_____ 10. Forms, reports, data filters, or queries are examples of this kind of database feature.

_____ 11. A measurement of the trustworthiness of the data in a database.

_____ 12. This is performed to prevent errors from entering a database.

TECHNOLOGY ILLUSTRATED: IDENTIFY THE PROCESS
What process is illustrated in this drawing? Identify the process and write a paragraph explaining it.

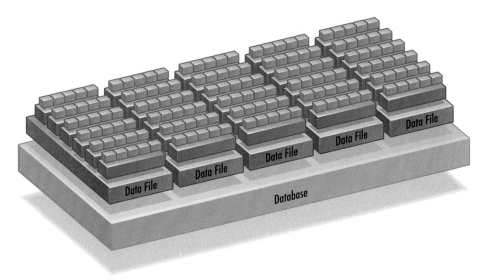

KNOWLEDGE CHECK: MULTIPLE CHOICE
Circle the letter of the best answer from those provided.

1. Modern information systems are underpinned by

   a. databases.
   b. spreadsheets.
   c. word processors.
   d. operating systems.

2. Primary keys must be

   a. text.
   b. numeric.
   c. unique.
   d. all of the above

3. Which of the following allows users to enter data?

    a. Reports
    b. Queries
    c. Forms
    d. Primary keys

4. A(n) _____ is a collection of related fields.

    a. record
    b. database
    c. entry
    d. field

5. Which of the following fields would be the best choice for a primary key?

    a. Birth date
    b. First name
    c. Last name
    d. Social Security number

6. Microsoft's DBMS is called

    a. Foxpro.
    b. Access.
    c. DB2.
    d. Oracle.

7. Querying a large database to identify customer preference trends would be called

    a. maintaining a data dictionary.
    b. data modeling.
    c. data mining.
    d. database administration.

8. SQL stands for

    a. structured query language.
    b. static query language.
    c. statistical quality language.
    d. statistical query language.

9. Which of the following types of information systems would be useful for automating an office?

    a. CIM
    b. OIS
    c. CAM
    d. HTTP

10. Placing records into a logical order using their key fields is called

a. listing.
b. organizing.
c. ordering.
d. sorting.

11. This type of database is used as a repository for information.

a. Operational database
b. Data warehouse
c. Flat file
d. Operational data system

12. A(n) _____ database would be used to keep track of daily orders, inventory, and deliveries at a furniture store.

a. data warehouse
b. operational
c. sales and marketing
d. SQL

13. _____ refers to a period of time during which the computer system is not functioning.

a. Development time
b. Maintenance span
c. Downtime
d. Latency

14. An operation performed upon a database that changes data is called a

a. transaction.
b. query.
c. filter.
d. report.

15. When ensuring data validation, a database might make sure that all the fields in a form are filled out.   This is called a(n)

a. redundancy check.
b. completeness check.
c. consistency check.
d. alphanumeric check.

THINGS THAT THINK: BRAINSTORMING NEW USES

In groups or individually, contemplate the following questions and develop as many answers as you can.

1. Web databases, such as those used by search engines to catalog the Internet, are becoming increasingly intelligent in interpreting queries written by nontechnical users. Go to several search engines that boast of easy-to-use advanced searching techniques and try them out. What other developments do you think may help databases become more intelligent and thus more useful?

2. Smart guns have been developed and are being tested by law enforcement agencies. The guns detect a chip that must be in close proximity to the gun in order for it to fire. Peace officers wear the chip in the form of a wristband or a ring; their weapons will be rendered useless if they are ever wrested away from them. In the future, it is possible that these chips could be injected beneath the skin, making them impossible to remove. If this advance in gun safety becomes commonplace, what advantages or disadvantage do you foresee? Brainstorm possible uses for this technology in other areas.

KEY PRINCIPLES: COMPLETION

Fill in the blanks with the appropriate words or phrases.

1. Database administrators typically set up _____ plans to mitigate the consequences of lost data.

2. _____ is a standardized format for entering database queries.

3. When choosing the _____ for a database, the numbers or text must be unique.

4. Information about the data stored in a database is called _____.

5. Altering and amending masses of data is called _____.

6. Matching data from fields in various record files, also called _____, is used when a database request requires data from more than one source.

7. The _____ is the person responsible for maintaining and updating the database and the underlying DBMS software.

8. The accuracy of the information provided to database users is referred to as _____.

9. A(n) _____ is the smallest element of data in a database.

10. _____ systems are slower to respond because all the records in the database must be searched sequentially.

11. If two or more users are attempting to update a record at the same time, the DBMS will implement a protection process called _____.

12. The process of making certain that data entered into the system is both correct and complete is referred to as _____.

13. Real-time systems use _____ processing.

14. Unreadable, incomplete, or damaged data indicates that _____ has occurred.

15. Electronic office is another term for a(n) _____.

TECH ARCHITECTURE: LABEL THE DRAWING
Identify the numbered components of the screens shown below.

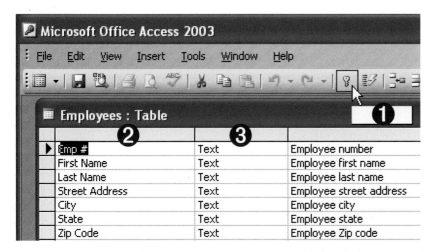

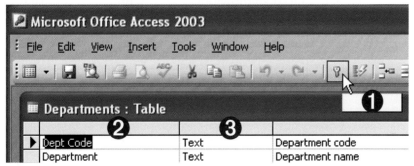

TECHNO LITERACY: RESEARCH AND WRITING
Develop appropriate written responses based on your research for each item.

1. What database management system (DBMS) would you choose?

   Imagine you are running your own home real estate business and need to purchase a database management system. Go to your local software supplier and price the various DBMS software packages. Study one application in detail through Web research. Write a summary describing the product, its capabilities, and whether or not you think it would be suitable for a real estate business. Compare this product to other similar products available in the marketplace.

2. What major features does Oracle's DBMS offer?

Go to www.oracle.com and study their DBMS products. Do a Web search for other non-Oracle sources of information about Oracle DBMS products. Does Oracle offer any features that its competitors do not? Does Oracle allow prospective customers to download a free demo? Is their software aimed at home PC-type or professional users? Write a summary of the information you gather, including answers to these questions.

3. How would you design a database to describe this course?

Create a database outline on paper with the entities that describe this course, including assignments, students, and grading. What types of records would you use? What fields would each record contain? What fields might be shared between records? Make sure that you identify the data type for each field. Do you think your database would be a useful resource for students and instructors if it was made available on a Web page? Would the content of your database pose any security risks?

4. Is online banking for you?

Investigate the features offered by an online banking service offered by a major bank. Would you prefer to do your banking via a Web page, a voice mail system, or by a drive down to the local branch office? Create a table that lists the pros and cons of each of these methods.

5. Identify a business that is dependent on databases.

Many businesses exist primarily to feed data into a database, process it, and retrieve it as valuable information. Can you think of a company in which practically every employee, and the very product of the business itself, is dependant upon a database? Describe in a written report how each employee interacts with the database, and show how the database forms the core of the overall operation of the organization.

TECHNOLOGY ISSUES: TEAM PROBLEM-SOLVING
In groups, brainstorm possible solutions to the issues presented.

1. In the near future, assume that most people will have access to high-speed Internet connections. You plan to run a dot-com service to provide downloadable music, e-books, and videos to the public for a fee. What kind of database would you use to do this? What kind of fee would you charge—a monthly subscription fee or a per use fee? How much do you think your customers would pay to download music?

2. You have been directed to price a database system for a network of ten workstations. A database license will be needed, along with two laser printers. You have technical staff able to perform the installation and setup, so you only need to price the software license and the printers. Research Web sites such as buy.com and gogocity.com and compare prices.

MINING DATA: INTERNET RESEARCH AND REPORTING

Conduct Internet searches to find the information described in the activities below. Write a brief report that summarizes your research results. Be sure to document your sources, using the MLA format.

1. It has long been a fear of privacy advocates that personal information will become a commodity, sold on the open market to the highest bidder. Investigate how companies obtain mailing lists and other customer information, and describe the kinds of companies that collect and sell this kind of information.

2. Electronic databases are the rule in most industries, but are not as common in some areas, such as medical records. Investigate the database situation at hospitals and medical facilities in your area. Do they use electronic databases, or are they still in the paper-file era? Are your medical records on the Internet? Do you think they will be some day?

3. With so much personal information stored in various Web databases, the crime of identity theft is on the rise. Research various online sources and write a summary that includes a definition of identity theft, statistics on the prevalence of identity theft, strategies for minimizing the risk of your identity being stolen, and the steps you should take if someone steals your identity.

TECHNOLOGY TIMELINE: PREDICTING NEXT STEPS

Look at the history of credit cards outlined in the timeline below. Research the topic and try to predict the next logical steps by completing the timeline through 2010.

1914   Western Union gives out metal cards providing credit privileges to preferred customers. These cards come to be known as "metal money."

1924   General Petroleum Corporation issues the first "metal money" for gasoline purchases.

1938   AT&T introduces the "Bell System Credit Card." Airlines and railroads soon reveal their own similar cards.

1959   Many banks offer the option of revolving credit, allowing people to make monthly payments on balances owed, rather than having to pay them at one time.

1966   Fourteen U.S. banks form Interlink, later known as Visa Card, a new association with the ability to exchange information on credit card transactions.

1980   ATM cards quickly become commonplace, replacing human bank tellers with machines.

2000   Smartcards grow dramatically in Europe and Asia, becoming the dominant form of electronic payment.

2001   Disposable credit cards good for one-use-only become popular for online consumer purchases.

2003   Orbiscom introduces ControlPay technology, which allows the primary credit card accountholder to control spending limits and locations for various family members.

ETHICAL DILEMMAS: GROUP DISCUSSION AND DEBATE

As a class or within an assigned group, discuss the following ethical dilemma.

Web sites often collect information about a user who has visited a site or has purchased something from the site. Sometimes this is accomplished by placing cookies on the hard drive of a user's computer that can be read the next time the user navigates to that site. Other times, a site requires a user to register some personal information in order to access "premium" features on the Web site. Many users offer this information without thinking about the privacy implications of sharing their personal data.

Because of consumer privacy concerns, more and more Web sites are posting a privacy policy, which typically indicates how they are storing site visitors' personal information, what they do with it, and whether they share it with other parties. However, they may also change this privacy policy from time to time or choose not to follow it. Have you noticed whether Web sites that you frequent have a privacy policy? Would you place more trust in a Web site that has a posted privacy policy? Would you no longer visit a Web site (or purchase from a Web site) if it did not have a privacy policy? Is it illegal or unethical for a company to change its privacy policy without notifying site users? What can you do if a company violates its own privacy policy? How would you recommend that privacy of consumer information be protected on Web sites?

ANSWERS TO TERMS CHECK AND KEY PRINCIPLES QUESTIONS

Terms Check: 1 – k; 2 – f; 3 – j; 4 – c; 5 – h; 6 – a; 7 – d; 8 – b; 9 – l; 10 – g; 11 – i; 12 – e

Key Principles: 1 – backup and recovery; 2 – Structured Query Language (SQL); 3 – primary key; 4 – metadata; 5 – database maintenance; 6 – joining; 7 – database administrator; 8 – data integrity; 9 – field; 10 – flat file; 11 – record locking; 12 – data validation; 13 – transactional; 14 – data corruption; 15 – office information system (OIS)

CHAPTER 9

UNDERSTANDING
INFORMATION SYSTEMS

UNDERSTANDING TECHNOLOGY

learning objectives

- Define information systems

- Explain why information systems are so widely used

- Identify the components of an information system

- Classify different types of information systems

- Discuss the steps in developing new information systems

key concepts

- What Is an Information System?

- Information Systems Classified by Function

- Considerations in Planning or Updating an Information System

- Factors in Choosing a New Information System

- Developing a New Information System

CYBER SCENARIO

Gino leaned back in his chair and watched his favorite TV show on his computer monitor, keeping the sound down so that it couldn't be heard outside his cubicle. As Gino sipped a soft drink, he thought about how much he loved these

mornings. His boss, Rebecca Stinson, was always an hour late on Thursdays. Gino wasn't too worried about being caught because he had instructed the company's facial recognition system to warn him when Rebecca arrived at the office.

Unfortunately for Gino, Rebecca arrived at the building entrance at 8:35 a.m., a full 25 minutes early. As she neared the entrance, digital cameras zoomed in on her face from three different angles. Facial recognition software created a three-dimensional model of her face, ran it through a database of authorized employees, and came up with a match. For the rest of the day, almost all doors would open automatically whenever Rebecca approached. But then she was the company's Chief Information Officer (CIO), so few doors were ever closed to her.

Gino's computer screen flashed a silent warning before his boss reached the elevator. Gino scrambled to get things in order as he gulped down the last of his soda. He jabbed a thumb at the cutoff button on his computer, replacing the TV show with his e-mail message box. Grabbing his handheld computer, he poked it into life and asked it to bring up the day's list of morning duties. Sometimes his handheld got touchy and refused to understand commands if his voice was too emotional, so he was careful to speak calmly.

First on the list was mail pickup, so Gino immediately headed for the mailroom. As he was picking up the mail, he turned around to find his boss watching him. Rebecca said, "Good morning," and Gino relaxed a bit. Still smiling, Rebecca reminded Gino that they had a busy day ahead. "No time for games today," she said. Gino could hear the mail clerk chuckling as he followed his boss out of the room. "How could she have known?" Gino muttered to himself.

Company information systems contain a wealth of data in text, audio, and image formats. These systems have the power to process the data into information that can be used to manage every operation of the organization, including performing tasks normally handled by humans, such as recognizing unauthorized intruders.

WHAT IS AN INFORMATION SYSTEM?

An information system is much more than computers or software. Recall from Chapter 8 that an information system (IS) is a combination of people, hardware, software, computer networks, and data that organizations use to manage daily and long-term operations. This can include using computerized information processing for taking orders, tracking inventory, and other transactions. Long-term operations include gathering and organizing the information necessary to make decisions about future growth and other strategic changes (see Figure 9-1).

Fast-food operations offer an excellent example of how information systems function. Cashiers take orders, enter them into computer workstations, and perform monetary transactions. The cash registers are actually sophisticated networked computers. They transmit work orders to the kitchen, where the orders are displayed on overhead terminals so that the cooks know what food to prepare (see Figure 9-2). The information system database automatically removes items from inventory as they are sold.

The information that the database processes can be used to create reports covering a variety of topics. With a few keystrokes, a restaurant owner can know the

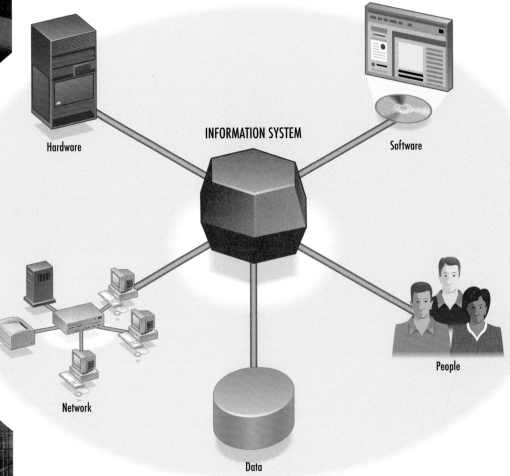

INFORMATION SYSTEM

Hardware

Software

Network

People

Data

F I G U R E   9 - 1 : An information system is a combination of people, hardware, software, computer networks, and data that organizations use to manage daily and long-term operations.

FIGURE 9-2: Fast-food workers use computer displays to fulfill customer orders. These computers are connected to an information system that records all parts of the transaction.

day's financial transactions, what items need to be reordered, and which products are selling well. Marketing people in company headquarters can use this information to increase the restaurant's competitiveness by deciding which products should be discontinued, promoted, or possibly sold at a reduced price.

Meeting Business Needs with Information Systems

Why do companies use information systems? The simple answer is that computerized information management increases productivity and efficiency, making companies more competitive. Computer-based information systems offer four key advantages over traditional (precomputer) information systems:

- **improved speed:** Companies are able to perform daily operations very quickly, reducing production times and increasing employee productivity.
- **improved efficiency:** Information systems can be used to design and manage more efficient production processes, saving time and money.
- **improved quality:** Computer-based information systems are less mistake-prone than traditional systems, enhancing product quality.
- **improved measurability:** Computers can be used to track all production factors, making it easier to sort through past data to find trends. This information can then be used to improve products and streamline the production process.

The Rise of Information Systems

The first computerized information systems appeared in the 1950s. They were designed to handle tedious tasks such as sorting mail, printing checks, creating phone bills, and storing demographic data for the U.S. Census Bureau. Some observers worried that computers would take jobs away from people, and in many cases they did. However, new jobs were also created, often requiring more highly trained and better paid individuals. People have now come to accept that computers are here to stay, and that information systems are an inevitable part of their daily lives.

Although we may not realize it, information systems are all around us. ATMs have only been available for two decades, but they now rule the consumer-banking world. Gas pumps take credit cards directly; there is no need to go inside the station to pay. Online shopping allows consumers to shop from the comfort of their own homes. At the grocery store, clerks only need to slide a product over a bar code reader to launch a series of important actions—recording the price, deducting the item from inventory, and ordering a replacement. All of these services are

examples of information systems in our daily lives. Comparing the speed of these electronic operations with the time they once took to perform manually shows why computerized information systems are so valuable.

Computerized information systems are continually expanding and becoming more comprehensive as they move into business and government activities that humans previously handled. The trend toward consolidation is one of the more striking features of this expansion. Older systems compartmentalized information and maintained separate databases for functions such as payroll, billing, sales, and work orders. Newer systems are merging these formerly separate databases, making them more accessible and increasing the number of ways that information can be manipulated. Nothing shows this trend toward consolidation more clearly than the Internet. The Internet is a gigantic information system, linking previously isolated governmental, educational, and business databases. This universal accessibility is one of the biggest factors behind the success of the Internet.

INFORMATION SYSTEMS CLASSIFIED BY FUNCTION

There are many different types of information systems, and the easiest way to differentiate them is by their function. Any system might be used by an individual running a PC or by thousands of employees at a Fortune 500 company. In either case, they provide the same service but on a different scale. The following are some common functional classifications for information systems:

- distribution management
- office information
- management information
- decision support
- executive support
- factory automation

Distribution Management Systems

Getting products to customers probably represents the greatest impact of information systems on business operations. **Distribution management systems** are designed to deliver products quicker, cheaper, and with fewer errors. Part of the system is an operational database, but the structure also encompasses such seemingly unrelated elements as the duties and schedules of forklift operators and truck drivers.

The major advantage provided by a distribution management system is the reduction of inventory overhead. Traditional systems involved the delivery and warehousing of inventory. The next generation of distribution systems was called just-in-time, and reduced the need to warehouse inventory by delivering it just before it would be used in the manufacturing process. Stockless systems represent the latest type of distribution management system. Savings in inventory overhead have steadily increased as these systems have evolved. Figure 9-3 illustrates a comparison of distribution systems.

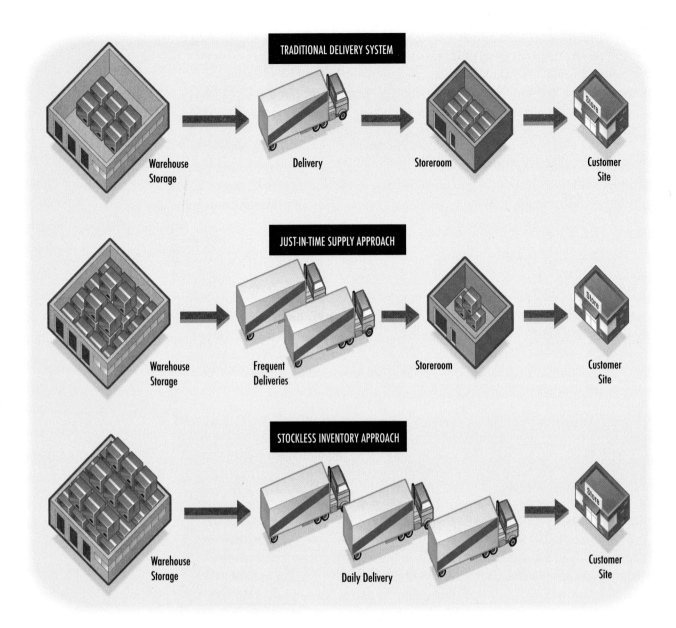

FIGURE 9-3: A Comparison of Inventory Distribution Systems. Note the differences in warehouse storage needs, delivery truck needs, and storeroom space needs.

Traditional Distribution Management

Mail-order companies, including publishers, were the typical users of traditional distribution systems. Inventory was maintained in bulk storage at the place of production, transported to wholesalers in various locations, and finally delivered to retail outlets. This system was slow, and it was often a month or more from the time books were off the presses to the final delivery of the product. This method resulted in large inventories of unsold products, reducing profitability.

Just-In-Time Distribution

In recent years companies have begun to focus on reducing inventories and the amount of time it takes to get a product from the factory to the consumer. Called **just-in-time distribution**, new computerized distribution management systems allow companies to produce products to match market demand. This shrinks inventories and increases profits. In publishing, this meant a change from large print runs to smaller and more frequent ones, reducing the size of inventories along the entire distribution chain.

Stockless Inventory

The most recent trend in distribution systems is a move to eliminate the local storage of products entirely. **Stockless inventory** systems work by making daily deliveries directly from the factory, allowing companies to keep their inventory and wasted production to a minimum, while increasing their responsiveness to customer needs. In publishing, this includes advances such as print-on-demand (POD), which allows bookstores to instantly print any paperback book from an electronic file, identical in quality to books printed using traditional processes.

Office Information Systems

Office information systems (OIS) are used to automate office work. These are systems that collect, store, and transmit data in a shared environment. An OIS typically provides the following office automation functions:

- maintaining standard operating procedures (SOP)
- connectivity
- electronic data processing (EDP)

Standard Operating Procedures

Standard operating procedures (SOP) are work instructions that act much like computer programs written for people. Workers follow the logical steps contained in SOPs in order to process information correctly. SOPs cover filling out forms, typing them into systems, creating reports, and transmitting the resulting documents to another office. Schools have SOPs to cover the class registration process. Registration forms are often filled out by hand and read into a database using a scanner. The database then produces a report informing students if they have been accepted into a class or placed on a waiting list.

Connectivity

Connectivity refers to the ability to link with other programs and devices. Connectivity allows office workers to move information faster and more accurately from one part of the information system to the next, without documents being lost or forgotten along the way. Connectivity is enhanced by computer networks that facilitate faxes, e-mail, and other forms of electronic document transmission.

Electronic Data Processing

Electronic data processing (EDP) is the use of computers to process data automatically. This function can take a variety of forms, from the creation of new documents to the production of paychecks using a payroll processing system. Transactional processing is used for most situations involving standardized data entry, such as fast-food restaurant ordering systems. Businesses handling large amounts of data input often use batch processing. For example, the banking industry uses batch processing to process the millions of checks and cash card transactions that need clearing every day. This is usually more efficient than updating the entire database every time a change is made.

Management Information Systems

With the exception of very small companies, nearly every business uses some form of a management information system (MIS). As the name suggests, an MIS exists to provide information that assists in the management of business operations. Management information systems typically integrate information from different company departments or functions into one database. It is this combining characteristic that enables the comprehensive reporting capabilities of an MIS. An MIS usually provides support to management in the form of regular reports, either on a periodic or an on-demand basis. Quarterly earnings, monthly cash flow, and other types of reports provide important information that helps managers improve productivity and profitability.

Decision Support Systems

Decision support systems (DSS) help managers make informed business judgments. A DSS is generally custom-built for each application. Spreadsheet programs and **expert system shells** (a type of artificial intelligence) are often used to create a new DSS. A DSS might exist independently of an OIS or MIS, but it is usually provided by the same software and database system.

Decision support systems do more than just track input data and print summary reports covering what happened during the previous month. One additional feature is called data modeling. **Data modeling** provides a simulation of a real-world situation built into a software application. With data modeling systems, users can input numeric data into "what-if" scenarios to predict future outcomes. For example, data modeling can be used to help a company decide whether to open a new branch office, or to determine loan payments at different rates of interest. The ability to visualize alternative scenarios is a valuable decision-making aid.

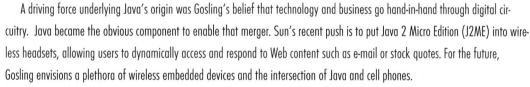

JAMES GOSLING, VICE PRESIDENT, SUN MICROSYSTEMS

James Gosling's name is prominent on the list of famous programmers. A Sun Microsystems fellow and vice president, Gosling is best known as the creator of Java.

Before his arrival at Sun in 1984, he is credited with building a multiprocessor version of Unix, multiple compilers, and mail systems. In addition, he also built the original "Emacs," a text and drawing editor for Unix systems, and helped to build a satellite data acquisition system. While earning a PhD in computer science from Carnegie-Mellon University in 1983, he worked as a principal on the

Andrew project, the high-speed, wireless infrastructure, now one of the largest installations of its type. His early activity at Sun as lead engineer of the NeWS window system led to the original design of the Java programming language and the implementation of its original compiler and virtual machine.

Java is based on the power of networks and the idea that the same software should run on many different kinds of computers, consumer gadgets, and other technology devices. Since its initial commercial release in 1995, Java technology has grown in popularity and usage because of its true portability. It is a platform that allows users to run applications on any compatible device that supports the Java platform, allowing programmers and users to do new things with Web pages that were never before possible.

Gosling did not develop Java as an individual pet project; its original name was "Oak," and it was part of a secret mission called "The Green Project." Gosling and a group of Sun employees were chartered to figure out the next "wave" of digitally controlled consumer devices and computers. Gosling recalls, "As we were building stuff, it became clear that one of the obstacles to the whole endeavor was the programming language and the tools we used to build the software. So my part of the project was to go off and solve the tool problem, and that's where Java came from. The vision was to build networks of big and little things connected together with Java as the concrete and nails."

A driving force underlying Java's origin was Gosling's belief that technology and business go hand-in-hand through digital circuitry. Java became the obvious component to enable that merger. Sun's recent push is to put Java 2 Micro Edition (J2ME) into wireless headsets, allowing users to dynamically access and respond to Web content such as e-mail or stock quotes. For the future, Gosling envisions a plethora of wireless embedded devices and the intersection of Java and cell phones.

In an interview with *Wired News*, Gosling maintains that his creation of Java started out as "something done for me and friends. It's almost a historical accident that I ended up doing what I did. We had no illusion of becoming widespread, and no worry about any particular goal. What's happened since then is nutty!" Gosling recalls that he had no idea the language his team was hammering away at would become an industry buzzword. "It was more of a matter of entertainment than creating a product."

Recently, Gosling is spending most of his time concentrating on developer tools that meet the needs and speeds of faster processors and more complex systems. His focus is on what can be done with tools to ease the use of these complex systems.

Sources: Sullivan, Tom, "James Gosling: Java," October 9, 2000, *Infoworld;* Gosling, James, "A Brief History of the Green Project," http://java.sun.com; TechTV News staff, "James Gosling, Java Guru," June 7, 2001.

Spreadsheets Used to Create DSS Applications

One of the key drivers of the personal computer revolution in the early 1980s was the popularity of spreadsheets as simple decision support systems. The spreadsheet is widely recognized as the "killer application" that drove early PC sales into the millions. People were using spreadsheets for "running the numbers," business jargon for performing what-if analyses on a DSS. Many people have convinced managers and lending institutions that their business proposals were sound investments using nothing but a PC and a spreadsheet application (see Figure 9-4).

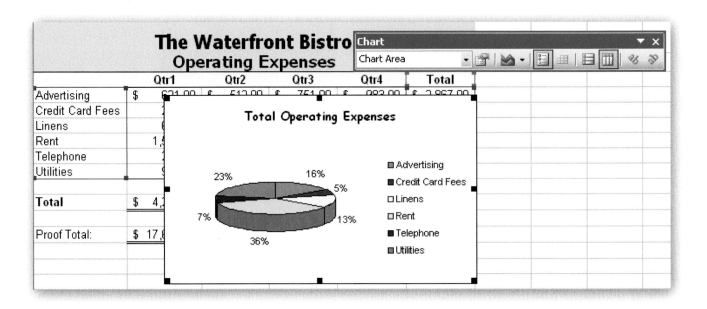

FIGURE 9-4: A spreadsheet program such as Excel 2003 can calculate elements of a business proposal, such as operating expenses, and display them in a chart.

Expert Systems

Expert systems provide much more sophisticated DSS data modeling methods. **Expert systems** attempt to model an expert's knowledge of a topic, such as a doctor or other professional (see Figure 9-5). An expert system can be queried using a set of rules called a **knowledge base**. The system will make recommendations after a conversational session in which the computer asks a set of focused questions. Expert systems exist to aid doctors in diagnosing rare diseases, to help geologists find oil and mineral deposits, and to troubleshoot network connections. They qualify as decision support systems, but they are also a major component of the field of artificial intelligence. For more information concerning expert systems, see the section on artificial intelligence in Chapter 12.

Online Analytical Processing

Online analytical processing (OLAP) systems are a new entry into the DSS arena. OLAP systems define and clarify methods of handling what-if questions posed to large databases, as well as to massively distributed data systems such as the Internet. Originating from a "white paper" commissioned by Arbor Software and written by Dr. E. F. Codd in 1993, this new software class has fostered the development of a variety of software packages. The field has yet to completely evolve, but the major thrust of the technology is focused on providing better ways to analyze the mass of data now pouring into databases, thus producing more useful results.

FIGURE 9-5: Doctors use expert systems to help them diagnose rare diseases.

Executive Support Systems

Executive support systems (ESS) function as an upper-management tool. They are similar to decision support systems but are generally less technical and broader in focus. Executive support systems attempt to bring together information from an entire organization, rather than focusing on any one department or group. An ESS uses this information to support strategic decision-making by facilitating the creation of high-level summary reports that executives can use to help make any number of important decisions. For example, an ESS is often used to handle accounting issues for corporations, such as cash flow, quarterly earnings, and dividends. In addition to knowing which burgers sell best, the CEO of a fast-food chain might want to know which locations are experiencing the best sales growth. This information could then be used to maximize profits by ensuring that outlets are only opened in the high-growth locations identified by the ESS.

Factory Automation

In addition to offices, information systems are frequently found in factories. Two major systems are used in factory automation: computer-aided manufacturing (CAM) and computer-integrated manufacturing (CIM). Statistical quality control (SQC) is another form of information system often used in plant operations.

Computer-Aided Manufacturing

Computer-aided manufacturing (CAM) involves the direct use of computerized systems to manufacture products. Robots used in automobile manufacturing

FIGURE 9-6: Automobile manufacturing plants commonly use robots as part of computer-aided manufacturing systems.

plants are a classic example of this technology. Even more common are systems that monitor and report on the progress of an assembly line. These CAM systems provide factory operators with information such as temperature readings, assembly line speeds, and quality test failure statistics. Any computerized system that directly aids in a manufacturing process is called a CAM system (see Figure 9-6).

Computer-Integrated Manufacturing

Computer-integrated manufacturing (CIM) offers much broader coverage than CAM systems. CIM systems focus not only on the factory floor, but also on the company as a whole. A CIM system connects the factory floor to the executive offices, the accounting department, and the sales staff, making information available to anyone who might need it. A much larger form of information system than a CAM, CIM systems impact everyone in a manufacturing company, from the president down to the mail clerks (see Figure 9-7).

In a furniture company employing CIM, factory sawmill lines would use individual CAM systems to help operators monitor and control production. These CAM systems would be networked to a centralized computer system tracking production progress, errors, and quotas. This information would be automatically sent to headquarters for evaluation. Orders would also be sent from the management information system telling the CAM lines what to produce and in what quantities.

FIGURE 9-7: Manufacturers of all types use computer-integrated manufacturing (CIM).

Statistical Quality Control

Statistical quality control (SQC) systems use a combination of data tracking and data modeling to build a picture of how well a factory is operating. An SQC tracks measurements of the quality of a final product and compares them to the conditions present throughout the manufacturing process. For example, a car manufacturer may discover that some supplied metal caused more defective parts than other metal, or that one shift of workers is generating better quality products than another group.

INFORMATION SYSTEMS CONSIDERATIONS

Planning or updating an information system is a process that organizations initiate in response to a variety of factors. Management may decide to "computerize" paper-based systems that worked well in the past but are no longer capable of keeping up with today's marketplace demands. In other cases, a company may have a computer system and databases that are only accessible to a few people with specialized skills. A new system may become necessary to accommodate the expansion of the business. For example, a small professional office (such as an optometrist) might join with several other offices to form a larger practice. Its

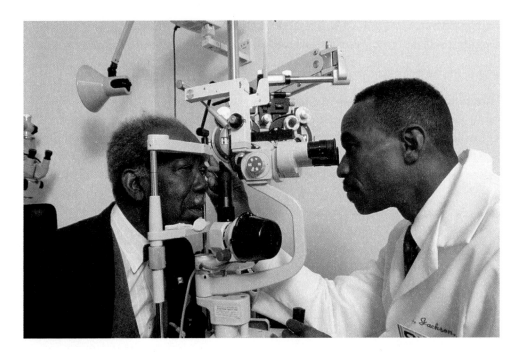

billing and receiving information may be on one computer database, while its payroll and inventory systems may still reside on paper forms. The larger practice could utilize a new information system to integrate all the functions and records of its member offices, allowing access to the practice's data from any workstation.

Impact of a New Information System

The impact of a new information system should be studied in order to determine its suitability. Replacing a traditional paper system can result in a difficult adjustment process for some employees. Sometimes a major information system upgrade has almost as dramatic an effect as did the switch from a paper to an electronic system. The major effects of upgrading or switching to a computer-based information system are

- expanded technical staff
- increased information technology costs
- increased profit margins
- enhanced product quality
- reduced clerical staff
- temporary disruption

While the impact of a new information system has both positive and negative effects, the negative effects are usually short term. Information systems should be perceived as investments in the future, and therefore they may take time to return their full value.

Expanded Technical Staff

In the short term, new technology requires additional technical personnel, such as technicians and programmers. The transition period can last a year or more at large companies, and the company payroll will increase dramatically. In addition to paying existing clerical staff to keep business rolling, the company must pay new technical staff to retrain the current staff so that they can operate the new system.

Increased Information Technology Costs

Computers are not like chairs or desks. They do not last for decades; they normally last only a few years before they are obsolete. Since there is a constant annual cost involved in keeping up with the latest technology, computers should be viewed as short-term purchases rather than fixed-cost investments. When pricing new systems, a common mistake of many managers is to forget to account for

I'm Hard at Work (Not)

Some people complain that today's technology makes it impossible to get away from their work. Perhaps they need to take a page from those who use that very same technology to escape the office—while leaving the impression that they're working harder than ever.

For years employees have known how to take advantage of a cell phone to make a business call from a tanning booth or a tennis club, or to use call-forwarding to take an office call on the boat. But the professional slackers have other tricks up their sleeves. To project the image of a nonstop worker, a person could use an e-mail timer to send messages long after the other office drones have gone home to bed. Some absentee employees reconfigure their instant messaging program to make it appear as if they are constantly online. Services such as Yahoo By Phone will deliver e-mail messages by computerized voice from any phone anywhere.

Using these tricks can convince people outside the office that you're hard at work. But how do you fool the person in the next cubicle? Try operating your office computer by remote control using a service such as GoToMyPC.com. It can move the cursor on your screen, open and close documents, and print them out on shared office computers. Everyone will assume you're just around the corner.

Such sly white-collar slacking gained notoriety when reporter Jason Blair brought shame upon *The New York Times* for fabricating stories. Part of his modus operandi was using e-mail and cell phones to file stories from places he had never visited. Technology keeps finding ways to keep workers connected to the office, but the savviest, or perhaps laziest, are quickly finding ways to use that technology to their own advantage.

Source: Spencer, Jane. "Slacking, Thanks to Computers," *Asian Wall Street Journal*, reprinted in the *Minneapolis Star Tribune*, July 8, 2003.

the cost of the inevitable upgrades that will be required in the years following the initial purchase.

Increased Profit Margins

The big payoff of any information system is the ability to do business faster. This takes time to materialize, and new systems usually aren't cost-effective for the first few years. Information systems may not always reduce a company's bottom line, but they do enable a company to grow and do more business than it would have without a system in place.

Enhanced Product Quality

Once an information system is fully functional, improvements in product quality should follow. For example, a company that manufactures computer printers should see several improvements by implementing an information system. Supplies will arrive more quickly and with fewer errors in the orders. If the information system includes quality elements, products will be superior to those produced using regular systems. Higher-quality products mean more satisfied customers and therefore increased sales—the ultimate goal of any business change.

Reduced Clerical Staff

One of management's goals in installing or upgrading an information system is to reduce clerical staff positions. As a general rule, computerized billing, order taking, and credit approval processes translate into a reduced need for personnel. Since employee salaries typically represent a company's largest single monthly expense, an efficient information system can cut costs significantly. However, the costs of additional computer hardware, software, and more technically capable employees cut into any savings.

Temporary Disruption

Another factor that people often fail to take into account is that disruptions to operations will almost certainly be experienced. On the technical side, hardware systems take time to perfect, and errors will emerge as the system is implemented. On the human side, switching systems is stressful for staff and management alike, as few people enjoy having to change the way they are used to doing things. Employees become comfortable with their jobs and they tend to avoid change, particularly the significant changes brought about by new computer-based information systems.

To Buy or To Develop?

Once the impact of a new system has been studied and a decision to proceed has been made, a new system must be purchased "off the shelf," or developed and brought into service.  The buy-or-develop decision is influenced heavily by the size of the company. Larger organizations usually have in-house IT staffs devoted to developing and maintaining information systems. Smaller organizations usually can't afford to pay employees to develop information systems, so they end up purchasing standard software packages, or subcontracting their information system development and support work. **Subcontracting** involves hiring a third party to handle the project, usually a consultant or a systems house. A **systems house** is a company that specializes in installing and supporting information systems. Systems houses are sometimes known as **systems integrators**.

As a company grows and its needs become more complicated, hiring a technician for system maintenance and support may become a necessity, since hourly consulting rates are much higher than a technician's salary calculated on an hourly basis. The amount paid to a consultant for one hour's work may be the same as the amount paid to an employee for a full day.

FACTORS IN CHOOSING A NEW INFORMATION SYSTEM

Deciding which information system to purchase is difficult, particularly for small organizations. In the early planning stages, managers may have only limited knowledge to guide them. It is not uncommon for nontechnical people to find themselves in charge of deciding which hardware and software combination they should purchase—without having any idea about how to make that decision. The following factors should be considered when choosing an information systems package:

- user interface design
- open versus closed system
- niche information system
- turnkey solutions
- system support

User Interface Design

One of the first things to examine is the system's user interface. The interface design should be user-friendly and intuitive. Critical information should be readily apparent. It is wise to examine a number of different interfaces before making this judgment. Information system software is expensive, and mistakes will be costly.

Open or Closed System?

Choosing between open- or closed-system formats is one of the most crucial decisions. An **open-system** format means that company IT staff can alter the system or hire a third party to take care of any necessary alterations. **Closed systems** must be serviced and supported by the original vendor. Because of this requirement, closed-system support services command a price that can surprise unwary buyers.

Niche Information Systems

Niche information systems exist to serve specially focused sets of customers. These packages are also commonly referred to as **vertical market** packages. An example of a niche system would be a package designed for dental offices. The system would include all needed forms and templates, such as those for invoices, patient records, and insurance claims. A major benefit of this type of information system is that it will serve an organization's needs well, without requiring a lot of technical know-how or staff training. The market for these specialized information systems is small, which means the price per system can be quite high. Another drawback is that vertical market packages often tend to lag technologically, and they may not be compatible with the latest operating systems.

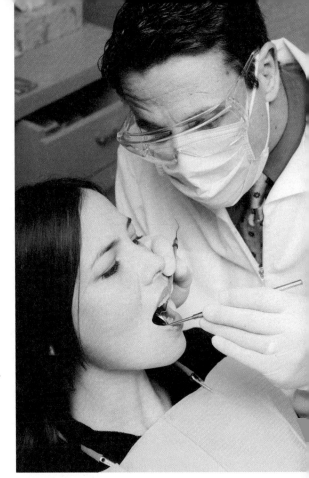

Turnkey Solutions

Turnkey solutions are usually out of the price range of small businesses. The name comes from the idea of being able to simply "turn the key" to get the system up and running. There should be no complications, and no technical skills are required. **Turnkey systems** are usually the best and the most expensive, as they are heavily customized and include the services of support people to tailor them to the exact needs of a business. Like any custom-built product, they tend to be a bit inflexible. It is very expensive to upgrade turnkey systems to take advantage of any improvements when the underlying technology changes.

System Support

The level of technical support is a key issue, whatever the system under consideration. Questions to be considered include whether or not installation, staff training, and on-site service and repair are included in the system package. If not, the cost of these services needs to be investigated and factored into any calculation of the total cost. All too often a call for technical assistance is likely to end up in a voice mail/holding pattern for hours, with the caller paying $20 a minute for assistance. The need for technical support and maintenance is a given, so it is important that the level of support be a known quantity before purchasers sign on the dotted line.

DEVELOPING A NEW INFORMATION SYSTEM

Identifying and assembling employees with the skills and expertise required to develop a new in-house information system is a necessary first step. A management group may be involved in answering questions and providing information in the early planning phases of the project, but programmers and/or software engineers handle the design and implementation of any new system.

Programmers specialize in the development of new software, while software engineers are highly skilled professionals with programming and teamwork training.

Their organized, professional application of the software development process is called **software engineering**.

Project Team

Because of their large size, information systems require the creation of a project team. A project team usually includes a project manager, who acts as the team leader. Sometimes the project manager also functions as a systems analyst, responsible for completing the systems analysis and making design recommendations. The rest of the project team includes software engineers and technicians. The software engineers deal with programming software, while technicians handle hardware issues.

The comprehensive process software engineers initiate is called the **system development life cycle (SDLC)**, a series of steps culminating in a completed information system.

System Development Life Cycle

FIGURE 9-8: The system development life cycle includes four major stages and substeps within each stage.

Creating a development plan and executing it has several stages, some of which have already been set in motion as part of the decision to proceed with the project. Figures 9-8 and 9-9 detail the steps in each stage.

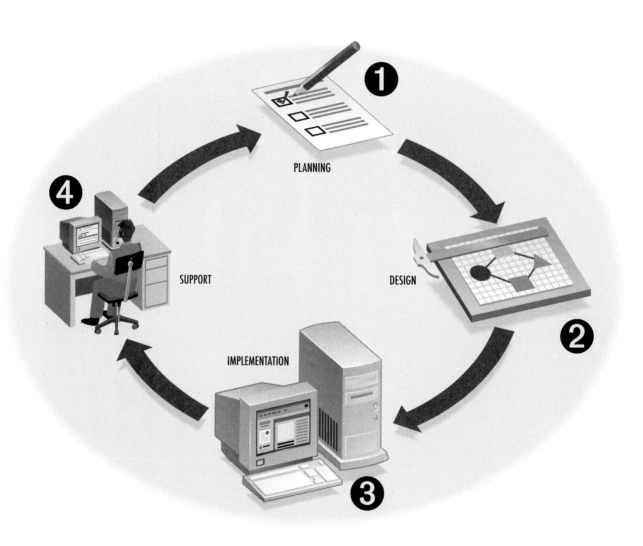

PLANNING

SUPPORT

DESIGN

IMPLEMENTATION

Return to Stage One

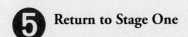 **Planning**
    a. Prepare a needs analysis.
    b. Conduct feasibility studies.
    c. Establish a project team.
    d. Create a project plan.

Support
    a. Identify technical support requirements.
    b. Provide for system updates.

Design
    a. Develop the functional specification.
    b. Develop the design specification.

Implementation
    a. Design a prototype.
    b. Develop the system.
    c. Purchase hardware and software.
    d. Install and test the system.
    e. Train the users.
    f. Approve the system.

FIGURE 9-9: The development of information systems follows a cycle that is ongoing.

Planning a System

To understand how the information system development process works, imagine a scenario involving an automobile manufacturing company named Big Engines, Inc. Big Engines' management decides that their old system isn't working well, and they see an opportunity to improve their current operations. After recognizing the need for a new system, they can either contact their company's own internal development team (if one exists), or they can contact an outside vendor.

Suppose Big Engines is considering an upgrade to their existing CIM. A **feasibility study** would be conducted to investigate how difficult the project might be to complete, and how much it might cost. A large automobile company like Big Engines is almost certain to have its own internal development team. However, the internal team may recommend hiring a systems house if the project is beyond their capabilities, or if the team is too busy handling existing problems.

If management decides to hire a systems house, a **request for proposal (RFP)** will be sent to one or more possible suppliers. The systems houses would then send representatives to determine what is required before quoting a price. In the case of larger, more expensive projects, systems houses might be asked to bid on the job, meaning that they must examine the proposal thoroughly before providing an estimated price for completion of the system. The lowest qualifying bidder meeting with company approval gets the job.

Project Plan

Part of the RFP involves the development of a **project plan**, which includes an estimate of how long the project will take to complete, an outline of the steps involved, and a list of deliverables. **Deliverables** are documents, services, hardware, and software that must be finished and delivered by a certain time and date in order to keep the project on schedule. Big Engines' project team must decide these requirements before the RFP is ready for release. Payments are usually based on the successful completion of project deliverables.

Project planning normally involves a large number of meetings. Systems analysts must meet regularly with potential system users and management personnel to learn exactly what they want and how their demands can be accomplished. Interviews, employee questionnaires, and simple observation of daily practices are all part of this process. Various project management tools are available to help schedule each phase of the project and to determine the priority of each step.

Project Management Tools

The project manager would probably use a Gantt chart and computer-aided software engineering (CASE) tools to handle large projects, such as a CIM system for auto manufacturing. **Gantt charts**, named after Henry Gantt, are bar charts showing the stages of a project and the order in which they must be completed (see Figure 9-10). Gantt charts graphically show critical steps and are used for scheduling purposes.

FIGURE 9-10: The Gantt chart shown might be used on a construction project.

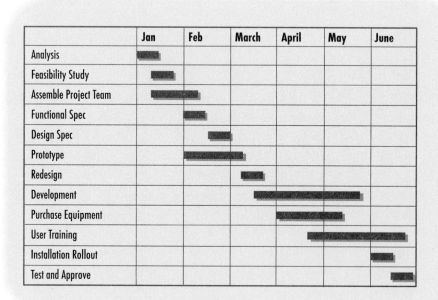

Setting realistic time frames is very important to the success of any project and is one of the more difficult tasks of project management.

CASE tools encompass a large group of sophisticated software packages that automate the design and development of an IS. These tools are used to carry out a project analysis, create a graphic specification, automatically generate and compile program code, test and debug the program(s), provide maintenance, and handle design changes during implementation. They also generate a project database that documents the information system using reports, graphs, models, and flowcharts of processes. Several software vendors sell packages that integrate an entire set of CASE tools. Most projects require additional custom programming, however, to closely fit the company's information system needs. Using CASE tools is generally referred to as **rapid application development (RAD)**.

TECH VISIONARY

Ever heard of Bill Gates and his impact on the world of personal computers? Of course. Ever heard of Hasso Plattner? His name is not nearly as recognizable, but Plattner has had a comparable impact on corporate computing.

Before Plattner came along, software for running a business needed to be custom-made and housed on high-priced mainframes. Plattner cofounded the small company SAP in a small town outside of Heidelberg, Germany, some 30 years ago. SAP has revolutionized the software industry by developing business programs that can be tailored to meet a company's needs and run on its own computers. In an industry ruled by American giants, Plattner's SAP became the world's third-largest software supplier.

Plattner is considered the charismatic visionary of SAP, a man with creative insight into software needs as well as a great marketer and deal-closer. He is a colorful man known for his bitter rivalry with Larry Ellison, the CEO of Oracle, the world's second-largest software company. This competitiveness extends to the yachting world, where the two captains of industry are equally competitive racing their sailboats. Plattner doesn't mind taking on Bill Gates either. Before a large audience at an SAP user conference in 2002, Plattner pleaded with Gates to adopt Java programming language so that software programs from different companies could work together more harmoniously. He used Ronald Reagan's words to Gorbachev, dramatically challenging, "Bill Gates, tear down that wall!"

A multibillionaire by the age of 59, Plattner decided in 2003 to step down as co-CEO of SAP to become chairman of its supervisory board. Granted, recent changes in German law will allow him to be much more involved in the company's activities compared to his counterparts on American supervisory boards. But Plattner says he is eager to be free of the tedium involved in running a company so that he will be able to focus all of his energy on technology and business strategy.

Sources: Hamm, Steve. "A Software Visionary Bows Out," *BusinessWeek,* March 31, 2003; McCright, John S. "Plattner Steps Down at SAP," *eWeek,* March 13, 2003; <http://www.eweek.com>.

Designing the System

A project is ready to move into the design stage once the project team has approved the plan, including the budget. The design process begins with the writing of the documentation, which covers functional and design specifications. In most cases, the project team creates the functional specification, describing what the system must be able to do. The company that wins the bid to do the project usually writes a second document, called the design specification, detailing the hardware and software necessary to execute the functions. The project leaders must approve both documents before work can proceed.

Functional Specification

The **functional specification** document is usually written first and states exactly what the information system must accomplish. For example, one part of the functional specification may require that 20 computer workstations be connected to a secure company database, with each workstation having Internet access. This document is only concerned with the functions the system will have to perform, not with the kind of computers or software that will be necessary to operate the system. One part of Big Engines' functional specification might demand that the CIM system automatically send a report back to the orders database every time a car is finished and driven off the factory floor.

Design Specification

The **design specification** spells out how the goals laid out in the functional specification will be reached. Hardware and software requirements are detailed, including

- operating system—Unix, IBM mainframe, etc.
- data model—object-oriented, relational, etc.
- authorized users—discussion of access issues

Part of this step requires the development of a data dictionary listing all the information that must be handled, and the types, names, and sizes these data elements require. As an auto parts company, Big Engines might want an inventory of all raw materials used in production. They would also want records providing ordering information for obtaining new parts from their suppliers. Most important would be their sales orders and customer records.

Another significant part of any design specification is deciding whether to use packaged (off-the-shelf) software or custom software. Big Engines might buy an off-the-shelf Oracle database and a CAM software package such as Wonderware®, and then employ a large consulting firm such as Deloitte Consulting or IBM to

Software Type	Commercial Example
database	Oracle, Access, IBM's DB2
operations/distribution	Peachtree®, QuickBooks®, Eclipse™
CAM/CIM	Wonderware, FactoryLink®

TABLE 9-1: Commonly Used Information Systems Software

use those products in the design and development of a custom information system. This software combination would be able to provide a good CIM system covering the entire operation.

In general, packaged software is cheaper and more reliable, but it may not solve all of a customer's needs. Custom software is more expensive and takes longer to develop, but it can be tailored to the exact needs of a buyer. Table 9-1 lists some commonly used commercial software packages for developing information systems.

Implementation

The project can move into its next phase, **implementation**, once the development team and the systems house develop the design specification and approve the plans. This step is where the actual work of putting the system together will be done, including creating a prototype and completing the programming. In most cases, implementing the new system is the longest, most difficult step in the process.

Prototype

A prototype may be created if the proposed system represents a major change or is significantly different from existing systems. A **prototype** is a miniprogram that demonstrates the user interface and functionality of the system. This step is sometimes skipped, but it is often worth the effort as it allows users to see what the final project will look like, often months before the completion date. Users often generate many suggestions for changes after they review the prototype. These suggestions will be easier to include if they are discovered at this early stage.

Development

This is the stage where the software programming is done, and the technicians ensure that the new computer hardware works. This phase involves discovering problems and spending long hours to solve them, and it requires hard work on the part of the development team. The information system will normally use an existing software package, but customization will be required to make everything work as desired. For example, an oil refinery and a grocery store might purchase the same "generic" information system package, but in both cases many modifications would have to be made to make the software meet their needs. A company that can use niche package software precisely tailored to their industry can save considerable time and money.

Hardware and Software Purchasing

All of the required hardware and software must be purchased and delivered before any system can be installed and considered up and running. In most cases, the software and service costs far outweigh the hardware costs, as the service requires many hours of highly skilled labor. Integrating all of the system's computers and software and getting the entire system to work as planned involves significant expenditures of financial and human resources.

Installation and Testing

Beta testing begins once the computers and software are installed and operating. **Beta testing** is a period during which the system is rigorously tested before it is completely trusted to function as designed. Any previously installed information systems are usually still in operation, and information from the old system can be moved to the new one during this time.

In the Big Engines case, the company would probably choose one of their many factories to test the system. All of the other factories would continue using the company's old system until the new one was deemed satisfactory. Once the new system has been approved, it would be installed in every plant, a process referred to as rolling out the system.

User Training

User training normally takes place at the same time as beta testing. System users must learn how to run the new software. This process can also result in the discovery of any errors not detected during the design and implementation process. A number of things can go wrong with an information system, including lost records, network errors, system crashes, or the accidental display of confidential information, such as employee salaries. All of these things can cause the development team to be called on to create an emergency patch, or correction, to the system. In the worst cases, errors may cause the team to go back to the planning stage to determine the origin of any problems.

Approval

Once an information system is installed and working, the committee or executive overseeing the purchase of the system must inspect, test, and approve it. This is normally done after the system has proved itself during a successful beta test period. Final approval is often tied to full payment being made to the suppliers. This can be a stressful time for everyone involved if a system has problems.

The Support Stage

A system goes into the support stage after it has been accepted and approved. It is quite possible that undetected errors might still exist, or that additional features may be requested. A **support contract** normally allows users to contact the sys-

tems house for technical support, training, and sometimes on-site troubleshooting. Even if the system was designed in-house, the responsible department often operates as an independent entity—sometimes even charging the department acquiring the system. The support stage continues until a new information system is proposed and developed, usually years later. At that point, the existing system is retired and no longer used.

Return to Stage One

The system development life cycle is referred to as a cycle because it operates in a circular fashion. Technology moves forward so fast that as soon as one process ends, a new development phase begins. If mistakes have been made the team might have to "go back to the blackboard" and return to the planning stage. This can happen for many reasons, including changes in funding, new technology, errors in the original plan, or other unforeseen difficulties. In any case, the circular methodology helps foster continual refinements and improvements in the process, which in the end benefit all participants.

ON THE HORIZON

Although the evolution of information systems technology tends to hold a rather steady and straight course with few dramatic breakthrough products, there are nevertheless some new directions in ways to deal with information. Companies are especially interested in new strategies that produce the greatest return on investment, including ways to identify and extract information from existing systems and innovative ways to capitalize on current technology.

Business Intelligence

Many companies have data warehouses brimming with information, with daily additions to the amount of information they contain. Product managers and marketing executives know that fantastic new products likely are hidden somewhere in these vast mountains of data, but the problem is in getting to the secrets locked away inside.

To solve this problem many companies are looking to new techniques, collectively called business intelligence, to sift through information warehouses to find the gold within. However, capturing customer information is only one part of the equation. Companies need help in making sense of the data, and this is a focus for information systems software vendors.

The Future Holds ... Simplicity

Simplification is one of the new tricks and tools emerging from information system support companies. Offering interesting new products will only overwhelm customers if the new software isn't easy to operate. Reliability is also an important concern. As the science of information systems matures, simplicity and reliability are at the forefront when it comes to developing new information system ideas.

Examples of products that have become simpler are legion within the broad spectrum of software, with networking solutions such as high-speed home access leading the list. Subscribers don't want to pay $200 for a professional installer, so software instructions are being created to take users through the installation process in less than an hour. The current customer base in the United States is fewer than 10 million households, but it is expected to rise dramatically, so the time is right for easy home installation without professional on-site help.

Customers are demanding simplicity, and voting with their dollars. People don't have the time to learn about new, complex, or awkward interfaces, and industry observers expect that the call for reliable, simple interfaces will expand from the general consumer market into the information systems market as well. The general trend toward smoother setup and installation for consumer software can be seen in products such as Windows XP.

Enterprise Integration Software

Rather than purchasing expensive new information systems, such as comprehensive customer relationship management (CRM) packages or collaborative software, some companies are opting for a new approach that helps them use their existing programs more effectively. Called enterprise integration software, these products link a multitude of different programs so that information can be shared and sent back and forth more easily. Buying integration software that can connect, for example, some 100 programs that previously did not link with each other can mean significant savings in both time and money.

A similar approach gaining popularity is subcontracting data storage and purchasing applications and Web site servicing. Industry researcher IDC predicts that the market for the outside vendor approach will balloon from $6.4 million in 2000 to as much as ten times that by 2005. Enterprise integration software can link several different programs to create a system similar to customer relationship management packages that allow information to be shared.

chapter
summary

What Is an Information System?

An **information system (IS)** is a combination of people, hardware, software, computer networks, and data that organizations use to manage daily and long-term operations. Computer-based information systems offer four key advantages over traditional (pre-computer) information systems: improved speed, efficiency, quality, and measurability.

Information Systems Classified by Function

Common information system functional classifications include **distribution management**, **office information**, **management information**, **decision support**, **executive support**, and **factory automation**. Within these categories are a number of different types of information systems, including **office information systems**

(OIS), **electronic data processing (EDP)**, **management information systems (MIS)**, **decision support systems (DSS)**, **online analytical processing (OLAP)**, and **executive support systems (ESS)**. There are two systems used in factory automation, computer-aided manufacturing (CAM) and computer-integrated manufacturing (CIM). **Statistical quality control (SQC)** is another form of information system often used in plant operations.

Information Systems Considerations

Upgrading or switching to a computer-based information system affects **technical staff**, **information technology costs**, **profit margins**, **product quality**, and **clerical staff**. Companies should also realize that there will be disruptions. Once the impact of a new system has been studied and a decision to proceed has been made, a new system must be purchased "off the shelf," or developed and brought into service. **Subcontracting** simply means hiring a third party to handle a project. A **systems house**, sometimes known as a **systems integrator**, is a company that specializes in installing and supporting information systems.

Factors in Choosing a New Information System

The following factors should be considered when choosing an information systems package: **user interface**

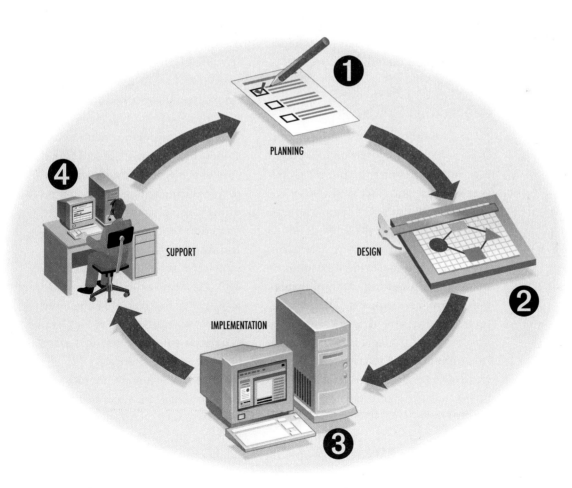

PLANNING

DESIGN

IMPLEMENTATION

SUPPORT

design, open versus closed system, niche information system, turnkey solutions, and system support.

Developing a New Information System

Because of their large size, information systems require the creation of a project team. Sometimes the project manager also functions as a **systems analyst**, responsible for completing the systems analysis and making design recommendations. Creating a **development plan** and executing it has four main stages: **planning**, **design**, **implementation**, and **support**. The process is circular, meaning that once the last stage is reached the planners return to the beginning and repeat the process. A **feasibility study** is conducted, investigating how difficult the project might be to complete and how much it might cost. If management decides to hire a systems house, a **request for proposal (RFP)** will be sent to one or more pos-

sible suppliers. In most cases, the project team creates a **functional specification**, describing what the system must be able to do. **Design specifications** detail the hardware and software necessary to execute the functions. A **prototype** is a miniprogram that demonstrates the user interface and functionality of the system. **Beta testing** is a period during which the system is rigorously tested before it is completely trusted to function as designed. **User training** normally takes place at the same time as beta testing. All of these things can cause the development team to be called on to create an emergency patch, or correction, to the system. A system goes into the **support stage** after it has been accepted and approved. A **support contract** normally allows users to contact the systems house for technical support, training, and sometimes on-site troubleshooting.

KEYTERMS

beta testing, 428

CASE tools, 424

closed system, 420

connectivity, 412

data modeling, 412

deliverable, 423

design specification, 426

distribution management systems, 409

electronic data processing (EDP), 412

executive support system (ESS), 415

expert systems, 414

expert system shells, 412

feasibility study, 423

functional specification, 426

Gantt chart, 424

implementation, 427

just-in-time distribution, 410

knowledge base, 414

niche information systems, 421

online analytical processing (OLAP), 414

open system, 420

project plan, 423

prototype, 427

rapid application development (RAD), 424

request for proposal (RFP), 423

software engineering, 422

standard operating procedures (SOP), 411

statistical quality control (SQC), 417

stockless inventory, 411

subcontracting, 420

support contract, 429

system development life cycle (SDLC), 422

systems house (systems integrator), 420

turnkey system, 421

vertical market, 421

Page numbers indicate where terms are first cited in the chapter. A complete list of key terms with definitions can be found in the Glossary at the end of the book.

chapter exercises

The following chapter exercises, along with new activities and information, are also offered in the *Computers: Understanding Technology* Internet Resource Center at www.emcp.com.

EXPLORING WINDOWS
In Tutorial 9, you learn how to customize some of the display settings in Windows to match your personal needs and preferences.

TERMS CHECK: MATCHING
Write the letter of the correct answer on the line before each numbered item.

a. functional specification
b. prototype
c. Gantt chart
d. beta testing
e. turnkey system
f. subcontracting
g. executive support system (ESS)
h. stockless inventory
i. user training
j. design specification
k. decision support systems (DSS)
l. connectivity

_____ 1. The process performed to ensure that a new information system is working properly.

_____ 2. The document describing the software and hardware needed for any new information system.

_____ 3. The practice of hiring technical consultants from other companies to help with information systems development.

_____ 4. A graphic depiction of the steps in an information system development schedule.

_____ 5. A procedure required with any new information system so that people can learn how to do their jobs.

_____ 6. A specialized information system geared to aid upper management.

_____ 7. Systems built to perform data modeling and provide "what-if" analysis.

_____ 8. An early step in information systems development, which allows people to see in advance what the final system will look like and how it will operate.

_____ 9. An expensive custom system that is easy to use and performs every function the user desires.

_____ 10. A document describing how a new information system will operate.

_____ 11. A new distribution strategy that uses an information system to maintain inventories with daily deliveries of product.

_____ 12. The degree to which computers can be linked for the sharing of resources and transmission of data.

TECHNOLOGY ILLUSTRATED: IDENTIFY THE PROCESS

What process is illustrated in this drawing? Identify the process and write a paragraph describing its use.

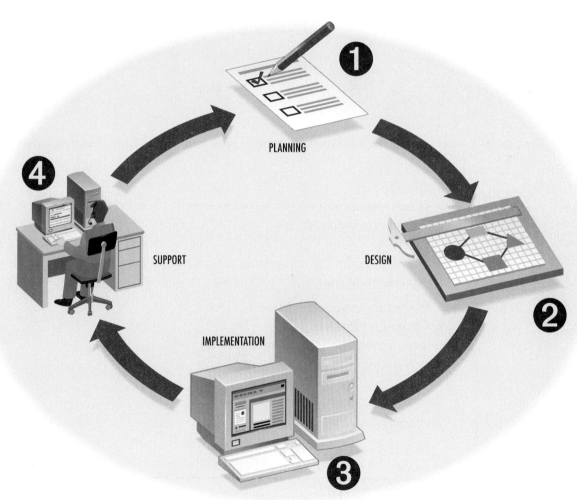

1 PLANNING

2 DESIGN

3 IMPLEMENTATION

4 SUPPORT

KNOWLEDGE CHECK: MULTIPLE CHOICE
Circle the letter of the best answer from those provided.

1. A type of information system with in-depth knowledge about a specific subject is called a(n)

   a. integrated information system.
   b. strategic information system.
   c. executive information system.
   d. expert system.

2. This type of information system is used to track measurements of final product quality.

   a. Quality control system (QCS)
   b. Process control system (PCS)
   c. Strategic information system (SIS)
   d. Statistical quality control (SQC)

3. An information system that connects the factory floor to company headquarters in a single seamless system is called a(n)

   a. CIM.
   b. CAM.
   c. EDP.
   d. DSS.

4. Which of the following are software applications that help in IS development?

   a. CASE tools
   b. Spreadsheets
   c. Design specifications
   d. Beta test operating systems

5. Which of the following steps would normally occur first when developing a new information system?

   a. Writing the design specification
   b. Creating a prototype
   c. Interviewing people to discover what they want
   d. Beta testing

6. Which of the following documents describes what a system needs to do, but not how it should be accomplished?

   a. Prototype
   b. Functional specification
   c. Design specification
   d. User manual

7. Which of the following describes a system for providing supplies to a factory at the last moment before production?

    a. Just-in-time delivery
    b. Stockless inventory
    c. Batch processing
    d. Transactional processing

8. This type of information system does not allow users to modify the software.

    a. Closed system
    b. Open system
    c. Niche information system
    d. Shareware

9. Systems houses are sometimes known as

    a. software houses.
    b. systems integrators.
    c. information system processors.
    d. applications management controllers.

10. Spreadsheets are often used for modeling data in a process called

    a. running the numbers.
    b. expert systems.
    c. data mining.
    d. batch processing.

11. A type of software used to coordinate a group project is called

    a. shareware.
    b. EDP.
    c. CASE tool.
    d. DSS.

12. A system that allows purchasers to make their own configuration changes is called a(n)

    a. closed system.
    b. open system.
    c. freeware.
    d. prototype.

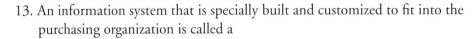

13. An information system that is specially built and customized to fit into the purchasing organization is called a

    a. prototype system.
    b. DSS.
    c. turnkey system.
    d. CAM system.

14. Which of the following types of system categories would fit an expert system?

    a. Prototype
    b. DSS
    c. Turnkey
    d. CAM

15. Which of the following trends is occurring in information systems and software in general?

    a. Simplicity
    b. Redundancy
    c. Opacity
    d. Obscurity

THINGS THAT THINK: BRAINSTORMING NEW USES

In groups or individually, contemplate the following questions and develop as many answers as you can.

1. One of the main benefits of system prototyping is that it allows users to see how the system will work long before development and testing is completed. Not only does this allow the project team to ensure that the system will meet the users' requirements, but it also makes the users feel more comfortable about the project. In what other industries would prototyping a product make sense?

2. Expert systems have been developed to determine the appropriate antibiotic for physicians to prescribe, to forecast the avalanche hazard for a particular area, and to determine whether to approve a credit application. Expert systems are particularly useful when determining whether the outcome may be costly or dangerous. Think of three other processes or decisions that would be made easier through the use of expert systems.

KEY PRINCIPLES: COMPLETION

Fill in the blanks with the appropriate words or phrases.

1. Systems that are heavily customized to meet the exact needs of a business are called _____.

2. A _____ demonstrates the user interface and functionality of the system to allow users to see what the final project will look like.

3. The ability to link with other programs and devices is called _____.

4. A set of rules called a _____ is used to query an expert system.

5. Because it must be serviced and supported by the original vendor, a _____ often costs more money than expected.

6. The _____ is a series of steps culminating in a completed information system.

7. _____ are documents, services, hardware, and software that must be finished and delivered by a certain time and date in order to keep the project on schedule.

8. Systems that help managers make informed business judgments are called _____.

9. _____ can be modified by a company's IT staff without involving the original vendor of the system.

10. _____ systems use a combination of data tracking and data modeling to build a picture of how well a factory is operating.

11. A project team member who makes design recommendations is called a(n) _____.

12. In order to determine how difficult a project will be to complete and estimate its cost, a(n) _____ is often conducted.

13. A _____ includes an estimate of the project timeline, an outline of the steps involved, and a list of deliverables.

14. Just-in-time and stockless inventory are two examples of _____.

15. Rigorous testing once the hardware and software are installed and operating is called _____.

TECH ARCHITECTURE: LABEL THE DRAWING
Identify the five components of an information system in the following illustration.

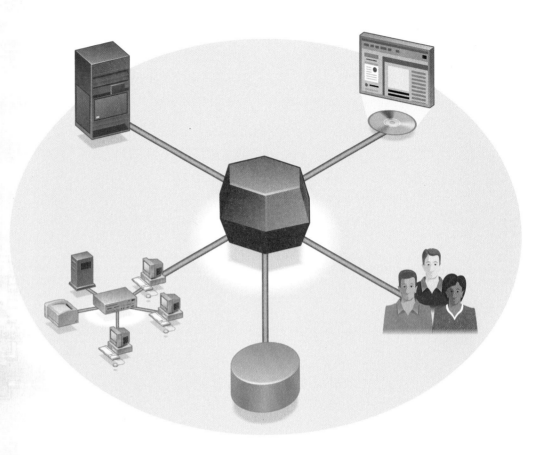

TECHNO LITERACY: RESEARCH AND WRITING
Develop appropriate written responses based on your research for each item.

1. How many information systems are tracking your actions right now?

   Research the different kinds of records stored on government and corporate information systems. What might the IRS, police, and government officials know about you from records in their information systems? Are your school records computerized? What type of information about you is kept by your school? Who is allowed to see your records? Are you allowed to see them?

2. Is there a company in your community that uses a noncomputerized information system?

   Find an information system that has yet to be converted to a computerized system. Describe the system and how it works. Find out from the system owners why they haven't moved to a computerized system and whether they have plans to do so in the future.

3. How was it done in the past?

Conduct research using the Internet and learning resource centers to find out how large information systems worked before the era of computerization. What kind of systems did large corporations use in the 1930s? Describe some of the methods they used and what kind of technology was employed.

TECHNOLOGY ISSUES: TEAM PROBLEM-SOLVING
In groups, brainstorm possible solutions to the issues presented.

1. You have been given the task of preparing a request for proposal (RFP) to send out to multiple systems houses for the development of a new information system. In order for your company to select the best systems house for the job, you will need to gather information about how each systems house will complete the project. What questions do you need to ask in the RFP to gather information about each systems house's project plan and deliverables? Is the timeline for completing the project or the price more important? What other factors do you need to consider before selecting the right systems house for the job?

2. Your class has decided to create an information system to track student contact information and assignment due dates for a large group project. Thinking about the steps in the system development life cycle (SDLC), outline the process you would follow to develop the information system. How should the class determine what information should be stored in the system? How will the class agree that the system meets its objectives?

MINING DATA: INTERNET RESEARCH AND REPORTING
Conduct Internet searches to find the information described in the activities below. Write a brief report summarizing your research results. Be sure to document your sources using the MLA format.

1. An information system operates on your school campus. Try to find out how that information system is organized. Can department assistants access any type of student information? Could they change data from their desks, using the right password? Is class schedule information kept separately from grades, parking tickets, library fines, and other types of information?

2. Imagine you are operating your own used-CD business using an information system running on a single computer. What features would you want it to have and what equipment would you want it to run on? How could you use this system to expand your business capabilities and increase sales?

3. Learn how an information system works at a local store by observing and asking questions during a visit. Does the system track inventory? Does it print receipts, give lists of new products to order, and allow for returns? What other features does it have? Is the owner happy with the system? Are there any other features the owner would like the system to have?

TECHNOLOGY TIMELINE: PREDICTING NEXT STEPS

Personal communications technology is growing pervasive, making it difficult to "hide" from family, friends, or employers. This trend is likely to continue as high-tech electronic gadgets bring us all into constant contact. Think of what might happen next as our communications capabilities expand. Add events to this timeline up to 2015.

1980   The first widely available cellular phone systems are offered to the public.

1993   The Internet takes off, and e-mail messages replace letters as a popular form of communication.

2000   Child location devices are introduced. Young children can call for help by pushing a button on their backpacks, and warnings can be sent if they leave their school area.

2001   E-mail messages sent via cellular phones become commonplace.

2002   Cell phones with digital cameras are available in the United States.

2003   Video instant messaging (VIM) is introduced, combining video and audio with instant text messaging.

ETHICAL DILEMMAS: GROUP DISCUSSION AND DEBATE

As a class or within an assigned group, discuss the following ethical dilemma.

When a company implements a new information system, some of management's goals for the project may include improved quality, increased profits, and reduced staff. The participation of current staff in the project is needed to ensure that the new system supports the business properly, but sometimes employees are reluctant to support the project for fear that their jobs are at stake. If staff is resistant to the changes that the new system will bring, the company may not successfully complete the project and realize its goals. Is it fair for management to expect staff to cooperate with the project if they may lose their jobs as a result of the successful implementation of the new system? Is it fair for staff to delay or sabotage the project for the sake of job security? What alternatives might management consider in order to keep employee morale high and complete the project successfully?

ANSWERS TO TERMS CHECK AND KEY PRINCIPLES QUESTIONS

Terms Check: 1 – d; 2 – j; 3 – f; 4 – c; 5 – i; 6 – g; 7 – k; 8 – b; 9 – e; 10 – a; 11 – h; 12 – l

Key Principles: 1 – turnkey systems; 2 – prototype; 3 – connectivity; 4 – knowledge base; 5 – closed system; 6 – system development life cycle (SDLC); 7 – deliverables; 8 – decision support systems (DSS); 9 – open systems; 10 – statistical quality control (SQC); 11 – systems analyst; 12 – feasibility study; 13 – project plan; 14 – distribution management systems; 15 – beta testing

Security Issues and Strategies

As we become increasingly dependent on computer systems to facilitate our jobs, our personal lives, and the infrastructures of our communities and country, the proper operation of computers grows correspondingly in importance. With the explosive growth of the Internet and networks in general, an enormous body of data and computers are now accessible by the general public—not all of whom are harmless. Companies today face security problems in three broad areas:

- network and Internet security risks
- computer viruses
- hardware and software security risks

NETWORK AND INTERNET SECURITY RISKS

Like the uncharted wilds, the Internet lacks borders, and it is this inherent openness that makes it so valuable and so vulnerable at the same time. Over its short life, the Internet has grown so quickly that the legal system has not been able to keep pace. Legal systems are not designed to adjust for rapid technological changes, and often a new technology is commonplace when laws and an enforcement body finally evolve to govern its use.

The security risks posed by networks and the Internet can be grouped into the following areas, each of which overlaps the others in terms of the technologies involved:

- unauthorized access
- information theft
- denial of service

Unauthorized Access: Hackers and Crackers

Most cases of unauthorized access to computers and networks are carried out by hackers. Recall from earlier chapters that hackers are defined by the behavior of "breaking and entering." Hackers tend to exploit sites and programs with poor security measures in place. For more challenging sites, they use sophisticated programs and strategies to gain entrance. When asked, many hackers claim they like to hack merely for the challenge of trying to defeat security measures. They rarely have a more malicious motive, and they generally do not aim to destroy or damage the sites that they invade. In fact, hackers dislike being identified with those who seek to cause damage. They call hackers with malicious or criminal intent **crackers**.

In recent years, hackers have become organized and thereby more powerful. When news events between two competing nations cause a flare-up of tensions, hackers tend to attack sites in the other nation. These cyber wars have yet to prove serious, but this may change in the future as we come to depend increasingly on the Net.

User IDs and Passwords

Most hackers focus on gaining entry over the Internet to a secure computer system by finding a working user ID and password combination. User IDs are easy to come by and are generally not secure information. Sending an e-mail, for example, may display the sender's user ID in the return address, making it very public. The only missing element then is the password. Hackers know from experience which passwords are common and they have programs (downloadable for free, of course) that generate thousands of likely passwords and try them automatically over a period of hours or days.

System Backdoors

Another unintentional entrance to networks and information systems is sometimes provided by programmers. A **system backdoor** is a user ID and password that provides the highest level of authorization. The "backdoor" often is created innocently in the early days of system development to allow programmers and other team members access to fix problems. Through either negligence or design, the user ID and password are sometimes left behind in the final version of the system. People who know about them can then enter the system, bypassing the security, perhaps years later when the existence of the backdoor has been forgotten.

Spoofing

A sophisticated way to break into a network via the Internet involves **spoofing**, which is the process of fooling another computer by pretending to send packets from a legitimate source. It works by altering the address that the system automatically puts on every message sent. The address is changed to one that the receiving computer is programmed to accept as a trusted source of information.

Spyware

Spyware is a type of software that allows an intruder to spy upon someone else's computer. This alarming technology takes advantage of loopholes in the Windows security systems and allows a stranger to witness and record another person's every mouse click and keystroke on the monitor as it occurs. For the spy, it looks as if a ghost is moving the mouse and typing in e-mail on his screen. For the victim, everything seems normal.

Information Theft

Information can be a company's most valuable possession. Think of a sales database, for example, listing all of a company's clients, with contact information and sales history. This database represents years of work and expensive research. A competitor who gains access to this information will have a huge advantage. He will know exactly how much to bid to gain a sale, which clients to call, and what products they like to buy. Stealing corporate information, a crime included in the category of industrial espionage, is unfortunately easy to do and difficult to detect.

Limited Security for Wireless Devices

The growing number of wireless devices has created a new opening for data theft. Wireless devices such as cameras, Web phones, networked computers, PDAs, and input and output peripherals are inherently less secure than wired devices. A normal wired

connection, such as a wire between a keyboard and a computer, cannot be as easily intercepted as a wireless radio transmission. To intercept company e-mails on a wireless LAN, all a competitor need do is park a computer-laden van outside the building and listen. This is far easier than splicing into a network that is connected by wires.

Denial of Service Attacks

One new type of computer crime generally attributed to organized hackers is the tactic known as denial of service (DoS). This simple, but highly effective form of attack by an organized worldwide team of hackers caused havoc for Yahoo.com, Amazon.com, CNN.com, and eBay.com over several days in the early part of 2001. In a **denial of service attack**, hundreds of hackers participate, each running a program that simply asks for the same information from a Web site over and over again— not just a few times, but thousands of times a second. The system soon is flooded and is essentially shut down (see Figure G-1).

COMPUTER VIRUSES

One of the most familiar forms of risk to computer security is the computer virus. Recall that a computer **virus** is a program, written by a hacker or cracker, which is designed to perform some kind of trick upon an unsuspecting victim. The trick performed

in some cases is mild, such as drawing an offensive image on the screen, or changing all of the characters in a document to another language. Sometimes the trick is much more severe, such as reformatting the hard drive and erasing all data, or damaging the motherboard so that it cannot operate properly.

A virus then is a form of computer vandalism. Most viruses are destructive and attack victims randomly, often causing millions of dollars in damage. A Computer Security Institute survey reported that 10.5 per 100 computers in business, government, and academic organizations experienced a virus attack in 2002, an increase of 950 percent from

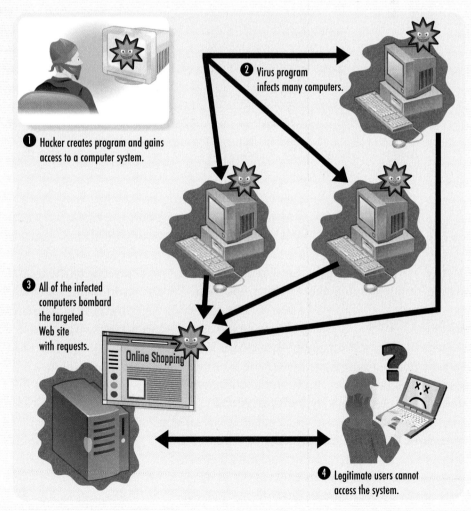

1 Hacker creates program and gains access to a computer system.

2 Virus program infects many computers.

3 All of the infected computers bombard the targeted Web site with requests.

Online Shopping

4 Legitimate users cannot access the system.

FIGURE G-1: Denial of service attacks bombard computers with messages, flooding the system and essentially shutting it down.

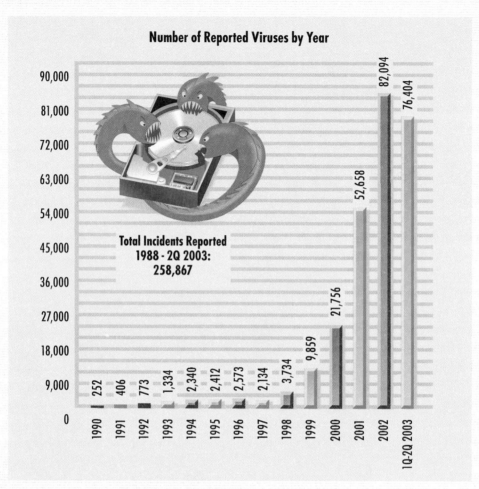

FIGURE G-2: Number of Reported Viruses By Year.
Source: CERT® Coordination Center, Carnegie Mellon Software Engineering Institute.

1996. Figure G-2 shows the rapid increase in virus reports from 1990 to 2003.

E-Mail Viruses

An e-mail virus is normally transmitted as an attachment to a message sent over the Internet. E-mail viruses execute when the victim clicks on the attachment. According to the International Computer Security Association, the majority of **viruses in the wild** (a term indicating successful viruses in common circulation) are e-mail attachment viruses (see Figure G-3). In recent years this type of virus has grown dramatically, overcoming the former leader, Microsoft Word macro viruses. The percentage of e-mail viruses is approaching 92 percent of the total, infecting millions of machines worldwide. New software to scan for e-mail viruses is in constant development, but new viruses appear every day. They are easy to create and they can spread across the globe in a few days if successful.

Macro Viruses

Another common form of virus transmission is by a **macro**, a small subprogram that allows users to customize and automate certain functions. A macro virus is written specifically for one program, such as Microsoft Word or Lotus Amipro, which then becomes infected when it opens a file with the virus stored in its macros.

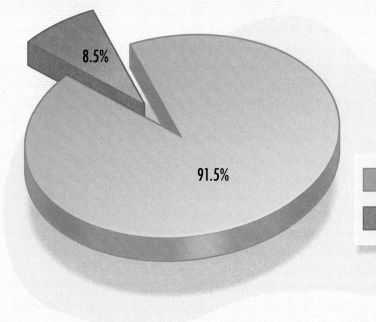

8.5%

91.5%

Email
Others

F I G U R E   G - 3 : Today, the overwhelming majority of viruses are transmitted via e-mail.

Boot Sector Viruses

The boot sector of a floppy disk or hard disk contains a variety of information, including how the disk is organized and whether it is capable of loading an operating system. When a disk is left in a drive and the computer reboots, the operating system automatically reads the boot sector to learn about that disk and to attempt to start any operating system on that disk. A boot sector virus is designed to alter the boot sector of a disk, so that whenever the boot sector is read by the operating system, the computer will automatically become infected. The virus on the infected disk or CD automatically transfers a copy of itself onto the hard disk.

Trojan Horse Viruses

Like its namesake from Greek legend, the **Trojan horse virus** hides inside another legitimate program or data file. These viruses are quite common with downloaded games and other types of shareware files such as screensavers. The program may install and

run without a problem, but unknown to the victim, a virus is included in the software, installing itself with the other files. These viruses may cause damage immediately, or they may delay acting for a time.

Software Worms

Software worms are often confused with viruses, but they operate in quite a different fashion. Rather than adding itself to another program and waiting for a user to execute an attachment or open a file with a macro, a **software worm** actively attempts to move and copy itself. Operating in most cases on the Internet, a worm uses spoofing techniques to fool computers into accepting and executing a copy. The worm then transmits itself to other machines and performs its prime function, whatever that may be. Today, worms are commonly used as hacking devices. They seek out computer systems to break into and leave a route for later entry by a hacker or cracker. Figure G-4 illustrates the operation of Code Red, an infamous worm that in 2001 burrowed its way into many servers via the Internet.

Virus Symptoms

How do you know if your computer has been infected by a virus? The signs of infection include, but are not limited to, the following events:

- Some of your files become corrupted and suddenly don't work properly.
- A specific program, very commonly Microsoft Word, does not operate properly.
- Programs or files have suddenly vanished.
- Unknown programs or other files appear on your hard drive.
- Strange messages or images display on your monitor.

- Your system has less available memory or disk space than it should.
- A disk or volume name has been changed.
- Unexpected sounds or music are played at random times.
- You receive the same e-mail message repeatedly from the same people.

PROTECTING COMPUTER SYSTEMS AND DATA

Our increasing reliance on computer-based systems means a corresponding rise in computer security threats. If online banking and shopping become the norm, for example, it only makes sense that bank

robbers and shoplifters would be online as well. The increasing complexity of the Internet and the constantly changing technologies also leave new gaps for cyber rogues to slip through. This section covers methods of safe-guarding computer systems.

Antivirus Software

Antivirus software packages such as Norton Antivirus are quite successful in detecting and cleaning off known viruses. The trouble with any antivirus software is that it can only detect viruses with known signatures. Newer viruses are harder to identify and remove. The Internet has helped greatly in this area, as it allows antivirus software to update itself over the Net. The process is normally free of charge and relatively painless for the user. If you use virus detection software, you should make it part of

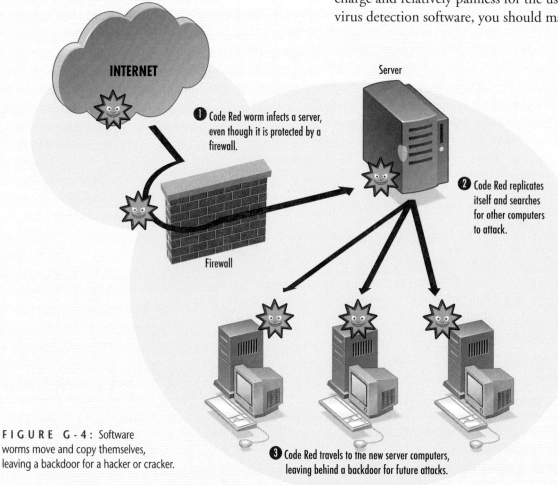

INTERNET

Server

❶ Code Red worm infects a server, even though it is protected by a firewall.

❷ Code Red replicates itself and searches for other computers to attack.

Firewall

FIGURE G-4: Software worms move and copy themselves, leaving a backdoor for a hacker or cracker.

❸ Code Red travels to the new server computers, leaving behind a backdoor for future attacks.

your routine to check for upgrades at least monthly. There are 10 to 20 new viruses reported daily, and your virus program must be upgraded constantly to protect against them.

Data Backups

One of the crucial elements of any prevention scheme is to be prepared for the worst. What if a fire burned up your company's offices and computers? Do all employees have recent backups on hand to replace their critical files? Backing up data and placing the backup in a safe spot is a necessary chore, because if antivirus software misses a bug or if a disaster occurs, you don't want to be left with nothing.

Disaster Recovery Plan

A disaster recovery plan is a safety system that allows a company to restore its systems after a complete loss of data. The elements of a typical disaster recovery plan include:

- data backup procedures
- remotely located backup copies
- redundant systems

Data Encryption

To prevent people from spying on sensitive transactions, such as the transmission of a user name and password across the Internet, companies use **data encryption** to scramble the information before it is transmitted. Data encryption schemes include an encryption key that is generated automatically and shared between the two computers that wish to communicate. This security can also work with cell phones and other forms of communication devices. Without this key, it is very difficult to break the encryption code.

Firewalls

Developed originally to prevent security breaches such as spoofing and hacking, firewalls run on computers that are attached directly to the Internet. The firewall will generally allow normal Web browser

operations, but will prevent many other types of communication. It works similar to a door bouncer at a club who checks IDs before allowing customers in. The firewall checks incoming data against a list of known, trusted sources. If a packet does not fit the profile of anything on the firewall's list, it is rejected.

User IDs and Passwords

A major player in nearly every computer security system is the user ID/password paradigm. The user ID is the known portion of the combination, the identification of the user relative to which account the user is seeking access. The password is the core security element that is used as authentication, proof that a user is who she says she is, and that she is authorized to access an account. The user ID is generally publicly known. The password is the secret part, the part that is sought by any hacker or other type of cyber criminal. ATM (automatic teller machine) cards, for example, are issued with PINs (personal identification numbers) that the customer types into a keypad similar to that on a telephone. PINs serve as passwords, while the ATM cards are the user ID.

Smart Cards

A possible solution to credit card security problems is the smart card. About the size of a credit card, smart cards are very popular in Asia and Europe, but somewhat rare thus far in the United States. Smart cards have an embedded chip in the plastic card that contains the encoded account number, just as the magnetic strip does on credit cards. The chip must come from the manufacturer, however, and can't be created easily.

Webcams

Webcams, available in standard size or the mini size, can be called either a security danger or a security solution, depending on how they are used. Costing less than one hundred dollars, wireless cameras the size of golf balls can transmit Web-ready, color video, and digital snapshots but need no more than a pinhole in a wall to peep through. The addition of a motion sensor, costing only a few dollars, allows them to transmit only when something is happening. Unfortunately, our privacy laws are quite lax in the area of preventing video surveillance. In 38 states, there are essentially no laws preventing someone from videotaping even a person's most private moments without his knowledge. Figure G-5 shows a popular type of webcam.

Biometric Authentication

Biometric identifiers are characteristic behaviors or physical attributes that are unique to individuals and can be used to authenticate their identity. Biometric identifiers that can be measured effectively by computers include voice, fingerprint, hand geometry,

FIGURE G-5: Many companies and retail firms use webcams as a security measure.

facial geometry, facial thermography, retinal patterns, iris patterns, and handwritten signatures. Many companies are now using biometric authentication systems to make sure that only authorized employees are allowed to enter secure areas, such as a research building. Biometric devices automatically recognize human beings in a variety of ways. Essentially, all of them focus on one characteristic behavior or body part and use a computer to compare known patterns against a measurement taken by the device. Fingerprint scanners simply make a digital image of a person's fingerprint, just as an optical scanner turns a photograph into a .gif file.

Computerized facial recognition (CFR) systems work in a variety of ways, but the primary goal is to recognize a human face by comparing it to existing scans of photos in a database. These systems are popular, particularly in Las Vegas casinos, which are among the most camera-laden environments on earth.

FUTURE SECURITY TECHNOLOGIES

New security strategies and intrusion detection devices are expected to dominate the computer industry news in the near future. Industry observers predict that biometric authentication systems will be incorporated into operating systems. Keystroke identification, a new area of biometric technology that measures typing rhythms, is another development to watch.

Quantum cryptography is a security technology still in the experimental stage. It is based on the physics principle that even observing a quantum phenomenon is enough to disrupt it. Using quantum devices to transmit light signals over fiber optic cable, two parties who wish to send a secret message can exchange their unprotected key as normal to start the sequence. If anyone observes the key, the system will be disturbed, and both sides will be aware of the security breach. If no one observes the key, then the transmission will continue normally, with complete security.

TUTORIAL 1

STARTING UP AND SHUTTING DOWN A PC

This tutorial shows how to start up a Windows PC and log on with a user name if required; it also explains the proper way to shut down a Windows-based PC to avoid data loss and file corruption.

Starting Up and Logging On

On a home computer with a single user, the Windows desktop may appear at start-up all by itself. On such a system there is no logon security; anyone may use the computer without identifying himself or herself.

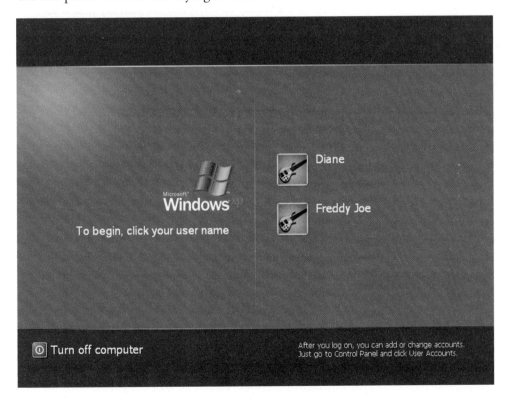

> In, out, up, down—what does it all mean? Logging on means connecting to the computer; logging in is the same thing, just different wording. Logging off means disconnecting, and logging out is the same thing.

On a home computer configured for multiple users, a Welcome screen appears at start-up with an icon for each user. Click the desired icon to log on. There's no security, because any guest can click an existing user's name to log on as that person.

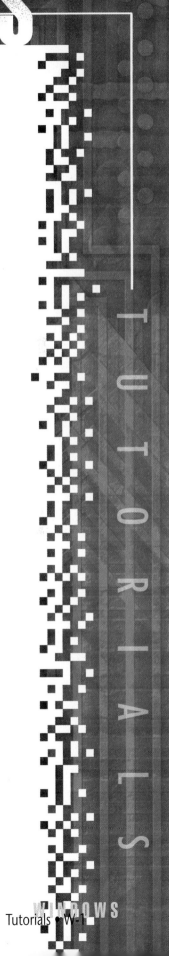

Such systems can be set up to require a password at the Welcome screen, so that a password prompt appears when someone clicks on one of the user names to log on. An optional Guest logon can also be configured so that someone who knows none of the passwords can still use the computer at least in a limited way.

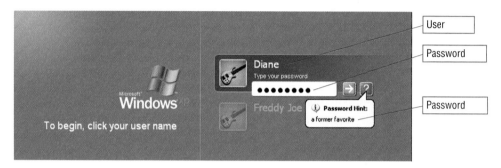

On a PC that is connected to a business or academic network, the Welcome screen may be disabled, such that the traditional Logon box appears like the ones in earlier Windows versions.

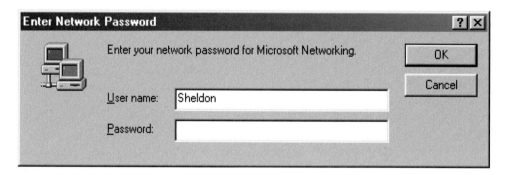

Steps

To log on at a traditional logon screen:

1. Click in the User name box, and type your user name.

2. Press Tab to move to the Password box, and type your password.

3. Click OK or press Enter.

In an environment where multiple users access the same computer, such as in a school, logging on (and off) is important for tracking purposes. On a network, logging on also connects the computer to the network using settings and permissions that are set up especially for that user. For example, there might be certain locations on a file server that become accessible through the network when a certain user logs on, but not when some other user logs on.

> You can change the Windows logon behavior through the User Accounts utility in the Control Panel. You can choose whether to use the Welcome screen or the traditional logon, and if you do use the Welcome screen, you can choose whether or not a particular user logon requires a password and what that password will be.

Logging Off

Logging off and shutting down are two separate operations, although shutting down also logs you off. Logging off simply tells the computer that a particular user is no longer sitting there. It doesn't shut down the PC.

Steps

To log off:

1. Choose Start, Log Off. If a confirmation box appears, click Log Off to confirm. The Log Off Windows dialog box appears.

2. Click Log Off. The Welcome screen reappears or the logon prompt reappears, depending on the way the PC is set up.

In Windows XP you can also use a feature called Fast User Switching to enable multiple users to be logged on at once to the same PC. This could be handy when one person is working on the PC and someone else comes up and wants a turn "just for a second." Instead of logging off as in step 2 above, the user could click Switch User and allow the other person to log on temporarily. Switch User leaves the original user's programs and data files open, whereas logging off closes them all.

Restarting and Shutting Down

In addition to logging off, you can also restart the PC, or you can shut it down completely. Restarting can help if you are experiencing errors or problems with Windows' operation. Shutting down completely is a good idea when you are going to be away from your PC for a while (say, 24 hours or more).

Steps

To shut down or restart:

1. Choose Start, Shut Down. A Shut Down Windows dialog box opens.

2. Open the drop-down list and choose either Restart or Shut Down (to turn off the PC.

3. Click OK.

On some systems, choosing Shut Down shuts off the PC's power; on other systems a message will appear onscreen about it being safe to turn the PC off now; press the PC's power button to complete the shut-down.

TUTORIAL 2

TAKING THE WINDOWS XP TOUR

The first time a computer runs after Windows XP is loaded, a window appears inviting you to take a tour of Windows XP. The multimedia tour highlights some of the newest features and includes music, narration, video, and interactivity. You can run the tour whenever and as often as you would like.

Steps

To view the tour:

1. Click the Start button to display the Start menu.

2. Point to All Programs. A submenu appears.

3. Point to Accessories. Another submenu appears.

4. Click Tour Windows XP. A welcome message appears, prompting you to select either the animated or nonanimated tour.

Animated or nonanimated? The animated tour can run almost totally unattended, while the nonanimated tour requires a mouse click to advance each screen. If you do not have sound support on your PC, choose the nonanimated version.

For these steps it is assumed you are choosing the animated method. If you are using the nonanimated method, explore the tour on your own from this point.

5. Click Play the animated tour... and then click Next. An introductory message displays, and after that a selection of tour features appears.

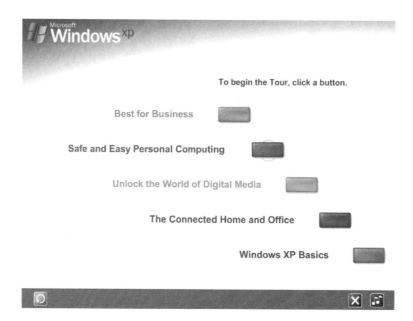

6. Click any item to begin the tour with information on the selected feature, or don't click anything and the tour will start at the beginning and run by itself.

Along the bottom of each tour window are three buttons you can click at any time to restart the tour, exit the tour, or turn the music on or off.

7.   Click the Exit button when you are finished to stop the presentation. It repeats itself continuously until you stop it.

TUTORIAL 3

RUNNING APPLICATIONS

A primary function of Microsoft Windows is to run applications. Without applications, there would be no reason for any of its other features such as networking, file management, and online connectivity. There are many ways of running an application; as you work in Windows you will choose the method that is the most appropriate for a given situation.

From the Start Menu

The Start menu provides a convenient central organizing location for shortcuts that run most of the installed applications.

Steps

To open the WordPad application from the Start menu:

1. Click the Start button to open the Start menu.

2. Point to All Programs. A submenu appears.

3. Point to Accessories. Another submenu appears.

4. Click WordPad. The WordPad application runs.

5. Click the Close (X) button in the top right corner of the WordPad window to close it.

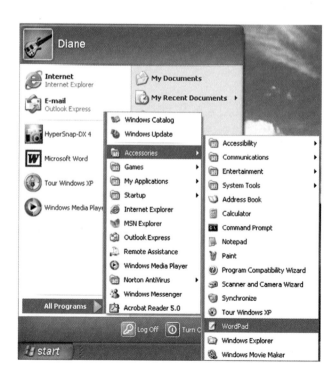

Notice in the above picture that in the leftmost column of the Start menu there are icons and names for six applications, including Microsoft Word. If you see a shortcut in this area for the application you want to run, you can click it here rather than working through the entire menu system.

From the Desktop Icons

Depending on your system's configuration, there may be certain icons on the Windows desktop. The Recycle Bin will be there in all cases, and there also may be icons for some installed applications.

Steps

To run an application from the desktop:

1. Double-click the application's icon on the desktop. The application runs.
2. Click the Close (X) button in the top right corner of the application's window to close it.

From the Run command

The Run command enables you to run an application that has no shortcut on the Start menu or the desktop. It is useful for running certain networking and troubleshooting utilities, for example, and MS-DOS-based applications. The Microsoft Configuration Utility is a very useful program for Windows troubleshooting, but it does not appear on the Start menu.

Steps

To run the Microsoft Configuration Utility:

1. Click the Start button to open the Start menu.
2. Click the Run command. The Run dialog box opens.
3. Type msconfig in the Open box.
4. Click OK. The application runs.
5. Click the Close (X) button to close the application.

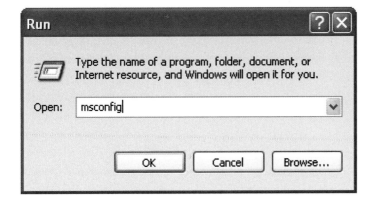

• • **TIP** • •
See Tutorial 11 to learn how to customize the Start menu, including customizing which shortcuts appear in its left column.

• • **TIP** • •
You can place shortcuts on the desktop yourself for the applications you use most frequently. There are many ways of doing this; here's one way. On the Start menu, right-click a shortcut and choose Copy. Then close the Start menu, so that you see the desktop, and press Ctrl+V to paste.

From a File Management Window

If you see an executable file (that is, the file that executes the application) while you are browsing a disk's contents in Windows Explorer or My Computer, you can start the application associated with it by double-clicking on it.

Steps

To run the WordPad application by browsing through the My Computer interface:

1. Click the Start button to open the Start menu.

2. Click My Computer to open the My Computer window.

3. Double-click the icon for the drive on which Windows is installed. (Ask your instructor which drive to use. If the instructor is not available, try drive C:.)

4. Double-click the Program Files folder.

5. If a message appears about the files being hidden, click Show the contents of this folder.

6. Double-click the Windows NT folder.

7. Double-click the Accessories folder. An icon for WordPad appears.

8. Double-click the WordPad icon. WordPad runs.

9. Click the Close (X) button on the WordPad window to close it.

It's a lot of work, isn't it? However, when you want to start an application that is on a CD or floppy disk, this may be your best bet.

TUTORIAL 4

WORKING WITH A WINDOW

Almost all content in Microsoft Windows appears in frames called windows. Each application runs in its own window, as does each file management interface such as My Computer. In addition, some applications show multiple individual documents in smaller windows within the larger application window.

In Tutorial 3 you saw two types of windows. The one for WordPad was an application window, and the one for My Computer was a file management window. Now let's look at what you can do with those windows after opening them.

Three Window States: Maximized, Minimized, and Restored

Every window is in one of three states at any given moment:

- Maximized: Fills the entire screen
- Minimized: Hidden except for its icon on the taskbar
- Restored: Open and visible, but not full-screen

You can switch among these three states with the buttons in the upper right corner of the window—not the red X (that's for closing the window)—but the other two. Why are there only two buttons, when there are three states? The Restore Down and Maximize buttons never appear simultaneously; a window has one or the other based on its current state.

When a window is restored, the buttons look like this:

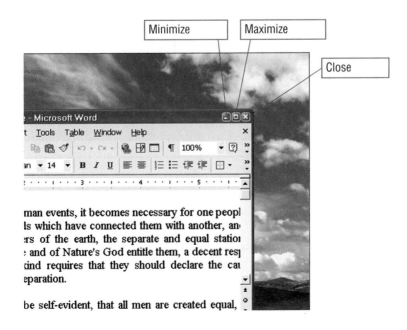

When a window is maximized, the buttons look like this:

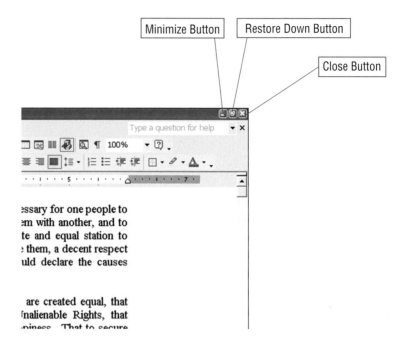

Minimize Button
Restore Down Button
Close Button

Steps

To see the action of these buttons:

1. Open the My Computer window. (Remember, to do this click the Start button and then click My Computer.)

2. Click the Maximize button on the My Computer window. (If the My Computer window is already maximized, step 2 is not necessary.)

3. Click the Minimize button on the My Computer window. It disappears except for its icon on the taskbar.

4. Click the My Computer icon on the taskbar. The window reappears, in maximized form.

5. Click the Restore Down icon on the My Computer window. The window returns to its non-maximized size.

6. Click the Close (X) button on the My Computer window. The window closes.

Move and Resize a Window

When a window is restored, there's some "breathing room" around it on the desktop. You can move the window around on the desktop, and/or you can change its size.

To move a window, drag its title bar. (That's the colored bar at the top.)

Title bar ———

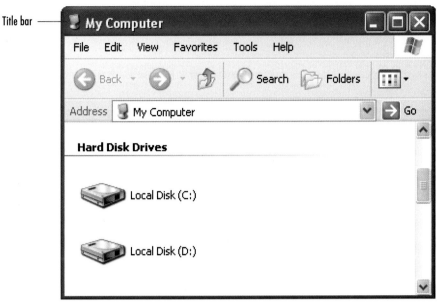

To resize a window, drag one of its borders. Most people prefer to drag the bottom right corner of a window to resize it, but you can drag any edge.

Steps

To move and resize a window:

1. Reopen the My Computer window.

2. Point to the title bar of the window.

3. Hold down the left mouse button and drag its title bar to move it to a different location onscreen. Release the mouse button at the new location.

4. Point to the bottom right corner of the window. The mouse pointer turns into a double-headed arrow.

5. Hold down the left mouse button and drag to change the window's size to approximately half of its original size. An outline shows what the new size will be. Release the mouse button when finished.

6. Resize the window again, this time making it so large that it almost takes up the entire screen.

7. Close the My Computer window, and then reopen it. Notice that Windows remembers its previous size and position.

8. Close the window again.

T U T O R I A L   5

BROWSING DISKS AND DEVICES USING MY COMPUTER

My Computer is the central location in the Windows interface for browsing disk contents. It lists all available local drives (and also some network drives).

Steps

To open My Computer:

1. Click the Start button.

2. Click My Computer. The My Computer window appears.

By default the My Computer window appears with two panes. At the right is the content of the selected drive, or the list of drives itself.

An optional Folders pane can be enabled that will show the organizational structure of the disks, including all levels of folders. Click the Folders button on the toolbar to toggle it on/off.

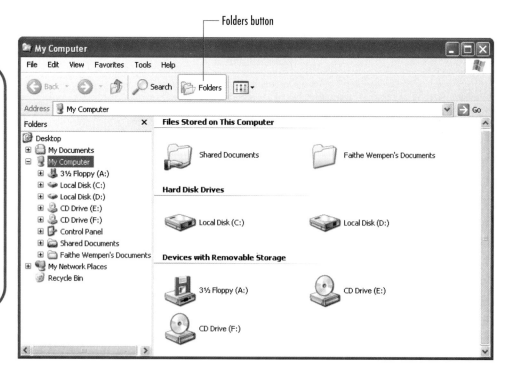

Folders button

Browse Disk Content

To see a disk's content, double-click that disk. The folders and files it contains appear in the right pane of My Computer. To see the content of a certain folder, double-click that folder's icon.

WINDOWS
W-12 • Tutorials

If the Folders pane appears, you can click a plus sign next to an icon to expand a list of the folders within that location. The list of drives and folders is commonly called a *folder tree* because the fully expanded hierarchy resembles the branches on a tree. When a "branch" of the file hierarchy is fully expanded, a minus sign appears next to it in the Folders pane; click the minus sign to collapse it.

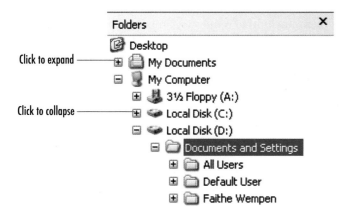

Move Back and Forward

Each time you select a different drive or folder, the new content replaces the previous content in the right pane of the My Computer window. To redisplay previous content, click the Back button. After you click Back, the Forward button becomes available; clicking Forward returns the display to the way it was before you clicked Back.

Move Up One Level

The folder structure of a drive can be many levels deep. The path to the top level of the disk is represented by a path statement that starts out with the drive letter and then lists the folders that you would travel through to arrive at that location. For example:

$$C:\backslash Windows\backslash System$$

The above path represents the System folder, which is stored within the Windows folder, which is stored on the C: drive. The folder to the left of another in the path—or above it in the folder tree—is called its *parent folder*. The folders within a parent folder are its *child folders*.

When you move up one level, you move to the immediate parent folder of the current folder. For example, to go up one level from the above path, you would go to:

$$C:\backslash Windows$$

 To go up one level, click the Up button on the toolbar. The parent folder's content is displayed at the right.

TUTORIAL 6

CREATING AND RENAMING FOLDERS

Have you wondered how all those folders came to exist on your hard disk? Windows itself created several of them, including Windows, Program Files, and Documents and Settings. Still others came into being when you installed various applications.

   You also can create your own folders. These can be used as organizers for storing files you create or acquire, such as digital camera pictures, word processing documents, and applications and data that you download from the Internet or receive as e-mail attachments.

Create a New Folder

A new folder can be created only in relation to an existing folder (or a drive's root folder), so you must start the folder-making process by displaying a particular location's content in the My Computer window (refer to Tutorial 5). Whatever location is displayed will be where the new folder will reside.

> • • • • • **TIP** • • • • •
> **Each drive's top level is its root folder. An analogy: when you walk into an office building, you first go into the lobby. At that point you are not in any particular office—you are simply in the building. The root folder of a drive is like that lobby. You're not in a folder yet—you're just "in the drive."**

Steps

To create a new folder:

1. Open My Computer and display the content of the folder in which you want to place the new one. (This can be the root folder of the drive or some other folder.)

2. Choose File, New, Folder. A new folder icon appears with the words New Folder selected below or to the right.

3. Type the desired name for the folder. Your typing replaces the New Folder text.

4. Press Enter. The new name is accepted and appears beneath the folder icon.

Correspondence

Folder names can be up to 255 characters and can include spaces and most punctuation symbols (but not reserved ones such as *, \, /, or ?). Windows will let you know if you have entered an unallowed character. Even though long names are possible, most people prefer to keep folder names relatively short (under 12 to 16 characters or so) to make it easier to refer to them and to make the display more tidy.

Rename a Folder

You can rename folders any time. However, use caution when renaming folders. If you rename a folder that a certain application relies on to operate, the application might not work anymore. When evaluating whether a folder can safely be renamed, ask these questions:

- Does the folder contain only data files, such as word processing documents, spreadsheets, and so on? If so, you can rename it safely. However, if a certain application has a default Save location set up for its data files, you may need to change it to the new folder name within that application.
- Is the folder stored within the Windows or Program Files folder? If so, do not rename it, or some application will probably stop working.
- Is the folder used to store the operating files for an application, or is it stored within the Windows or Program Files folder? If so, do not rename it, or the application will probably stop working.

Steps

To rename a folder:

1. Click the folder once to select it.

2. Press F2. The name becomes editable.

3. Type a new name, or edit the existing one.

4. Press Enter.

TUTORIAL 7

COPYING AND MOVING FILES AND FOLDERS

In the last several tutorials you learned how to use My Computer to view disk content and create folder structures within the file system. Now that you know how the file system works, you're ready to start manipulating its content.

You can move and copy files and folders to other locations—that is, to other disks or other folders on the same disk or to a different disk. You might move a file to archive it, for example, or copy a file in order to create a backup copy.

Drag-and-Drop Moving/Copying

One easy way of moving or copying is to simply select and drag the file or folder to the desired location. The desired location must be visible (or at least an icon for it must be visible) either in a window or on the Folders tree.

Steps

To move or copy a file or folder using drag-and-drop:

1. Open My Computer, and display the location of the file(s) and/or folder(s) you want to move or copy.

2. If the Folders list does not appear already, click the Folders button.

3. Expand the folder tree if needed (refer to Tutorial 5) so that the destination disk or folder's icon is visible on the tree.

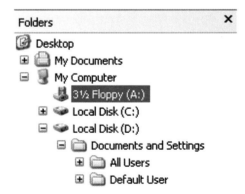

4. Select the file(s) and/or folder(s) you want to move or copy.

To select multiple contiguous files or folders at once, click the first one and then hold down Shift while you scroll down (or up) through the list; then click the last one. For noncontiguous selection, hold down Ctrl as you click individually on each desired file or folder.

5. If you are moving a file or folder, hold down the Shift key; if you are copying, hold down the Ctrl key.

6. Drag the selected files/folders to the destination and drop them there. You'll see a plus sign on the arrow, as shown below, if you are copying; an absence of a plus sign means you are moving.

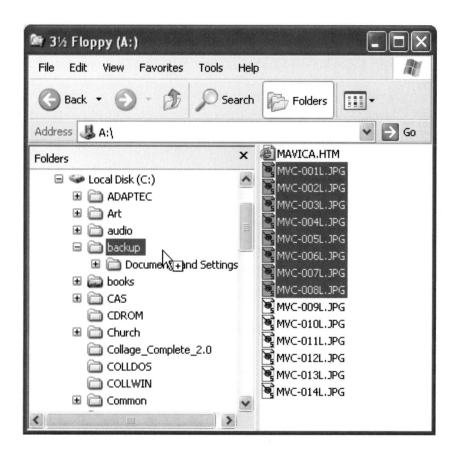

What happens if you do not hold down any keys in step 5? It depends on the relationship between the original location and the destination. If they are on different drives, the default is to copy. If they are on the same drive, the default is to move.

Clipboard Moving/Copying

The drag-and-drop method works well if both the original location and the destination can be viewed onscreen at once. If that's not possible (or not convenient at the moment), you can fall back to the Clipboard method of moving and copying. This involves the Cut, Copy, and Paste commands.

To move a file or folder, you select it and use the Cut command; then you display the destination location and use the Paste command. Copying is the same thing except you use Copy instead of Cut. The advantage here is that you don't have to paste immediately after the cut/copy operation, so both locations need not appear onscreen simultaneously.

The Clipboard is a temporary holding area common to all Windows applications and to Windows itself. Items are placed on the Clipboard with Cut and Copy operations, and inserted from the Clipboard with the Paste operation.

Steps

To move or copy files or folders with the Clipboard:

1. Open My Computer, and select the file(s) and/or folder(s) you want to move or copy.

2. To move the file(s) and/or folder(s), choose Edit, Cut. To copy, choose Edit, Copy.

Edit	
Undo Copy	Ctrl+Z
Cut	Ctrl+X
Copy	Ctrl+C
Paste	Ctrl+V
Paste Shortcut	
Copy To Folder...	
Move To Folder...	
Select All	Ctrl+A
Invert Selection	

3. In My Computer, display the destination location.

4. Choose Edit, Paste.

The above steps illustrate one method of issuing the Cut, Copy, and Paste commands, but there are many alternative methods, as listed in Table 7.1. Feel free to select the most convenient method for a given situation.

You might also have noticed the Move to Folder and Copy to Folder choices on the Edit menu. These provide yet another alternative method of moving and copying. Each opens a dialog box where you can select a destination folder for the moved or copied files. Experiment with these commands on your own.

	Menu	Keyboard	Mouse
Cut	Edit, Cut	Ctrl+X	Right-click selection and choose Cut
Copy	Edit, Copy	Ctrl+C	Right-click selection and choose Copy
Paste	Edit, Paste	Ctrl+V	Right-click destination and choose Paste

TABLE 7.1: Cut, Copy, and Paste Methods

TUTORIAL 8

DELETING AND RESTORING FILES IN THE RECYCLE BIN

Imagine what would happen if every time you wanted to throw away a piece of paper, you set it on fire. You can probably see two immediate problems: 1) it would be extremely time-consuming, and 2) there would be no way to "dig through the trash" to recover something that you deleted too hastily. A much better way—and the way that you probably practice—is to collect unwanted paper in a wastebasket, and then once a week or so, set all of your trash out for garbage collection.

In Windows, file and folder deletion works on that same principle. The Recycle Bin is like a wastebasket in your computer "office." Rather than immediately destroying files that you delete, Windows places them in the Recycle Bin, a temporary holding area. It then waits until you either execute the Empty Recycle Bin command or run low on hard disk space before it permanently deletes the items.

> • • • • • **TIP** • • • • •
> The Recycle Bin works only on local hard disks. It does not work
> with removable disks or network locations.

Delete a File or Folder

To delete a file or folder such that it goes into the Recycle Bin, select it and then do any of the following:

- Press the Delete key on the keyboard.
- Choose File, Delete.
- Right-click the selected file(s) and choose Delete.

Depending on how your PC is set up, you might see a confirmation message or not. If you do, click Yes.

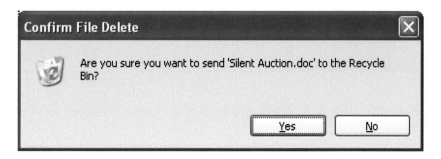

Tutorials • W-19

WINDOWS

Restore a Deleted File or Folder

Suppose you made a mistake in deleting a certain file. You can recover it by opening the Recycle Bin and retrieving it.

Steps

To restore a deleted file or folder:

1. Double-click the Recycle Bin icon on the desktop. The Recycle Bin window opens.

2. Locate the file to be retrieved and select it.

3. Choose File, Restore or click Restore This Item.

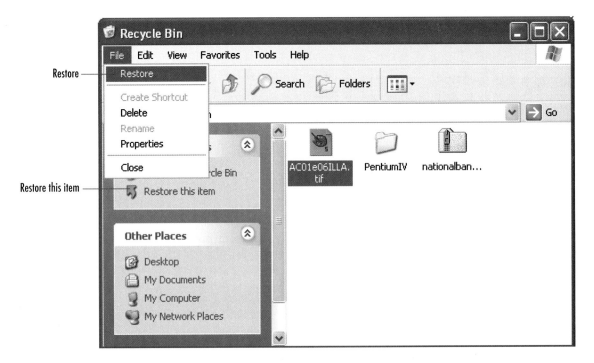

The file or folder disappears from the Recycle Bin. If you then open its original location in My Computer, you will see it there.

Occasionally you may run into an issue where you have multiple copies of the same file in the Recycle Bin, perhaps from different original locations or with different dates. How can you tell them apart? One way is to right-click one and

choose Properties; a Properties box appears letting you know the date it was created, the date it was deleted, its size, and the folder it was deleted from.

Empty the Recycle Bin

If you have plenty of free hard disk space, it's okay to let files build up in the Recycle Bin indefinitely. Windows will automatically start deleting the oldest ones whenever disk space becomes an issue. However, some people like to keep things orderly by regularly emptying the Recycle Bin. Privacy is one motivator; another is that if you have only a few items in the Recycle Bin, it becomes much easier to locate and restore any files that you accidentally delete.

You can empty the Recycle Bin from the desktop without having to open the Recycle Bin window. Just right-click it and choose Empty Recycle Bin:

If the Recycle Bin is already open, you can empty it by choosing File, Empty Recycle Bin. (This doesn't work if you have any files selected in the Recycle Bin; deselect all files first.)

T U T O R I A L   9

CHANGING DISPLAY SETTINGS

Customization is a valuable concept. It lets different users have different ideas of what constitutes the "perfect" settings, in everything from salad bars to automobiles. Windows has many customization options, and some of the most important ones deal with the display settings.

Display Resolution and Color Depth

The *display resolution* is the number of pixels—that is, colored dots—that comprise the display. The higher the resolution, the smaller the icons, text, menus, and dialog boxes will appear. Windows XP has a minimum resolution of 800 x 600 pixels, which is appropriate for small monitors (15"). If you have a larger monitor, you may wish to operate Windows in a higher resolution; it is a personal preference issue.

Color depth is the number of colors that Windows and applications can use to comprise the display. At a high color depth, photos look more realistic, but system performance may be slightly better at a lower color depth. Color depth is measured by the number of binary digits (bits) required to uniquely describe each color. A color depth of 32-bit would use 2^{32} binary digits for each color, for example.

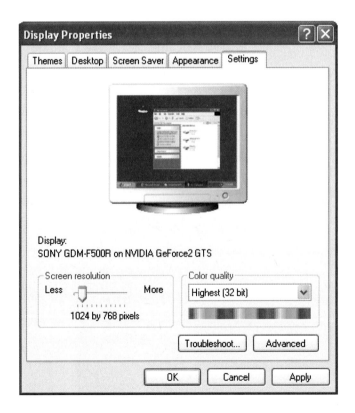

Steps

To change the resolution and color depth:

1. Right-click the desktop and choose Properties. The Display Properties dialog box appears.

2. Click the Settings tab.

3. Drag the Screen resolution slider to change the resolution if desired.

4. Open the Color quality list and choose a different color depth if desired.

5. Click OK. If a confirmation prompt appears, respond to it with Yes or OK, depending on its wording.

Appearance Themes

Appearance themes change the style of the windows, menus, dialog boxes, and buttons. By default, Windows XP comes with two themes: Windows Classic and Windows XP. Windows Classic makes the display look like earlier versions, which can be helpful for someone who is anxious about upgrading. You can also create your own themes or download more themes from the Internet.

Steps

To apply an appearance theme:

1. Right-click the desktop and choose Properties. The Display Properties dialog box appears.

2. Click the Themes tab.

3. Open the Theme list and choose the desired theme.

4. Click OK to apply the theme and close the dialog box.

Desktop Image

In the default Windows XP theme settings, you see a picture of a sunny meadow as your desktop. You can choose a different picture or turn off the picture altogether for a solid color background (blue, by default).

Steps

To change the desktop image:

1. Right-click the desktop and choose Properties. The Display Properties dialog box appears.

2. Click the Desktop tab.

3. Click on the name of a picture to select it, or click None to choose not to use a picture.

4. Click OK.

Color Scheme

Windows XP's default theme is available in three color schemes: Blue, Olive, and Silver. You can select a different color in the Appearance section of the Display Properties dialog box.

Steps

To choose a different color scheme:

1. Right-click the desktop and choose Properties. The Display Properties dialog box appears.

2. Click the Appearance tab.

3. Open the Color scheme list and choose a color scheme.

4. Click OK.

> Users of previous Windows versions may wonder where all the color choices went. They're still there, but they're not available with the Windows XP display style. On the Appearance tab shown above, open the Windows and Buttons setting and choose Windows Classic Style. Then open the Color Scheme list and there will be many more color scheme choices.

TUTORIAL 10

INSTALLING AND REMOVING SOFTWARE

Although Windows does have some important utilities built in, its main purpose is to run software that you buy separately. Some of the software you can buy for Windows includes office suites (word processor, spreadsheet, database), Web site creation applications, programming tools, and games.

Installing and removing software is not difficult, but it's important that you do it the right way. You can't simply copy the files for an application to your hard disk to install it, and you can't simply delete its files to remove an application. Windows maintains a configuration database called the Registry that stores information about which applications are installed and where their files are stored. By using the proper procedures for installing and removing software, you allow Windows to update its Registry to reflect the change.

Installing Software

Most software comes on self-running CD-ROM. To install it, simply insert the CD and follow the prompts that appear. If the Setup program does not begin automatically, you can locate and run the Setup program in My Computer.

Steps

To run the Setup program:

1. With the CD inserted, open My Computer.

2. Double-click the CD icon. The Setup program may start automatically at this point. If it does not, the content of the CD will appear.

3. Locate and double-click the Setup.exe file. The Setup program starts.

4. Follow the prompts to complete the setup.

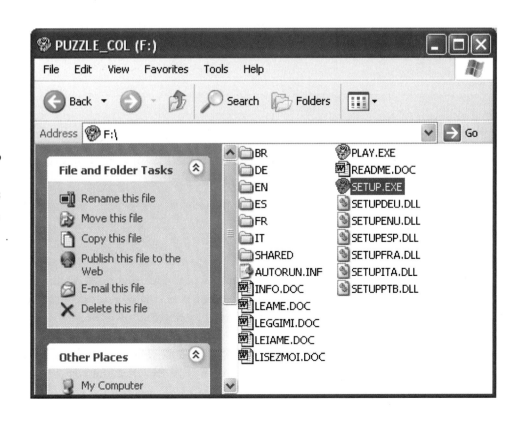

If you cannot find a Setup.exe file, you can direct Windows to locate and run the Setup program for you.

Steps

To direct Windows to locate and run the Setup program:

1. Choose Start, Control Panel.

2. Click Add or Remove Programs (or double-click it if you're using the Classic view of the Control Panel). The Add or Remove Programs dialog box opens.

3. Click the Add New Programs icon at the left.

4. Click the CD or Floppy button. Windows searches all CDs and floppies for the Setup utility, and runs it.

5. Follow the prompts to complete the setup.

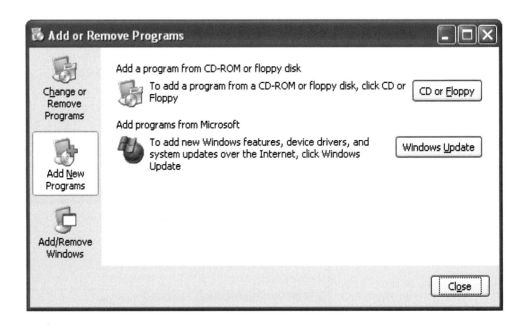

During installation, you might be asked to choose which type of install you want. The best choice is usually Typical.

Removing Software

Removing software that you don't use is not essential, but it frees up space on your hard disk. In addition, if the installed software was loading some portion of itself automatically at startup, removing it will prevent that from happening and will free up some RAM.

If an application has a Remove or Uninstall option on the Start menu, you should use it to remove the software. Otherwise, use options on the Control Panel.

Steps

To remove software via options on the Control Panel:

1. Choose Start, Control Panel.

2. Click Add or Remove Programs (or double-click it if you're using the Classic view of the Control Panel). The Add or Remove Programs dialog box opens.

3. Click Change or Remove Programs if it is not already selected.

4. Click the application to remove.

5. Click the Remove (or Change/Remove) button.

Some applications have separate buttons for the Change and Remove functions; others have a single Change/Remove button that opens a maintenance utility from which you can do either activity. Still others have no Change functionality at all, and have only a Remove button.

6. Follow the prompts that appear. The procedure differs depending on the application.

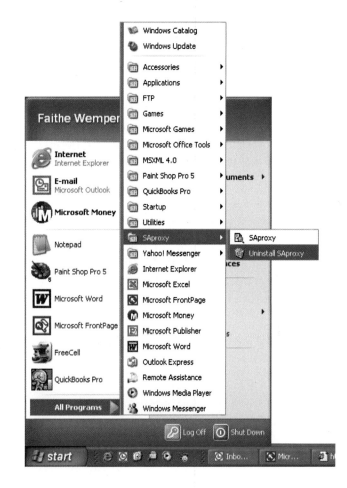

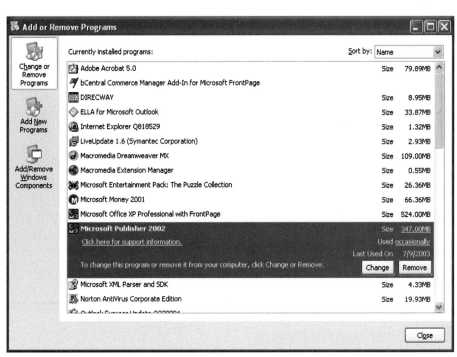

TUTORIAL 11

CUSTOMIZING THE START MENU

The Start Menu is highly customizable in Windows XP. Not only can you rearrange, add, and delete application shortcuts, but you can also change the structure of the underlying menu itself.

Pin a Shortcut to the Start Menu

You might have already noticed that the applications you use most often appear at the top level of the Start Menu's organizational system, directly above the Start button. The shortcuts in this area change depending on your usage.

Notice also that above these changing shortcuts are two additional ones, for Internet and E-mail. These are shortcuts to whatever e-mail and Web applications you have configured as the default ones. You can place other shortcuts in that area as well, to make them a permanent part of the Start Menu's top level. This is known as pinning the shortcut to the Start Menu.

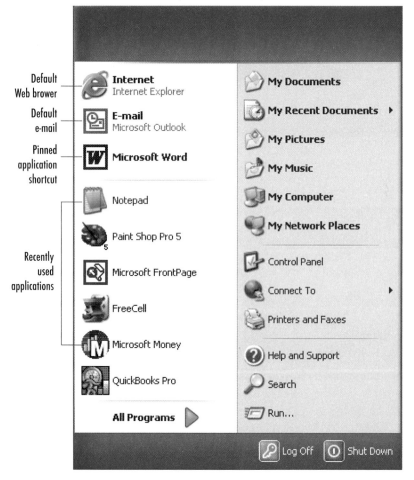

Default Web browser

Default e-mail

Pinned application shortcut

Recently used applications

Steps

To pin a shortcut to the Start Menu:

1. Right-click the application's icon.
2. Choose Pin to Start menu.

To unpin a shortcut:

1. Right-click a pinned shortcut.
2. Choose Unpin from Start menu.

Reorganize the All Programs Menu

When you choose Start, All Programs, a menu appears containing shortcuts for installed applications. Some of these have their own folders (submenus); others appear directly on the first level of the All Programs menu.

To move shortcuts and folders around on the All Programs menu, simply drag-and-drop the items. If you need to open a submenu, pause on it with the dragged item and it will open within a second or two.

To delete a shortcut from the All Programs menu, right-click it and choose Delete. This does not uninstall the application; it simply removes its shortcut. You can still start the application using other shortcuts (for example, on the desktop) or by browsing for the executable file in My Computer.

For more extensive reorganization, you must open the All Programs menu in the My Computer window. From there you can create new folders (which will be submenus) for organizing. This works because All Programs is actually just a folder on your hard disk, and the shortcuts on the menu are merely shortcut icons stored in it.

Open
Pin to Start menu
Send To ▶
Cut
Copy
Create Shortcut
Delete
Rename
Sort by Name
Properties

Steps

To open the All Programs menu:

1. Click the Start button.

2. Right-click All Programs and choose Open All Users. The Start Menu window opens in My Computer.

3. Double-click the Programs folder. The contents of the All Programs menu appears.

4. Add, delete, and arrange folders and shortcuts as desired. You learned in earlier tutorials how to create and delete folders and how to move and copy files.

5. Check your work by opening the Start, All Programs menu. When you are satisfied, close the My Computer window.

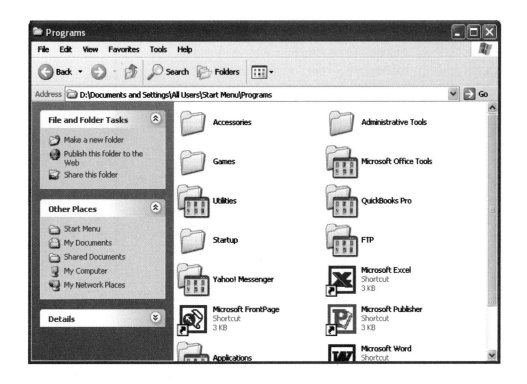

Choosing Which Items to Show

On the right side of the Start Menu are icons for commonly used shortcuts such as My Documents, My Computer, Control Panel, and so on. You can use the Advanced settings in the Start Menu's Properties to control which of these icons appears and whether it appears as a submenu or a shortcut to a folder.

Steps

To choose the Start Menu's top-level content:

1. Right-click the taskbar and choose Properties. The Taskbar and Start Menu Properties dialog box opens.

2. Click the Start Menu tab.

3. Click the Customize button next to Start Menu. The Customize Start Menu dialog box opens.

4. Click the Advanced tab.

5. In the Start menu items section, scroll through the list and select the desired settings for each item. For example, you can make the Control Panel not appear at all, appear as a shortcut to a folder (the default), or appear with its contents displayed as a submenu.

6. Click OK, then OK again to close all dialog boxes.

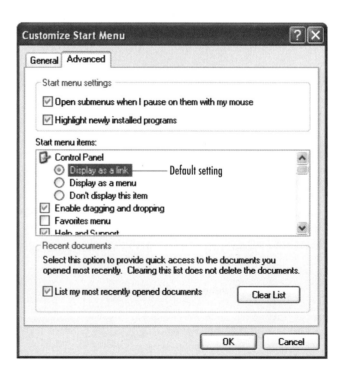

Using the Windows Classic Start Menu

If you have recently upgraded from an earlier Windows version, you might prefer to go back to the Classic Start menu style.

Steps

To revert to the Classic Start menu style:

1. Right-click the taskbar and choose Properties. The Taskbar and Start Menu Properties dialog box opens.

2. Click the Start Menu tab.

3. Click the Classic Start menu option.

4. Click OK.

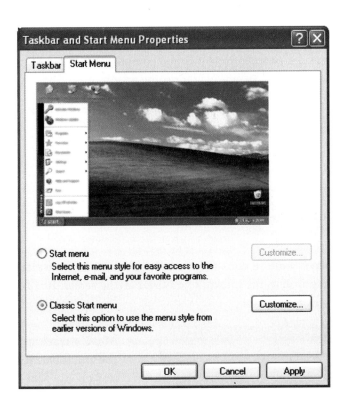

TUTORIAL 12

PLAYING A MUSIC CD OR DVD MOVIE

Windows Media Player is a music and video player that comes free with Windows XP. It will play a wide variety of music and video clip types, including the popular MP3, WMA, WAV, MOV, and AVI formats.

> Windows Media Player does not support certain MPEG-type video clips, but you can buy a codec (a piece of software that acts as a converter) that will allow it to do so. See the Help system in Windows Media Player for pointers to third-party add-ons.

Play an Audio CD

To play an audio CD, simply insert it in the computer's CD drive. It should start playing immediately. If it does not play for some reason, use Windows Media Player to start it.

Steps

To start an audio CD with Windows Media Player:

1. Choose Start, All Programs, Windows Media Player.

2. Choose Play, CD Audio and then click the icon for the drive containing the audio CD.

As the CD plays, you can click the Now Playing button to display a graphic that moves in response to the music. The Now Playing screen also shows a track list. From this screen you can:

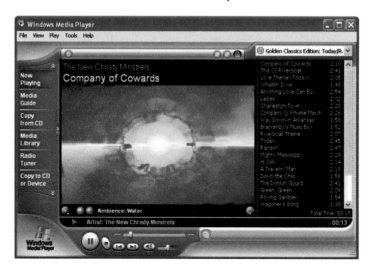

- **Move a track up or down in the track list.** Right-click it and choose Move Up or Move Down.
- **Skip certain tracks.** Select the track(s) to skip, then right-click the selection and choose Disable Selected Track(s).
- **Pause or stop the player.** Use the buttons at the bottom of the window. They work just like buttons on a cassette tape player or stereo CD player.

Play a DVD Movie

Most computers that come with a DVD drive also come with extra software that works with that drive to play DVD movies. One popular brand is WinDVD. Such software is usually more full-featured than Windows Media Player, so you may prefer to use it if available. However, in the absence of a third-party DVD movie player utility, Windows Media Player will serve.

Steps

To play a DVD movie in Windows Media Player:

1. Insert the DVD movie in the drive. It may start playing automatically, or you may see a window like this:

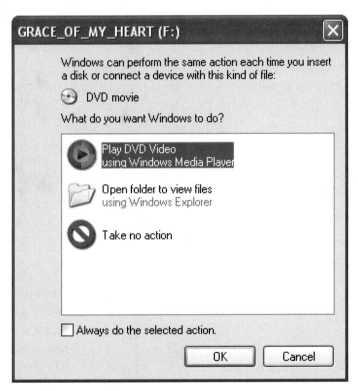

2. If you see the above window, click OK to play the movie in Windows Media Player.

If you see a message that Windows Media Player cannot play the movie, click the More Details hyperlink in the message box to find out why. You might not have an MPEG decoder installed on your PC. This can either be a hardware board or a software utility, and it usually comes with the DVD drive. Its purpose is to decode and decompress the movie data and display it on your monitor.

TUTORIAL 13

BURNING A CD-R

Most new computers have at least one writable CD drive. With earlier versions of Windows, a third-party utility was necessary to use these drives for writing ("burning") a CD, but Windows XP has this writing functionality built in. The procedure for creating a CD depends on what kind of CD you want—data or music.

Nearly all writable CD drives can use either CD-Recordable (CD-R) or CD-ReWritable (CD-RW) discs. CD-R discs are cheaper but can be written to only once. CD-RW discs are more expensive, but the contents can be changed after the initial write. The steps here assume you are using CD-R media.

Creating a Data CD

CD is a great medium for creating backups of important files. A CD can hold about 700 MB of data, which is the storage capacity of about 485 floppy disks.

Steps

To copy files to a writable CD:

1. Insert a blank CD-R in the drive. If a window appears asking what you want to do, click Open writable CD folder using Windows Explorer and then click OK.

2. Open My Computer and select the files/folders you want to copy.

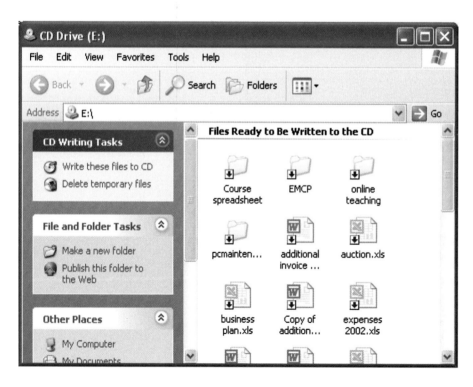

3. Do either of the following:

   - If you opened a window for the CD drive in step 1, drag and drop the files from My Computer to the CD drive's window.
   - Right-click the selected files and choose Send To and then choose the CD drive from the list of locations.

4. When you are finished selecting the files/folders for the CD, display the CD drive's contents in My Computer and click Write these files to CD.

5. A CD Writing Wizard appears, prompting you for a CD name. This will be the volume label for the CD. The default is today's date. Change it if desired.

6. Click Next.

7. Wait for the files to be written to the CD. Try not to use the computer while it is writing, to minimize the possibility of write errors.

8. When the writing is done, a confirmation appears and the CD ejects. Click Finish.

Creating an Audio CD

There are two kinds of music CDs: MP3 and CD Audio. MP3 files are audio files designed to be played on a computer, while CD Audio (CDA) files are designed to be played on an audio CD player. MP3 files take up much less space, so you can fit many more of them on a single disc. However, you can't play an MP3 CD on regular stereo equipment.

If you want to place MP3 files on a CD, treat it as if it were a data disc (see the preceding section). If you want to make an audio CD that will play in regular stereos, however, you must use a special utility such as Windows Media Player to convert the digital audio clips (for example, MP3 and WMA files) into CDA format and write them to the CD.

Steps

To create an audio CD that will play in regular stereos:

1. Insert a blank CD-R in the drive. If a window appears asking what you want to do, click Cancel.

2. Open Windows Media Player.

These steps assume that you have your digital audio clips already cataloged in the Media Library of Windows Media Player. If you do not, choose Tools, Search for Media Files and allow Windows Media Player to find and organize your clips before proceeding.

3. Click Copy to CD or Device.

4. Under the Music to Copy heading, open the drop-down list and choose All Audio. (Or choose some subset of All Audio if desired, such as a particular playlist.)

5. Click the checkbox next to the Title heading to clear the checkbox for all clips.

6. Scroll through the list of clips and place a checkmark next to the clips you want to copy to the CD. When the maximum amount of content has been selected for the disc's capacity, the next clip you select will cause the message *Will not fit* to display in the status.

7. When you are done selecting clips, click the Copy Music button.

If warnings appear about digital licenses, you may be attempting to copy a clip that cannot be copied due to its licensing restrictions.

TUTORIAL 14

WORKING WITH ANTIVIRUS SOFTWARE

One of the most important actions you can take to protect your computer and your data is to install and update reliable antivirus software. Popular antivirus programs include Norton Antivirus, McAfee VirusScan, InoculateIT, and PC-illin.

Antivirus software contains a list of virus definitions that describe the identifying characteristics of various viruses and provide program instructions for removing them and fixing the damage they cause (when possible). New computer viruses are created daily, so it is important to update your antivirus software definitions at least once a week. Most antivirus programs automatically check for updates and install them for you.

Because antivirus software is only as good as the most recent update, companies that manufacture this software sell the product on a subscription basis. When you buy the software you pay for a certain amount of time during which you will receive updates (usually 12 months); after that time, you must pay again.

Installing Antivirus Software

Antivirus software installs like any other software (refer to Tutorial 10). It can be installed from CD or from an Internet download. Many antivirus applications offer free limited-time trials, so you can experiment with several different programs before you decide which one works best for your needs. (You should have only one installed at a time, however; uninstall one before installing another.)

The most popular antivirus software is Symantec's Norton Antivirus. Go to www.symantec.com to request a free trial.

Using Antivirus Software

Antivirus software runs itself. It starts automatically when you start Windows, and it monitors all activity and reports any viruses it finds. It even schedules its own full system scans to occur at periodic intervals (such as weekly). You can make changes to its configuration settings if desired, but the default settings are usually acceptable.

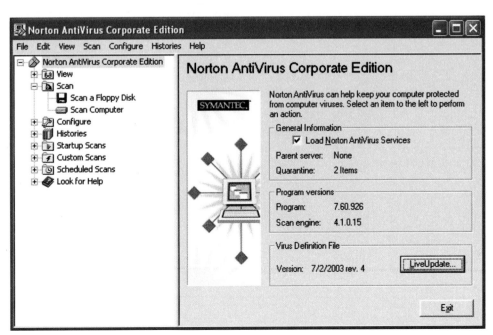

You can tell that the antivirus software is running because an icon for it will appear in the notification area (next to the clock in the bottom right corner). You can double-click the icon to open its configuration window.

Updating Virus Definitions

It is absolutely essential to update virus definitions regularly, but most antivirus programs update themselves automatically every week. You can also specifically request an update—for example, if you read in the news about a new virus threat but your update is not scheduled for several days. For Norton Antivirus, the LiveUpdate utility updates the virus definitions; you can access it by clicking LiveUpdate in the application's configuration box shown above. Other utilities have different update procedures.

Temporarily Disabling Virus Protection

Sometimes antivirus software interferes with the installation of other software because it thinks that the new software is a system threat. If you encounter this problem, you can temporarily disable the antivirus program. To do so, right-click its icon in the notification area and choose Disable, Exit, or whatever command seems as if it would close, pause, or otherwise disable the antivirus software. The exact command depends on the application. As shown in the figure below, you could select Enable File System Realtime Protection to remove the checkmark next to it, temporarily disabling it. After the new software has been installed, you can then re-enable the antivirus software.

TUTORIAL 15

FINDING AND FIXING DISK ERRORS

Disk errors occur when the "table of contents" for the disk becomes out of sync with the actual content. When the operating system expects to find a certain piece of data in a certain spot but it isn't there, problems occur. A disk error can trigger lockups, program termination, out-of-memory errors, and many other types of errors that appear on the surface to be unrelated to disk storage. One disk error can also set up the conditions for another to occur, further compounding the problem.

Disk errors result from an application (or Windows itself) not shutting down properly. The shutdown process saves open files and updates the disk's FAT or MFT (its table of contents) with the newest information. If that orderly shutdown does not occur, a file's actual content, storage location, size, and/or properties may not match its description —and a disk error occurs. The most common cause of improper shutdown is loss of electrical power; the second most common cause is a user shutting down the PC by pressing its Power button rather than using the Start, Shut Down command (the correct method).

> A disk under Windows XP can have any of several file systems in use. Disks that use the FAT or FAT32 file system keep track of disk contents in a File Allocation Table (FAT) . Disks that use the NTFS file system keep track of disk contents in a Master File Table (MFT).

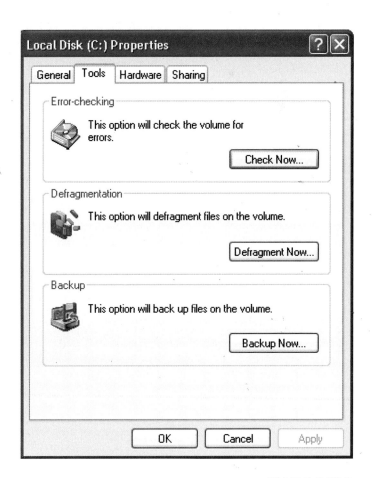

Windows 9x and MS-DOS have a utility called Scan Disk that finds and fixes disk errors. Windows 2000 and XP have a similar utility called Check Disk.

Steps

To run Check Disk:

1. In My Computer, right-click the hard disk icon and choose Properties.

2. Click the Tools tab.

3. Click the Check Now button. The Check Disk Local Disk dialog box opens.

4. (Optional) If you want any errors to be automatically repaired (recommended), click in the *Automatically fix file system errors* checkbox.

5. (Optional) If you want a surface scan as well as a logical check, click in the *Scan for and attempt recovery of bad sectors* checkbox.

In most cases a surface scan is not necessary, and it makes the test take much longer (up to several hours). You should include a surface scan in the test only if you are getting error messages about problems reading or writing to the disk.

6. Click Start.

7. Wait for the tests to finish. Try not to use the computer while they are running, because if the disk content changes, the tests might restart themselves.

8. A box appears letting you know when the check is complete. Click OK.

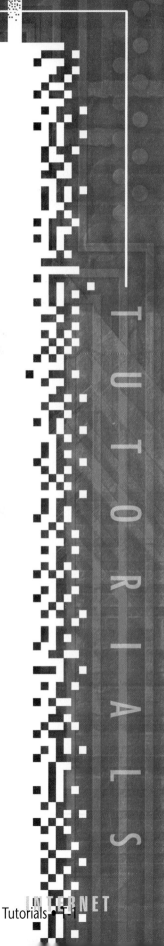

T U T O R I A L   1

BROWSING THE WEB USING WEB ADDRESSES

The Internet is a collection of computers around the world connected together through telephone lines, cables, satellites, and other telecommunications media. The World Wide Web, called the Web, is a part of the Internet that contains Web pages consisting of text, sounds, video, and graphics that link to other related Web pages. These links are called hyperlinks. Many Web pages are stored in a language called HTML (Hypertext Markup Language) which can be viewed on any computer regardless of the operating system platform (Macintosh, Windows, UNIX, Linux, and so on).

Connecting to the Web

To connect to the Internet and view Web pages you will need the following resources:

1. A computer with a modem or network connection to a server with Internet access.

2. Browser software, such as Internet Explorer or Netscape, that provides the interface for viewing Web pages.

3. An account with an ISP (Internet Service Provider) if you are using a computer that is not connected to a network server. An ISP sells Internet access usually by charging a monthly fee for a set time period. The ISP has the computers, network equipment, and modems to allow multiple users to connect at the same time.

In the steps that follow you will explore Web sites on the Internet using Web addresses in Microsoft Internet Explorer version 6.0 operating in the Windows XP Professional environment. If you are using another operating system, Web browser, or a different version of Internet Explorer, you may need to alter these instructions slightly.

Steps

1. Double-click the Shortcut to Internet icon on the desktop, or click the Start button and then click Internet at the pop-up menu.

If you are completing this tutorial using your computer at home, you may need to enter your user name and password and click OK to connect through a dial-up connection to your ISP.

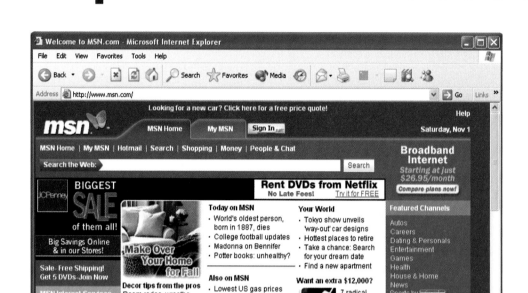

FIGURE T-1 Internet Explorer Window with msn.com Web page

The Internet Explorer window appears with a Web page displayed in the window as shown in Figure T-1. (The default Web page shown when Internet Explorer first opens may vary from the msn.com page shown.)

2. Move the mouse pointer over the current entry in the Address text box, and then click the left mouse button.

Clicking the left mouse button selects the entire address and changes the white arrow pointer to an I-beam which indicates you can type text and/or move the insertion point using the arrow keys on the keyboard.

3. Type usatoday.com and then press Enter.

The USA Today home page appears in the window. Watch the status bar for messages displaying the status of loading the page. When the page has finished displaying all of its text, graphics, and other components, the status bar displays the word "Done."

The entry in the Address text box is called a URL (Uniform Resource Locator). URLs are the addressing method used to identify Web pages. After pressing Enter, notice the browser automatically inserted *http://* in front of the address you typed: *http* stands for HyperText Transfer Protocol which is the communications standard used for transferring data within the Web.

4. Move the mouse pointer over the underlined headings displayed at the left side of the USA Today page.

Notice the pointer changes shape to a white hand with the index finger pointing upward when it is positioned over underlined text. When the pointer takes this shape, it means you can click the left mouse button to jump to a related Web page (called a *hyperlink*).

5. Click the left mouse button over News Briefs.

In a few seconds the News page is displayed with the current day's top stories and links to full coverage articles.

6. Click the Back button ⬅ Back on the toolbar to return to the previous page.

7. Click the Forward button ➡ on the toolbar to redisplay the News page (the page viewed prior to clicking Back).

Notice the Back and Forward buttons on the toolbar include down-pointing arrows. Click the down-pointing arrow and then click a Web site name in the drop-down list to jump to a page previously viewed.

8. Click the mouse pointer over the entry in the Address text box, type **microsoft.com**, and then press Enter.

9. Click one of the hyperlinks on the Microsoft home page to jump to a topic that interests you.

10. Continue exploring Web pages by typing URLs in the Address text box, clicking hyperlinks, the Back button, and the Forward button on the toolbar.

11. When you have finished exploring the Web, click the Close button ☒ at the right end of the title bar to exit Internet Explorer. If necessary, disconnect from your ISP if you are not continuing on to Tutorial 2.

If you want to browse the Web by *topic*, rather than addresses, click the Search button on the toolbar. Click in the *What are you looking for?* text box, type the topic you are interested in, and then click the Search button. You will learn more about searching in Tutorial 2.

TUTORIAL 2

CONDUCTING A BASIC SEARCH

In the previous Internet topic, Web sites were explored by keying the Web address (URL) for a specific company. Another method used to find information is by entering a keyword or a phrase and then browsing through a series of Web pages that were found. Several search engines are available to assist users with locating Web sites by topic. A search engine is a company that uses specialized software to continually scan the Web to index and catalog the information that is published. These companies have created Web sites where the user begins a search by typing the word or phrase they would like to find information on. The search engine then lists the Web pages that contain the word or phrase as links, which are called hits. Some search engines maintain category indices where the user clicks through a series of categories and subcategories until they reach the desired list of Web pages.

In this topic you will find information on the Web by entering keywords and then conduct another search by browsing through a list of categories.

What are you looking for?

Type your question below. For best results, use complete sentences.

space station facts|

Sample question:

→ Where can I read about the history of Puerto Rico?

You may also want to...

🔍 Search this computer for files

☑ Change preferences

❓ Learn more about Search Companion

Search

Steps

1. Start Internet Explorer and then Maximize the Internet Explorer window if it is not already maximized. If necessary, connect to your ISP and enter your user name and password.

2. Click the Search button 🔍 Search on the Internet Explorer toolbar.

The Search Companion pane opens at the left side of the Internet Explorer window. A white text box containing the prompt *Please type your query here, and then press <Enter>.* is positioned below the question *What are you looking for?* Help text displays above the white text box to assist you with phrasing a question.

3. Click over the text *Please type your query here, and then press <Enter>.*, type **space station facts**, and then click the Search button.

By default, the search engine msn.com is used to locate Web pages related to the search phrase. A list of hyperlinked Web pages displays in the Internet Explorer window that msn.com has indexed to the phrase you typed.

4. Click one of the links in the Internet Explorer window to view a related Web page.

5. Click the Back button to return to the Search results list and then click another link to view another Web page.

Another way to search for information is to use a search engine's category index. In the next steps, you will close the Search companion pane, type the URL for a search engine, and then browse the category index.

6. Click the Search button on the Internet Explorer toolbar to close the Search companion pane.

If you prefer to use the full screen for viewing Web pages, close the search companion pane and then go directly to the search engine's URL.

7. Type **yahoo.com** in the Address text box and then press Enter.

Yahoo! is a popular search engine that maintains category indices and can also be used to search for a topic by keywords.

8. Scroll down the Yahoo! Web page and then click Science.

9. Scroll down the Yahoo! directory page for the Science category and then click Space.

10. Scroll down the Yahoo! directory page for the Science > Space category and then click Space Stations.

11. Click International Space Station (ISS) on the Space Stations category page.

12. Click one of the links that is of interest to you on the International Space Station category page to read about this international project.

13. Click the Back button on the Internet Explorer toolbar, click another link from the International Space Station category page, and then view the Web page.

14. Close Internet Explorer. If necessary, disconnect from your ISP if you are not continuing on to Tutorial 3.

Business & Economy
B2B, Finance, Shopping, Jobs...

Computers & Internet
Internet, WWW, Software, Games...

News & Media
Newspapers, TV, Radio...

Entertainment
Movies, Humor, Music...

Recreation & Sports
Sports, Travel, Autos, Outdoors...

Health
Diseases, Drugs, Fitness...

Government
Elections, Military, Law, Taxes...

- **Research** (192)
- **Science and Technology Policy** (52)
- **Science on Postage Stamps** (6)
- **Space** (1511) NEW!
- **Space@**
- **Web Directories** (39)

- **Space Elevators** (13)
- **Space Environment** (65)
- **Space Physics** (30)
- **Space Stations** (50)
- **Spacecraft** (443)
- **Web Directories** (8)

URLs for other popular Search Engines	
Excite	http://www.excite.com
Google	http://www.google.com
WebCrawler	http://www.webcrawler.com

TUTORIAL 3

CONDUCTING AN ADVANCED SEARCH

The number of Web sites that an individual will see in a list as the result of a search request can be overwhelming. It is not uncommon to see thousands of hits result from searching by a few keywords. The challenge when searching for information on the Internet is to reduce the number of hits to the smallest possible number. Including a search operator with the keywords refines a search by limiting the sites that are displayed based on where or how the keywords are placed. Search operators vary between search engines so it is best to view links to advanced search information for a search engine prior to using operators.

In this topic you will find information on the Web using Boolean operators, specifying a time period, and filtering by a domain in an advanced search page.

Steps

1. Start Internet Explorer. If necessary, connect to your ISP and enter your username and password.

2. Type **webcrawler.com** in the Address text box and then press Enter.

3. Type **endangered species** in the Search text box and then click the Search button.

In a few seconds linked Web pages display with the total number of sites found from searching the index provided at the top of the search results list.

4. Scroll down the search results list and read the titles and descriptions of the Web pages found.

In the next steps you will refine the list to display only those pages that contain information about birds that are endangered.

5. Scroll to the top of the page and then click Advanced Search.

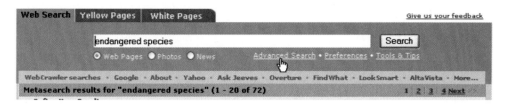

6. Click Get more information on Boolean searches in the Use Boolean Terms section of the Advanced Search page.

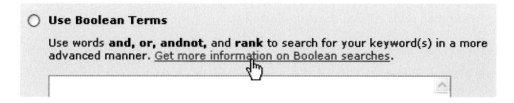

A WebCrawler window opens with information on the available Boolean keywords and includes examples of how to conduct a search using Boolean logic. Boolean keywords are especially useful for narrowing search requests by adding to the keyword list and specifying whether to include or exclude Web pages containing the keyword in the search results list.

7. Read the information on Boolean Searches in the WebCrawler window and then close the window.

8. Click in the white text box below Use Boolean Terms, type **endangered AND species AND birds**, and then click the Search button.

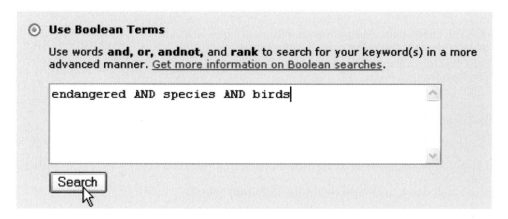

9. Scroll down the search results page. Notice the Web pages listed are different than those on the first list you viewed.

In the next steps you will further refine your search by specifying a time period for published information and a domain filter.

10. Click the Advanced Search link.

11. Click in the white text box below Use Boolean Terms, type **endangered AND species AND birds**.

12. If necessary scroll down the Advanced Search page to the Last Page Update section below Additional Search Criteria.

13. Click the *after* check box in the Last Page Update section.

14. Click the down-pointing arrow next to the month list box in the *after* section and then click *September* at the drop-down list.

15. Click the down-pointing arrow next to the year list box in the *after* section and then click *2002* at the drop-down list.

Additional Search Criteria

LAST PAGE UPDATE   Use **After** to find results updated after a certain date. Use **Before** to find results updated before a certain date. Fill out both fields to find results updated between two dates.

☑ after   September ▾   01 ▾   2002 ▾

☐ before   November ▾   01 ▾   2003 ▾

16. If necessary, scroll down the Advanced Search page to the Domain Filter section.

17. Click the in the white text box next to the Include Results From list box in the Domain Filter section and then type **.gov**.

DOMAIN FILTER   You can use generic domain names like **.com**, **.gov** and **.edu**, or you can include a specific domain name like **anycompany.com**.

Include Results From ▾   .gov

Domain names using .gov are restricted to government funded departments and agencies.

18. Scroll to the bottom of the Advanced Search page then click the Search button.

19. Scroll down and view the list of Web sites found.

20. Close Internet Explorer. If necessary, disconnect from your ISP if you are not continuing on with Tutorial 4.

TUTORIAL 4

SHOPPING ON THE WEB

The ability to shop at any time throughout the day, browse a variety of products within minutes, and compare prices among vendors with just a few mouse clicks is making online shopping a popular choice. *E-tailing*, the selling of retail goods on the Internet, is what most individuals think of when the term *e-commerce* is used. Companies that brought e-tailing to mainstream popularity are Dell Computers and bookseller Amazon.com. Most e-tailers use secure Web site servers that automatically encrypt personal data such as a credit card number as it is transmitted. This provides protection for both the consumer and the e-tailer. A secure Web site is indicated with a URL that begins with *https* rather than http. Encryption involves the use of Secure Sockets Layer (SSL) technology that scrambles information into an unbreakable code before it is sent over the Internet. To indicate that an active Web site is secure, Internet Explorer displays an icon of a closed lock in the status bar and Netscape displays an unbroken key.

In this topic you will browse an e-tailer's secure Web site and identify the security and privacy features.

Steps

1. Start Internet Explorer. If necessary, connect to your ISP and enter your user name and password.

2. Type **amazon.com** in the Address text box and then press Enter.

Amazon.com began selling books online in 1995 and is considered to be one of the pioneers in e-tailing.

3. Click SEE MORE STORES at the right end of the tab names just below the Amazon.com logo.

4. Scroll down the store directory page and then click Gift Certificates in the Gifts & Registries list.

5. Click the Order gift certificates button below Gift Certificates for Friends & Family

Note: In the next steps you will proceed to order a gift certificate in order to look at the visual clues that identify a secure Web server. However, you will not complete an actual transaction.

6. Click the Order e-mail gift certificates button.

7. Read the information on the Web page regarding the safe shopping guarantee and then click the link that says Click here to continue your order on our secure server.

8. Scroll to the bottom of the Web page and then click the Privacy Notice link.

> Having difficulties? We're here to help. Please <u>e-mail us</u> with your questions.

<u>Conditions of Use</u> | <u>Privacy Notice</u> © 1996-2003, Amazon.com, Inc. or its affiliates

9. Read the information on the Amazon.com Privacy Notice page.

Security is not just about keeping credit card information safe but is also about protecting a buyer's personal information. If an e-tailer does not have a link to a page that informs the buyer how information is stored and shared, then the site should be avoided.

10. Type **landsend.com** in the Address text box and then press Enter.

11. If necessary, scroll down the page and then click the Policies link at the left side of the page below Our Company.

12. Read the Privacy Policy information that is displayed, click the link to Security Policy, and then read the information about security policies at Lands' End.

13. Read the information and consider the differences, if any, in the policies for Lands' End and Amazon.com. Which company provides more comprehensive information about privacy and security?

14. Close Internet Explorer. If necessary, disconnect from your ISP if you are not continuing on to Tutorial 5.

Cavaet Emptor!

The trading principle, "Let the Buyer Beware" is just as applicable to electronic commerce as it is to face-to-face shopping. Buyers need to be prudent about verifying product and vendor reliability. The Better Business Bureau's site at **http://www.bbb.org** is a great place to start.

TUTORIAL 5

DOWNLOADING INFORMATION FROM THE WEB

If you find a Web site that contains information on a topic that you want to save for future use, you can either print a hard copy of the Web page(s), or you can save it as a file on your computer. If you want to save only a portion of the text on the Web page, select the text with the mouse and then copy it to the Clipboard. Once the text is stored in the Clipboard, it can be pasted into WordPad or Microsoft Word and then saved as a document. A graphic or other multimedia component on a Web page also can be downloaded and saved as a file.

In this topic you will save an entire Web page as a file, select text from a Web page to copy and paste, and then save a graphic image as a file.

Steps

1. Start Internet Explorer. If necessary, connect to your ISP and enter your user-name and password.

2. Type **loc.gov** in the Address text box and then press Enter.

3. Click the link to American Memory US History & Culture.

4. At the American Memory page, click the link to Today in History.

5. Click File on the Menu bar and then click Save As.

6. Click the down-pointing arrow next to the *Save in* list box and then change to the drive and/or folder that you would like to use to store the Web page, for example, 3½ Floppy (A:).

7. With the default name Today in History [current date] in the File name text box, click the Save button in the Save Web Page dialog box.

A progress box appears as the Web page elements are downloaded and saved locally. To view the Web page at a later time, start Internet Explorer, click File and then click Open. Click the Browse button in the Open dialog box, navigate to the drive and/or folder where the Web page is stored, and then double-click the Web page name in the list box.

8. With Today in History still the active page, position the mouse pointer slightly left of the first character in the first paragraph of text until the pointer changes to the I-beam pointer I and then drag the mouse down and right to the end of the first paragraph as shown. *Note: Your text will vary from the text shown if you are viewing* Today in History *on a date other than November 1st.*

On **November 1**, 1897, the first Library of Congress building opened its doors to the public. Previously, the Library had been housed in the Congressional Reading Room in the U.S. Capitol. I

9. Click Edit on the Menu bar and then click Copy.

The selected text is saved to the Windows Clipboard. To save the text permanently, open a software application such as WordPad or Microsoft Word, paste the text, edit or format as required, and then save it as a document.

10. Click Start, point to All Programs, point to Accessories, and then click WordPad.

11. At a blank document window, click Edit on the Menu bar; then click Paste.

12. Click the Save button on the toolbar. Change the drive and/or folder as required in the Save in text box, type **Today in History** in the File name text box and then click the Save button.

13. Click File and then click Exit to close the document and exit WordPad.

When WordPad closes, you should automatically be returned to the Internet Explorer window. If necessary, click the button on the taskbar representing Internet Explorer to restore the window.

14. Click Back on the toolbar to return to the American Memory page.

15. Move the mouse pointer over the picture of the American flag superimposed on an open book at the top of the page and then right-click.

16. Click Save Picture As from the shortcut menu.

17. At the Save Picture dialog box, click the down-pointing arrow next to the Save in list box and then change to the drive and/or folder that you would like to use to store the graphic file, for example, 3½ Floppy (A:).

18. With the default name *amtitle* in the File name text box, click the Save button.

19. Close Internet Explorer. If necessary, disconnect from your ISP if you are not continuing on to Tutorial 6.

A graphic does not have to be saved as a file—right-click a picture on a Web page and Copy it to the Clipboard. Paste the image into a document using the Edit, Paste command if you simply want to copy an image and do not need it saved as a separate file.

TUTORIAL 6

REFERENCE RESOURCES ON THE WEB

A search engine can return a large number of hits as the result of a search request by keyword(s) or phrase even when search operators are included to reduce the list of Web pages. Although using the Internet to locate information is fast and very accessible, extra time needs to be taken to assess the reliability and accuracy of the online information. Information on the Internet can be comprised of opinions, stories, statistics, or facts. The context with which information is presented may be designed to inform the reader or persuade the reader to accept an opinion or buy a product or service. A considerable amount of time to filter through the hits to find the credible information can be avoided by using one of the many reference resources available on the Web. Reference resources are portals to information that has been evaluated prior to being linked through the resource site.

In this topic you will use two reference resource sites to locate employment information on the Internet.

Steps

1. Start Internet Explorer. If necessary, connect to your ISP and enter your user-name and password.

2. Key **lii.org** in the Address text box and then press Enter.

The Librarians' Index to the Internet contains over 7,800 Internet resources selected and evaluated by librarians. The index was originally funded by the U.S. Institute of Museum and Library Services and is now maintained through funding from the Library of California.

3. Click in the Search text box, type "**job search**" and then click the Search LII.ORG button. *Be sure to include the opening and closing quotes.*

4. Scroll through the list of Web links found. Click one of the links that interests you.

5. Click the Back button on the Internet Explorer toolbar, scroll to the bottom of the search results page and then click the *Jobs Topics Page* link.

6. Click the Job Listings link in the Jobs Popular Topics list on the Business, Finance, & Jobs page.

7. Click Information Technology on the Job Listings General Resources page.

The Results banner displays the multi-level search that has just been completed.

8. Type **ipl.org** in the Address text box and then press Enter.

The Internet Public Library is hosted by the School of Information & Library Studies of the University of Michigan. The site contains a rich resource of library services to Internet users.

- Job Hunting
- Job Listings
- Labor Statistics
- Labor Unions

General Resources

- Aerospace Industry
- African Americans
- California
- Education
- Government
- Graphic Arts
- Health
- Hispanic Americans
- Information Technology
- International
- Journalism

The Librarians' Index to the Internet and the Internet Public Library are just two of many reference resources. Go to your favorite search engine page and type **reference resources** to find more!

9. Point to Business in the Subject Collections list and then click Employment in the Business & Economics list.

10. Scroll down the list of links provided for the category *Employment* and then click a link to a site that interests you.

11. Close Internet Explorer. If necessary, disconnect from your ISP if you are not continuing on to Tutorial 7.

TUTORIAL 7

COMMUNICATING USING INSTANT MESSAGING

Instant messaging (IM) is similar to an online chat with the exception that there are fewer participants engaged in a conversation that is not able to be viewed by everyone who is online. IM runs in the background while you are working on your computer. When a message arrives or one of your contacts goes online, a pop-up screen informs you. In a default installation of Microsoft Windows XP, Windows Messenger is installed and activated upon start-up. To send and receive instant messages with another individual you need to have a .NET Passport, and the IM address of your friend added to your contacts list.

In this topic you will open Windows Messenger, obtain a .NET Passport, add a contact to your contacts list, and send and receive a message to another student.

Steps

Note: Check with your instructor before completing this topic to find out which student in the class you will be partnered with for sending and receiving an instant message.

1. Click Start, point to All Programs, and then click Windows Messenger. If necessary, connect to your ISP by entering your user name and password.

If Windows Messenger has already been set up for a user with a .NET Passport account, Windows attempts to log on the user with the e-mail address of the .NET Passport. You may be prompted for your password if the password has not been stored. If the log-on is successful go to step 5. New users of Windows Messenger should proceed to step 2.

2. At the Windows Messenger dialog box, click over the text Click here to sign in.

3. At the .NET Messenger Service dialog box, click Get a .NET Passport. *Note: If you have a Hotmail or MSN account, you already have a Passport—sign in by typing your e-mail address and password and then proceed to step 5.*

4. Click Next at the first .NET Passport Wizard dialog box and then follow the prompts in the wizard dialog boxes to set up a .NET Passport account. When you have completed the wizard you will be signed in and returned to the Windows Messenger window.

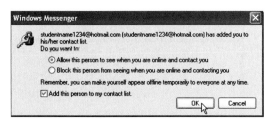

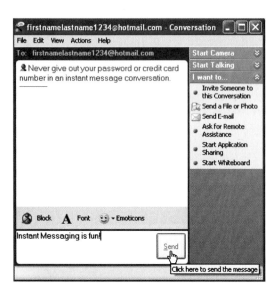

You may use an existing e-mail address as your Passport, or, you may prefer to set up an MSN Hotmail account for purposes of using Windows Messenger.

5. For the remaining steps you will be working with your instant messaging partner. Decide between you which student will add the other as a contact and only one student should complete steps 5-8. At the Windows Messenger window, click *Add a Contact* in the *I want to* section.

6. With *By e-mail address or sign-in name* selected in the *How do you want to add a contact?* section of the Add a Contact dialog box, click Next.

7. Type the e-mail address of the student with whom you have been partnered for this topic in the *Please type your contact's complete e-mail address* text box, and then click Next.

8. Click Finish at the last Add a Contact dialog box that says you have successfully added *[e-mail address]* to your list.

9. The student that did not add the contact should complete this step. At the Windows Messenger dialog box informing you that *[student name]* has added you to his/her contacts list, click OK to accept *Allow this person to see when you are online and contact you* and *Add this person to my contact list*.

10. In the *Online* section of the Windows Messenger window, double-click the e-mail address of the student with whom you have been partnered.

A Conversation window opens in which you type message text to send and read the other person's replies.

11. With the insertion point positioned in the message text box at the bottom of the Conversation window, type **Instant Messaging is fun!** and then click the Send button.

The other student receives an alert on his or her computer as soon as the message is received.

12. Send a few more messages back and forth to each other.

13. When you are finished using Windows Messenger, click the Close button on the Conversation window title bar.

14. Click the Windows Messenger – Signed In icon 👤 on the taskbar next to the current time and then click *Sign Out* at the pop-up menu.

glossary

3D modeling programs Programs that allow users to create the illusion of depth in objects drawn on the computer

3D video card A graphics video card that excels at drawing three-dimensional images used in computer games and/or animation applications

802.11 protocol A protocol for wireless LAN technology that specifies an over-the-air interface between the wireless client device and a server, or between two wireless devices; approved by the IEEE in 1997

802.11a Revision of the 802.11 protocol for wireless LAN technology, approved in 2001, which offers transfer rates of up to 54 Mbps when devices are at a range within 60 feet of the primary access point or hub, 22 Mbps at longer distances

802.11b First major revision of 802.11 protocol for wireless LAN technology, approved in 1999, relatively low cost and with a faster transfer rate of 5.5-11 Mbps at a range up to 250 feet; popular in home and small office wireless networks

802.11g Approved in June 2003, this protocol for wireless LAN technology operates in the same frequency range as 802.11b but with transfer rates similar to 802.11a; also called **wireless 3G**

A

Accelerated Graphics Port (AGP) bus A bus that increases the speed at which graphics (including 3-D graphics) and video can be transmitted and accessed by the computer

Acceptable Use Policy (AUP) A set of guidelines schools and other organizations develop to inform their internal users about standards of computer and Internet behavior and the procedure for reporting violations

access time The time a storage device spends locating a particular file

active desktop An onscreen desktop that can contain icons linked to the Web

active-matrix display A type of monitor display in which separate transistors control each color pixel, allowing viewing from any angle

adapter (add-in, add-on) board An expansion board that can be installed on the motherboard to add capabilities to a computer.

address A specific location in memory where an instruction or data is stored. The computer assigns an address to each location so the instruction or data can be quickly located and retrieved when needed.

Advanced Research Projects Agency (ARPA) A government agency created by President Eisenhower to fund and coordinate defense-related research

aggregation software E-commerce software application that combines online activities to provide one-stop shopping for consumers

algorithm A series of precise steps to solve a given programming problem

alphanumeric Containing letters and numbers; may contain special characters

alphanumeric check A check made by database input forms to make sure that the value entered into a field is either letters or numbers, only

alpha product A prototype of software under development that the development team uses for testing purposes

American Standard Code for Information Interchange (ASCII) A coding scheme used on most computers, including personal computers, to represent data. ASCII makes it possible for data in this form to be transferred from one computer to another computer.

amplifier (repeater) An electronic device that receives signals along a network, amplifies the signals, and resends them along the network

analog Continuous, not broken into bits; said of telephone signals, sound waves, temperatures, and all other signals that are not discrete

analog signals Signals composed of continuous waves transmitted at a certain frequency range over a medium, such as a telephone line

android A term used to describe a robot designed to seem human

anti-aliasing The process of progressively lightening or darkening pixels along the edge of an image to produce the effect of a smooth edge

antivirus program A software program for personal computers that seeks out and destroys any viruses found on a computer. To keep up with the proliferation of new computer viruses, antivirus programs need to be constantly updated.

applet A small application program, generally one created using the Java programming language, that performs specific functions; applets are used to extend the capabilities of Web pages

application developer A person whose job is to adapt software for use within a new system

application development The use of commercial software to develop an information system for a specific organization

application service provider (ASP) A private company that leases applications software to customers over the Internet

application software Programs that enable a user to perform specific tasks. Examples of application software include word processors, database programs, spreadsheets, and desktop publishing.

applied ethics The application of normative ethical beliefs to controversial real-life issues

arithmetic/logic unit (ALU) The part of the CPU that carries out the instructions and performs the actual arithmetic and logical operations on the data. Arithmetic operations the ALU can perform are addition, subtraction, multiplication, and division. The ALU can also compare data items.

ARPANet A wide area network (WAN) created in 1969 that enabled research institutes and universities engaged in government research projects to collaborate by sharing information

artificial intelligence (AI) The science of using computers to simulate intelligent mental activities or physical behaviors such as problem solving, learning, and natural language processing

ASCII A coding scheme used on many personal computers and on various midrange servers

assembly language A low-level programming language that is derived directly from the binary instructions (machine language) understood by the CPU

asynchronous transmission A data transmission method in which control bits surround each byte of data. An extra bit, called a start bit, is added at the front of the character to signal its beginning and another bit, the stop bit, is added at the end of the character to indicate its end. There is also the errorchecking bit called a parity bit.

attribute The term for a field in a relational database

audio data Relating to sound, including speech and music

audio input The process of entering (recording) speech, music, and/or sound effects into a computer

audio mail Sound attachments that can be sent with e-mails

audio perception The capability of a computer system to hear sounds in its environment and to understand what it is hearing. Speech recognition is one example of this technology.

authentication The process of identifying an individual based on a username and password

automated clearinghouse An automated entity established for the purpose of transferring funds electronically from one account to another account

avatar An on-screen persona or a virtual body given to a player in a game in order to create a virtual reality

AVI (.avi) A Windows movie media format

B

B2B broker A business that assists other businesses by searching for, and locating, products and vendors

B2B infomediary (information intermediary) An e-commerce business that sets up an electronic hub using the same interface, protocols, and other technologies as other e-commerce buyers and sellers in a particular industry. The hub provides both buyers and sellers with special services, such as allowing sellers to find buyers.

B2B service A type of business organization that provides services to businesses over the Internet

B2B vendor A business that uses electronic commerce to sell products to customers. An example is an automotive parts manufacturer that produces and sells (vends) auto parts and components to automobile companies, such as Ford Motor Company and General Motors Corporation.

back end The database management system (DBMS), the software that manipulates and manages a database.

backup A second copy kept of valuable data

backup and recovery A key part of database management that makes sure data is backed up and recoverable in case power interruptions or equipment failure causes data loss

backup utility Software that allows the user to make copies of the contents of disks or tapes

backward compatibility Being able to work with earlier versions of a program or earlier models of computers

bandwidth The number of bits that can be transferred per second over a given medium in a network

banner A type of advertisement that takes up an approximately one-inch high slice of a Web page. Clicking on the banner activates a link to a vendor's site.

bar code reader An electronic device that uses photo technology to read the lines in a bar code. The lines and spaces contain symbols that the computer translates into information.

baseband A type of coaxial cable about 3/8 inch thick having a single channel for transmitting digital signals at about 10 mbps and often used in computer networks

BASIC A programming language designed in the 1960s as a learning language for new programmers

basic input/output system (BIOS) A program that boots (starts) a computer when it is turned on and controls communications with the keyboard, disk drives, and other components

batch-processing The accumulating of a large amount of data to process at once, rather than doing it immediately, as requests come into the system

bay A site within the system unit where a device, such as a floppy disk drive, hard disk drive, or CD-ROM drive is installed

beta-testing One of the last steps in software development that involves allowing outside people to use the software to see if it works as designed

beta version A prerelease version of a piece of software distributed so that users can test it to evaluate features and to identify any existing bugs

bezier curve A straight line or curve that is described by its tangents; programs using bezier curves make it possible to create curved lines, to join them together, and to modify the curvature of lines

binary number Base 2 numbers written as strings of 1s and 0s

binary strings Sequences of binary symbols

binary system A number system with a base of 2. Unlike the familiar base 10 decimal system, the binary system uses only two numbers (0 and 1).

biometric device A device that measures some unique feature of the human anatomy, or a human behavioral trait, that can be used to identify or distinguish individuals

biometric identifier An identifiable physical or behavioral trait that can be measured by a biometric device and used to identify individual people

biotechnology The application of computer processing or technical processes to the science of living organisms

bit (binary digit) The smallest unit of data a computer can understand and act on

bit depth The number of bits used in a graphics expansion board to store information about each pixel

bitmap A storage technique in which scanned text or a photo is stored as a matrix of rows and columns of dots

bitmap-based graphics A computerized process of displaying images in which the program treats the image as a large collection of pixels, each of which is stored in its own location; the image is created by specifying the color of each pixel

bits per second (bps) A measure of the number of bits (the fundamental digital unit, which can be either a 0 or a 1) that can be transmitted in a second's time; the usual measure of bandwidth

blind link A hyperlink that directs a Web browser to an unexpected result or location, such as a link that triggers an undesired download

blog Frequently updated journals, or logs, containing chronological entries of personal thoughts and Web links posted on a Web page

Bluetooth A technology that uses infrared light signals to send information

boot drive The disk drive that houses the operating system

booting The procedure for starting or restarting a computer

boot sector The sector of a floppy disk or hard disk containing information about how the disk is organized and whether it is capable of loading an operating system

boot sector virus A virus designed to alter the boot sector of a disk so that whenever the operating system reads the boot sector, the computer will automatically become infected

bridge Hardware and/or software that allows for communication between two networks that are *similar*

bring-your-own-access (BYOA) A developing trend in marketing Internet services where large portals such as AOL, MSN, and Yahoo! will combine essential content with services and then charge customers a monthly access fee.

broadband A type of coaxial cable having several channels, each of which can carry about 10 mbps and which is often used for cable television transmissions

broadband medium A communications medium capable of carrying a large amount of data at fast speeds

broadband modem (cable modem) A modem capable of handling fast transmission speeds

broker *See B2B broker.*

browser A software application that enables a person to access sites on the World Wide Web that may include an e-mail or newsgroup program

browsing (surfing) Accessing and moving about the Web using a browser

buffer A temporary storage place to which part of data to be displayed, printed, or transmitted is written

bug A term coined by Grace Hopper meaning any kind of computer error

bus A collection of tiny wires through which data, in the form of 0s and 1s, is transmitted from one part of the computer to another

bus bandwidth A term that refers to the amount of data (as 0s and 1s) that can travel along a bus (a tiny collection of wires) from one part of the computer to another

business-to-business electronic commerce (B2B) Buying and selling of products and services between businesses over the Internet

business-to-consumer electronic commerce (B2C) Buying and selling of products and services between sellers and customers over the Internet

bus topology A type of network layout in which all computers are linked by means of a single line of cable, called a bus, with two endpoints. All communications travel the length of the bus. As they pass, each computer checks to see if it is the assigned destination point.

bus width A measure of the size of a bus; determines the number of bits the computer can transmit or receive at one time

button A graphical element that, when selected with the mouse or keyboard, causes a particular action to occur within a software program

byte A combination of eight bits (0s and 1s) that represents a letter of the alphabet, a number, or a special character inside a computer. There are enough different combinations of bits (0s and 1s) in an eight-bit byte to represent 256 different characters.

C

C A programming language developed in the 1970s. Newer versions of C are used to write most of the software sold to the public.

C# A new version of the C++ programming language developed by Microsoft

C++ An object-oriented version of the C programming language developed in the 1980s

cable modem (broadband modem) A special type of modem that provides fast transmission speeds

cache memory A dedicated holding area in RAM in which the data and instructions most recently called from RAM by the processor are temporarily stored

Carnivore A controversial FBI program designed to target and monitor e-mail communications for illegal activity

carpal tunnel syndrome The condition of weakness, pain, or numbness resulting from pressure on the median nerve in the wrist; the syndrome is associated with repetitive motion, such as typing or using the mouse

CASE tools A set of software tools that aid in the project management of software development

cathode ray tube (CRT) monitor A large, sealed glass tube housed in a plastic case; the most common type of monitor for desktop computers

CD-burner (CD-writer) A device that uses lasers to record and read data to and from an optical disc

CD drive A drive that can read nearly any kind of data recorded on an optical disc, including text, graphics, video clips, and sound

CD-R (compact disc-recordable) A disc technology that allows a user to write data onto a compact disc. The disc can be written on only once, cannot be erased, but can be read from an unlimited number of times.

CD-ROM (compact disc-read-only memory) A disc technology in which data is permanently recorded on an optical disc and can be read many times, but the data cannot be changed

CD-RW (compact disc-rewritable) A newer type of optical disc storage technology that uses an erasable disc on which a user can write multiple times

cell In a spreadsheet, the intersection of one row and one column into which text, numbers, formulas, links, or other elements may be entered

cellular technology An increasingly popular technology that allows people to communicate without having to be connected via wired phone lines or cables. Using cellular technologies, communication can occur between people almost anywhere in the world

central processing unit (CPU) The part of a computer that interprets and carries out instructions that operate the computer and manages the computer's devices and resources. The CPU consists of components, each of which performs specific functions.

certificate program Intensive education course offered primarily by large IT companies such as Microsoft and Cisco, intended to train an individual for a particular job working with a specific type of product

CG FX (computer graphic special effects) special effects created for movies with computer graphics

chart A visual representation of data that often makes the data easier to read and understand. A chart displays data in graphical rather than numerical form.

charting Preparing a visual representation of data, particularly numerical information, to make the data easier to understand

chat room (chat group) An online area, provided by an online service or an Internet host, where people can meet, exchange ideas and information, and interact socially

check box A box containing multiple options you can turn on or off. You can activate a particular option in the box by clicking on the option. When an option is activated, a check mark appears beside the option. Unlike option buttons where you can select only one option, check boxes allow you to choose multiple options.

chip A thin wafer of silicon containing electronic circuitry that performs various functions, such as mathematical calculations, storage, or controlling computer devices

ciphertext Unreadable, coded information produced by the process of encryption from a user's personal or financial information. Ciphertext ensures that consumers' privacy rights will not be violated when they enter personal data to complete online transactions.

client A smaller computer, terminal, or workstation capable of sending data to and from a larger computer (host computer) in a network

client/server architecture A type of network architecture in which a personal computer, workstation, or terminal (called a *client*) is used to send information or a request to another computer (called a *server*) which then relays the information back to the user's client computer, or to another computer (another *client*)

clip art Professionally designed graphic images sold for use in word processing and other types of documents; collections are sometimes included in a software program.

clock cycle The time between two ticks of a computer's system clock. A typical personal computer goes through millions or even billions of clock cycles per second.

clock speed The pace of the microprocessor's internal clock, which determines how fast operations are processed within the CPU; clock speed is measured in megahertz (MHz).

closed system A hardware or software system that must be serviced and supported by the original vendor

closed system architecture A system, either hardware or software, with a design that does not easily allow other companies to build additions to the system

cluster A group of two or more sectors on a disk which is the smallest unit of storage space used to store data

coaxial cable A type of wire that consists of an insulated center wire and grounded by a shield of braided wire

COBOL A business application-oriented programming language developed in the 1960s

coding A term used by programmers to refer to the act of writing source code

cognitive science A broad discipline dedicated to the study of the human mind

cold boot Process of starting a computer by turning on the unit's power switch

collaborative commerce Joint planning among companies to create common objectives, such as mutual sales or operational goals. It allows a business realtime access to information about partner firms' inventories, product designs, and work schedules.

command-line interface A user interface, like the one created by the DOS operating system, that makes use of typed commands

comments Notes written by programmers in the source code of their programs. Comments help later readers comprehend the meaning of the program.

commercial software Programs created and sold to the public on a retail basis by software developers such as Microsoft, Sun Microsystems, and Corel

Common Gateway Interface (CGI) script A programming language used on Web sites to allow the tracking of traffic and the production of dynamic Web pages

communications device A device that makes it possible for a user to communicate with another computer and to exchange instructions, data, and information with other computer users

communications medium A medium, such a telephone line, used for carrying data or information between computers and networks

communications satellite A solar-powered electronic device that contains a number of small, specialized radios called *transponders* that receive signals from transmission stations on the ground called *earth stations*, amplifies the signals, and then transmits the signals to the appropriate locations

communications software Software that allows your properly equipped computer to communicate with other similarly equipped computers. You can send and receive electronic messages, visit various Web sites, locate and retrieve information stored on other computers, electronically transmit large files, and much more.

compact disc A plastic disc 4.75 inches in diameter and about 1/20 of an inch thick; information and data are stored on compact discs through laser technologies

compiler A type of language-translating software that translates an entire program into machine language before the program will run

completeness check A database accuracy element that requires every field to be filled in completely

computer An electronic device capable of interpreting and executing program instructions and data and performing the required operations to produce the desired results

computer-aided design (CAD) software A sophisticated kind of productivity software providing tools that enable professionals to create architectural, engineering, product, and scientific designs

computer-aided manufacturing (CAM) A computer information system that directly manages factory production

computer codes of ethics Standards for ethical use of computers put forward by computer professional organizations

computer engineering Area of study focusing on hardware design

computer ethics The adapting of traditional ethical thought and behavior to issues involving computers and computer technology. Computer Ethics is a newly formed branch of Applied Ethics.

computer graphics special effects (CG FX) Techniques used to make computer animated movies and special effects

computer information systems (CIS) An educational degree or area of study that is application-oriented, requiring both business and computer science courses. Students learn programming, usually aimed at application development with existing software products rather than the creation of new software products.

computer-integrated manufacturing (CIM) A computer information system that manages production and connects the factory floor to every level of management

computerized facial recognition (CFR) A computer system capable of comparing facial images to a database of known individuals and recognizing people

computer programmer Person whose profession is to write sets of coded instructions that direct a computer's operations

computer science Area of study focusing on writing, or programming, new software

computer system System unit along with input devices, output devices, and storage devices

computer virus A bit of programming code, created as a prank or as a malicious action, that secretly affects other programs and causes unintended consequences

concentrator A communications device that enables data to be transmitted from only one device at a time over a communications medium

connectivity Refers to the ability to link with other programs and devices

consistency check A database check that ensures data is accurate by checking it against known data

consultant An individual or a company with highly skilled IT workers that completes projects for other organizations

consumer profiles A set of information about customers' lifestyle and buying habits that marketers use to more effectively target and sell their goods

context sensitive Capable of "sensing" the user's needs based on what the user is doing; said of software

control unit The part of the CPU that directs and coordinates the overall operation of the computer system. It interprets each program instruction in a program, and then initiates the action needed to carry out the instruction.

conversation speech biometrics A technology developed by IBM capable of recognizing a person's voice even though the database may not include the exact words spoken

cookies Small programs placed on a computer's hard drive by Web sites. Cookies can remember passwords and User IDs, avoiding the necessity of having to enter this data each time the site containing the cookie is visited.

coprocessor A special type of dedicated processor designed to perform certain kinds of processing, such as processing large amounts of numerical data

copyright The legal protection of an individual's or business's original work, such as applications software, music, and books, that prohibits others from duplicating or illegally using such work or products. An artist or author whose work is copyrighted has the right to charge others for its use.

corrupted file A file that has been scrambled so the data is unreadable. Accidents involving power loss, viruses, or poor software design can cause corruption of files

crack The altering of a software product to remove copy protection

crackers A term coined by computer hackers for those who intentionally enter into (or hack) computer systems to damage them

crash The halting or shutting down of a program due to a major error

crash bug A run-time error that causes a program to stop running, or crash

creating The development of a document, such as a letter or memo, by entering text and numbers, inserting graphical images, and performing other actions using one or more input devices, such as a keyboard or mouse

credit account A customer's promise to pay for online purchases upon receipt of a periodic statement from the seller. When online purchases are made, each purchase is charged to the customer's credit account.

crossovers The result of combining the most successful variations (mutations) of potential design solutions into a new design; the new design is called a crossover

cross-platform compatibility The capacity of a software package to run on more than one operating system/type of computer

cross-platform operating system An operating system capable of being used on more than one type of computer

customer relationship management (CRM) This term refers to all aspects of interaction a company has with its customers and suppliers. Such software can help companies keep track of customers, develop detailed consumer profiles, and offer customers just the products they want to buy.

customized software See customized program.

custom program (customized software) A specialized software program written by a programmer to meet a company's special requirements

cyberspace A term used to describe the virtual environment of the Internet

cyber war Attacks by groups of international hackers against sites in a competing country

D

data Raw, unprocessed information

database A computer application in which data is organized and stored in a way that allows for specific data to be accessed, retrieved, and used

database administration A combination of application development, technical support, and technical training; includes maintaining and fixing databases

database administrator A critical job that involves the continuous management of a database management system (DBMS)

database file A collection of related records

database key A single field that can be used to search for a given record

database maintenance The constant requirement for altering and amending masses of data contained in a database

database management approach A procedure for the development of databases

database management system (DBMS) Software that allows a user to create and manage a computerized database, and to create reports from stored data

database object An element within an object-oriented database, such as a report or a table

database response time The length of time it takes a database to respond to a request from a user; a critical measurement in rating the performance of any database

database server A computer that stores data in a database and provides authorized users with access to information in a database

data browsing The process of moving through a database file, examining each record and looking for information

data communications specialist A computer professional responsible for developing, implementing, and maintaining computer networks

data compression A process of shrinking the storage size of a body of data, usually stored as a disk file. Data compression techniques work by removing redundant information.

data contamination The spread of incorrect information throughout a database and into other databases, diminishing the usefulness of the systems

data corruption The process of data becoming unreadable, incomplete, or damaged

data-destructive virus A virus designed to destroy data either by erasing or corrupting files so that they are unreadable or by formatting the entire drive so it is blank

data dictionary A descriptive listing of all the data values in an Information system

Data Encryption Standard (DES) A secret key encryption system used by the United States government to protect sensitive information transmitted over the Internet

data entry operator A person whose job it is to keep the information in a database current and accurate

data filter A condition that narrows down a large list of records

data integrity A measurement of database correctness and validity

data mining A technique used by programmers to collate and extract meaningful data from a data warehouse. Data mining software allows data warehouse users to see as much data detail or summarization as they need to aid them in making decisions.

data model Defines the structure of information to be contained in a database, how the database will use the information, and how the different items in the database relate to each other

data modeling A practice often used in Decision Support Systems and other forms of IS to represent a scenario and allow for "what-if" type analysis of various management options

data processing (information processing) The actions performed through transactions with a database

data register A reserved location in main memory for storing data being processed or being used in a specific processing application

data transfer rate The speed at which data is transferred from memory or from a storage device to the CPU

data validation A strict process that ensures the entry of valid data into a database

data warehouse A collection of related databases that have been stored together so that needed data can be retrieved, analyzed, and readily available for decisionmaking

dead code Any source code within the final version of a released software product that is "commented out" and therefore not part of the actual working program

debugger A utility that help a programmer remove errors from software

decision statement The decision points in a program and the different actions that can be performed depending on conditions

decision support system (DSS) An information system designed to model possible future outcomes and thus aid in the decision-making process of corporate management

decoding The activity of translating or determining the meaning of coded instructions

dedicated server A server that performs one or more specific functions

default option An option that has been programmed into a program by the software publisher under the assumption that that option is the one most likely to be chosen

defragmenting The process used by a defragmenter utility to reorganize files and unused disk space allowing the operating system to locate and access stored files and data more quickly

deliverable A document, service, hardware component, or software program that must be finished and delivered by a certain time and date in order to keep a project on schedule

denial of service (DS) attack A form of online attack, usually performed by hackers, in which a Web site is brought down by overloading it with false requests for data

design specification A document specifically states how a program development project will be completed

desktop A screen on which graphical elements such as icons, buttons, windows, links, and dialog boxes are displayed

desktop computer A personal computer system designed to fit on the top of a desk

desktop publishing (DTP) software A type of software that enables a user to produce documents that closely resemble those done by printing companies

development service providers (DSPs) Online software development packages that allow software developers in geographically separate locations to work together on the same software

dexterity Hand-eye coordination

diagnostic utility A utility program that assesses a computer's components and system software programs and creates a report identifying problems

dialog box An element in a graphical user interface that displays a rectangular box providing information to a user and/or requesting

information from a user. Usually, a dialog box is displayed temporarily and disappears once the user has entered the requested information.

dial-up access A method for accessing the Internet in which a user can connect to the Internet using a computer and a modem to dial into an ISP or online service over a standard telephone line

dial-up modem A modem (electronic device) that converts digital signals into analog form so they can be sent using an analog communication medium

dictionary A reference work containing an alphabetical listing of words with definitions plus the word's meaning, pronunciation, and usage

digital Composed of discrete bits (1s and 0s) understood by computers

digital cable A technology capable of offering a wide selection of television stations, typically more than 200, with the capability of expanding to 2,000 stations

digital camera A type of camera that record and store images, including people, scenery, documents, and products in a digitized form that can be entered into and stored by a computer

digital cash A system that allows a customer to pay for online purchases by transmitting a number from one computer to another computer. Issued by a bank, each digital cash number represents a specified amount of real money.

digital divide A term created to describe the gap between those who have access to computers and the Internet and those who do not

digital ink technology Process in which a digitizer (a grid of tiny wires) is laid under or over an LCD screen to create a magnetic field that can capture the movement of a special-purpose pen and record the movement on the LCD screen; the effect is like writing on paper with liquid ink

digital media A digital transmitting, receiving, or other form of media

Digital Millenium Copyright Act of 1998 Legislation updating copyright protection to bring it in line with the technical changes brought about by computer technology. This law generally prohibits people from taking action to break down software encryption programs and other safeguards that copyright holders have established to control access to their works, including DVDs, software, and digitized books and music.

digital signal An electrical current representing a 1 or 0 in a computer

digital signature A code attached to an online transaction that uniquely identifies the sender

Digital Subscriber Line (DSL) A high-speed Internet connection

digitizing The process of converting analog information to digital information

digitizing pen An electronic pen device, resembling a standard writing pen, used with a drawing tablet to simulate drawing on paper

direct access A storage technique that allows a computer to immediately locate and retrieve a program, information, or data similar to the way music stored on a CD-ROM can accessed

directory A special kind of file that allows other files to be grouped together logically

directory tree A structure maintained by the operating system that organizes disk files into a hierarchy of folders (directories)

disaster recovery plan A safety system that allows a company to restore its systems after a complete loss of data; generally includes procedures for data backup, remotelystored backup copies, and redundant systems

disk defragmenter A utility program that scans hard or floppy disks and reorganizes files and unused disk space, allowing the operating system to locate and access files and data more quickly

disk drive A storage device that houses a secondary storage medium such as a floppy or hard disk

disk pack A vertically aligned group of hard disks mounted inside a disk drive on a large computer system. When activated, electromagnetic read/write heads record information and/or read stored data by moving inward and outward between the disks.

disk scanner A utility that examines hard or floppy disks and their contents to identify potential problems, such as bad sectors

disk server A type of server that enables users to access programs, data, and other resources just as easily as if the resources were stored on their individual user computers

disk toolkit Software that contains utilities programs that let users identify and correct various problems on a hard or floppy disk

display device The screen, or monitor, of a personal computer

display goggles A type of monitor presently used for computer games that may become a standard feature of some of the new mobile computer devices such as belt-top computers or other systems worn on the body

display window A rectangular area of the screen used to display a program, data, or information

distance learning The electronic transfer of information from a college or publisher's host computer system to a student's computer at a remote site and the transmission of required responses from the student's computer to the host computer system. A course presented in this manner is called an *online course.*

distributed computing (grid computing) model The next generation of software as services; also the shared processing of a computing project among several computers, particularly on the Web

distributed database A relatively new type of database model where databases function in a networked environment, with each computer storing a portion of the total amount of data in the network

distribution management systems A common application of information systems involving the transportation of goods from the manufacturer to the customer

divide-and-conquer approach A methodology for software development that breaks down large problems into small ones

DNA sequence An arrangement of nucleic acids within a DNA (deoxyribonucleic acid) molecule.

docking station A laptop computer accessory that provides additional ports plus (typically) a charger for the laptop's battery, extra disk drives, and other peripherals

documentation Any written manual, specification or commentary upon a computer system

document object model (DOM) A newer version of HTML that allows object-oriented Web page development

domain name A portion of an Internet address, such as .com or .edu, that is used to segment Internet addresses into broad categories

domain suffix The part of a URL that comes last and identifies the type of organization

dot-com companies A term used to describe Web-based e-commerce companies with Web sites in the .com domain

dot-matrix printer An impact printer that forms and prints characters in a manner similar to the way numbers appear on a football scoreboard

dot pitch The distance between the centers of pixels on a display

dots per inch (dpi) A measurement in which resolution (text and image quality) is expressed as the number of dots occupying one square inch

Double Data Rate SDRAM (DDR SDRAM) A type of RAM chip that can transfer data twice as fast as SDRAM because it reads twice as much data during each clock cycle

download To transmit data, such as a digitized text file, sound, or picture, from a remote site to one's own computer via a network

downtime Time in which the system is unavailable

draft quality A print quality acceptable for most inhouse needs, but not for professional-looking documents

drawing program Software that enables a user to create images that can be easily modified by providing an intuitive interface through which a user can draw pictures, make sketches, crate various shapes, and edit images

drawing tablet A tablet with wires under the surface that, when used with a digitizing pen, allows the user to create and capture drawings that can be entered and stored on a computer

driver A small program that enables the computer to communicate with devices connected to it, such as a keyboard or a printer

dual-scan display A type of display in which a single transistor controls an entire column or row of the display's tiny electrodes

dumb scanner A scanner that can only capture and input a scanned image. Once entered into a computer, the image cannot be edited or altered

dumb terminal A terminal that has no processor of its own and that is used for input and output, often to and from a mainframe or minicomputer

DVD (digital versatile disc) A type of optical disc, available in a variety of formats

DVD-R (digital versatile disc-recordable) Can be recorded only one time

DVD-ROM (digital versatile disc-read-only memory) An extremely high capacity disc capable of holding several gigabytes of data, such as a movie or the entire contents of a telephone book listing every resident in the United States.

DVD-RW (digital versatile disc-rewritable) Allows recorded data to be erased and recorded over numerous times without damaging the disc

dwell time The amount of time a given key is depressed during a keystroke

Dynamic HTML (DHTML) A general term used to describe a variety of new features in HTML programming that allow for more responsive, graphically interesting Web page development

Dynamic RAM (DRAM) A type of RAM chip that eventually loses its contents without a continuous supply of electrical energy

dynamic routing A capability of the Internet to send a given packet via a different route depending on traffic circumstances

E

earth stations Transmission stations on the ground

EBCDIC A coding scheme used mainly on large servers and mainframe computers

editing The process of altering the content or format of an existing document

educational and reference software Programs that facilitate learning, such as software designed to enable a user to learn algebra, or that provide reference information, such as encyclopedias and dictionaries

efficiency The allocation of resources required to achieve specific organizational goals

electronic bulletin board system (BBS) An Internet application consisting of an electronically stored list of messages that can be accessed and read by anyone having access to the bulletin board. A user having access can post messages, read existing messages, or delete messages.

electronic chip A small electrical device consisting of tiny transistors and other circuit parts on a pierce of semiconductor material; also called integrated circuit

electronic commerce (e-commerce) A set of business Internet technologies in which business information, products, services, and payments are exchanged between sellers and customers and between businesses

electronic commerce venue A Web site where ecommerce transactions occur. The Web provides a variety of venues that allow visitors to move from place to place to search for, find, purchase, and pay for information, products, and services.

electronic data interchange (EDI) Companies' use of computer networks to buy, sell, or otherwise exchange information with each other electronically

electronic data processing (EDP) An old term for an information system

electronic funds transfer (EFT) A general term for the transfer of money over the Internet

electronic mail (e-mail) A text, voice, or video message sent or received remotely, over a computer network or the system by which such a message is sent

electronic office Another name for an OIS (office information system)

electronic signature (digital signature, e-signature) A code attached to an e-mail that uniquely identifies the sender of the message

electronic spreadsheet A productivity program that provides a user with a means of organizing, calculating, and presenting financial, statistical, and other numeric information. Spreadsheets are used to manipulate numbers electronically instead of using a pencil and paper.

electronic wallet (e-wallet) A software application that stores a user's personal, credit card, and shipping information. The application may store one set of user information or multiple sets that allow a user to choose which credit card or shipping information will apply to a certain purchase.

e-mail attachment A file that is associated with a text e-mail message

e-mail software Software that allows a user to create, send, receive, print, store, forward, and delete e-mail messages and to attach files to messages being sent

e-mail virus A virus transmitted to victims via an email attachment

embedded computer A specialized computer, usually housed on a single chip, that is part of a larger system, device, or machine

encryption The process of converting readable information, or plaintext, into unreadable information, or ciphertext, to prevent unauthorized access and usage

encryption key A special type of encryption code used to encrypt (encode) information being transmitted over the Internet

encyclopedia A comprehensive reference work containing detailed articles on a broad range of subjects

entertainment software Programs that provide fun as well as challenges; includes interactive computer games, videos, and music

entity A person, place, thing, or event in a database

ergonomics The study of the interaction between humans and the equipment they use

espionage virus A virus that does no damage, but allows someone to enter the system later for the purpose of stealing data or spying on the work of a competitor

e-tailer An individual or company that carries out business-to-consumer e-commerce over the Web

Ethernet A bus topology type used by many local area networks

ethics Rules we use to determine the right and wrong things to do in our lives

executable statement A statement within a program that, when run by the program, performs an action

executing The CPU process of performing an operation specified in a program instruction

execution time (E-time) The time required for the arithmetic/logic unit to decode and execute an instruction

executive support system (ESS) An information system tailored to the needs of upper management

expansion board (add-on board or add-in board) An electronic circuit board that can be inserted onto the motherboard inside a computer to add new capabilities to a computer. Examples include sound boards, video boards, graphics boards, and boards that allow you to capture and enter photos into your computer.

expansion bus A motherboard component that provides for communication between the processor and peripheral devices

expansion slot An opening in a computer motherboard where an expansion board can be inserted (installed)

expert system An information system that uses artificial Intelligence (AI) techniques to simulate the judgment of a human professional

expert system shell A type of artificial intelligence

exporting Saving a data file with a different file format

Extended Binary Coded Decimal Interchange Code (EBCDIC) A coding scheme used mainly on mainframe computers

Extensible HTML (XHTML) An improvement on the HTML scripting language that allows Web designers to use HTML and XML together in programming Web pages

Extensible Markup Language (XML) An improved Web language that not only defines the content of a Web page but also organizes data so that computers can communicate with each other directly, without human intervention

external modem A modem that works in the same fashion as an internal modem, but is a stand-alone device connected by cable to a computer's motherboard

extranet A network that makes certain kinds of information available to users within the organization and other kinds of information available to outsiders, such as companies doing business with the organization

F

facial geometry A biometric identifier that uses the structure of a person's face to recognize individuals

facial recognition technology *See computerized facial recognition.*

facial thermography A biometric identifier that uses the arrangement of capillaries in person's face to recognize individuals

facsimile (fax) machine An electronic device that can send and receive copies (facsimiles, or faxes) of documents through a telephone line

fair use The right by law to use copyrighted materials under certain conditions

fax An electronic document that is transmitted or received over a telephone line using a fax machine or fax/modem board

fax/modem board An add-on board that serves as a modem and provides many of the features of a standalone fax machine

fax program Software needed to send and receive a fax; allows users to compose, send, receive, print, and store faxes

feasibility study A study conducted to investigate how difficult a project might be to complete and how much it might cost

fetching The CPU process of retrieving instructions or data from memory for execution

Fiber Distributed Data Interface (FDDI) A type of network software for ring networks dispersed over a large area and connected by fiber optic cables. The software links the dispersed networks together using a protocol that passes a token over long distances.

fiber-optic cable A cable consisting of optical fibers that allows data to be transmitted as light signals through tiny hair-like glass fibers

field In a table created by a database management system application, a column into which one kind of information about an entity, such as name or address, is entered

file A named body of data that resides on a storage medium

file allocation table (FAT) A section of a disk that keeps track of the disk's contents

file compression The process of shrinking the size of a file so it occupies less disk space

file compression program A utility program that greatly reduces the size of a file, and thus, the space needed to store or transmit the file

file extension A period (.) and a set of characters following a file name which identifies the type of file

file manager An operating system function that performs basic file management functions, including keeping track of used and unused disk storage space and allowing a user to view stored files and to format, copy, rename, delete, and sort stored files

file processing Manipulation of the data within a database

file server A special type of computer that allows other computers to share its resources

file specification An optional additional element in a URL that indicates the name of a file or file folder. It is typed after the domain suffix.

File Transfer Protocol (FTP) A transmission standard that enables a user to send and receive large files, such as reports, over the Internet

filtering programs Software that can prevent access to sites, keep track of sites visited, limit connection time, record keystrokes, prevent downloading, and allow users to view only those sites that have been accessed

financial electronic data interchange (FEDI) A form of EDI technology used to transmit payments and associated remittance information electronically among a payer, payee, and their respective banks.

find A software program feature that allows a user to quickly locate a number or a particular type of text within a file

fingerprint scanner A biometric device that reads, records, and recognizes fingerprints

firewall Software and hardware systems that place an invisible wall around the internal network, protecting it from unauthorized material from the Internet

flaming The act of transmitting negative comments to someone via the Internet

Flash A commonly used format for online downloadable movies

flash memory (flash ROM) A type of read-only memory that can quickly be erased and reprogrammed, or updated

flat file Traditional data file storage system that lacks the ability to interrelate data in an organizational structure because it contains only one table or file

flat-panel display A type of computer monitor that allows display units to be smaller, thinner, and lighter so they can be used with small computers, such as notebook computers, personal digital assistants (PDAs), and other devices

flight time The amount of time between keystrokes

floppy disk (diskette or **disk)** A secondary storage medium consisting of a thin, circular mylar wafer, sandwiched between two sheets of cleaning tissue inside a rigid plastic case

floppy disk drive A secondary storage device capable of recording information to, and reading information from, a small disk placed inside the device

flowchart A graphic representation of a programming algorithm

footer In word processing, a line or more of repeated text such as a page number and a document's title that appears at the bottom of the document's pages

foot mouse A foot-controlled mouse that allows a user with carpal tunnel syndrome or other hand or wrist injuries to use a computer

form In a database management system, a document used for entering information to be stored in one or more linked records

format (noun) The appearance of a document, for example, page margins, the spacing between lines, and text alignment between the margins; (verb) to change the appearance of a document

formatting The procedure of preparing a disk for use during which the disk surface is arranged into tracks, sectors, and clusters

formula Any mathematical equation or an equation entered into a cell in a spreadsheet or database

FORTRAN A programming language developed in the 1960s and used primarily for the solving of math and science problems

frame A single still image. Many frames, shown together in rapid succession, create the illusion of movement we call a movie

frame rate The number of frames that a system is capable of producing and displaying per second. If this number falls much below 20 frames per second, video begins to appear choppy.

freehand tool A tool in a drawing program that allows users to draw an irregular line on the screen that is then automatically transformed into adjustable bezier curves

free market A competitive market that allows individuals, businesses, and organizations to freely make decisions and engage in practices affecting their success or failure

freeware A computer program that is provided free to users by its creator but for which the creator usually retains the copyright

frequency range A span of changes reflected in the transmission of voice or sound signals

front end The interface program of a database, through which the user enters data and requests information

full-duplex transmission The simultaneous transmission of information of data in both directions at the same time

functional specification A document that describes what an information system must do, but not exactly how it is supposed to do it

fuzzy logic An artificial intelligence term that relates to the use of inexact conditions and criteria. Most logic requires exact information to operate.

G

Gantt chart A chart that identifies critical steps in the completion of a system development project

garbage in—garbage out (GIGO) A database related proverb meaning that if errors are entered into a database, it will produce erroneous output; also refers to all situations involving incorrect user input into a computer

gateway Hardware and/or software that allows communication between *dissimilar* networks

general-purpose computer A computer that allows the user to perform a range of complex processes and calculations

genetic algorithm An artificial intelligence design concept that uses tiny, evolutionary changes to solve a problem by trying many solutions, testing them, and selecting the best, then trying more variations of the best survivors of each successive generation

geosynchronous orbit The path of a satellite orbiting the earth at the same speed as the earth's rotation, making the satellite appear stationary when viewed from the ground

GIF (.gif) files A file format that provides compressed bitmap images. Gif files are capable of limited animation.

gigabyte Unit of memory equal to 1,073,741,824 bytes

gigahertz A frequency of one billion times a second

global economy A term for an economic system in which companies can sell their goods and compete for customers throughout the world

Global Unique Identifier (GUID) An Internet tracking device using unique identification numbers that can be coded into both hardware and software

grammar checker A part of a program or a standalone application that automatically searches for errors in grammar, usage, capitalization, or punctuation and suggests correct alternatives

graphic (graphical image) Computer-generated picture produced on a computer screen, paper, or film, ranging from a simple line or bar chart to a detailed and colorful image or picture

graphical user interface (GUI) A computer interface that enables a user to control the computer and launch commands by pointing and clicking at graphical objects such as windows, icons, and menu items

graphics adapter Converts digital signals into text that is immediately displayed on the monitor screen

graphics board An add-on electronic board or card designed specifically for handling image-intensive applications, such as Web pages and computer-aided design programs

graphics card An add-on card that enables a computer to capture and display graphical images

graphics coprocessor A chip designed specifically for processing image-intensive applications, such as Web pages and computer-aided design programs

graphics data Still images, including photographs, mathematical charts, and drawings

graphics-intensive A term describing applications that use most of the CPU power to draw images on the screen

graphics tablet A flat tablet used together with a penlike stylus or a crosshair cursor. To capture an image, the user grasps a stylus or crosshair cursor and traces an image or drawing placed on the tablet surface.

grid A matrix formed by the intersections of rows and columns, as in a spreadsheet

groupware Communications software that allows groups of people on a network to share information and to collaborate on various projects, such as designing a new product or preparing employee manuals

H

hacker An individual who attempts to break into computer security systems

hacking code Writing code without carefully planning and structuring the program

half-duplex transmission A transmission method in which transmissions can flow in both directions but not at the same time

hand geometry A type of biometric identifier based on the shape of one's hand

hand geometry system A biometric device that recognizes individuals based on the structure of their hands

handheld computer A personal computer small enough to fit into a person's hand

handheld scanner A small scanner used for scanning small or curved areas

hard copy A permanent version of output, such as a letter printed on paper

hard disk A secondary storage medium consisting of one or more rigid metal platters (disks) mounted on a metal shaft and sealed in a container, called a disk drive, that contains an access mechanism used to write and read data

hard drive A device for reading and writing to the magnetic storage medium known as a hard disk; consists of one or more rigid metal platters (disks) mounted on a metal shaft in a container that contains an access mechanism

hardware All physical components that comprise the system unit and other devices connected to it, such as a keyboard or monitor. These external connected devices are collectively referred to as *peripheral devices* because they are outside, or peripheral to, the computer itself.

hardware design The specification of computer hardware such as CPUs, video cards, and memory chips; as a career, it is part electrical engineering and part programming and requires advanced skills

hardware-destructive virus A very rare form of virus capable of damaging specific hardware through excessive misuse

header In word processing, a line or more of repeated text such as a page number and a document's title that appears at the top of the document's pages

hertz A unit of measure that refers to the number of cycles per second

High-Capacity FD (HiFD) disk drive A type of floppy disk drive capable of holding large amounts of data

high-definition television (HDTV) A newer type of television technology that uses digital signals instead of analog signals to display high-quality pictures on the screen

high-level language An English-like computer language used for writing application programs

home page The first page usually displayed when a user accesses a Web site. A home page often contains links to other pages at that site or to other Web sites

host (or host computer) A large-capacity computer to which other computers are connected in a network

hot plugging The procedure of disconnecting one device and connecting another device to a computer while the computer is still running

hot swapping The capability of switching back and forth among various types of PCMCIA cards while a notebook or similar computer is running

hub An electronic device used in a local area network that links groups of computers to one another and allows computers to communicate with one another. A hub coordinates the traffic of messages being sent and received by computers connected to the network.

hybrid A type of database that combines more than one data model

hybrid topology A combination of networks having different topologies, such as a star network and a ring network

hyperlink (link) An address that links to a document or to a Web page

hypertext document A Web document created using a Web language, such as HTML or XML, that contains one or more hyperlinks (links) to other Web documents or sites

Hypertext Markup Language (HTML) A set of codes used to create pages for the World Wide Web; codes specify typefaces, images, and links within text.

Hypertext Transfer Protocol (HTTP) The communications standard used to transfer documents on the World Wide Web

I

IBM OS/2 A graphical user interface operating system developed by IBM that can run application programs native to it and also application programs written for DOS and Windows systems

icon A graphic symbol that represents a software program, a command, or a feature

identify theft The stealing of an individual's personal information, such as social security number and credit card numbers, via hacking into a database on the Internet

if-then statement A decision statement in a programming language that decides upon two or more possible courses of action

IM *See instant messaging.*

image-editing program Software that allows a user to touch up, modify, and enhance image quality

immersiveness A virtual reality term that is a measurement of how convincing a virtual environment is, how "immersed" the user feels in the environment

impact printer A printer that prints much like a typewriter, by striking an inked ribbon against the paper

implementation The phase of a project in which the actual work of putting the system together is done, including creating a prototype and completing the programming

importing The act of loading a file that uses a different data file type than the application normally requires

individual application software Programs individuals use at work or at home

industrial espionage The stealing of corporate information

Industry Standard Architecture (ISA) bus The most common type of expansion bus that allows devices such as a mouse or modem to communicate with the processor

inference engine A software component of an expert system that processes input and a knowledge base to make logical conclusions

infinite loop A software bug that involves the creation of a loop with no endpoint, and which may cause the computer to crash

infomediary *See B2B infomediary.*

information Data that has been processed to make it useful for a specific purpose, such as making a decision

information processing (data processing) The manipulation of data according to instructions in a computer program

information processing cycle A cycle during which information is entered, processed, output, and/or stored by a computer

information retrieval The process of obtaining information stored on the Internet or on another computer

information system A system involving hardware, software, data, people, and procedures that is usually used to help manage a company

information theft The illegal copying and use of information such as financial or product design data

infrared A type of radiation similar to light with a wavelength outside the visible spectrum; used in TV remote controls and in wireless handheld computers to send data

infrared technology A communications technology that provides for wireless links between PCs and other computing devices, such as keyboards and printers

ink-jet printer A nonimpact printer that forms images by spraying thousands of tiny droplets of electrically charged ink onto a page. The printed images are in dot-matrix format, but of a higher quality than images printed by dot-matrix printers.

input Data that is read into a computer or other device or the act of reading in such data

input device Any hardware component that enables a computer user to enter data and programs into a computer system. Keyboards, point-and-click devices, and scanners are among the more popular input devices, and a desktop or laptop computer system may include one or more input devices.

instant messaging (IM) A form of communicating online in real time that causes pop-up windows to interrupt users when a message is received

instruction cycle *See machine cycle.*

instruction register A memory location (register) where instructions being used for processing are stored

instruction time (I-time) The amount of time required to fetch an instruction from a register

integrated circuit A small electronic device consisting of tiny transistors and other circuit parts on a piece of semiconductor material

integrated software A combination of applications programs bundled as a single package

intellectual property Creative endeavors that are claimed as the personal property of the person who created them

intelligent agent A program or interface to a program that behaves intelligently, attempting to make complex operations easier and faster for a user by employing artificial intelligence techniques

intelligent scanner A scanner that uses optical character recognition (OCR) software to create an image that can be manipulated (edited or altered) with a word processor or other application program

interdependence The relationship between businesses and the outside vendors who help create, market, and distribute their products

interface The connection between a user and software, between two hardware devices, or between two applications

interface card An expansion card or board that allows a computer to interact (interface) with another device or computer

interface program *See front end.*

internal modem A type of modem inserted into an expansion slot on the computer's motherboard

Internet (Net) A worldwide network of computers linked together via communications software and media for the purpose of sharing information. It is the largest and best-known network in the world.

Internet appliance A device with limited function that can be connected to the Internet from the home or other remote location

Internet-enabled cell phone (smart phone) Allows users to transmit and receive e-mail messages and photos and browse through Web sites designed for display on the phone

Internet Protocol (IP) A set of standards for the sending and receiving of information over the Internet

Internet Protocol (IP) address A numeric address, similar to a phone number, that locates a specific computer on the Internet. URLs are translated to IP addresses when connections are made.

Internet service provider (ISP) An organization that has a permanent connection to the Internet and provides temporary access to individuals and others for free or for a fee

Internet telephone service (Voice over IP) A service that allows two or more people with sufficiently good connections to use the Internet to make telephone calls around the world without long-distance telephone charges; users at each end of the connection must download and install a shareware program

Internet2 A new type of Internet currently being planned and developed that, when fully operational, will enable large research universities in the U.S. to collaborate and share huge amounts of complex scientific information at amazing speeds

interpreter A type of language-translating software that reads, translates, and executes one instruction at a time

intrabusiness electronic commerce A Web-based technology that allows a business to handle transactions that occur within the business. Although no revenues are generated, increased efficiency enables the business to save money by lower its operating costs.

intranet A network normally belonging to a large business or organization that is accessible only by the business or organization's members, employees, or other authorized users

iris pattern A type of biometric identifier based on the unique design of one's iris

iris recognition system A biometric device capable of identifying individuals through the unique patterns of their irises

ISDN line A special digital telephone line that can be used to dial into the Internet and transmit and receive information at very high speeds, ranging from 64 kbps (64,000 bits per second) to 128 kbps. An ISDN line requires the use of a special ISDN modem.

J

Java® A third-generation programming language used to write full-scale applications and small applications, known as applets, for use on the World Wide Web

JavaScript A scripting language developed by Sun Microsystems

Java Virtual Machine (JVM) Part of the Java programming language that converts the general Java instructions into commands that a device or computer can understand

Jaz® cartridge A removable hard disk manufactured by Iomega Corporation that offers 1GB of storage

joining A process that allows a query to pull up data from more than one record source by matching data from fields in various record files

joystick An input device (named after the control lever used to fly older fighter planes) consisting of a small box that contains a vertical lever that, when pushed in a certain direction, moves the graphics cursor correspondingly on the screen. It is often used for computer games.

JPEG (.jpg or .jpeg) A file format for still images on the Internet

just-in-time distribution Computerized distribution management systems that allow companies to produce products to match market demand in order to shrink inventories and increase profits

just-in-time (JIT) manufacturing/delivery Strategies that provide for the manufacture of products in time for delivery, and for the delivery of products at the exact time they are needed

K

kernel An operating system program that manages computer components, peripheral devices, and memory. It also maintains the system clock and loads other operating system and application programs as they are required.

kerning In word processing and page layout programs, the space between the letters of a word

key An attribute that can be used to identify a set of information and therefore provide a means to search a database

keyboard An electronically controlled hardware component used to enter alphanumeric data (letters, numbers, and special characters). The keys on most keyboards are arranged similarly to those on a typewriter.

keystroke identification A biometric identifier that recognizes people by how quickly they type different sequences of keys

keyword (search term) A word used to tell a search engine what information to look for on the Web

kilobyte Unit of memory equal to 1,024 bytes

knowbots Intelligent software agents that filter and retrieve information found on the Internet

knowledge base A specially structured database of information used by an expert system to make intelligent decisions

knowledge engineer An individual that creates knowledge bases

L

LAN connection A way to connect to the Internet by connecting users to an ISP on a direct wire at speeds 20 or more times faster than can be achieved through a dial-up modem

land Flat, unburned area on a compact disc

landscape format A printing format in which a printed page is wider than it is tall

language generations A way of categorizing computer languages by type through grouping them in the chronological order in which they were developed

language translator A special type of program needed to translate (convert) high-level language programs into machine-language programs so they can be executed by the computer

laptop computer A computer small enough to be placed on a lap or carried by its user from place to place

laser printer A nonimpact printer that produces output of exceptional quality using a technology similar to that of photocopy machines

leading In word processing and page layout programs, the space between lines of type

legacy database An old, large database that has been updated and maintained for years, and which may contain helpful, undiscovered information

legal issues Actions or behaviors concerned with the keeping or breaking of the law. Illegal actions or behaviors include theft, fraud, drug trafficking, and spreading a virus over the Internet.

legal software Programs designed to help a user analyze, plan, and prepare a variety of legal documents, including wills and trusts

letter quality A print quality preferred for important business letters and documents; available with a variety of printers including laser printers

Level 1 cache A type of cache memory that is built into the architecture of microprocessor chips, providing faster access to the instructions and data residing in cache memory

Level 2 cache A type of cache memory that, in current processors, may be built into the architecture of microprocessor chips; on older computers, it may consist of high-speed SRAM chips placed on the motherboard or on a card inserted into a slot in the computer

Level 3 cache A type of cache memory that is available on computers that have level 2 cache, or advanced transfer cache, and is separate from the microprocessor.

link *See hyperlink.*

Linux An operating system based on AT&T's UNIX and developed by a Finnish programmer named Linus Torvalds. Unlike most other operating systems, the original version is a nonproprietary operating system and is available for free to the public.

liquid crystal display (LDC) A display device in which liquid crystals are sandwiched between two sheets of material

local area network (LAN) A computer network physically confined to a relatively small geographical area, such as a single building or a college campus

local bus A high-speed bus that connects devices such as disk drives to the CPU

local environment The environment that encompasses local customers, suppliers, competitors, stockholders, and local regulators with which the business must interact

local ISP An Internet service provider that typically provides users with one or more telephone numbers they can use to dial-up the ISP's network computer

local online shopping Online shopping limited to those Web sites of stores or services located in close proximity to the customer

locomotion Broad movements such as walking

logic (time) bomb A virus that is triggered by an event or the passing of a certain time

logic error In programming, an incorrect instruction stated in correct syntax

logic statements Programming statements that describe conditions by which a decision should be made; for example: "If the light is red, then stop the car."

looping The process of repeating instructions in a computer program

low-level language A computer language that is more like machine language than English

M

machine code Low-level computer languages that are closer in form to the thought processes used by computers, written in binary language consisting of 1s and 0s

machine cycle A cycle used by a computer during which four basic operations are performed: (1) fetching an instruction, (2) decoding the instruction, (3) executing the instruction, and (4) storing the result

machine language A program consists entirely of 0s and 1s that a computer can understand and execute quickly

machine-to-machine (M2M) e-commerce Computers communicating directly with each other with no human intervention, thus automating many routine business transactions such as reordering supplies when inventories run low

Macintosh OS The first profitable graphical user interface released with Apple's Macintosh computers in 1984. With its impressive graphics and ease of use, it quickly became the model for other GUIs.

macro A sequence of instructions designed to accomplish a specific task and generally executed by issuing a single command

macro virus A form of virus that infects the data files of commonly used applications such as word processors and spreadsheets

magnetic disk storage Secondary storage that provides for the storage of programs, data, and information on a magnetic storage medium, such as magnetic disk or magnetic tape

magnetic storage device A storage device that works by applying electrical charges to iron filings on magnetic storage media so that each filing represents a 0 or a 1

magnetic tape storage A type of secondary storage for large computer systems that uses removable reels of magnetic tape. The tape contains tracks, each of which contains metallic particles that are magnetized, or not magnetized, to represent 0 and 1 bits.

mailing list An Internet application that allows people interested in a topic to communicate via e-mail with others sharing their interests

mail server A computer used to facilitate the sending and receiving of electronic mail messages

main memory Addressable storage locations directly controlled by the central processing unit (CPU) used to store programs while they are being executed and data while it is being processed

main menu *See menu bar.*

mainframe computer A large, powerful, expensive computer system capable of accommodating hundreds of users doing different computing tasks

management information systems (MIS) An information system that turns raw data into information so that managers can make knowledgeable decisions

math coprocessor A special type of coprocessor dedicated to processing numerical data

matrix A rectangular arrangement of elements into rows and columns

megabyte Unit of memory equal to 1,048,576 bytes

megahertz Millions of cycles per second; a unit used for measuring clock speed in computers

memory A place for temporary storage of data, programs, or instructions

memory access time The amount of time required for the processor to access (read) data, instructions, and information from memory

memory resident A characteristic describing programs, including operating systems, that remain in memory while the computer is in operation

mental interfaces Systems that read the minds of their users by monitoring brainwave activity and react by controlling the computer

menu An on-screen set of options from which a user can make selections by clicking the option with a mouse or by typing one or more keystrokes

menu bar A horizontal or vertical bar that shows the highest-level command options

merchant account (e-commerce account) An account in which money is held until an online transaction has been completed. E-tailers pay a monthly fee to maintain this account plus a commission on each transaction.

metabrowser A Web browser that allows the user to put all of her favorite sites onto one page and thus reduce the number of clicks it takes to check those favorite sites daily

metadata Information that helps explain the nature of other data

metalanguage A language for describing other languages

metropolitan area network (MAN) A wide-area network limited to a specific geographical area, such as a city or town

microcomputer (personal computer, PC) Relatively small, affordable computers intended to be operated by an individual user

micro payment A software system that enables buyers to purchase low-cost items such as newspapers over the Internet

microprocessor (processor or CPU [central processing unit]) chip A single integrated circuit chip containing millions of electrical transistors, packed onto a surface smaller than a postage stamp, that processes data in a computer

microwave system A communications technology that transmits data in the form of high-frequency radio signals through the atmosphere from one microwave station to another microwave station, or from a microwave station to a satellite and then back to earth to another microwave station

middleware The system that connects the user interface of a microcomputer to the database engine of a mainframe

midrange server A powerful computer capable of accommodating hundreds of client computers or terminals (users) at the same time; formerly known as minicomputers

minicomputer A large and powerful computer capable of accommodating hundreds of users at the same time.

mirrored hard drive A drive containing duplicate data from another hard drive so that if one fails, the data isn't lost

MMORPG (Massively Multiplayer Online Role-Playing Game) A type of virtual reality online game that can involve thousands of players

mobile commerce (m-commerce) The carrying out of e-commerce activities through the use of small portable computers such as wrist or handheld computers

modem A hardware device that translates signals from digital to analog and from analog to digital, making it possible for digital computers to communicate over analog telephone lines

modem board A circuit board that enables a computer to communicate via telephone lines and other communications media

moderator An individual charged with maintaining order and civility in a virtual environment, such as a chat room

modular code Code created in modules, with each module handling separate components of a program

modularity A measurement of how well written software is, based upon how well divided the source code is into modules

molecular storage A type of storage in which programs and data are represented by tiny molecules

monitor The screen, or display, on which computer output appears

monochrome one-color display capability

Moore's law Not really a law, but rather the prediction that the number of transistors that can be packed on a chip will double every two years while the price decreases by half

moral realism A school of ethical thought that believes ethical principles have solid objective foundations and are not based on subjective human reasoning

moral relativism A school of ethical thought that believes ethical principles are not absolute and unchanging, but subjective and variable from society to society, from situation to situation, or from individual to individual

motherboard The main circuit board inside a personal computer to which other circuit boards can be connected. It contains electrical pathways, called traces, etched onto it that allow data to move from one component to another.

mouse An input device that, when moved about on a flat surface, causes a pointer on the screen to move in the same direction

mouse pad A rubberized pad with a smooth fabric surface that facilitates use of a mouse

mouse pointer A type of cursor resembling a small on-screen arrow, movements of which correspond to movements made with a mouse

MOV (.mov) An Apple movie media format

MP3 A popular file format used for storing digital music

MPEG (.mpeg) A commonly used file format for storing compressed video files; the movie equivalent of the MP3 music format

MPEG2 The high-quality movie format DVD players use

multifunction device (MFD) A piece of equipment that provides a variety of capabilities including scanning, copying, printing, and sometimes faxing

multimedia The use of sound, images, video and or text mixed together to create a work or presentation

multimedia authoring software Program that allows a user to create stand-alone multimedia products

multimedia database A database model that allows the storage of pictures, movies, sounds, and hyperlinked fields.

multimedia developer Graphic artist, digital sound editor, or animation specialist who creates and enhances Web content with images, sounds, and movies

multimedia development The use of computers to create and enhance Web content with images, sounds, and movies

multipartite virus Viruses that have the ability to attack in several different ways

multiplexer An electronic device that increases the efficiency of a network system by allowing 8, 16, 32, or more low-speed devices to share simultaneously a single high-speed communications medium

multipoint videoconferencing system A videoconferencing system that allows three or more participants to sit in a virtual conference room and communicate as though they were seated next to each other

multitasking The ability of an operating system to run more than one software program at a time

multi-user computer system A computer system that can accommodate many users concurrently

multi-user operating system An operating system designed for use with large computer systems and capable of handling several users at the same time

Musical Instrument Digital Interface (MIDI) A type of data file for instrumental music

mutations Random variations in the designs generated by genetic algorithms

N

nanobots Microscopic robots

narrowband medium A communications medium capable of carrying a smaller amount of data at slow speeds

national environment An environment in which a business interacts with national suppliers, federal agencies, competitors, and national regulators

National ISP A large Internet service provider that provides telephone numbers in most major cities. Their larger size than local ISPs often allows them to provide more services and technical support for users than local ISPs.

National Science Foundation Network (NSFnet) A wide area network developed to assume the civilian functions of the U.S. Department of Defense's ARPANet in case of nuclear attack

native format A file format that is specific to the application being used

natural interface An interface between human and machine that more closely approximates the normal communications between people

natural-language interface An interface that would allow programmers to describe what they want using natural (human) language rather than writing programs in highly structured programming languages

natural-language processing (NLP) A type of speech recognition software being developed that will, when perfected, enable a computer system to understand any person's language

navigation The science of moving a mobile robot through an environment

netiquette A term used to describe polite behavior online

NetWare Developed by Novell, Incorporated, Netware is a popular and widely used operating system for microcomputer-based personal computers.

network A group of two or more computers, software, and other devices that are connected by means of one or more communications media

network administration The operation and maintenance of a company network, including a LAN, WAN, network segment, intranet, or interactions with the Internet

network administrator Person whose job is to oversee and maintain a company's network

network architecture The way a network is designed and built, just as an architect might design a new building or other facility

network interface board A circuit board that allows for communication between the computer and a network

network operating system (NOS) An operating system that allows client computers to communicate back and forth over a network with a host computer, called a network server

network server A large and powerful computer to which smaller computers are connected in a network, and which manages all user activity occurring on the network

network sniffer A software package that displays network traffic data such as which resources are being used or which Web sites are being visited

network topology The way computers and peripherals are configured to form networks

neural network An artificial intelligence technology that mimics the way nerve cells are connected in the human brain. Information is supplied to the neural network to train it to recognize certain patterns, resulting in a program capable of making predictions, such as weather forecasts and fluctuations of stock values.

newsgroup An online environment that allows users to exchange written information on a variety of subjects

niche information systems Information systems focused on particular sets of customers; a system designed for dental offices would be an example

node A component connected to a network server, such as a personal computer or a printer

nonimpact printer A printer that uses electricity, heat, laser technology, or photographic techniques to produce output

nonprocedural Said of programming languages, such as scripting languages, that explain what the computer should do in English-like terms but not precisely how the computer should do it

nonresident A characteristic describing a program that does not reside in memory while the computer is running, but instead resides on a storage medium, such as a hard disk, until needed

nonvolatile A type of computer storage specifically designed to hold information, even when the power is switched off; examples include hard disk and CD-ROM

normalization A process performed in a relational database to eliminate duplication of data (redundancy)

normative ethics Determining a standard or "norm" of ethical rule that underlies ethical behavior

notebook computer A lightweight portable computer that can fit inside a briefcase

NTSC converter A device connected to both a computer and a TV that converts the computer's digital signal into an analog signal that can be displayed on the television screen

nuisance virus A virus that usually does no real damage but is rather just an inconvenience

numeric Consisting of numbers only

O

object A programming term indicating a single element that contains both data and the code to manipulate the data

object-based graphics Pictures constructed in programs by means of creating, editing, and combining mathematically defined geometric shapes

object linking and embedding (OLE) A feature of Windows operating systems and applications that allows material from one application to be ported into a document created in another application and linked in such a way that when the material is updated in the originating application, it is automatically updated in the application into which it has been ported

object-oriented database A database that stores data in the form of objects; each object contains both the data related to the object and the actions that the user might want to perform on that object

object-oriented programming (OOP) language A newer basis for programming language design developed in the 1980s

office information system (OIS) An information system dedicated to automating an office environment

online Connected to a network such as the Internet

online analytical processing (OLAP) A new class of software that is focused on providing better ways to analyze the mass of data in large databases and massively distributed data systems such as the Internet in order to produce more useful results

online auction A peer-to-peer online transaction venue where consumers can place items for sale, bid on auctioned items, or (in some cases) buy items outright. An example of a popular online auction site is eBay.

online banking The process of using a computer, modem, and an Internet connection to conduct routine banking transactions. A user can make arrangements with the bank that will allow her to pay bills, transfer funds among various accounts, and transact other financial activities.

online catalog A virtual presentation of information about products and services similar to a traditional paper catalog. Online catalogs can include multimedia, such as voice, animation, and video clips.

online course A course of study, such as English or psychology, offered over the Internet by a college or a textbook publisher

online discussion Communication using the services of a chat room that allows users to communicate back and forth with each other

online marketplace An electronic hub using the same interface, protocols, and other technologies as other e-commerce buyers and sellers in a particular industry. An online marketplace provides both buyers and sellers with special services, such as allowing s sellers to find buyers.

online service A business that provides users with Internet access, and also offers special features such as online news, weather reports, financial news, and sporting news

online shopping (**electronic shopping** or **e-shopping**) Using a computer, modem, browser, and Internet access to locate, examine, purchase, sell, and pay for products over the Internet. Online shopping can be worldwide or local.

online shopping mall A collection of stores found at a single Web site. The stores share an electronic marketing environment including servers, software, and payment systems.

online store (**virtual store**) Similar to a walk-in store, a seller's Web site where customers can locate, examine, purchase, and pay for products and services

online superstore Online stores that offer an extensive array of products, from candy bars to household appliances

online transactional processing (OLTP) A form of transactional processing used at e-commerce Web sites that require fast, always-on processing

on-screen desktop An on-screen work area on which graphical elements such as icons, buttons, windows, links, and dialog boxes are displayed

open-source software program Sets of rules and standards for developing application programs that will run on any type of computer

open system With an open system, the company IT staff can alter the system or hire a third party to take care of any necessary alterations

open system architecture A product, hardware, or software design that allows other companies to easily connect their products to it

Open Systems Interconnection (OSI) model A set of communications protocols defined by the International Standards Organization based in Geneva, Switzerland, and adopted by the United Nations

operating environment An onscreen visual interface on top of an underlying DOS kernel that makes using a computer easier

operating system A type of software that creates a user interface and supports the workings of computer devices and software programs that perform specific jobs

operational database A database that aids in the daily operations of an organization

optical character recognition (OCR) Software that allows a captured image to be manipulated (edited or altered) with a word processor or other application program

optical disc A secondary storage medium on which data is recorded and read by two lasers: a high-density laser that records data by burning tiny indentations, or pits, onto the disc surface, and a low intensity laser that reads stored data from the disc into the computer.

optical mouse A type of mouse that contains no mouse ball and instead uses a light-based sensor to track movement. This mouse can be moved around on nearly any smooth surface, except glass, and thus no mouse pad is required.

optical reader A type of optical scanner installed by many retailers at checkout stations

optical scanner (scanner) A light-sensing electronic device that can read and capture printed text and images, such as photographs and drawings, and convert them into a digital form a computer can understand. Once scanned, the text or image can be displayed on the screen, edited, printed, stored on a disk, inserted into another document, or sent as an attachment to an e-mail message.

option button (radio button) A type of button used with a graphical user interface and resembling buttons on a standard radio that enables you to choose from among a set of options

OS/2 An operating system produced by IBM in response to the popularity of Microsoft Windows and the Apple Mac OS operating system

output Information that is written or displayed as a result of computer processing; also the act of writing or displaying such data

output device Any hardware device that makes information available to a user, such as a monitor or printer

output medium Any medium or material on which information is recorded, such as paper

outsourcing Using an outside company or organization to perform programming or other activities for a company or organization

P

packet Data that has been divided into small blocks and sent over the Internet to a specific destination where the blocks are reassembled

packet-switching The process of breaking up a message into parts called packets and directing the packets to their final Internet destination where they are reassembled

page scanner A type of scanner, resembling a tabletop copy machine, on which pages being scanned (copied) are either laid face down on the scanner's glass surface or fed through the scanner by means of a side-feed device

painting program Software that allows a user to create images in bit-map form and also to color and edit an image one bit at a time

Palm OS An operating system produced by Palm, Incorporated for use with the company's handheld personal digital assistants (PDAs)

palmtop computer A computer small enough to fit into a pocket

parallel port A slot (opening) for connecting printers, scanners, and other devices. A parallel port can transmit data eight bits at a time.

parallel processing A processing action in which two or more processors work concurrently on segments of a lengthy application, thus dramatically increasing processing capability

parallel transmission A transmission method in which a group of 8 bits representing a single byte (plus one bit called a *parity bit*) are transmitted at the same time over separate paths

parity bit An extra bit added to a byte, character, or word to ensure that there is always either a predetermined even number of bits or an odd number of bits. If data should be lost, errors can be identified by checking the number of bits.

passive-matrix display A type of display in which a single transistor controls an entire column or row of the display's tiny electrodes.

password A secret code of letters and numbers used to prevent access to a computer system by unauthorized people

patent An award made to inventors that allows them ownership of their invention. An inventor whose work is patented has the right to charge others for the use of the invention

pathname The entire URL (Web address) describing where information can be found

PC Card A type of expansion board developed specifically for the smaller PCs. A PC card plugs into the side of a notebook or portable computer.

PCMCIA card (PC card) A type of expansion board (card) developed for use with small computers such as notebook and other small computers

PCMCIA modem A modem that can be inserted into a PCMCIA slot in a notebook or other portable computer

PDF (.pdf) A popular platform-independent file format for the storage of high-resolution printable documents such as tax return forms; PDF documents may contain text, graphics, video, and sound in the QuickTime video format

peer-to-peer architecture A network design in which each PC or workstation comprising the network has equivalent capabilities and responsibilities

peer-to-peer (P2P) file sharing A way to use the Internet that allows people to download material directly from other users' hard drives rather than from files located on Web servers

peer-to-peer online transaction A type of businessto- consumer online transaction that allows individuals to sell, buy, trade, or share goods with each other

pen computer A computer equipped with pattern recognition circuitry so that it can recognize human handwriting as a form of data input

performance monitor A set of operating system instructions that monitor the computer system's overall performance

Peripheral Component Interconnect (PCI) bus A type of bus that allows for the connection of sound cards, video cards, and network cards to a computer system

peripheral device A device, such as a printer or disk drive, connected to and controlled by a computer but external to the computer's central processing unit (CPU)

Perl (Practical Extraction and Reporting Language) A popular script language that is similar to C, but with powerful text-processing abilities

permanent storage A type of storage that consists of devices and media used to record information and data permanently so it can later be retrieved, edited, modified, displayed, or printed

permanent storage medium A storage medium on which information and data can be permanently recorded, such as a floppy disk

persistent cookies Software codes that have the potential to reside on computers for years and can be used to track user Web access histories

personal computer A single-user computer capable of performing its own input, processing, output, and storage

personal digital assistant (PDA) A handheld, wireless computer, also known as a handheld PC or HPC, used for such purposes as storing schedules, calendars, and telephone numbers and for sending e-mail or connecting to the Internet

personal finance software Programs that assist users with paying bills, balancing checkbooks, keeping track of income and expenses, and other financial activities

personal identification number (PIN) A password that is all numeric and can be typed in using a keypad such as the one on a telephone

personal information management (PIM) A function of the Pocket PC operating system that enables a user to prepare and store personal and business notes, as well as access schedules, contact lists, calendars, task lists, and to access and use the Internet

person-to-person payment system An Internet service that allows consumers to transfer money through a credit card or a bank account

petaflop A measure of speed equivalent to one quadrillion calculations per second

photograph printer A unique high-quality ink-jet printer designed to print high-quality color photographs in addition to other types of print output.

pipelining A technique for improving microprocessor performance that enables the computer to begin executing another instruction as soon as the previous instruction reaches the next phase of the machine cycle

pit A tiny indentation burned by laser into the surface of a compact disc to represent information, data, or programs

pitch The quality of sound reflected in the sound's loudness, intensity, and clarity

pixel The smallest picture element that a computer monitor or other device can display and from which graphic images are built

pixelated Jagged slopes or curves in graphics images, resulting from low resolution (limited dot-per-inch capability)

plagiarism The unlawful use of another's ideas or written work

plaintext Readable information entered into a computer that is then converted to ciphertext, or unreadable, coded information in the process of encryption

platform Compatible computers from one or more manufacturers; the two popular platforms for personal computers are PCs and Macintoshes.

plotter A hard-copy output device used to output special kinds of hard copy, including architectural drawings, charts, maps, diagrams, and other images

plug-in A downloadable software addition, often used to distribute additional Web browser capabilities

Pocket PC A scaled down version of Microsoft's operating system designed for use on a small handheld computer from Microsoft Corporation called the PocketPC

point-to-point videoconferencing system A videoconferencing system in which each party's computer has a video camera, microphone, and speakers that allow their voices and images to be carried over the network, appearing in a window on the other participant's monitor

polling protocol A network protocol that continually polls all workstations to determine if there are messages to be sent or received by each workstation

polymorphic virus A virus that can alter itself to prevent antivirus software from detecting it

pop-up window A screen that jumps into the foreground of a Web page, usually during surfing. These windows are oftentimes advertisements.

port (interface) A plug-in slot on a computer to which you can connect a device, such as a printer or, in the case of accessing the Internet, a telephone line

portal A Web site that offers a variety of Internet services, such as search engines, news, weather, sports, yellow pages, and online stores and shopping malls

portable computer A computer small enough to be carried around

portrait format A format in which a printed page is taller than it is wide

Post Office Protocol (POP) A protocol in the recipient's communications software that allows a recipient to retrieve an e-mail message.

Post Office Protocol (POP) server A special type of server that holds e-mail messages until they are accessed and read by recipients of the messages

power-on self test (POST) A chip containing instructions that check the physical components of the computer system to make certain they are working properly when the computer is turned on

power spike A jump up or down in the level of power provided to a computer system, potentially damaging the hardware

power supply A source of electrical energy that enables the computer to function

presentation graphics software An application program that allows one to create a computerized presentation of slides

primary key A database key that uniquely identifies every record in a table

printer The most common type of hard-copy output device that produces output in a permanent form

printing The action of producing a document or file in hard-copy form on paper or plastic film

print server A type of server that allows multiple users to share the same printer

print spooler A program within an operating system that increases a computer's efficiency by placing a document to be printed in memory buffers where they reside until a printer is ready to print it

print spooling A printing technique in which a document to be printed is placed in a buffer instead of being sent to the printer. The document is held in the buffer until the printer is ready to print it, thereby enabling the printer to print at its own speed. When a document is placed in a buffer, the CPU is free to begin executing the next instruction or carry out the next command by the user.

privacy statement An e-tailer's written promise that the merchant will protect the confidentiality of any information revealed by a customer

problem solving Analyzing a problem and using logical processes to find a solution to it

processor The brain of the computer, consisting of the arithmetic/logic unit and the control unit

procurement The activity of searching for, finding, and purchasing materials, supplies, products, and services at the best prices and assuring that they are delivered in a timely manner

product developer Companies that manufacture new hardware and software products for the general market

productivity In business, the degree and turn-over of a company's output

productivity (application) software Programs that allow users to perform specific tasks, such as creating documents, preparing income tax returns, managing finances, sending and receiving messages over the Internet, and designing new products. Productivity software enables a user to be more "productive."

profitability The difference between the revenues derived from the sale of products and services and the costs of producing them. Profitability is essential if a firm is to survive in the long term.

program A set of instructions to be executed by a computer; types of programs include applications and operating systems.

programming languages Coding systems, containing smaller vocabularies and simpler syntax than human (natural) languages, that are used to write programs

project management software Software that allows a user to plan, design, schedule, and control a project, thus facilitating the effective and efficient management of complex projects

project plan An estimate of how long a project will take to complete, along with an outline of the steps involved and a list of deliverables

prompt A symbol, character or phrase that appears on-screen to inform the user that the computer is ready to accept input

proprietary software Software owned by an individual or business that cannot be used or copied without permission

protocol A set of rules and procedures for exchanging information between network devices and computers

prototype An initial "demo" version of a product or information system that allows people to get an idea of the final product's capabilities

pseudocode Programming code that is more English-like than a programming language, and therefore easier to read, but is more structured and simplistic than English

public access network (PAN) A wide-area network operated and maintained by a large company, such as AT&T, MCI, or US

Sprint, that provides voice and data communications capabilities to customers for a fee

public key encryption A form of data encryption that uses two encryption keys, a public encryption key known by all authorized users, and a secret encryption key known only by the sender or the receiver

pull-down menu (submenu) A menu containing various lower-level options associated with main menu options

pure-play A category of e-commerce companies created solely to solicit business on the Web

Q

quality The value (or perceived value) of a firm's products and services. Everyone expects products and services purchased to be of value, at least in proportion to the prices paid.

quality assurance (QA) The task of making sure that products meet with quality standards before being released to the public

quantum cryptography An encryption technology that attempts to keep the starting encryption key secret by using quantum devices to transmit the starting key via light signals over fiber-optic cable. If anyone observes the key, the system will be disturbed, the sender and receiver will be aware of the security breach, and the starting key can be changed.

query A request for information from a database

Query by Example (QBE) A standard for querying, or asking for particular information from, a database management system

query tools Tools in a database management system that help users narrow down the amount of information that needs to be searched

R

Rambus DRAM (RDRAM) A new memory design that achieves higher data transfer speeds; expensive to manufacture

random-access Because each RAM location has an individual address, the computer can go directly to the instructions and data it needs rather than searching each individual location one after another sequentially

random-access memory (RAM) A computer chip or group of chips containing the temporary, or volatile, memory in which programs and data are stored while being used by a computer

range check A database validity check that makes sure a field value entered by the user is within specified limits

rapid application development (RAD) A set of techniques and practices designed to increase the speed of software development

raster image An image composed of a collection of black, white, or colored pixels; the most commonly used file format is the Tag Image File Format (TIF or TIFF)

raster image-based graphics *See bitmap-based graphics*

read-only memory (ROM) A computer chip on the motherboard of a computer containing permanent, or nonvolatile, memory that stores instructions

real time At the present moment; occurring now; live

real-time system An information system that is in communication with real world events directly and must operate fast enough to keep up with real world events. Examples are CAM systems, traffic control systems, and elevator systems.

record In a table created by a database management system application, a row providing information about one entity, such as an individual or organization

recordable Capable of having files of information stored on, or written to

record-locking A process used by database to ensure that errors do not occur when two users access the same record

redundancy The duplication of data in different locations within a database

redundant system A duplicate system that is part of a disaster recovery plan; one part of a redundant system might be a mirrored hard drive that could be used to replace a damaged or corrupted hard drive

refresh rate The number of times per second a monitor's screen is redrawn

regional ISP An Internet service provider that serves one or more states

register A component of the ALU that temporarily holds instructions and data

relational database A type of database in which various tables can be linked (or related) in a way that allows you to retrieve data from more than one table. Tables must have a common data field, such as a product number.

removable storage medium A secondary storage medium, such as a floppy disk or a CD-ROM, that can be removed by the user and replaced by another medium

repeater (amplifier) An electronic device that receives signals along a network, amplifies the signals, and resends the amplified signals along the network

repetitive motion injuries A category of injury that involves the overuse and subsequent damage of joints and nerves

report A database output that is often printed, such as a utility bill or a school transcript

request for proposal (RFP) The solicitation of a plan for an information system sent to possible suppliers, inviting them to send representatives to determine what is required before quoting a price

resolution A measurement of the sharpness of an image displayed on a computer monitor or other output device; resolution is measured in dots per inch (dpi), both vertically and horizontally, with higher resolution achieved by more dots per inch.

retinal pattern A type of biometric identifier based on the unique composition or design of one's retina in the eye

retinal recognition system A biometric device that uses the unique retinal patterns of individuals to identify them

rewritable Capable of having files of information stored on and overwritten, or restored

ring topology A network layout in which there is no host computer and each computer or workstation is connected to two other computers. Communications are passed in one direction from the source computer to the destination. If one computer isn't working, that computer is bypassed.

RISC A shortened set of instructions that increase the speed and performance of a microprocessor

robotics The science of creating machines capable of independent movement and action

rotating backups A system of maintaining multiple backup copies of data in which the oldest copy is erased and reused every time the system is backed up

router An electronic device typically used in large networks, including the Internet, to ensure that messages are sent to their intended destinations

routine (function) A section of code containing instructions for a specific purpose

RPG A programming language commonly used in business environments; an acronym for Report Program Generator

RSA A popular public encryption technology used to transmit data over the Internet. It is named for its developers, Rivest, Shamir, and Adleman.

run-time error Program mistake that occurs when an application is running

run-time version A limited version of a supporting program that's bundled with an application program. An example is an early version of Microsoft's Excel that included a version of Microsoft Windows for those users who didn't yet have Windows.

S

sampling Measuring the pitch, frequency, and volume of a sound

sampling rate The number of times per second that digital measurements of a sound are taken

saving The process of storing a copy of the displayed document to a secondary storage medium such as a floppy disk or hard disk. Once saved, a document (or portion of a document) can be retrieved and reused. Saving a document requires specifying the drive and assigning the document a file name.

script language (scripting language) A large variety of languages that are interpreted rather than compiled. Script languages are often used to write special functions into Web pages, as the transmission of a script is faster than a binary plug-in.

scroll bar Rectangular bars at the side or bottom of a window that enable a user to see and work with other portions of the document by moving the small arrows at the tips of a scroll bar or by dragging the small box between the two arrows

SCSI An abbreviation for small computer system interface, pronounced *scuzzy*; a parallel interface system used by most Apple Macintosh computers, some PCs, and some UNIX systems for connecting peripheral devices to a computer; provides for faster transmission rates than standard serial and parallel ports; multiple devices can be attached to a single SCSI port

search engine A software program that enables a user to search for, locate, and retrieve specific information on the Internet about any topic

search operator Logic statement used by search engines to locate information on the Web; three of the most common are AND, OR, and NOT

secondary storage (auxiliary storage or external storage) Hardware devices and media that enable the permanent storage of important information such as computer programs, files, and data and that allow the stored data to be reentered and reused. External, nonvolatile storage that stores program instructions and data even after the user switches off the power

secret key encryption An encryption method in which both the customer and the business use the same encryption key to encrypt and decrypt the data

sector A numbered section or portion of a disk similar to a slice of pie on which programs, data, and information is stored

Secure Sockets Layer (SSL) An encryption protocol used for secure servers. SSL is commonly found on sites that involve financial transactions, such as the use of credit card information.

security measures Methods used by a database management system to protect and safeguard data

SELECT command The basic query command supported by SQL, which asks a database to return records that match specified criteria

semiconductor A type of material that is neither a good conductor of electricity (like copper) nor a good insulator (such as rubber) and therefore does not interfere with the flow of electricity in a chip's circuits; most commonly used is silicon, a type of purified glass

sequential access A storage technology whereby stored data can be retrieved only in the order in which it is physically stored, just as musical selections on a cassette tape are recorded and accessed one after the other

serial port (communications [COM] port) A port (opening) for connecting devices such as the keyboard, mouse, and modem to a computer. Serial ports transmit data one bit at a time.

serial transmission A data transmission method in which all the bits (0s and 1s) that comprise the data are transmitted one bit after another in a continuous line

server A computer and its associated storage devices that are accessed remotely over a network by users

service Intangible actions that satisfy consumer or business needs. Good service results in goodwill. *Goodwill* may be defined as the desire of a consumer or business to want to do business with an organization with which the customer or business is treated well. *See also B2B service.*

set-top box A popular type of Internet appliance placed on top of or near a television set

shareware Software developed by an individual or software publisher who retains ownership of the product and makes it publicly available for a small "contribution" fee

shopping agent (bot) Software that works for shoppers by locating Web sites that offer products specified by a user and does comparison-shopping to find the best bargain

shopping cart (shopping basket) An icon that allows a customer to electronically select products for purchase at an online shopping site

signature verification system A biometric device that recognizes individuals via their handwriting

SIM card A storage medium used with some digital cameras for storing pictures

Simple Mail Transfer Protocol (SMTP) A communications protocol installed on an ISP's or online service's mail server that determines how each message is to be routed through the Internet and then sends the message

simplex transmission A directional protocol that allows transmissions to flow in only one direction; that is, messages can be either sent or received but not both

single sign-on (SSO) technology A security design that eliminates the problem of users having an ID and password for each application or system they access

single-user computer system A personal computer system that can accommodate a single (one) user at a time; the type of computer system found in homes and in small businesses and offices

site analysis A business or organization's ongoing evaluation of an e-commerce Web site and its activity

site license A contract that allows an organization to load or use copies of a piece of software on a specified maximum number of machines

situational ethics Another name for the school of ethical thought called moral relativism

slide A document created using presentation graphics software that may contain text, graphics, images, sound, and other elements that can help capture and hold an audience's attention.

slide show A group of slides comprise a presentation. A slide show may include any number of individual slides.

smart card A small plastic card that stores personal and financial data on a tiny microprocessor embedded in the card. When the card is inserted into an electronic card reader, information on the card is read and, when appropriate, updated.

soft copy A temporary version of output, typically the display of data on a computer screen

software Programs containing instructions that direct the operation of the computer system and the written documentation that explains how to use the programs. Two main types of software are system software and application software.

software development life cycle (SDLC) The circular series of steps that any software development project goes through

software engineer Person whose profession is to design and build computer programs

software engineering The organized, professional application of the software development process by programmers and software engineers

software piracy The act of copying or using a piece of software without the legal right to do so

software suite (integrated software) A combination of applications programs bundled as a single package. A software suite may contain applications such as word processing, spreadsheet, database, and possibly other programs.

software worm A program that actively transmits copies of itself over the Internet, using up resources and causing other problems

sort A feature of many application programs, such as word processing programs and database management systems, that enables the user to organize selected information in a particular way, as, for example, alphabetically or by date

sound board A type of expansion board that allows voice input by means of a microphone and sound output via speakers

sound digitizing card A computer hardware component capable of reproducing sound from a variety of digital file types

source code A computer program written in a programming language, but not yet turned into executable machine language by a compiler

spam Similar to junk mail, an unsolicited e-mail message sent to computer users by a business or individual to promote products or services

spam blocker A utility program that allows users to block incoming spam messages

speaker-dependent program A particular speech recognition program whereby the computer captures and stores your own voice as you speak words slowly and clearly into the microphone

speaker headset A miniature version of larger speakers frequently used with portable devices, including music CD players

speaker-independent program A particular speech recognition program that contains a built-in vocabulary of prerecorded word patterns. The computer can recognize only spoken words that match a word contained in the built-in list of vocabulary words.

speakers Computer devices that output sound; applications for which speakers are particularly important include computer games, multimedia distance learning programs, audio e-mail, and video-conferencing.

special-function keyboard A type of keyboard designed for specific applications involving simplified, rapid data input

specifications A detailed set of requirements for a software product to be developed

speech recognition (voice recognition) A computer system's capability to recognize and capture spoken words using a speech recognition program

spelling checker A part of a program or a standalone application that automatically searches for spelling errors and suggests correctly spelled alternatives **splitter** A device used with a cable modem in which one part connects to the television cable and the other part connects to the cable modem

spoofing A practice by which a program masquerades as a legitimate source of data on a network in order to get a remote computer to accept its transmissions

spreadsheet An application program used primarily for financial analyses and record keeping, resembling on the screen the paper with rows and columns used by accountants

spyware Software used to view the screen of an individual remotely, and possibly without the person's knowledge

standard operating procedures (SOPs) Work instructions that act much like computer programs written for people

start bit A bit that signals the beginning of a character during asynchronous transmission

star topology (hub-and-spoke topology) A network topology in which multiple computers and peripheral devices are linked to a central computer, called a host, in a point-to-point configuration

Static RAM (SRAM) A type of RAM that is faster and more reliable than the more common dynamic RAM

statistical quality control (SQC) A methodology used by manufacturing companies to maintain quality by vigilantly performing statistical analysis upon their production error rates

stealth virus A rare and sophisticated virus that attempts to "hide" from anti-virus software by covering up its identifiable characteristics

stereoscopic Said of vision that allows depth perception and the detection of movement

stockless inventory A new model for distribution management that involves daily deliveries to the customer

stop bit A bit that signals the end of a character during asynchronous transmission

storage A permanent recording of information, data, and programs on a permanent storage medium, such as floppy disk, so they can be used again and again

storage device A hardware component that houses a secondary storage medium

storage medium A medium, such as magnetic disk or magnetic tape, on which data is recorded (stored), similar to the way a VCR is used for recording a television program on the tape inside a cassette

storage register Special areas of main memory used to store program instructions being executed and data being processed

stored program concept A storage concept that allows a program to be entered a single time and used again and again

storefront An e-tailer's home page, a computerized version of a brick and mortar retail store, on which the e-tailer lists or shows products, descriptions, and prices of the merchandise

storing The activity of permanently saving instructions and data for future use

storyboard Sketches of the pages or frames as they will appear in the final work; used to plan sequential page-based multimedia or movie-based multimedia

streaming techniques (webcasting) An alternative to downloading a piece of music or a video, streaming sends a continuous stream of data to the receiving computer where it is immediately displayed.

structured programming A set of procedural rules for creating software that is written in a readable, standardized format, and which is broken into coherent structures

Structured Query Language (SQL) A standard for querying, or asking for particular information from, a database management system

style A special shortcut feature in an application program that allows text to be formatted in a single step

style error An error in writing source code that does not keep the program from working, but does make it more difficult to read

style sheet A predefined set of formats, such as rightjustified, 10-point Helvetica bold italic with 12-point leading, that can be automatically applied to selected text

stylus A sharp, pointed instrument used for writing or marking

subcontracting Hiring a third party to handle a project, usually a consultant or a systems house

supercomputer Fastest, most powerful, and most expensive type of computer designed for multiple users

SuperDisk drive A high-capacity storage device manufactured by Iomega Corporation

supply chain (value chain) A series of activities a company performs to achieve its goals at various stages of the production process. The value added at each stage contributes to profit and enhances the product's value as well as the company's competitive position in the market.

support contract A contract that allows users to contact the systems house for technical support, training, and sometimes on-site troubleshooting

surfing The process of exploring the Internet in search of something specific, or just anything interesting

surge protectors A type of power strip that contains electronics that try to modulate and "smooth out" spikes in the power supply

synch byte Bytes of data signaling the beginning and end of blocks of data during synchronous transmission

Synchronous DRAM (SDRAM) A high-speed random-access memory (RAM) technology that can synchronize itself with the clock speed of the microprocessor's data bus

synchronous transmission A transmission method that provides a fast and efficient way of sending data in which blocks of bytes are wrapped in start and stop bytes called synch bytes

SyncLink DRAM (SLDRAM) A type of RAM chip that enables the CPUs in new PCs to access data at speeds equal to the speed of some earlier mainframe computers

syntax The structure of a language

syntax error An error that violates the rules of a programming language. Syntax errors are listed by a compiler when it attempts to translate a program from source code into machine language.

system backdoor A secret, sometimes forgotten entry point into an otherwise secure system; oftentimes left behind by the original programmers, accidentally or on purpose

system bus Connects the processor (CPU) to main memory, providing the CPU with fast access to data stored in RAM

system clock A small electronic chip inside a computer that synchronizes or controls the timing of all computer operations. The clock generates evenly spaced pulses that synchronize the flow of information through the computer's internal communications channels.

system development life cycle (SDLC) The comprehensive process software engineers initiate, a series of steps culminating in a completed information system

systems analyst Person whose profession is to study and evaluate computer operations and procedures used to accomplish specific goals

systems house (systems integrator) Company that specializes in installing, customizing, and supporting information systems; also sometimes called a systems integrator

Systems Network Architecture (SNA) A networking program that uses a polling protocol for transmitting data. Workstations are asked one by one if they have a message to transmit. A "yes" response allows the message to be sent, and then the next workstation is polled.

system software A type of software consisting of a set of programs that control the operations of a computer system, including starting the computer, processing applications, formatting disks, and copying files; it also controls all components and devices that comprise the computer system.

system unit The main part of a personal computer system that contains the motherboard and other components necessary for processing information

T

T line A permanent connection between two points set up by a telephone company and typically leased by a business to connect geographically distant offices. A leased "T" line is always active and dedicated for use only by the leasing business that pays a monthly fee for use of the line.

T1 line A high-speed telephone line that allows for both voice and data transmission and can carry data at a speed of 1.544 megabits per second

T3 line A high-speed telephone line capable of carrying data at speeds of up to 44.7 megabits per second

tab A subset of options, each of which is labeled as if it were a manila folder within a file drawer. The name of the subset of options is displayed in a tab at the top of the folder. Clicking on the tab brings the particular group of options to the front of the dialog box.

table In relational databases, a file consisting of rows and columns

tablet PC A type of notebook computer that has a liquid crystal display (LCD) screen on which the user can write using a special-purpose pen, or stylus

tactile perception The science of making a computer understand what is it touching

tangents Straight lines that are perpendicular to and bisect a line

tape cartridge A secondary storage technology used with personal computers mainly for backing up the contents of a hard drive. The tape is housed in a small plastic container (the cartridge) that also contains a tape reel and a take-up reel.

tape drive A device that records and reads data to and from a reel of magnetic tape. Many large businesses and organizations use this sequential-access storage medium for backing up important programs and data.

tax preparation software Programs designed to aid a taxpayer in analyzing federal and state tax status and to prepare and transmit tax returns

technical sales A career involving educating potential customers about a product so that they want to buy it

technical servicing The installation and maintenance of hardware and software

technical support Career that involves responding to customers' phone and e-mail requests for assistance with computer-related products

technical training Career that involves teaching individuals how to use computer systems

technical writing Career that involves writing user manuals, training materials, and textbooks for hardware and software products

technician Person whose job is to repair and maintain computer equipment and systems and install software on a company's computers

telecommunications The combined use of computer hardware and communications software for sending and receiving information over communications media, including phone lines and other types of media

telecommuting (telework) An Internet application that enables workers to perform their work activities at home instead of at the workplace by using their computers, communications software, and a telephone line; also called **teleworking**

telematics A wireless technology that will be incorporated into cars so that drivers can access their corporate networks while commuting

template A previously created and stored form

terabyte A unit of memory measurement equal to approximately 1 trillion bytes

terminal An input/output device, consisting of a keyboard and monitor, typically used with multi-user computer systems

testing harness A standard set of tests that a software product must pass before being released to the public

text A common data storage format made up of characters, such as a name or an address

text box A type of dialog box used for typing information that will allow the computer to continue or complete a task

text data Alphabetic letters, numbers, and special characters, typically entered to produce output such as letters, e-mail messages, and reports

texture A bitmap used to cover the surface of a virtual object in a virtual environment such as a game

thin-film transistor (TFT) display A type of display unit, often used with notebook computers, in which separate transistors control each pixel, allowing viewing from any angle

throughput A measure of a computer's overall performance

time-sharing A system by means of which several users are allowed to access and work with a computer system by rationing time to users who are connected simultaneously

title bar A rectangular area at the top of a window in which the window's name is displayed

token ring protocol A type of protocol that sends an electronic signal, called a token, carrying both an address and a message around a token ring network quickly

toner An ink-like powder used in a laser printer

toolbar A type of menu on which sets of icons are displayed that represent actions unique to the software and ones frequently employed by users. The number and kinds of icons often vary among programs and among different versions of the same program.

top-down design Envisioning a programming project in its entirety by viewing larger elements and then the smaller elements contained within them; often documented using an outline format

touch pad An input device that enables a user to enter data and make selections by moving a finger across the pad

touch screen An input device that allows the user to choose options by pressing a finger (or fingers) on the appropriate part of the screen

trace Electrical pathway etched onto a motherboard that connects internal computer components

track A numbered concentric circle on a magnetic disk, or groups of lines along the length of magnetic tape, along which programs and data are stored

trackball An input device consisting of a plastic sphere sitting on rollers, inset in a small external case, or in many portable computers, in the same unit as the keyboard. The user moves the ball with her fingers or palm to position an on-screen cursor.

transaction A business activity central to the nature of an enterprise, such as the sale of a product, the flight of an airline, or the recording of a grade

transactional database A database that operates on a give-and-take basis, doing what is asked of it immediately

transactional processing A type of data processing that is done continuously, as each activity occurs, and tends to be done with smaller databases or with operational databases that require all information to be very current

transceiver A device that sends messages along the bus in either direction

Transmission Control Protocol/Internet Protocol (TCP/IP) A communications protocol used to define the technique of packet switching on the Internet. The *TCP* portion divides the information into packets and then numbers each packet so that the message can be reconstructed at the receiving end. The *IP* portion sends each packet on its way by specifying the address of both the sending and receiving computers so that the packets can be routed to the correct computer.

transponder A device contained in a communication satellite that receives signals from transmission stations on the ground

tree diagram A diagram that shows the links between the planned pages of hypertext page-based multimedia

Trojan horse virus A computer virus that gets the victim to install and use it by masquerading as a legitimate program

true color A term that refers to a graphics device using at least 24 bits to represent each pixel so that up to 16 million unique colors can be represented to accommodate the complex shades and hues of our natural world

tunneling A security technology used by a virtual private network to safeguard data that enables one network to send its data via another network's connections

tuples Records in a relational database

Turing Test An experiment proposed by Alan Turing and originally called The Imitation Game whereby a human being interacts with an entity in a closed room, asking questions and receiving responses, and must determine whether the entity is human or a computer

turnkey system An information system that is tailored to the customer's needs and thus is easy to use

tutorial A form of instruction in which students are guided step-by-step through the learning process

twisted-pair cable A communications medium consisting of two independently insulated wires twisted around one another. One of the wires carries the information while the other wire is grounded and absorbs any interference that may be present on the line.

U

Unicode A data coding scheme that can accommodate a larger array of letters and symbols than ASCII; uses two bytes, or 16 binary digits, and can represent 65,536 separate characters

Uniform Resource Locator (URL) An Internet address

uninstaller A utility program for removing (deleting) software programs and any associated entries in the system files

Uninterruptible Power Supply (UPS) A device that provides a battery backup for a computer in the event of a blackout

Universal Product Code (UPC) A type of code printed on products and packages consisting of lines and spaces that a computer translates into a number. The computer then uses this number to find information about the product or package, such as its name and price, in a computerized database.

Universal Serial Bus (USB) port A type of port that is widely used for connecting high-speed modems, scanners, and digital cameras to a computer. A single USB port can accommodate several peripheral devices connected together in sequence.

UNIX An operating system developed by programmers at Bell Laboratories originally designed for large computer systems including minicomputers, mainframes, and supercomputers

unzipped Said of a compressed file in which the compression process has been reversed to create a new file that is full size again

user ID Also called username; a unique combination of characters (letters and numbers) identifying an individual computer user

user interface A set of instructions that allow the software to communicate with the user and, in turn, the user to communicate with the software. The manner in which the user enters data and commands and in which information and processing options are presented is controlled by the program's interface.

user name (user ID) A unique combination of characters (letters and numbers) identifying an individual computer user

utility program A type of program that performs a specific and helpful task, such as checking for viruses, uninstalling programs, and deleting data no longer needed

utility software Programs that perform specific tasks, such as managing a monitor, disk drives, printers, and other devices. In addition to utility software that is included with the operating system, a separate utility program, such as an antivirus program, can be installed in a computer.

V

value Data, such as a number, entered into a specific cell in a spreadsheet program

value added network (VAN) A network in which a business uses the facilities of large communications companies to provide subscribers with additional services, such as providing subscribers with access to various network databases, electronic mail, and online advertising and shopping.

variable In a computer program, a data object used to hold values such as numbers or text

vector-based graphics *See object-based graphics*

vendor *See B2B vendor.*

vertical application software A complete package of programs that work together to perform core business functions for a large organization

vertical market Specially focused sets of customers. *See niche information systems*

video Consists of motion images, similar to those seen on a television or movie screen

video board (graphics board, video adapter) An add-in circuit board that enhances the quality of pictures and images displayed on the monitor's screen

video capture card An add-on card which, when inserted in an expansion slot, converts an analog video signal into a digital signal

video card (graphics card, video adapter) A circuit board residing on the motherboard inside the system unit that converts the digital signals produced by the computer into analog signals and sends them through a cable to the monitor

videoconference A meeting between two or more participants at different sites, using computer networks and videoconferencing software

videoconferencing software Programs that make videoconferencing applications possible

video data Refers to moving pictures and images, such as a videoconference, film clip, or full-length movie

video digitizing card A piece of hardware that allows users to capture and digitize video images and sound from such sources as television, videotape recorders, and camcorders

video editing software Software that allows users to edit sound and video and output it in various digital formats

video input An input technology that occurs by using a special type of video camera attached to the computer and plugged into a video capture card in an expansion slot, which converts analog video signals into digital signals

video port A port (connection) for connecting a monitor to the system unit. The port may be built into the computer's system unit or provided by a video card placed in an expansion slot.

virtual age A term applied to the present era in which computers and their ability to simulate reality are a powerful economic force

virtual private network (VPN) A type of wide area network (WAN) whereby a company has each branch office set up a local Internet connection through which company networking traffic is routed. This type of network uses encryption and other security technologies to ensure that only authorized users can access it and that the data cannot be intercepted.

virtual reality (VR) A gamelike form of interface that puts the user into a very realistic alternate world; used for 3D design work and gaming

virus A program that is designed to harm computer systems and/or annoy users. Most viruses are sent as e-mail attachments.

viruses in the wild Successful viruses in common circulation

vision-input system A type of input technology that enables users to see, and avoid, obstacles that may be in their pathway

Visual Basic (VB) A language developed by Microsoft in the 1990s that is popular with programmers who want to rapidly develop Windows interface software

Visual Basic Script (VBScript) A script form of Visual Basic that can be used to create sophisticated Web pages

visual perception The science of making a computer understand what it sees with an electronic eye (camera)

voice input Technology that allows users to enter data by talking to the computer through a microphone

voice output Technology that allows spoken words and sounds to be to be heard via a computer's speakers

voice recognition Programs that recognize preprogrammed words stored in a database

voice verification system A biometric device that recognizes people via their voice patterns

volatile A type of computer memory whereby stored instructions and data are lost if the power is switched off

W

warm boot Process of restarting a computer while power is on; clears the memory and reloads the operating system

wave (.wav) file A file type used to reproduce any kind of sound; is not a compressed format

wearable computer A type of computer that can be worn on a person's body, thereby providing the user with access to mobile communicating capabilities and to information access via the Internet

Web administrator Person who is responsible for developing and maintaining a Web site; also called a Web master

Web appliance A simplified computer device that connects the user to the Internet, where programs and other applications are available at Web site; Web appliances do not store and run programs themselves.

Web browser (browser) Software that allows users to move from one location to another on the Web and to access and retrieve Web pages

webcam A tiny camera, sometimes wireless, that transmits still or video images to a computer continuously. Webcams are often hooked to the Internet so that the images can be viewed by anyone.

Web databases Databases associated with Web pages

Web-enabled cell phone (smart phone) A phone that allows a user to transmit and receive e-mail messages and browse through Web sites designed for display on the phone

Web host A company that allows individuals or other companies to use their Web server to store Web pages. Examples of Web hosts include Internet service providers, communications companies, and online shopping malls.

Web master *See Web administrator.*

Web page An electronic document stored at a location of the Web. The document can contain text, images, sound and video and may provide links to other Web pages.

Web page trap A Web page that is specifically built to fire advertisements at users in a bewildering array and attempts to keep them from leaving the site

WebRing A managed ring of links between Web sites that allows a surfer to move through many topically similar sites

Web server A computer that allows users to access and use the Internet and World Wide Web

Web site A collection of Web pages associated with a given topic or company on a single host system

webtop Technology that allows individuals and businesses to lease and access software through a Web browser

wide area network (WAN) A network that spans a large geographical area

Wi-Fi (802.11 protocol) A protocol for wireless communication that specifies an over-the-air interface between the wireless client device and a server, or between two wireless devices

Windows 2000 Professional A Microsoft operating system designed for use with business desktop and notebook computers and containing the power as well as many of the features of the earlier Windows NT

Windows 2000 Server A Windows-based operating system specifically designed for use on a network server

Windows 3.x The first versions of Microsoft's Windows operating systems, including Windows 3.0, 3.2, and 3.11

Windows 95 The release of the Microsoft Windows operating system that followed Windows 3.11, and offered Internet access and a new interface

Windows 98 An upgrade of the earlier Windows 95 operating system that offered improved Internet access

Windows CE An operating system, similar in appearance to the Windows 98 operating system, used for personal digital assistants or handheld PCs

Windows Millennium Edition (Me) A 1999 version of Microsoft Windows designed for users of less powerful PCs, such as those found in homes and small businesses.

Windows NT A powerful operating system, released in 1993, and designed for executing large applications in networked environments

Windows NT Server One of Microsoft's earlier entries into the client/server market that supports multitasking operations

Windows Server 2003 Microsoft's latest release of its server operating systems, available in four editions: Standard, Enterprise, Datacenter, and Web

Windows XP An operating system from Microsoft Corporation, released in 2001 and designed for the latest computers that are fast, powerful, and have lots of memory and hard disk space

Windows XP Server An operating system version designed for a typical client/server business network capable of handling electronic commerce applications

Wired Equivalent Privacy (WEP) A security protocol for wireless networks

wireless 3G The third generation of wireless communication technology; offers high-speed data transfer between devices such as Web-enabled cell phones and the Internet

Wireless Application Protocol (WAP) A protocol commonly used with low-bandwidth, wireless systems, such as cell phone networks

Wireless Markup Language (WML) A standardized language included in the Wireless Application Protocol (WAP) that converts an HTML-coded page to Wireless Markup Language (WML), removes the graphics, and then sends the text to the wireless device, where it is displayed on the device's screen.

wireless service provider (WSP) A business that provides wireless Internet access to subscribers using wireless Internet devices

wizard An application or part of an application that guides the user, step-by-step, through the completion of a task or that anticipates what a user might want to do and performs all or part of a task automatically

word A group of bits or bytes that a computer can manipulate or process as a unit

word processing A type of computer application that allows the user to create, edit, manipulate, format, store, and print a variety of documents, including letters, memos, announcements, and brochures

word size The number of bits a processor can interpret and execute at a given time

workgroup application software Programs that enable people at separate PC workstations to collaborate on a single document or project, such as designing a new automobile engine

workstation A high-performance single-user computer with advanced input, output, and storage components and that can be networked with other workstations and larger computers

worldwide online shopping Online shopping in which a customer goes online to find the best buys regardless of the location of the seller

World Wide Web (the Web) A global system of linked computer networks that allows users to jump from one site to another by way of programmed links on Web pages

WORM (write once, read many) disc A type of optical laser disc that provides very high capacity storage that is often used by companies to store huge amounts of data, particularly images

X

XHTML (Extensible HTML) A scripting language comprised of elements of HTML and XML used in Web page programming

XML (Extensible Markup Language) A scripting language that not only defines the content of a Web page but also organizes data so that computers can communicate with each other directly, without human intervention

Z

Zip drive A high-capacity floppy disk manufactured by Iomega Corporation

zip file A compressed file format, unrelated to Zip drives; commonly used for the downloading of large files over the Internet to speed up the process

index

new nations under, 210
policy and development issues with, 339-341, 346
research over, 315
searching for information on, 332-334, 345
security risks and, G: 1
updating antivirus software over, G: 6
viruses and, 186-187
Web page viewing and, 327-332
Internet appliances, 23, 182
Internet applications: newer, 345-346
Internet Assigned Numbers Authority, 260
Internet Corporation for Assigned Names and Numbers, 325
Internet-enabled cell phones, 25, 28, 30
Internet Explorer, 173, 179, 237
Internet 2 framework, 328
Internet Protocol, 287, 289
Internet protocol (IP) addresses, 323, 324, 345
Internet relay chat, 311
Internet Security Foundation, 25
Internet service providers, 21, 236, 284, 308, 319, 344
    free connections through, 337-338
    free hosting from, F: 2
    installing hardware and connecting to, 321-322
Internet telephone services, 336, 345
Internet2, 328, 342-343
Internet usage: top countries with, 319, 320
Internic, F: 5
Interpreters, 189, 194
Intranets, 275-276, 293
Inventory Distribution Systems: comparison of, 410
Inventory overhead: reduction of, 409
Inventory tracking systems, 375
Iomega Corporation, 127
IP. See Internet Protocol
IRC. See Internet relay chat
IS. See Information system
ISA bus. See Industry Standard Architecture bus
ISDN. See Integrated Services Digital Network
ISDN line, 292
ISPs. See Internet service providers
IT. See Information technology

J

Japan: global positioning systems in, 156
Java, 189, 345, 413
Java applets, 328, 345
Java Jacket, 23
Java 2 Micro Edition, 413
Jaz cartridge, 127
Jivkova, Svetla, 291
Jobs, Steven, 107
Joining, 370
Joysticks, 52, 54, 86

J-Phone Co. Ltd., 28
J2ME. See Java 2 Micro Edition
Jumbo! Web site, 212
Jupitermedia Corporation, 10
Just-in-time, 409, 410-411

K

Kavehrad, Moshen, 291
KaZaA, 335
KDE, 182
Kernel, 156
Kerning, 215
Keyboard drivers, 158
Keyboards, 16, 17, 19, 86, 87
    cordless, 270
    for notebook computers, A: 5
    types of, 48-49
    virtual, 57
Key feature option menus, 162-164
Keys, 368, 390
Keystroke identification, G: 8
Keywords, 333, 345, 379
Kilby, Jack S., 62
Kilobytes, 75
Kirtas Technologies, 70
Knowbots, 207
Knowledge base, 414
Kurzweil, Ray, 343

L

Lag time, 391
LAN. See Local area network
LAN connection, 320, 345
Lands, 128, 140
Landscape format, 112
Language translators, 185, 189, 194
Laptop computers, 23
Large computer systems
    magnetic storage devices for, 134
    optical storage devices for, 135
Laser printers, 116-117, 139, A: 4
LCD. See Liquid crystal display
Leading: adjusting, 215
Learning tutorials, 234, 236, 244
LeBerge, Stephen, 240
Lee, Edward A., 228
Legacy databases: access to, 388
Legal software, 231, 243
Legislation: against Internet pornography, E: 6
Letter quality, 113
Level 1 cache, 77
Level 2 cache, 77
Level 3 cache, 77
Liebenberg, Louis, 137
LightPointe Communications, 290
Line charts, 221
Link option: with Google, 244
Links: adding to Web pages, F: 4
Links feature: in database programs, 225
Linux, 182, 190-191
Liquid crystal display, 23, 24, 106
Lisa computer, 107, 160

Local area network, 10, 128, 239, 272-273, 293
Local area network protocols, 286
Local Internet service providers, 320
Logical topologies: physical topologies versus, 279
Lotus Amipro, G: 4
Lotus Development, 213
Lotus 1-2-3, 218
Lotus Software, 235
Lucas, George, 107
Lucent Technologies, 290
Lucidity Institute, 240
Lycos, 238

M

Machine cycle, 69
Machine language, 63
Macintosh computers, 171
Macintosh OS, 20, 161, 179, 283
Macintosh OS 9, 179
Macintosh OS X, 21, 179
MacPaint, 217
Macromedia Dreamweaver, F: 3
Macromedia Flash Player, 328, 329
Macromedia FreeHand, 232
Macros
    in spreadsheets, 220-221
    viruses and, G: 4
MA4-TC (Xybernaut Corporation), 110
Magnetic disk storage, 134, 140
Magnetic storage devices, 122, 140
    for large computer systems, 134
Magnetic tape storage, 134, 140
Mailing lists, 312
Mail server, 287
Mainframe computers, 7, 21, 26-27, 34
Main memory, 72
    selecting, A: 3
Main menu, 162
MAN. See Metropolitan area network
Management information systems, 365, 390, 412, 432, 433
Markup language, 327
Massachusetts Institute of Technology (MIT), 171, 313
Matador, 189
Math coprocessor, 70
McAfee, 186
McAfee VirusScan, 186, 187
McCaw, Craig, 165
McDonald's Corp., 289
Medical databases: nationwide, 389
Medical records, 389
Medium, 74
Megabytes, 75
Memory, 18
    cache, 76-77, 88
    comparisons of, 76
    managing, 157-158
Memory access time, 78
Memory boards, 87
Memory resident, 156

Memory Stick, 78
Menu, 162
Menu bar, 162
Message boards, 312
Metabrowsers, 324, 345
Metadata, 370-371, 390
Metalanguage, 327
Metcalfe, Robert, 265
Metcalfe's Law, 265
Metropolitan area network, 274, 293
MFDs. *See* Multifunction devices
Microcomputers, 7
Microphones, 19, 57
Microprocessors, 18, 87
    performance improvements with, 71-72
    selecting, A: 3
Microsoft Access, 221, 368, 370
Microsoft Corporation, 30-31, 165, 175, 177, 179, 209
Microsoft Encarta, 234
Microsoft FrontPage, F: 3
Microsoft Internet Explorer, 322
Microsoft LAN Manager, 283
Microsoft .NET Initiative, 184-185, 194
Microsoft Network, 11, 178, 319
Microsoft Office, 227
Microsoft Office programs: Web pages from, F: 3-4
Microsoft Outlook, 308, 310
Microsoft Outlook Express, 308
Microsoft PowerPoint, 226
Microsoft Tablet PC operating system, 24
Microsoft Windows 3.x, 171-172
Microsoft Windows 95, 172
Microsoft Windows 98, 172-174
Microsoft Windows 2000, 272, 283
Microsoft Windows 2000 Professional, 176
Microsoft Windows 2000 Server, 181
Microsoft Windows CE, 182, 183
Microsoft Windows CE .NET, 185
Microsoft Windows Imaging, 233
Microsoft Windows Media Player, 318
Microsoft Windows Millennium Edition (Me), 176
Microsoft Windows Mobile 2003, 183-184
Microsoft Windows NT, 283
Microsoft Windows NT Server, 180
Microsoft Windows NT (Workstation), 174
Microsoft Windows operating system, 20, 156-157, B: 1
    entertainment software programs with, 231-232
Microsoft Windows Paint, 232
Microsoft Windows Server 2003, 181
Microsoft Windows Sound Recorder, 57
Microsoft Windows XP, 21, 283
    desktop, 159
Microsoft Windows XP Professional, 177-180, 272
    desktop, 178
Microsoft Wireless Optical Desktop, 51

Microsoft Word, 63, 213, G: 4
    installing, B: 2-3
Microwave systems, 268, 292
MIDI (Musical Instrument Digital Interface) keyboards, 118
Midrange servers, 21, 25-26, 34
Minicomputers, 26, 34
Mining data, 149
MIS. *See* Management information systems
MITS Altair, 165
MMC. *See* MultiMediaCard
Mobile devices, 3
Modem boards, 79
Modems, 20, 261-262, 319
    cable, 266, 322
Moderated environments, 339, 346
Moderator, 339
Monitors, 16, 87, 103-106, 108-111, 138
    buying, A: 4
    ergonomics for, 109-110
    improvements in, 136
    performance and quality factors for, 106, 108-109
Monochrome, 104, 138
Monsters Inc., 107
Moore, Gordon, 53
Moore's Law, 53
Moral realism, E: 1
Moral relativism, E: 1
Mosaic, 211
Motherboard, 18, 66-67, 87
Mouse (mice), 16, 17, 19, 50, 86, 87, 161, 270
Mouse pad, 50, 51
Mouse pointer, 50Movies
    downloading, 335
    high-speed downloads of, 328
    illegal digital copies of, 318
MPEG, 318
MP4 format, 318
MP3 (Moving Pictures Expert Group III), 317
MP3 music files, 335
MP3 players, 317
MSN. *See* Microsoft Network
MSN TV Service, 23, 319
Multifunction devices, 119, 120, 139
MultiMediaCard, 78
Multimedia databases, 374
Multimedia data model, 390
Multimedia files, 346
Multiplexers, 282, 294
Multipoint videoconferencing system, 239
Multitasking, 158, 174
Multithreading, 72
Multi-user computer system, 17
Multi-user operating system, 181
Music: downloading, 185, 232, 317, 335, E: 5

N

Nanobots, 343
Nanotechnology, 84

Nantero Inc., 84
Napster, 334, 335, E: 5
Narrowband medium, 260
National Human Genome Research Institute, 9
National Internet service providers, 320
Natural language processing, 153, 241
NBEA Computer Education Task Force Code of Ethics for Information Systems, E:8
.NET Initiative (Microsoft), 184-185, 194
Netiquette, 338, 339, 346
Netscape Communications, 324
Netscape Navigator, 179, 238, 324
NetWare (Novell), 180, 283
Netware6, 283
Network and communications hardware, 279-283
Network architecture, 292
Network classifications, 271-276
    by architecture, 271-272
    by coverage, 272-275
    by users, 275-276
Network hardware, 293-294
Networking: over the Web, 259
Networking ants, 267
Networking operating system, 283
Network interface boards, 79
Network interface cards, 282-283
Network repeaters, 280
Networks, 10
    home, 47
    security risks with, G: 1
Network server, 25
Network software, 283
Network topologies, 277-279, 293
    bus, 277
    hybrid, 278
    physical versus logical, 276
    ring, 278
    star, 277-278
NewObjects Fusion, F: 3
Neworking components, 259
Newsgroups, 314
Newton (Apple), 121
New York Times home page
    copyright notice on, 341
NeXT software, 107
Niche information system, 421, 434
NICs. *See* Network interface cards
NLP. *See* Natural language processing
Node, 277
Nonimpact printers, 112, 139
Nonresident operating system parts, 156
Nonvolatile random-access memory, 84
Nonvolatile ROM chips, 77
Normalization, 383
Normative ethics, E: 1
North Korea: hacking in, 324
Norton Antivirus, G: 6, 186
Norton SystemWorks (Symantec), 186
Norton Utilities Disk Doctor, 188
NOS. *See* Networking operating system

Notebook computers, 10, 23, 83
  buying, A: 4-6
  pointers with, 52
NOT search operator, 334
Novell Corporation, 180, 283
NRAM. *See* Nonvolatile random-access
  memory
NTSC converter, 111
Number formatting: in spreadsheets, 220
Numeric data types, 363
Numeric keypad: on keyboard, 49

O

Object linking and embedding, 228
Object-oriented databases, 373
Object-oriented data model, 390
OCR. *See* Optical character recognition
Octopus, 324
Office information system, 365,
  411-412, 432
Off-the-shelf software, 426
OIS. *See* Office information system
OLAP. *See* Online analytical processing
OLE. *See* Object linking and embedding
OLTP. *See* Online transactional processing
Olympus, 77
On-demand computing, 30
OnePage, 324
Online analytical processing, 414, 433
Online courses, 316
Online gambling, 317
Online games, 316
Online help, 162, 170-171
Online shopping, 318, 408
Online shopping sites, 376
Online transactional processing, 386
Online transactions, 392
Open Source Development Labs, 182
Open-source software program, 182
Open-system format, 420
Open systems, 434
Open Systems Interconnection
  model, 284
Operating environments, 171
Operating systems, 20, 33, 154-156, 192
  installing/upgrading, B: 1
  Macintosh, UNIX and OS/2, 194
  new user interface design for, 190
  PC, 155, 171-175, 177-180, 193
  server, 180-182, 194
  wireless, 182-184, 194
Operational databases, 372, 374, 375, 390
Operation Lindburgh, 383
Optical character recognition, 55, 119
Optical disc data, 130
Optical disc drive, 140
Optical discs, 140
  increased storage capacity for, 136
  types and storage capacities of, 129
Optical fibers: higher-speed, 290-291
Optical laser disks, 140
Optical mouse, 51

Optical readers, 56
Optical scanners, 55-57, 86
Optical storage devices, 128-133
  for large computer systems, 135
Option buttons: in dialog boxes, 168-169
Oracle, 182, 367, 368, 425
Ordnance Engineering Corporation, 13
OR search operator, 334
OS. *See* Operating systems
OS/2 (IBM), 171-172, 180
OSI model. *See* Open Systems
  Interconnection model
OTM Technologies, 85
Output, 16, 33, 86, 102
  types of, 102-103
Output devices, 19, 33, 103, 138
  buying, A: 4
Output medium, 103, 138
Outsourcing production, 97

P

Packard, David, 29
Packets, 326, 345
Packet-switching, 326, 345
PageMaker, 218
Pagers, 10
pages per minute, 115
Painting programs, 232, 243-244
Palm Computing, 121
Palm handheld, 54
Palm Inc., 183
Palm OS, 182, 183
PalmPilot, 121, 183, 257
Palmtops, 24
PAN. *See* Public access network
Paradox (Corel), 221
Paragraph formatting, 215
Parallel ports, 80, A: 3, A: 4
Parallel processing, 72
Parallel transmission, 262-263, 292
Parity bit, 263, 285
Passive-matrix display, 106
Passwords, 159, 160, 276, G: 2, G: 7
Paterson, Tim, 175
Pathnames, 325, 345
Pattern recognition software, 241
PC cards, 80, 88
PCI bus. *See* Peripheral Component
  Interconnect bus
PC Magazine, 137
PCMCIA card (PC card), 79
PCMCIA (Personal Computer Memory
  Card International Association)
  modem, 262
PC operating systems, 171-175, 177-180,
  193
  OS/2, 180
  Windows 95, 172
  Windows 98, 172-174
  Windows Millennium Edition, 176
  Windows NT, 174
  Windows 2000 Professional, 176

Windows 3.x, 171-172
Windows XP Professional, 177-180
PCs. *See* Personal computers
PC Suite, 211
PDAs. *See* Personal digital assistants
Peachtree, 209
Peer-to-peer architecture, 271, 272, 293
Peer-to-peer file sharing, 334-335, 345
Pen computers, 24
Pens, 54, 86
Pentium 4, 67, 71, 85
Pentium M, 70
Performance monitor, 159
Peripheral Component Interconnect
  bus, 82
Peripheral devices, 17, 33
Permanent storage, 120, 122
Personal and social issues: and computer
  ethics, E: 2
Personal computers, 7, 21, 22-24, 33-34
  architecture, A: 2-3
  buying and installing, A: 1-8
  commonly used operating systems
    for, 155
  history behind, 165
Personal computer system: complete, A: 2
Personal digital assistants, 10, 24, 28, 30,
  54, 183, 270, 319
Personal ethical guidelines: need for, E: 7-8
Personal finance software, 229, 243
Personal identification numbers, G: 7
Petaflop, 27
Pew Internet and American Life Project,
  266, 267
Photograph printers, 115-116
Physical topologies: logical topologies
  versus, 279
Pie charts, 221
PINs. *See* Personal identification numbers
Pipelining, 72
Piracy, 242
  software, 185, 209
Pitch, 260
Pits, 128, 140
Pixar Animation Studios, 107
Pixels, 28, 55, 60, 104, 108, 139
PKZIP, 188
Plagiarism, 44
Planning, 434
Platform, 155, 192
Plattner, Hasso, 425
Plotters, 117-118
Plug-and-play (PnP) features, B: 3
Plug-ins, 328-329, 345
Pocket Excel, 183
Pocket PC, 24, 182
Pocket PC operating system, 183
Pocket PC 2003, 183
Pocket Word, 183
POD. *See* Print-on-demand
Pointers, 52
Pointing devices: for notebook
  computers, A: 5

Synchronous DRAM, 75, 108
Synchronous transmission, 285-286, 294
SyncLink DRAM, 75
System backdoors, G: 2
System board, 87
System bus, 81-82
System catalog, 371
System clock, 69-70
System components: connecting, B: 3-4
System development life cycle, 422-424,
    426-429, 429
System performance monitoring, 159
Systems analysts, 376, 390, 424, 434
Systems house, 420, 433
Systems integrators, 420, 433
Systems Network Architecture, 287
System software, 20, 33, 154, 192
    user-friendly, 190
System support, 434
System unit ports: locating, B: 4
System units, 16, 18, 33, 65-66, 87, A: 2
    expansion boards/devices installed
        inside, B: 4-5

T

Tables: in relational databases, 372
Tablet PC, 23
Tablets, 54, 86
Tabs: in dialog boxes, 168
Tape backups, 381, 391
Tape cartridges, 123, 128, 140
Tape drives, 128
Task Scheduler, 331
Tax preparation software, 230-231, 243
TCP. See Transmission Control Protocol
TCP/IP. See Transmission Control
    Protocol/Internet Protocol
Technical staffs: information systems and,
    418, 433
Technical support: for information
    systems, 421
TEKPAD (Traditional Ecological Know-
    ledge Prior Art Database), 372
Telecommunications, 259, 292
Telecommunications media: connection
    speeds for, 322
Telecommuting, 314
Teledesic project, 165
Telematics, 31
Telephone connections to Internet:
    alternatives to, 322-323
Telephone services: Internet, 336, 345
Telesurgery, 383
Television displays, 111
Telework, 314
Templates, 214, 226
Terabyte, 27, 76
Terminals, 26
Testing: information system, 428
Texas Instruments, 62

Text, 102, 138
    creating, 214
    data, 14, 33
    editing, 214-215
    formatting, 215-216
Text boxes: in dialog boxes, 169-170
TFT. See Thin-film transistor
Thermometer: digital, 6
Thin-film transistor, 106
3COM Corporation, 265
Threshold, 74
Throughput, 157
Tiger Team, 25
Timken Company, 10
Title bar, 166
TiVO, 190
T lines (T1 and T3), 267, 292
Token ring protocol, 286
Token ring technology, 278
Toner, 117
Toolbars, 164
Topologies
    bus, 293
    hybrid, 293
    ring, 293
    star, 293
Torvalds, Linus, 182
Toshiba, 77
Touch pads, 52, 86
Touch screens, 52, 86
Toyota Corporation: Linux operating
    system adopted by, 191
ToySmart, E: 3
Toy Story, 107
Toy Story 2, 107
Tracer, 85
Traces, 66
Trackballs, 51, 86
Track pad, 52
Tracks, 124, 140
Transaction, 365
Transactional processing, 385-386, 392
Transceiver, 277
Transistors, 53
Transmission Control Protocol, 328
Transmission Control Protocol/Internet
    Protocol, 287, 294
Transponders, 268
Trelix, 235
Trojan horse viruses, G: 5
True color, 108
Tuples, 372
Turnkey solutions, 434
Turnkey systems, 421
Tutorials, 234, 236, 244
Tuvalu, 260
Twisted-pair cable, 264, 292
Type I cards, 79
Type II cards, 79

U

Unauthorized access, G: 1-3
Unicode, 64, 65, 87

Uniform Commercial Code, E: 7
Uniform (or Universal) Resource Locators,
    313, 323, 324, 345, F: 3
    obtaining, F: 5
    path of, 326
    submitting to search engines, F: 5
Uninstallers, 187
United Nations, 284
United Parcel Service (UPS), 56
Universal Product Code, 55
Universal Serial Bus, 82
Universal Serial Bus port, 80, A: 3, A: 4
University of Phoenix: home page,
    316, 317
UNIX operating system, 181, 283
UNIX-X Windows, 171
Unpacking computer system, A: 7
Unzipped files, 308
UPC. See Universal Product Code
Upgrading: operating system, B: 1
URLs. See Uniform (or Universal)
    Resource Locators
U.S. Census Bureau, 407
U.S. Copyright Act, E: 5
USB. See Universal Serial Bus
USB devices: with Windows 98, 174
USB port. See Universal Serial Bus port
User-friendly system software, 190
User IDs, 160, 276, G: 2, G: 7
User interfaces, 160-164, 166-171,
    192-193
    command-line interfaces, 160
    design of, 420, 433
    graphical user interfaces, 160-164,
        166-171
    new designs for, 190
User name, 159-160
User response, 86
User training, 434
    and information systems, 428
Utilities software, 20, 33
    improved, 190
Utility programs, 185-186, 194
    kinds of, 187

V

Value added networks, 274, 293, 319, 344
Values, 218
VANs. See Value added networks
Vehicle Information and Communication
    System (Japan), 156
Verizon Communications, 283
Versatility: with computers, 8, 32
Vertical application software, 208, 242
Vertical market packages, 421
Video, 103
    streaming, 336
    viewing over Internet, 317-318
Video adapter, 79, 104
Video board, 79
Video camera, 59
Video capture card, 58
Video card, 104, 108

Videoconferences, 239, 244, 291
Videoconferencing software, 239, 244
Video data, 14, 33
Video digitizer, 59
Video input, 58
    applications for, 59-60
    devices, 87
Video output, 138
Video ports, 80
Video surveillance, G: 8
Virtual casinos, 317
Virtual keyboards, 57
Virtual private network, 274, 293
Virtual reality, 316
Viruses, 186-187, 340-341, 346, E: 5,
    G: 3-6
    boot sector, G: 5
    e-mail, G: 4
    macro, G: 4
    reported number of, by year, G: 4
    symptoms of, G: 5-6
    Trojan horse, G: 5
Virus scanning software, 341, 346
VisiCalc, 235
VKB Inc., 57
v-nations, 210
Voice input, 57
Voice output, 119, 139
Voice over IP, 336
Voice recognition programs, 57
Volatile memory, 75
Voting: electronic, 318
VPen, 85
VPN. *See* Virtual private network
VRAM, 108

W

WAN. *See* Wide area network
WAP. *See* Wireless application protocols
Warm boot, 156
Warranties: for computer systems, A: 7
Wearable computers, 23
Wearable displays, 110-111
Web authoring programs, 227, F: 3
Web browsers, 21, 172, 179, 237,
    323-324, F: 3
Webcams, 336-337, 346, G: 8
Webcasting, 336, 346
WebCrawler, 238
WebCT, 211, 316
Web databases, 376, 390
Web Edition: Windows Server 2003, 181
Web-hosting services: free, F: 2
Web links, 327, 345

Weblogs, 312
Web pages, F: 1, 12
    images added to, F: 4
    links added to, F: 4
    software chosen for building of, F: 3
    viewing, 327, 345
Web page traps: escaping, 331
Web phone, 319
Web protocols, 287
Web Publishing Wizard: with Windows
    98, 173
WebRings, 331-332, 345
Web sites, 327, 345
    building, F: 1-6
    evaluating, F: 5-6
    organizing, F: 2-3
    planning, F: 2-5
    privacy policies on, 402
Web site servicing: subcontracting, 431
Webster's Dictionary, 234
Webster's New World Dictionary of
    Computer Terms, 234
WebTV. *See* MSN TV Service
"What if" calculations, 218, 219
Wide area network protocols, 287
Wide area networks, 10, 239, 272,
    274-275, 293
Wi-Fi protocol (802.11), 289
Wi-Fi (wireless) connections, 184, 323
WinZip, 188
Wired communications media, 263-264
Wired computers, 28, 34
Wired News, 413
Wireless Application Protocol, 287-289, 294
Wireless capability: with notebook
    computers, A: 5-6
Wireless communications media, 267-271
Wireless computers, 28, 34
Wireless device operating systems,
    182-184, 194
Wireless devices
    expanding use of, 30
    limited security for, G: 2-3
Wireless 3G, 289
Wireless Internet connections, 323, 345
Wireless keyboard and mouse, 51
Wireless operating systems, 182-184
Wireless service provider, 270
Wizards, 214, 226
WMV format, 318
Wonderware, 426
Word: and microprocessors, 71
Word processing, 213-216
    creating text, 214

editing text, 214-215
    formatting text, 215-216
    programs, 214
    saving and printing, 216
Word processors, 213, 242
Word Pro (Lotus Development), 213
Word size, 71
Workgroup application software, 208, 242
Workplace: privacy issues and, E: 4
Workplace computer usage: mon-
    itoring, 150
Workplace technologies, 101
Workstations, 21, 25, 34
World Wide Web, 12, 33, 172, 294, 332
    future of, 343
    history behind, 313
    networking over, 259
    protocols used by, 287
Worms, G: 5
WORM (write once, read many) disks,
    135, 140
Wozniak, Steve, 107
WRAM, 108
WSP. *See* Wireless service provider
WWW. *See* World Wide Web
WYSISYG (what you see is what you
    get), 313

X

Xerox Corporation, 137, 160
Xerox PARC research center, 107, 265
X83 (Lexmark), 120
Ximian Evolution, 191
XML. *See* Extensible Markup Language
Xybernaut Corporation, 110

Y

Yahoo!, 238
    WebRing home page, 332
Yahoo By Phone, 418
Yahoo.com, G: 3
Yahoo Messenger, 311
Yamamoto, Keijiro, 28

Z

Zip disk, 125
Zip drive, 20, 125
Zip files, 188, 308
Z-learning, 240
Zoomer, 121

photo credits

Chapter 1: *Page 3* Japack Company/CORBIS, LWA-Dann Tardif/CORBIS; *Page 4 counterclockwise from top* PhotoDisc/Getty Images, Charles O'Rear/CORBIS, Reuters NewMedia Inc./CORBIS, Courtesy of Hewlett-Packard Company; *Figure 1-1* Royalty-Free/CORBIS (digital thermometer), Courtesy of Intel Corporation, Encore; *Figure 1-2* Bettmann/CORBIS; *Page 8* Roger Ressmeyer/CORBIS, Cameron/CORBIS; *Page 9* PhotoDisc; *Page 12* PhotoDisc; *Figure 1-9* Donofrio Studios; *Figure 1-10* AP Photo/Kathy Willens; *Figure 1-12* Encore; *Figure 1-13* Encore; *Figure 1-14* Encore; *Figure 1-15* Encore; *Figure 1-16* Encore; *Figure 1-18* Courtesy of International Business Machines Corporation; *Figure 1-19* Encore; *Figure 1-20* Copyright 2003 Motorola, Inc.; *Figure 1-21* Copyright 2003 Motorola, Inc.; *Figure 1-22* AFP/CORBIS; *Figure 1-23* Courtesy of Hewlett-Packard Company; *Figure 1-24* Copyright 2003 Motorola, Inc.; *Figure 1-25* Courtesy of International Business Machines Corporation; *Figure 1-26* Courtesy of Hewlett-Packard Company; *Figure 1-27* Royalty-Free/CORBIS; *Figure 1-28* Courtesy of International Business Machines Corporation; *Figure 1-29* Courtesy of Hewlett-Packard Company, Copyright 2003 Motorola, Inc., Copyright 2003 Motorola, Inc.; *Page 30* PARROT PASCAL/CORBIS SYGMA; *Page 31* Copyright 2003 Motorola, Inc.; *Page 33* C/B Productions/CORBIS, PhotoDisc; *Page 34* Encore, Courtesy of Hewlett-Packard Company; **Chapter 2:** *Page 47* Royalty-Free/CORBIS, Ricki Rosen/CORBIS SABA; *Page 48* Digital Stock; *Figure 2-1* Bob Rowen/CORBIS; *Figure 2-2* Durand Patrick/CORBIS SYGMA; *Figure 2-3* Encore; *Figure 2-5* Courtesy of Microsoft Corporation; *Figure 2-6* Courtesy of Microsoft Corporation; *Figure 2-7* Encore; *Figure 2-8* Courtesy of www.freeimages.co.uk; *Figure 2-9* Courtesy of Hewlett-Packard Company; *Page 53* Roger Ressmeyer/CORBIS; *Figure 2-10* Courtesy of: Think Outside; *Figure 2-11* Courtesy of Handspring™, Courtesy of Hewlett-Packard Company; *Figure 2-12* Encore, Courtesy of Hewlett-Packard Company; *Figure 2-14* Ted Horowitz/CORBIS; *Figure 2-15* Donofrio Studios; *Page 57* Courtesy of Siemans AG; *Figure 2-16* Royalty-Free/CORBIS, Encore; *Figure 2-18* Courtesy of Eastman Kodak Company, Courtesy of Epsom America, Courtesy of www.freeimages.co.uk; *Page 62* Roger Ressmeyer/CORBIS; *Figure 2-23* Encore; *Figure 2-24* Encore; *Figure 2-25* Courtesy of Intel Corporation; *Figure 2-26* Courtesy of Intel Corporation; *Figure 2-31* AFP/CORBIS, Courtesy of Intel Corporation; *Figure 2-32* AFP/CORBIS *Figure 2-33* Encore; *Figure 2-34* U.S. Robotics, OvisLink Corporation, Cisco Systems, AVM; *Figure 2-35* Encore; *Page 82* PhotoDisc; *Figure 2-37* Encore; *Page 84* Courtesy of International Business Machines Corporation; *Page 86* Palm, Inc., Courtesy of Microsoft Corporation, Courtesy of www.freeimages.co.uk; *Page 87* Brand X Pictures; *Page 88* Courtesy of Hewlett-Packard Company; **Chapter 3:** *Page 101* Chuck Savage/CORBIS; *Page 102* Royalty-Free/CORBIS, AFP/CORBIS; *Figure 3-1* Courtesy of NEC Mitsubishi Electronics Display of America; *Figure 3-2* Courtesy of ViewSonic Corporation; *Figure 3-6* Encore; *Figure 3-7* Courtesy of Dell Computer; *Page 107* Reuters NewMedia Inc./CORBIS; *Figure 3-10* Forestier Yves/CORBIS SYGMA, Reuters NewMedia Inc./CORBIS, AFP/CORBIS; *Figure 3-11* Touhig Sion/CORBIS SYGMA; *Figure 3-15* Courtesy of Hewlett-Packard Company; *Figure 3-16* Courtesy of Hewlett-Packard Company; *Figure 3-17* Encore; *Figure 3-18* Ariel Skelley/CORBIS; *Figure 3-19* Courtesy of Brother International; *Figure 3-20* Toshiba America; *Page 121* Maiman Rick/CORBIS SYGMA; *Figure 3-23* Encore; *Figure 3-27* Courtesy of Iomega; *Figure 3-28* Courtesy of Sony; *Figure 3-32* Encore; *Figure 3-33* eProformance; *Page 136* Courtesy of Lucent Technologies; *Page 137* Roger Ressmeyer/CORBIS; *Page 138* Encore; *Page 140* Superstock, Encore; **Chapter 4:** *Page 153* Royalty-Free/CORBIS; *Figure 4-6* Courtesy of Apple Computers; *Page 165* Lynn Goldsmith/CORBIS; *Figure 4-31* Courtesy of Sun Microsystems, Inc; *Page 175* Courtesy of Tim Paterson; *Page 182* James A. Sugar/CORBIS, Reuters NewMedia Inc./CORBIS; *Figure 4-32* Reuters NewMedia Inc./CORBIS; *Figure 4-33* Palm, Inc; *Figure 4-34* Steve Prezant/CORBIS, Nokia; *Page 191* Courtesy of Toyota Motor Sales, USA, Inc; **Chapter 5:** *Page 207* Owen Franken/CORBIS, Reuters NewMedia Inc./CORBIS; *Page 208* Digital Stock; *Page 209* Darren Modricker/CORBIS; *Figure 5-1* Encore, Courtesy of Adobe Systems Incorporated; *Page 211* Digital Stock; *Page 213* Digital Stock; *Figure 5-7* Donofrio Studios; *Page 221* PhotoDisc; *Page 225* Rob Lewine/CORBIS; *Figure 5-19* Royalty-Free/CORBIS; *Figure 5-20* David Sailors/CORBIS; *Page 230* Rob Lewine/CORBIS; *Page 231* Royalty-Free/CORBIS, Digital Stock; *Figure 5-22* Royalty-Free/CORBIS; *Figure 5-25* Microsoft Encarta; *Page 235* Louis Fabian Bachrach; *Page 237* PhotoDisc; *Figure 5-30* Steve Chenn/CORBIS; *Page 240* Wartenberg/Picture Press/CORBIS; *Page 241* Reuters NewMedia Inc./CORBIS; *Page 242* Joe Bator/CORBIS; **Chapter 6:** *Page 257* Ariel Skelley/CORBIS; *Page 265* Nogues Alain/CORBIS SYGMA *Figure 6-22* Courtesy of U.S. Robotics; *Figure 6-23* Courtesy of Cisco Systems; *Figure 6-25* Courtesy of Cisco Systems; *Figure 6-26* Encore; *Page 289* PhotoDisc, Copyright 2003 Motorola Inc.; *Page 290* Digital Art/CORBIS; *Page 294* Courtesy of U.S. Robotics; **Chapter 7:** *Page 307* Chuck Savage/CORBIS; *Page 313* AFP/CORBIS; *Figure 7-10* Reuters NewMedia Inc./CORBIS; *Page 323* Joyce Choo/CORBIS, T. Kevin Smyth/CORBIS; *Page 340* Images.com/CORBIS; *Figure 7-26* Reuters NewMedia Inc./CORBIS, Koopman/CORBIS; *Page 342* AFP/CORBIS; *Page 345* Courtesy of Hewlett-Packard Company; **Chapter 8:** *Page 360* Steve Chenn/CORBIS; *Page 361* Bettmann/CORBIS, Annebicque Bernard/CORBIS SYGMA; *Page 365* Reuters NewMedia Inc./CORBIS; *Figure 8-3* Lester Lefkowitz/CORBIS; *Page 367* Najlah Feanny/CORBIS SABA; *Figure 8-7* Bob Krist/CORBIS; *Page 374* Reuters NewMedia Inc./CORBIS; *Figure 8-9* Bob Rowan, Progressive Image/CORBIS; *Figure 8-10* Underwood & Underwood/CORBIS; *Figure 8-15* Eric K. K. Yu/CORBIS; *Figure 8-16* Royalty-Free/CORBIS; *Page 385* Donald C. Johnson/CORBIS; *Page 386* Jose Luis Pelaez, Inc./CORBIS; *Page 388* Royalty-Free/CORBIS; *Page 389* Chuck Savage/CORBIS; **Chapter 9:** *Page 405* Reuters NewMedia Inc./CORBIS; *Figure 9-2* Baldev/CORBIS SYGMA; *Page 408* Owaki - Kulla/CORBIS, Mary Ann Kulla/The Stock Market; *Page 409* Royalty-Free/CORBIS; *Page 411* James Leynse/CORBIS; *Page 412* Ariel Skelley/CORBIS; *Page 413* Courtesy of Sun Microsystems Inc.; *Figure 9-5* Jose Luis Pelaez, Inc./CORBIS; *Figure 9-6* Charles O'Rear/CORBIS; *Figure 9-7* Brownie Harris/CORBIS; *Page 417* Jacques M. Chenet/CORBIS; *Page 419* Peter Vadnai/CORBIS, Setboun/CORBIS; *Page 420* Chuck Savage/CORBIS; *Page 421* Ken Kaminesky/CORBIS, Chuck Savage/CORBIS; *Page 428* Attal Serge/CORBIS SYGMA; *Page 429* Royalty-Free/CORBIS; *Page 430* Charles Gupton/CORBIS; *Page 432* Brownie Harris/CORBIS